PHOTOGRAPHIC ARCHITECTURE

IN THE TWENTIETH CENTURY

PHOTOGRAPHIC ARCHITECTURE
IN THE TWENTIETH CENTURY

CLAIRE ZIMMERMAN

University of Minnesota Press
Minneapolis • London

This book is supported by a grant from the
Graham Foundation for Advanced Studies in the Fine Arts.

The University of Minnesota Press gratefully acknowledges the
financial assistance provided for the publication of this book from
the Office of the Vice President for Research, University of Michigan.

Published by the University of Minnesota Press
111 Third Avenue South, Suite 290
Minneapolis, MN 55401-2520
http://www.upress.umn.edu

Library of Congress Cataloging-in-Publication Data
Zimmerman, Claire.
Photographic architecture in the twentieth century / Claire Zimmerman.
Includes bibliographical references and index.
ISBN 978-0-8166-8334-5 (hc)
ISBN 978-0-8166-8335-2 (pb)
1. Architecture and photography. 2. Architectural photography—History—20th century.
3. Architecture, Modern—20th century. I. Title.
NA2543.P46Z56 2014o
720.1'08—dc23 2014003744
Printed in the United States of America on acid-free paper

20 19 18 17 16 15 14 10 9 8 7 6 5 4 3 2 1

Dedicated to

two Rachels and two Marthas,

babies and mothers

CONTENTS

PREFACE

The roots of this study go back to my years as an undergraduate student majoring in architecture at the University of Pennsylvania. Two distinct experiences from that time stand out in my memory. The first occurred in a warm classroom in Hayden Hall, as I gazed sleepily on dim slides of heroic European buildings and wondered what on earth I was doing studying these spatially replete objects in such an impoverished manner. The perversity of studying architecture through two-dimensional images struck me powerfully at the time and left an impression that has only now been partially exorcised. Now that we use much more sophisticated tools to accomplish the same tasks, we can expect students of architecture to ask an opposite question when faced with dazzling arrays of computer-generated animated models on screen projections: How can such visually replete images ever be matched by the poverty of our current habits of construction? In both cases, the disjunction remains as problematic today as it was years ago.

The second experience at Penn came from the teaching of a remarkable drawing instructor named Frank Kawasaki. A man of few words, Frank believed more in the power of doing than of saying, or so we believed. Classes were conducted at an array of sites, most of which were quite difficult to draw, where Frank would give one-on-one instruction in a concentrated but abbreviated manner. Sitting next to me one day in the Penn stadium, he explained the idea that the way a building appears ought to bear some correspondence to how it was made. I found this a novel idea at the time (it seemed to me that buildings, more than anything else, are there to tell stories), particularly when Frank noted the ethical ramifications of this idea—or the way in which the idea had been endowed with ethical connotations going back to nineteenth-century structural rationalism but residing more presently for him in twentieth-century functionalism. It was impossible to tell whether he believed that buildings should tell of their own structural and programmatic identity through external representation, but his laconic manner conveyed the debate to me in a few short sentences. With hindsight, I appreciate his proximity to debates that remain deep in a past to which I had no direct access (other than through his instruction) and that I have had to recover through the very means that seemed to me so impoverished back in Philadelphia: texts and images, as well as buildings themselves.

This book marries these two concerns in a study of twentieth-century modernism and its photographs. One of my purposes in writing *Photographic Architecture in the Twentieth Century* was to clear a field for the consideration of contemporary challenges in imaging architecture—of the ways that architecture adapts to the demands of its own marketing structures. Although it hazards a few comments on contemporary conditions, the book is primarily a historical study of a past condition of architecture that can be experienced today only as history or revival. It cannot be lived anew.

PHOTOGRAPHIC ARCHITECTURE
IN THE TWENTIETH CENTURY

The very same bourgeois culture

that fabricates history also oversees

its silencing.

—MARK JARZOMBEK

INTRODUCTION

BEYOND VISIBILITY

MODERN ARCHITECTURE IN THE PHOTOGRAPHIC IMAGE

The British architectural historian and critic Reyner Banham is reputed to have started the chain of events that led to this book. He did so most evidently in Buffalo, New York, although the events really began somewhere in England in the 1940s or 1950s, well before I was born and well before 1986, when the following words were printed:

> And this brings up a matter of extraordinary historical importance that goes well beyond any scandals about leaking roofs: . . . insofar as the International Style was copied from American industrial prototypes and models, it must be the first architectural movement in the history of the art based almost exclusively on photographic evidence rather than on the ancient and previously unavoidable techniques of personal inspection and measured drawing. . . . the power of the photographs comes from the fact that, like the works of engineering they represented, they were understood to be the product of the scientific application of natural laws. . . . The photographs represented a truth as apparently objective and modern as that of the functional structures they portrayed.[1]

The charge embedded in this text then passed in rapid succession through the hands of other scholars a decade later, changing its shape in the process. It arrived in my hands around 2001, although I had been ready for some time.[2] I took it up in earnest only after encountering some relics myself: the silver gelatin prints of well-known early projects by Ludwig Mies van der Rohe (1886–1969). These photographs were interleaved with more recent copy prints in the research files of the Mies Archive at the Museum of Modern Art. The idea of an "original" photographic print is paradoxical; its existence presents historians of photography with a familiar conundrum nevertheless. In this case, the "original" Mies photographs stood out from all the other prints with which they were filed. First, they were often mounted on the dull-blue matte board that was ubiquitous in the museum's photographic collections at the time. Second, they had been made from large-scale glass negatives, and had therefore a crispness and precision of detail that was not present in later copy prints made from them. (No glass negatives of these projects survive in the MoMA archive; some are presumed smashed in the bombing that obliterated the Berliner Bildbericht photographic agency, on Eisenacher Street in the Schöneberg section of Berlin sometime in late 1943 or 1944; others suffered unknown fates and may still reappear.) The unpublished photographs were particularly useful, allowing me to construct a full spatial sequence of most of the Tugendhat House in my mind, thus duplicating a way of studying architecture that was common for much of the twentieth century. Banham's account had pushed me through the then miraculously open door of the Mies Archive into this book.[3]

By studying how and what modern architecture, as a shared discursive practice —as a movement—gained from the agency of photographic images and their framing sites (journals, books, exhibitions, and illustrated lectures), we can construct an alternative history. Unlike new architectural discoveries and new tools, photography was used covertly, not boldly declared. This book therefore represents an act of historical recovery. Architects and their champions in academia and the press consistently denied the importance of the medium. Photographs evidently threatened the integrity of architecture in a way that construction technique and modern consciousness did not. But as the twentieth century ended and the comparative simplicity of analog photography was replaced by the juggernaut of the digital, defense through denial has proven inadequate. Indeed, since this project began, the development of picture theory, or *Bilddiskurs*, has transformed its objects more than once. Narrating that story now suggests some of its implications in the present.

Just two years separate François Arago's official announcement of photography's invention by Nicéphore Niépce and Louis Daguerre in 1839 from the death of Karl Friedrich Schinkel, often regarded as the first modern architect, in 1841. Thanks to the relatively slow technological development of photography, buildings provided ideally stable subjects for early photographers and the slow emulsions with which they worked, making architecture a frequent subject of experimental pictures.[4] British polymath William Henry Fox Talbot's first official photograph, his "philosophical window," provides a graphic example (Figure I.1); so did Niépce take his first picture of the building in which his apparatus was housed.[5]

Architecture and photography were both characterized by dual agendas in the second half of the nineteenth century. Buildings designed by architects fulfilled pragmatic needs dictated by program or function, as they translated social and cultural values into concrete objects. Photographs, visual marvels of new chemical and technical processes, were also carriers of a new kind of aesthetic experience. The visual richness of photographs often seemed like a mere by-product of their scientific utility, just as rich representational programs turned use into spectacle in major public buildings of the nineteenth century. The Paris Opéra, for example, gave visible expression to the program for an opera house, one that relied on and emerged from historical precedents and functional demands, but endowing this program with unprecedented opulence (Figure I.2).

Perhaps in connection with the dual operation of architecture and photography—one operation connected to utility, the other to aesthetic representation—both practices reflected related conceptual approaches to visible appearance and signification as decades passed.[6] This parallelism appeared relatively early in the nineteenth century. In the case of architecture, we might look to Schinkel, who used plaster render over brick construction to achieve maximal visible clarity on building exteriors by articulating them with neoclassical order and detail. This was not fakery; Schinkel connected visible formal representation to an ethical project when he denoted such articulation as primary, noting, "Everything essential must remain

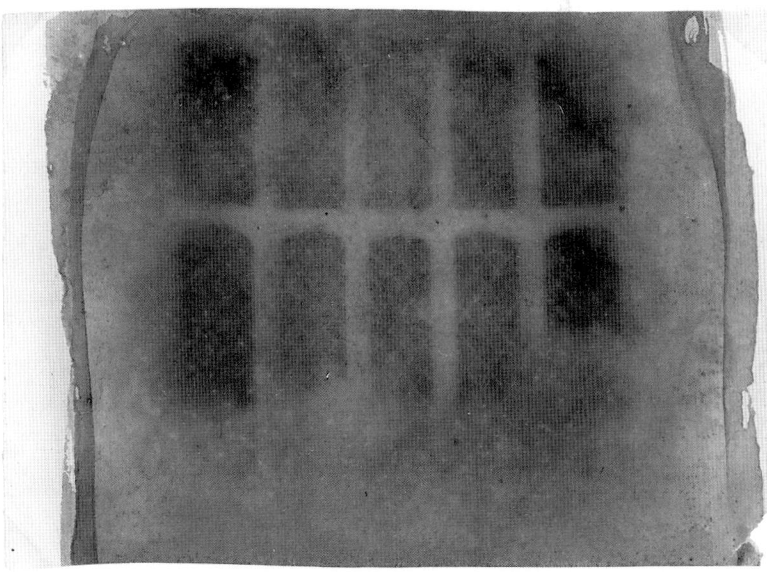

Figure I.1. William Henry Fox Talbot, *The Oriel Window, South Gallery, Lacock Abbey*, 1835 or 1839. Photogenic drawing negative, 3¼ × 4$\frac{3}{16}$ inches. The Metropolitan Museum of Art, The Rubel Collection, Purchase, Ann Tenenbaum and Thomas H. Lee and Anonymous Gifts, 1997 (1997.382.1). Image copyright The Metropolitan Museum of Art.

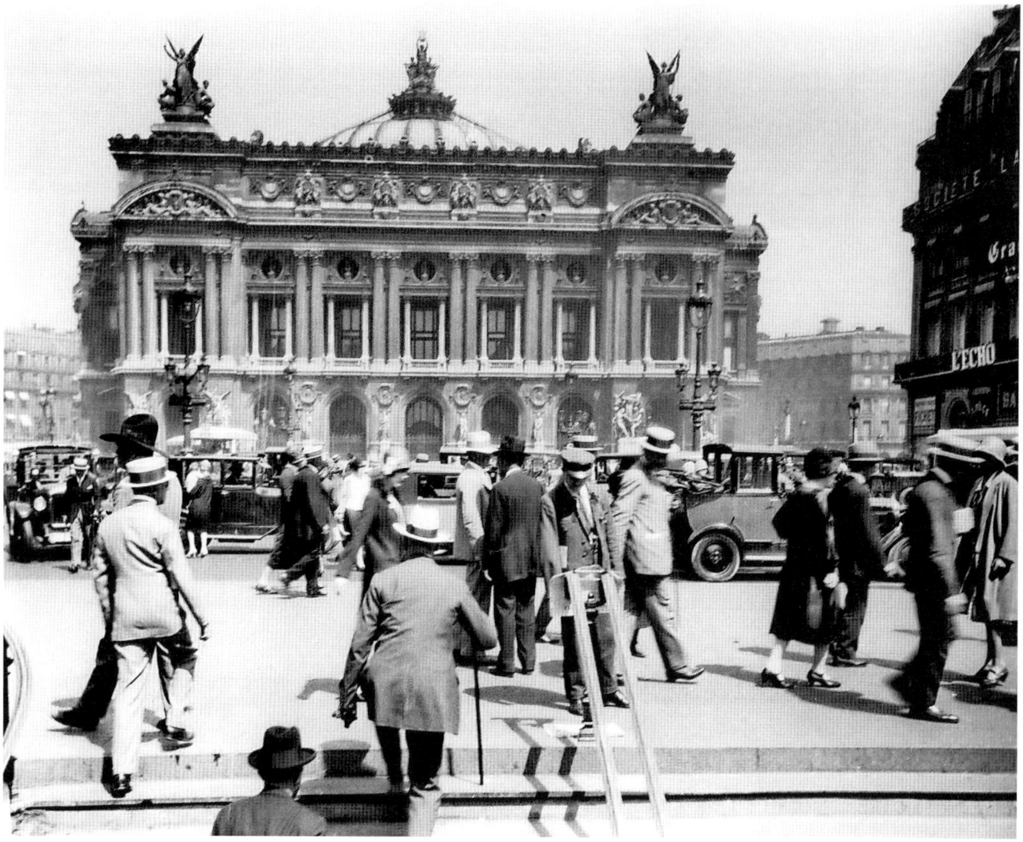

Figure I.2. The Paris Opéra, undated. Building: Charles Garnier. Photograph: Delmaet and Durandelle. Clarence Ward Archive, Department of Image Collections, National Gallery of Art Library, Washington D.C.

visible."[7] Similarly, in *The Pencil of Nature*, Fox Talbot asserted the remarkable veracity of photographic images as testimony to the order of nature.[8] Within two separate arenas of activity, appearance was connected to the assertion of visible truth. Rationalism and objectivity were the shared obligations of art, science, and social representation in both fields; equally important were mythological corollaries between photography and architecture that allowed each to function as mythmaking sign as well as scientific artifact.

As time passed, transparency (of form, construction, and cultural meaning) emerged as a recurrent concern of modern architects. As problematic as it would turn out to be in many respects, this idea became closely affiliated with core discourses of German modern architecture and its subsequent expansion in the United States and the United Kingdom after World War II. These discourses subsumed functionalism, rationalism, formalism, and related attempts to balance pragmatic, scientific, and aesthetic priorities in architecture. In this inclusiveness, we may identify one of the binding threads of modernism as a general category. In turn, photographs provided a format for the dissemination of information about buildings that was demonstrably more effective than lithographic drawings. Mass printing of photographic images of architecture changed the conditions of architectural commerce just as steel, concrete, and plate glass changed building construction in the same decades. Within modernist praxis, a relationship between photographic image and built object emerged, developed as a result of commercial protocols, and turned back on itself, as imaging strategies began to have explicitly architectural effects. The task of this study is to historicize those effects, and to make them relevant to the present and future.

Before photography, buildings and the architectural drawings that brought them into being and broadcast their presence carried on a complex and nuanced dialogue. We might begin here by understanding both building and drawing as alternate forms of representation; we might categorize both as "functions" of the broadest class of visual representation, the image.[9] This is not to ignore the other aspects of buildings, beyond that of form. It is, rather, to allow architectural form to enter into a field in which other formal manifestations also exist—to place architecture, as it were, within a larger field of representations. After the arrival of photography, architectural representations multiplied further, as they populated every stage of the creation of buildings, from drawing before the fact to construction itself to photography of construction to photographs taken for publication after the building was completed. The expansion of these forms of representation means that we can explore how photography changed the game for building in the twentieth century more easily, partly because photographs added yet another kind of image to the many genres of drawing and building that already existed. In addition, however, the new kind of image that photographs constituted exceeded existing categories of analysis and therefore required new ones, such as those provided by Banham in 1960 and by others since.

This book seeks to develop these earlier insights, focusing first on the interaction between the Weimar "New Building"—one development of interwar modern architecture—and the photographic image. This interaction remained central after World War II, despite the fact that the Neues Bauen was far more complex and nuanced than the pictures of it that survived the war, and that other developments of the interwar period were forgotten or left aside. Thanks to the persistence and durability of its photographs—their potent "afterlives"—this version of modernism monopolized more airtime than others in the ensuing history of architecture.[10] This study examines that history and analyzes some of its effects. It must be emphasized at the outset: this is *not* a book about architectural photographers. There will be no substitution of Ezra Stoller or Julius Shulman for Mies or Neutra here, for what sense would there be in casting down the architectural deity only to erect a photographic one in his (not her) place? Nor is it a history of architecture as a form of representation independent from its modes of appearance, as Neil Levine has recently written.[11] The book focuses on the interface between Western modern architecture and its image, reading the complex shadow play taking place on that surface over a period of some fifty years.[12]

Within a group of focused *sondages* beginning before World War I and concluding with Banham in the 1960s, the book emphasizes moments of particular instability in the developing economies of modern architecture. It is not a comprehensive history but a diagnostic exercise, locating volatile moments in the emergence and development of a new communicative vehicle for architecture and using those as case studies in a stepped historical narrative. Other analyses might narrate similar moments using different buildings and pictures. The unstable moments detailed here, however, usefully recast our understanding of the dynamic relationship between two media, both for understanding the past and for constructing the present. The dynamic relationship between pictures and buildings might be referred to by the general blanket term *photographic architecture*, here narrated in relation to the German neo-avant-gardes and explorations of themes such as abstraction, idealism, and hard-line functionalism.

PHOTOGRAPHIC ARCHITECTURE

Evidence, visible appearance, and truth constructions in photography and architecture became more causal and direct as the twentieth century advanced, shaping both media as mass publics formed around them. As Beatriz Colomina noted in 1994, "Emerging systems of communication that came to define twentieth-century culture—the mass media— . . . are the true site within which modern architecture is produced and with which it directly engages."[13] We might add here that the relationship between media and image discussed by Hans Belting has yet to appear in the architectural history of modernism, although the present study moves in this direction, lodging as it does between the hard stuff of buildings and the ephemera of photographic images.[14] As used here, the term *photographic architecture* includes photographic influence within building design as well as the infrastructure of commercial architectural photography. But it is not merely a container term. Photographic architecture also signals the commercial networks of professional architecture within which photographs circulated. I intend it as a general category that assembles the components of architecture's engagement with photographic processes. The term shuttles between buildings, pictures of buildings, and audiences—perhaps similar to Belting's definition of "a 'medium' in the sense of a vector, agent, *dispositif*," that transmits neither building nor picture but rather the synergetic combination of the two. Belting notes further: "I do not speak of images *as* media, as is often done, but instead of their need *for* and use *of* media in order to be transmitted to us and become visible to us. The same images may even migrate in history from one medium to another, or they may accumulate features and traces of several media in one and the same place."[15] In the history of architecture, the opposition between building and image that is so frequently part of our historiography complicates analysis. Nevertheless, it has become increasingly clear that buildings interact with other systems of information; they do not stand apart from them.

Engagements between photographs and buildings in the age of mass photographic printing were particularly intense from the mid-1920s to the 1970s and had a decisive impact on the history of both.[16] Buildings were important in the early development of photography, both because they did not move and because their sharp edges and clear geometries had a compelling effect in photographic images.[17] This book focuses on the disciplinary history of architecture, however, recasting it in relation to the matrix through and in which it came into existence—that of texts and discourse from a range of fields, of photographic images, and of commercial relationships.[18]

As noted, photographic architecture, if it describes a mass medium that brokers relationships between architecture and pictures, is here broken out into two major topics of investigation, each of which includes subtopics. The first concerns the fabric of buildings themselves, as photographic procedures, proliferating photographic images, and new imaging technology influenced architectural design. The visual practices that were part of photography entered into the design procedures of architects, resulting in new architectural concepts that were manifested in constructed projects, even if these were not always immediately evident to the public.[19] In cases analyzed here in parts I and III, photography expanded the boundaries of professional practice from the inside out. Wall-sized photographic murals, highly reflective stone surfaces, and plate glass joined the indexical or evidentiary image to the building, but the investigation that follows reveals that more conceptual interpretations of photographic ideas were also present from the 1920s onward.

The second trajectory here concerns the architectural photograph. Architectural photography regulated architectural commerce in late industrial society, having consequential effects on the reception and production of new architecture and channeling discourse in particular directions. Some of these effects are recounted in parts II and III. In both trajectories, photographic modes and habits of seeing penetrated architectural practice. This interpenetration created a number of corollary effects. The two modes of photographic architecture discussed here are complicated by the fact that one of them—photographs of architecture—was also the primary means by which information about buildings was transmitted, and that photographs often conceal as much as they reveal. A question that is considered throughout the book concerns the degree to which it is possible to separate these two aspects of photographic architecture from one another, and what is gained in historical knowledge by doing so. That which is held separate also blends together.

Photographs of buildings are photographs of built representations—which means that we might understand them as mediated images that mediate yet other sorts of images—a case of *mise en abyme* if ever there was one. The book begins from the understanding that one of the primary tasks of modern architecture from the nineteenth century was to provide adequate sites for the images of a society to appear in and through its buildings.[20] This burden of representation on buildings was both challenged and mixed up by the capaciousness of photography, a capaciousness that differed fundamentally from that of the architectural drawing. The story of modern architecture is in part the story of confusion between different orders of representation—between the built image and the photographic image of that construction. Thus grand civic architecture of the late nineteenth century such as that of the Paris Opéra (Figure I.2) conjured bourgeois French nationhood in cultural artifacts that both housed and enacted cultural self-presentation. Such three-dimensional architectural images were constructed at full scale on sites and projected in rendered drawings that depicted the three-dimensional built representations in two-dimensional drawn ones. The Opéra was also systematically photographed during the course of its construction; thus photographs joined drawing and building in rich modes of representation. But just as the Opéra was both a representation itself and a subject of further representation, so does the history of modern architecture reflect an increasingly self-conscious acceptance of both modes on the part of architects and their interpreters. Buildings were both depicted and depictions. The introduction of a term such as *photographic architecture* accommodates the simultaneity with which architecture was both representation and subject for representation and constructs the analytical framework within which to consider doubling of three-dimensional object and two-dimensional photograph more precisely.[21] We might move back in time briefly to locate an earlier moment in this developing relationship, one that anticipates the invention of the photographic image.[22]

If architects and historians often identify Schinkel as the first modern architect, they also note that he worked out important tenets of modern architectural practice after visiting English factories in 1826, where new construction technology had streamlined the production of goods (Figures I.3a, I.3b).[23] Whether Schinkel's priority is meaningful or not (there are others who also reflect the early development of modernism), the focus here is on work in which an intensive dialogue between

a

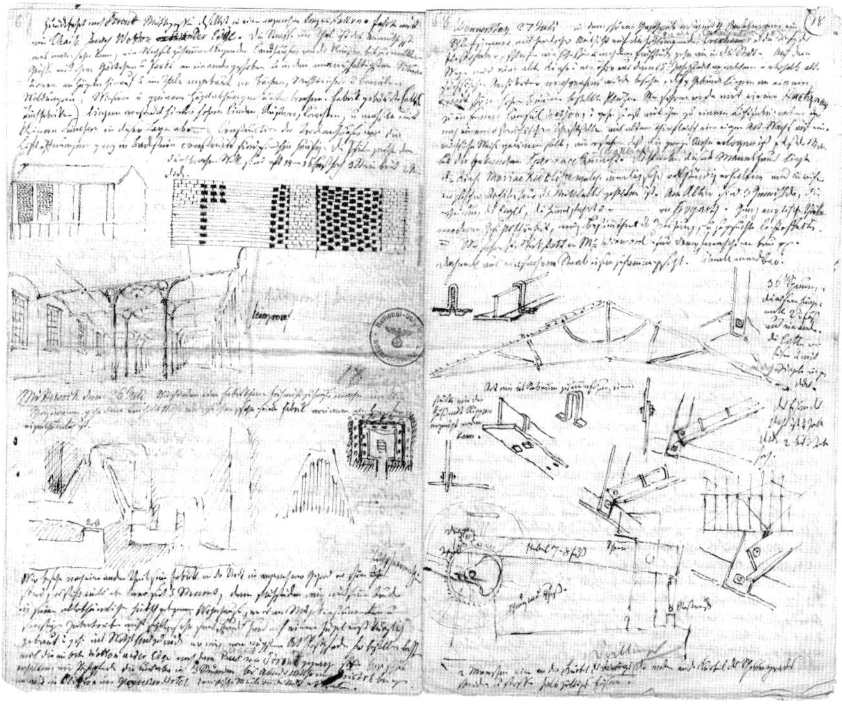

b

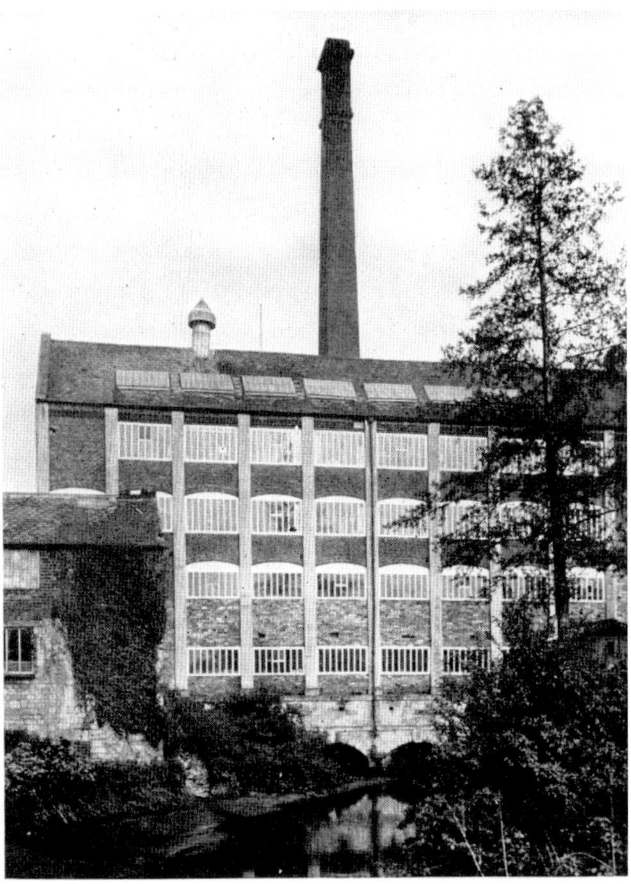

Figure I.3. (a) Karl Friedrich Schinkel, sketches of English factories, 1826, including the Stanley Mill. Photograph: bpk, Berlin/Zentralarchiv, Staatliche Museen, Berlin/Art Resource, NY. (b) Stanley Mill, Ryeford, England. Photograph: Eric de Maré; published in J. M. Richards, *The Functional Tradition in Early Industrial Buildings* (London: Architectural Press, 1958).

construction and representation took place, as it often did in Schinkel's work. Other important strains in modernism differ from the ones studied here, such as those that accompanied architectural expressionism.[24] But one persistent and well-developed genealogy leads from Schinkel through Peter Behrens to Walter Gropius and Ludwig Mies van der Rohe. This line underpins one of the most often repeated accounts of architectural modernism as a discourse between rationalism and the metaphysics of form. I make no claims for the superiority of this strain, nor do I defend its exaggerated profile in architectural history, for there are many ways to be, or not to be, modern. Rather, this book tracks interactions between formalist architectural practice as it originated in German architecture and the new modes of representation by which it came to claim status as a modern project. The very dominance of narratives such as formalism in the history of architecture rests partly on the success with which they adapted to the new protocols of photography, both commercial and conceptual. Some of the mechanisms of that process are revealed here.

Examples help define the new term *photographic architecture.* The engineering of frame construction systems (first metal, then concrete) in the last quarter of the nineteenth century created non-load-bearing facades that invited the installation of walls as giant picture surfaces. To suggest that frame construction invited these surfaces into architecture in a new way is to claim that facades were or should be reflections of interior constructional conditions. This is an assumption bounded in time. The idea of the facade as a literal indicator—an index—of the construction within is only as old as the eighteenth century; for Alberti, for example, it was not so. We find the idea taking on revolutionary significance in a building like Schinkel's Bauakademie (1835–36), in which functionalism and structural rationalism transposed from those same British factories created a signifying architecture that announced its own constructional condition through a carefully designed, communicative facade. But the pictorial facades of metal- or concrete-framed buildings gradually moved toward photographic effects, not merely pictorial ones, thanks to the increased use of reflective plate glass as a facade material. The Leipzigerstrasse Tietz Department Store (Bruno Sehring, 1900) facade, for example, is an early hybrid of this type (Figure I.4). Large expanses of glass display goods framed incongruously by three bays of ornamented stone; a masonry spandrel runs across the top.

Increasingly sophisticated examples of glass-fronted buildings can be found in the work of Otto Wagner and his school in Austria-Hungary (Figure I.5). They appear again in yet more extreme versions with greater expanses of glass in unbuilt projects of the early 1920s, such as Ludwig Mies van der Rohe's well-known Friedrichstrasse Skyscraper scheme. This project crystallized the discoveries of the previous decades, endowing glass with new independence as a building material. Other examples

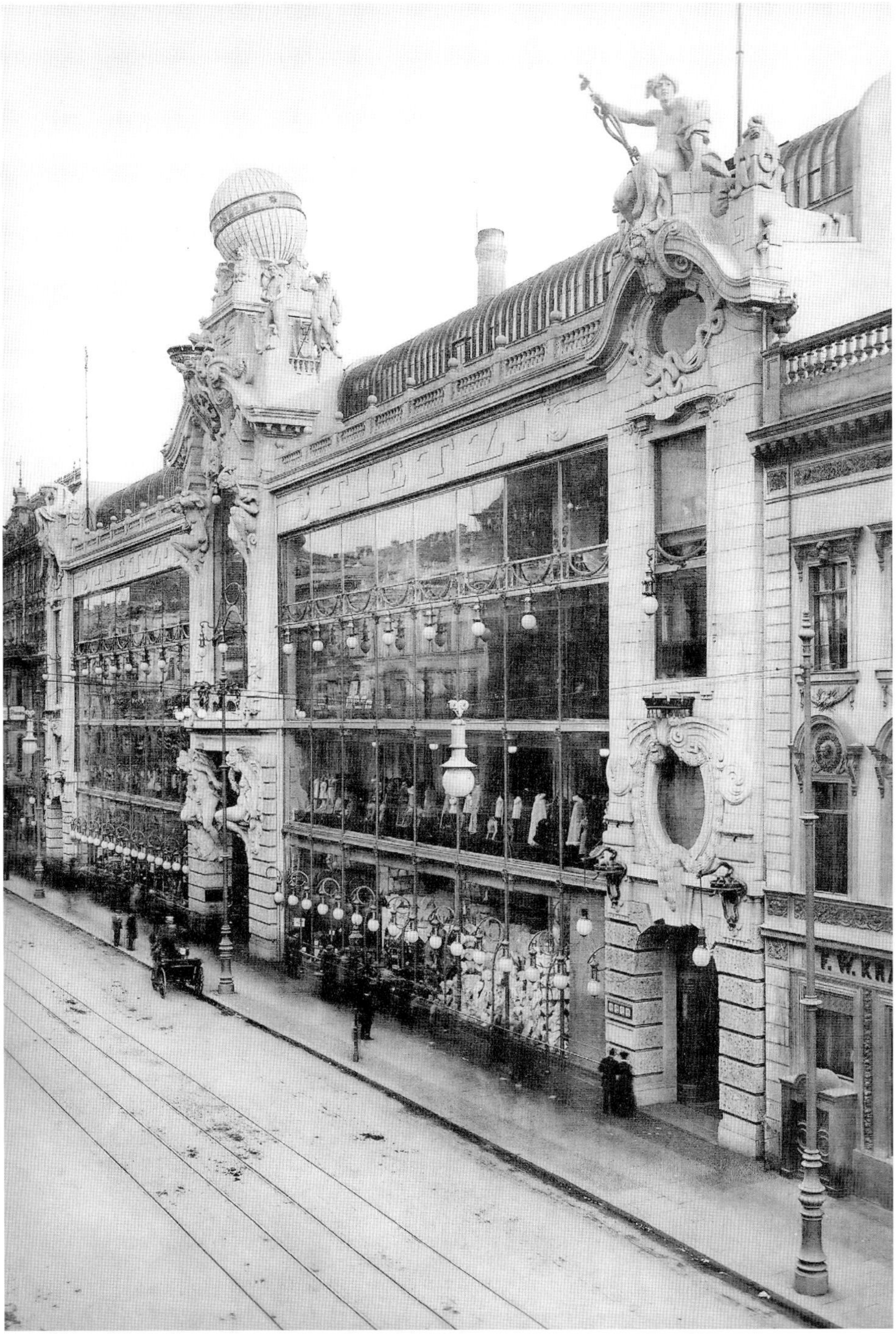

Figure I.4. Warenhaus Tietz, Leipzigerstrasse, Berlin, 1900. Building: Bruno Sehring. From Peter Gössel and Gabriele Leuthäuser, *Architektur des 20. Jahrhunderts* (Cologne: Taschen, 1990), 61.

submitted to the same competition provide useful comparanda for a project that was in many respects unique. But earlier attempts to use glass facades as reflective picture surfaces were common before the 1920s, in glass-fronted or partially glass-fronted buildings. The remarkable department store design of István Benkó-Medgyaszay, with its luminous translucent glass curtain wall, was published in *Der Architekt* in 1902, more than twenty years before Mies's similar commercial buildings on Friedrichstrasse/Leipzigerstrasse in Berlin (Figure I.6). Subsequent developments turned plate glass into a ubiquitous surface for modern buildings, making it appear as if the history of twentieth-century high-rise architecture culminated in the realization of Mies's 1920s dream, whether in the same architect's Seagram Building (1957), in the John Hancock Tower (1976) in Boston, or in any number of glass-sheathed towers from legions of late modernists that have sprung up like mushrooms since.[25]

Another issue concerns parallel methodologies. Photography was a proximate cultural practice that provided a specific model for modern architecture. It com-

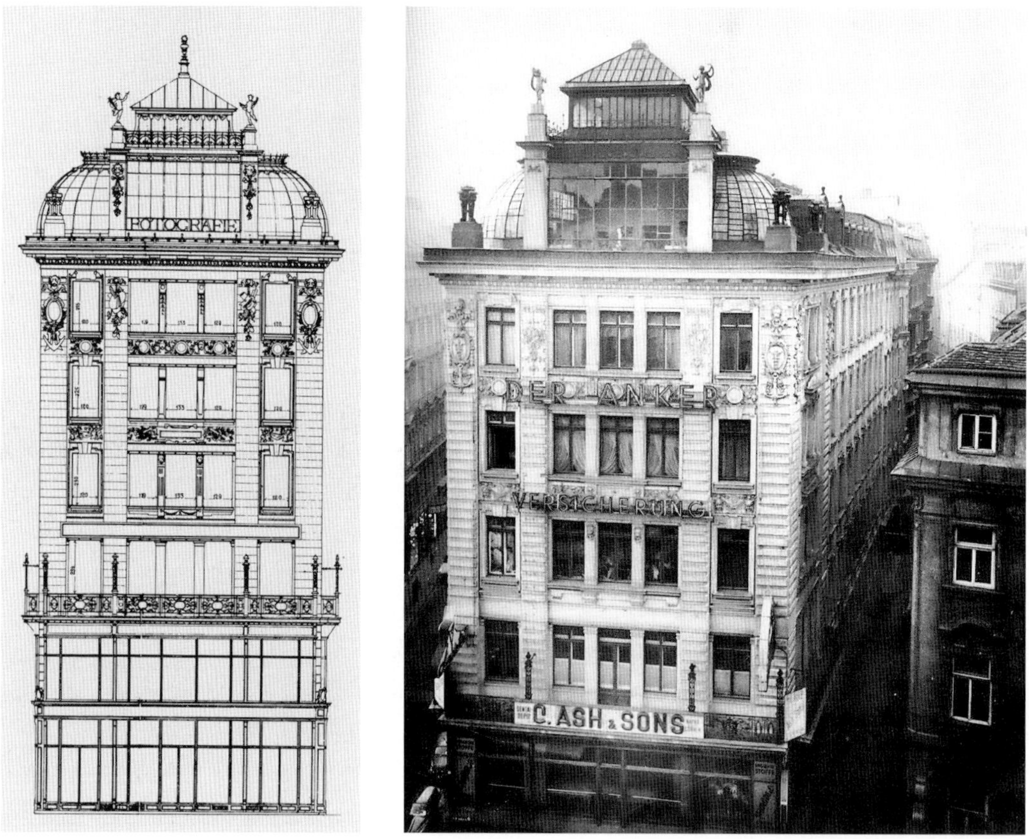

Figure I.5. Ankerhaus (with photo atelier on roof), Vienna, 1895. Building: Otto Wagner. Photograph: Josef Dapra.

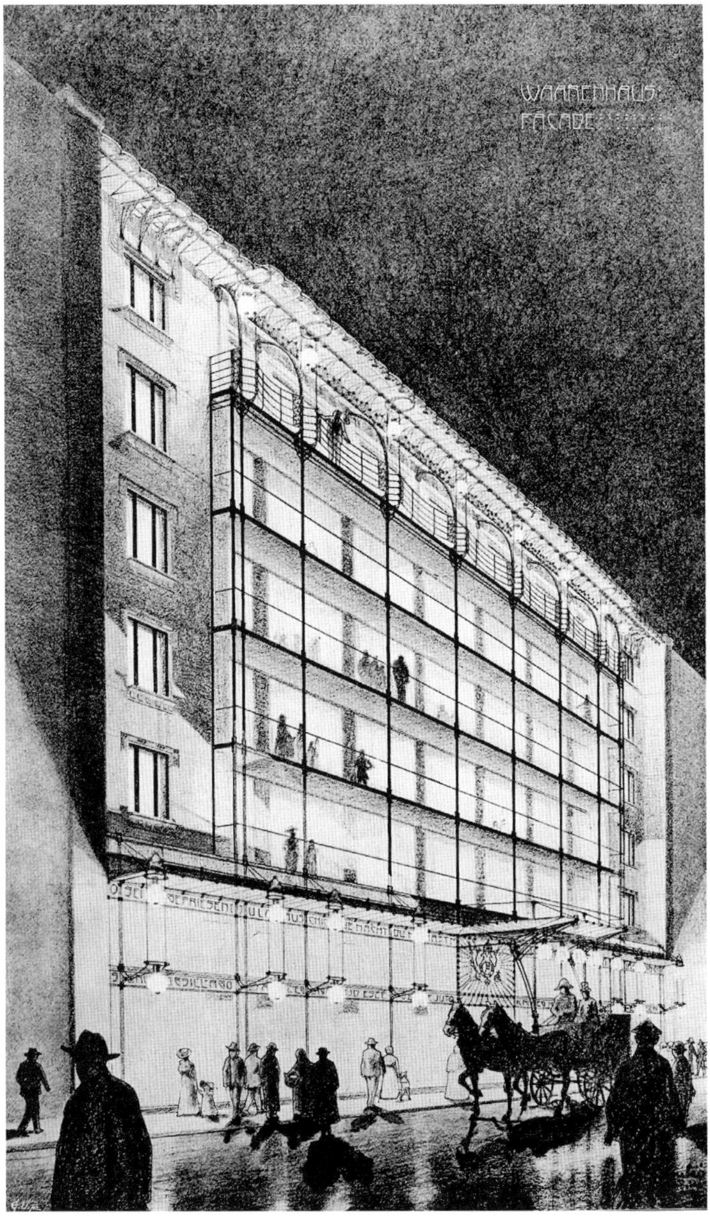

Figure I.6. Design for a department store, 1902, István Benkó-Medgyaszay. From *Der Architekt* 8 (1902).

bined the demand for aesthetic judgment with the certitude of scientific method. Photography provided a visible demonstration of how to make art that might also wield the incontrovertible authority of science. This is not to say that it was the only such disciplinary practice that influenced architects in the twentieth century, or that it had no precedents. The combination of science and art that emerged as a defining characteristic of photography at the end of the nineteenth century was also part of architecture's internal history since the Renaissance. But by 1890, the internal history of architecture no longer served the needs of the architectural profession in the way that it had throughout the nineteenth century. To meet the ongoing challenges of an industrialized society, architecture needed to be updated in conceptual as well as in practical terms. Whether the parameters of photography provided the source for a set of core ideas about architectural modernism or the same ideas emerged in both practices through concordance with deeper methodological drives from nineteenth-century European society is a question that does not affect the conclusions offered here; indeed, it may be a question for a different book. This one is concerned with the superficies—the place where connections between two media became most evident in external appearance—and the ways in which visible external appearance offered a reliable index for architectural meaning, or the ways in which it didn't.

PHOTOGRAPHY INTO BUILDING

The increase in published photographs of architecture intersected with artistic currents in Germany and Eastern Europe in the periods preceding and following World War I. Interest in abstraction filtered from adjacent practices such as painting, sculpture, and the performing arts into architecture during the same period. Cubism and Soviet modern art were particularly influential among architects, with figures such as Kazimir Malevich and El Lissitzky moving between art and architectural projects. As abstraction became a focus of art practices in other media, so were modern architects confronted by the challenge to create architectural abstraction—by no means an easy task, thanks to the concreteness and physicality of buildings. This challenge differed from and ran counter to the representational modalities of much nineteenth-century architecture, as briefly described above. In fact, the drive for architectural abstraction conflicted with many ideas on which modern architecture had been based, ideas such as structural rationalism and formal expression. In exploring the ramifications of abstraction for architecture, a group of modern architects attempted to expand known varieties of spatial experience in a limited number of experimental projects. These experiments resulted, paradoxically, in richly embodied multisensory environments, discussed in chapters 2 and 3. After 1933, these fledgling attempts to define architectural abstraction as intensified spatial experience were largely lost from view—in part because only some aspects of such multisensory architecture were retained in the black-and-white photographs that became ever more important for communicating ideas within Europe and to the rest of the world.

Architectural photographs of newly constructed buildings, in contrast to the spatial experiments described above, depicted abstraction in architecture in the terms provided by black-and-white photography: as a matter of pictorial composition, geometry, lack of color, and absence of context. The aesthetic offering provided by photographs replaced multisensory architectural investigations of abstraction that had been simmering throughout the second half of the Weimar years in buildings such as Mies's famous pavilion in Barcelona (1929) and El Lissitzky's Abstrakt Kabinett (1927) in Hannover.[26] Photography played a critical role in communicating the idea of an abstract architecture to audiences with the means available to the photograph—not those present in the building. In the process, the photograph helped make modern architecture adequate to its own cultural moment—despite the losses that accompanied the substitution of photographic abstraction for earlier, short-lived experiments in a manner of architectural "abstraction." Photographs of interwar modernism were active agents in constructing ideas about modern architecture for distant sites, including the United States after World War II. Abstract architecture worked precisely against the abstraction of the photographic image, by using imaging strategies in conjunction with other sensory inputs in three dimensions, bringing them into the world in which physical forces acted on the material stuff of building.

Banham noted similarities between photography and architecture in the passage quoted at the beginning of this chapter. Photographs resulted from a scientific procedure involving chemical processes. They also provided a new way of seeing the world that was described in aesthetic and narrative terms—and both aspects of photography were evident from the beginning.[27] While the scientific basis of photography was accepted from the outset, the status of the photograph as aesthetic product or mythmaker was initially contested. Practitioners of neither the fine nor the literary arts initially endorsed the new medium unilaterally. Despite this, photography combined science and aesthetics in a way that echoes in the history and theory of architecture. But if architects and theorists of modern architecture adopted the hybrid model of science and aesthetics that also governed photography, we can at least ask whether it was in emulation or simply because both photography and modern architecture shared a common nineteenth-century frame of reference.[28] It is likely that their status between fine and applied art ensured the need to draw upon both disciplinary frameworks. Recent scholarship on the history of objectivity in science underpins this point.[29] But connections between photography and architecture, while they may rest on deep foundations of knowledge practices founded during the Enlightenment, were also manifest in the most superficial ways. Within the day-to-day operations of two media that were closely interrelated from the first invention of photography, common concerns did not need to travel abstractly through the channels of nineteenth-century science. The surfaces of photographic images and the surfaces of articulated building masses shared many common representational concerns that were important to the degree that they were self-evident. And while architectural theorists were steeped in Enlightenment thought, the audiences for buildings were not uniformly so. Instead, they were mostly equipped with seeing eyes and walking feet. Many of those who constituted architecture's publics were more concerned with visible appearance and bodily experience than they were with historical underpinnings.

VISIBLE APPEARANCE

Despite the effort to affiliate architecture with space, material, and experience, the strain of modernism under scrutiny here placed a premium on the appearance of things, and on photographs as they trafficked that appearance. The question of how appearance (whether of buildings or their images) reflected architectural "essence" was not easily answered, however, although it had been central to architectural debate for some time. Photography merely brings attention to an issue that troubled architecture with particular intensity after frame construction began to remove tectonic indicators from building facades. Just as Schinkel created the appearance of stone construction even when he had to use plaster or stucco to imitate its presence, so did later modernists follow his example, opting for the appearance of new constructional realities even when they had to be simulated.

Tension between the core of constructional fabric or conceptual idea and the shell of external appearance was fundamental to debates about modernism. These concerned photography insofar as the medium's own evidentiary aspect implied some correspondence between visible appearance and the identity of an object. For some modern architects, the appearance of truth in the external form (the "image") of a building was frequently more important than how it might be gained. Many saw the problem of construction as merely a logistical step toward the realization of the designed image. Construction was circumstantial in light of the ever-accelerating pace of technical evolution and technological improvement. Photography thus became an essential adjunct to the presentation of new formal and constructional ideas regardless of tectonic realities; photographs appeared to document constructions, but the appearance could not be verified, at least not within the framework of information exchange in which photographs were presented and consumed.

As the twentieth century advanced, the accelerating use of photography for the dissemination of ideas about architecture produced increasingly ambivalent responses among professional architects. While they needed photography to advance their practices, they were also committed to distinguishing their product (architecture) from its vehicle of communication (photography). This reflects architects' thinking about medium specificity; it also follows a basic tenet of successful markets in capitalism: that the product (mass-produced though it may be) is best marketed as being uniquely suited to the need it addresses, a need that cannot be satisfied by any other good. Architects maintained their control over architectural products and their market by downplaying the importance of photography and photographers in terms of architectural representation, at the same time valuing photographers' skill in monetary terms that led to the establishment of a substantial professional subspecialty well before World War II. By emphasizing the architectural qualities that photographs were unable to communicate, architects could point to the unique medium of their discipline. Thus the "spin" that accompanied commercial photography of architecture ran counter to Walter Benjamin's notion of aura diminishing in proportion to the growth of mechanical reproduction. Commercial photographs of architecture were accompanied by text and captioning that helped enhance the cult status of the buildings represented by offering photographs as visible tokens of invisible riches to be gleaned only through direct experience. This effect partly reflected the need to ensure architecture's market niche in relation to both commercial and cultural capital.

Among other criticisms, modern architects often disparaged photography because it failed to account for what were arguably defining characteristics (or the specific medium) of modern architecture: the crafting of space, the confrontation with material, the display of structure through expressive construction. How might architecture survive in a media-directed society, when the chief instrument of information transmission evacuated the very qualities that distinguished architecture from other art practices? Books and journal articles are filled with resentment for the very medium that made architectural work globally portable in the first place. In these accounts, photography is often charged and convicted in one breath; accused of pretending to the status of true representation, it is pronounced guilty as charged, as a medium capable only of approximating architectural effects, not of representing them with fidelity. The same sorts of conversations recurred throughout the history of twentieth-century photography; they recur even today, amplified, if anything, by the digital age.[30] The complaints hinge on the consequences of translating three dimensions into two—and thus relate to other recurrent debates about representation from antiquity to the present. They result partly from the conflation of one image with another: the image that is the building differs in kind from the image that is an architectural photograph. But as they had done before, architects used the distance between photographs and buildings to strategic advantage. The flexibility of photographic representation and reception allowed modern architecture to settle anywhere, equally at home in any location.[31]

An opposition has been presented in the passages above. Photographic architecture, I have suggested, subtends two major topics: architectural photography and photographic influences in building design and execution. The former served a number of purposes but was also a means for importing pictorial abstraction into thinking about building. The latter included a variety of experiments in the possible interplay between space and image, enriching the modes of architectural experience in relation to interiors and urban space. An opposition between architectural photography and new constructive practices in building underlies the chapters that follow. But the investigation is precisely that: any easy opposition will be confounded as many times as it is confirmed in the pages ahead, as the two forms of photographic architecture collude in new spatial products and new representations—indeed, as clear boundaries between them disappear and reappear. The opposition merely offers a dialectic within which the book unfolds, a structure for the investigations that follow rather than an end point to the analysis. The two streams do not remain separated; architectural photography and photographic effects in building acted upon one another in mutually constitutive ways, moving seamlessly between raw visibility and the relay of ideas associated with appearance, and making photographs testify to that which could not be seen but only imagined.[32]

This book narrates a relationship between one strand of modern architecture and its chief public interface over the period in which magazines and books were the main instruments of storytelling (present and past) in architecture. It is unevenly staged, by intention. The early chapters sketch the murky beginnings of the relationship as pioneered by those who first used photographs to erect new analytical models for architecture: architectural historians and theorists. The middle chapters deal in greater detail with the blossoming of the relationship in synergies (functional and dysfunctional) between buildings and photographs in Germany between the two world wars. The later chapters, faced with the implosion of continental Europe and the related explosion of architecture and its pictures after the second of these wars, glance off some important, diagnostic episodes in the later stages of the relationship. These unfolded just before the relationship between architecture and photography gave way to new synergies between digitally fabricated images and digitally fabricated building designs (and now, more recently, digitally fabricated buildings). Much more could be written to round out the narrative presented here. But it is my hope that this account includes just enough to make one historical trajectory clearer, and to allow the reader to pose the next set of questions that follow on from this material.

PART I ARCHITECTURE AFTER PHOTOGRAPHY

An observation of image architecture, or depicted architecture, necessarily leads into an intermedial zone of art. Influences from one branch of the fine arts, architecture, can be detected on another, painting. This observation also shows how the reverse may be true—relationships appear that lead from painted architecture to realized buildings developed from them. . . .
Such projected architecture is realized "unhindered by thoughts of the impossibility of their execution" (J. Burckhardt).

—PAUL ZUCKER,
SPATIAL REPRESENTATION AND PICTORIAL ARCHITECTURE IN THE FLORENTINE QUATTROCENTO

1. *BILDARCHITEKTUREN*

ARCHITECTURAL SURFACE, CIRCA 1914

What roles did the mass-produced photographic image play in the study, practice and presentation of architecture in the age of photography, and since? To address this question, we might turn to the beginning of the twentieth century, when an early interaction between photographic mass media and buildings can be identified in two different contexts that allow the arguments of this book to commence. One of these is dealt with in this chapter; the other heads the second part of the book.

Commercial photography of architecture emerged in the wake of photographic mass printing, altering the specialized genre of architectural photography that had unofficially existed since Nicéphore Niépce and William Henry Fox Talbot first captured buildings in early photographic images. A change in the character of architectural photographers, from highly skilled but rather arcane documentarians into commercial service providers, around the turn of the century is significant, but should not be oversold. Photographers of all sorts were pressured by the demands of markets, as François Brunet and Robin Kelsey have shown.[1] Nevertheless, the architectural photographer in the twentieth century did respond to somewhat different pressures from those experienced earlier, and this changed the way that two-dimensional media showcased buildings, as well as changing audience response. The most wide-reaching of these changes were inaugurated by the mass-printed images that appeared in architectural publications as early as 1881, but with greater frequency after 1895. The first way in which architectural practice and architectural photography interacted occurred in commercial advertising imagery, whether disguised by the format of the architectural monograph or scholarly article or not. This development underpins part II of the present book; its earliest development is surveyed in chapter 4.

The second way in which the two media interacted was less fraught with tension between art and commerce and more obviously tied to new creative developments in practice and academic study. It prompts the first of a series of historiographical interjections that recur in this narrative, in which scholars of architecture studied intermediality early in the twentieth-century history of architecture. Their reflections are often incisive, appearing in print in a variety of sites, from newspapers to books. Whether their words were read and understood by practitioners of architecture or those training future professionals in the field is less clear.

In the first fifteen years of the twentieth century, a group of young architectural historians grew interested in the phenomenon of *Bildarchitekturen*, or picture architecture. These historians explored the pictorial surface in architecture a short decade or so after the mass-printed photograph began to appear in journals and published monographs with regularity. A new pictorial consciousness related the appearance of photographic reproductions in studies on architecture to the content of study itself: the pictorial surfaces of buildings (Figure 1.1). At the same time, pictures and texts related to ongoing experiments with architectural surface in new building, through shared source material and architectural discourse, and thanks to the new prominence of frame construction methods that left facades free to host images rather than display tectonic necessities. The synergy between architects and historians at this time suggests a model of activist history that also motivates this study.

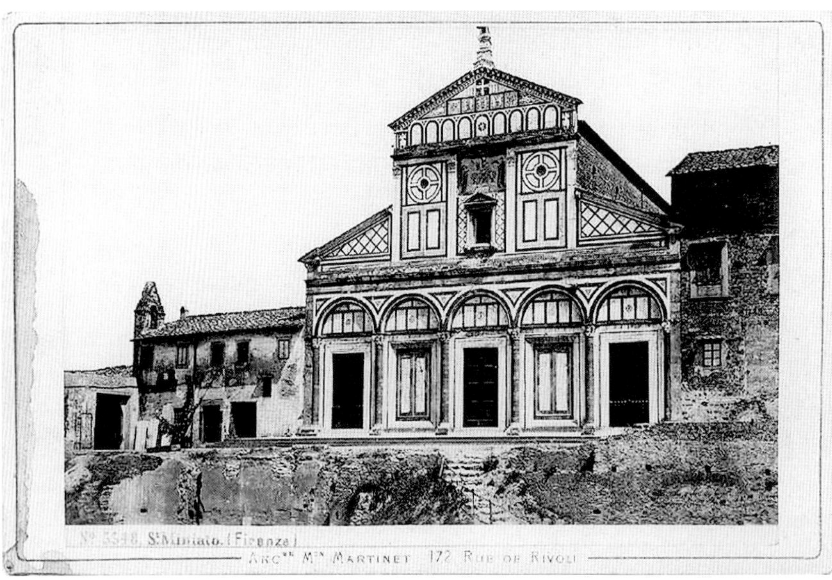

Figure 1.1. San Miniato al Monte, Florence, Italy, twelfth century or later. Photograph: Giorgio Sommer (1834–1914).

The early flirtation between photographic mass media and buildings at the beginning of the twentieth century launched a lasting relationship. Why would one ask questions of it now? What more is to be gained by asking such questions historically, at a moment when the notion of "kissing architecture" presents intermediality as a contemporary mandate?[2] The purpose of tracing a historical arc here (at least back to the eve of the 1914 war) is to suggest that intermediality in architecture (subtending images transferred to or reflected on building surfaces, and published photographs of architecture) had one effect once photographs allowed buildings to be seen in new ways, and that it has a different effect today. Originally a phenomenon of the late nineteenth and early twentieth centuries, the persistence of photographic architecture now is status quo or even nostalgic, rather than disruptive, and this is a consequential difference. Photographic-architectural intermediality in its initial appearance was calibrated by the invention of photography and then of mass printing, and punctuated by the traumatic history of the twentieth century, beginning with the Soviet Revolution and World War I. Buildings as giant picture surfaces, whether for still or moving images, summon a number of important disciplinary questions today—not necessarily because they are catalytic forces, but rather as witness to the long-standing and now habitual commodification of (consumer) desire itself. An artist such as Pipilotti Rist both critiques and enters into this relation with large-scale displays at MoMA and elsewhere. Despite widespread embrace of screen/image surface, however, the divide between screen experience and physical experience (largely following geopolitical and economic gradients) is perhaps more dramatic than ever before, even as it is also reframed by the ever-increasing interpenetration of one form into the other, at least for a significant percentage of the public.[3] Sylvia Lavin's theorization of architecture's mandates today is in productive tension with this history, which in turn recontextualizes current propositions about intermediality within the ongoing popularization or massification of culture over the *longue durée*, and the accompanying acceptance of protocols that were formerly subject to debate. Contemporary pictures in and of architecture tend to be much larger and more numerous than earlier ones. This upshift in modes of spectatorship shifts the address of photoreproductive images from individuals to groups, enhancing (one hopes) visual literacy in the present, even as it enforces the relay effects of photographic images overall.

A NOTE ON ARCHITECTURAL SURFACE AND FRAME CONSTRUCTION

The structural frame in metal or concrete released architectural surfaces from structural constraints in the last two decades of the nineteenth century. Building facades no longer had to hold up floor joists and roof beams. Rather, facades might hang from the structural cages of metal (or concrete) with which high-rise buildings began to be constructed at this time. This became a conceptual issue as much as a constructional one for modern architects. It also coincided with the appearance of the mass-printed photograph, as noted above. Photographs of buildings appeared in the mass media as architects began to use facades as large-scale pictures without structural restrictions—or, more important, without the obligation to represent structure.[4] Distinct and separate, architectural surfaces and mass-printed photographs of buildings were related nevertheless by the professional practice of architecture. Architects explored new facade technologies even as they also worked to remain competitive under changing advertising and market conditions that required extensive photography of their work. As the twentieth century unfolded, the complex fictions devised by nineteenth-century theorists such as Gottfried Semper to historicize facades and ornamental building surfaces might be abandoned. As building facades were increasingly freed of conventional tectonic restrictions, they began to be used for a broader set of representational tasks. This historical circumstance underpins the discussion in this chapter.

The development of the steel frame for multistory construction has been analyzed by successive generations of architectural historians. Recent publications have placed primary texts and secondary analysis at historians' disposal, revealing that the conceptual underpinnings of metallic frame architecture developed alongside the technology itself.[5] The development of a new way of building evolved in conjunction with new ways of thinking about the past.[6] This research has clarified the extent to which the development of a new structural system also required the development of new building envelopes and new theories to account for both structure and skin.

Frame construction created the conditions under which one kind of photographic architecture could come into being in the 1920s, by allowing building facades to become picture surfaces that did not necessarily carry structural loads. The degree to which architects were able to exploit this potential varied significantly and grew slowly over the next decades. Looking back in time, we might note that buildings had been used as picture surfaces throughout the history of architecture; Renaissance facades, for example, included ornamental pictures, as did nineteenth-century buildings. How did these differ from the metallic or concrete frame buildings of the early twentieth century? A superficial historical comparison helps clarify the distinction and previews buildings dealt with more fully below, pending a fuller etiology of this condition.

The differences between the facade of a pre-Renaissance building such as San Miniato al Monte (eleventh to twelfth centuries) in Florence (Figure 1.1) and a photograph of Mies's (1886–1969) Glass Skyscraper of 1922 in a large glass model

(Figure 7.4) appear obvious at first glance. First, San Miniato's front facade is at least partially load-bearing; its inlaid marble surface masks and is supported by masonry behind, where the Glass Skyscraper was conceived with no exterior bearing wall whatsoever and was to have been supported on an array of columns distributed throughout the floor plate. Second, the depths of the facades themselves differ. The sectional articulation of frieze courses and columns at San Miniato contrasts with the apparent flatness of the glass facade. Third, while both facades have an ornamental aspect, in that they create pictures on surfaces, the sources of their ornament differ radically. The Florentine building is covered in stylized geometric and curvilinear ornament inlaid in varied tones of marble; the Glass Skyscraper would have been ornamented by the reflections of sky, city, and city dwellers in a continuously changing array of reflections overlaid on the occupants of the offices visible through the glass facade. Both buildings presuppose that ornament emerges from other conditions of construction, particularly building materials. Not applied to finish off a masonry shell and render it adequate to its context, however, the skin of the Glass Skyscraper was to be ornamented by events outside itself, yet intrinsic to the interaction among construction material, method of building, and site. The privileging of qualities intrinsic to building material became a recurrent theme in modernist aesthetics in architecture; we will find it recurring in tension with its opposite—dematerialized form—in the pages ahead.

Chronologically closer to the Glass Skyscraper is the Majolica House of 1898–99 by Otto Wagner (1841–1918) in Vienna. Wagner's facade is covered in floral ornament of glazed colored tile under an overhanging cornice and a running series of lion's-head ornaments. As at San Miniato, ornament is symmetrical around a central axis running invisibly down the centerline of the facade. It is a load-bearing masonry building that comprises a single large-scale picture on its main street facade, despite the articulation of ornamental motifs around the rhythm of the windows, and it is notably flatter than most buildings built in Vienna at the time, even by Wagner himself. Wagner's facade is pictorial, and while little about it specifically recalls photography as a possible source for the architect's ideas, nevertheless it marks a transition between conventional masonry construction and the incipient changes made possible by the structural frame. Earlier buildings, and a later one at Neustiftgasse 40, made this emergent structural condition even more clear, as did Wagner's Post Office Savings Bank (1904–6). Perhaps most striking for its early date was a building by Wagner's former employee Max Fabiani. His Portois and Fix Building (1899–1900) in Vienna was fronted by a flat surface of glass ceramic tile decorated with an abstract pattern. Wagner's similar experiments in plate-glass facades occurred in at least two buildings: Warenhaus Neumann in the Kärntner Strasse and the Ankerhaus am Graben (both 1895), both in Vienna. Both buildings have plate-glass facades on the first two levels; above this the walls were built of conventional masonry supported by their metallic frames.[7] The Glass Skyscraper points to a new aspect of building in modernity, however, in which the architect deploys the mutable conditions of a site as part of a building design, complete with chance and accidental event. The Glass Skyscraper may be the closest we get to Dada architecture, and it was, in its day, disruptive of accepted norms.[8]

The point of this comparison is not to heighten the contrast between medieval and modern buildings, but rather to highlight particular qualities of twentieth-century design that differentiate its modes from earlier ones. Technological factors such as the steel frame and the development of plate-glass wall surfaces certainly played a major role in this differentiation. The claim put forward here, however, is that technological changes to the building industry joined with alterations to the visual language of contemporary society to produce a new set of expectations for buildings. Photography (and subsequently film) was essential to those alterations, but even more significant was its proliferation and distribution through the popular and professional presses. Photographs were not just new sorts of images—they also became available in unprecedented quantities at this time. Plate glass such as that projected for the Glass Skyscraper allowed a similar sort of visual vocabulary to that of photographs and cinematic imagery to also populate architectural surfaces. And yet plate glass provides only one of many ways that new pictorial modes altered the field of expectations for modern buildings. Others are discussed throughout this chapter and the chapters to follow; these too created the disruptions that we associate with the very notion of modernity.

PICTORIAL FACADES AND ARCHITECTURAL HISTORY

The relationship between photography and architecture quickened when photographs of buildings began to be found readily in newspapers, journals, and books and were no longer singular, hand-produced deposits of silver emulsion on thick paper. Books that featured photographs interleaved with text in the 1880s gave way to the more critical collation of printing plate and halftone image around 1895. From 1889, when Adolph Goldschmidt interleaved plates of printed photographs in his study of medieval artists from Lübeck, and generally during the years preceding the war of 1914–18, photography (and then film) began to alter the modalities of art history substantially.[9] By the beginning of the war, photographs had altered the research modes of historians of buildings as well as historians of painting and sculpture. The close ties between practice and the academic study of architecture that existed in Germany before World War I also linked architectural photography, new building, and architectural history, revealing topics of concern for practitioners within historical accounts. How then did a new means of communicating information about buildings in widespread printed formats influence the study of architecture? To answer that question, a digression into Weimar developments sets the stage.

Siegfried Kracauer's essay on Berlin's neobaroque movie palaces, "Cult of Distraction," appeared in Kracauer's *Frankfurter Zeitung* column long after World War I in 1926.[10] It introduces this subject in more detail. The essay focused not on architecture but on the placement of the screens in film palaces of the 1920s.[11] It helps illuminate how projected images were understood at the time. In "Cult of Distraction" the author reflected on optical immersion in projected mobile images rather than still ones. The conjuncture of architecture and screen image in the movie palace may have impressed Kracauer both as a journalist and as an architect, albeit a lapsed one. In any case, in commenting on this conjuncture, his essay considers the relation of flat images to three-dimensional construction.

In "Cult of Distraction," Kracauer described the "motley sequence of externalities" that accompanied film projection in his day, referring to the abundance of architectural ornament and the supplement of musical performance and colored lights in movie palaces (Figure 1.2). He recommended that ornamental detail be removed from the interior of the movie palace along with other distracting ancillary sensory stimuli. For Kracauer, the ancillary aspects of the film palace were pure distraction: "Like *life buoys*, the refractions of the spotlights and the musical accompaniment keep the spectator above water. The penchant for distraction demands and finds an answer in the display of pure externality." He went on to liken the distracted experience found in movie palaces to the increase in mass media with which contemporary city dwellers were bombarded: "Hence the irrefutable tendency, particularly in Berlin, to turn all forms of entertainment into revues and, parallel with this tendency, the increasing number of illustrations in the daily press and in periodical publications." Instead, Kracauer advocated for a blank interior where the visual spectacle could unfold in front of the viewer without interruption. The intensity of pure opticality might then hurtle the viewer into "the abyss" of a fully disembodied yet communal experience of optical immersion. Kracauer saw the purification of the movie palace interior not as a necessary or logical development of the cinema type but seemingly as a means by which a population might come to terms with its own urban condition of atomy yet also see itself as a community of similar subjects. He was also proposing a soundless, optically intense engagement in film viewing. He was, in effect, refunctioning existing empathy theory for film viewing, differing notably from empathy theorists such as Heinrich Wölfflin. Kracauer described a communal mass-cultural experience, not a singular high-art one.

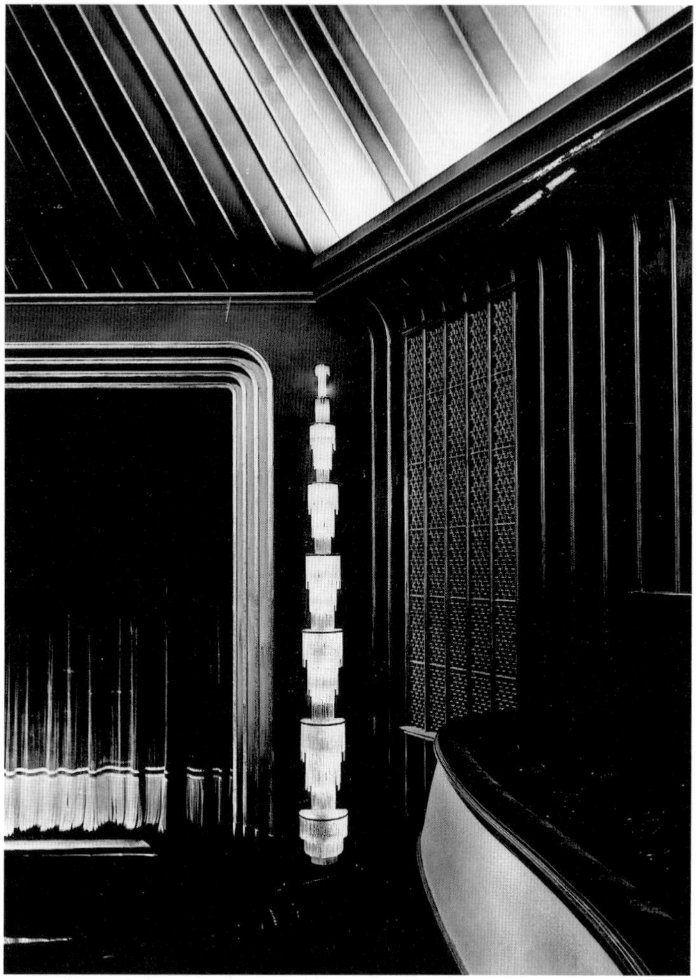

Figure 1.2. Capitol Theater, Berlin. Design: Hans Poelzig (1869–1936). From Paul Zucker, *Theater und Lichtspielhäuser* (Berlin: Wasmuth, 1926), 135. Photograph: Architekturmuseum TU Berlin, inventory number F 1669.

Here Kracauer's contribution to architectural intermediality becomes more apparent. He noted that the great potential of film was reduced, watered-down, by the viewing conditions in movie palaces:

> The *two-dimensionality* of film produces the illusion of the physical world without any need for supplementation. But if scenes of real physicality are nevertheless displayed alongside the movie, the latter recedes into the flat surface and the deception is exposed. The proximity of action that has spatial depth destroys the spatiality of what is shown on the screen. By its very existence, film demands that the world it reflects be the only one; it should be wrested from every three-dimensional surrounding, or it will fail as an illusion.[12]

The intensity of the filmic experience is enhanced by Kracauer's desire to remove architecture from the theater. The spectacle projected on the film screen, he suggested, becomes properly activated through dramatic contrast on the other side of the screen. Optical fullness would be activated by sensory vacuum in the auditorium.

These claims relate back to an earlier period of Kracauer's formation with which this chapter is largely concerned, when he himself was still tied to the world of professional architectural practice and historical study. In addition to obliquely referencing empathy theory, the screen experience hinted at in "Cult of Distraction" reflects Alois Riegl's distinction between haptic and optic perception, where the viewer experiences a range of effects within the limits of two-dimensional cognition. "Cult of Distraction" suggested that architecture was both the frame and the mediator of immersive experience—equally reflecting Riegl's distinction between frame and fill. Kracauer's formation as an architectural historian illuminates his idea of optical immersion and wider interest in the possible roles of architectural surfaces *as surfaces of immersion*, into which I will dip briefly now.

Kracauer was one of a group of young architectural historians who studied building surfaces in architecture, in graphic design, and in urban morphology, and who were trained just before the war of 1914–18. These young historians focused on different kinds of material objects, from cities to buildings to two-dimensional representations and surface applications. Students of nineteenth-century scholars such as Goldschmidt, Karl Frey, Wölfflin, and Richard Borrmann, they also played significant roles in twentieth-century architecture and cultural studies. They all extended the legacy of Riegl in the investigation of surface application and expression, a legacy that was particularly strong in the wake of Wilhelm Worringer's influential *Abstraction and Empathy* of 1908.[13] These young historians are assembled here in relation to a thematic link connecting their first major research projects—the link of architectural surface. This means that ornamental surfaces, representational surfaces, and the surfaces of building masses are gathered into one enclosure for the purposes of historical comparison here.

Walter Curt Behrendt, the later editor of *Die Form*, studied architectural surface at the urban scale, as a space-defining plane in city development. He published his dissertation on the urban street facade, "The Unified Street Facade in City Building" in 1911.[14] The next year, Adolf Behne (1885–1948) published his dissertation on marble inlay in medieval Italian churches (Figure 1.3), as the medieval architectural historian Paul Frankl (1878–1962) published a book on painted glass surfaces in south German architecture of the fifteenth century, from a dissertation defended in 1910.[15] Also in 1912, Paul Zucker (1888–1971) completed his dissertation on the spatial effects of perspectival wall painting from the Florentine Quattrocento and published two books, the second an expanded version of his dissertation.[16] Walter Müller-Wulckow (1886–1964), later editor of the popular Blauen Bücher

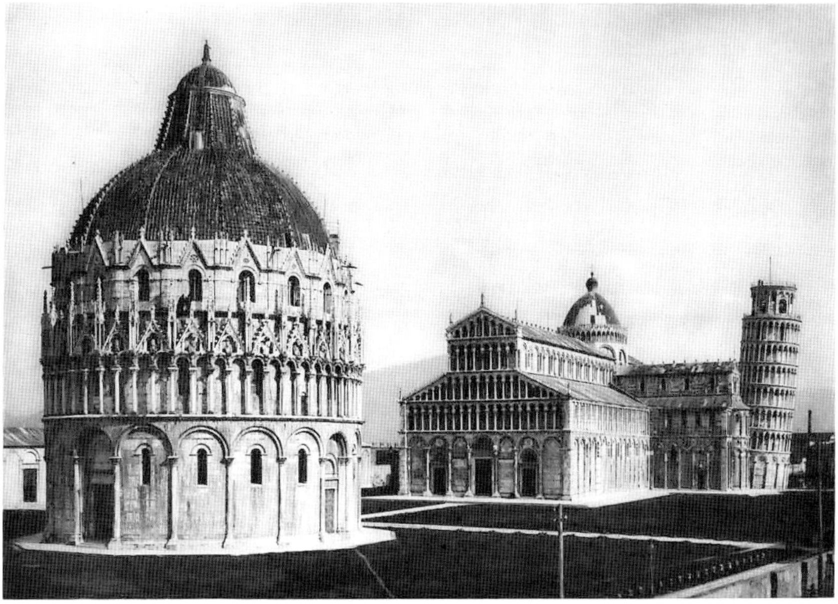

Figure 1.3. Duomo, Pisa, Italy. From I. B. Supino (1858–1940), *Arte pisana* (Florence: Fratelli Alinari, 1904).

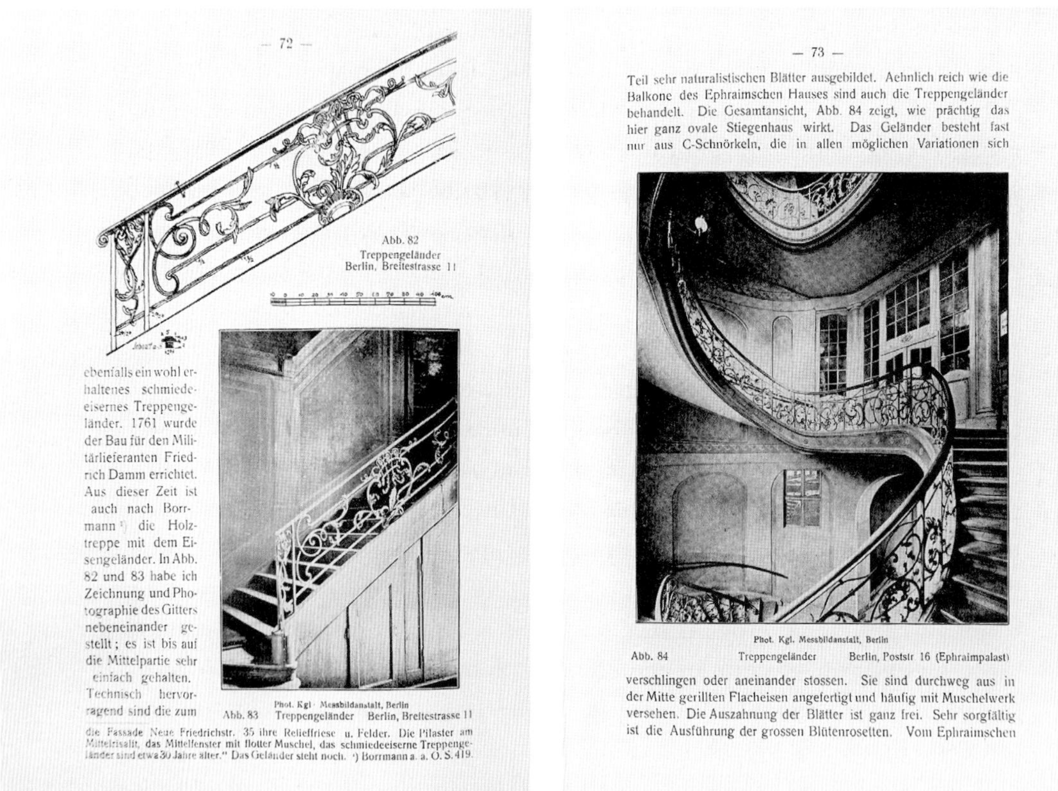

— 72 —

Abb. 82
Treppengeländer
Berlin, Breitestrasse 11

ebenfalls ein wohl erhaltenes schmiedeeisernes Treppengeländer. 1761 wurde der Bau für den Militärlieferanten Friedrich Damm errichtet. Aus dieser Zeit ist auch nach Borrmann[1]) die Holztreppe mit dem Eisengeländer. In Abb. 82 und 83 habe ich Zeichnung und Photographie des Gitters nebeneinander gestellt; es ist bis auf die Mittelpartie sehr einfach gehalten. Technisch hervorragend sind die zum

Phot. Kgl· Messbildanstalt, Berlin
Abb. 83 Treppengeländer Berlin, Breitestrasse 11

die Fassade Neue Friedrichstr. 35 ihre Relieffriese u. Felder. Die Pilaster am Mittelrisalit, das Mittelfenster mit flotter Muschel, das schmiedeeiserne Treppengeländer sind etwa 30 Jahre älter." Das Geländer steht noch. [1]) Borrmann a. a. O. S. 419.

— 73 —

Teil sehr naturalistischen Blätter ausgebildet. Aehnlich reich wie die Balkone des Ephraimschen Hauses sind auch die Treppengeländer behandelt. Die Gesamtansicht, Abb. 84 zeigt, wie prächtig das hier ganz ovale Stiegenhaus wirkt. Das Geländer besteht fast nur aus C-Schnörkeln, die in allen möglichen Variationen sich

Phot. Kgl. Messbildanstalt, Berlin
Abb. 84 Treppengeländer Berlin, Poststr 16 (Ephraimpalast)

verschlingen oder aneinander stossen. Sie sind durchweg aus in der Mitte gerillten Flacheisen angefertigt und häufig mit Muschelwerk versehen. Die Auszahnung der Blätter ist ganz frei. Sehr sorgfältig ist die Ausführung der grossen Blütenrosetten. Vom Ephraimschen

Figure 1.4. Siegfried Kracauer, *Die Entwicklung der Schmiedekunst in Berlin, Potsdam und einigen Städten der Mark vom 17. Jahrhundert bis zum Beginn des 19. Jahrhunderts* (Berlin: Gebrüder Mann, 1997 [1915]), 72–73.

series, wrote a dissertation on "the construction of images of architecture in German graphic art of the fifteenth century" in 1911; it was published in 1914.[17] Kracauer's own book, on baroque wrought-iron ornamented surfaces in Brandenburg and Berlin, appeared in 1915 from a dissertation completed the year before (Figure 1.4). Zucker researched pictures on architecture, Behne representational surfaces of buildings, Behrendt space-defining surfaces at the urban scale, Frankl ephemeral architectural surfaces, and Müller-Wulckow graphic depictions of architecture (Figure 1.5).

These works divide into two groups: studies of building surfaces and studies of the representation of architecture in two dimensions. These are by no means the same, but they share certain concerns. Intermediality is the term that might unite this body of work today, but Zucker used a similar term, as seen in the epigraph to this chapter. In German, this is "*Zwischenland der Kunst.*"[18]

These six authors focused on pictorial or representational surfaces, ornamental surfaces, and mass-bounding/membranous surfaces. Some focus on graphic surfaces, some on the ephemerality of surface treatments. Because a focus on image surfaces on or in building—*Bildarchitektur*—is common to these early researches, we might explore how photography reflected a common set of concerns. Mapping contemporary preoccupations onto historical investigations, as Gottfried Semper had already done when (among other pursuits) he wrote a conceptual history of metallic frame construction in the mid-nineteenth century, these scholars used contemporary architecture as a guide to historical study in their earliest research, to limited effect. These are early studies, flawed as scholarly works but valuable as diagnostic devices. Among them, interest had shifted away from the investigation of ornament as an index of construction history or stylistic evolution, as explored by Semper and Riegl, to interest in surface representations that might, or might not, provide an index to anything at all—construction or style included—but that might serve another purpose altogether. Architectural representation (whether in books or on buildings) can be distinguished from the reality of building in a new way in these books—through surface appearance. As the mediatization of urban life unfolded around them, they used it to help frame historical questions. We might consider them early activist historians—writing optimistically "operative history," as Manfredo Tafuri later dubbed such practices.

Perhaps thanks to spatial theories of architectural form that came to dominate the history of architecture during the Weimar period and after, these kinds of investigations died out after 1918—and indeed, these scholars went on to do very different kinds of work. Architectural historians embraced spatially oriented studies, as in the work of Herman Sörgel, Sigfried Giedion, and Siegfried Ebeling, all building on the earlier spatial theory of August Schmarsow and others.[19] Among the many

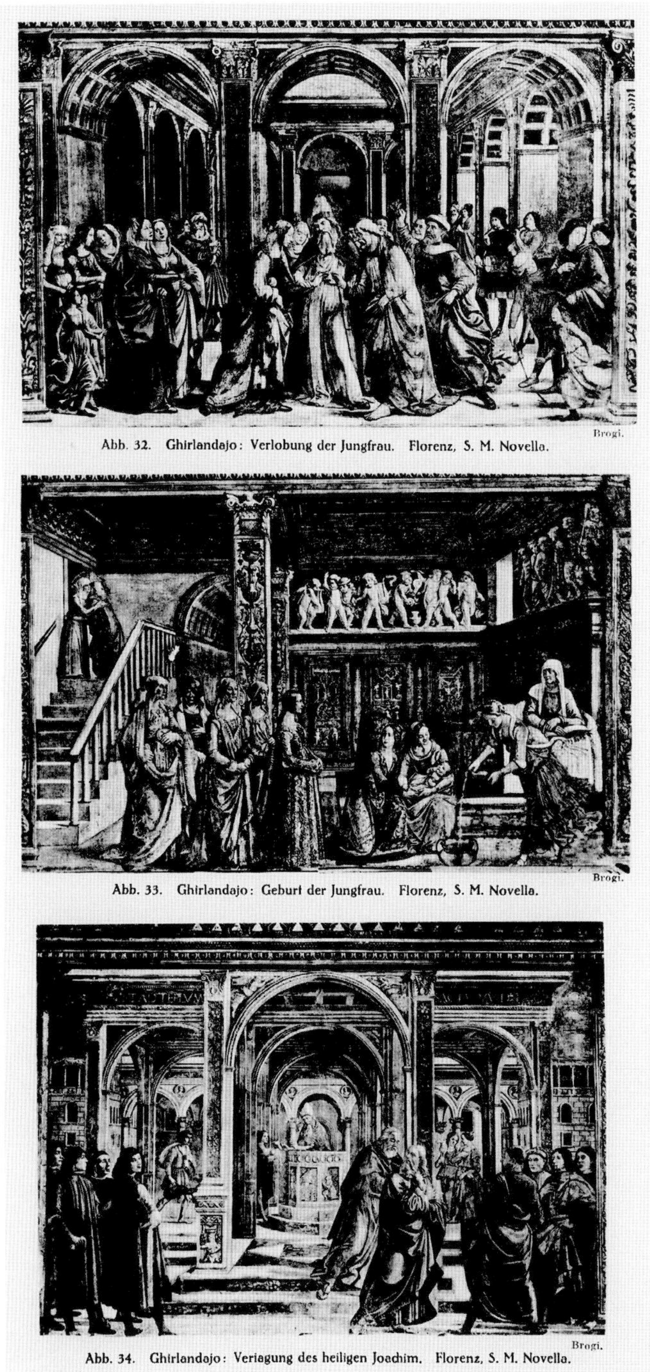

Figure 1.5. Plate x from Paul Zucker, *Raumdarstellung u. Bildarchitekturen bei den Florentiner Malern der ersten Hälfte des Quattrocento* (Leipzig: Klinkhardt & Biermann, 1912).

dissertations written in German-speaking lands at this time, these six can be affiliated thematically. But they are also united in another way: all of their authors later became prominent in fields affiliated with architecture—in history, theory, and publishing.[20] Their early focus on pictorial architectural surface appears to reflect the development of photography almost osmotically, conjuring a notion of intermedial architecture that is evident particularly in Zucker's writing. This early work alters the history of mass media and architecture, relocating photographic intermediality to the period before World War I.

A brief summary of three research studies exposes architectural and photographic correlates. Paul Zucker (1889–1971), a student of Borrmann at the Technische Hochschule in Berlin, completed a study of representations of space in Florentine painting that he expanded as *Raumdarstellung und Bildarchitekturen im Florentiner Quattrocento* and published in 1913. The book was illustrated with forty-one photographs arranged on separate plates that were bound in with the text (Figure 1.5). Wall painting and low-relief panels were the subjects, specifically murals that depicted spatial constructions on interior walls of churches through one-point perspective. Zucker first placed these spatial projections into a chronological stylistic framework and then analyzed how they affected cognition of their architectural surroundings (through the "rhythm" of the architecture depicted in the painting). He described his findings succinctly on three fronts: "The conquest of space through painting and relief, the rhythmicization [Rhythmisierung] of composition through the use of architectural settings, and finally the relationship of the represented architecture to real buildings and excavations of that time."[21] His goal as articulated in *Raumdarstellung* was to investigate a period when clearly defined formal or constructional goals ran up against technical constraints that could not be immediately overcome. His hypothesis: that such formal goals had been first explored in projected spatial representations, from which site they subsequently affected new building. By assembling a catalog of architectural painting (of architecture), Zucker posited a theory about the agency of flat images on the billboards of Renaissance interiors for future building. He did this in 1912–13.

Zucker was also interested in the psychology of perception and empathy theory, and he analyzed Florentine wall painting by considering how spatial projection worked with and altered spatial perception. Zucker described a recursive relationship between depicted architecture and the further development of new building. He began his dissertation with the words quoted in the epigraph to this chapter, cited more fully here:

> An observation of image architecture, or depicted architecture, necessarily leads into an intermedial zone of art. Influences from one branch of the fine arts, architecture, can be detected on another, painting. This observation also shows how the reverse may be true—relationships appear that lead from painted architecture to realized buildings developed from them. Critically speaking, the analysis of such a border condition is particularly fruitful, because projective developments appear there that are elsewhere impeded or precluded by technical considerations. The laws of statistics or budget shortfalls do not interrupt ideal intentions and creative principles; painted architecture appears more clearly than that which has been constructed. Such projected architecture is realized "unhindered by thoughts of the impossibility of their execution" (J. Burckhardt). . . . It is thus possible and probable that the characteristic inner distinguishing features of a style already express conditions that it is not yet capable of realizing fully in its own expressive form—that in a hybrid form a new anticipatory sense is already expressed, through which the boundaries between individual branches of art are blurred, and where new style characteristics develop first in the more "mobile" ['beweglichste'] manifestation.[22]

Zucker interprets painted images of architecture as the testing ground for new ideas. Although his notes are steeped in references to empathy (Lipps, Schmarsow, Wölfflin), his own interest turned toward a projective use for these pictures, away from the discourse of medium specificity that later became a hallmark of modernism. Zucker's words in 1912–13 anticipated Kracauer's comments on ideal conditions of visual perception that appeared more than a decade later; both were evidently invested in the future action that different sorts of images might impel in the viewer and in the interaction between media rather than their isolation by discipline or medium.

In exploring the architecture of painted murals, Zucker noted that tectonic representation becomes ornamental when depicted on a surface: "Just as a ground plan, by virtue of the tectonic laws embodied in it, can become ornamental in and of itself, so does the objectivity [Sachlichkeit] of spatial definition within a painting work the same way, that is, surrounding architectural elements become ornamental through the principle of equilibrium of the mechanical forces they embody." This static equilibrium Zucker denoted as "struktiv-ornamental," arguing that it then dictated the lines of action that can unfold within the narrative of the painting. Here he interpreted the architectural backdrop, in effect, as the primary compositional agent within the painting, but denoted it as ornamental thanks to the rhythm and regularity that it imposed on a surface—and the fact that its effects are purely visual. What represents a tectonic reality is in itself merely a visible ornamental effect.

Adolf Behne (1885–1948) completed his doctorate at the Friedrich-Wilhelms Universität Berlin in September 1912. Adolph Goldschmidt had arrived in Berlin in 1912 to replace Wölfflin when he left for Munich and was a reader for a dissertation that was probably supervised by Karl Frey. In his dissertation and first book on marble inlay in Tuscan architecture from the eleventh to the thirteenth centuries, Behne explored the relationship between surface treatment and structural expression. Titled *Der Inkrustationsstil in Toscana* and published in 1912, the book analyzed buildings revetted in ornamental marble, such as the Duomo at Pisa and San Miniato al Monte in Florence (Figure 1.1).

Behne began with the Pisan Duomo, where Near Eastern and Byzantine precedents could be traced in the marble inlay of the building's interior and exterior (Figure 1.3). These, he claimed, were organically designed and represented a new indigenous invention that borrowed and translated earlier models in a new context. In the words of Kai Gutschow, "Pisa's mosaics were 'organic' in their comprehensiveness, they were tectonic and haptic, and all the pieces were subordinated to a higher idea."[23] The schematic decoration of the exterior surface roughly corresponded with the building's structural reality, as much through the mechanics of construction as through any conscious representational program. But the purpose of the facade inlay was not to represent structural realities, but rather to sublate them into an ornamental representational program. The facade represented a structural reality that was beyond the view of the beholder.

Behne turned to marble inlay on Florentine buildings later in his book, where a markedly different decorative approach developed. Behne referred to the "complete cladding [Verkleidung] of the architecture" in a surface (Oberfläche) in which "a game" of geometric forms and pure abstraction was played out. The structure beneath was wholly hidden; no connection between structure and ornamental surface could be reliably made from the representational program of the facade. Rather,

> the dress [Kleid] that is laid over the architecture gives to a certain degree a substitute for the absent structure, marking the essential lines of construction through dark lines inlaid in white marble. . . . Nevertheless, it would be false to imagine that the inlay is ruled by the idea of showing the structure most clearly. The system that the decorator followed is much more purely decorative. It has to do with a game with geometric forms. . . . Horizontals, verticals, arches, diagonals are ordered in a purely abstract game with rectangles, triangles, rhomboids.[24]

The inlaid facade of the Florence Baptistery narrativizes constructional forces on a flat surface. In the case of San Miniato: "The architecture is flat throughout. The end gable shows not the slightest deviation from an even surface. The archivolts, the string courses, the window frames are without any profile. The large fields of the intercolumniations are smooth. In short, the architecture declares itself in its particularity through color alone."[25] Like the Baptistery exterior, but unlike the Pisan examples, this architecture is oriented to surface appearance rather than stylized representation of construction.

In noting that there was no direct correspondence between structure and surface cladding in Florentine buildings, Behne emphasized instead a fictional correspondence between structural forces acting beneath the skin and markings on the skin. He emphasized the representational role of architectural surface in tandem with the independence of skin from structure. Figural representation belonged to the task of art itself, to the identification and development of the *Kunstwollen* of a particular era; its relationship to material reality was, in this case, purely secondary.

Taking up a central issue in the development of modern architecture, Behne showed how the physical delamination of exterior cladding from structure allowed buildings to take on more aggressively representational roles. The narratives they related might float free from building tectonics. In doing so, they contravened the principles of structural rationalism that were to become foundational in nineteenth-century architectural theory. At the turn of the century, German-speaking architects began to question whether, or how, structure should be mirrored or represented on building exteriors, so that the outside told the story of the building's structural performance, as Eugène-Emmanuel Viollet-le-Duc had instructed. Different iterations of this debate played out over the course of the late nineteenth and early twentieth centuries, as architects attempted to determine the degree to which a building's representation and its static realities might or should be connected.[26]

As he was writing his dissertation, Behne was already also writing criticism, relating art historical study to a popular readership. His later work focused on contemporary architecture. And indeed, as he was researching Tuscan marble inlay, he wrote an article about Peter Behrens's design for the crematorium at Hagen (1905–8) (Figure 1.6).[27] Behne's marble study was in dialogue with Behrens's new use of an old technique: marble decorative cladding or incrustation that stylized a nominal tectonic diagram in surface treatment. Behne explored antecedents of a revival style that had become popular just after the turn of the century. His continuing engagement with contemporary art and architecture illustrate interests that were consistently wider than art historical. The marble study gave way to criticism of twentieth-century architecture: we see here Behne's interest in the prehistory of a present condition.

To conclude we might turn to Kracauer. His later 1920s cultural commentaries reflected ambivalence about architectural ornament and his interest in ephemeral surface and its optical effects. But Kracauer's dissertation on baroque wrought-iron architectural ornament already contained an approach to the articulated ornamental surface.[28] This little-known book may narrate his first optical encounter with architectural surfaces. His later writing on glass surfaces creates an interesting dialogue with this earlier analysis of ornamental fields—not by repeating the same ideas, but through a shared focus on the way in which marks fill and animate a sheetlike or planar surface.[29] We can juxtapose the early sublimation of ornamental surface here with his later comments on the film palace and glass curtain walls.[30]

Kracauer published his dissertation in 1915 under the supervision of Richard Borrmann.[31] Titled *Die Entwicklung der Schmiedekunst in Berlin, Potsdam und einigen Städten der Mark vom 17. Jahrhundert bis zum Beginn des 19. Jahrhunderts* (The development of the art of forging in Berlin, Potsdam and some cities of the mark from the seventeenth century to the beginning of the nineteenth century), it contained studies of balcony railings, gates, fences, lampposts, grave markers, signage brackets and frames, and window grilles (many carefully drawn by the author) (Figure 1.4).[32] Kracauer confined his examples from architectural interiors to lobbies or transitional spaces such as stairways, as if he were gradually backing

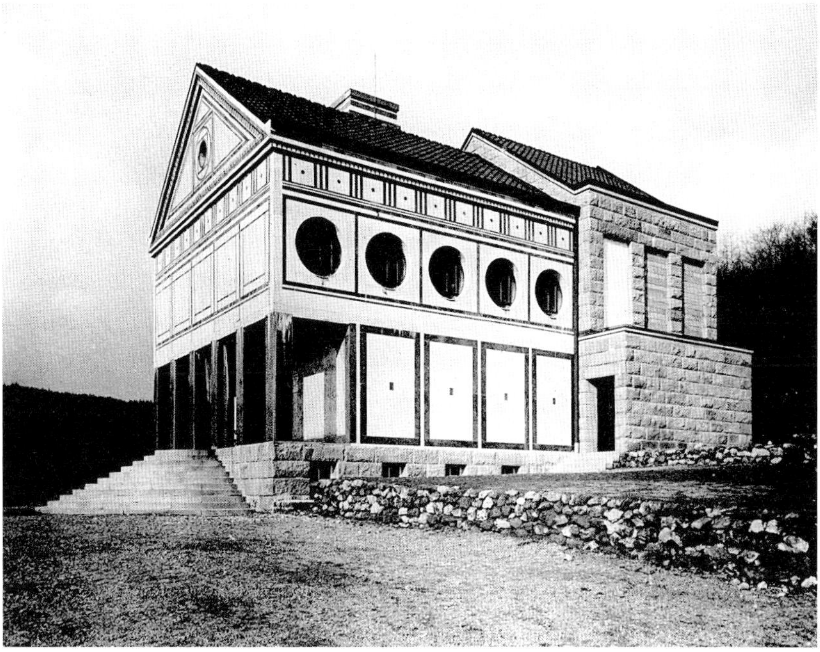

Figure 1.6. Crematorium at Hagen, Hagen-Delstern, Germany, 1905–8. Building: Peter Behrens. Photograph: Foto Marburg/Art Resource, NY.

down the stairs, out of the edifice, and onto the street—where his real locus of interest lay. Although the dissertation includes smaller-scale architectural elements like lampposts, much of it concerns surfaces with the minimal depth of a wrought-iron stick (Stab) and maximal length—like fabrics or screens, they are both sheetlike and see-through at the same time, and they have no conceptual boundary. They are also adjunct or supplementary to architecture; in the case of court boundary fences (Hofabschlussgitter), Kracauer notes that "they close off the court and tie the wings of the building together architectonically without hindering the view to the main building."[33] They could (in theory) be infinitely long fences—like the extruded sheets of plate glass manufactured after 1914.[34] Kracauer's focus on eighteenth-century material reflected a contemporaneous revival that resulted in works like *Um 1800* by Paul Mebes, just as Behne reflected on the marble inlay of contemporary architects in his study of the past.[35] After a careful description of the material of study, accompanied by photographs and measured drawings also executed by the author, Kracauer focused on the transformation of ornamental motifs from French precedents into a local Prussian genre.

Before considering the specific Prussian contribution to the development of wrought-iron ornament, it is worth noting that one aspect of Kracauer's study is particularly striking. He examined a group of artisans using a material—metal—that would become associated with industrialization, but in a nonindustrialized fashion. Wrought iron was self-supporting in accordance with its own structural properties.

It was, in effect, a structural building material used in a nonstructural application, thus confounding existing hierarchies of architectural form developed by earlier scholars, notably Semper and Bötticher.[36] In that sense, Kracauer's study, like that of Behne, shows Riegl's influence.[37] Kracauer also bypassed the qualitative distinction between works of applied art and works of fine art, a distinction that became widespread within art history despite or after Riegl. In tracing the development of wrought-iron ornament, Kracauer noted the importance of the general development of art ("Gesamtentwicklung der Kunst") within a given period.[38] In other words, he was interested in history as the autonomous development of style, or formalism, but also in the role of material and technique in the development of this history.

While indebted to Rieglian analysis, Kracauer also drew on Georg Simmel's 1907–8 essays on ornament, which showed how the decorative arts participate in defining collective experience, connecting individual and mass subject in immediately accessible art forms.[39] In describing the "indigenous" wrought-iron ornament in Berlin and Potsdam that developed from French models, he noted how the "ornamentation of the surface" (Schmückung der Fläche) replaced the use of centralized motifs (Schmuckzentrum) such as the monogram or crown. The result was a looser and more regular treatment across the extent of the ornamental surface. Conventional motifs were softened and transformed through adaptation from distant originals to new surface fields. Kracauer wrote: "The monogram . . . loses the meaning that it had in the baroque as a decorative piece. As in this particular example, so generally. It becomes one among many coordinated scrolled embellishments, when earlier it created a decorative center and was the ornamental point of the grille surface, as it were. The typical form of the baroque crown is dissolved into shell-like ornamentation."[40] The network (Netzwerk) of ornamental fields became repetitive and rhythmic, losing hierarchical subdivision and residual references to ornamental stone construction evident in earlier versions.[41] Like Zucker and Behne, Kracauer found rhythmic implications for visual appearance in decorative surface.

Kracauer relied on surface appearance to provide the clues for its own analysis. In his later work, freed from the disciplinary constraints of *Bauforschung*, he transferred the investigation from one of research into the past (in his dissertation) to one with a contemporary focus (in his critical work of the 1920s). But as he did so, the raw material of his investigations also shifted from architecture and the decorative arts to more ephemeral image surfaces that were beginning to receive the same intense scrutiny that wrought-iron or remnant colored marble surfaces had received from nineteenth century archaeologists—the new surfaces of photograph and film screen. In his later work Kracauer substituted the unknown future for the unknown past, producing a kind of therapeutic projective historical materialism—the nineteenth century overlaid on the twentieth. Implicit in Kracauer's intellectual development is the proposition that mass media might be considered twentieth-century extensions or equivalents of applied art.

To summarize: Zucker, Behne, and Kracauer investigated different aspects of surface construction. One was concerned with painted projections on architectural surfaces, one with decorative inlay to create surfaces, and one with ornamental yet transparent bounding surfaces. All three interpreted architectural surfaces as sites of representation capable of adding depth to purely superficial construction—whether virtually through perspectival projection, as in the case of Zucker, or more metaphorically through optical effects, in the cases of Kracauer and Behne.

The latter investigated two complementary aspects of surface construction. One was concerned with building facades, the other with ornamental surfaces with a singular architectural function—that of establishing boundary or enclosure. Both treated their materials of study in relation to representation in architectural contexts. For Behne, representation and construction were affiliated but not the same; it was incumbent on architects to devise "organic" systems of representation, regardless of tectonic constraint, but still indexed to it. If Behne's material remained necessarily tied to the question of tectonic representation, Kracauer, by contrast, selected a body of material that allowed his analysis to float free of any structural datum beyond that of a membrane or boundary. Like Behne and Zucker, he also called attention to artistic evolution over time, suggesting that the transportation of motifs and manufacturing techniques carried with it an increasing freedom of interpretation from one site to the next. A meaningful distortion rendered existing technologies and representational strategies adequate to a new context.

These six explorations, of which I have discussed only three here, occupy a historical cul-de-sac, a dead end without immediate successors in architecture culture. In relation to what came before them, they trace a shift from histories of ornament on surfaces to a focus on different modes or potentials of architectural surface itself. Their work reflects the importance of new technologies for surfacing metallic-framed or masonry buildings that had recently (or not so recently) become available to architects, such as plate glass, cast metal, and glazed terra-cotta. In relation to what followed them, such studies (although not their authors) appear as a line dropped from the ongoing history of architecture, partly as a result of the interruption of World War I and partly as a result of shifting research focuses after the war.[42] In fact, this was not the case. The theorization of the architectural image surface found in these sources locates the early appearance of an obsession that would endure throughout the twentieth century.

What bearing did this interest in the surfaces of architecture have more locally, in the years around World War I, on the increasing regularity with which photography had begun to insert itself into the practice, study, and marketing of architecture? Frederic Schwartz has suggested that a conjuncture between the history of art and photographic habits of seeing can be found in the work of art historians Hans Sedlmayr, Wilhelm Pinder, and others. Similarly, Kracauer bridged the divide of the century, was trained in nineteenth-century traditions of German *Bauforschung*, and left those to become a critic of mass society and its cultural expression. He and other early twentieth-century historians incorporated new paradigms of visual perception into their research, at least partially influenced by modes of optical perception that were identified with photography. Perhaps the best-known example of this is Sedlmayr's article on the Macchia of Brueghel.[43]

Ornamental screens, painted wall murals, architectural inlay, glass painting, and graphic art were linked partly by the means through which these became objects of modern historical attention: photography and photomechanical processes. In the cases described here, these young scholars turned their attention to surfaces that were both deep and shallow, both virtual and material. They looked with particular intensity at the surfaces of buildings insofar as they contained different kinds of images. But, importantly, they did so through the vehicle of copy images. Incipient interest in new forms of image architecture relates to the contemporary context of architecture, but also to the increasing presence of photography in the city and in the consciousness of its inhabitants. This media presence both produced and resulted from the growing discourse on abstraction and realism in both art and building design in the years before 1933.

Before concluding, we might look back at the books themselves. At a moment when photomechanical processes were growing more flexible, authors might print photomechanical images together with text and drawing on one printing plate, as Kracauer elected to do in his small book on wrought iron. The quality of these photographs was initially somewhat lower than that found in books with plates of photographic reproductions. In Zucker's book, for example, lithographic plates printed on thick paper were then bound between text pages (Figure 1.5). Behne's book is most mysterious: it had no plates at all, despite the fact that Behne wrote in detail about architectural ornament at Pisa, for example, as well as other sites. His footnotes led the reader to a range of illustrated books that preceded his own. Thus in reading Behne's study, one is forced to consult other books. Earlier illustrated books provide a clue to the transition that was taking place in the work discussed here—the transition between photography as a new tool of study and photographic presentation as a potential model for architectural historical investigation—an optical format that brought with it a new kind of visual attention.

Adolph Goldschmidt, for example, one of the readers for Behne's dissertation, illustrated his *Lubecker Malerei und Plastik bis 1530* of 1889 with photo engravings (subheaded *mit 43 Lichtdrucktafeln von Joh. Nohring in Lubeck*) (Figure 1.7) fully twenty years before the developments narrated above. Photographic reproductions imposed a different set of habits on scholars, perhaps most graphically demonstrated in Heinrich Wölfflin's celebrated slide comparison lectures.[44] Behne, Zucker, and Kracauer defined comparative research projects for which photography provided an invaluable methodological tool. Without the photographic format to assist him, Zucker, for example, would have found it nearly impossible to construct the chronological sequence that constitutes an important aspect of his argument. Although Behne did not publish photographs of the buildings he studied, his text suggests that photography was essential to his analysis.

There is more to be said about the publishing choices (or regimes) imposed on these young scholars; for the moment, however, the point is merely to note that photographic tools were sources of attention in and of themselves by the beginning of World War I. Perhaps we witness a desire on the part of these scholars, in their first (and in some cases last) focused scholarly projects, to question modes of study and visual attention that were being embraced nearly wholesale by their mentors.

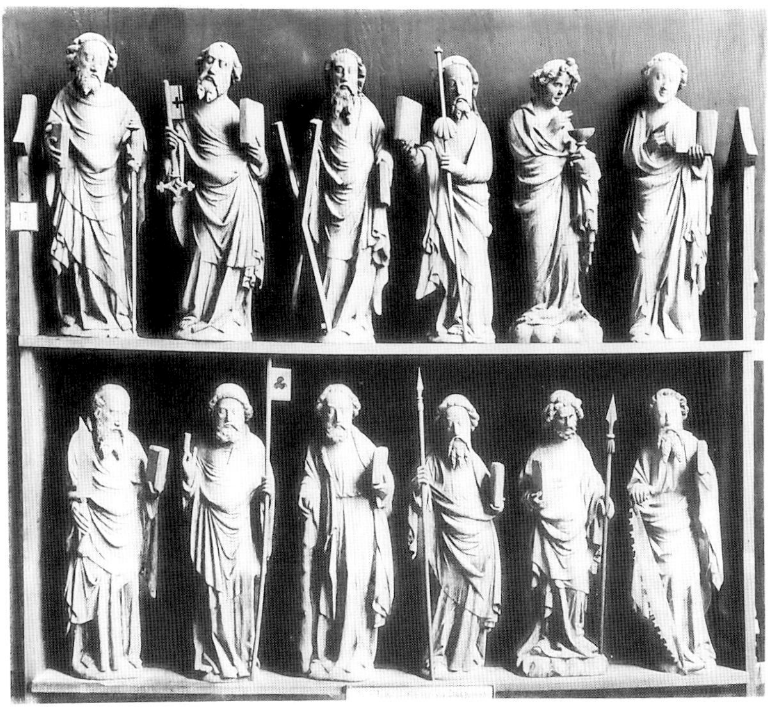

Figure 1.7. Plate 9 from Adolph Goldschmidt, *Lubecker Malerei und Plastik bis 1530 mit 43 Lichtdrucktafeln von Joh. Nohring in Lubeck* (Lubeck, 1889).

In any case, the method of Goldschmidt—using photography as a "straight" tool of comparative analysis—is not the same as that of Zucker, Behne, or Kracauer. In each case, and that of the three others not discussed in detail here (Behrendt, Frankl, and Müller-Wulckow), photography has shifted the focus of attention not to surface ornament but to the image of building that appears in the optical depth of surface treatments.

This body of work illuminates the transition from the nineteenth to the twentieth century in both architecture and its academic history and suggests how photography affected modes of attention in architecture. It provides rare insight into a historical moment when surface ornamentation and frame construction overlapped in revealing ways, in continuity with earlier developments but also distinct from them. Kracauer's study of ornamental surface and the similar work of his contemporaries was executed as modern architects began to proscribe ornament in new building, particularly in German-speaking countries. Adolf Loos's "Ornament and Crime" (1908–10) is the best-known document of this rejection of ornament, but Loos's arguments were echoed by Karl Grosz in the 1912 yearbook of the German Werkbund; similar arguments were soon to become a leitmotif of modernism.

The studies of a group of young scholars (no doubt encouraged or germinated by their professors) responded to this crisis in representational ornament, one also present in art history from Wilhelm Worringer's *Abstraction and Empathy* of 1908—a book closely related to these studies, particularly that of Behne. These early works connected contemporary problems of surface articulation and pictorial architecture to the systematic study of earlier ones, at the same time posing a new set of questions. Instead of tracing the history of fabrication as retained in surface traces, as Semper had done, they reflect an interest in optical experience and reception, in the artistic consciousness of the artists and artisans who produced these surfaces, and in the society that received them. This is not the same shift in modes of attention that took place in the latter half of the nineteenth century; it is, rather, a new focus on optical richness resulting in part from constructed flatness.

These studies explore intermedial effects in architecture—effects that reflected a new set of technical capacities and new ways of seeing and conceiving space. Although not unprecedented (as the work they studied shows), this scholarship reflected consciousness of modes of representation that were neither fish nor fowl in terms inherited from the nineteenth century or accepted in the twentieth. Images materialized on flat surfaces without reference to adjacent structural forces, but through the agency of authors communicating ideas optically, in relation to building construction. Just as imaging techniques and industrialized construction methods produced new architecture, so conceptual ideas about surface imagery penetrated scholarship as well. This is a preliminary photographic architecture, in which the projection of spatial effects through optical means became a powerful force in discourse on built things and representation.

After World War I a parallel line of research into theories of space (Raumforschung) that emerged from formalist art history was incorporated into postwar accounts of modern architecture to a much greater degree. Theorization of both topics—surface and space—resumed after the war, as Kracauer's later work shows. But only one of them—spatial theory—appears to have subsequently crossed the larger divide constituted by World War II to remain part of the official history of modernism, perhaps thanks to the concerted efforts of Sigfried Giedion, Walter Gropius, Henry-Russell Hitchcock, and Philip Johnson.[45] Thus a vein of historical study that took surface treatment and its narrative potential as guiding focuses disappeared from later historical accounts—possibly damage that was collateral to the rejection of surface effects that we find Gropius voicing in relation to photography in his 1920s publications.[46] It might also be useful to point here to the mutual constitution of surface and space—appreciated by figures such as Siegfried Ebeling, but evidently not by all.

To be sure, differentiated systems of construction that included building surface, such as Le Corbusier's "Five Points," became staples of architectural modernism. Despite the fact that facade architecture and building skin were part of these systems, however, research into surface effects on building facades did not survive as a key component of modernist theory, particularly not in relation to intermedial effects. Instead, the schism between Otto Wagner, a proponent of representational surface on buildings, and Adolf Loos left the latter largely in command of later debate. Advocating a building exterior that shows nothing of the building's interior richness—neither its structure nor its spatial arrangement—Loos severed connections between surfaces and picture making in a reduction that has had wide ramifications in modernism. Loos's rejection of pictorialism on architectural surface was linked to his opposition to the Viennese Secessionist movement. What it meant for the subsequent history of modern architecture, however, was a closure of possibility.

We might briefly return to Kracauer in 1927 to connect this chapter to those that follow. In his reviews of the Werkbund exhibition "The Dwelling" in the *Frankfurter Zeitung,* he wrote a memorable description of the translucent walls of the Glass Room (see Figures 2.10 and 2.11) that has recently been rediscovered by scholars. Located in the Materials Exhibition at one of three separate sites in the city of Stuttgart, the Glass Room displayed the products of the German plate-glass industry (Deutches Spiegelglasverein) in a striking composition of highly polished glass walls asymmetrically distributed within the anonymous space of the exhibition hall.

Ludwig Mies van der Rohe and Lilly Reich designed the installation, which featured plate glass in different widths, different degrees of transparency or translucency, and different tints.[47] The installation was treated as a series of "rooms" that made reference to domestic projects of the sort that Mies would realize later in a series of houses, some with enclosed courtyards. One space was evidently a living room, adjoined by a slot of space for a winter garden; another contained a desk; yet others served as foyers for entry and exit. Finally, one boxlike space enclosed entirely by glass contained a sculpture: inaccessible to the visitor, this container seemed to imply that abstract pictorial art had finally found a corollary in three dimensions.[48]

The installation made an impression on Kracauer, who saw it when he visited the Stuttgart exhibition in 1927. His comments in 1927 contrast with his reflections on film screens in "Cult of Distraction" of the previous year, discussed at the beginning of this chapter. He wrote:

> In the hall exhibitions there is a strangely conceived room by Mies van der Rohe and Lilly Reich. Its walls are composed of milky and dark-colored glass sheets. A glass box, transparent, the nearby rooms penetrate into it. Every device and every movement within them conjures shadow games on the wall, bodiless silhouettes float through the air and mix with the reflections from the glass room itself. The conjuring of this ephemeral glass ghost that wanders like kaleidoscopic light reflexes indicates that the design of the new dwelling doesn't signify final fulfillment, that blithely installing water faucets and striking the decoration from cast-iron stoves is insufficient. However kitschy the stricken ornament was, what is left when it is stripped away offers no replacement. The new buildings are apparently compensatory, meaning that they are timely constructive foreordinations of elements cleansed of bad excess; and certainly these remnant compositions reflect contemporary society. . . . the building skeleton is not an end in itself, but the necessary through-passage to a new amplitude that needs no more deductions and today can only be witnessed negatively through grief. It will first take on flesh, when man steps out of the glass.[49]

Plate glass is not an emblem of the future, but rather a placeholder for a new architecture that might escape the reductions of capitalism, reductions that Kracauer, like the critic Ernst Bloch, the dramatist Bertolt Brecht, the historian Behne, and, later, the architect Rudolf Schwarz, associated with the Neues Bauen.[50] But what gives plate glass this status as a blank placeholder for future realities? Its pictorial capacities, akin to those of the film screen or the photographic negative, are somehow both projective of future possibilities and inadequate in and of themselves. They require, according to Kracauer, a more tangible and significant reason for being. They require content that appears in his remarks as a set of compelling, if transitory, images—harbingers of the future. In this case, the emptying out of all ancillary detail, which Kracauer called for in his assessment of the baroque movie palace, merely left a blank space that had not yet been filled with meaningful imagery.

If this is activist history, then we need to reckon up. What were the stakes in relation to architectural history and production? If this group of scholars brought contemporary concerns to their study of the past, why should this surprise us? More to the point, what might this history add to all the other, subsequent discussions about the activist role of the historian? Did it help architects such as Bruno Taut incorporate new media into architectural projects, as in the "Monument to Iron" (Figure 1.8), in which Taut included large photographs and screen projections in an exhibition pavilion?[51] Kracauer, Behne, and Zucker brought future and past together as a way of reckoning with the novelty of their own time—not by way of familiarizing it through past precedent. To quote Wilhelm Worringer, the historian must "infer the immaterial conditions to which this [lifeless historical material] owes its origin. That constitutes an inference leading into the unknown, the unknowable, one for which there is nothing but an intuitive basis."[52] All three went on from studies of pictorial architecture to a concern with screen environments: Kracauer focused on film itself, Behne on the interaction between film and architecture, and Zucker on both—joining books on theaters and film palaces to work on the *Stadtbild,* or city image, along with a remarkable essay on time in architectural representation.

In Kracauer's case, we wind up at the edge of an abyss in 1926–27—either the optical abyss of unmediated screen immersion, where we began, or at the abyss of the future, in architecture that had not yet found vividness as at the Stuttgart exhibition. In either case, Kracauer's reflections drew on his insights into the history of ornamental surface, suggesting that Weimar culture had come up against its own limit—that technology had moved in advance of the possibility of thinking it. One might remember that Kracauer studied Kant closely in the years between his wrought-iron book and his Stuttgart reports, in the process teaching *The Critique of Pure Reason* to a young Theodor Adorno on Saturday afternoons. According to the latter, Kracauer sought for ontological insights within the epistemological investigations found in texts and other material phenomena that were then subject to systematization. Material representation provided one through-point to ontological speculation. Surfaces of glass, of screen, or even of wrought iron are then literal and metaphorical wormholes—not windows—into some other mode of thought, one that has not yet been articulated in words.

Kracauer used the Glass Room as an opportunity to reflect on issues concerning the Neues Bauen. He did not consider the installation as a representative example of the work of a group of progressive architects; rather, he saw it as a project that

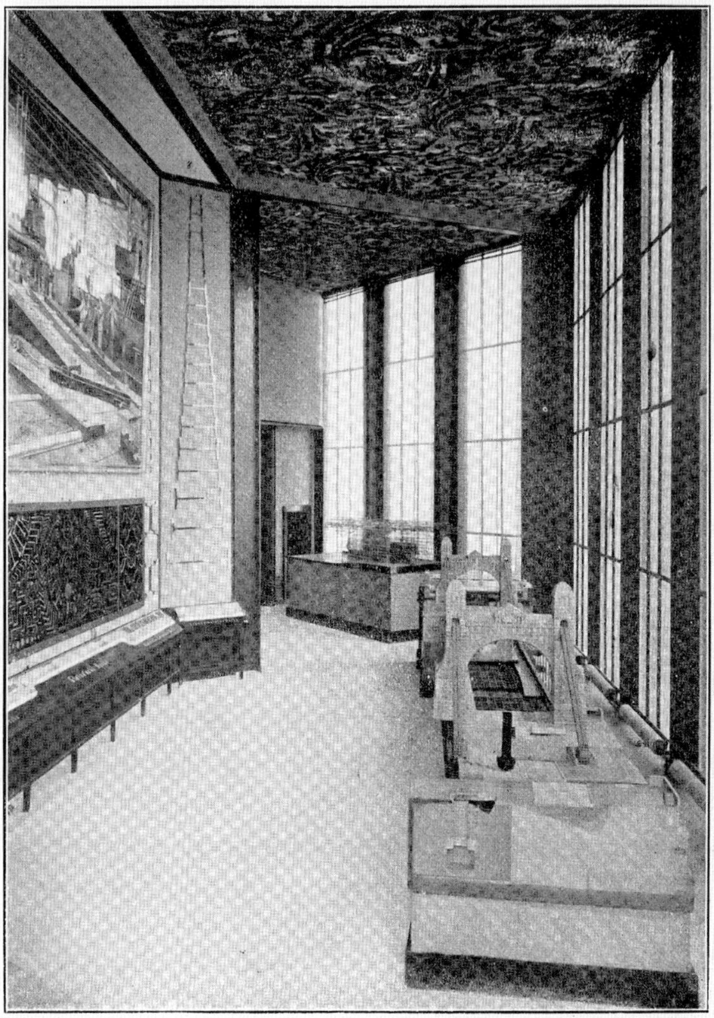

Figure 1.8. "Monument to Iron," ground-floor backlit photomural display, International Building Exposition, Leipzig, 1913, with cinema upstairs. Building: Bruno Taut. From *Der Industriebau* 4, no. 11 (November 15, 1913): 151.

allowed one to understand problems that contemporary architecture faced at the time. The means by which the Glass Room achieved this subtle critique, Kracauer implied, were the reflective glass walls that made the visitor intensely conscious of the play of reflected mobile images that danced across the surfaces of the room, overlaid on one another through layers of transparent or translucent material. In his description, the replacement of conventional building facades by plate glass represented the stripping away of ornament from modern architecture in general. This excision in turn portrayed something lacking, both in the Neues Bauen and in the populations that inhabited modern buildings. It represented a kind of death that had not yet been replaced by new life.

Surprising contradictions and common themes, however, link Kracauer's description of the movie screen in "Cult of Distraction" with his review of the Glass Room of the following year.[53] In the first, Kracauer asserted that the experience of viewing film would be properly fulfilled only when all distraction had been removed, enabling the viewer to fall into the abyss of the screen, optically or metaphorically. In the second, the situation was reversed: the ornament was gone, and what remained now denoted a state of lack. Kracauer described how the structural skeleton of the new architecture could "first take on flesh when man steps out of the glass" on which his reflection was still just a ghostly projection. What Kracauer mourned at Stuttgart—the stripping away of ornament from interior design—he had anticipated in the film palace but one year before. The reconciliation of these two contrasting positions rests in his studied ambivalence about many of the phenomena of modern urban society on which he commented frequently. It also lies in his projective thought—finding cultural matters in a state of general indecision, he described modernity as something anticipated, not yet reached. To paraphrase Kracauer in "The Hotel Lobby," we are also those who wait; neither the film palace nor the architecture of the Neues Bauen had reached a state of readiness adequate to the challenges they had the capacity to address.

Scholars have rediscovered the Glass Room in the past fifteen years through a series of black-and-white photographs by Walter Lutkat, a local architectural photographer who photographed installations in the new materials component of the Werkbund exhibition in 1927.[54] Kracauer's comments on the pictorial qualities of plate glass make the reader aware of a particular case where pictures of architecture such as those described by Zucker coincided with architecture itself. Plate glass gave rise to transitory images on buildings; as a result, architecture and representation collapsed into one surface. In this case (as in many others in the history of modernism), we are compelled to appreciate this fact about the Glass Room by looking at photographs. In the process, we look at pictures of architecture that makes pictures.

At the very beginning of this story of modern architecture and photography, the two media overlap and interpenetrate, both in architectural history and in the products of Weimar architecture.

What is real is the continual *change* of form: *form is only a snapshot view of a transition*. Therefore, here again, our perception manages to solidify into discontinuous images the fluid continuity of the real. When the successive images do not differ from each other too much, we consider them all as the waxing and waning of a single *mean* image, or as the deformation of this image in different directions. And to this mean we really allude when we speak of the *essence* of a thing, or of the thing itself.

—HENRI BERGSON,
CREATIVE EVOLUTION

2. PHOTOGRAPHY INTO BUILDING
MIES IN BARCELONA

Between the closing of the Stuttgart exhibition of 1927, "The Dwelling," and its Glass Room and the hasty completion of one of the most well-known buildings of the Weimar period less than two years elapsed. Many of the same concerns that surfaced in Stuttgart were also addressed in Mies's and Lilly Reich's work at the Barcelona International Exposition of 1929. Perhaps the most notable repetition was found in the glass architecture of the so-called Barcelona Pavilion, or the German Pavilion at Barcelona (Figures 2.1–2.5). The building was referred to in German as a *Repräsentationspavillon,* a building with a symbolic or representational function. Embedded in the German word is an idea about display and public symbolism that has no corollary in English usage but that suggests the importance of visual presentation.

Like the Glass Room, the Barcelona Pavilion contains sheets of colored glass in varying widths and tonalities, all polished to high reflectivity. In these the visitor sees him- or herself as well as other visitors to the building. In addition, two kinds of green marble in separate wall segments and a sheet of onyx supplement the glass and complete the enclosure of the building. Other space-defining elements include wall-height red silk curtains, a large black carpet, and two pools of water set into the travertine floor of the pavilion's podium. This plinth negotiates the grade change between the front entry of the pavilion, a meter or so above the plaza in front of it, and the back, where the building's floor is roughly at ground level. Luxurious materials rich in surface effects show substances often overlaid with reflections—the

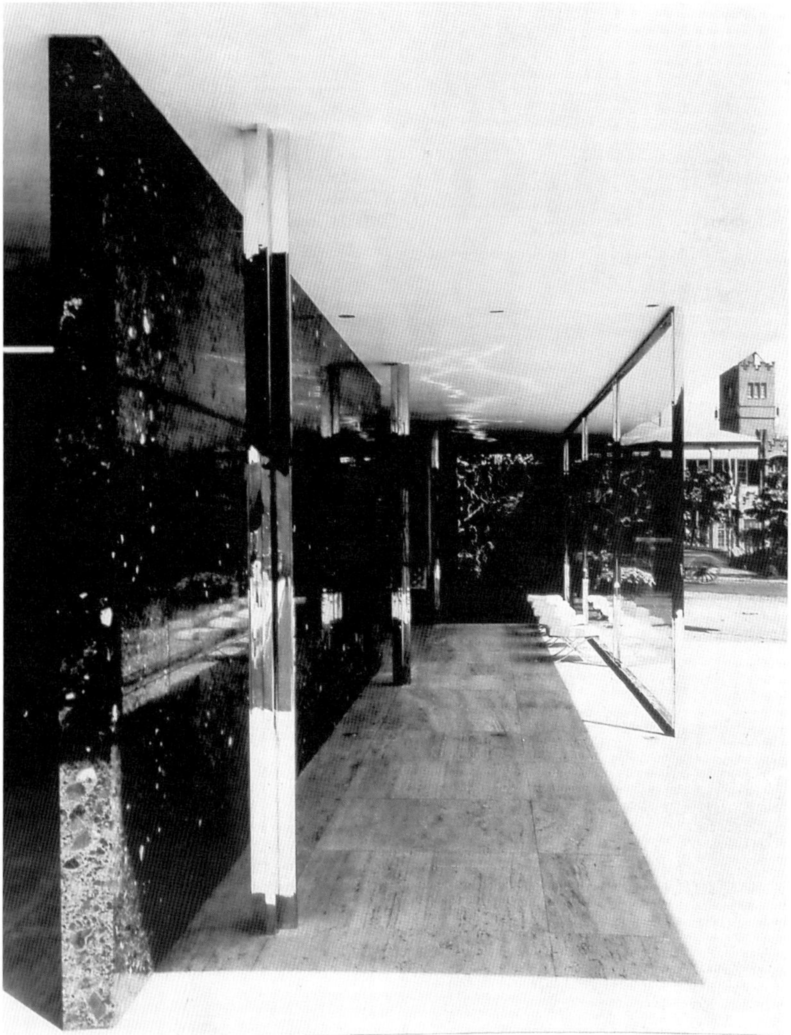

Figure 2.1. Entry, Barcelona Pavilion, 1929. Building: Ludwig Mies van der Rohe. Photograph: Berliner Bildbericht. Mies van der Rohe Archive, The Museum of Modern Art, New York; Gift of the architect; digital image copyright The Museum of Modern Art/Licensed by SCALA/Art Resource, NY.

colored planes of glass, the veined or patterned marble, the surface of water hosting smooth or troubled reflections of the sky overhead, surrounding walls, or visitors. Traversing the building, the visitor is accompanied by mobile reflections that track progress through space, making an optical experience architectural and suggesting ways in which the building might be considered a piece of photographic or filmic architecture. All of this was newly revealed in the 1986 reconstruction of the building (Figure 2.6)—a reconstruction in large part carried out thanks to the influence of the original set of black-and-white photographs of the building.

Two definitions of the term *photographic architecture* were suggested in the introduction: one in which photographic effects alter architectural design

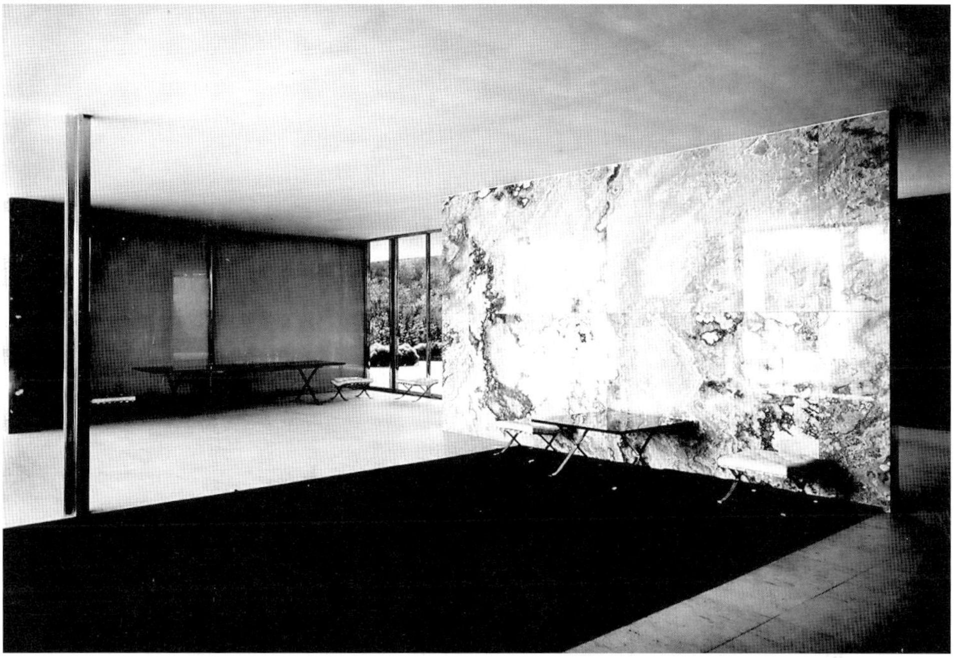

Figure 2.2. Interior, Barcelona Pavilion, 1929. Photograph: Berliner Bildbericht. Mies van der Rohe Archive, The Museum of Modern Art, New York; Gift of the architect; digital image copyright The Museum of Modern Art/Licensed by SCALA/Art Resource, NY.

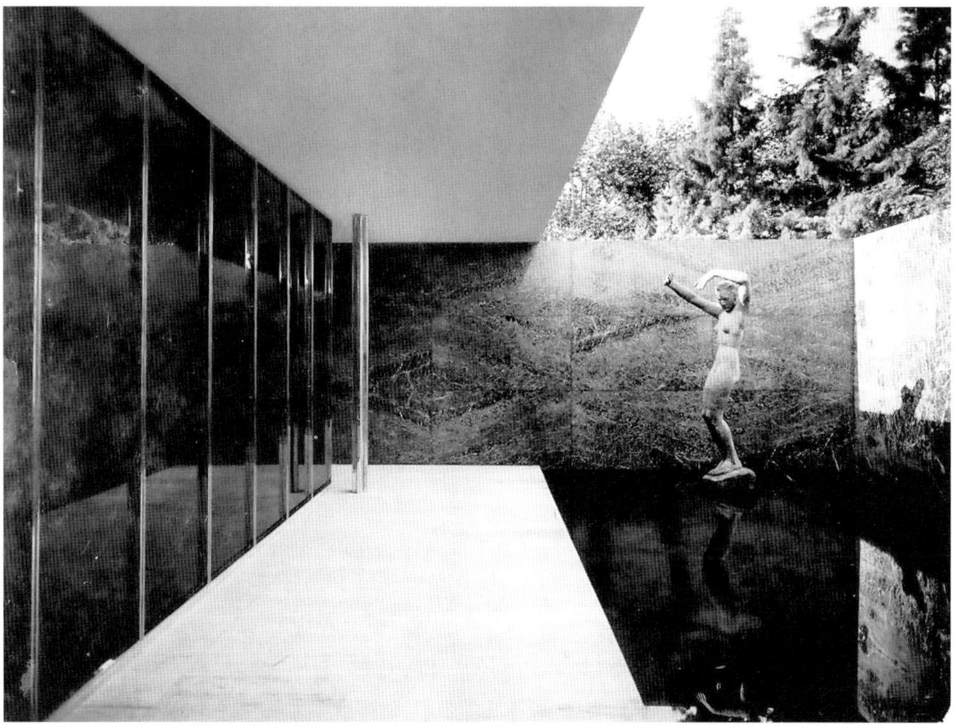

Figure 2.3. Courtyard pool and Kolbe's *Morning*, Barcelona Pavilion, 1929. Photograph: Berliner Bildbericht. Mies van der Rohe Archive, The Museum of Modern Art, New York; Gift of the architect; digital image copyright The Museum of Modern Art/Licensed by SCALA/Art Resource, NY.

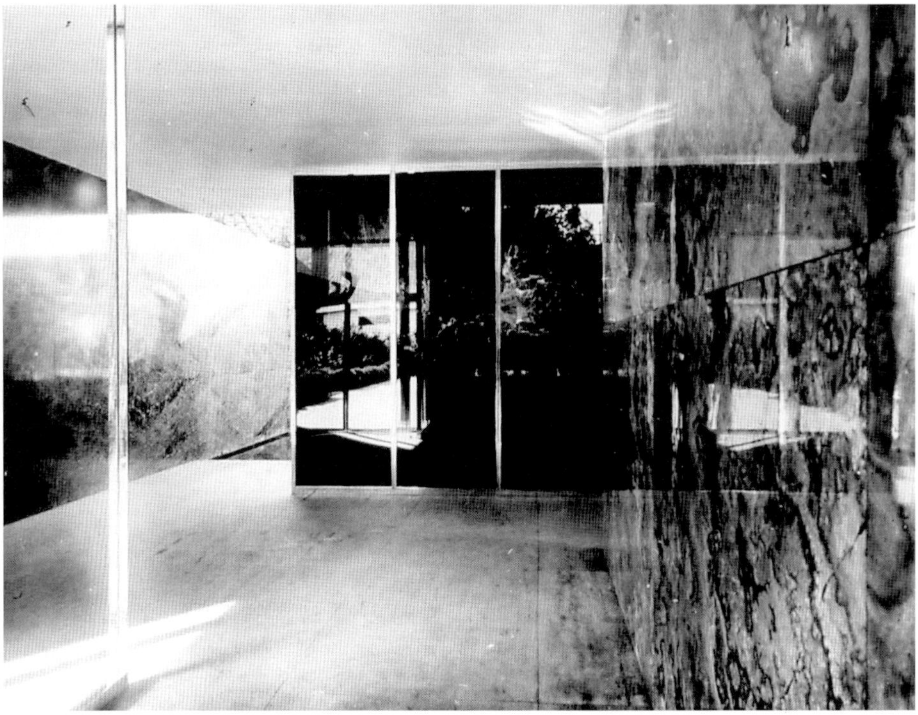

Figure 2.4. Rear entry, Barcelona Pavilion, 1929. Photograph: City of Barcelona Municipal Archives.

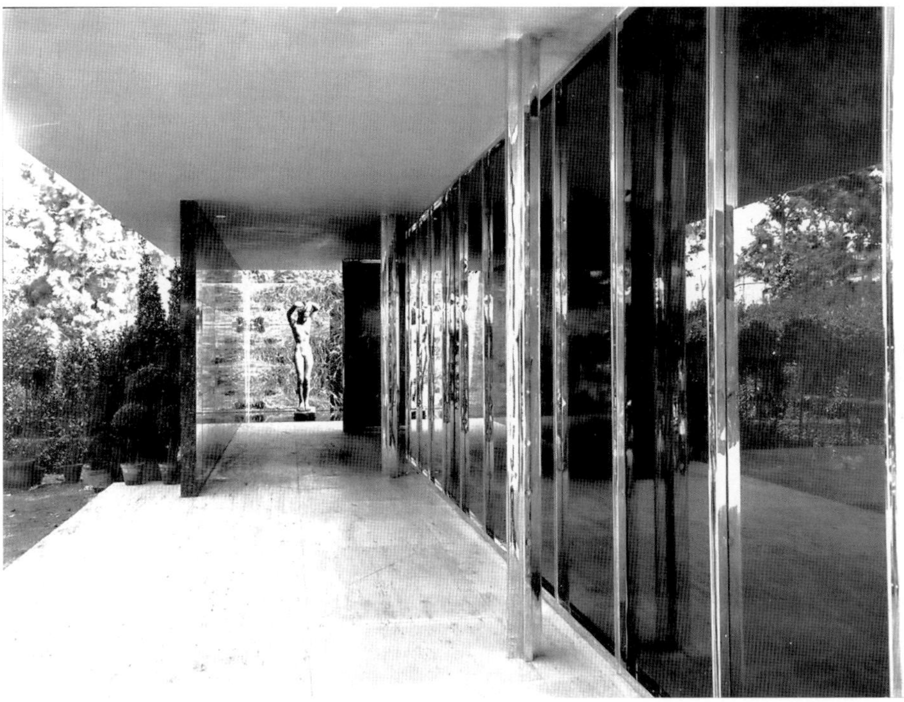

Figure 2.5. Rear passage with Kolbe's *Morning*, Barcelona Pavilion, 1929. Photograph: Berliner Bildbericht. Mies van der Rohe Archive, The Museum of Modern Art, New York; Gift of the architect; digital image copyright The Museum of Modern Art/Licensed by SCALA/Art Resource, NY.

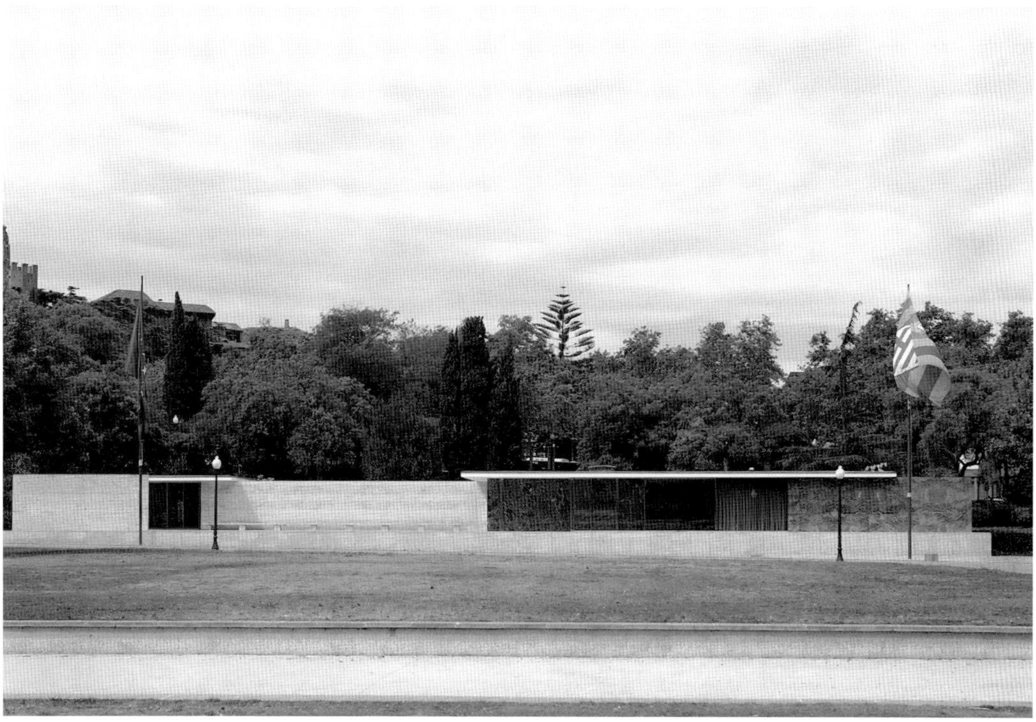

Figure 2.6. Exterior, Barcelona Pavilion. Photograph: Liao Yusheng, 2011.

practices and one in which the border between a building and its public is policed by the architectural photograph. Subsequent chapters will focus on the latter, on architectural photography as it helped create a manner of architecture that was confined to projective inhabitation by viewers and that contributed to one notion of architectural abstraction. This chapter deals instead with the first definition of photographic architecture as it took shape in the paradoxical idea of constructed abstraction.

Studies carried out largely in the context or the wake of major exhibitions on the architect in 2001, however, have shown how cinematic viewing influenced Mies's work, underlining as well the architect's use of montage, a practice pursued in architecture, photographic media, and film.[1] Given the proximity between photography and film at the beginning of the 1920s, it may not be worth arguing about priority. Mies and Lilly Reich evidently responded to both in their Barcelona designs. Mies's work had been transformed by contact with the *G* group, and by Hans Richter in particular. Film was critical to Mies's design practice in the second half of the 1920s, as a number of projects and textual evidence show. A study concerned primarily with Mies's design process might well focus on film as a central theme in his work. But this book is not focused on Mies primarily, or on the further (re)construction of an architectural canon around his work, but rather on the network effect of photographic media in architecture.[2]

Photography had a contradictory influence on Mies, as well as on others. A new medium subject to artistic exploration in the hands of László Moholy-Nagy or El Lissitzky, it was also an increasingly powerful commercial medium by which architects advertised their work in journals, magazines, monographs, and newspapers. In this commercial sphere, film did not yet compete in the 1920s—nor, it may be said, did it come to compete with printed media later (although the National Socialists made a concerted attempt to use film to direct public perception), in the sense of providing architects with a commercial marketplace similar to that of the architectural journal. The experimental aspects of new media often coincided with commercial ones in interwar avant-garde practices. Architectural photography provides a useful datum—a through-line that connects experimental avant-gardism with the architectural market. Architects benefited from the experimental approaches that were shown in exhibitions such as "Film und Foto" in 1929, but they were also ambivalent about the increasing commercial power of photographic images. There was an early and recurrent tension between the potential of photographic media for new architectural ideas and the burden of representation placed upon the architectural photograph. This tension formed the substrate for interactive discourse.

The nature of the spatial proposition made at Barcelona was at least partly visible, if not fully comprehended, through its original black-and-white photographs. The 1986 reconstruction threw the agency of photography into sharper relief against the spatial effects of the building (admittedly now a Mercedes to Mies's Volkswagen Beetle). This has in turn made it possible to posit some of the differences between spatial abstraction and photographic abstraction. The Barcelona Pavilion has provided an invaluable time capsule with this temporal sequence: building (1929–30), set of photographs (1930–86), building (1986–present). The rich materiality briefly described above and well-known from other literature on the Barcelona Pavilion can now be juxtaposed more easily with the spatial sequence that is prescribed by the design itself and that appeared in architectural photographs and the building's mute plan. This chapter focuses on the relay between the original building, the first photographs, and the 1986 reconstruction that made the building newly visible and comprehensible as a spatial entity.[3]

Peeling away a layer of photographic abstraction, a more complex notion of architectural abstraction appears in this building. The chapter explores this idea in Weimar Germany, one that was inspired in part by Russian precedents. Other works by Mies and experiments by architects and artists interested in the same topic proposed an aesthetic abstraction that differed from the negative definition of the term that was associated with the deleterious effects of industrial capital as pointed out by authors from Simmel to Kracauer. In flat media, aesthetic abstraction was posited generally on projective sensory experience imagined through the two-dimensional surface. The search for a corollary construct in architecture was complicated by the substitution of the body for the eyes. If pictorial abstraction hinged on the tension created by the viewer's interface with a two-dimensional surface behind which an intense optical experience hovered, it was not immediately clear what might happen when that surface was removed. Painterly abstraction suspended the real in favor of a cosmic ideal, a precursor to the "virtual reality" of the human imagination. If tension between a transparent planar surface and projected depth was essential to painterly abstraction, how might architecture find a corollary in constructed space, and to what end?

Architectural abstraction appeared in Mies's work through a host of bodily and optical engagements. Although he was not the only architect interested in experimentation in this direction, Mies was the most successful in translating one compelling version of abstraction into constructed buildings. This chapter shuttles between the construction of the original Barcelona Pavilion and its 1986 reconstruction, but it also turns to other unconstructed or ephemeral projects focused on similar ends. Not all were by Mies. The chapter concludes with a reflection on the paradoxical difference between architectural abstraction as built and the photography that could not, by definition, translate that effort into a flat image. Collaterally, this chapter details the apparent shortcomings of photography for architecture. To include it in a book on photography's influential impact on modern architecture is not whimsical; the chapter identifies the sorts of alterations that necessarily took place as spatial ideas were translated into pictorial ones, a core issue for this study.

ARCHITECTURAL PHOTOGRAPHS AND OPTICAL EXPERIENCE IN THE PAVILION

Visual experience at the Barcelona Pavilion was calibrated by bodily experience carefully choreographed in the building's design. The architectural photographs correlate to this choreography well; not only do they allow the viewer to "walk through" the building, but they also show how particular moments in the plan might be considered visual opportunities, or three-dimensional pictures. In a plan of the pavilion that includes the station points for each photograph imposed over the circulation pattern of the building (Figure 2.7), directional changes coincide with the locations from which photographs were also made, with just one exception. The photographs thus reflect the plan strategies of the building. Whether the architects suggested these particular station points for the camera is not definitively known; in any case, these points appear as likely places from which to take pictures. As one mounts the stairs

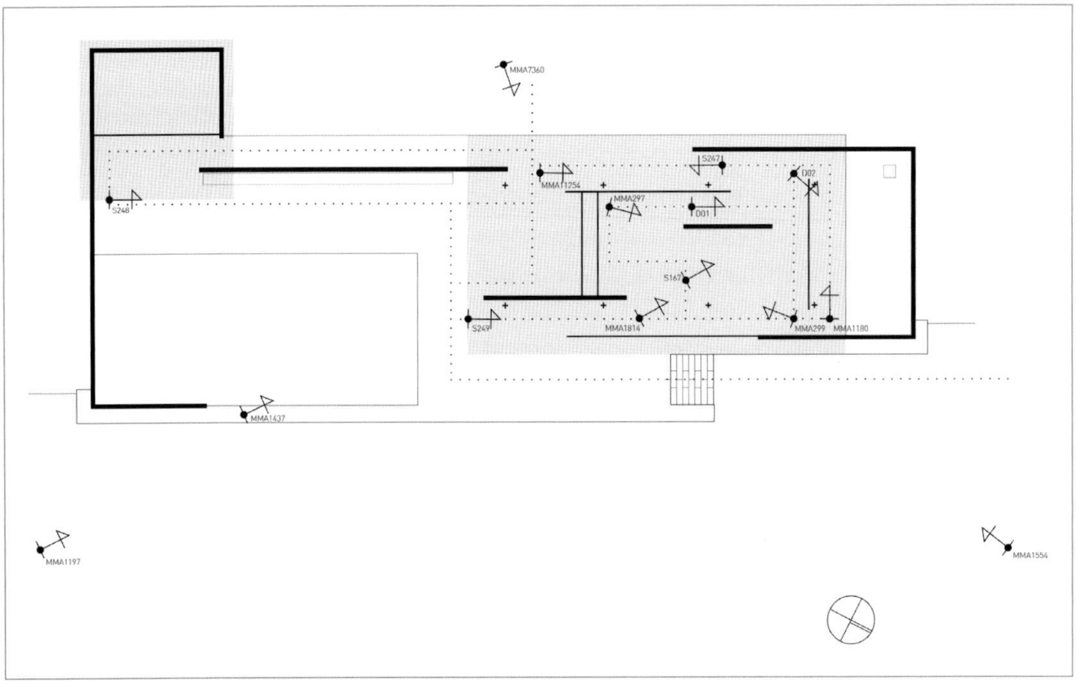

Figure 2.7. Plan of Barcelona Pavilion, showing location of photographs and coincidence with major directional shifts and visual tableaux. Plan drawn by Sara Dean and Joss Kiely.

to the podium, for example, and turns to enter the building, one tends to pause at the entry to survey the space ahead. Here in 1929, the cameraman set up his machine and took a picture.

On at least one occasion, Mies sent his photographers a sketch showing his preferred standpoint for a photograph.[4] But regardless of the architect's role in the process, these moments in plan are obvious points from which to take pictures. A plan laid out so clearly around a coordinated sequence of changing visual tableaux indicates the importance of pictorial concerns within design itself. Whether we affiliate this to a pictorial interest or a specifically photographic or filmic one may be merely a question of interpretive preference (a preference with clear ideological associations). But this design reflects contemporary developments in photography and film, partly through biographical and formal connections to Hans Richter and others, even while reflecting a pictorial tradition based in nineteenth-century architecture. This argument can best be elaborated contextually, through a consideration of specific developments contemporaneous with the pavilion.

Two summary observations are relevant here: Mies's plans are spatial choreographies, and the movement patterns laid down in them were carefully calibrated against particular viewing moments in a manner that recalls other visual experiments of the European avant-garde. Recent scholarship has emphasized similar points.[5] Just as Robin Evans describes the pavilion as making conscious the act of seeing, Detlef Mertins describes it as a machine for making pictures—pictures that problematized the accepted limits of architectural reality.[6] In Mertins's view, Mies's abstraction destabilizes the subject, mapping multiple images onto one another and, in the process, substituting spatial mutability for stability.[7] Similarly, Maria Gough describes how El Lissitzky's Abstrakt Kabinett (1927) and its close precedent the Raum für konstruktive Kunst in Dresden (1926) destabilize the occupant through visual disorientation (Figure 2.8). Lissitzky's related *optische Dynamik* (a kind of early version of op art) renders subjects perceptively active but also disarms them cognitively, precisely by presenting them with unfamiliar perceptual experiences. Gough describes new modes of spatial experience integrated with visual innovations of the previous century in the two *Demonstrationsräume* (demonstration spaces), such that architecture was overlaid with and impregnated by media practices (film and photography) and with ideas about the physiological constitution of vision.[8]

Mies achieved a similar effect by using reflective glass in combination with more traditional building materials (such as marble) that were mounted and framed in unfamiliar ways. The reflective pictorial qualities of glass impregnated architecture with filmic and photographic correlates. The glass walls of Mies's Weimar projects reflected the occupants. They resonate with the idea not only of a physiologically constituted subject but also of a psychologically constituted one. Gough makes a similar point for Lissitzky's project, in which the surfaces of the walls were articulated with vertical baffles, or fins, painted in black, gray, and white—occupants do not see their own reflections, but they become conscious of their corporeality by the

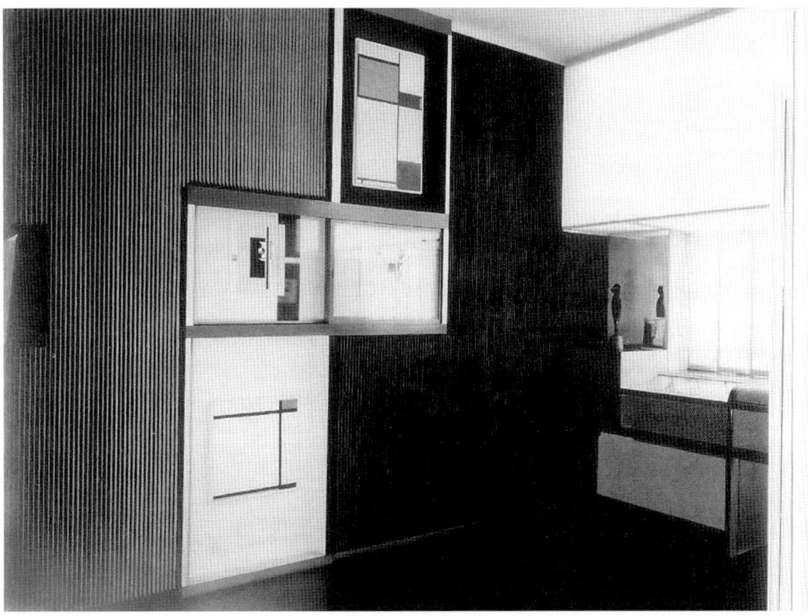

Figure 2.8. Abstrakt Kabinett, Hannover, 1927. Design: El Lissitzky. Photograph copyright 2012 Artists Rights Society (ARS), New York.

coloration of the wall, which changes according to each viewer's standpoint: from one side gray; from another, black; head-on, white.[9]

We can supplement Mertins's and Gough's arguments by recalling the importance of vision relative to movement to those who move through this building. The correlation of visual tableaux and rhythmic movement within Mies's architecture highlights the multisensory experience proposed there. By "visual tableau" I mean a place in the building that is framed or set up as an image, a kind of staging area that might prompt a moment of visual reckoning, causing the mover to pause, look, turn, and move on. While the photographs of the pavilion capture these image tableaux, which confronted the visitor at strategic moments, they do so only in part, as the reconstruction has shown. In contrast, the ways of moving through Mies's buildings seem somewhat static or overdetermined from the buildings' plans. But we might simply consider the seemingly exaggerated simplification of the plans in relation to the complexity created by the materials, their visual mutability, and their montage qualities.[10] If the spatial choreographies are hieratic, excessively ritualized and rhythmic, this is offset by visual abundance or complexity. A wider context develops these points in relation to photographic and architectural abstraction.

MIES'S MAJOR PROJECTS OF THE 1920S AND THEIR TECTONIC PRECEDENTS

The Barcelona Pavilion and the Tugendhat House are major constructed projects that are identified with architectural abstraction as a function of spatial modes introduced here, but they are also part of a much larger body of work. They are so well-known that a short description suffices to supplement the information given thus far. Mies was appointed director of the Barcelona exhibition in 1928. He himself selected the site for the "Pavilion of German Representation" (rejecting one offered by the Spanish authorities), a critical decision for what became a contextual, site-dependent building. Located at the terminus of an important cross-axis partway up the exposition's ceremonial spine, the building was shielded quietly behind a screen of Ionic columns at the end of a long plaza.[11] Reference to a pendant building at the other end of the plaza—the neo-Renaissance Pavilion of the City of Barcelona—echoed gently in the two enclosing end walls of Mies's project, remnant traces of an eviscerated neoclassicism.

The architectural elements of Mies's pavilion included walls of four varieties of stone (slabs of two green marbles, travertine, and *onyx dorée,* all supported by metallic frames), tinted glass (green, gray, white, and clear), and columns of chrome-covered metal. The plan of the building displayed structure clearly disengaged from enclosing walls, an effect that is easy to overlook in the building itself.[12] Marble-clad and glass walls choreographed an uninterrupted spatial sequence punctuated by the slim lines of the cruciform columns set against walls of intense reflectivity.

The absence of the pavilion's steel-and-glass doors (left out of nearly all original photography) was critical to the reading of spatial continuity, further defamiliarizing the experience of this building by eliminating the division between inside and out. Within the display of slick yet ornamental surfaces, an oversized statue of a woman (Georg Kolbe's *Morning*, or *Dawn*) provided a figural reference somewhere between cult image and modern icon, appearing in reflected surfaces throughout the building. Her arms raised gracefully from the midst of a dark pool in the building's rear court, the statue transposed its classical prototype from hieratic deity into evocative but elusive nude.[13] A larger pool greeted the visitor in the building's outer court, open to the street from the raised podium on which the whole structure stood; in this case lily pads growing in the water and creepers trailing down the wall behind provided other recognizable figures counterposed against the abstractly rendered fields of water and textured stone.[14]

General Commissioner Georg von Schnitzler articulated the government's intentions for the Barcelona fair as reflecting "our desire to be absolutely truthful, giving voice to the spirit of a new era." As Dietrich Neumann has shown, Schnitzler was essential to the completion of this commission, seen by many as an unnecessary luxury that supplemented the displays of German products in nearby pavilions.[15] Germany also sought to develop new markets in Spain and the Americas through this exhibition. The pavilion was chiefly representational; as a symbolic building, it was intended to broadcast the idea of a newly democratic Germany. The aesthetic and spatial achievements of the pavilion existed within a sociopolitical framework, where the building symbolized Germany's progressive stance in both cultural and material terms. Mies's goals were probably somewhat different.

Commissioned at roughly the same time as the Barcelona exhibition, the Tugendhat House in Brno was completed in late 1930, with a larger budget and a more specific program.[16] The house presents a single story to the street. A curved milk-glass volume to the left of an open carport shields its entry; a distant view of Brno's picturesque fortress lies directly ahead, framed by an opening in the building mass. Inside, the main living level is one floor below the entry, its large open space subdivided into separate spatial zones by a single onyx wall, a nearly semicircular wall of ebony, cruciform columns, and floor-to-ceiling silk curtains in muted tones.[17] The abolition of space-enclosing walls allows each individual spatial cell to benefit from continuity with surrounding spaces. Transparency between spaces extends outside thanks to the enormous sheets of plate glass that bound the living area from the garden, two of which sink completely into the wall below. The living area is simultaneously interior and exterior; curtain "walls" allow for further spatial mutability. This quality contrasts with the spatial fluidity of the Barcelona Pavilion; the two buildings project very different aspects of Mies's system of design.[18]

The relationship between landscape and architecture at Tugendhat was a theme of Mies's work, further developed in the unbuilt Gericke House (1932), as Barry Bergdoll has shown.[19] In contemporaneous debates on architectural modernism, the building was invoked to signal the move away from radical functionalism toward a vision of architecture raised to the "realm of the spirit," in the words of the critic Walter Riezler. It thus also marks the point at which Mies's common cause with more politically motivated German modernists, from Gropius to Taut, began to weaken.[20] Its relationship to photography will be discussed further in chapter 3.

INVISIBLE HISTORY

The Barcelona Pavilion was dismantled in early 1930. After World War II, photographs of the building became newly important, as buildings in Germany and Eastern Europe became increasingly inaccessible to many from the West. Conversely, Eastern Europeans had increasing difficulty traveling to Western sites after 1938 or 1939. The pavilion was inaccessible to both simply by virtue of its having been dismantled. Like Frank Lloyd Wright's Larkin Building or H. H. Richardson's Marshall Field Warehouse, its photographic existence was especially influential because there was no "control" in the form of a building on a site to which the photographs might be compared. As a result, qualities that resulted from particular characteristics of photographic representation—including the effects of the wide-angle lens; the subtraction of color, materiality, and facture; miniaturization; and compositional choices—were difficult to distinguish from building as a physical construct on a site.

This chapter distinguishes abstract effects of photography from architectural effects. Architectural photographs of both the Barcelona Pavilion and the Tugendhat House draw from abstract composition in photography, painting, and graphic art. But architectural effects are harder to characterize with the term *abstract.* If I do so here, it is with the understanding that architectural abstraction is a placeholder for a range of experimental practices that are also potentially subject to further parsing. To use one blanket term here is to define a precinct within which to work. Within that precinct we might include photography, film, choreography (dance), drama, and music, as well as visual arts such as painting, as contributing to architectural design. An act of recovery shows how these media entered into the fabric of architectural practice itself; photographs of buildings do not necessarily aid in this understanding, and they often retard it. Just as the sequence of Barcelona Pavilion photographs tell us obliquely about what *cannot* be seen there—the choreography of the building and its particular experiential effects—so other architectural photographs often do the same. The history of the pavilion now allows for comparison between what was seen before—photographs—and after the 1986 reconstruction of the building.

While photography supplied the flat surface and virtual space that made it possible to bring buildings into comparison with painterly and graphic abstractions, photographs also helped obscure other fruitful investigations related to this concept that could enter architecture only paradoxically. Retrieving an idea of architectural abstraction during the 1920s reveals a rich set of experiments that were crafted in close dialogue with a community of artists, filmmakers, photographers, and performing artists. It also clarifies the active agency that photography assumed in the translation of concepts that became particularly important in the years following World War II.

A small group of Weimar architects responded to the challenge to architecture implicitly presented by two-dimensional abstraction in other art practices. These architects sought modern architecture beyond advances in technology and mass production, implicitly acknowledging buildings as public representation. New conceptions of subjective experience that had emerged from nineteenth-century physiological and psychological aesthetics awaited exploration in spatial practices, particularly design, despite earlier experiments. In architecture, perceptual psychology could be used to counter technological imperatives (such as industrialization or prefabrication) with equally compelling (and positivist) scientific ones based on perceptual experience. As ideas about human subjectivity circulated in the first decades of the new century, they tended to return architectural decisions to the realm of aesthetic judgment.[21]

Among the group of experimenters whose work is adumbrated here, we might number El Lissitzky, Marcel Breuer, Erich Buchholz, Walter Dexel, Alfred Gellhorn, Hannes Meyer, Ludwig Mies van der Rohe, Farkas Molnar, László Moholy-Nagy, Lilly Reich, and Bruno Taut, as well as others who sought to construct new spatial and material experiences with architectural matter. Artists such as Kurt Schwitters and more mainstream professionals such as Walter Gropius and Erich Mendelsohn, and, from an older generation, Peter Behrens and Hans Poelzig, also participated in these developments to greater or lesser extents. Gropius, for example, aware of the potential of architectural abstraction, was nevertheless committed to work at the Bauhaus that balanced aesthetic concerns with technological and economic ones. This resulted in an ambivalence that he shared with others, and that has troubled modern and contemporary architecture for decades. Projects associated with the early experiments of the artists and architects cited above are already well-known, but they have not yet been analyzed in relation to architectural abstraction and its dialogue with other art practices. Core participants in this dialogue were Mies, Taut, Moholy-Nagy, and Lissitzky.

ABSTRACTION AND MODERN ARCHITECTURE

Two-dimensional visual abstraction may have prompted the idea that intensified opticality might be experienced differently in combination with three-dimensional space. De Stijl painters first sought to transpose painterly abstraction into building, where visual strategies derived from the work of theosophist M. H. J. Schoenmaekers were applied to interiors. Schemes proposed by Theo van Doesburg or Piet Mondrian demanded heightened attentiveness from occupants, partly through unprecedented spatial configurations like those found in selected projects by Mies and El Lissitzky, as we will see below. But these experiments, in projects such as the Café Aubette or the Interior for Ida Bienert, were relatively mute in architectural terms: they depended on color surfaces applied to existing spatial containers. De Stijl experiments were tied mostly to painting in ways that made them restrictive to architectural experiment, specifically through a primary emphasis on surface application of color.

Manfredo Tafuri and Francesco Dal Co examined this contradiction within the broader problematic of abstraction in the 1920s:

> But we have seen that abstraction is a flight from the real, and the question arises as to whether the effort to rejoin reality . . . was not destined to fail precisely because of its own premises. . . . tension toward the real was valid only so long as it remained just that, so long as it did not pretend to arrive at concrete results.[22]

Tafuri and Dal Co implied that abstraction did not translate from painting to architecture simply because the tension of a viewing plane was intrinsic to the very concept. If the highly charged surface-to-depth relationships found in de Stijl or even in suprematist painting, for example, were to be re-created for a medium with no such tension between viewing plane and spatial depth, another means had to be found to produce an aesthetic experience similarly based on creating new perceptual horizons. Architecture could not simply imitate the tropes of two-dimensional art; it had to carve out a new mode of experience for itself. But what were the desired characteristics of such a project? Among the effects sought by Weimar avant-gardists in architecture we might number profound sensory defamiliarization and a heightening of bodily consciousness. By creating an "abstract" architecture, architects might deliver a new utopia in the present, one based on bodily experience in concert with visual or perceptual disruption. This experimentation occupied a brief period in the interwar years; it can be distinguished from the photographic records that circulated later. Architects may have taken the spatial suggestions of painting as cues, but the translation of those into analogous three-dimensional constructions was another matter entirely.[23] To map Mies's attempt to do so, we return once more to the Stuttgart exhibition of 1927, and to the two new paradigms of steel frame and glass cell.

STEEL FRAME AND GLASS CELL

By the time "The Dwelling" opened in 1927, Mies had assumed an important role in German architecture. He made at least two breakthroughs there. The first was the steel frame of his large apartment building on the summit of the hill, often billed as the first use of a metallic frame in a multiunit domestic building in Germany. The lightweight dividing walls between spaces within a single unit in the building could change, but the structural grid of the frame was fixed in place (Figure 2.9). The second was the Glass Room discussed by Siegfried Kracauer in his reviews in the *Frankfurter Zeitung* and in the previous chapter, in which wall-height plate-glass partition walls were placed freely in space. Through the opposition between a structural grid and a set of mutable spatial dividers, Mies then launched a series of spatial

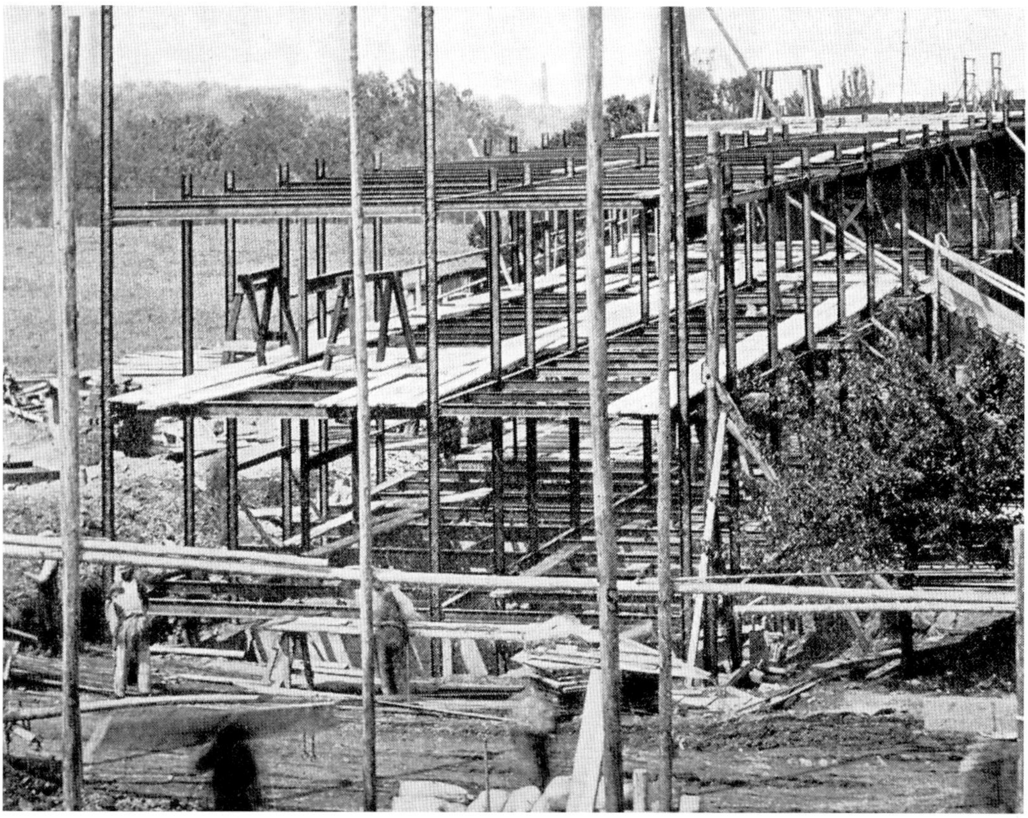

Figure 2.9. Weissenhof apartment building under construction, 1927.
Building: Ludwig Mies van der Rohe. Photograph: unknown.

experiments, distinct from but in play with those of the avant-garde in architecture and other media.

Mies had had his first personal contact with Le Corbusier at "The Dwelling," and the opposition between structural grid and spatial partition in two of his projects there shared certain characteristics with Le Corbusier's "Five Points for a new Architecture."[24] These five components (supporting *pilotis,* free plan, free facade, ribbon window roof garden) encouraged chance adjacencies and conjunctures in building design.[25] After 1927, Mies joined the structural system of the steel-framed apartment block to the spatial planning of the Glass Room. The spatial arrangement developed in the Barcelona and Brno projects—a fixed grid of supports and a mutable composition of spatial dividers—was already nascent in these earlier projects and recurred in Mies's 1920s and 1930s projects. It appeared briefly in his American

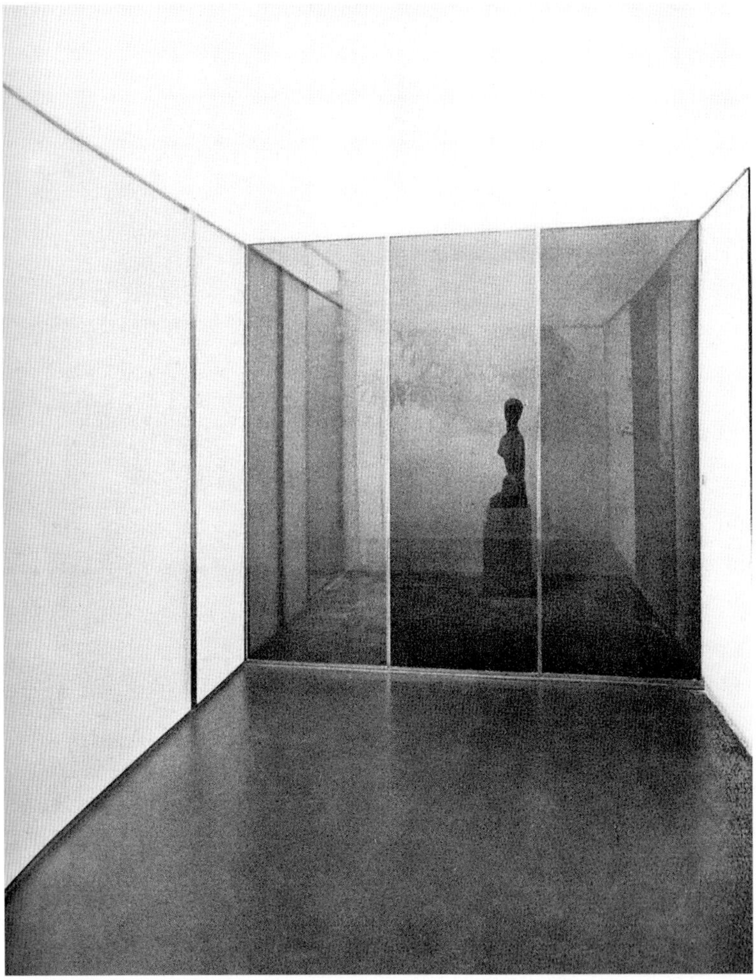

Figure 2.10. Plate-glass installation in the materials show (Materialienschau), "The Dwelling," Stuttgart, 1927. Interior: Ludwig Mies van der Rohe and Lilly Reich. Photograph: Walter Lutkat. Mies van der Rohe Archive, The Museum of Modern Art, New York; Gift of the architect; digital image copyright The Museum of Modern Art/ Licensed by SCALA/ Art Resource, NY.

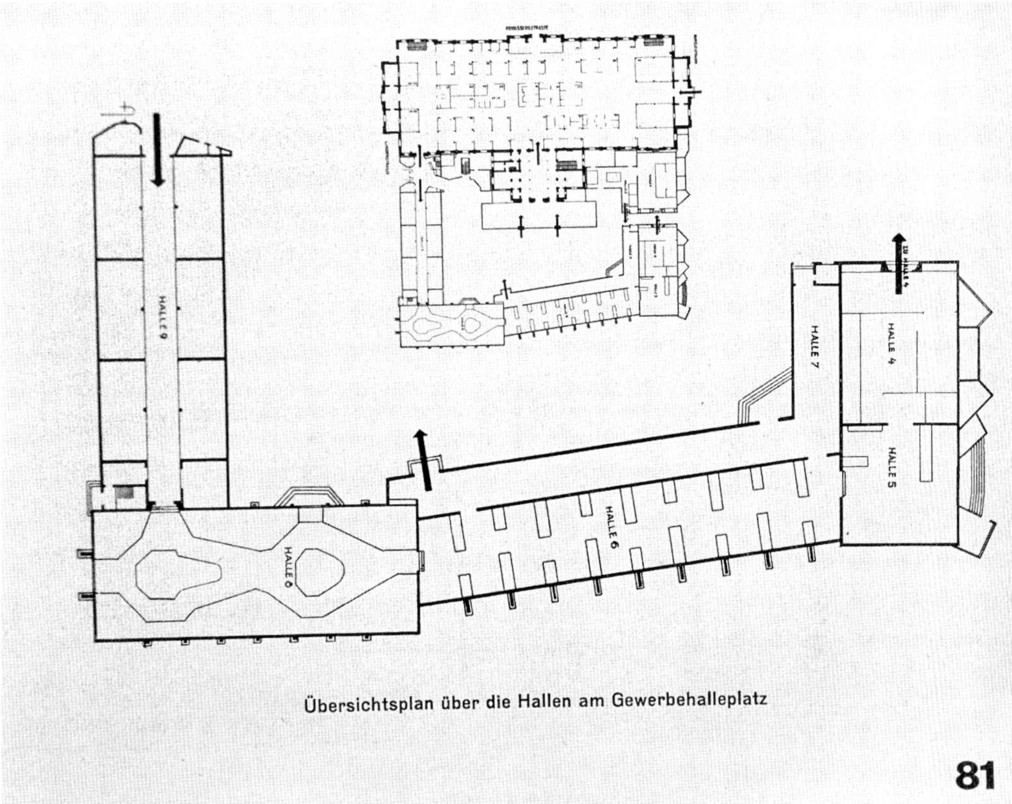

Figure 2.11. Materials show (Materialienschau), "The Dwelling," in the Gewerbehalle in downtown Stuttgart, 1927. Plan of plate-glass installation on right. From *The Dwelling*.

work, before he began to use the steel frame to incorporate spatial enclosure—where a unitary system replaced the early dualism of structure versus enclosure.[26]

In contrast, Mies and his collaborator Lilly Reich used freely composed spatial dividers within a rectangular spatial envelope in the Glass Room of 1927, described in chapter 1 (Figures 2.10, 2.11). A circulation path threaded around full-height glass partitions, mimicking the bourgeois home with entry vestibules, dining room, living room, study, winter garden, and one cell of inaccessible space occupied by a Wilhelm Lehmbruck bust. Reflective tinted plate glass showed visitors their own reflections, extending Mies's investigations of 1921 and 1922 in his unbuilt glass skyscraper projects. These earlier projects suggest the degree to which he had absorbed the imaginative potential of other media, such as montage, for architecture. In Stuttgart, an earlier interest in glass was deployed within a simulated habitation; this was a decidedly spatial investigation that recalls Mies's interest in Siegfried Ebeling and suggests an early encounter with Ebeling's theories as published in *Raum als Membran* that has been recounted by Fritz Neumeyer.[27]

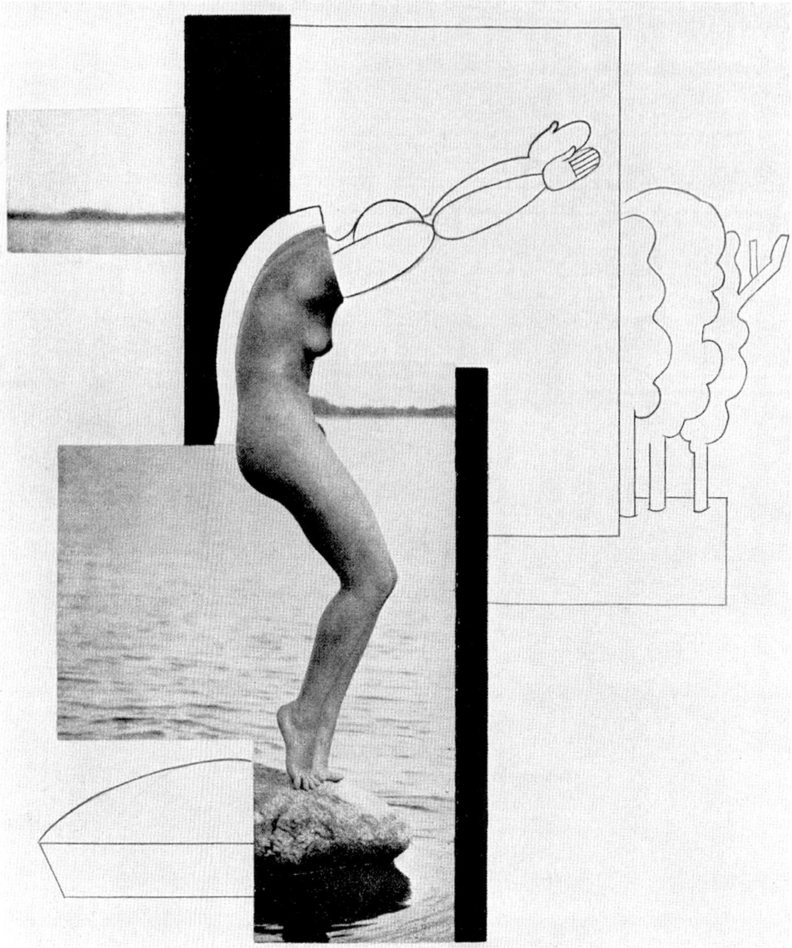

Figure 2.12. Untitled collage, circa 1927. Artist: Willi Baumeister. Reproduced courtesy Stiftung Kunstmuseum Stuttgart.

The glass-enclosed inaccessible space containing the Lehmbruck sculpture in the Glass Room may well concretize the virtual space of painterly abstraction, restricting casual entry or passage through. It provided a motif that would recur with subtle differences in Mies's subsequent work. Photographs of the Glass Room published in *Die Form* in 1928 were placed in close proximity to Lissitzky's Abstrakt Kabinett, with a covering article by curator Alexander Dorner that overlapped the first page of photographs of the Glass Room.[28] Mies's project continued and illustrated the text, where the author deftly noted correspondences between the two projects. Dorner wrote that constructivist compositions had the character of "architectural fantasies" that sought to spring the bounds of the two-dimensional surface into real construction. Lissitzky's exhibition room was transitional; it began the escape from two dimensions into three, activating the wall surface itself: the short metal fins already alluded to dissolved the planarity of the wall surfaces throughout the gallery.[29] In the Glass Room, Mies used plate glass to accomplish a similar task.[30]

The realism of the Lehmbruck sculpture amid unadorned sheets of glass recalls the photographic fragments and blank spaces of photomontages by Mies's Stuttgart collaborator Willi Baumeister (Figure 2.12) or by László Moholy-Nagy. Taken together with the Glass Room and the installation at Hannover, these delineate a theme around the (generally nude) female body enclosed in inaccessible space—a theme common to Weimar art at this time, sometimes with political dimensions, as in the work of Hannah Höch. Gesturing to the virtual space of painterly abstraction, inaccessible architectural spaces also signal the general conceptual space of representation by concretizing them in visible objects. Photographs of the Glass Room installation show the Lehmbruck overlaid by one or more planes of tinted glass, as the architecture itself provided additional collage elements.[31]

The Naum Gabo installation in Lissitzky's Hannover exhibition room was too small to allow a visitor to enter; in other respects it was similar to Mies's vitrine—or so the placement in *Die Form* encouraged the reader to believe. The figurine belonged to the miniaturized world of the glass vitrine that contained it (Figure 2.13). But a visitor might have entered the chamber designed by Mies if physical access had been granted. Physical accessibility was established by visual connection but denied by the blunt refusal of entry.[32] The disjunction between sight and access recalls similar visual strategies used by Karl Friedrich Schinkel.[33] But it equally recalls the *Schaufenster,* or show window, featured so prominently in books like Arthur Korn's *Glas im Bau und als Gebrauchsgegenstand* (1929) and throughout the pages of Wilhelmine- and Weimar-era periodicals.[34] Hannes Meyer satirized the vitrine as an instrument of capitalist representation as early as 1925.[35] Thus Mies's use of the vitrine, now enlarged to

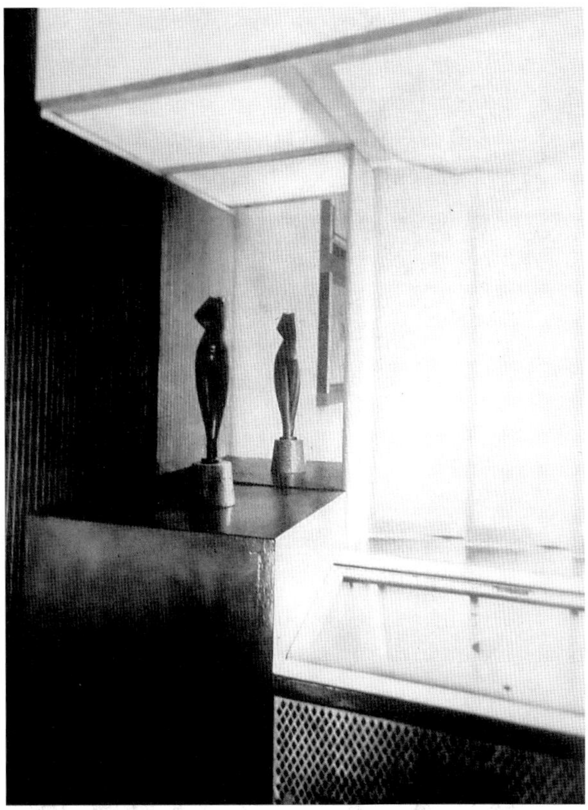

Figure 2.13. Abstrakt Kabinett, Hannover, 1927, with Naum Gabo's *Modell für "Rotierender Brunnen,"* 1925. From *Die Form*, 1927. Photograph copyright 2012 Artists Rights Society (ARS), New York.

the scale of human occupation, returns also to the capitalist abstraction that worried aesthetic practice throughout the Weimar years. Ebeling described how architecture might address this condition of capitalism, writing, "Architecture, evolving on a broad working basis, relates to the human body more directly than ever, as a creative form that is increasing infinitely within the sphere of a magical environment; from being the handmaid of the technical arts, it has become once more the queen, and has to define the task of industry." Mies transformed the *Schaufenster* in the Glass Room and elsewhere; in the process, architecture sublated industrial production for a new purpose. "Industry," Ebeling went on, will thank architecture "for a new sphere of activity that expands its previous technical and intellectual boundaries."[36] The same can be said of the chrome or zinc that wraps the metallic columns in Mies's projects of these years. The wrappers are not products of industry but rather products of industry disciplined by architecture.

Pushing through the two-dimensional surface of glass for a three-dimensional spatial construct, Mies also used glass surfaces to establish something analogous to the surface tension of the abstract canvas, embedded in construction. Thus he supplemented his earlier use of this material in unbuilt montage projects with a literal use of glass as membrane, as Ebeling formulated it. This did not represent a final answer to the question of how to find architectural corollaries for abstract painting, sculpture, and graphic art, nor should we assume that flat art provided the motivating force behind all architectural experimentation. The cell in the Glass Room was, I think, rather a notation for a larger project of abstract architecture, supplying a directive for future work. In any case, the next project brought the mobile occupant into the space of the glass vitrine itself.

MIES'S SPATIAL MODES

Within the internal conflicts of progressive Weimar architecture circles, Mies took an independent direction in the years following 1927 that may have proceeded from a variety of causes: his connections to the power structure of the Werkbund; his interest in gaining desirable commissions with adequate budgets; his doubts about reductive or politicized approaches to architecture, in contrast to his own interest in the "spiritual" and organic approach of Ebeling; fealty to his earlier avant-garde connections around the journal *G;* or some combination thereof. His work in the period 1926 to 1931 illustrates a clearly articulated design method and a specific approach to architectural plan making. The method relates to the work of Hans Richter and Adolphe Appia, two formative influences on his early career. Richter, especially, may have helped Mies develop certain consistent parameters for design, partly derived from the determining conditions of photography and film.[37]

Responding to other artists and the media in which they worked, Mies developed new architectural proposals. Drawing (whether consciously or not) on the still-influential notion of the *Gesamtkunstwerk* and the potential to create synesthetic architecture, Mies began to design projects in which unprecedented spatial and material constructs were found.[38] The idea of medium specificity that underpinned the concept of the *Gesamtkunstwerk* raises the difficulty of identifying the single medium specific to architecture. This conflict remained for the most part unresolved in modernism; in any case, Mies marshaled a broad range of effects under the mantle of building. Broadly underpinned by Immanuel Kant's notion of the sublime as an experience of thorough aesthetic defamiliarization, more proximate sources on the recalibration of sensory experience can be located in the ideas of Ebeling, but also in the work of others with whom Mies came into contact: Goethe, Nietzsche, Georg Simmel, Richter, Appia, Lissitzky, and many others.[39] In this gambit, the architect developed his new architectural approaches.

Mies's work at this time enacted a mode of experience in space that had previously been available only virtually, in the experiments of Russian constructivists, suprematists, and de Stijl and Bauhaus artists, and in the pioneering film work of Richter and Viking Eggeling. The architect absorbed new media and new artistic approaches and transformed them.[40] These design modes would occupy him for the next decade in some of his most important work. They addressed a number of important issues. On one hand, a consistent structural or tectonic approach developed around the regular steel frame. This then allowed Mies to distinguish structure from enclosure; walls that no longer provided structural support (or exclusive structural support) could be used instead to develop innovative spaces and spatial sequences.

On the other hand, and not solely in response to the steel frame, Mies developed a way of organizing plans in which movement through adjacent spaces was carefully choreographed in relation to apertures, entries, and changes of direction. By 1927 several varied approaches to architectural space coexisted but had not yet been fully integrated with one another. The Esters and Lange Houses that Mies designed in Krefeld (1927–30), in which the spatial sequence was extremely sophisticated, were constructed using a complex and inelegant structural system, not the simple cage of the Stuttgart building. After 1927, however, Mies had developed a single system, one subject to remarkable variety in execution. His interest in spatial sequence and his emphasis on conceptual clarity (structure versus enclosure) were brought together in a series of projects. These may be distinguished from one another by the architect's use of separate manners of design in projects that look formally similar in other respects.

These might be referred to as new design modes that would occupy him in the remaining decade of his life in Germany and his first years in the United States. Early projects such as the Eliat House (1925) (unbuilt), the Wolf House (1927), the Esters and Lange Houses, and the Stuttgart projects of 1927 show components that would also characterize his later work but are not as fully integrated as they became later, in a wide range of projects, built and unbuilt.[41] In work between 1929 and 1942, Mies pursued a number of different spatial modes using consistent design elements. The use of the musical term *modes* indicates the spatial duration of architectural experience and suggests affinities with other arts that unfold over time. Thus the concept of modes deployed here designates temporal aspects of architecture. In an insightful work on the poet Octavio Paz, the literary historian Rachel Phillips describes a similar procedure as follows: "Music is the art form which accepts structure as form itself, and the musical mind *par excellence* is aware of the relationship of parts to each other and of these parts to the whole. . . . Thus a mode is at once a closed system and a flexible tool."[42] This description recalls Mies's way of designing. Leaving aside the notion of medium specificity that came to dominate other artistic discourse, and to which architecture was ill suited by its internal procedures, its methods, and its component parts, the term *spatial modes* is commensurate with the intradisciplinary nature of his interests.

The design system that Mies developed provided a substantial degree of flexibility that led to different investigations. As Phillips notes in regard to Paz: "The relationship of notes to each other within each mode is a given factor, but the mood created by each mode differs. . . . in effect the tensions set up by the differing relationship of notes create the varying moods of each individual mode."[43] Between 1929 and 1942 Mies created a series of spatial modes derived from a single set of tools that then created varying spatial character. The notion of consistent tools applied to the widest variety of requirements is a core modernist idea that also characterized other artistic responses to mass society and communal or universalist discourse. More than a "kit of parts," it is rather a systems approach applied to the practice of design itself.

The first of Mies's spatial modes is denoted here *rhythmic space*; the second, *montage space*. A third, which I use in chapter 3 to characterize the development of the Tugendhat House, is *panoramic space*. Each connects to a notion of photographic or filmic cognition in conjunction with bodily movement. These modes appeared with the two most important constructed projects of these years: the pavilion in Barcelona and the large house for the Tugendhat family in Brno; they sometimes overlapped and coexisted within the same projects, but all recurred in built and unbuilt projects of the late 1920s and the 1930s. Similar modes may perhaps be detected in the unbuilt as well as the constructed work of these years.

Although this analysis is largely limited to the sphere of constructed architecture and its photographic representation,[44] the unbuilt projects of the period from the early 1920s until 1942 are nevertheless important to this interpretation of Miesian design. Part of the topography of Mies's practice, this large body of work shows how techniques adapted from photography, film, theater, and dance appeared in projects, whether built or unbuilt. Influences from new media parallel and connect to Mies's and Reich's interests in new construction materials such as large plate-glass sheets (wall height and more than five feet in width). They also relate to the way in which Mies delineated a clear frame within which to place his own work, as well as to his choreographic interests.

Working backward from the two major discoveries at Weissenhof—the steel construction frame and the system of freely composed spatial dividers of the Glass Room—a third discovery prior to 1927 revealed the montage possibilities afforded by both frame construction and plate glass as early as the skyscraper projects of 1921 and 1922. The pairing of the two Stuttgart innovations seems like a clear dualism between structure and enclosure.[45] One system did the structural work and provided a conceptual as well as a constructional ordering system (one easily adapted to particular exceptions); another partitioned the space and provided the confrontation with material that was characteristic of Mies's architecture. The definition of systems that combined freedom and order was a long-standing theme in German philosophy, dating back to Kant's efforts to establish moral laws and a *sensus communis*.[46] But other, earlier influences acting on the architect complicate the idea of a binary system in Mies's architecture.[47] Specifically, his interest in glass effects was not solely limited to its role in cladding a frame or directing circulation. Plate glass offered the opportunity to create wholly new effects and experiences. The objectives that contributed to Mies's new spatial modes were related to the new technological imperatives of steel structure and plate glass but derived from the spatial, material, and experiential possibilities those materials provided "on the ground."[48]

The Miesian plan of the 1920s and 1930s was confusing; its apparent clarity as a diagram gave little indication of what it instantiated experientially. Corbusian plans look complicated and the buildings they represent *are* complicated; the opposite might be said for an architect like Louis Kahn. Mies's plans look homogeneous, but the buildings that sprang from them are not. Mies's plans are especially inarticulate next to their constructed reality, diminishing the notion of any pure "spatial" effect and increasing the importance of material rendition, circulation patterns, building function, and detailing. In addition, the contrariness of the plan renders other forms of representation more critical in the analysis of Mies's work. Discussions of "Miesian space" as a vacant, totalizing, universal construct are puzzling in this regard.

Descriptions of the vast spaces produced during his American period, in buildings like Crown Hall and the New National Gallery, gave rise to this term. In the German period, by contrast, Mies's unprecedented uses of clear and colored plate glass produced intimately replete spaces.

Functional differences in the Barcelona Pavilion were subsumed by formal similarity (the dimensional similarity of solid and glass wall planes, each playing a different functional role). "*Nonfunctional*" differences were dealt with similarly; the differences among various kinds of marble in the building, for example, were offset by similarities of finish, size, and detail. Similarly, different kinds of plate glass produced different visual effects—but all remained the same in one dimension (height) and similar, or related, in their other dimension (width), and all (even the milk-glass box) had a similar highly polished surface. Thus, where Le Corbusier's architecture might be described as highly articulated, we might instead introduce the term *isotopic* to describe Mies's architecture of this period. The architect used dimensional and constructional sameness to highlight difference of architectural/spatial effect, stabilizing and delimiting a fixed frame within which his architecture operated.

RHYTHMIC SPACE

Turning to the occupation of these buildings, the interplay of movement and image tableaux appears widely in Mies's work at this time, but it is especially clear at Barcelona. Conjunctures between movement shifts shown in plan and particularly important vantage points for viewing through the building recur throughout the 1920s. At the Esters, Lange, and Wolf Houses (1925–30), picture windows, doorways, or interior tableaux of some kind often calibrated directional changes in plan.[49] At the Barcelona Pavilion, patterns of movement were similar, as noted above. With the elimination of conventional windows and walls, shifts in orientation and viewing were structured not around viewing apertures per se but around openings or particular image tableaux framed by rectangular planes or located at particularly charged places in the building's spatial sequence.

Approaching the pavilion from its back entrance, or crossing between the building and the large pool, a passage runs along the back wall toward the Kolbe statue and pool. A turn of the head (and body) reveals this ensemble, picturesquely framed like a piece of statuary in a classical garden (Figure 2.5). Similar moments occur throughout the pavilion, as movement through the building reveals the sculpture from several vantage points, the full surface of the onyx wall from front and back angles, the pools, the travertine bench, or the corridor-like vistas that traverse both long sides of the building, either in combination or alone. Other similar moments abound in Mies's work of this period—movement through space calibrated by specific visual experiences.[50] This rhythmic occupation recalls the dance movement associated with eurhythmy by the Swiss choreographer Émile Jaques-Dalcroze, staged by Appia, in which a similar correlation among body movement, set, and music was intended to create a kind of bodily and spiritual harmony.

Going back to the Esters and Lange commissions of 1925, one finds a similarly rhythmic back-and-forth around walls and across adjacent spaces, with frequent changes of direction calibrated to landscape views or architectural tableaux. Tracing the plan of the Esters House, for example, brings one into the building along the long east-facing wall that fronts the house (Figure 2.14). From the front entrance an immediate 180-degree turn brings one back along the other side of the same wall, straight into the hall. Turns of the body of 90 or 180 degrees order the passage through the hall, the study (Herrenzimmer), the dining room, into the parlor (Damenzimmer) or the nursery, or to the garden terrace. Continuing leads directly to Esters's study; penetration of other realms, such as the dining room, requires instead another 180-degree turn from the hall back to the north. Further movement to the garden terrace requires, first, a turn of 90 degrees down the length of the dining room, then another 90-degree turn out the terrace door. A final 90-degree turn brings one face-to-face with the garden. But to enter the garden (to substitute physical presence for visual connection) one must descend yet another short flight of steps, or turn 90 degrees, walk along the garden terrace, descend more steps, and

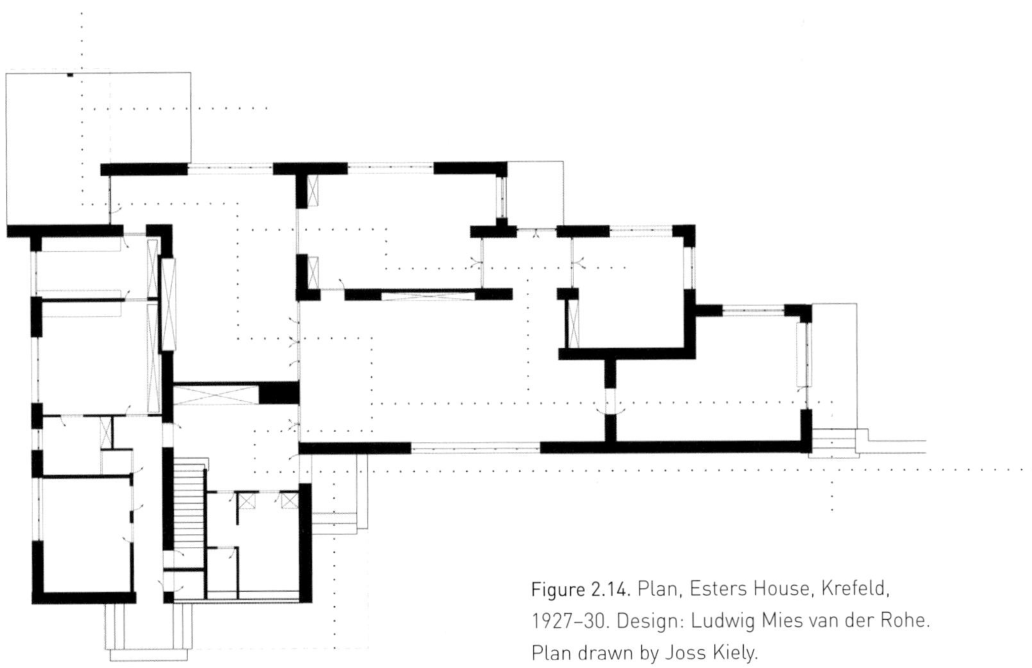

Figure 2.14. Plan, Esters House, Krefeld, 1927–30. Design: Ludwig Mies van der Rohe. Plan drawn by Joss Kiely.

turn yet again, before entering the garden proper. The construction of this house required a complex metallic frame under the building's brick outer garment; the system was not yet working elegantly.[51]

Tracing paths of movement through other plans of the period 1927 to 1942, one meets similar choreographed movement patterns laid out in space. The technique was to all appearances an important one in Mies's thinking at this time. Schinkel's plans exhibit a similar interest in highly orchestrated movement coordinated with (but also distinguished from) viewing axes; these were almost certainly important in the genesis of Mies's plans, as others have noted.[52] In addition, Mies's familiarity with Adolphe Appia's set design and choreography of 1912–13 at Hellerau has been noted repeatedly, generally accompanied by photographs of one or more of Appia's sets.[53] Appia's designs displayed similar, predetermined, ritualized patterns of movement through the space of the stage, particularly in the series of "rhythmic designs" dating from Appia's earliest collaboration with Jaques-Dalcroze in 1909, but also in his slightly later sets for Hellerau from the years just before World War I. Many of Appia's stage designs dated to the 1910s prefigure Miesian circulation patterns (Figure 2.15). Like concrete manifestations of the patterns later suggested in Mies's plans, Appia's sets simply excluded the constricting addition of exterior walls and roof, which were deferred to the shell of the performance space, Heinrich Tessenow's Festhalle of 1911.

Most interestingly, the formal relation between Appia's theatrical choreographies and Mies's designs is echoed in more substantive affiliations between their projects. Appia revised stage design technique to make the set complement the actor's performance dramaturgically, but also in a bodily sense. Appia noted, in describing a design for a scene from *Siegfried*: "How are we to present a forest on stage? . . . [The stage director] will think of the forest as an atmosphere around and about the performer; an atmosphere which can be realized only in relation to living and moving beings on which he must focus. . . . We shall no longer try to give the illusion of a forest, but the illusion of a man in the atmosphere of a forest."[54] The theatrical experience was to be purified in a mise-en-scène in which performance and movement were only minimally supplemented by set and lighting—all growing as if organically from the core provided by the actor's work.[55]

A similar reduction to essentials characterized Mies's early architectural projects such as the Concrete Office Building and the glass skyscraper projects, translated into architectural terms. Mies's notion of purified *Bauen,* or building construction, was that of building stripped back to essential elements that then accrue to themselves the additions necessary for functional completion.[56] These different forms of production, from Appia to Mies, shared what many modernists shared: the redefinition

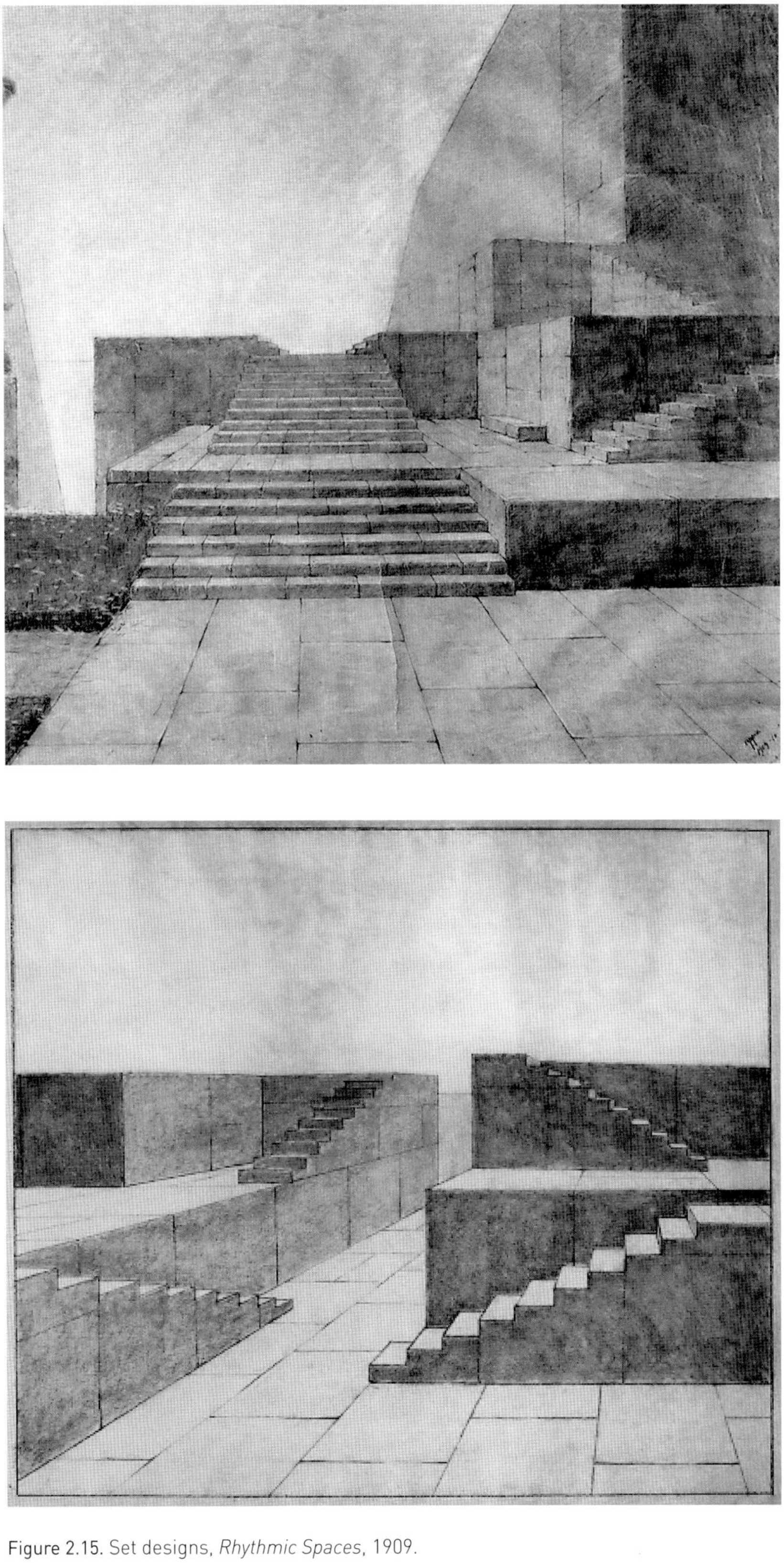

Figure 2.15. Set designs, *Rhythmic Spaces*, 1909.
Designer: Adolphe Appia. Swiss Theatre Collection, Berne.

of their artistic goals according to new constructs of subjectivity. But affiliations between theatrical performance and architectural inhabitation were a leitmotif of modern architecture in the period before World War I; they remain a recurrent theme throughout the development of modern architecture.[57] The similarity between the choreographies of Appia's set designs and those of Mies's building plans is the hieratic, regularized movement back and forth across a space where movement is keyed to visual experiences.

Manfredo Tafuri reflected on connections between the theatrical design of Appia and the building design of Mies in his essay "The Stage as 'Virtual City': From Fuchs to the Totaltheater."[58] After drawing the parallel between these two figures, Tafuri noted:

> The theater dreamed of by Appia for a community that needs no theaters to realize itself was to have, however, another fleeting expression. In 1929 in the Barcelona Pavilion, Mies van der Rohe constructed a scenic space whose neutrality shares profound similarities with that of the rhythmical geometries of the sets of Appia and Craig.[59]

Tafuri construed absence and emptiness as constitutive of the pavilion's meaning, and his interpretation has been influential. One might, however, interpret the *programmatic* emptiness of the building as precisely providing the opportunity for its *experiential* fullness.[60] Similarly, the lack of program requirements placed the pavilion on "equal footing" with other cultural products, such as paintings, sculptures, and objects of graphic art, elevating architecture to the status of the programmatically useless but semantically full. In any case, the stripping away of theatrical ritual from the conventional stage in Appia's work and the interweaving of choreographic technique in the Miesian plan bring the two conceptions into closer proximity.

The strategy of carving out, of establishing level datums of ceiling and floor as fixed conditions within which architectural space developed, recalls the operations of de Stijl designers in the early 1920s and the work of Theo van Doesburg most notably. Mies's work represented perhaps the most successful realization of de Stijl's written propositions for an abstract architecture to date, as Van Doesburg appears to have appreciated.[61] But unlike de Stijl, Mies followed the emptying out of space—the negative project of modern architecture—with the positive act of filling it again. These buildings were not filled with designed objects. Mies filled his cleared planes with the means for a synesthetic experience made possible by the use of modern industrial methods deployed in concert with old materials: marble, colored glass, metal, water, fabric. This achievement followed Mies to the United States, even while his particular architectural strategies, once he arrived, deflected radically to his new context.

Paradoxically, Appia's stripping away of physical barriers between the audience and the stage was not paralleled in any similar stripping away of barriers between the eurhythmic body and the unschooled body of the casual spectator. If anything, the new artifices of eurhythmics called for a trained elite corps, a "cult without gods" that left the spectator behind.[62] A question might then be posed in relation to Miesian space: If choreographical or theatrical modes—in their original settings highly self-conscious—begin to influence our experience of architecture, then in what ways do those modes register themselves in the experience of the visitor? Are we to agree with Tafuri that the visitor to the Barcelona Pavilion "is obliged to perform a pantomime that reproduces the wandering in the urban labyrinth of sign-beings among signs having no sense"? Or might this question be considered less abstractly, without the gloss of post–World War II theory, as a sequence of experiences hinged to specific sensory affect intended to act on the occupant?

Rhythm was a broad focus of interest in the late Wilhelmine and Weimar years, in particular across the intersection of modern dance performance and architecture. Rudolf Laban, Mary Wigman, and Oskar Schlemmer, in addition to Jaques-Dalcroze and Appia explored dance movement in relation to space and form.[63] Rhythmic movement was central to modernist performance, particularly to Jaques-Dalcroze's system of dance, which took its name from the Greek *eurhythmy.* Likewise, Laban created *Ausdrucktanz* (expression-dance) and developed a new form of notation for recording movement in space, in which irregular (nonrhythmic) movement was nevertheless recorded systematically—a notation system installing structure within free movement. As Debra McCall has noted, Laban's training as artist and architect contributed to his conception of "movement as architecture in space."[64] Rhythm provided a point of connectivity between body and mind, recalling philosophy of becoming from Henri Bergson, dynamic movement from eurhythmics, and rationalized movement through space from the world of architecture. Mies, more than any other architect of his day, integrated rhythmic movement into architectural planning through his particular plan-making strategies.

Connections between theatrical design and modern architecture date back to Schinkel at least and were a recurring theme in interwar modern architecture, of which Mies was well aware.[65] As noted, a concern for rhythm was central to dance, but the same concern had ramifications in other cultural realms as well. The economic historian Karl Bücher's popular *Arbeit und Rhythmus* of 1896 signaled the importance of rhythm and music to worker performance and productivity, counterposing industrial production and aesthetic production, the second taming the first.[66] Willy Drost's 1919 *Die Lehre vom Rhythmus in der heutigen Ästhetik der bildenden*

Künste surveyed rhythm in art, and frequent references to rhythm in writings by Weimar artists and critics abounded.[67] For Mies, this discourse appears to have applied directly to architecture in the rhythmic choreography of the architectural plan, regardless of whether Mies knew Drost's book. Applying the self-consciousness of performance practices to the design of a building plan also instilled a heightened self-consciousness in visitors to the building. This was especially appropriate for the Barcelona Pavilion, a building with a purpose that was primarily ritual and representational (even theatrical). Mies also used the opportunity of creating ritualized movement through the building as a counterpoint to the disjunctive optical experience provided by the montage of planes that inhabited the building, to which we now turn.

MONTAGE SPACE

The use of independent architectural elements, such as slabs of marble and sheets of glass starkly juxtaposed, recalls montage practices in both photography and film. The adaptation of these techniques was a distinctive feature of Mies's work, beginning with the glass skyscraper projects of the 1920s, where faceted glass surfaces created discontinuous reflections from the surrounding contexts. In the exploration of the relationship between montage and architecture, the question of rhythm was also still in play. The two themes, rhythm and montage, were closely interrelated in Mies's work of this period. Choreographed movement through space was a thread connecting disconnected elements of architectural montage sequences, sequences that are easiest to analyze in the constructed work. The interplay between connectivity and disjunction in relation to buildings of the late 1920s and 1930s can be seen in the changing visual tableaux that were orchestrated by consistent parameters, easiest to see in the Barcelona Pavilion.

Robin Evans described the space of Mies's architecture, for example, as "sheath-like," always sandwiched between ceiling and floor slab. Evans noted: "Vision is not so much confined as impeded. . . . you are left with a variegated, horizontal strip in middle ground, sandwiched between two broad, blank bands above and below. Mies is often criticized for pressing architectural space between flat, horizontal sheets. That is all he ever did." In summing up his findings, Evans stated, "By virtue of its optical properties, and of its disembodied physicality, the pavilion always draws us away from consciousness of it as a thing, and draws us towards consciousness of the way we see it."[68] Other critics have also dwelled at length on the visual effects of the pavilion's walls/surfaces.[69] All agree, however, that the polished surfaces of the building are surfaces on which some virtual visual experience takes place, and in which extravagant optical illusion tracks the visitor's movements through space.

Connections between the pavilion and avant-garde film of the period recall Mies's close connection with Hans Richter in the early 1920s.[70]

Richter and other Dadaists invoked the term *universal language* in the 1920s to describe their vocabulary of design.[71] The term has always had a kind of troubling resonance in Mies studies, drifting loose from early contextual references after World War II and becoming conflated with the architect's later, American work on clear-span structures.[72] But in Weimar culture it had a very different meaning, where the search for universal language came from nineteenth-century philosophy of language and was pursued in a variety of disciplines. Richter's abstract film reflects ideas extrapolated from theories of universal language that he recorded in a pamphlet titled *Universelle Sprache,* which he coauthored with Viking Eggeling in 1920.[73] Describing universal language in visual and experiential terms that superseded the use of written or spoken language, Richter saw it as a subtly differentiated, dramatically replete vocabulary of interreferential forms and substances in which proportional variation of shape and form moved within the stable datum of the film frame and the void space it appeared to contain. In viewing Richter's films, we see a direct corollary between the filmstrip as a never-varying formal parameter and Mies's own insistence on two absolutely level planes of floor and ceiling. The objects distributed throughout Miesian space—luminous wall, gray transparent/reflective wall, green marbles, *onyx dorée,* and others—function analogously to the moving planes of one of Richter's early abstract films, such as *Rhythmus 21* (1921) (Figure 2.16).[74] The uniformity of the floor-to-ceiling condition for Mies did not reflect a lack of interest in the section as a device of architectural planning so much as an attempt to stabilize the frame within which certain architectural effects might be obtained. Close connections between these two artists and the appearance and content of their work in the early 1920s suggest that they were aiming for similar goals within the restrictions of their media.

Spatial sequence and rhythm constituted important scenographic elements for Richter. The formal language of *Rhythmus 21* bears striking similarities to the Barcelona Pavilion. One common thread that runs between Richter's early abstract films (made at the same time that *G* appeared under the editorship of Richter and Mies) and later buildings by Mies lies in the manner in which they unfolded: in *Rhythmus 21,* Richter arranged a mobile sequence of abstract planes that either move toward the viewer or suggest movement through space; Mies orchestrated the movement of the occupants of his buildings through a sequence of plane-defined spaces. Richter's films depict spatial experience without the delimiting condition of ceiling, surrounding walls, and exterior context, but within the limits of the film frame itself. This condition may help explain the rigidity of Mies's floor and ceiling planes. If one

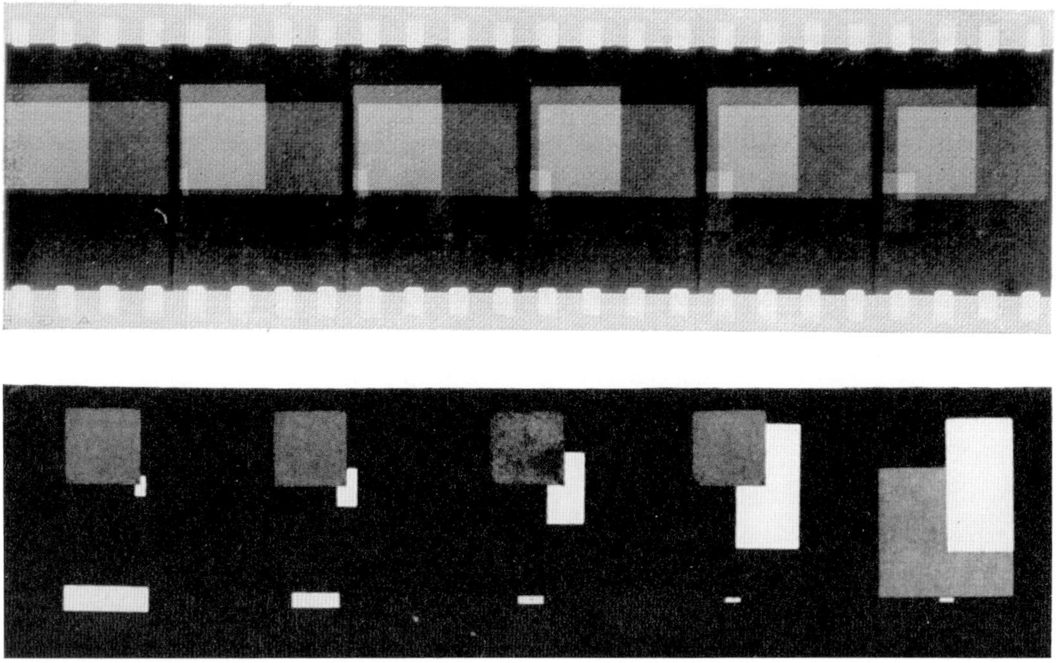

Figure 2.16. Hans Richter, film stills, *Rhythmus 21*, 1921.

understands the ceiling and floor planes as delimiting a cleared space that Mies then filled with planes, the filmic parallel becomes more comprehensible, and Mies's possible debt to Richter clearer. Mies used the floor and ceiling as fixed datums against which an intensified perceptual experience played out.

Richter's work in abstract film in the early 1920s used rhythm as a central organizing motif. By 1929 Richter had codified some of the principles of his film theory in the primer published to coincide with the 1929 "Film und Foto" exhibition. In a section titled "Jetzt der Rhythmus" in *Filmgegner von heute, Filmfreunde von morgen,* Richter explained the importance of rhythm for filmmaking: "Rhythm is the basic form, the skeleton of a film—insofar as it is art. . . . Here one must attend to: 1. the length of a montage sequence; 2. the direction of movement; 3. the tempo; 4. finally, the power [of the sequence], whose effect differs according to the size of its tone and form. Rhythm in film means nothing less than the artistic, clearly ordered sequence of movements."[75] Richter's abstract film, where discrete sequences of continually moving assemblages of rectangles follow one another in an ordered train, suggests restless movement forward and backward, in and out of the frame in space. This recalls Appia's striation of the stage through back-and-forth movements, just as it also describes Mies's plan choreography of the late 1920s. Standish Lawder, in his book on Cubist cinema, described *Rhythm 21* as "a work in which the content was essentially rhythm, the formal vocabulary was elemental geometry, the structural principle was the counterpoint of contrasting opposites, and in which space and time became interdependent." Lawder went on to describe the bulk of the film as follows:

> Sections of the film use a larger number of design elements, all rectangular in configuration, and introduce dissolves of one composition into another. By expanding and diminishing the size of these individual forms, a pictorial composition of constant imbalance is created. As one form swells to the foreground, another sinks into the distance, others merge, interpenetrate, or overlap. No single form seems to move in isolated activity. . . . the movements of each form seem inexorably linked to movement elsewhere on the screen.[76]

Malcolm Turvey described these early films "as balancing disorder with order, spontaneity with intentionality, chance with pattern. For while on a macro-level they create a strong impression of order, on a micro-, moment-by-moment level, they are surprising and unpredictable."[77] Both these descriptions also apply to Mies's work of the mid- to late 1920s with minimum revision. From the Glass Room through the Barcelona Pavilion and into the work of the 1930s, Mies used rectangular forms, rhythmic movement, a balance of regular order with freely distributed space-defining elements. Mies's 1942 Museum for a Small City is one of the last projects he composed using this design method, with the added element of canvases and statuary in a dynamically balanced architectural performance. This form of contrast is quite different from the dyad structure–enclosure that has often characterized analyses of Mies's work. Turvey and Lawder, although by no means in total agreement in other respects, have both identified visual contrast as a goal of Richter's film work. Similarly, Mies's architecture relied on experiential variation and contrast, both within the spatial "sheath" provided by ceiling and floor and outside it. The frame of floor and ceiling and the dimensional similarity of individual elements created sharp contrast, as the visual character of reflective tinted plate glass differs from polished Tinian marble and thick curtains of red silk.

The theme of rhythm that played out in the back-and-forth movement of the Miesian plan of this period connects Appia, Richter, and Mies.[78] An idea of equilibrium or harmonious balance is implied in Appia's eurhythmics and Richter's notion of rhythm. Also a foundational principle of neoplastic aesthetics (with which both Richter and Mies had direct contact, through their encounters with Theo van Doesburg in the early 1920s) and Gestalt psychology, the notion of equilibrium was directly keyed to sensory and perceptual possibilities inherent to the individual subject. When reflecting back on his early period, Richter noted that he and Eggeling had based their work on "species-wide laws of human perception" and that "all of these discoveries became meaningful in the light of our belief that a precise polar interrelationship of opposites was the key to an order, and once we understood this order we knew we could control this new freedom."[79] Appia had noted much earlier, in 1912, that equilibrium is a function of controlling what he called the "reciprocity of the senses":

> Within the same individual a sort of equilibrium is attained in regard to the sum of his powers: if one sense strengthens, another grows weaker, but it is evident that their overall power, which determines a personality, remains the same. It follows that we can only influence our senses in their *reciprocal* relations: the variations in sensory response are unlimited and they distinguish one person from another far more than we tend to assume.
>
> With regard to education . . . how should we proceed if we require access *directly* to the student's senses themselves in order to harmonise their relative value? It is particularly here that the differences in personality will be felt; for there can be no intermediary between instruction and the senses. . . . In the first instance the individual must discover his own senses; he must become *aware* of the reciprocity of his senses; only then can he attempt to bring them into harmonious play.[80]

Appia described the action of sensory stimuli on individuals and suggested that equilibrium regulates disparities between individual experiences—in effect, he suggested, like Richter, that equilibrium in the human subject follows the "species-wide laws" that Richter referred to many years later. Thus the "universal language" of form rests on the notion that such laws could be codified for individual subjects.

Rhythmic movement in relation to montage elements struck critics of Mies's work when it was first completed.[81] The occupant undergoes a carefully scripted sequence of visual and spatial experiences that also recalls the idea of equilibrium, partly through regular movement through space, as if its systematic traversal would finally result in a kind of balanced occupation. If any architectural plan is a performance score delimiting movement patterns in space, then Mies's plans describe a particular kind of movement, related to the rhythmic syncopation of visual and experiential moments. Equilibrium occurs when movements through the plan are punctuated by corresponding visual experiences that accompany directional shifts. While the movement patterns in his plans attest Mies's close attention to Schinkel's similar organization of plans and landscapes, nevertheless Mies updated his nineteenth-century precedent by integrating a particular way of moving through space with contemporary ideas about stagecraft, performance, and filmic experience.[82]

CONCLUSION

How fully was Mies's architecture organized around the possibility of creating cosmically charged environments that called up an idea related to painterly and graphic abstraction and applied it to building? There are many features in his work that make clear his consciousness of the importance of the issue and the various means with which he helped form them. Just as no architect before him had succeeded in fully resolving the paradox of constructed reality versus projected space, so Mies cannot be said to have solved a problem that had no solution. Instead, Mies's architecture, as constructed, was clearly embedded in the discourses with which he was closely involved and through which he sought means to realize certain apparently extraphysical propositions through physical means. In this he was eminently successful, even if this success has had to be recuperated and posed in contrast to the enormous influence of the photographs of his work.

Perhaps the most interesting part of the process outlined here lies in the very seamlessness with which two media infiltrated one another in at least two ways. The ways in which photography and film influenced Mies's work as an architect reveal how the tradition-bound practice of architecture adapted itself to modernization, at least in one important case.[83] These modes of investigation represent newly retrieved developments whose mechanisms remained temporarily obscured for many years. Indeed, if Mies's architectural investigations were conceptually rarified and segregated from the rhetoric of social reform that accompanied much architecture of the 1920s, they also represent one of the most ambitious attempts to reintegrate architecture into contemporary cultural life. This might be considered the central task that modern architects set for themselves in the wake of critical judgments of the historicizing architecture of the later nineteenth century, not just a response to that century's overriding call for modernization. Mies's success in both modernizing the conceptual basis of architecture and neutralizing the threat of historicism is evident in his continuing importance to the field, both to historians and to practicing architects. While he is not alone in this achievement, his particular case bears closer examination in a cross-medial sense—in other words, in relation to cultural practices beyond the limits of architecture. Subsequent chapters shift ground to consider the photographic documentation of Mies's work of the late 1920s.

In a world where things and experiences are fantastically mutable the house remains a relatively rigid, multi-celled spatial entity. Its base is either fixed or loosely connected to the ground through which manifold forces flow. Its remaining surfaces come into contact with a thinner medium that is penetrated by rays of light of variable quality, alternating periodically. The friction between these two sets of forces plays out in the hollow space of the house, entering into a *law-governed* interaction—mental and physiological—with the inhabitants inside. The degree of harmonious balance between these three components determines the character and quality of the architecture.

— SIEGFRIED EBELING,
SPACE AS MEMBRANE

3. ARCHITECTURAL ABSTRACTION
THE TUGENDHAT PHOTOGRAPHS

The main group of photographs of Ludwig Mies van der Rohe's Tugendhat House in Brno constitutes a single (although multistranded) spatial narrative similar to the one recommended by Wilhelm Lotz in an article on architectural photography in *Die Form* in 1929.[1] One can trace a route right through the building: approach along the street from the south on the opposite side (Figure 3.1);[2] turn to view the distant Spilberk on the Brno skyline through the framed aperture between the entry and the garage; turn again to approach the front door and enter the building (Figure 3.2); turn again within the foyer to descend the tight curve of the semicircular stairs (Figure 3.3); turn during the descent to arrive at the door to the main salon; view the broad space of the living floor several times (Figure 3.4); look back through the door just entered; choose first to move toward the office directly ahead; move through the office and into the library; view the back corner of the library, with table and reading niche; turn to view the onyx wall (Figure 3.5) through the office from the back corner of the space (do not look into that corner, where the hidden vault lies); move straight ahead back into the space of the office, turning to look back at the milk-glass diaphragm between living and service areas and the entry door to its right (Figure 3.6); continue past the onyx wall straight along the glass edge of the winter garden; look back (Figure 3.7); look along the full-height glass panes fronting the garden, over the seating area; turn in passing to look back at the seating area and onyx wall; move along the inside of the garden windows (two perhaps sunken into the floor); continue along this edge, turning to glimpse the grand piano behind the onyx wall (but ignoring the small aperture behind which the film projector lives); look back at and through the glass walls of the winter garden, head-on (Figure 3.8); move further beyond the dining "room" and look back again (Figure 3.9); move further and look back along the entire inside length of the garden wall; move out the terrace door and onto the terrace; look into the terrace corner, with table and chairs (Figure 3.10); move out and look back at the facade (Figure 3.11); look down the garden stairs; descend the garden stairs, glance sweeping the garden facade; turn, look back at the stairs; move further into the garden and look back; move further and glance at the side of the winter garden (Figure 3.12); move down to the bottom of the garden and view the rear facade (Figure 3.13). Repeat this process with curtains in various closed or half-open positions on the main floor (Figures 3.14, 3.15), and in various kinds of weather.

Like the Barcelona Pavilion photographs, those of the Tugendhat House relay information filtered through and adjusted by the camera's lens. The mode of spatial design may owe more to film than to photography, but regardless of the genesis of Mies's design, the means by which it has entered architecture culture since has been overwhelmingly that of the architectural photograph. The series of photographs described above might be seen as projecting a book or film, or transposing a filmic architecture into a format that would allow it to circulate widely in the architectural press. A monograph similar to Erich Mendelsohn's *Neues Haus—Neue Welt* of 1932 may have been intended for the Tugendhat House, which would explain the existence of more than eighty different views of the building, requiring more than eighty glass negatives that measured approximately eighteen by twenty-four centimeters each, a total of more than 3.45 square meters of photographically sensitized glass.

Chapter 2 argued that architectural photography introduced two-dimensional abstraction into architectural discourse and that architectural abstraction was a considerably more complex construct. The Tugendhat House allows further development of the first of these claims. A concept ambivalently imported from the painterly avant-garde into architecture appears to have exercised significant influence there—not solely in pictures but in buildings as well. Photographs of Mies's buildings conveyed ideas about architecture through the means available at the time of their making. Representational abstraction in architectural photography, however, differed from investigations by Mies and others into the possibilities of "abstract" architecture in three dimensions, as noted in the preceding chapter.

Despite the potential practical utility that eighty individual photographs might serve in conveying information about a building, architectural photographs effected profound alterations to their contents. Perception of space through the photographic

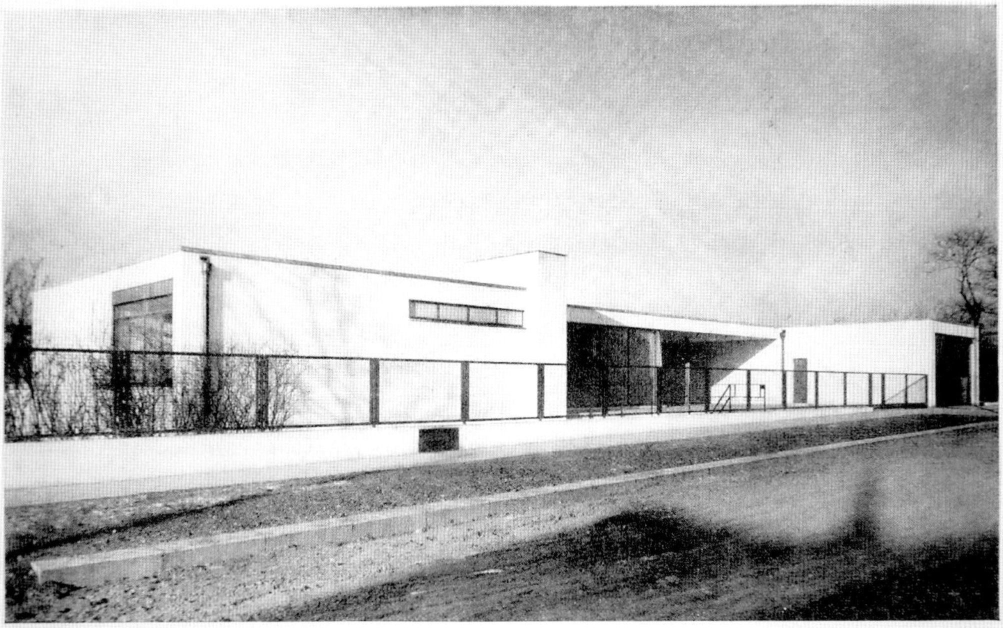

Eingang von der Straße, das Wohngeschoß liegt unterhalb der Straße nach dem Garten zu
Entrée sur la rue; l'étage réservé à l'habitation est situé sous la rue et donne sur le jardin
Entrance from the street. The groundfloor is below the level of the roadway, facing the garden

Figure 3.1. Street view, Tugendhat House, Brno, Czechoslovakia, 1931. Building: Ludwig Mies van der Rohe. Photograph: Atelier de Sandalo. As published in *Die Form* 6 in 1931.

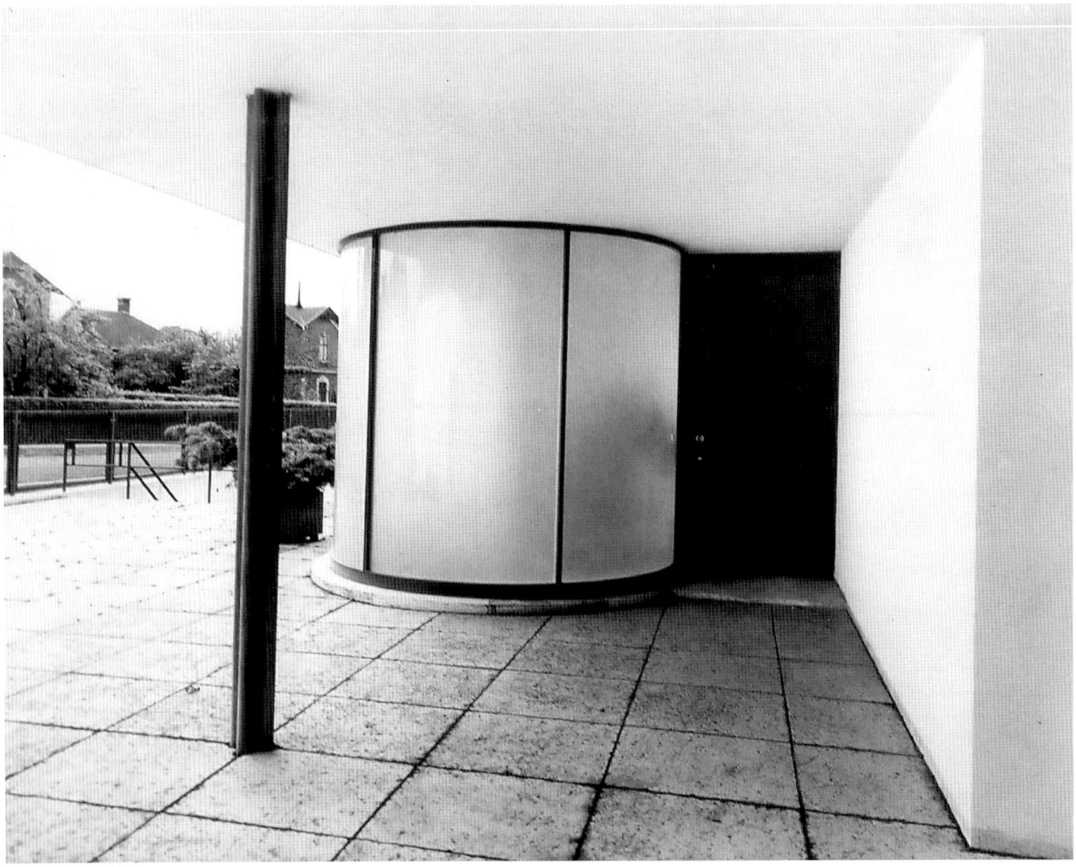

Figure 3.2. Entry, Tugendhat House. Photograph: Atelier de Sandalo. Mies van der Rohe Archive, The Museum of Modern Art, New York; Gift of the architect; digital image copyright The Museum of Modern Art/Licensed by SCALA/Art Resource, NY.

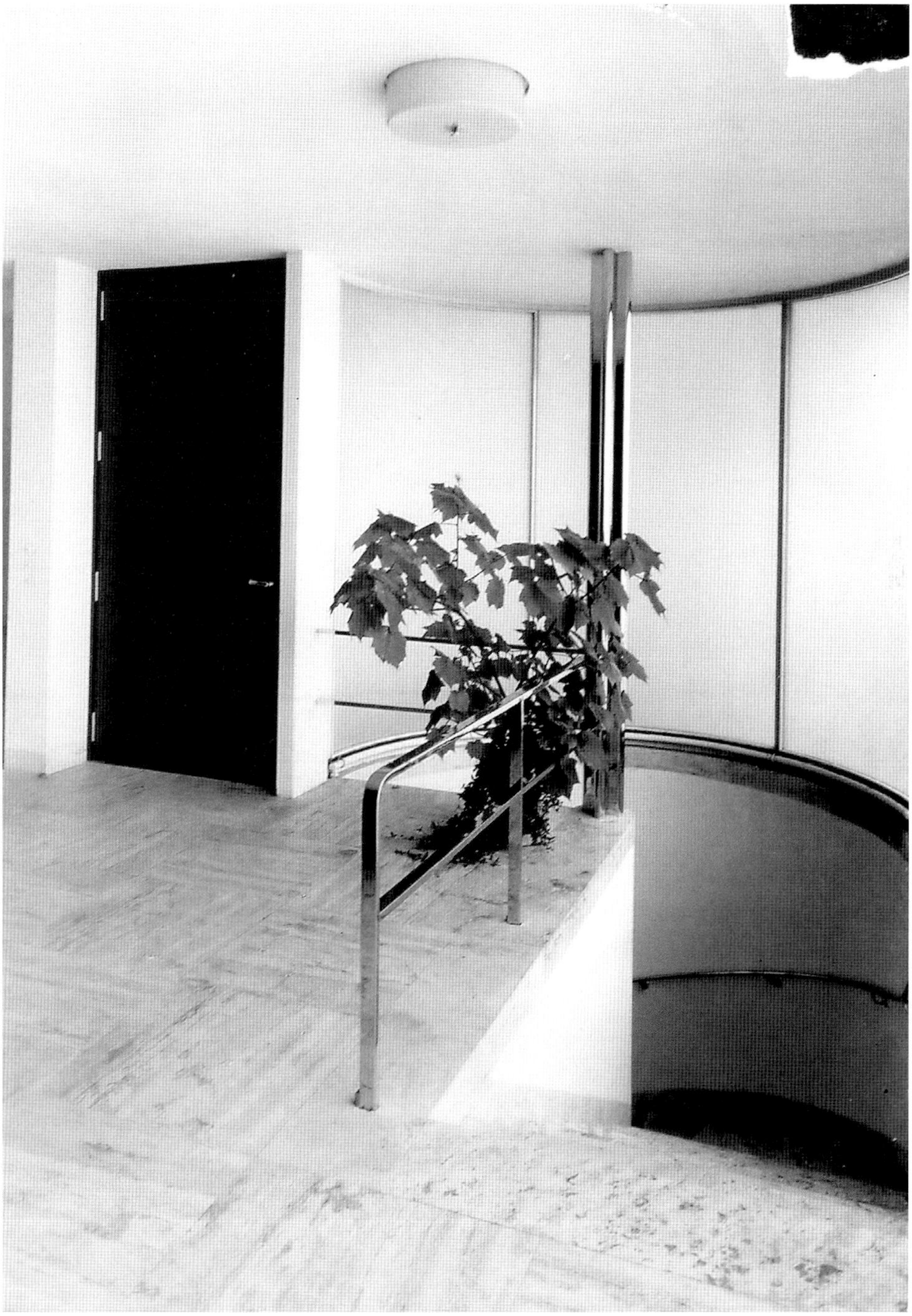

Figure 3.3. Foyer and stair, Tugendhat House. Photograph: Atelier de Sandalo. Mies van der Rohe Archive, The Museum of Modern Art, New York; Gift of the architect; digital image copyright The Museum of Modern Art/Licensed by SCALA/Art Resource, NY.

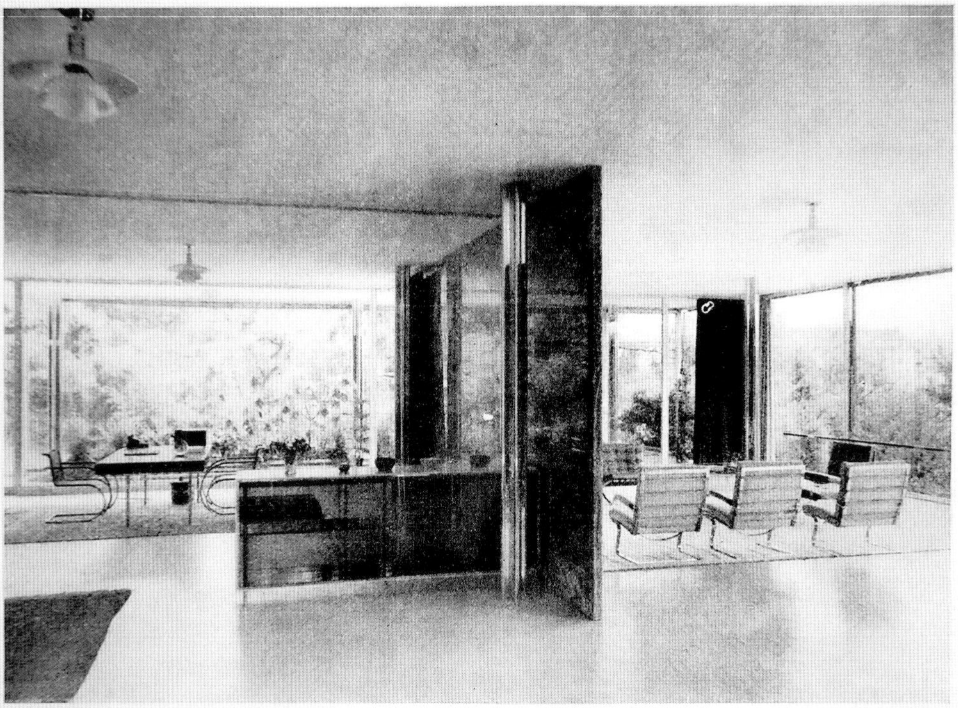

Blick nach der Schmalseite mit Wintergarten. Im Vordergrund honiggelbe Onyxwand
Perspective s'ouvrant sur le côté étroit de l'immeuble au long duquel on voit le jardin d'hiver. A l'avant-plan, paroi d'onyx jaune miel
View towards wintergarden showing honey coloured onyx partition

Figure 3.4. Main salon, Tugendhat House. Photograph: Atelier de Sandalo. As published in *Die Form* 6 in 1931.

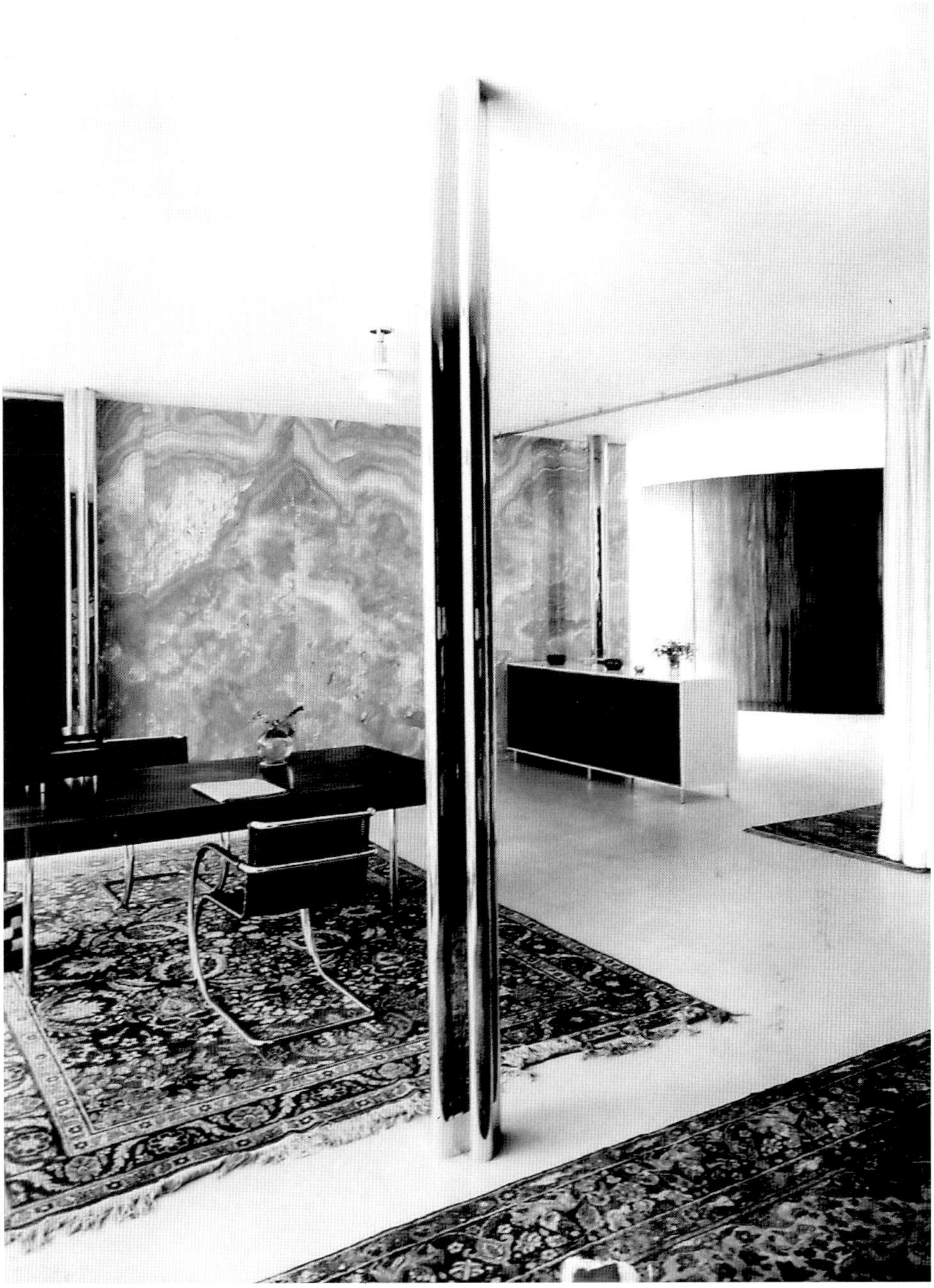

Figure 3.5. Study, from library, Tugendhat House. Photograph: Atelier de Sandalo. Mies van der Rohe Archive, The Museum of Modern Art, New York; Gift of the architect; digital image copyright The Museum of Modern Art/Licensed by SCALA/Art Resource, NY.

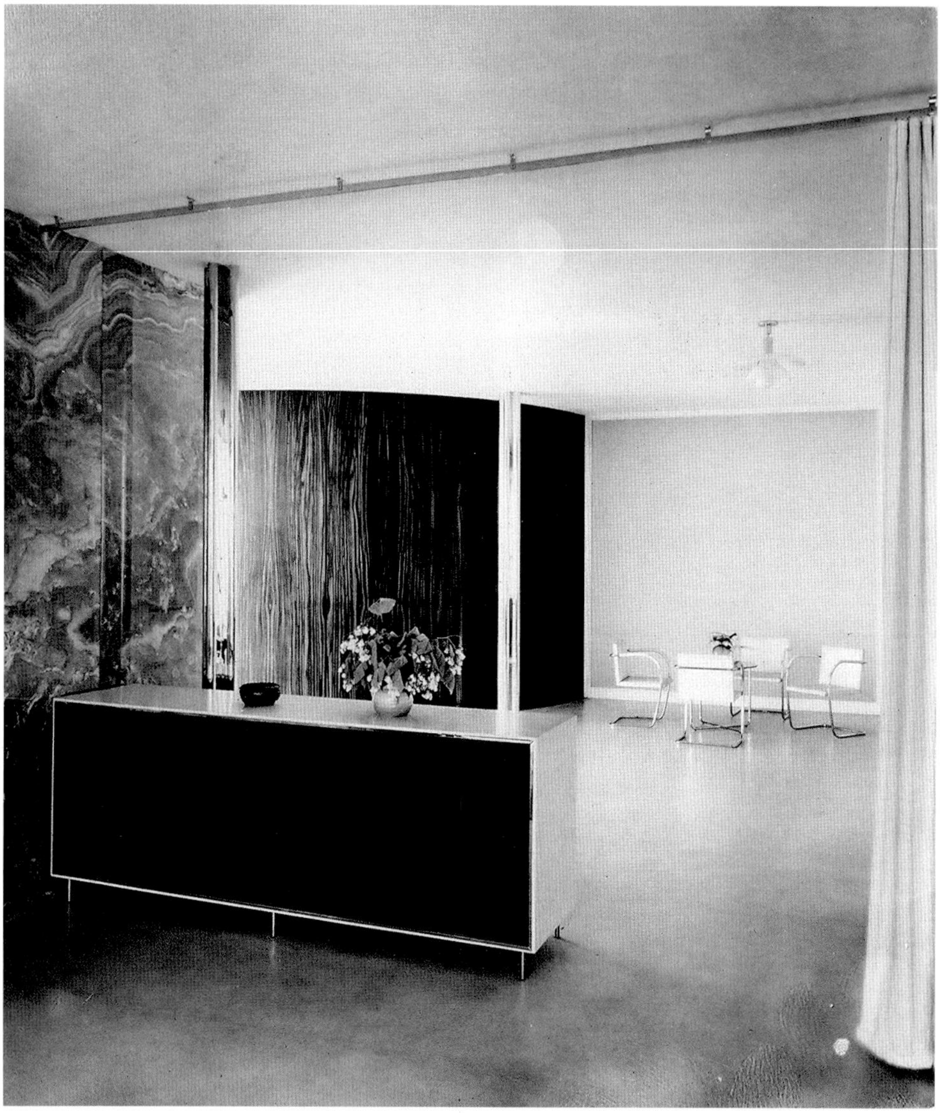

Figure 3.6. Study, looking back toward entry, Tugendhat House. Photograph: Atelier de Sandalo. Mies van der Rohe Archive, The Museum of Modern Art, New York; Gift of the architect; digital image copyright The Museum of Modern Art/Licensed by SCALA/Art Resource, NY.

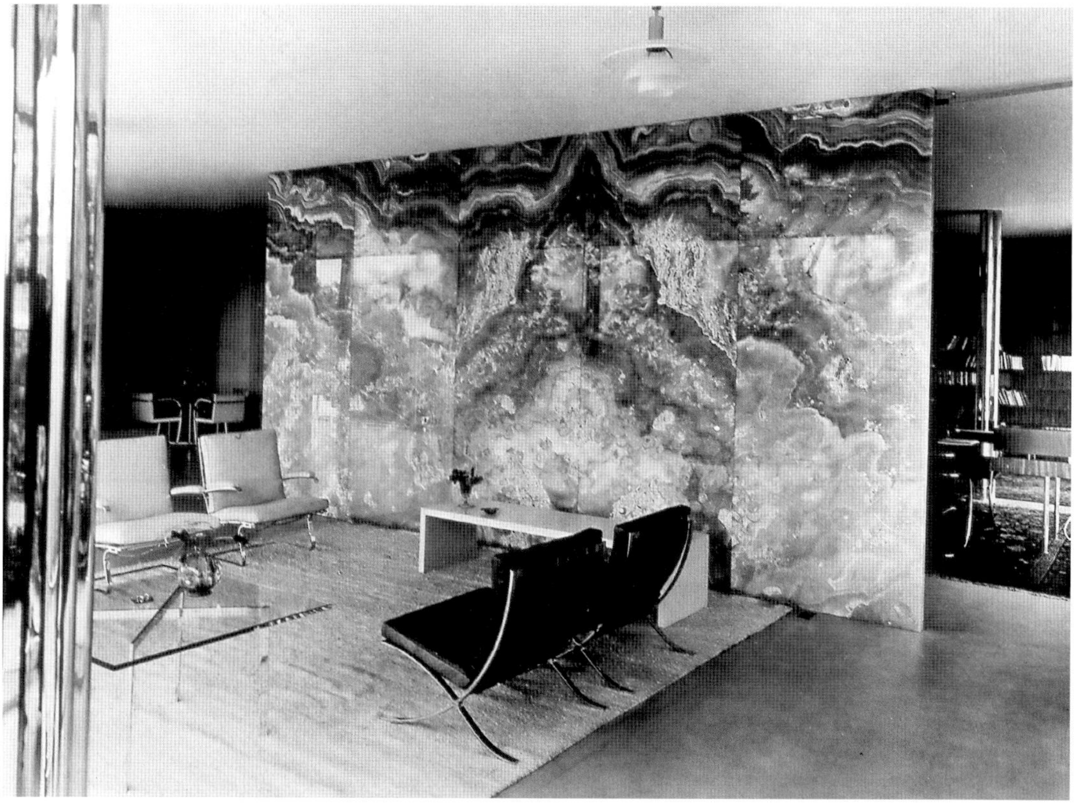

Figure 3.7. Onyx wall and seating area, Tugendhat House. Photograph: Atelier de Sandalo. Mies van der Rohe Archive, The Museum of Modern Art, New York; Gift of the architect; digital image copyright The Museum of Modern Art/Licensed by SCALA/Art Resource, NY.

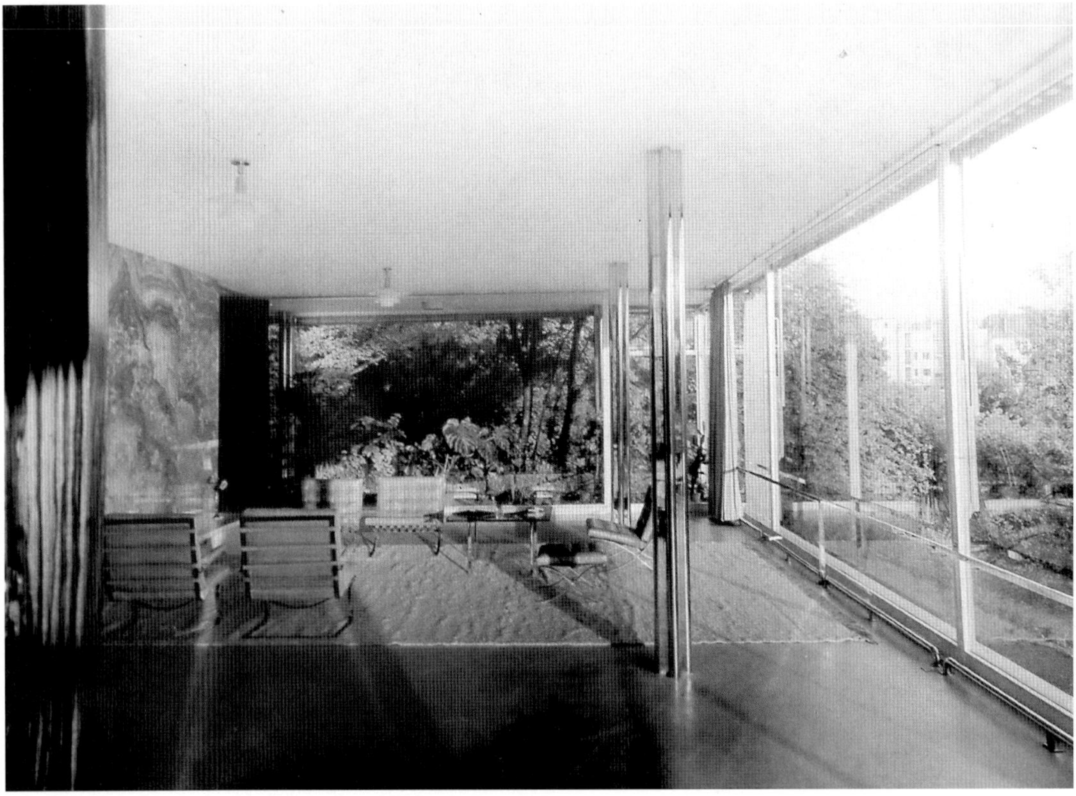

Figure 3.8. From dining area toward living area, Tugendhat House. Photograph: Atelier de Sandalo. As published in *Die Form* 6 in 1931.

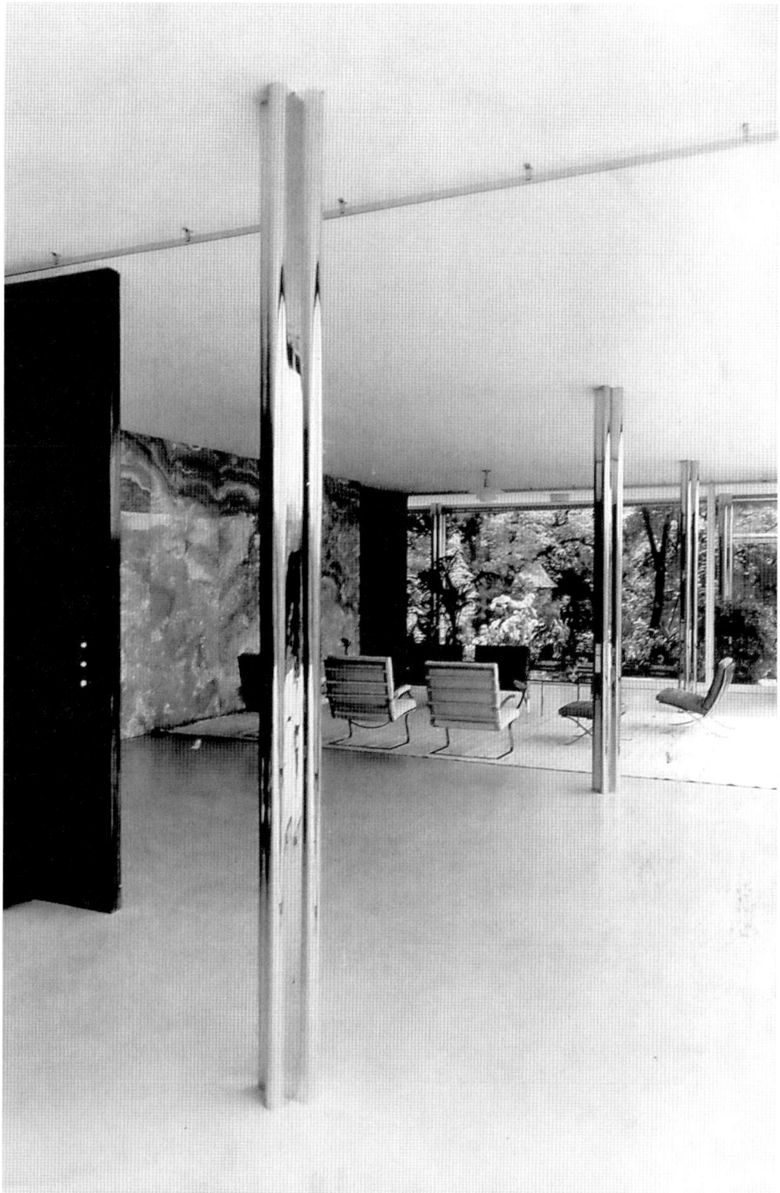

Figure 3.9. Edge of dining area with column, Tugendhat House. Photograph: Atelier de Sandalo. Mies van der Rohe Archive, The Museum of Modern Art, New York; Gift of the architect; digital image copyright The Museum of Modern Art/Licensed by SCALA/Art Resource, NY.

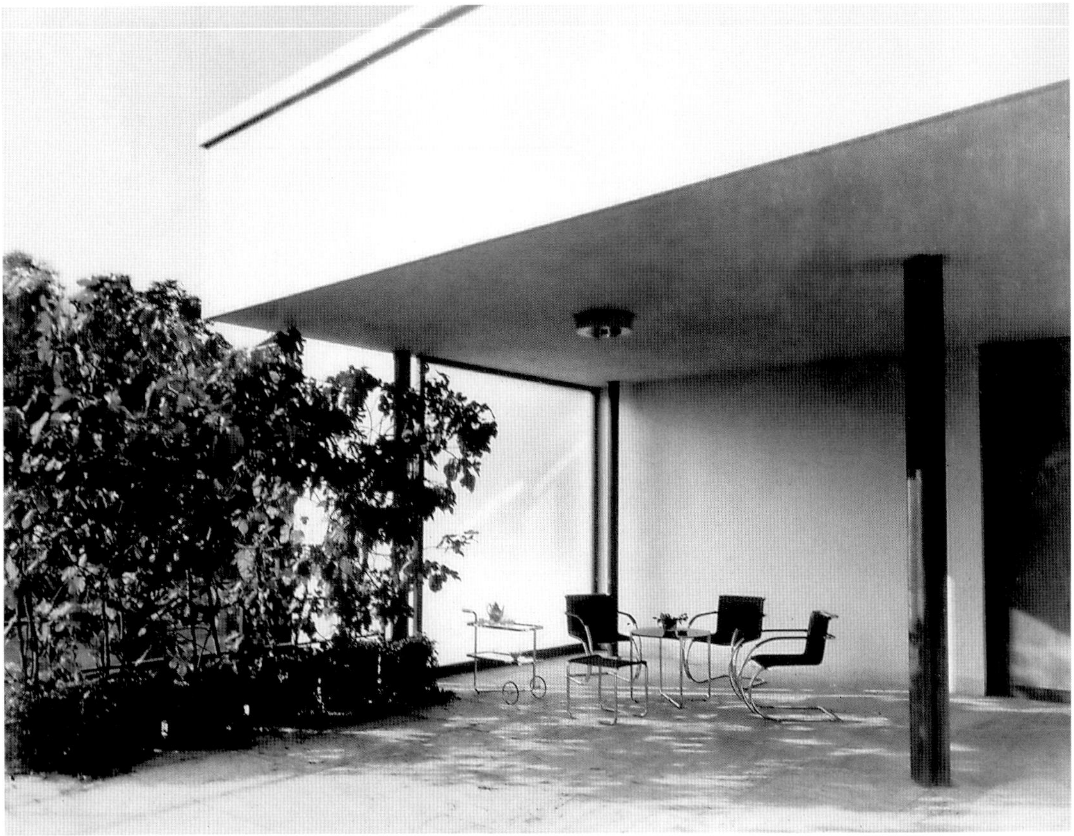

Figure 3.10. Terrace, Tugendhat House. Photograph: Atelier de Sandalo. Mies van der Rohe Archive, The Museum of Modern Art, New York; Gift of the architect; digital image copyright The Museum of Modern Art/Licensed by SCALA/Art Resource, NY.

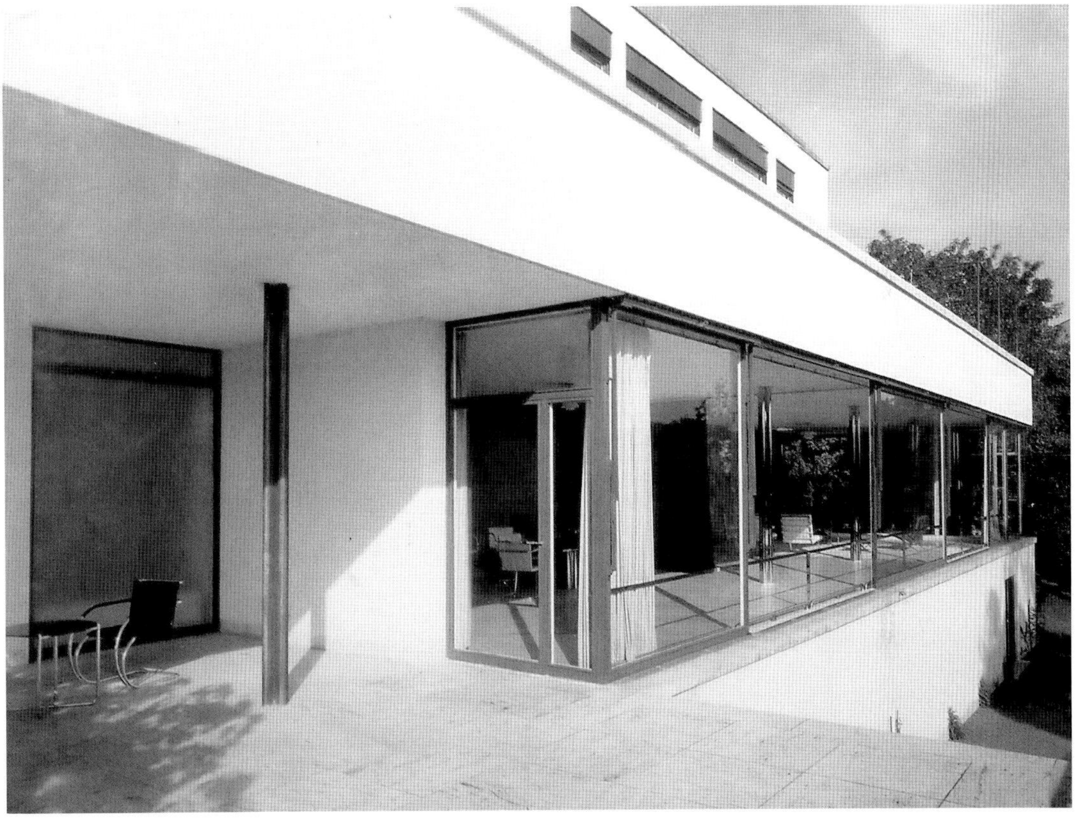

Figure 3.11. Garden facade from terrace, Tugendhat House. Photograph: Atelier de Sandalo. Mies van der Rohe Archive, The Museum of Modern Art, New York; Gift of the architect; digital image copyright The Museum of Modern Art/Licensed by SCALA/Art Resource, NY.

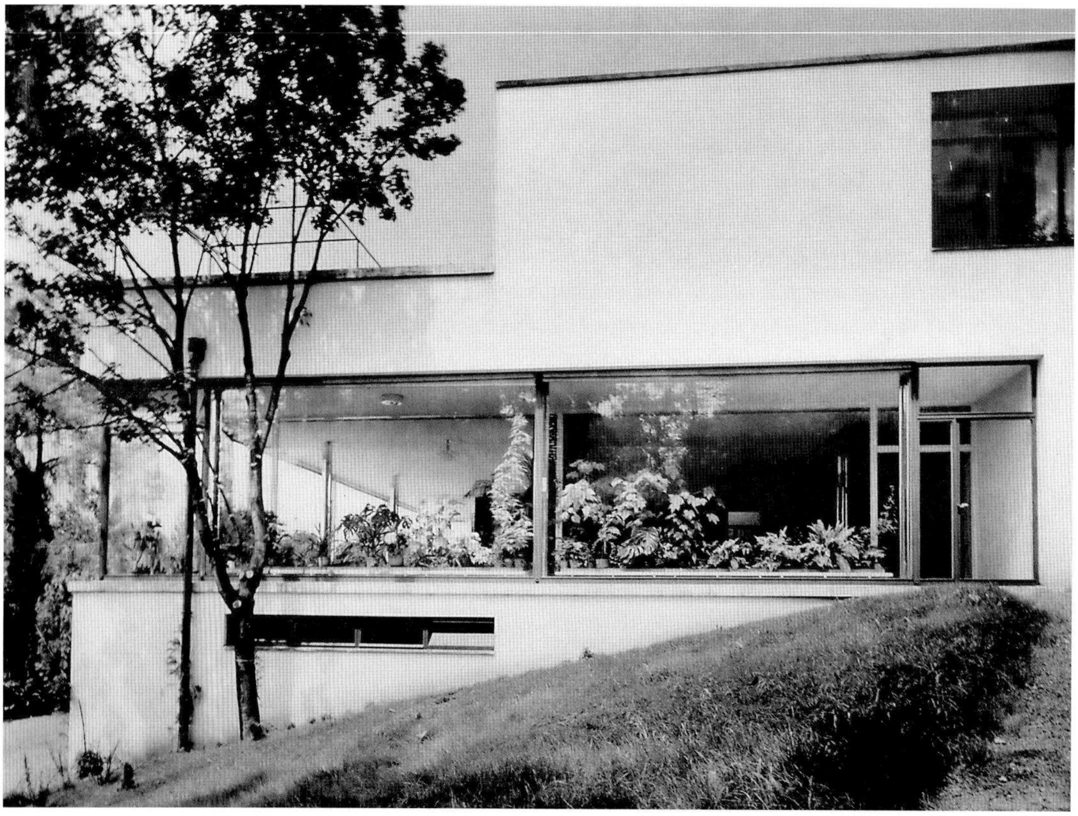

Figure 3.12. Side facade with winter garden wall, Tugendhat House. Photograph: Atelier de Sandalo. Mies van der Rohe Archive, The Museum of Modern Art, New York; Gift of the architect; digital image copyright The Museum of Modern Art/Licensed by SCALA/Art Resource, NY.

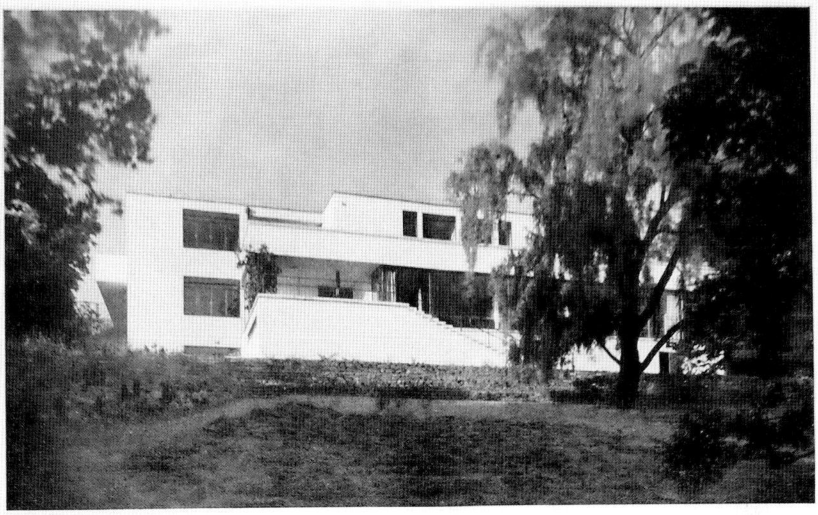

Haus Tugendhat in Brünn. Architekt Ludwig Mies van der Rohe, Berlin
Ansicht des Hauses von der Gartenseite her. Der Eingang von der Straße mündet im Obergeschoß
Aspect de la maison vue du jardin. L'entrée donnant accès de la rue débouche à l'étage pupérieur
The house as seen from the garden. The entrance from the street leads into the upper floor

Stahlskelettbau mit Steineisendecken
Ausmauerung der Außenwände halbsteinstarkes Mauerwerk, verputzt, mit Isolierung durch Torfoleumplatten
Im Wohngeschoß Luftheizung, im Obergeschoß und in den kleineren Räumen Warmwasserheizung
Im Obergeschoß Fenestra-Fenster
Construction à squelette d'acier avec plancher en béton de pierre armé
Les murs extérieurs sont en maçonnage de l'épaisseur d'une demi-brique, crépis et isolés par un système de plaques en torfoleum (huile de tourbe)
L'étage réservé à l'habitation est chauffé à l'air chaud; l'étage supérieur et les pièces de moindre superficie sont chauffés à l'eau chaude
Steel frame construction with re-inforced concrete ceilings
Brickwork of outer walls, half a brick thick, plastered, insolated by means of "Torfoleum" sheets, an insolating material made chiefly of peat, i. e. "Torf" in German
Central hot air heating in groundfloor; central warm water heating in upper floor, and in all smaller rooms

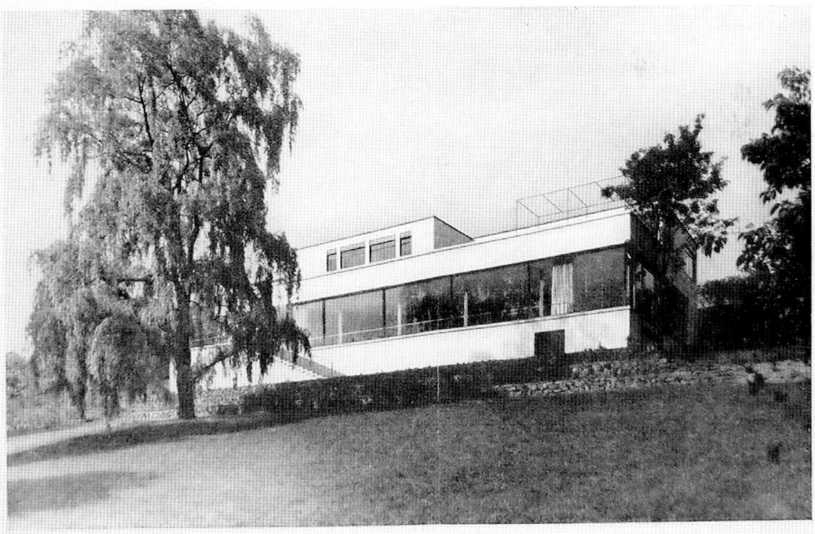

323

Figure 3.13. Views from garden, Tugendhat House. Photographs: Atelier de Sandalo. As published in *Die Form* 6 in 1931.

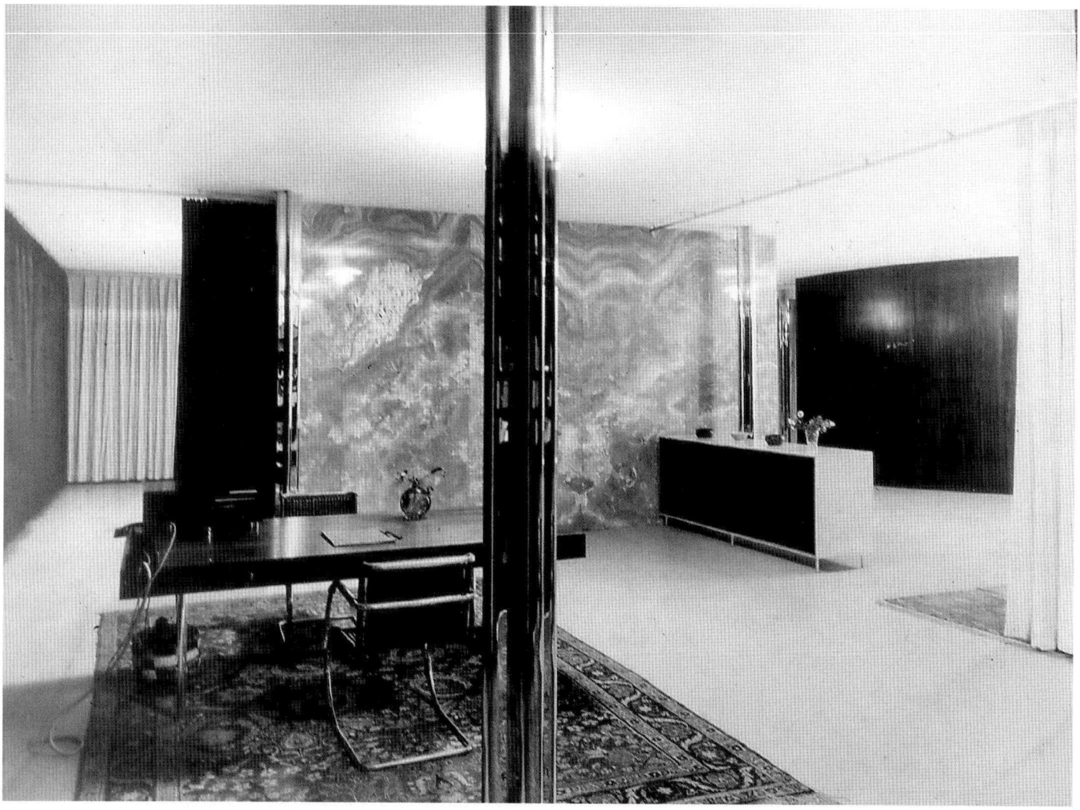

Figure 3.14. From library toward onyx wall (curtains closed), Tugendhat House. Photograph: Atelier de Sandalo. Mies van der Rohe Archive, The Museum of Modern Art, New York; Gift of the architect; digital image copyright The Museum of Modern Art/Licensed by SCALA/Art Resource, NY.

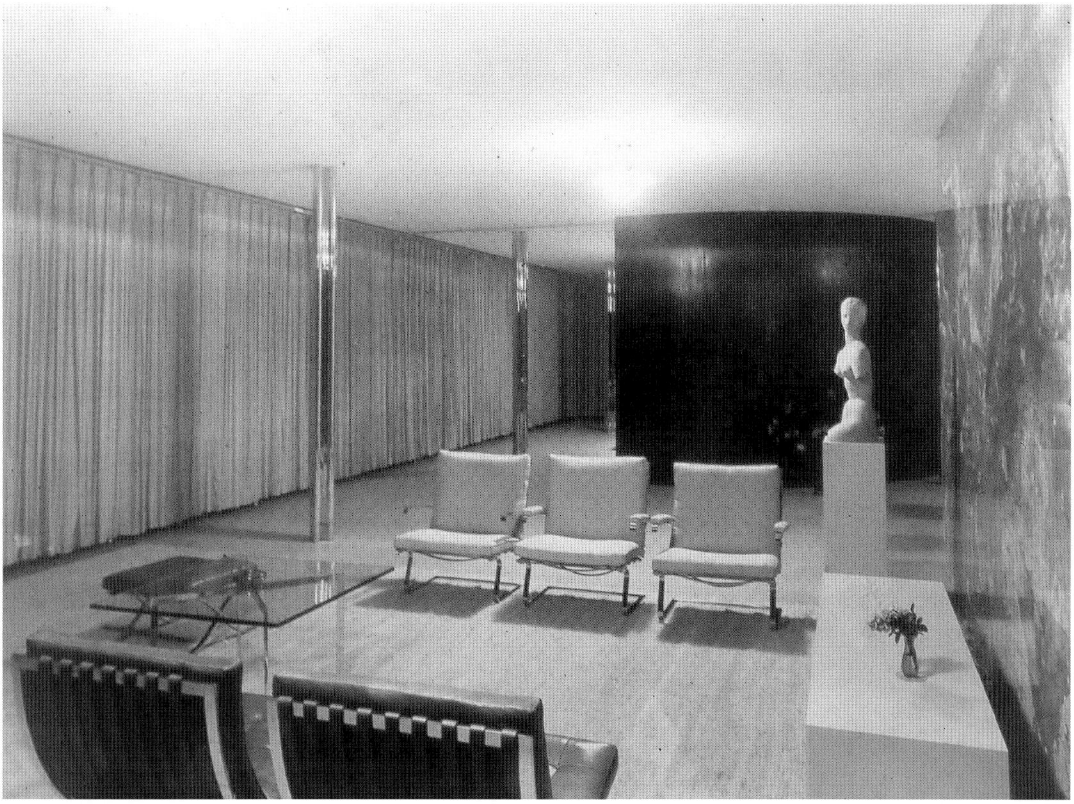

Figure 3.15. Seating area with Lehmbruck bust (curtains closed), Tugendhat House. Photograph: Atelier de Sandalo. Mies van der Rohe Archive, The Museum of Modern Art, New York; Gift of the architect; digital image copyright The Museum of Modern Art/Licensed by SCALA/Art Resource, NY.

image differed profoundly from spatial perception on-site. Yet spatial constructs traveled widely in individual photographs all the same, spreading wordless and formless images of modern architecture that were coded with implications that differed substantially from the images that buildings on sites constituted. After 1937, Mies had to make a new professional practice in the United States with the help of these photographs of prior architectural work. The architect was thrown back on a different set of buildings from those he left in Europe, to make his future with the aid of pictorial buildings, or photographic architecture.

As noted, Mies was interested in photography and film as new media with potential for architectural design, but he did not attempt to manage the commercial or trade presses, at least not at this phase of his career. Mies's design work benefited from both media, to judge from his skillful use of reflection, montage, and choreography in buildings. Photographic or filmic effects within the fabric of buildings differ from the photographic effects in which architectural photography enframed them. If the Tugendhat House was mostly learned about photographically (as it was, even before 1938, when Czechoslovakia was annexed by Germany), then the differences between photographs and buildings were as consequential for architects who came after as for Mies himself, building a new practice in Chicago.

PANORAMIC SPACE

The extensive photographic coverage of the house accords with two possible modes of architectural photography that Lotz recommended in his essay on the subject, when he described the "approximation of filmic representation" through which "one senses the house in its corporeality through the overview of five exposures."[3] This quasi-filmic model for architectural photography reflects the close affiliations between the two media at this time and recalls the quote from Henri Bergson at the opening of chapter 2.

Sensory abundance combined with carefully scripted movement characterized the Glass Room and the Barcelona Pavilion. As noted, the circulation and the visual and material excess around which they were organized were punctuated by moments of directional change or turning—the moments at which photographs were often taken. A trio of modal elements were used to characterize Mies's work in the late 1920s: ritualized patterns of movement constructed around rhythmic intervals, visual overlay that can be characterized best as a form of architectural montage, and calibration points or intervals from which the briefly arrested body in motion apprehends a new visual moment, an image or image tableau.

These modal elements might be supplemented in the case of the Tugendhat

House.[4] With movement patterns similar to those in the pavilion, the spaces of the main living level are considerably more fluid. While the main level is separated into zones that correspond to those of the traditional bourgeois home (salon, dining room, library, study), there are no "rooms" in the traditional sense at all; the space is articulated through the placement of furniture, curtains, and planar spatial dividers.[5] It is also visually open and navigable along multiple routes. This partly reflects its use as a private house whose inhabitants move freely between the spatial zones of the living floor.

The structuring of views also differs from those of the pavilion and of Mies's earlier Esters, Lange, and Wolf Houses. Instead of framed tableaux defined by architectural elements, views at Tugendhat are continuous and open-ended. The glass walls of the living room and the lack of enclosing interior walls keep wide exterior views in sight from almost every vantage point. The city view out the window is horizontal and wide-ranging. The Tugendhat House could best be described as "panoramic," an adjective that can also be applied to a number of the horizontally oriented photographs of the house (Figure 3.4).

During the development of the Brno project, Mies became involved with the German League for Independent Film (Deutsche Liga für unabhängigen Film), an outgrowth of his activities in connection with *G*. In addition, Fritz Tugendhat was an avid amateur photographer (trained in the expensive Autochrome technique for producing color photographs) and a filmmaker. The house was equipped with a basement darkroom in addition to the projection booth. Films were perhaps projected onto the white silk curtains in the main living area, curtains that screened the reflective plate-glass windows that continually played the film of the Tugendhat family's life throughout the day. As Mies deployed filmic, photographic, and pictorial techniques at the Barcelona Pavilion, the Tugendhat commission allowed him to further explore filmic architecture, a mode of design that reflected the constant run of daily life in the house, in marked contrast to the episodic visitations of an exhibition pavilion. Here we see the impact of building function or program on a coherent system of design.

The series of photographs described at the beginning of this chapter was intended to give an animated impression of a spatial sequence. Yet the Tugendhat book, if one was planned, never appeared. Nor was the long sequence of photographs published in its entirety anywhere else. As the photographs appeared in the press over time, an increasingly narrow set of pictures was published again and again. Those proffered the public view of the house that is often considered. Here, however, the entire corpus of photographs provides a larger analytical framework for study.

MODERN ARCHITECTURE AND PHOTOGRAPHY IN BRNO

At the time of the Tugendhat House's construction, Brno was the center of a regional wave of modern building in Moravia that competed with Prague architectural culture, considered more cosmopolitan than that of its smaller neighbor.[6] In 1928 the city hosted an important public exhibition, the "Exhibition of Contemporary Culture," to display architectural modernism and innovations in industrial design. The exhibition grounds on the outskirts of Brno included a large number of newly constructed modern buildings (depicted on another exhibition poster for 1929; Figure 3.16) when Mies paid his first visit in the last week of September 1928. The "Exhibition of Contemporary Culture," just about to close its doors at the time of Mies's visit, included a number of interesting projects, part of the wave of modernism spreading throughout Central and Eastern Europe in the 1920s. Bohuslav Fuchs built a steel-and-glass pavilion for the municipal gasworks, in addition to the City of Brno Pavilion; equally modern was the Moravian Pavilion by Vlastislav Chroust.[7]

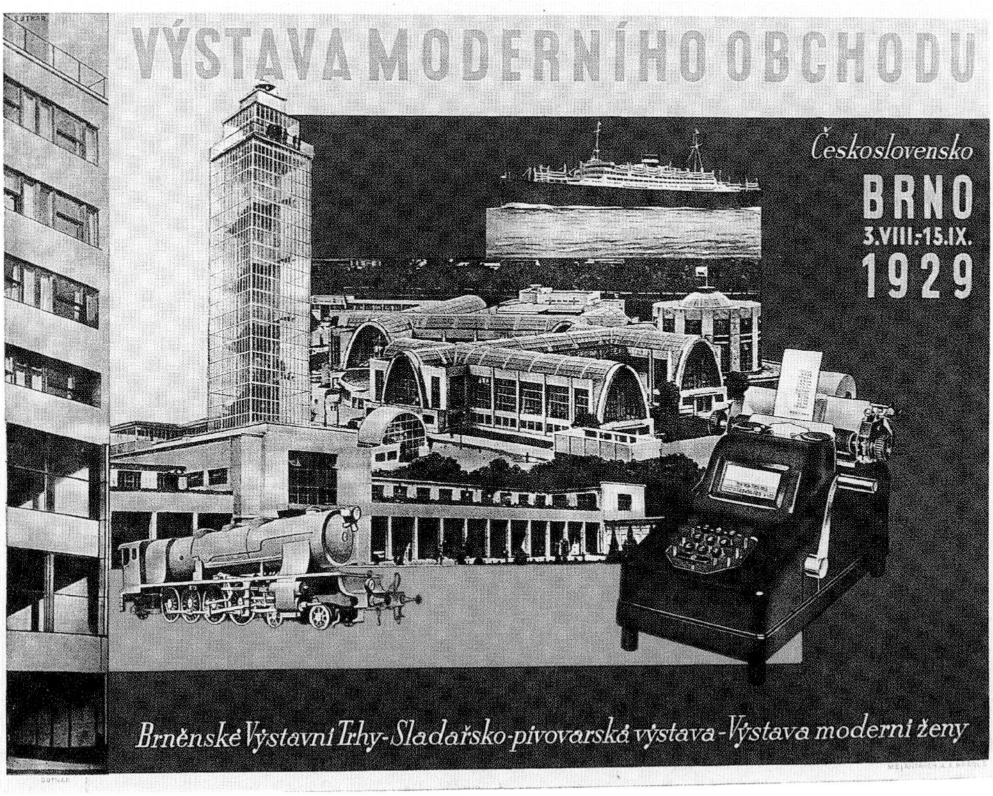

Figure 3.16. Poster for Brno modern architecture fair, 1929. Designer: L. Sutnar. Collection of the Museum of the City of Brno, Czech Republic.

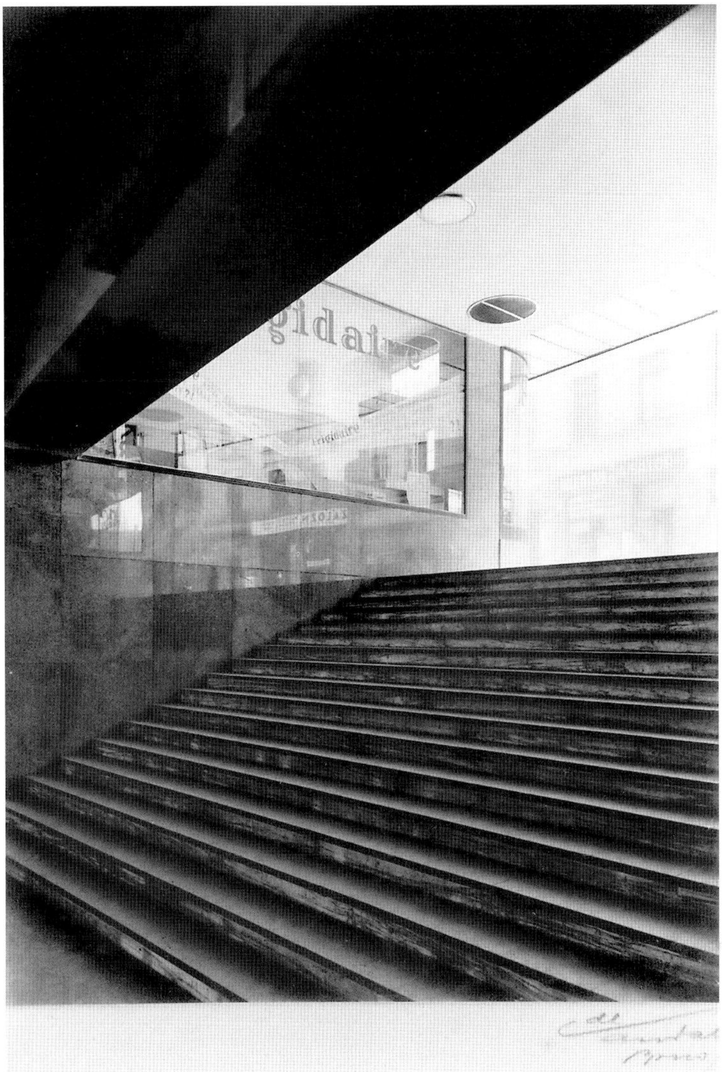

Figure 3.17. Moravian Bank, Brno, Czechoslovakia, 1928–30. Building: Bohuslav Fuchs and Arnost Wiesner. Photograph: Atelier de Sandalo. Collection of the Museum of the City of Brno, Czech Republic.

A glass-clad observation tower and a concrete-ribbed exhibition building were also part of the exhibition grounds; on a separate site, a small housing colony similar to the Weissenhofsiedlung in Stuttgart included a number of interesting modern buildings. Fuchs was also constructing some of his most important projects at the time, including the Moravian Bank of 1928–30 (with Arnost Wiesner) (Figure 3.17) and the Masaryk Student Dormitory of 1929–30 (Figures 3.18a, 3.18b).[8] While the Tugendhats' choice of Mies as their architect had as much to do with Grete Tugendhat's six-year residence in Berlin as with any rejection of local talent, nevertheless Mies entered an architectural context that was already well versed in modern architecture, even if not entirely predisposed to Miesian modernism.[9]

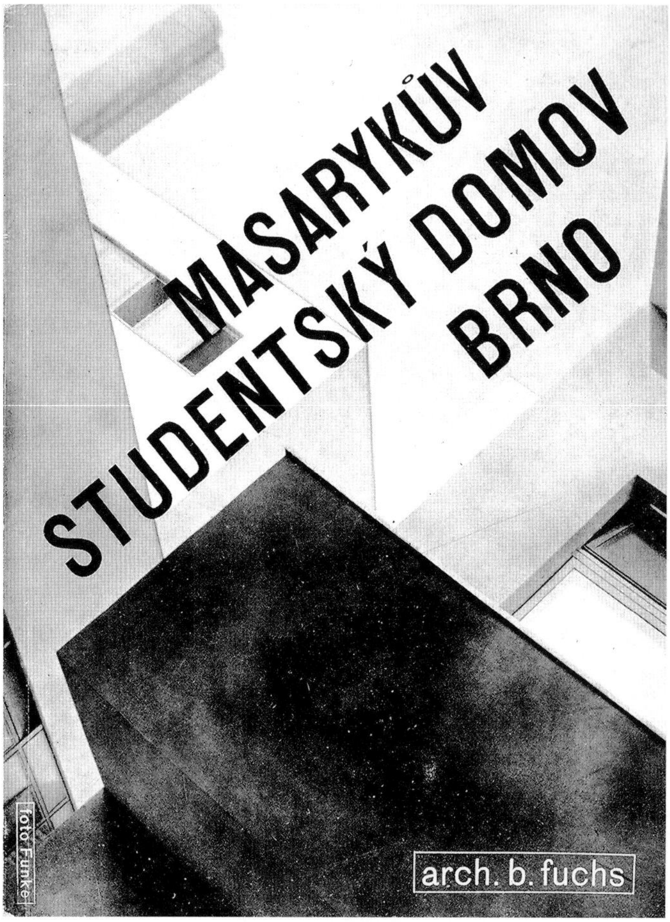

a

Figure 3.18. Masaryk Student Dormitory, Brno, Czechoslovakia, 1929–30. Building: Bohuslav Fuchs. (a) *Masarykův Studentský Domov Brno* (1929), cover. Photograph: Jaromír Funke. (b) Front of dormitory. Photograph: Atelier de Sandalo. Collection of the Museum of the City of Brno, Czech Republic.

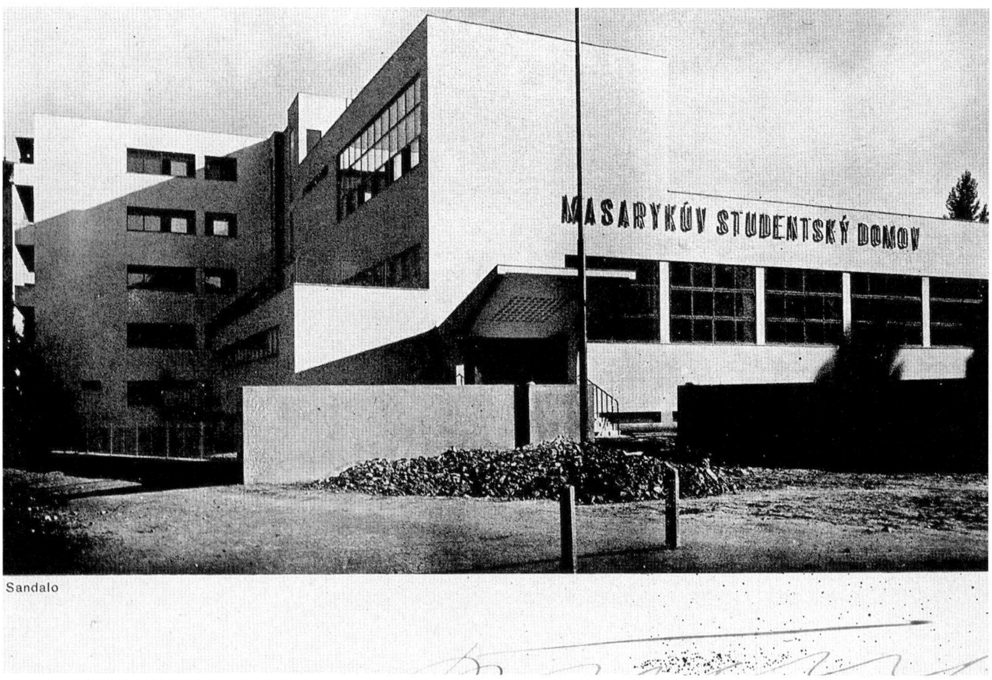

b

The majority of the formal architectural photographs of the Tugendhat House are credited "Atelier de Sandalo," a Brno firm established by Rudolf de Sandalo (1869–1932, formerly Sandola) after 1902.[10] De Sandalo was a German-speaking Czech citizen; his son, also named Rudolf de Sandalo (1899–?), was merely a tolerated alien (despite being born in Czech territory, he appears never to have gained Czech citizenship). Until 1918, Moravian Brno was part of the Austro-Hungarian Empire, and German culture was prominent in the region. After 1918, when Moravia gained independence as part of Czechoslovakia, anti-German reaction resulted in a preference for local or non-German governance at all levels. As a result, the elder Rudolf de Sandalo lost his position on the Brno Chamber of Commerce, where he had previously represented the city's professional photographers.

The architectural press in Moravia at this time was split between German- and Czech-language publications; the de Sandalos advertised their office in both.[11] The studio was well-known locally, already acting as the house photographers of Bohuslav Fuchs, one of the best-known modern architects practicing in Brno, and equally active in commissions from other local architects. In 1930, the firm advertised its specialty in the photography of modern buildings, a reflection of the burgeoning of modernism in the Moravian capital. De Sandalo fils opened an office in Prague after his father's death and subsequently photographed Albert Speer's Reichskanzlei in Berlin in 1939. Judging from the number of de Sandalo photographs published in local architectural journals such as *Forum*,[12] de Sandalo father and son were among the busiest architectural photographers in Brno, in spite of significant local competition.[13]

The atelier's work for architects in and around Brno was characterized by creative photographic composition within a modernist idiom. Still, its work was firmly tied to professional standards for the photography of buildings. The firm specialized in the photography of modern architecture after the Tugendhat commission. Abstract composition and utilitarian spaces characterize a striking series of photographs for Fuchs's Municipal Baths complex of 1927 in Brno. Figure 3.19 fluctuates between rendering vertiginously deep space and a circular composition of rays emanating from a central point not quite central to the image field.[14] In the same series, several photographs depict the mechanical equipment, generally dramatically lit and evocatively framed.[15] Some of these were included in a typophoto-collage attributed to Fuchs in the Brno City Museum, a playful collage of different architectural elements (Figure 3.20).[16] The work of the de Sandalo firm collapsed conventional distinctions between high and low art, a goal of artists and designers in the interwar years.

But despite the bold compositions of the Atelier de Sandalo, a comparison with a contemporaneous photographer shows how firmly grounded they were in

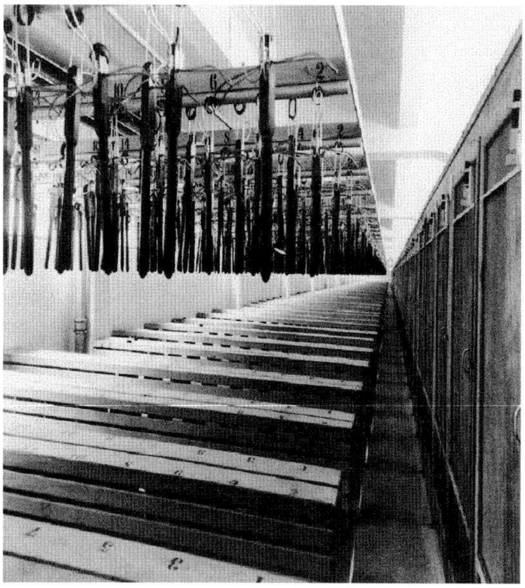

Figure 3.19. Garderobe, Municipal Baths, Brno, Czechoslovakia, 1927. Building: Bohuslav Fuchs. Photograph: Atelier de Sandalo. Collection of the Museum of the City of Brno, Czech Republic.

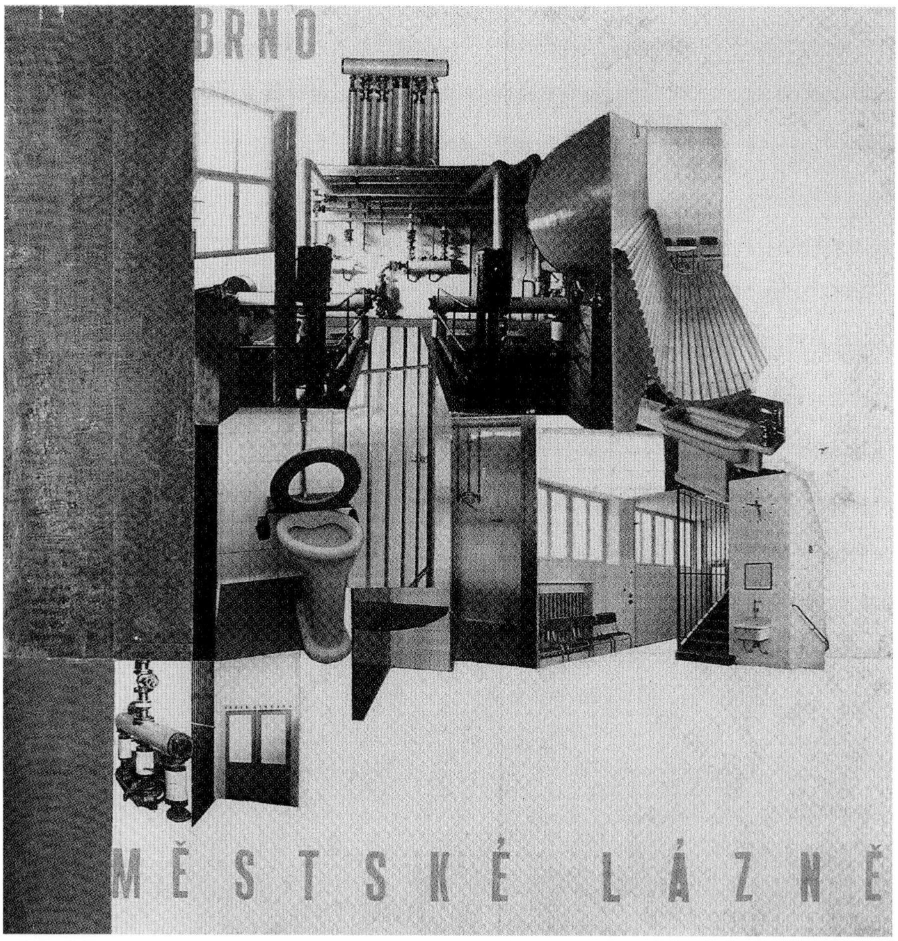

Figure 3.20. Photocollage, Municipal Baths, Brno, 1927. Collection of the Museum of the City of Brno, Czech Republic.

conventions of architectural photography. The firm photographed Fuchs's Masaryk Student Dormitory in Brno in 1930 (Figure 3.18b). The avant-garde photographer Jaromír Funke collaborated with Atelier de Sandalo on a photographic book.[17] The Funke photographs published there are classic avant-garde photographic compositions deploying unconventional camera angles in diagonally composed photographs (Figure 3.18a). The conventions of architectural photography versus the new norms of avant-garde practice distinguish the de Sandalo from the Funke pictures, so effectively juxtaposed in the book. An insistence on a normative view—on the myth of the camera as biological eye—still governs the production of the professional architectural photographs, all Neues Sehen rhetoric aside. The implied subject is an occupant or a passerby, equipped not just with camera vision but with wide-angle vision, with the kind of boring-in, supercharged X-ray vision that shoots the building off into depth but does not upset the standpoint of the observer's body. If the architectural photographer was a technical expert supplied with the tools of his trade, he was also a craftsman attempting to disguise not just the terms of translation but also the very fact that translation had occurred at all.

The de Sandalo firm photographed the Tugendhat House in the winter of 1930–31 and again in spring and/or summer 1931. In the initial set of photographs, virtually all shot with a wide-angle lens, the house seems barely occupied, and the Lehmbruck statue is not yet in place in the main salon. The later photographs, taken when the winter was over, include a minimum of household accoutrements; the house never looks fully occupied in the de Sandalo pictures, in contrast to the family photographs published by Daniela Hammer-Tugendhat. Only a small number document the private rooms of the Tugendhat family; even fewer describe the service spaces in the house. A number of rooms were apparently not photographed at all, or these photographs do not survive. The living quarters of the house staff, the substantial mechanical works in the basement that powered the electric windows, and Fritz Tugendhat's film projection room and darkroom are not included in the sets of photographs archived in Brno, Vienna, and New York. Instead, a detailed incremental documentation of the street facade, the entry sequence leading into the main living space, the main living space itself, the sequence leading out and down into the garden, and, finally, the view from the garden back up to the house has been briefly described above, along with the possible plan for a monograph similar to Erich Mendelsohn's *Neues Haus—Neue Welt* (1932) or Bruno Taut's *Ein Wohnhaus* (1927). The office correspondence files for the Tugendhat House were not included with the office material transferred to Chicago in 1963, so few archival records for the building remain.[18]

THE SEQUENCE OF PHOTOGRAPHS

In addition to the continuous series of interconnected views, other photographs stand alone, not part of a running sequence. The de Sandalo photographer found creative ways to render information about the house in ways that correlated well to the architecture. The tools of the photographer included various technical instruments but also tropes such as approximation, exaggeration, and compensation that are typical in architectural photography (see chapter 4). In the Tugendhat photographs, pictorial abstraction serves as a primary compensatory attribute of pictures that distort particular material qualities of space but that nevertheless convey compelling visual ideas about a modern building.

Roughly half of the eighty known views of the house document the main salon or living area of the middle floor, one level below grade on the street side, and one level above the basement on the garden side. The remaining half of the photos are divided roughly as follows: an equal number of views of the front facade/entry approach and of spaces on the upper level, a slightly larger number of views taken from various places in the garden, a much smaller number of views of the upper terrace, and two photographs of service spaces (kitchen and pantry). The photographs can also be divided into two uneven groups, the first consisting of all the pictures that document the most public, representational (or representative) routes through the house, and the remainder, that show semiprivate or fully private zones. Those in the second group do not overlap or extend one another for the most part.[19] Broken down by compositional motif, other formal groupings among the eighty prints also exist. Front and back views of the whole building, while depicting different architectural features, are mostly similar raking three-quarter views from the southwest (garden) or southeast (street front).[20] These overall views are conventional; it is more difficult to interpret them in terms of two-dimensional composition and easy to see them as transparent to what they represent—a piece of architecture. Nevertheless, differences in the set show how an architectural photograph turns from a document into a rhetorically laden image. Before continuing this line of inquiry, I turn to general techniques used in making these pictures.

SPACE OCCUPIED VERSUS SPACE DEPICTED

A comparison between the Tugendhat House and its photographs reveals differences consistent with other modern buildings. The photographs are cool black-and-white compositions. Horizontally extensive, they pull away from the camera, describing deep interior spaces or remote exterior blocks. The subsequent experience of the building itself comes as something of a surprise, not only because it appears dimensionally different, but because the experience differs in some other important respects as well. The main living floor, for example, seems dry and warm—full of texture—in contrast with the slick, cool surface of the photographic prints. The space, as stuff (in the German sense of *Stoff,* material), is palpable. The proportions and edges of individually programmed spaces—library, living room, music room, dining room—are clearly legible, and in comparison to the prints, they seem spatially full, square, and generous. The warmth of materials and the quality of light supplied by the extensive windows give the space a tactile presence; it is almost like cotton wool, fluffy. The spaces also seem to be distributed more evenly throughout the space of the main floor than appears to be the case in pictures.

The differences between the space occupied and the space depicted in photographs reflect a proportional discrepancy, because the relative dimensions of the space were altered in the photographs. This is an effect of the wide-angle lens. The extension in our perception of depth (a function of early photography exacerbated by the wide-angle lenses in widespread use after 1890) in turn alters the proportions among height, width, and depth, rendering the Tugendhat House in photographs lower and longer than we find the building itself. In addition, the wide-angle lens distorts unevenly, stretching the foreground around all 360 degrees and leaving the middle ground and background progressively less distorted in proportion to their distance away from the camera. This characteristic distortion of the foreground brings elements in the middle ground and background into apparently closer proximity to one another than they would appear on-site. Because the more extremely distorted foreground pushes both middle- and background objects away, these objects also appear to lie further back in space. The objects look smaller, and the distances between them appear correspondingly smaller. In short, the wide-angle lens stretches unevenly, elongating the space closest to the camera and compressing the space behind.

A distortion in depth perception destabilizes proportional relationships for the image field as a whole.[21] The photographs of the house describe a novel spatial construct, different in its most basic characteristics: overall shape and relationship of its parts. This difference is critical to understanding the relationship between photography and architecture. The alteration of proportional relationships is one of the basic operations of transferring visual information from three dimensions to two, a basic schism between two forms of representation. In the photographic image, the foreground is brought closer, the background pushed further away, its objects shrunken in relation to the space in front of them. The spatiality of the photographs and the viewing context are quite different from the architecture as experienced on-site.

This describes the general effect of the wide-angle lens. The photographs of the Tugendhat House were taken with a large wooden view camera on a tripod that required a level setup and depended on ambient lighting conditions. They are generally stable across their horizontal axis, because they are taken from a level standpoint. The horizontality of the photographs, whether in vertical or horizontal format prints, contributes to the normative perspectival character advocated by experts in architectural photography at the time. This insistent perspectivalism is also a basic characteristic of Miesian architecture, both in the architect's representational preferences and in terms of the insistence of the two horizontal planes of ceiling and floor that keep space bounded within the perspective frame. The abstract composition of many of these views is thus joined by two possibly contradictory qualities: the consistency of a level standpoint and exaggerated depth. As clearly as the photographs are two-dimensional compositions drawn from the architecture, they nevertheless also always return to the implied normative subject who sees from a height of one meter with the depth of a camera eye. In other words, they register building and occupant at once.

The apparent veracity of the photographic image contradicts the spatial distortion caused by the camera. The difference between what we *see* in the photographic image and what we *get* on-site is variable and hard to distinguish with certainty. Technical conditions of the photograph are often difficult to pin down. Pictures produced by different lens selections are rarely immediately apparent to the viewer, and, in general, the photographic image does not reveal the conditions of its own making. This unhinging of knowledge or certainty from artifact is one of the most significant operations of photography, what Roland Barthes described as the "pure spectatorial consciousness" of the photograph.[22] It is particularly in force in an architectural context. No matter what one *knows* about the wide-angle lens or about the projection of space from architectural plans, the picture works against that knowledge, declaring itself a document containing accurate information about space. Thus the spatial information depicted in the photographic image can act on the creation of new projects, inspiring architects to strive for the spacious grandeur of the wide-angle lens.[23] Further analysis indicates some of the stakes.

A winter view of the street facade was shot in bright late-afternoon sun. Raking sunlight casts the exaggerated shadows of bare branches (the branches themselves were cropped out of the photograph) onto the near front facade, the entry is cast into dark shadow, and the oversized shadow of a house across the street dominates the broad strip of unpaved road that engulfs the lower third of the picture (Figure 3.1). Low sunlight casts ghosts of invisible objects onto the surfaces of the photograph. In this view the pallid, undifferentiated sky is the only surprise; it would seem to belong to a different picture. In another view of the same side of the building, the photographer created a more dramatic mise-en-scène by darkening the already lowering winter sky along the top edge of the image, particularly in the top right corner (Figure 3.21). The house, by contrast, is framed in a nimbus of burned-in white. Atmospheric effects distinguish both, but darkroom work has made the second a more striking picture.

A group of compositionally similar photographs that contrast with these typical views focus on the semicylindrical glass volume at the entry to the house. In four exposures (shot in the spring or summer of 1931) different formal compositions accompany the relay of architectural information. A nearly head-on shot of the doorway (Figure 3.2) exists in two prints cropped differently. Geometric shapes arranged within the field of the photograph include a white trapezoid, a black door, a slick gray panelized cylinder syncopated by black lines and the distorted reflections of things inside and out, a striated gray column, and a floor grid splayed at an angle stretching a net of lines into the depth of the picture. The street appears almost like a window onto another scene or a montage fragment added to the edge of the composition. Together with the door hardware, the small window frame in the top

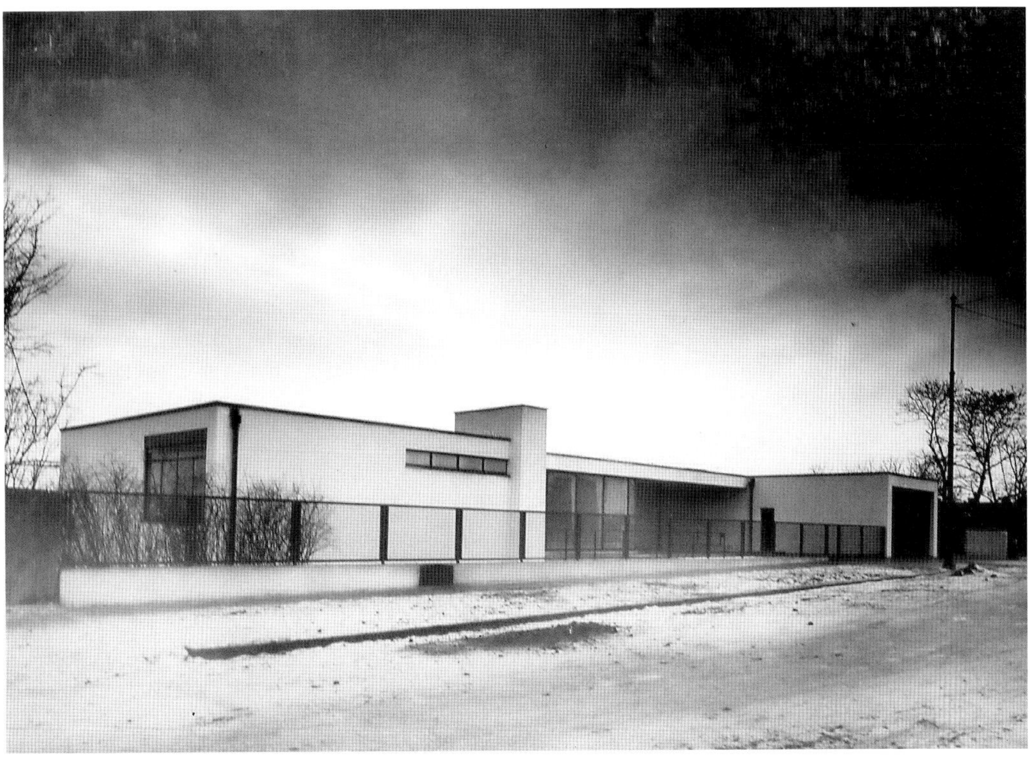

Figure 3.21. Alternate street view, Tugendhat House. Photograph: Atelier de Sandalo. Mies van der Rohe Archive, The Museum of Modern Art, New York; Gift of the architect; digital image copyright The Museum of Modern Art/Licensed by SCALA/Art Resource, NY.

right-hand corner, the socle on which the milk-glass cylinder and the walls sit, the mullions of the cylinder itself, and the texture and staining of travertine floor slabs, these details ground a concrete construct. They play against the abstract compositional structure like the photographic fragments in a Moholy-Nagy photocollage.

The camera was placed directly facing the doorway, but its lens was turned slightly to the left. It might be mistaken for a one-point perspective.[24] One of two "vanishing points" is far to the right in the middle of the front door; the second is far off to the left, cut off by the edge of the photograph. The floor grid is off the horizontal by about fifteen degrees. Neither a head-on nor a raking diagonal view, this is rather a pragmatic combination of the two. It suspends the cylinder, rectangle, trapezoid, and column in a net of radiating lines that hie off to the left-hand street edge. The photographer made the picture more dynamic and spatially flatter by turning the camera away from the center so that the perspective grid of the floor does not coincide with the geometry of the frame, but rather extends obliquely off to the left-hand side. It describes an angled cut across a gridded matrix. The photographer compensated for the exaggerated depth of the wide-angle lens by shifting off the perspectival grid of the architecture. He may also have wished to avoid the need to shift the camera back to the left in order to capture a wider field to the left of the image center. In this case, turning the tripod would have obviated the need to shift the back of the camera—or reduced the degree of the shift, also reducing the corner vignetting that often occurs as the edge of the image field approaches the cylinder of the lens casing itself. The result is a dynamic photograph that partakes of the visual force of single-point perspective while avoiding the potential problems it might have created.[25]

Two versions of the entry are depicted in Figure 3.2; they are similar but not the same. One is photographic, and one was available on-site.[26] Both versions are nevertheless present in the photographic image; photographs of architecture are doubly referential, buildings not necessarily so. Distinguishing the photograph from the entry in Brno are lack of color, two-dimensionality, adjusted lighting (either in the negative or in printing out), lens distortion, lack of copresence between viewer and space, and atmosphere. The similarities between the building on-site and the picture are confined to formal similarity and perspectival resemblance. If you stand where the photographer stood, you will see something quite like what you see in the picture. The similarities and differences serve to point out a difference in kind.

A third group of photographs are dominated by one of the cross-shaped columns. While top and bottom are cropped out in some views, pictures that show them are more successful, partly thanks to depth of field (see chapter 4). Photographs with truncated columns too close to the camera are significantly out of focus; they pull away from other elements in the pictures (Figure 3.14). But the floor and ceiling plane also provide a field in which the architectural staffage of the images floats. In a group of Mondrian's neoplastic paintings, strong black verticals and horizontals stop short of the edge of the canvas, separating the painting from its frame and counteracting the spatial illusionism of a cropped edge. When vertical elements stop short of the frame in these photographs, they similarly demarcate the space of the picture from surrounding context.[27] The floor and ceiling of the Tugendhat House separate the interior from its surroundings (in the process highlighting its spatial continuity with the outside) and delineate a space potentially continuous with, but also cut off from, a viewer of photographs. This perspectival space is familiar, potentially continuous with our own; but the abstract, purified components of the picture separate the viewer equally clearly. A tension between perspective and abstraction is critical to this series of photographs, as in photography of interwar modernism generally.

In Figure 3.9 there is a foreground column, a slanted crossing axis of the curtain rail in the ceiling, and a black rectangle edging the dining room, punctuated by the three white dots of electrical switch buttons. Remaining detail falls into a single broad horizontal swath sandwiched between ceiling and floor from the edge of the dining room to the right-hand edge of the photograph. This splayed rectangle contains columns, chairs, rug, onyx wall, and winter garden, joined in a highly detailed background. The column and curtain rail cross at an angle—a motif common in the 1920s, like that in a print from the Kestner-Mappe (1922–23) by Moholy-Nagy.[28] Formal abstraction would have been even easier for the photographer to capture: the ground glass of the camera inverted the view, rendering it both easier to abstract and more like the Moholy-Nagy print or a host of similar abstract compositions of the period (Figures 3.22, 3.23). Like the photograph, Moholy's print was similarly spatial, with geometric elements floating in a free space of indeterminate depth.

The consistency of views in which the camera stakes a frontal or near-frontal position at Tugendhat required occasional adjustments from the photographer, especially when the camera was set up close to walls or other barriers, as in the entry photograph described above. In Figure 3.24 the negative plate was roughly parallel to the wall opposite the tripod; because this lies to the extreme far left of the space depicted, the photographer again turned the camera slightly to the right, yielding an angled view of the space. In this case, the discrepancy between the vanishing point and the center of the image field shows how he shifted the camera back to the right; although no vignetting is apparent at the edges of the photograph, nevertheless the lower right-hand corner is distorted. The resulting picture, off center in its framing,

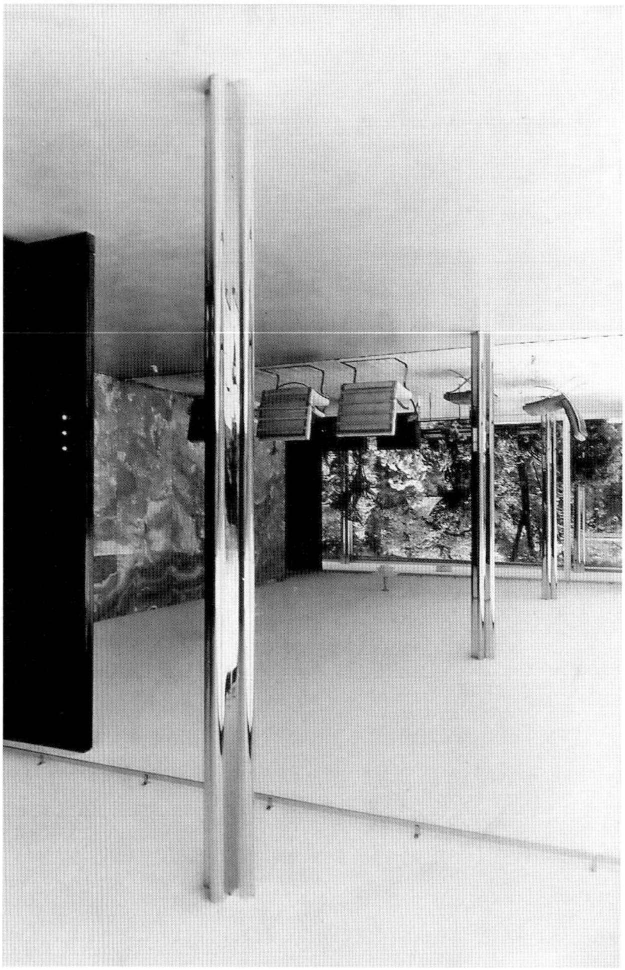

Figure 3.22. Inverted photograph of Figure 3.9. Mies van der Rohe Archive, The Museum of Modern Art, New York; Gift of the architect; digital image copyright The Museum of Modern Art/Licensed by SCALA/Art Resource, NY.

reveals more to the right of the vanishing point and less to the left. The little girls occupy the image center (but not the perspectival center), framed between the two columns marching past them. This dual-centered picture is one of the most interesting compositions used by modernist architectural photographers, allowing visual asymmetry and conventional symmetry at the same time (children as image center).

These photographs depict a photographic Tugendhat House quite different from that on-site. Who created this new virtual spatial construct? It was a group effort, achieved by the collaboration of an architect (a constellation of actors might be represented in this single figure, including all those involved in the making of the building), a photographer, and a field camera equipped with black-and-white film and a wide-angle lens. We turn now to a debate that erupted when the building was first in use.

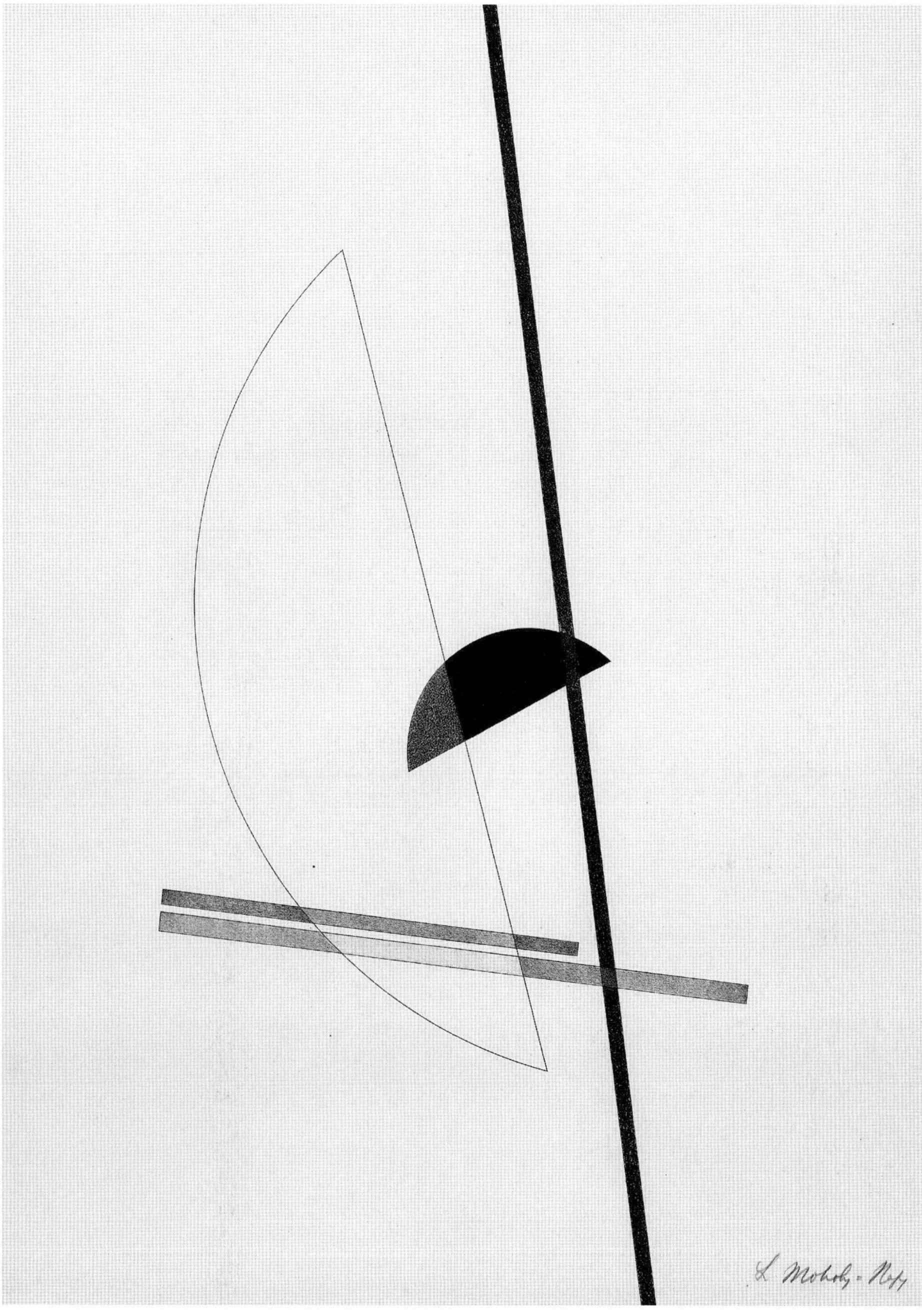

Figure 3.23. László Moholy-Nagy, lithograph from the Sixth Kestner Mappe, *VI Konstruktionen*, 1922–23. Sprengel Museum Hannover. Photograph: Michael Herling/Aline Gwose; copyright 2012 Artists Rights Society (ARS), New York/VG Bild-Kunst, Bonn.

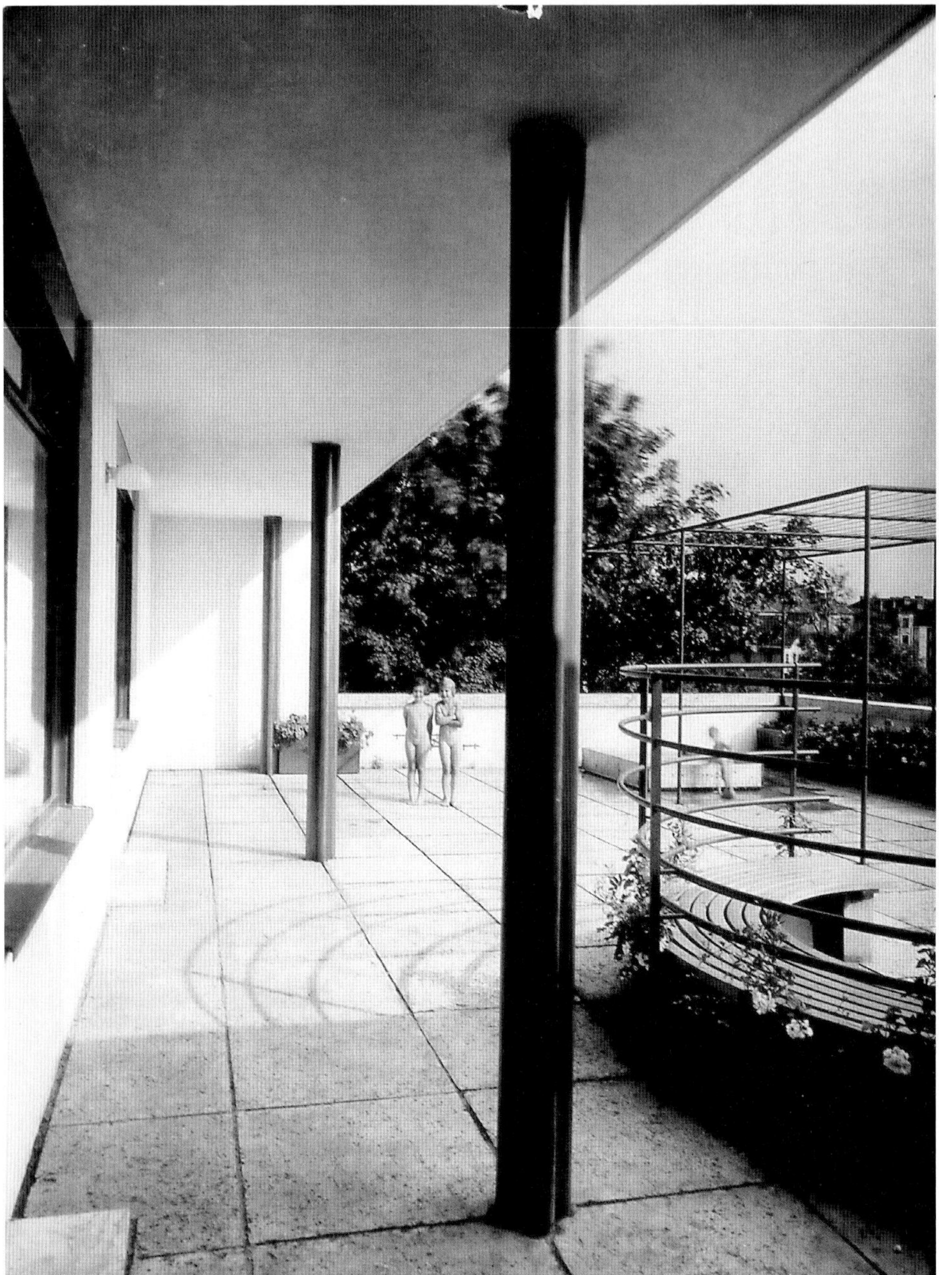

Figure 3.24. Upper terrace, Tugendhat House. Photograph: Atelier de Sandalo. As published in *Die Form* 6 in 1931.

CAN ONE LIVE IN THE TUGENDHAT HOUSE?

In 1931 a polemical debate about the house took place. "Can one live in the Tugendhat House?" was the title of an essay by Justus Bier that appeared in the October 1931 issue of *Die Form,* where the first photographs of the house had been published in September.[29] In his contribution, Bier described the house as a showpiece, not a domestic space, eliciting a defense from *Die Form*'s editor, Walter Riezler. In the journal's November issue, Marxist critic Roger Ginsburger and Riezler continued the debate. Fritz and Grete Tugendhat rebutted Bier and Ginsburger, describing the house as an ideal home. Ludwig Hilberseimer echoed their views in another defense of the commission.[30]

Fritz Tugendhat suggested that "Mr. Bier, who perhaps knows the house only from a few flat photographs, . . . speaks only of the large main space—without thinking that this is just a piece of the house organism."[31] In fact, although Ginsburger had not visited the house, Bier probably had. Nevertheless, Bier's critique of the building's monumentality and "representative style . . . intended . . . for impersonal spaces" that forced residents to live "as if on display" recalls the distensive grandeur of the photographs printed in *Die Form* the previous month, to which Bier no doubt referred in his comments. The famous Tugendhat debate appears to have been as much a conversation carried on at cross-purposes as a dissenting ideological critique of Mies's architecture for its expense and luxuriousness, and for its failure to engage with the central concerns of the Neues Bauen and the newly born Congrès International d'Architecture Moderne (CIAM). The most compelling evidence for this claim, however, is not simply to be found in periodicals. It comes from comparing the Tugendhat House photographs with a visit to the remarkably different Tugendhat House.

In *Die Form,* the de Sandalo photographs were used to describe the house as a remarkable achievement of modern architecture—and as impersonal, monumental, and grand, redolent of retrograde social values. The Tugendhat House debate is relevant because the virtual stretching performed by the camera, which turned this building into a set of flat surfaces rendered in slick black-and-white emulsion, resulted directly from the moving of an object from the private to the public realm. This was equally a desire to transform it into something that could go anywhere and serve many viewers ready to invest themselves in an optical projection into architecture.[32] To those interested in the transformative social potential of modernism, the Tugendhat House offered only a countermodel. Its photographs projected a strangely distilled, purely visual experience of luxurious architecture far out of reach of the masses. But the printed page, sacrificing the sensorial effects so important to Mies, offered in exchange a compensating breadth of circulation. Fundamental alterations to the building were only partly camouflaged in the photographs, which then propagated their own terms of discussion tangentially related to architectural experience on a site. The qualities captured by photographs allowed the house to be condemned for lack of social responsibility, despite the fact that the qualities *not* captured by the camera represented new terrain for modern architecture in its unfolding relationship to new media. But published buildings become subject to social projection if not social practice. We should also note that architects in the late 1920s and early 1930s could mine new territory in architecture in limited ways: through unbuilt work, through short-term exhibition installations, or through commissions from wealthy patrons who provided them with freedom in design and execution. Mies here simply replayed one of the central dilemmas of modern architecture: how to be aesthetically progressive without being socially or politically progressive, at a time when many aspired to commit to both.

Before concluding, we might imagine moving through the space of these pictures. In movies shot with a wide-angle lens, a figure approaching the camera from a distance moves with exaggerated slowness until reaching a certain point, the point at which middle ground gives gradually over into foreground. At that point the pace picks up, and the figure hurtles with unexpected speed past the camera and out of the frame of the shot. Were we to imagine a figure entering these pictures, the figure might be excessively small, as are the two little girls in the depth of the picture on the upper terrace. Or it might be close to the camera and excessively large. Or, more likely, it might occupy some of the extra space that the wide-angle lens has added to the middle distance. Conversely, if we consider the subject implicit in the camera's station point (what Barthes calls the *operator*), that subject is not required to scale canted surfaces, fly like a bird, or assume the position of a worm. The subject of these pictures walks firmly on flat surfaces, viewing architectural space with gravity, but equally through the distending prosthesis of the wide-angle lens.[33]

When Theo van Doesburg described the new space of abstract film, he identified depth as its distinguishing characteristic. Within this spatial depth, the filmgoer would find new experiential dimensions, the kind of optical experience that led Karel Teige to call Man Ray "the Columbus of the new continent of optical poesy."[34] We can locate architectural photography, in interwar modernism at least, in the realm of *Zukunftglauben,* of futuristic utopianism. On this topic van Doesburg wrote about the filmic surface at a time when film and photography were understood to belong to the same order of product: "It is just this surface that must be burst, that beyond it the new deep, the space-time continuum, may be discovered. There and nowhere else lies the constructive sphere of creative film! The polydimensional space that sculptors have vainly tried to create ever since Michelangelo's Deposition will finally come to life through the means provided by refined film technique."[35] His reference to Michelangelo's *Entombment of Christ* corrects the impression of unexplored, limitless terrain: the space of these photographs, as much as it instantiates "a new deep," or "a new depth," does so fully within the parameters understood as belonging to perspective vision.[36] But in them, this same system, a system that Erwin Panofsky described as "objectivity carried over into the domain of the phenomenal," has been subjected to internal disruption from the lens, not always detectable and often easy to overlook.[37] This new depth, what we might also describe as the new space of the surface of architectural representation, draws us empathetically into a place our bodies could never in fact occupy, without undergoing their own dimensional and temporal extension. The new depth of the architectural photograph turns out, in this case, to be something like a wormhole, a transport zone—but only that—into the modernist spatial utopia of perceptual enlightenment. Its promise—fully architectural; its means—graphic and two-dimensional. Its attraction—precisely that it distances the concrete, imposing the viewing regimen of the visual arts onto architecture, shooting that which we *can* grasp with all senses off into the domain of the virtual.

It is hardly surprising to find photographs of modern buildings projecting features we also associate with modern architecture. But the differences between the photograph and the building also raise the question of what gave rise to what. It has long been noted that certain characteristics of modern architecture have their roots in photographic representations of architecture. The Tugendhat prints fit well into the International Style—the promotion of ubiquitous, acontextual architecture that could be transferred with little alteration from place to place. But this is not epiphenomenal. The very notion of the International Style was derived precisely from photographs like these, ambivalently wrapped up in the development of photographic abstraction, and the projection of architectural abstraction as enacted in and by photography. In the catalog to the MoMA exhibition that gave rise to the label "International Style," Alfred Barr noted at the outset, "And as in this book the text itself is intended as an introduction to the illustrations, one need scarcely speak at length about them."[38] As Sigfried Giedion and others had asserted previously, the language of images differed from that of words; it was far more direct and thought to require no textual translation.[39] We might turn briefly to this claim now.

SURFACE TENSION AND PROJECTED SPACE

Wilhelm Worringer, Wassily Kandinsky, Theo van Doesburg, Kazimir Malevich, and El Lissitzky wrote about painterly abstraction. As noted in chapter 2, the idea often rested on the notion of limitless space in tension with a clear limit—the limit of the canvas, or the two-dimensional surface. The lack of tension between surface and space meant that architectural abstraction appeared differently, despite the assistance provided by plate glass, which Mies had explored in 1927. The comparison in chapter 2 between the exhibition rooms designed by Lissitzky and projects designed by Mies illustrated approximate and analogous attempts to transpose painterly abstraction into a corollary construct in architecture—in the case of Lissitzky and Mies, through two inaccessible cells containing sculpture in space. Other aspects of both installations also translated something like pictorial abstraction into embodied architectural experience. In Mies's case, these experiments resulted in the synesthetic experience of the Barcelona Pavilion. This chapter, however, is concerned with how a different sort of two-dimensional abstraction entered modern architecture through architectural photographs.

It is possible that the interwar modern movement in architecture foundered on its inability to realize the potential of pictorial abstraction as depicted in suprematist and neoplastic painting, and even in cubist simultaneity, in architectural constructions. The work of Lissitzky, Mies, and others suggests otherwise, although the years in which European architects were free to investigate such ideas quickly ended after 1933. Architectural photography provided a timely solution to the challenge of abstraction, reinstating the flat surface as a site on which space was projected. It brought a familiar tension to the apprehension of architecture—the tension between surface plane and depth. At the same time, it appeared to offer incontrovertible evidence of constructed realities. It thus connected projective painterly composition to constructed space, marrying ideal construct and real thing. In its most skillful manifestations, as in the photographs of Mies's Tugendhat House, the architectural photograph represented the nonexistent space of a virtually abstract architecture better and more simply than it had ever been represented before.

The problems that plagued both photography and architecture in relation to the concept of abstraction as it developed among the avant-gardes in the periods immediately preceding and following World War I were similar. Both photography and architecture are anchored in physical space: architecture in constructing space, photography in recording and interpreting it. Although architects and photographers pursued abstraction in the 1920s and 1930s, both also shared a paradoxical relationship to ideas received from painting and graphic arts. The notion that each medium had a specific character based on its format and practices ran counter to the equally strong notion that the arts were bound together by general concepts such as artistic will, or *Kunstwollen*. Photography and architecture each made creative adjustments to its own existing modalities to confront the challenge presented by medium specificity and pictorial abstraction. Photographers pursued abstraction in the deep, liquid space of the photogram, through the destabilization of visual conventions in the New Vision or the New Objectivity, and with newly invented photographic techniques such as those pioneered by Étienne-Jules Marey and Eadweard Muybridge.[40]

Architects, in turn, explored abstraction in visionary architectural projects, as pursued in two-dimensional representation over a broad historical span.[41] But in addition, in the modern period architects began to relocate desires analogous to those found in painterly projection into bodily experience of space; the play between flat surface and projected depth began to appear in architecture as a play between physical phenomena in space and their internal sensory effect on the occupant, drawing as much from music and performance as from visual art, as described in chapter 2.[42] It was a small but critical jump from the notion of an aphysical abstract space (as depicted in painting) to the conception of that space as internal to human consciousness and the physicality of the brain: an understanding that the abstract space of modern art was, in effect, the internal space of the mind. Architects sought to make productive use of this understanding, which was initially based on nineteenth-century discoveries about the physiological basis of human perception but nevertheless seemed to negate the scientific determinism intrinsic to its earlier formulation. In other words, the notion of an internal world of human consciousness out of reach of scientific rationalism countered the understanding of human perception as a matter of quantifiable scientific method—the science of human physiology—with an antirational opposite. Thus the avant-garde undid the determinism of the nineteenth century and replaced it with the myths of intrinsic essence and spiritualized aesthetics.[43]

But equally important for the argument here is the fact that architecture in the modern period relied on architectural photography for its dissemination. And the inevitable distance between a building and its photographic image returned architecture to the two-dimensional surface that mediated pictorial perception. The virtual space of architectural photography rendered construction both abstract and concrete at the same time. By supplying evidence of existing construction, it showed the viewer how the promised utopia of abstract (painterly) space could be brought into existence and yet still remain out of reach. At the same time, architectural photography helped obscure the profitable line of architectural investigation described in chapter 2. Architectural photographs privileged visual perception over other sensory modes, imposing a viewing regimen that subtracted many of architecture's specific attributes. The influence of abstract form is seen in postwar International Style architecture, where the photographs of the Weimar period exercised a significant influence over new work.

To return to the limited test case provided by Mies van der Rohe, the small group of photographs of the Barcelona Pavilion and the large group of photographs of the Tugendhat House are test cases for hypotheses about architectural photography at the end of the 1920s in Germany. The photographs of the Tugendhat House describe a different spatiality, using a different visual model, from the architecture of the Tugendhat House. The same is true in a different sense of the Barcelona project. To understand the significance of this difference for modern architecture, we can pose a few questions to the remaining chapters of this study. How did pictures project an architectural reality that then acted on architects and their broadly defined clientele in the European culture world and subsequently? The spatiality of photographic architecture, at least in Mies's case, projected a space almost entirely empty of figures and depleted of incidental objects of habitation, described by textured shades of gray, black, and white, with a palpable immediacy in the foreground and a distant density in the background. This was not the world in which architects executed their working drawings and built their ideas for clients. Instead, it was a conceptual world in which the dreams of utopic modernism entered the world of architecture with relative ease, in which architectural abstraction might be explored and developed in a two-dimensional mode, with cool, unchanging photographs leaving their built counterpart alone and in peace to fight the messy battles of budget shortfalls, good or poor construction, inhabitation, aging, and other trials of history—but also to mediate the domain of a new and unfamiliar kind of "abstract" experience—all by itself. We have not had to think abstraction and sensory or embodied intensification in the same sentence: a closer look at the Weimar period suggests that we might.

PART II ARCHITECTS AND ARCHITECTURAL PHOTOGRAPHS

The tendency to make the sign independent of the object . . . is the guiding principle of the whole of modern art, which arose as the antithesis of naturalism. It is inseparable from the pioneering endeavor of this art and does not depend on the biographical features of the individual practitioners.

—ROMAN JAKOBSON,
"THE CONTOURS
OF THE SAFE
CONDUCT"

4. TYPE-PHOTO

ARCHITECTURAL PHOTOGRAPHY IN GERMANY

This chapter turns to architectural photography as a professional commercial practice that emerged after the advent of the mass-printed photograph. Compositional rules of thumb that governed the photography of the interwar period resulted from a long tradition of picture making that preceded the invention of photography. Andreas Haus has suggested how modern architecture and modern photography worked synergistically, infiltrating existing pictorial modes into effective photographs that combined the geometry of cameras with the geometry of modern architecture itself.[1] Most likely, age-old compositional rules and new technical protocols both contributed to the persuasiveness of photographic images such as those of the Tugendhat House discussed in chapter 3. Both were characteristics of the subdiscipline of architectural photography to which I now turn. The commercial market for photographs of buildings played a role in the scripting of modern architecture's history, and to understand that better, we might review some of its practices.

Architectural photographers defined clear operational parameters that made their profession a subdiscipline of professional photography before the end of the nineteenth century.[2] Many photographers learned by doing rather than by studying from books and articles, but their conclusions can be tracked through photographic publications. A literature and a set of rules regularized professional practices, orienting the developing medium in relation to existing aesthetic precedents. Habits of painterly composition underpinned by theories of the picturesque were imported into architectural photography well before mass printing techniques made photographs into popular illustrations.[3] Photographers of architecture nevertheless encountered recurring challenges in relaying three-dimensional experience through two-dimensional surfaces. They developed techniques that were then disseminated in photographs, in illustrated primers, and in journal articles actively circulating in the first decades of the twentieth century. The rules devised to address these challenges also had ramifications throughout the subsequent development of the profession, and discussion of these rules will therefore recur in subsequent chapters. They are reviewed here as basic elements of architecture's visual language in the twentieth century.

Before the advent of mass-printed photographs, nineteenth-century architectural photography was most frequently used to document historic or culturally important buildings or construction processes, or for journalistic purposes, as numerous sources detail.[4] The representational or historicist architecture of that century was replete with complex detail; photography could document this richly ornamented work efficiently and impressively. The Paris Opéra was one of the first construction sites to have a photographer included on staff for construction administration, an early instance in which a building's photographic documentation was understood to be part of its creation. The photographs taken by Louis-Émile Durandelle (1838–1917) recorded the progress of construction, serving as administrative devices as well as illustrations.[5]

The early "documentary" use of photographs contrasts with the later use of architectural photographs to advertise new buildings to audiences and clients. This rapidly became architectural photography's primary role after the turn of the century and the development of mass printing, as Robert Elwall and others have pointed out.[6] Photographs then joined other kinds of flat representations such as architectural renderings produced by architects to advertise their work in journals and books. Although orthographic drawings such as plans and sections were considered technical documents, it was generally assumed that all readers might understand and decipher information relayed in photographs, and this accessibility was thought likely to increase interest in architecture and expand stylistic knowledge.[7] Unlike drawings, photographs provided visible evidence of a construction on a site. Once the camera could practically document completed buildings for publication, renderings became more properly projective, depicting unbuilt projects for competition juries, clients, and public audiences, or depicting idealized versions of built work. At the same time, photography tied architects down to a standard of visual evidence that was more easily evaded in drawn renderings, where it was easier to show buildings as they had been designed and imagined, not as they were constructed.

As both media changed in response to technological innovations that occurred after 1880, photography was linked to architectural practice in at least two ways. First, architects could use photographs as references for new building designs with increasing ease, as it became possible to take or purchase photographs of models from distant places. Second, after 1895 they could disseminate photographs of their buildings easily and increasingly inexpensively in the press, spreading more vivid pictures of newly constructed buildings than had been possible with earlier printing techniques, often partly based on photographs.[8] Henry Hobson Richardson (1838–86) assembled a large collection of architectural photographs in order to use historical details from European precedents with greater accuracy. In the 1870s, Richardson was also one of the first to publish photographs of his work in journals.[9] By the close of the century the halftone screen had made it possible to print photographs and text cheaply from the same printing plates in magazines, newspapers, and journals. Photographs replaced lithographs and etchings (themselves often based on single photographic views) in the mass media, becoming the state-of-the-art tool for architects' publications.[10] The development of mass printing turned photography from elite hobby to widespread communications device. In addition, the ubiquity of photography increased with the production of inexpensive handheld cameras and roll film at the turn of the century, a development that culminated in the flexible "point and shoot" Leica of the 1920s, the machine that turned cameras into tools of avant-garde image making.

Gradually, photography began to affect the way in which architects might approach other forms of representation such as drawing and building. The architectural photograph soon became commercially expedient, if not absolutely necessary, for architects in practice. Only the most recalcitrant modernists, such as the Viennese architect Adolf Loos (1870–1933), openly disavowed the value of photography, noting that it was unfit to the task of architectural representation.[11] And even Loos accepted photography, in fact if not in word; photographs of his projects were disseminated through architectural journals and books. That he took liberties retouching, cutting, and using montage in photographs of his built work is in no way surprising. His manipulation of the photographic image adds to his published comments expressing doubt about the value of photography's claim to truthful representation from the start.[12]

To be a modern architect in the twentieth century, then, required that one's work be photographed and published, as scholars pointed out long ago.[13] The profession therefore had to adapt to the demands of photographic imaging, although it took decades to work out how best this new medium might benefit architects and their practices. As photography became more familiar, architects found ways to assert the inadequacy of the photograph to its subject at the same time that they reaped the benefits of widespread dissemination of photographic images of architecture in the commercial press. Among other uses, photography could promote the idea that certain things could not be photographed. Photography helped define modern architecture by providing a way for the public to experience buildings visually, even as texts, captions, and photographs themselves also helped deliver the message that buildings were more than visual images, and that their ineffable material qualities could not be conveyed in two dimensions. In this way, photography spread information but also qualified it, establishing hierarchies of value for buildings in cultural and capital markets.

As the costs of cameras, film, and mass printing gradually fell over the course of the twentieth century, commercial architectural photographs grew increasingly numerous. This was by no means an even progression—technology moved in fits and starts, accelerated by historical events such as World War II, not progressing smoothly along a line of continuous development. In fact, as the ubiquity of printed photographic images grew, the quality of the pictures themselves grew ever more variable. When we compare the velvety photogravure of the photographs in Sigfried Giedion's 1931 French monograph on Walter Gropius issued by the publishing house of G. Crés with the more cheaply printed images in Giedion's later monograph on the same architect from 1954 and then that work's reprint in 1992, the difference is visibly striking, if invisible in secondary reproduction.[14] Different genres or types emerged, from documentary photographs to art photographs to pictures for commercial advertising. For each type, recursions into architectural practice can also be identified. As photographic images proliferated, the value of any single image also fell, just as the process of understanding architecture through them became more habitual as time went by.

ARCHITECTURAL PHOTOGRAPHY AS A PROFESSIONAL SUBFIELD IN GERMANY BEFORE THE WAR OF 1914–18

A professional niche market for architectural photography had emerged in Germany by the 1910s, as can be seen in publications such as a series of volumes from the Wasmuth publishing house, particularly Max Creutz's edited volumes of *Architektur des XX. Jahrhunderts,* including the *Sonderheften* on new buildings such as those of the Tietz company (Figure 4.1).[15] Such monographic publications may relate to the bound folios of photographs that were produced throughout the latter half of the nineteenth century, particularly in Berlin; Alan Powers notes that such publications revive a tradition of publication from the Renaissance.[16] Two examples demonstrate different contexts for architectural photography at the time. Gartenstadt Staaken (architect Paul Schmitthenner) was a new residential development in Berlin-Spandau; a generously illustrated photo book from Wasmuth in 1917 reflected the importance of its style, its architect, and his practice. The Tietz department store chain, on the other hand, employed different architects to produce a series of buildings in different cities, so that the publications focused on the firm itself and architecture insofar as it represented the name of Tietz and the quality of the department stores, designed by architects such as Joseph Olbrich.

The 1920s witnessed the development of a new relationship between architecture and photography, but the latter medium was already more than seventy-five years old by 1920, and interactions between the two were well established. The explosion of photographic reproduction made possible with new printing processes developed in the last two decades of the nineteenth century changed the contexts in which photographs were seen, and this too made the period from 1880 to 1920 especially dynamic.[17] Photographs provided base material for woodcuts (photoxylography) or lithographs from midcentury, before the development of the autotype (also known as the collotype) and the halftone, two printing technologies that allowed photographs to be mass printed on pages with text by the last decade of the century.[18] Many of these developments appeared first in France, not Germany.

Architectural photographs had been used throughout the second half of the nineteenth century for public propaganda in relation to the construction of monuments like the Eiffel Tower in Paris in 1889 or such projects as the urban modifications carried out by Baron Haussmann in the 1870s. They were also the means for historical documentary projects affiliated with the new field of preservation, used by figures such as Prosper Merimée (followed by Eugène-Emmanuel Viollet-le-Duc as director of the Commission des Monuments Historiques) for the Missions Héliographiques, a fascinating untapped image archive not seen in full until the 1980s.[19] Documentary and ethnographic projects were widespread throughout the second half of the

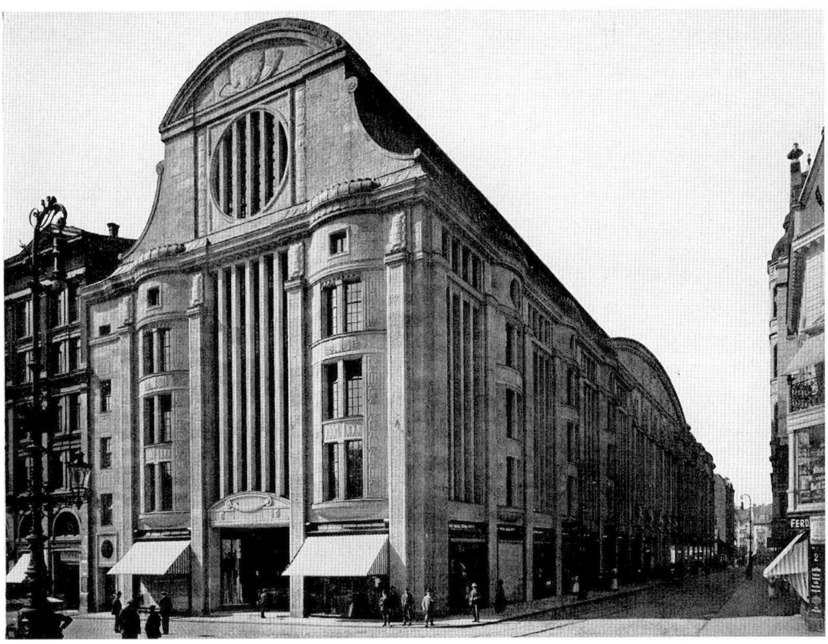

Figure 4.1. Warenhaus Tietz, Elberfeld, 1912. Architect: Wilhelm Kreis. From Max Creutz, ed., *Wilhelm Kreis: Kaufhausneubau L. Tietz A.G. in Elberfeld* (Berlin: Ernst Wasmuth, 1912), 14.

century, resulting in large photographic collections held by wealthy individuals like Karl Ernst Osthaus, commercial firms, and government entities, including museums. An international group of topographic photographers who documented buildings and cities at this time included Charles Marville, Frederick Evans, Frédéric Boissonas, Franz Stoedtner, Eadweard Muybridge, the Alinari brothers, and the topographic photographers of the American western exploration. These photographers worked with restrictive technical constraints such as wet plate processes and mobile darkrooms. The conditions under which they worked partially defined their products and meant that at an early stage photography differentiated itself from both art and science by combining the two with a high degree of craft. Others made photographs for specialized purposes such as exploration, mineral prospecting, mapmaking, the art market, or forensic examination.[20]

The commercial business in architectural photography that grew more noticeable in the years leading up to World War I was, however, quite distinct from earlier precedents. Commercial architectural photography was a form of advertising that grew out of earlier architectural advertisement (primarily lithographic or print based) combined with photography, suddenly available with the frequency and in the quantity of other mass-printed media.[21] Mass-printed photographs of architecture in journals and books reflect both continuity and difference in the transition from the nineteenth to the twentieth century. On one hand, architectural photographs were produced for a range of new purposes in the new century; on the other, visual continuities between different forms of architectural advertising tended to mask the distinctions between them. The genres of photography in which buildings appeared continued to grow more numerous throughout the first decades of the twentieth century. These included "soft" advertising incorporated into books, journals, and newspapers as illustrations to scholarly or popular articles; self-advertising in the architects' own publications; and product advertisement in ads paid for and published by the building industry. Photographs might benefit the architect of the building that was photographed, the client for whom the building had been designed, the building supplier or contractor, or all three. They were sometimes commissioned by the journal that wished to publish the building or produced by staff photographers who worked for publishers or journals.[22] By the mid-1920s commercial photographic images of buildings appeared in a variety of publications in which the same sorts of pictures might be adapted for different purposes. By the 1950s, the same photographs were being used to advertise a building product and to supplement the presentation of the architect's work.

Commercial architectural photography has two distinct ancestries. One lies in commercial advertising as it developed before the invention of mass photographic printing, when printed lithographs and other graphic devices accompanied architectural advertisements or advertisements for general products connected such products to buildings, often through the trademarks or logos of companies or their offices (see Figure 5.4).[23] In these kinds of advertisements we expect to find continuities in the advertising copy, in graphic design, and in the venues that published them, as the transition between graphic illustration and photography unfolded.[24]

Large-format photographs of buildings, landscapes, or cities from the topographic tradition constitute a second important precursor to commercial architectural photography of the early twentieth century. In these cases, although the materiality of the photographic image changed substantially from original studio print to mass-printed copy, nevertheless compositional norms or standards often remained relatively constant.[25] The photographs looked similar, even as their object quality, their textual framing, and their placement changed in fundamental ways. Nineteenth-century photographs, valued for novelty, craftsmanship, and the sheer difficulty that accompanied their capture, and issued in limited sets of copies, shifted to become twentieth-century tokens available in multiple copies in an accelerated market for products oriented to present and future. Continuity in the visible image accompanied difference in the way it began to circulate in the market for cultural products. Compositional similarity between different stages in the development of photography reflects an underlying pattern language that goes back to picturesque precedents, whether in landscape painting or in pictorialist photography.[26]

Within this new practice, formed from commercial and aesthetic precedents from the nineteenth century, a set of conventions developed. These were codified in handbooks, primers, and journal articles for professionals. Theorists, philosophers, and historians also reflected upon them. A cross section of this literature reveals a number of recurrent themes. Photographers and writers were concerned about a basic dilemma: photographs were considered to be more authoritative, in factual terms, than other sorts of images. But photographs were manifestly ill suited to render ineffable qualities of spatial occupation with any degree of reliability. Architects faced the difficulty of coming to rely on a form of communication that appeared more veracious than existing modes of representation but that combined this promise of veracity with thoroughgoing deception. Throughout the entire history of photography in architecture, the same debates repeated themselves. Photographs were evidence, and yet they were unreliable, duplicitous, misleading, and deceptive. In reciting these issues, however, professionals in the fields of photography and architecture did not confine themselves to repeating truisms such as these. Instead, they applied their expertise to finding solutions to the many problems that photography brought to professional architectural practice, even as they capitalized on all the new potential that it also brought.

This potential was rich indeed. Photographs made architecture attractive precisely because they were not buildings, but were instead portable, small-scale, mass-printable images that might offer imaginative possibilities that were unavailable in constructed architecture to audiences in different places. Photographs, even as they "deceived" modern consumers of architecture, also gave producers and consumers an entirely new perspective on buildings, one that differed fundamentally from earlier printed devices that broadcast architecture in the press. Mario Carpo and Richard Wittman have both made convincing arguments regarding how print media altered architectural practice long before the twentieth century, so that media circulation is not the primary alteration here.[27]

And yet photography changed the game for architecture. The photographic image functions differently from the perspective rendering or the orthographic drawing or, indeed, the architectural model. That functionality bears some description. Recurrent themes from literature on architectural photography relate to rhetorical tropes: early twentieth-century writers mentioned the need to deploy approximation, exaggeration, and visual intensification as tools for crafting successful architectural photographs, precisely to compensate for their deficiencies in relation to constructed objects. The photograph might not represent, but it might approximate. It might exaggerate certain properties (in the photograph) in an attempt to relay different but related qualities of architecture, since those were beyond reach in a two-dimensional image. It might compensate the viewer for one sort of deficiency by enhancing and intensifying visual experience itself.

Other rhetorical devices that feature both in the literature and in photographs themselves include synecdoche and metonymy: the photographic image may represent only one part of a larger whole (synecdoche), or the attributes visible in photographs become signifiers for a host of attributes that are not visible or are only partially visible (metonymy). These and other tropes appear in the literature reviewed below. This material thematizes aspects of architectural imaging that will recur in the history of modern architecture, introduced here in a synoptic review of the practice. The most frequently discussed topics included the distortion of depth and the pros and cons of including scale figures in photographs of architecture.

Conventions for architectural photographs codified in handbooks and journal articles on the subject in the years before World War I supply a vocabulary for this new kind of visual communication. They included guidelines for equipment, lighting, lens choice, camera siting, and picture composition. The problem of depth perception in photographic images was also of primary importance for the representation of architectural space, as was the question of scale figures.[28] Publications on the subject offer insight into the problems that photographers faced when trying to provide adequate information about buildings in the limited format of publication with the equipment available at the time. Often trained in the field, photographers learned through apprenticeship, not from books or formal schooling, so the contents of these publications do not necessarily correspond to any specific professional practice.[29] Practical norms recorded in handbooks may not unlock the mysteries behind corpora of photographs. We might rather see them in this light: as theoretical recommendations for an idealized professional practice that often unfolded in decidedly nonideal terms.[30] Nevertheless, the handbooks provide an overview of common practices and are useful indices of the field in the early stages of its development. By reviewing this material we gain awareness of the technical limits of field photography, of the compositional norms that predominated among architectural photographers, and of common attitudes toward framing, lighting, and staffage. Reflections on depth and color perception also provide clues to the translation from building site to printed page as it was understood at the time.

Hans Schmidt's *Die Architektur-Photographie: Unter besonderer Berücksichtigung der Plastik und des Kunstgewerbes* (Architectural photography: with particular reference to sculpture and the decorative arts) (1902) gives a cross section of professional architectural photography at the turn of the century.[31] Schmidt's book of "practical rules for the general principles of the discipline" provided rules of thumb that echoed existing norms for painting or drawing, filtered through a pragmatic, documentary approach to the production of record photographs of buildings. Guidelines from Schmidt's handbook recur in other literature on architectural photography. A summary of the most important information allows us to understand the conventions of the practice in the period before the war. Many of these conventions remained in place throughout the interwar years and beyond. As the technical parameters for architectural photography changed over the century, picture-making conventions remained relatively stable, at least for commercial practices, or changed at a much slower pace than the conventions of other photographic genres. This initial survey thus provides a reference point for later discussions.

EQUIPMENT

Schmidt's recommendations for photographic equipment balanced image quality against portability, suggesting that the photographer use a field camera with a large negative plate of eighteen by twenty-four centimeters (close to eight by ten inches), the largest standard size for architectural photographs throughout the Weimar years (Figure 4.2). This produced a negative with precise detail that could be contact printed to produce the sharpest possible picture. Such cameras required that architectural photographers carry large sheets of coated glass with them to building sites up until the beginning of World War II in 1939, after which smaller-format plastic

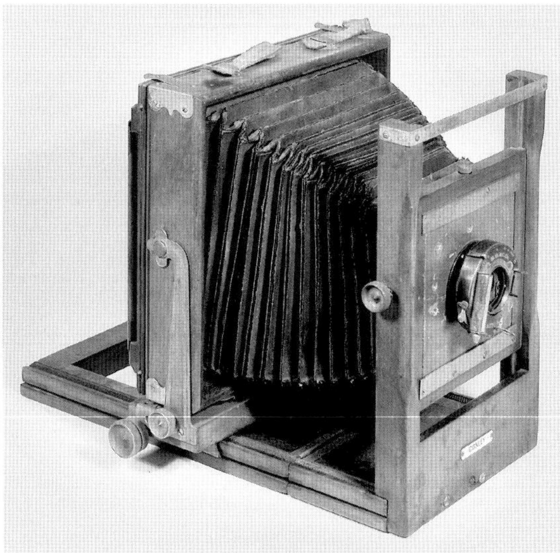

Figure 4.2. Field camera for photographing architecture, circa 1902. Photograph copyright Larry Pierce (http://www.piercevaubel.com).

films came into more frequent use in professional architectural photography. Glass negatives would sometimes be recycled—cleaned and recoated—to save materials and expense.[32] The cameras were portable wooden field cameras set up on tripods. The photographer exposed the film from underneath a hood that covered the ground-glass screen through which the latent photograph could be seen. This projected image would appear inverted and in reverse; the photographer thus composed each picture while looking at the subject upside down and backward. Although photographers internalized this constraint through force of habit, nevertheless it emphasized composition at the expense of narrative content, which remains difficult to recognize when seen upside down. Perhaps unrelated, writers often emphasized the importance of composition in their guidelines for taking photographs.[33]

Writers on photography also complained about the distorting effects of the wide-angle lens, at the same time noting its necessary use for the photography of buildings. Complaints about distorting lenses focused on the overemphasis on deep space that often resulted from their use. Recommendations for the careful disclosure of scale relationships reveal the importance these writers placed on architectural photography as a means of faithfully portraying architectural information. Aesthetic concerns were generally balanced against concerns regarding accurate communication about architecture. Like other writers on the subject, Schmidt recommended that photographers use the longest focal length possible, and that they place the camera at the farthest practical distance from the object or space to be photographed. The former ensured a larger area of focus; the latter gave the photographer greater control over image composition and reduced the visual distortion that wide-angle lenses brought with them.

STANDPOINT AND IMAGE COMPOSITION

The placement of the camera was the first step toward taking a picture. The raking diagonal view (sometimes supplemented by head-on views) was the preferred viewpoint for architectural photographs. It was important to mimic the standpoint of a casual observer, because "pictures taken from a hard-to-reach standpoint always have something unnatural about them."[34] Schmidt discouraged excessive camera height, sometimes necessary in the photographing of tall buildings, suggesting that the camera be set up one meter above the ground. The aim of the photographer was the naturalistic representation of architectural space as if seen by an observer on-site. Photographs of Schmitthenner's Gartenstadt Staaken (1917) or of one of the Tietz department stores illustrate this approach, despite the distortion involved in photographing large urban buildings from tight spaces in the latter example (Figures 4.1, 4.3). Schmidt's text, like other primers on architectural photography at this time, emphasized the importance of a standpoint that was not "unnatural" and that any casual observer might assume.

Under the subheading "Some Aesthetic Rules," Schmidt included the following guidelines. After recommending the raking diagonal, he went on to note that in certain situations—streets, colonnades, interiors, "and especially in the case of objects that pull strongly into depth" (überhaupt bei sich stark in die Tiefe ziehenden Objekten)— a frontal standpoint is required. But on no condition should the photographer assume a position on the symmetrical middle axis; the camera should always be set to one side or the other.[35] Only when the two sides of the space/object are notably different may the camera be placed directly on the centerline of the space. In addition, in interior photography, one side of the enclosed space should always include the connection between wall and ceiling: "The total lack of such [closure] makes itself felt as tremendously disturbing, in that the whole shows no limit to itself. . . . A picture must always have a fitting conclusion, and may never be a vault without supports."[36] We might recall this condition with respect to the Tugendhat House and its columns, discussed in chapter 3. He concluded this point with a positive example of how pictures may be fittingly framed by an arched doorway or other aperture, as Figure 4.4, another example from Gartenstadt Staaken, illustrates.

Schmidt instructed the photographer to keep the foreground as narrow as reasonably possible, except when trying to show a building perched on an elevated site. In such cases, Schmidt implied that the picture represents an important fact about the architecture—its high siting—through an exaggerated foreground and a low camera height. These are analogous photographic techniques that are meant to suggest specific architectural qualities. This approach—of using analogous techniques to approximate architectural effects—will recur in other photographic literature. In this case, the photographer uses the camera to approximate an accurate record of its subject precisely through exaggeration, as paradoxical as that may appear. The fact of being sited on a high piece of ground can be intimated through the analogous (but quite different) motif of an exaggerated foreground produced partly with

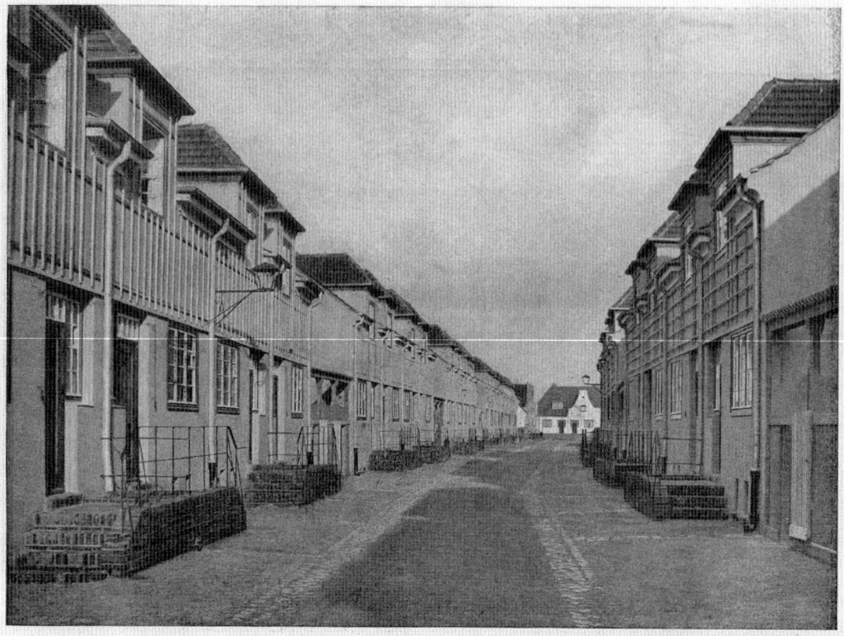

Einfamilienhausstraße „Am Pfarrhof". Im Hintergrunde die Einmündung auf den kleinen Platz

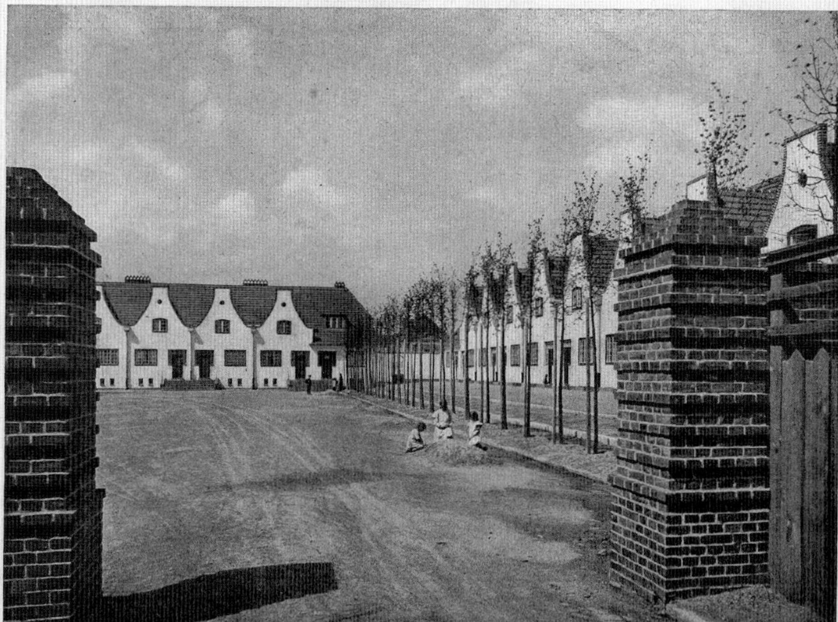

„Kleiner Platz" mit Einfamilien-Reihenhäusern

Figure 4.3. Gartenstadt Staaken, Berlin-Spandau, 1914–17. Architect: Paul Schmitthenner. Photograph: Wasmuth-Verlag.

a wide-angle lens and a low camera angle. These two devices—exaggeration and approximation—constitute two consistent guidelines for architectural photography throughout the century to follow.

Pointers for successful image composition and appropriate staffage featured regularly in literature on architectural photography throughout the 1910s and 1920s. Writers often noted the reduced control over lighting that architectural photographers enjoyed and recommended against shooting in bright sunlight.[37] Opting for the raking diagonal, they dwelled on the balancing of focal length, standpoint, and the judicious use of the wide-angle lens required to capture a "natural" view.[38] Schmidt emphasized that lack of color increased the importance of image composition: "Since the photograph doesn't represent the color of the original, it is only really effective through the course of the lines themselves. A handsome perspective is thus far more decisive for the general worth of a photographic image than is the case with painting."[39]

Schmidt noted the reduced control over lighting conditions that an architectural photographer enjoys in comparison with a studio photographer: "In architectural photography particularly we cannot create effects through the nuanced distribution of light and shadow since we have only limited control here, in contrast to portrait photography. Thus we must take great pains to create effects through perspective."[40] Thus architectural photographers were already understood to be compensating for challenges intrinsic to the medium of photography—lack of color and uncontrolled lighting in the field. By paying close attention to the formal composition of the image, they might make up for other missing qualities. A picture that was deficient in some respects in relation to its object might nevertheless be enhanced in other ways by photographic technique. A good photograph could approximate the rich panoply of effects that prevailed "on the ground," translating a built object into something like an analogous representation but compensating for lack

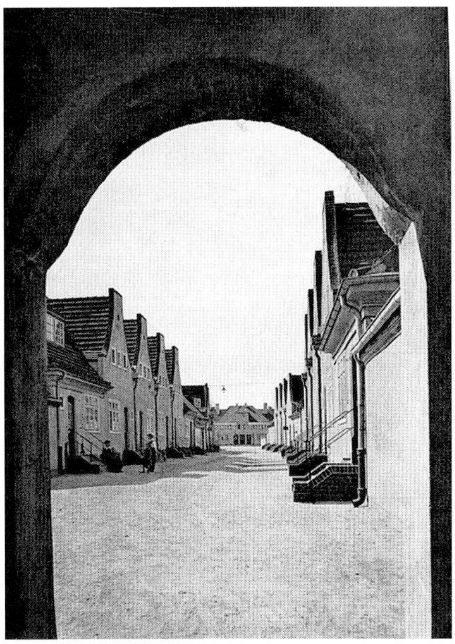

Figure 4.4. Gartenstadt Staaken, Berlin–Spandau, 1914–17. Architect: Paul Schmitthenner. Photograph: Wasmuth-Verlag.

of copresence in space with some visual intensification within the picture. This intensification constitutes a third trope based on the idea that the photograph might compensate for its own deficiencies.

Approximation, exaggeration, and intensification: these are three compensatory poles of architectural photography as it entered the twentieth century. To summarize: the photograph must compensate the viewer for lack of presence on-site with elements and staging that intensify visual experience and suggest immanent presence, regardless of how they may differ from their subject. How did these three aspects appear in photographic images? The use of a low camera angle for buildings sited on hills has already been mentioned, as has the use of a framing element such as a doorway or window aperture that closes the composition, creates high contrast between dark and light, exaggerates the size of the foreground, and places the viewer within the photograph yet set off from its "interior" space. Other similar devices might include an emphasis on formal abstraction within the picture and the adoption of a synecdochic approach in which the part-to-whole relationship of a building element supplies a stand-in for larger views. In the pages ahead, other examples that emphasize how exaggeration, intensification, and approximation were used to compensate visitors for lack of spatiality will be reviewed in light of these early texts.

SCALE

The question of scale potentially affected all three of these modes of response (exaggeration, approximation, intensification) by installing a control within the space of the photograph that tethered visual appearances to an object of known size. In considering the use of scale figures, we might review the different rhetorical devices of architectural photographs that have already been introduced. Intensification, exaggeration, and approximation were manners of architectural photographic rhetoric. Other techniques known from the history of rhetoric that also find a place in the architectural photograph include metonymy and synecdoche, as noted above. Other mechanical techniques of architectural photographs also reviewed above proceed from rules of thumb that govern staffage and composition, including framing, lighting, lens choice, and printing techniques. All of these devices relate to the photographer's effort to produce a persuasive image, perhaps the central task of this sort of photography. When the inclusion of scale figures in a picture would work against a photograph's other rhetorical tasks, we can assume that they were often omitted. The choice to use scale figures or not was also an ideological one, although its ideological indices were not entirely fixed, nor can we necessarily make claims about them.

Scale figures in architectural photographs generally help the viewer infer building size, whether the figures are human or mechanical (a car will do, as in Figure 5.1). Human figures in photographs of Gartenstadt Staaken, for example, clarify building scale while narrating ideas about community (Gemeinschaft). The well-known motorcars that adorned later pictures of the Weissenhofsiedlung, by contrast, supply a contrasting narrative element equally loaded with a preference for machine technologies. But the absence of both cars and people is a common feature of architectural photography, even to the present day. This absence may have roots in the earlier history of photography, when slow photographic emulsions required absolute stillness on the part of subjects. But the continued exclusion of figures throughout the post–World War I period cannot be explained solely by technical limitations of photography that no longer pertained. By the turn of the century, exposure times were fast enough to allow for the inclusion of adults and even fidgety children. Instead, we might consider the riddle of architectural photographs that specifically *withhold* the cues that help the viewer to understand accurately the absolute size of a building, as an object in space on a specific site. Why would architectural photography embrace such a restriction, if its intended purpose were to relay information about the real-life scale of its subject?

Carl Franck, writing in the *Photographische Rundschau und Mitteilungen* in 1915, noted:

> Some believe that every picture should include staffage, particularly one or more people, even if only some passing schoolchildren. Everyone knows how fully such embellishments can spoil the effect of an otherwise successful picture. Certainly, from time to time the enlivening of a street or a square is very appealing, but it must also really be an enlivening, it must not be more or less obtrusive people spread around. Better no staffage than such a one that looks all too much like sham.[41]

Whether for scenographic or aesthetic reasons, the absence of figures was often seen as a positive choice, an intentional practice with intended results. At its most obvious, it drew the viewer's attention to the space and object, not the human being.[42]

Many photographers nevertheless included figures in their pictures. Those interested in situating architecture in relation to narrative depictions of everyday life frequently used scale figures. Photographs of *Heimatstil* architecture, as the setting for a communal, tradition-bound lifestyle such as that proffered by Schmitthenner and his Wasmuth photographer (possibly Arthur Köster), were more likely to include figures. In other cases, figures could be put to didactic use, to instruct the viewer about the intended use of a given building.[43] These demonstrations of inhabitation constitute interesting exceptions to a general rule that became only more prevalent as time went on, despite the fact that it was always subject to challenge.[44] Coarsely formulated, the difference concerns whether photography should emphasize the building or the use being made of the building. Architects were divided on this question; photographers, perhaps less so.

DEPTH PERCEPTION

Photographs were said to distort most noticeably in their representation of depth. Willi Warstat, in his 1909 *Allgemeine Ästhetik der photographischen Kunst auf psychologischer Grundlage,* asserted that the camera records proportional relationships in two dimensions, height and width, with relative reliability. In the third dimension, however, in its record of depth, the photographic negative is highly unreliable:

> But differences that require no further explanation, between the eye on the one hand and the photographic plate on the other, appear to all with respect to the reproduction of the third dimension, the dimension of depth. It has certainly come to the attention of every photographer that the photographic camera doesn't handle distance as well as the human eye. Every photographer will have had the experience—sometime in the course of his career—that objects that seem not so far away from his eye appear as if pushed disproportionately far back into the distance.[45]

Warstat's reflections on the differences between spatial perception and photographic recording occupy the first section of his book, which was volume 65 in the *Encyklopedie der Photographie.* The book was a general treatise on photography in relation to pictorial art, specifically painting. Warstat claimed that the natural shortcomings of the photographic negative could be ameliorated through skillful production of the positive image, and he assigned photography its place among the other arts, each medium-specific and all seen in relation to an aesthetic standard derived from painting.[46]

Warstat ascribed the distortion of depth perception in photography to a number of causes, analyzing differences between photographic lenses and human vision. The cues by which we understand depth with binocular vision on-site include quantity of detail, constant eye movement, and tonal variation in the object of view, Warstat noted. These cues are suppressed in cognition of the black-and-white photograph, which records all detail without editing, limits eye movement in the third dimension (depth), and distorts many of the color and tonal values by which we also read depth. Thus the photographer must address the shortcomings of the photographic plate and the camera lens by adopting certain compositional conventions and darkroom practices engineered to compensate for what Warstat understood to be inherent limitations of the medium. Compensation again emerges as an overriding mandate placed on architectural photography.

METONYMY, NOT MEANING

In literary theory, the idea of metonymy refers to the attribute of a thing when used to refer to the thing itself. The classic example of literary metonymy is the use of a feature to describe a larger construct: "black hat" as a reference to a man who habitually wears a black hat, or "Blackbeard" for a man with a black beard. Roman Jakobson relates this phenomenon to a visual model: "In a poetic world governed by metonymy the outlines of things are blurred and the various aspects of one single object turn into independent objects in their own right."[47] Physical contiguity allows an object to be conflated with an aspect of itself. This idea applies well to individual architectural photographs that are taken as representatives of whole buildings. These sorts of images are carriers of meaning that are *contiguous to* but distinctly separate from the constructions they represent. They engender meanings that are hinged to the original construction but float free from that construction precisely because they emerge from a two-dimensional picture surface.

In the context of German culture battles of the 1920s, photographs broke free in different directions. Returning to the material of chapter 3, the Tugendhat House in photographs was both a positive model for aesthetic expansion and a negative model in relation to the social obligations of modern architecture. Similarly, for all the positive propaganda provided by the Berliner Bildbericht photographs of the Barcelona Pavilion, right-wing journals also published countless negative images targeting building developments of the Neues Bauen like the pavilion itself and the Weissenhofsiedlung in Stuttgart (Figure 6.12).[48] These were then metonymic in two senses: they implied an overall condition for the building depicted (of decrepitude or shoddy construction) and, by extension, that such a condition also applied to the enterprise that had produced this sort of building in the first place: the Neues Bauen.

Metonymy provides one category of signification for architectural photographs—an important one, but not the only rhetorical model that could be usefully applied here (synecdoche is another, as noted). Models from the study of rhetoric in language are not precisely transferable to photography, but they highlight the gap between *any* precisely fixed meaning and the appearance of a photograph. This gap may be the single most important aspect of the relationship between buildings, photographs of buildings, and publications. Not only does any given photograph present merely a single "aspect" of a building: subject to metonymic interpretation, it can create associations that differ significantly from those created by other pictures of the same building, leading to logical contradictions. Changing interpretations over time also make the mutability of the architectural photograph evident, as Juan Pablo Bonta's study of the photographs of the Barcelona Pavilion made clear many years ago, and as we will see at the start of the next chapter in the case of the Bauhaus. If we return to the suggestion that photographs are images of images, and place this idea into the current discussion, it would appear that the flexibility that attends the interpretation of any aesthetic object is multiplied by at least three things in the case of photographs of architecture. First, the process of fixing complex three-dimensional objects in photographs results in serial single views that may relay significantly different meanings for the same objects. Second, the process of making a photograph can obscure the representational qualities of a piece of architecture, particularly when the building has been designed with the idea of resemblance already in mind (as in the case of revivalism, or buildings that reference other buildings). Third, the repeated publication of a single iconic picture of a building is accompanied by changing interpretations over time that further destabilize the idea that a photograph might *mean* anything at all. We can at this point take the notion of fixed meaning out of consideration altogether (if it was ever there) and note that photographs of architecture are not in the business of making meaning. Rather, they are used to make associations, to suggest, to imply, to misdirect, to entice—in short, to sell the viewer on something that has been decided outside the frame of the image—something that is, in this case, beyond the visible surface.

In the case of the Barcelona Pavilion, the building is a monument of modern architecture not *in spite of* its survival in photographs but precisely *because* photography protected it from the fierce ideological battles of its day—a fact it shares with many other buildings. But at the Tugendhat House, I have argued, photographs produced the opposite effect, sparking a critique of the building that rested on qualities discernible in photographic images but not on-site. How can this be? How can photographs create a given dispute in one case and prevent a very similar dispute from occurring in another? There are circumstantial issues related to the short life of the Barcelona building, which meant that the "original" could not be checked against the "copy" after January 1930; these might be used to explain this discrepancy. But more than that, the discrepancy underscores the flexibility of commercial photographic images of architecture that has just been outlined. The value of the photograph was its endless flexibility—partly because it was seen to have no intrinsic art value of its own (despite the artistry involved), but to have the attributes of a descriptive language, even a polemical one, that might be scripted at the will of the author. There was no confusion that the photographs of the pavilion were not architecture. They were propaganda agents for architecture, for Mies, and for Germany (at least for a while). Part of their lasting value emerged from their ability to suspend, not determine, fixed meaning.[49] And in this, many photographs of buildings followed in their wake.

INTERWAR ARCHITECTURAL PHOTOGRAPHY

Professional architectural photographers remained tied to standards of verisimilitude in the Weimar period, unlike pictorial photographers and members of the avant-garde. Such standards were updated in reference to the "New Vision," but, on the whole, architectural photographers produced standard compositions for the trade presses of the building industry and for the architectural press as the 1920s passed. Notable exceptions include Albert Renger-Patzsch, who photographed buildings designed by his friend Rudolf Schwarz using more adventurous visual tropes, and Arthur Köster, who performed a similar service for Erich Mendelsohn. An important article on architectural photography signaled some confusion on the matter of objective (sachlich) representation of buildings in 1929. The editor of the Werkbund journal *Die Form,* Wilhelm Lotz, called for architectural photography to be "solely the medium of the impression of the object" (nur Mittler des Eindrucks des Objekts). In the same essay, however, he also demanded that architectural photographs offer "a clear and objective representation of the object" (eine klare und sachliche Darstellung des Objekts).[50] Whether the photograph offered "an impression" or an "objective representation" seems to have been a general question among architects and critics that remained unanswered at this time. Architectural photographs were expected to fulfill both requirements, despite potential contradictions between "representation" (Darstellung) and "impression" (Eindruck). A shift of emphasis between Weimar and earlier photographs of architecture from picture making to clarity of representation suggests, however, that expectations were changing, no matter how much photographs stayed the same. What emerged in the 1920s, perhaps in relation to this shift, was a strong ambivalence about the architectural photograph.

Lotz's article, embedded in a journal dedicated to new trends in the arts, raises a question. Discourse on art practices had changed substantially between 1902 and 1929, but it is less clear that this had affected standards for the professional photography of buildings. Standard compositional formats such as the three-quarter raking view persisted in Weimar architectural photography, even as technical innovations, particularly in lens design, altered photographs more generally. On the whole, architects tended to discourage innovation, preferring photographic neutrality to a distinctive artistic signature in all but a few well-known cases. They often saw skillfully composed photographic compositions as distractions from the "straight" relay of architectural information. They generally preferred to regard the photograph as a transparent window—albeit an imperfectly designed one—through which the public might gain access to a building, thus reaching back beyond the visual self-consciousness of the nineteenth century, all the way back to Alberti, for a canonical standard.[51] The craft of architectural photography, invested in technological change but not necessarily in conceptual change, diverged from the field of architecture, invested in conceptual change with or without technological change.[52]

The most innovative architectural photographers working in Weimar Germany and much of Central Europe, while conversant with the rules of thumb of the discipline, were also aware of New Vision photography, in which artists explored photography as a means for new visual experiences. These photographers and artists, most notably figures such as Aleksandr Rodchenko and László Moholy-Nagy, used radical points of view and abstract composition to reconfigure visual experience throughout the 1920s according to new protocols. In some cases, architectural photographers found creative ways to deploy new compositional modes within the constraints of commercial practice. In other cases, however, their techniques exhibited innovations specific to the technical and disciplinary limits of their distinct professional field.

Perhaps most notable of these Weimar-period photographers was Köster in Berlin, whose work has recently been analyzed in two German monographs. Between 1919 and 1926 Köster was a staff photographer at the Wasmuth publishing house. After 1926 he established an independent photographic practice in Berlin, operated with his brother and then his nephew. By the end of the 1920s, he was the most important photographer of the Berlin architectural scene, personally endorsed by members of The Ring (Zehnerring), the group of progressive architects based in Berlin.

Köster's repeat clients among architects of the Weimar period included Mendelsohn, but also Otto Haesler in Celle and Mies.[53] Where Köster's work tended to eschew unconventional camera angles, nevertheless he broke many of the rules of architectural photography as laid down by Schmidt and others. He used human figures and cars to people (and scale) his photographs, and in other respects he practiced a kind of dramatic scenography that included backlighting street facades and photographing on bright sunny days with skies full of fluffy white clouds. On the other hand, he also frequently framed his subject through an aperture, often from the building itself, as in his remarkable pictures of Mendelsohn's Luckenwalde hat factory of 1921–23 (Figure 4.5). Köster's practice led to new trends in the architectural photography of the Neues Bauen. In the process, he explored the pictorial capacities of architectural photography in relation to new rhetorical possibilities.[54]

Photographs of buildings were and remained evidentiary documents in the Weimar period; they supplied basic information about buildings. They were also pictures, altering spatial perception in visible ways, as remaining chapters explore. Finally, they were small-scale, portable indices of a kind of visual experience that had become increasingly prominent in urban experience at several levels in the years of the new century. Photographic or indexical images had become increasingly common "texts" of a public visual literacy after the 1890s, combined with signage (elec-

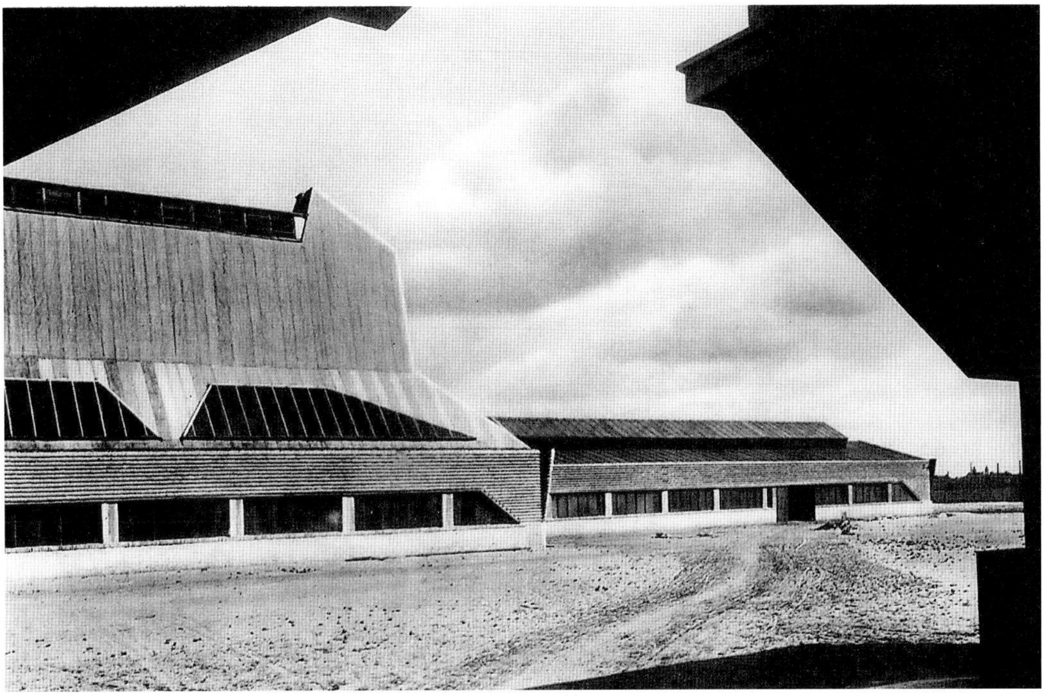

Figure 4.5. Hat factory, Luckenwalde, 1921–23. Architect: Erich Mendelsohn. Photograph: Arthur Köster; copyright VG Bild-Kunst Bonn/Germany, 2012.

trified or not) and graphic devices such as advertising during the Weimar years. Rolf Sachsse has pointed out something like a confusion of tongues in architectural photography, in which picture-postcard views were used to depict radically modern buildings, or strictly "technical reproductions" were used to describe architectural monuments. Deploying a linguistic metaphor, Sachsse notes that this hybridization resembles the "slang use of grammatical terms"—or, in other words, attempts to talk to the street, but with the language of the palace.[55] This mixed mode of address is, however, common in modernity, where new visual forms from high art slowly become popularized in the mass media, where they retain just the scent of their former site. Furthermore, although Sachsse interprets this hybridity in terms of social class (grammar versus slang), we might allow that the visual modes of photography deployed existing compositional motifs quite promiscuously, without any regard to prior conventional meaning. Not modes of speech, they are more like words and letters, waiting in limbo for new combinations to come to life, where they can begin their metonymic work.

We might now supplement this review of the professional conventions of architectural photography by turning to particular instances in which architectural photographs were particularly effective: in publications and exhibitions.

Not style problems, but building problems are foundational to the new building art. Thus the surprising accord of the external formal appearance [Erscheinungsform] of this new international building art can be apprehended. . . . It is highly differentiated through regional and national particularities and through the persona of the creator, but on the whole the product of the same conditions. From there proceeds the unity of its exterior form. Its spiritual connectivity surmounts all borders.

—LUDWIG HILBERSEIMER,
INTERNATIONALE NEUE BAUKUNST

5. AURA DEFERRED

BAUHAUSBAUTEN DESSAU

By January 1926, the new building of the Dessau Bauhaus was under construction; before it was complete, the photographer and publicist Lucia Moholy began to take pictures.[1] She continued after construction was complete, photographing the school's exterior and the houses for the Bauhaus masters located nearby. Among her photographs is a well-known picture of the studio wing of the Bauhaus (Figure 5.1). The camera rakes across the corner of the building, capturing the floors of the studios inside their transparent glass skin, cast-iron radiators sitting incongruously on visible concrete slabs in a building that appears naked, not merely glass-walled. Around the corner, a car parked in shadow is framed by the unpaved road that runs under the bridge connecting classrooms to studios, theater, and dormitories, and containing the office of Bauhaus director Walter Gropius, also the architect of the entire complex.

Published in 1930 in *Bauhausbauten Dessau* by Gropius and László Moholy-Nagy, this picture was closely associated with the Bauhaus as a locus of artistic experimentation as years passed. A decade after Gropius's book appeared, Sigfried Giedion compared the photograph to a cubist painting, printing it opposite Picasso's *L'Arlésienne* (1912–13) (Figure 5.2). Giedion's caption in *Space, Time and Architecture* (1941) noted how the painting used the "cubist device of simultaneity—showing two aspects of a single object at the same time." The Bauhaus photograph on the facing page was captioned: "In this case it is the interior and the exterior of a building which are presented simultaneously. The extensive transparent areas, by

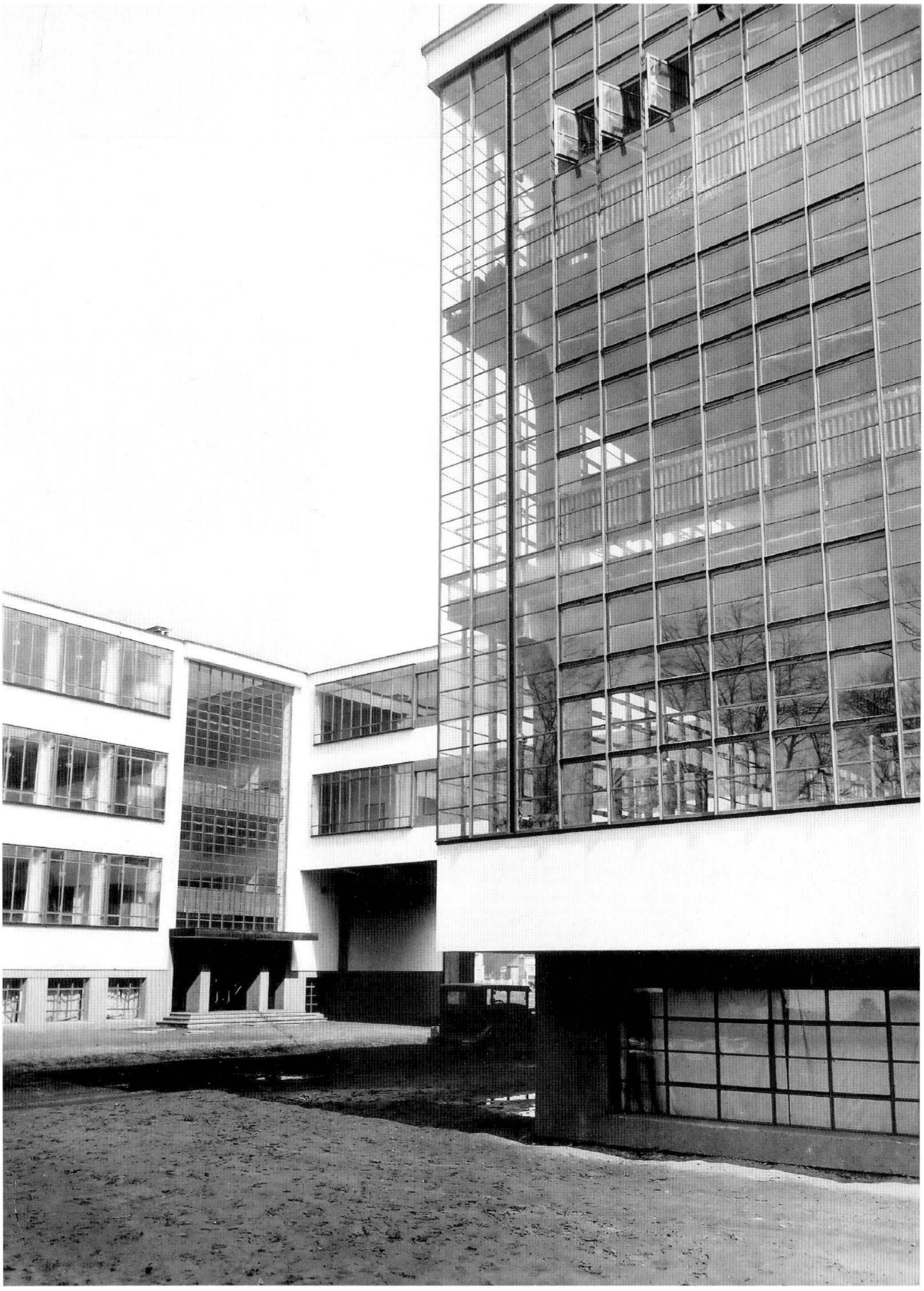

Figure 5.1. Studio wing, the Bauhaus, Dessau, 1926. Architect: Walter Gropius. Photograph: Lucia Moholy. Copyright 2012 Artists Rights Society (ARS), New York/VG Bild-Kunst, Bonn.

dematerializing the corners, permit the hovering relations of planes and the kind of 'overlapping' which appears in contemporary painting."[2] Giedion's caption described the building as the architectural rendition of a painterly achievement (one nearly fifteen years old when the Bauhaus was built), almost as if architecture itself had provided no relevant discourse for the building or the photograph, which went unremarked.

Giedion related cubist "simultaneity" to architectural transparency in the passages quoted above. Cubist simultaneity recalled a mode of painting from the 1910s in which time and visual cognition overlap, collapsing the tiny gap between seeing one side of an object and seeing another, recording movement around objects in a single view. Cubist painting transformed perception over time—architectural perception, one might say—into an image. Architectural transparency as described here demonstrated an opposite idea—that of seeing many things at once from a single stationary point. Simultaneity in architecture here suggests a single moment of seeing one thing through another, not dynamic experience but rather a quality of the view or glance. If Giedion (and cubism) "architecturalized" painting, he appeared

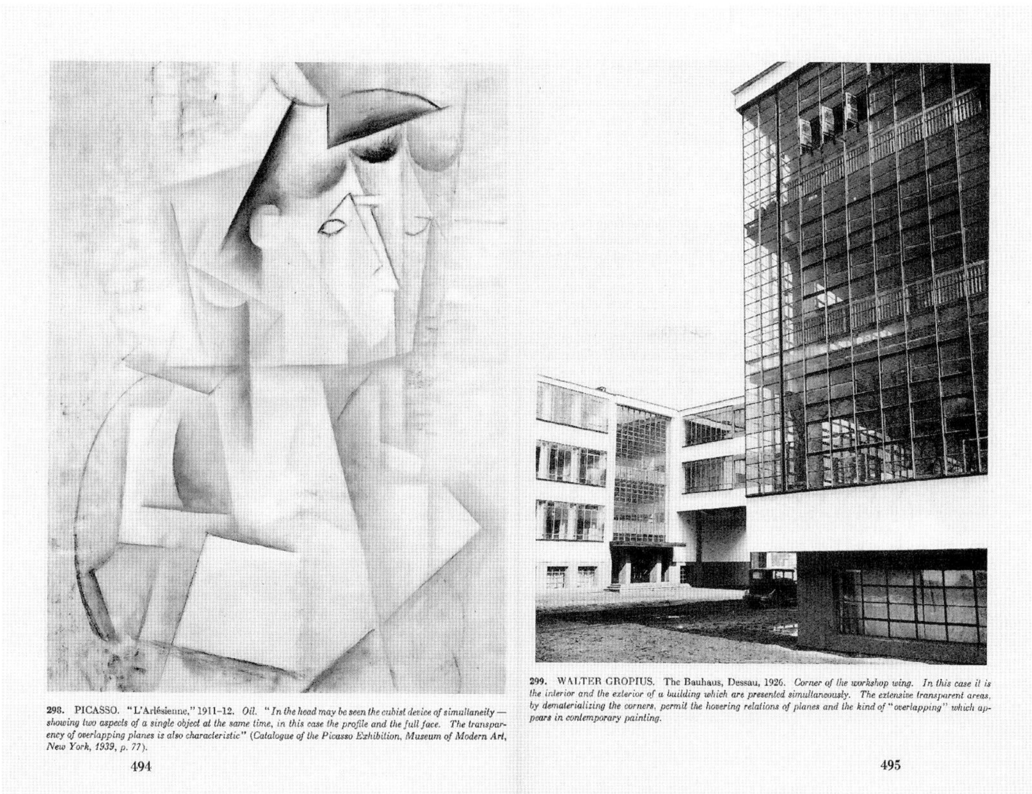
298. PICASSO. "L'Arlésienne," 1911–12. *Oil.* "*In the head may be seen the cubist device of simultaneity — showing two aspects of a single object at the same time, in this case the profile and the full face. The transparency of overlapping planes is also characteristic*" (*Catalogue of the Picasso Exhibition, Museum of Modern Art, New York, 1939, p. 77*).

494

299. WALTER GROPIUS. The Bauhaus, Dessau, 1926. *Corner of the workshop wing. In this case it is the interior and the exterior of a building which are presented simultaneously. The extensive transparent areas, by dematerializing the corners, permit the hovering relations of planes and the kind of "overlapping" which appears in contemporary painting.*

495

Figure 5.2. Two-page spread from Sigfried Giedion, *Space, Time and Architecture: The Growth of a New Tradition*, 3rd ed. (Cambridge, Mass.: Harvard University Press, 1959), 494–95.

to reduce architecture—through the device of an architectural photograph—to a matter of visual cognition. Giedion's interpretation of simultaneity collapsed the Bauhaus into something that could be apprehended in a single photographic image.

CAPTION AND TEXT

Giedion's creative correlation between *L'Arlésienne* and the Bauhaus corner was part of a campaign for modernism during World War II that differed from the campaigns of ten years earlier, when the Bauhaus was newly built. But this example shows how easily photographs could slip into new editorial frames. Published in the most widely used and frequently reprinted textbook on modern architecture, this photograph became perhaps the best-known photograph of the Bauhaus building. The building was henceforth tied to cubism by Giedion's text, a pedigree for subsequent architectural discourse that persists today.[3]

It comes as something of a surprise, then, to compare Gropius's caption for this photograph in his 1930 book with that of his close associate. Gropius wrote:

> the corner of the workshop building allows the construction frame of concrete pillars and massive decks to be clearly recognized. for the first time the problem of the dissolution of the wall through spanning a continuous glass skin in front of the bearing skeleton of the building is carried through to its logical conclusion. the cantilever of the decks over the cellar provides a double advantage: the statically efficient and therefore economical shortening of the distance from outer columns to middle columns on the interior and the usefulness of the whole glass facade in front of the columns as well as between, for work spaces for the workshops. low heating units along the whole width of the glass wall. window curtains under the floor decks along the whole glass wall to protect against the rays of the sun.[4]

Giedion emphasized the achievement of this building in relation to the mandates of painting. Gropius, a decade earlier (before the election of a National Socialist government in 1933 and the outbreak of war in 1939), emphasized its technical performance in relation to function, program, and construction. His words suggest the importance of evaluating the building by correlating what was visible with what had been constructed. Cantilevered floor decks, innovative glass skin, and concrete structural frame represented substantial achievements, but the visibility of the achievements was perhaps even more important than the technological innovations they represented. Technology that was for the most part more than twenty years old was brought to the surface and put on display.[5]

These two publications and the differences between them show how text and layout helped establish the meaning of architectural photographs, through terms that

Roland Barthes has described as relay or anchorage.[6] But as *Bauhausbauten Dessau* and *Space, Time and Architecture* demonstrate, captions and layout never lock down the meaning of a photograph entirely. To those trained outside the framework established by Giedion's influential textbook (i.e., roughly after the early 1980s in the United States), the association of the Bauhaus corner with a cubist painting of many years earlier may seem oddly self-serving. Glass curtain walls came into being for many reasons other than the elusive idea of simultaneity mentioned by Giedion, which was instead closely connected to his evolving historical interests. Text and captions tell us about the context in which a photograph circulates—they do not limit its potential meanings elsewhere, despite any burdens of history.

Another difference can be found between these two publications of the same photograph. In *Bauhausbauten Dessau* the plate with the Bauhaus corner photograph was credited to Lucia Moholy as photographer. In *Space, Time and Architecture*, Moholy's name was missing, and Gropius received sole credit for the building as well as the picture. There may be a circumstantial explanation for this omission. Lucia Moholy had departed Germany in 1934 after the arrest of her partner, Communist politician Theodor Neubauer, by the Gestapo. She left her negatives in the care of Gropius, who had them shipped to the United States without informing Moholy herself, despite the fact that both were in England in 1934 before Gropius moved on to the United States.[7] Perhaps her name was omitted from Giedion's book because any legal or proprietary rights appeared to have been suspended in a new legal context (the United States), or because photographer and architect disagreed about the ownership of the image, or simply because Moholy did not know of the publication. In fact, photographers' credits frequently did not accompany published architectural photographs at this time. Captions often, but not always, named the architect alone, a fact that reinforced the tendency to treat photographs of architecture as transparent windows onto the buildings they depicted rather than as two-dimensional compositions produced by highly skilled visual technicians, craftsmen, or even artists.

Extrapolating from this single photographic image and its sites of publication, we might hazard three relevant frames with which to analyze a published architectural photograph: compositional and technical characteristics of the photograph; the textual framing provided by caption and graphic design; and the strategic interpretation of the picture by architects and critics, achieved through omissions such as the one just narrated or through adjacent textual commentary that appeared in print.[8] These three frames of photograph, caption, and textual explication allow us to examine how architectural photography interacted with modern architecture at this time; Bauhaus images provide a challenging case study.[9] The photograph, its publication in a journal, magazine, exhibition catalog, or book, and the commentary on its publication provide three registers for analysis that were, however, not entirely discrete or separate from one another, as a brief narration of Bauhaus history shows. The image of the Bauhaus was a function of all of these, and others.

TRADEMARK BUILDINGS

The Bauhaus building and the 1927 exhibition discussed in the next chapter help reveal the varied tasks to which architectural photography was applied in the mid-1920s. New modern buildings by a wide variety of architects were published regularly in the Weimar press, but the program of the Neues Bauen deployed a smaller group in media publications, both nationally and internationally. In certain cases buildings were enlisted to advance modernist polemics from the moment of their inception; in other cases buildings emerged over time as important symbols of modern architecture. The Dessau Bauhaus belonged to the first group. It was designed and built after the institution had already been threatened with closure in Weimar, when the conservative city government elected to terminate funding for the school. After this defeat, which was discussed in the press, Gropius safeguarded the future of the institution as best he could, using the much-celebrated Dessau building as a showpiece. A publicity campaign heavily reliant on photography promoted the building as signifier for the institution.

Visual associations between buildings and institutions existed well before the twentieth century. Advertising already connected commercial establishments to products in the nineteenth century; examples such as the Parisian Printemps, Germany's Wertheim and Tietz chains (Figure 4.1), and the Schlesinger and Mayer department store in Chicago by Louis Sullivan all used buildings to identify and sell brands. Long before the Bauhaus association between a building and its educational products, precedents existed. The building itself might be treated as a constructed advertisement or three-dimensional image, with logos, signage, or distinctive sculptural embellishment appended to the architecture. The image of the building (whether drawn, engraved, or photographed) might appear in commercial advertisements in the trade presses. Documentary photographs of the building might be used to affiliate its image with a commissioning client and architect in a more subtle form of advertisement in the architectural press. In the latter two cases, two-dimensional images presented three-dimensional ones.[10]

The Turbine Hall (1908–10), built in Berlin-Moabit for the Allgemeine Elektricitäts Gesellschaft (AEG) by Gropius's former employer Peter Behrens, provides a precedent for the Bauhaus. The Turbine Hall bore the AEG trademark, which was inscribed into the building's pediment-like facade. But the building was also itself a trademark: photographs and drawings affiliated its image with other graphic information used by AEG to promote its products (Figure 5.3).[11] Part of the goal of the AEG's design campaign concerned brand identification, whereby German products might be associated with product quality through the unifying symbol of the trademark.[12] In addition, the symbolic form, or image, of the factory building allied product quality with the self-respect and social relevance of workers. This is by no means identical to the branding of a hotel or department store; nevertheless, the building functioned as an image (a three-dimensional one) in both cases.

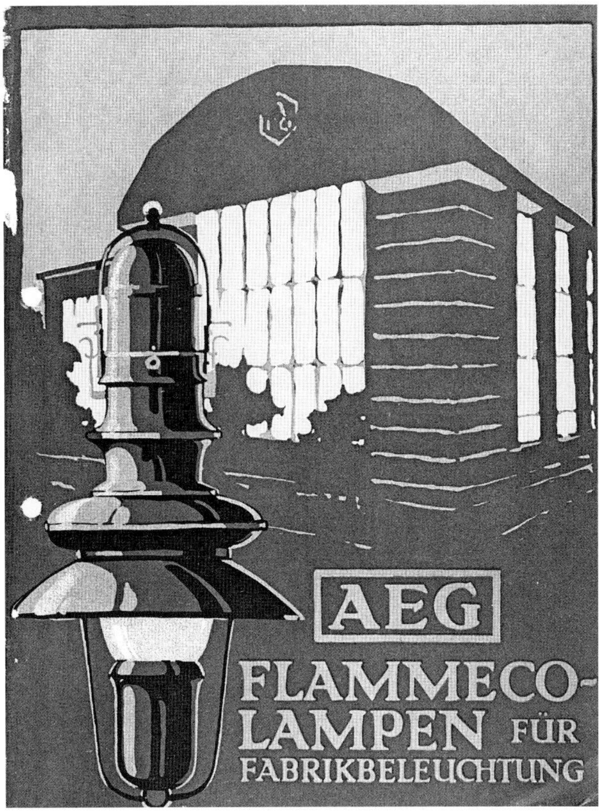

Figure 5.3. Turbine Hall, Berlin, 1909, in an advertising poster for AEG lighting. Architect: Peter Behrens. Source: Tilmann Buddensieg, *Industriekultur: Peter Behrens und die AEG, 1907–1914* (Berlin: Mann, 1979).

The AEG building provides a relevant precedent because the Bauhaus repeated many of its tropes. The Turbine Hall has been interpreted as a factory masquerading as a temple, as if the values associated with sacral architecture might be actively bestowed upon the occupants of the factory. Work was thus to be metaphorically ennobled through architectural form: the formal shell of the building acted as a communicative sign, whether the symbolism was pagan or Christian (Karl Scheffler referred to this building as a "cathedral of work"). Similarly, the Bauhaus was a school wearing the garb of a factory: the "product" was educated talent, and the elevation of workers at the Turbine Hall was here replaced by the desire to bring art into line with industrial production. The school was the concretization of ideas formulated by members of the German Werkbund who also supported the AEG project, among them Behrens.[13] The Bauhaus adopted the form of the factory, just as the factory (Behren's Turbine Hall) had adopted the form of a temple. That the Bauhaus building was long interpreted as a functionalist manifesto is one of its great achievements (or deceptions). In the case of the Bauhaus, functionalism is chiefly a citation.

Contemporary with the Bauhaus, Erich Mendelsohn's design for the renovation

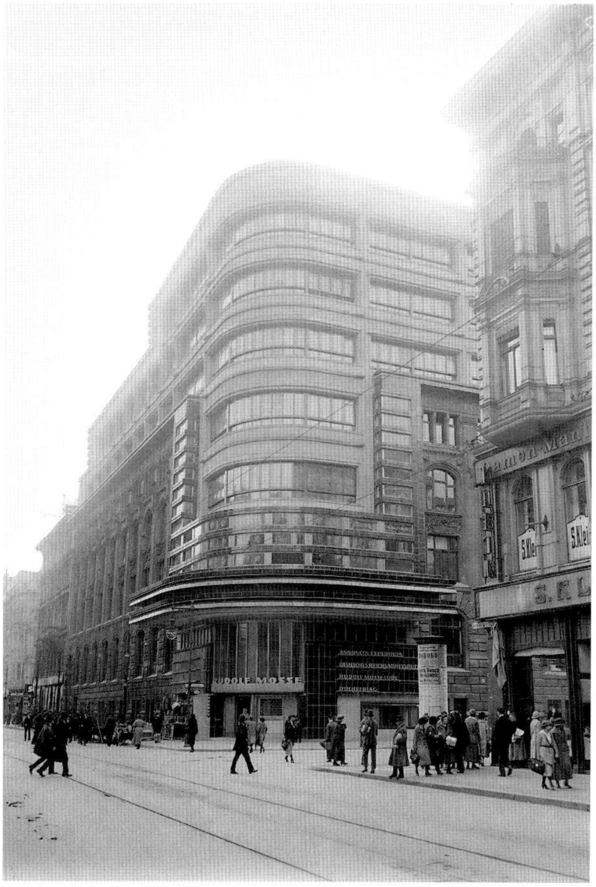

Figure 5.4. The Rudolf Mosse Publishing House, Berlin, rebuilt to a design by Erich Mendelsohn, 1920. Photograph: Bundesarchiv Bildarchiv.

of the Rudolf Mosse publishing company in Berlin also conjoined a building and a corporation. An earlier building on the same site had been heavily damaged in the factional street fighting that followed World War I in 1919. As rebuilt by Mendelsohn, the corner of the Mossehaus, as it was called, became synonymous with the Mosse brand (Figure 5.4). The newly reconstructed corner became a trademark for the company, its image (whether in photographs or drawings) used in commercial advertising and other marketing materials.[14] The photographs of the Mossehaus, like those of the Bauhaus, reinforced a strong associative link between a building and an institution. The form of the new building, with its distinctive rounded corner and damaged original fabric, created a three-dimensional trademark considerably more concrete than a graphic sign. Photographs of the building captured this three-dimensional image in two dimensions. Historian Sabine Hake has traced the graphic presence of the Mosse Verlag in printed matter circulating in Berlin, insightfully showing how the Mossehaus corner was used to associate the publishing house with a newly democratic Germany. The choice of Erich Mendelsohn as the architect recalled a set of political associations as well.[15] Similarly, the Dessau Bauhaus also embodied a program with specific political connotations and was advertised that way from the start (Figure 5.5).[16]

We might then turn to the history of the Bauhaus.[17] In Dessau, the commission for the new building was awarded to Gropius's private architectural practice in 1925. The school was first housed in temporary quarters while Gropius designed the new building and supervised its construction, with the official opening in December 1926.[18] Gropius completed the commission together with a set of houses for the Bauhaus masters; other buildings in the city of Dessau followed, specifically the Törten-Siedlung and the Arbeitsamt. Shortly after the Bauhaus arrived in Dessau, Gropius saw history beginning to repeat itself as the city government moved to the right. He left the directorship to return to private practice in Berlin in 1928, having led the institution since its founding in 1919. He suggested his own replacement: the Bauhaus master and Swiss architect Hannes Meyer.

When Meyer became director in spring of 1928, the Bauhaus enjoyed continued support from the mayor of Dessau, Fritz Hesse, regardless of opposing factions in the regional government. Hesse had been instrumental in bringing the Bauhaus to Dessau in 1925. His support did not initially waver, in spite of local pressure.

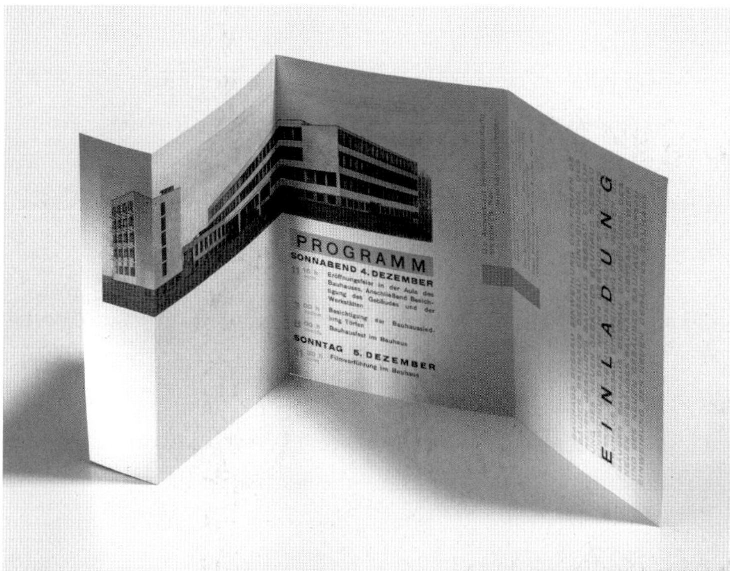

Figure 5.5. Invitation to the opening of the Dessau Bauhaus, December 4, 1926. Designer: Herbert Bayer. Photographs copyright 2012 Artists Rights Society (ARS), New York/VG Bild-Kunst, Bonn.

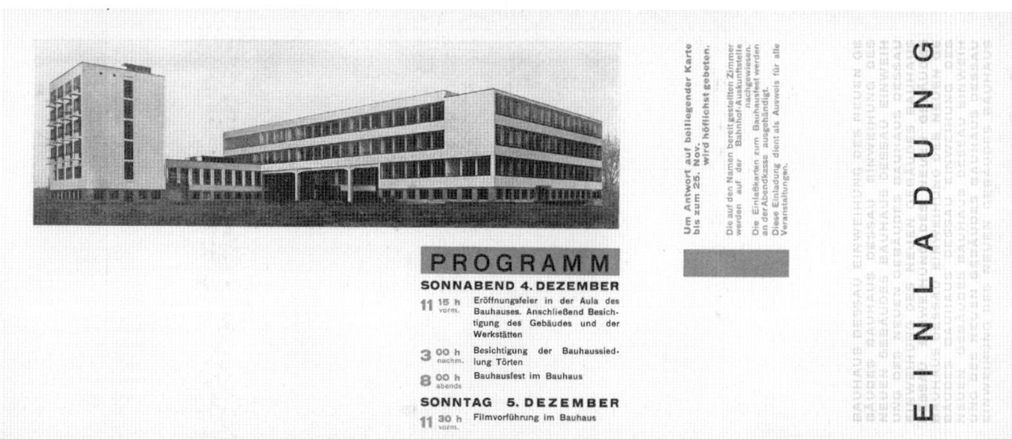

After receiving the appointment as director, Meyer attempted to address local criticism by increasing profitability through the production of industrially designed products. Here he followed through on an issue that had underpinned public support for the Bauhaus since Weimar days. His approach to education, as noted by Magdalena Droste and Rainer Wick, emphasized connectivity between architecture and social life; in this sense his focus was broadly democratic, aimed at the larger social collective, not the smaller field of artists and designers who dominated Bauhaus life.

Meyer also revised the Bauhaus curriculum, broadening the spectrum of disciplines taught through visiting lectures and separating subspecialties at the expense of the integrated medium- and workshop-based teaching that preceded his arrival in 1927. In this, he extended the long-articulated mission of the Bauhaus: to integrate art and life following a long-standing avant-garde aim. But in so doing, Meyer diminished the formerly central role of painting within the curriculum.[19] Wassily Kandinsky, Paul Klee, Josef Albers, Lyonel Feininger, and former director Gropius soon opposed the new director and the emphasis on mass production that resulted from his leadership. Meyer's dismissal in 1930 was attributed to his politicization of the Bauhaus. His poor relationships with powerful members of the faculty were also consequential, as he noted in his public letter of response: "At the Adriatic, V. Kandinsky stretched out on the sand with relief: it was all over."[20] By 1930 Meyer had left the Bauhaus for the Soviet Union and was replaced by Ludwig Mies van der Rohe, who remained director when the institution was closed down in Dessau and then briefly reopened in Berlin, finally closing its doors permanently in 1933.

The building was often conflated or identified with photographs of its Dessau building from the opening festivities of 1926, but the nature of the identification changed substantially after the institution closed its doors and entered the arena of history.[21] As photographs taken and distributed before 1928 were spreading more widely throughout the national and international press, Meyer appears to have been ambivalent about the branding of the institution through its architecture.[22] For the brief period from 1928 to 1930 under his directorship, the active association of the building and the institution ceased. After Gropius departed, Meyer stopped using dedicated photographs of the Bauhaus and its earlier products to promote the institution. Instead, in his *Junge Menschen kommt ans Bauhaus!* brochure of 1929, he included photographs of Bauhaus products, of Bauhaus staff, and of activities at the school in which the building was merely a backdrop. In exhibitions of Bauhaus products that traveled throughout Europe, he omitted pictures of the building and of earlier products, focusing on the task he had begun by showcasing new Bauhaus work only.[23] Gropius's monograph *Bauhausbauten Dessau* was edited and produced at precisely this time—appearing in 1930, the same year that Meyer left the Bauhaus for the Soviet Union. Gropius was able to address his successor's criticisms of the pre-1928 Bauhaus in print.[24] After Meyer's departure and the publication of *Bauhausbauten Dessau*, the image of the institution and that of its building again adhered to one another closely, a situation that continues to the present, despite changing views of the institution over the intervening years.

The association of the Bauhaus with its image, while similar in kind to the examples discussed above, differed from them as well. The Turbine Hall was affiliated with sacred architecture in order to deliver a particular message to its users and the public. The Bauhaus building represented the institution of Bauhaus learning in a different way. Not only a factory for education, the building demonstrated the sort of activities that went on within it. The simplicity of its massing; the order and dynamic asymmetry associated with its pinwheeling form; particular parts of the building, such as the studio wing, with its glass sheathing and naked concrete structure; the bridge spanning a city street to connect the four discrete functional volumes of the building (classroom, dormitory, theater, studio)—all of these parts were in some sense demonstrative. Either they displayed the activities housed within them literally (as in the studio wing or the staff offices bridging studio and classroom) or they demonstrated the values of Bauhaus design more metaphorically (pinwheeling form as dynamic asymmetry; transparency).

Gropius stated that the building exemplified processes or design values promoted at the school, such as the "self-reflexive life functions" of the architect. It is not clear whether this was his intention in 1925 or a retroactive claim of 1930, responding to Meyer's criticisms: Meyer had openly espoused "life functions" as the focus of the designer's work. In Gropius's case, the building was more likely a formal and operational (functional) demonstration that would allow architecture to effectively "figure" the institution. The Dessau Bauhaus as designed by Gropius was in that sense an image-building: a building intended to display its meaning didactically through visible form, to be memorable, to give formal shape to functional intention. The tendency of students and faculty to use the Bauhaus building as subject matter for their photographs, or as a stage set for their theatrical productions, further demonstrates how much the building and its products were inseparable in the minds of users, hinting at the recursive nature of a building that, in a sense, demonstrated its own intended results.

MOHOLY AND BAYER

From 1926 to 1930, different kinds of photographs of the Dessau Bauhaus proliferated. Construction photographs, documentary architectural photographs, reportage of the building in use, scenographic pictures of the Bauhaus as stage set, "New

Vision" photographs with innovative composition and dramatic lighting, and snapshots by *Bauhäusler* and visitors all attest an unusually varied use of photography for a single building. This variety resulted in part from the notoriety of the school as a locus of experiment, but it also reflected a growing interest in photographic representation and photographic publicity at the time. László Moholy-Nagy's early writings, worked up in collaboration with his wife, began an investigation that would culminate in later work.[25] The essays "Production-Reproduction" (1922) and "Typophoto" (1925) outline new tasks for photography in the presentation of information and the creation of new optical experiences.[26] According to Lucia's notes, they worked jointly on "Production-Reproduction," which came out in the magazine *De Stijl* under Moholy-Nagy's sole authorship in 1922.[27] After their move to Weimar, the couple's activities diverged along the lines described in the 1922 manifesto: she reproduced the work of the Bauhaus for publication; he produced "New Vision" photography in contact with other members of the Weimar avant-garde. Lucia Moholy became increasingly involved in photography and in producing published material for the Bauhaus, although her contribution is difficult to verify, since her name was left out of all but one of the Bauhaus books. To pursue this work, she apprenticed with a local professional photographer in Weimar and subsequently attended the Leipzig Hochschule für Graphik und Buchkunst in 1925–26, where she studied technologies of reproduction for publishing (Reproduktionstechnik). By 1926, the professional skills she had gained from her experience in photography, editing, and bookselling were united in the technical production of photographically illustrated publications.[28]

In the series of fourteen Bauhaus books that began to appear in 1924, Moholy is mentioned in the fourteenth volume, Moholy-Nagy's *Von Material zu Architektur*.[29] Although this series began in Weimar, her role as Bauhaus publicist appears to have grown more important in Dessau, when one of the products of the Bauhaus was the building itself. During the Dessau period, Moholy executed most of her architectural photography, trained in Leipzig, and worked on the inaugural issue of the Bauhaus magazine.[30] Leaving the Bauhaus with Gropius in 1928, she and her husband returned to Berlin; within a year, they had separated and begun new phases of their lives.[31]

Moholy's Dessau photographs included exterior views of the Bauhaus building and interior and exterior views of the nearby masters' houses. For nearly all subjects she used the standard three-quarter raking or head-on views characteristic of conventional architectural photography (Figures 5.6, 5.7); she also took a series of photographs through apertures or other framing elements (Figures 5.8, 5.9).[32] Many of the photographs were carefully composed and unconventional in their framing

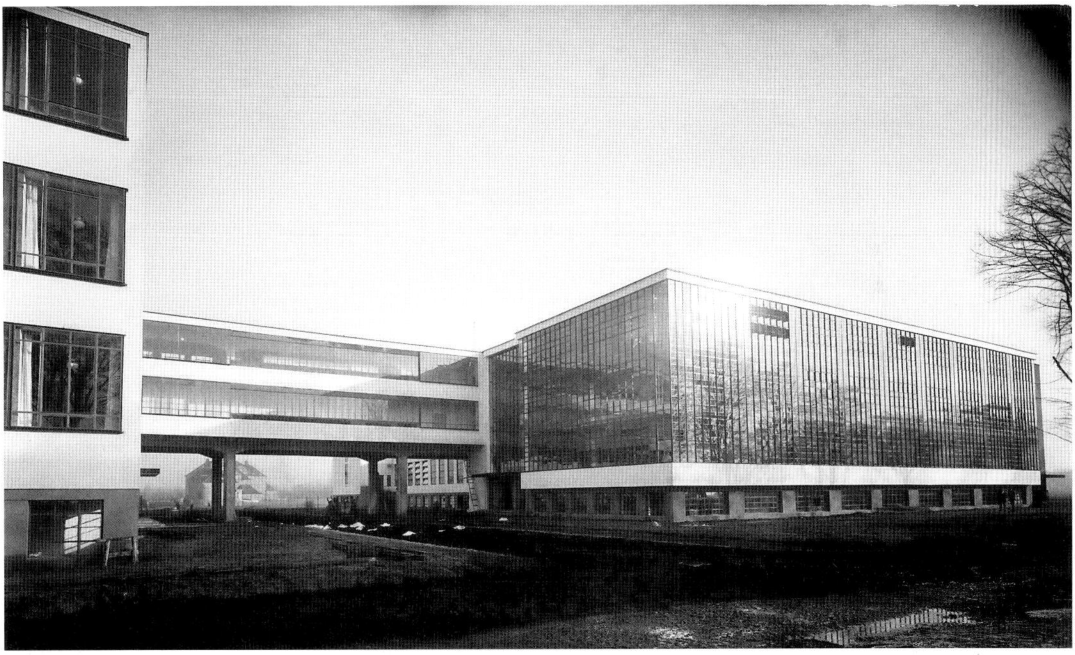

Figure 5.6. The Bauhaus from the northwest, Dessau, 1926. Photograph: Lucia Moholy. Copyright 2012 Artists Rights Society (ARS), New York/VG Bild-Kunst, Bonn.

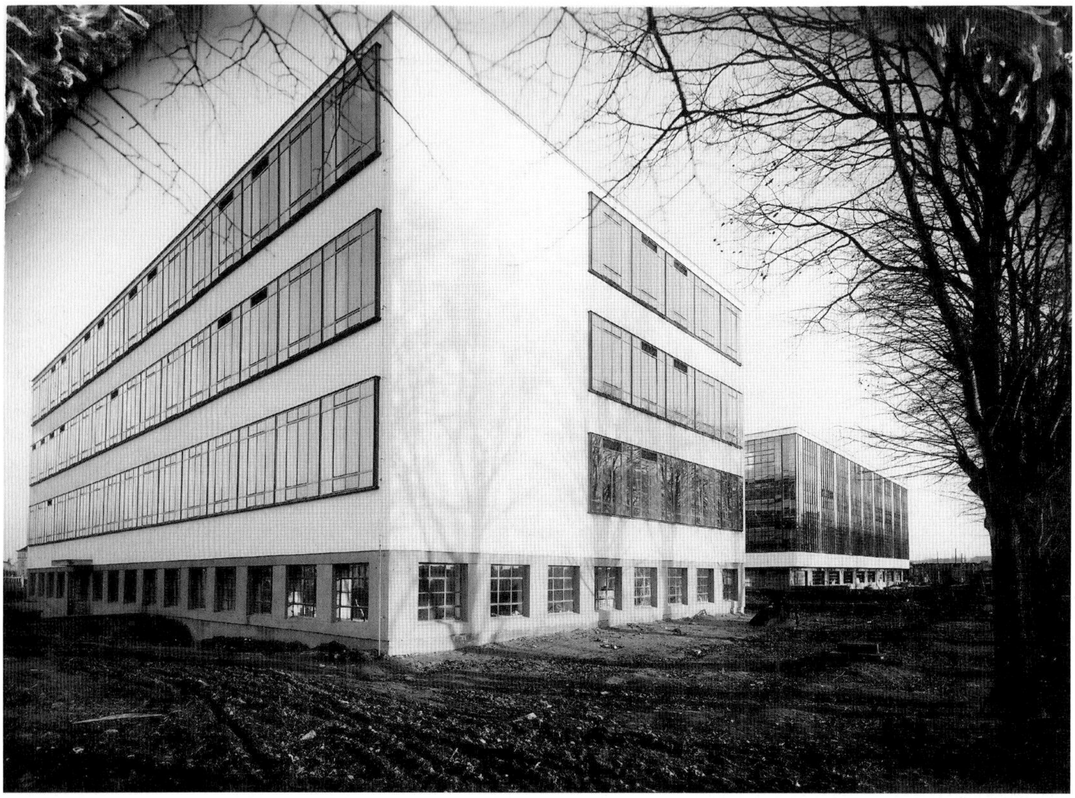

Figure 5.7. The Bauhaus from the northwest, Dessau, 1926. Photograph: Lucia Moholy. Copyright 2012 Artists Rights Society (ARS), New York/VG Bild-Kunst, Bonn.

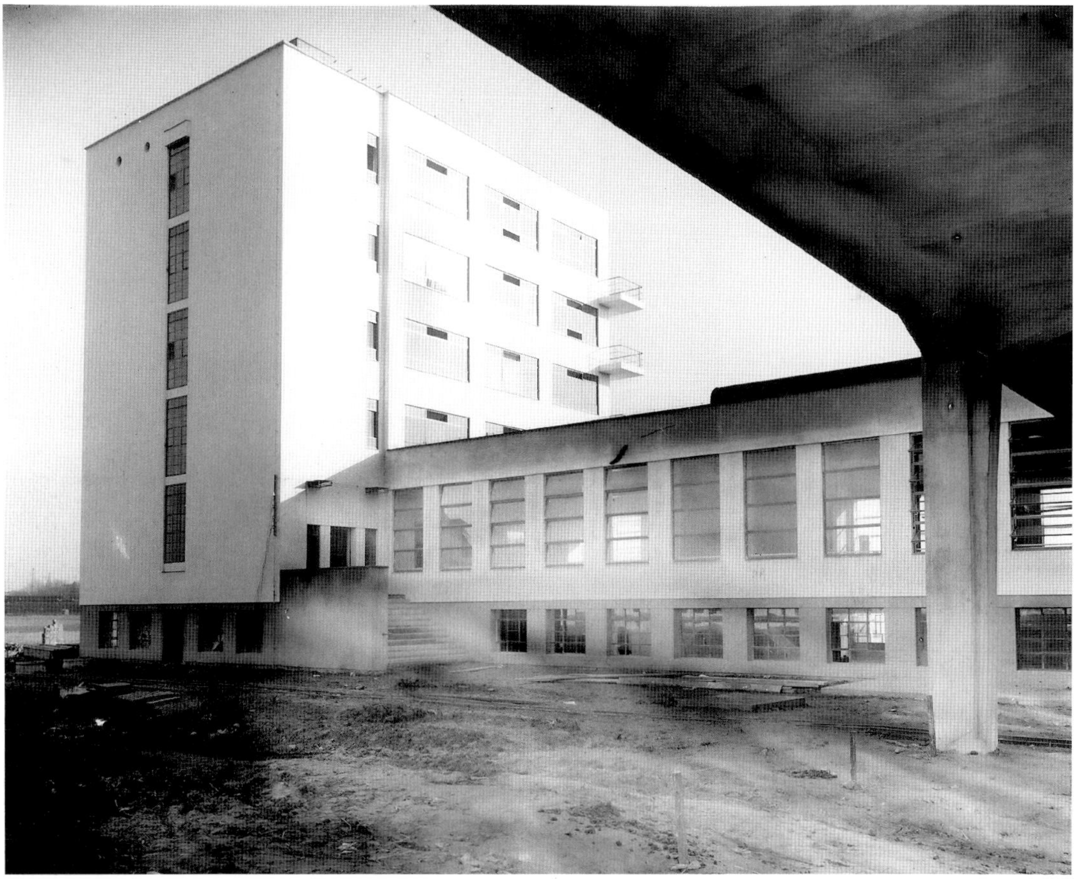

Figure 5.8. View from underpass toward dormitory, the Bauhaus, Dessau, 1926. Photograph: Lucia Moholy. Copyright 2012 Artists Rights Society (ARS), New York/VG Bild-Kunst, Bonn.

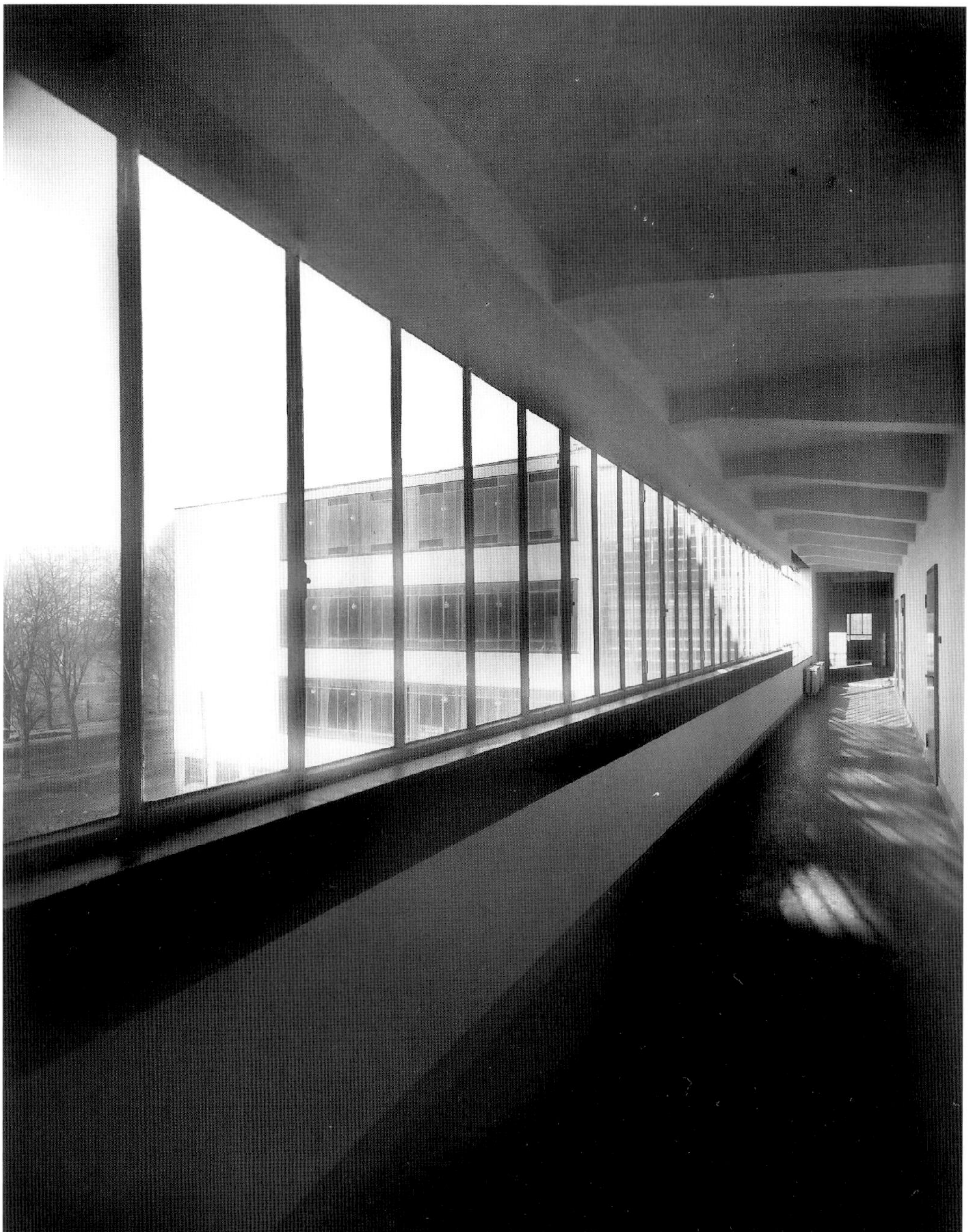

Figure 5.9. Bridge, the Bauhaus, Dessau, 1926. Photograph: Lucia Moholy. Copyright 2012 Artists Rights Society (ARS), New York/VG Bild-Kunst, Bonn.

and/or composition, including the raking view of the workshop corner discussed at the outset of this chapter.[33] A number of partial views were doubly framed by architecture, a gesture to photography itself.[34]

Moholy's photographs appeared in the first issue of *bauhaus* magazine, produced by Moholy and Moholy-Nagy—with his name appearing, hers not. In it, the photographs of the building are accompanied by a separate textual description (Figure 5.10). Photograph and text are juxtaposed and framed by a black band that separates them from a third element, Gropius's chronicle of the move from Weimar to Dessau and his celebration of their new patron city. In *bauhaus* 1, two texts and one set of photographs run as parallel "texts" presenting different facets of the institution. The first is narrative description; the next, visual description through photographs; the third, narrative chronology. In each of these sections, information from one account supplements the next. Each genre of information commands its own sphere of action but contributes to the other two, acting as a reinforcement of but also as a check on the other. The visual "text" of the photographs has a minimum of captioning information; writing is a different kind of text and occupies its own space.

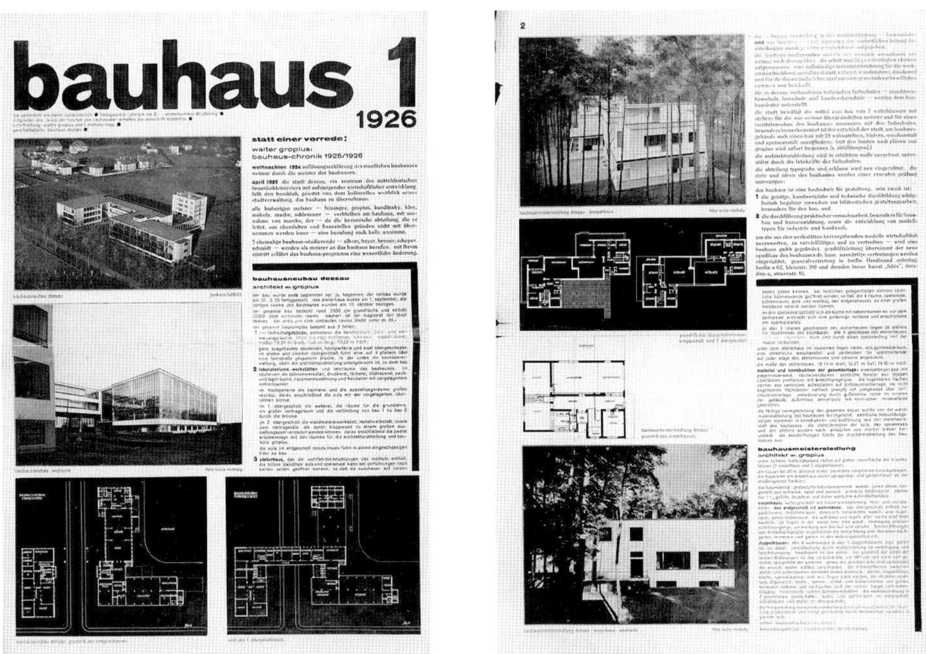
bauhaus 1
1926
statt einer vorrede:
walter gropius:
bauhaus-chronik 1925/1926
bauhausneubau dessau
architekt w. gropius
bauhausmeistersiedlung
architekt w. gropius

Figure 5.10. Lucia Moholy and László Moholy-Nagy, eds., *bauhaus* 1 (1926).
Photograph copyright 2012 Artists Rights Society (ARS), New York/VG Bild-Kunst, Bonn.

It is tempting to connect this approach to graphic production to a conscious attitude toward the presentation of information. Moholy had studied philosophy at Prague University, and her attitude toward media may reflect the influence of the philosopher-scientist Ernst Mach, as some scholars have noted. Moholy had learned of Mach's theories of relational representation as a student and had shared these ideas with Moholy-Nagy. According to Mach's theories, different forms of representation are accorded parity of appearance for the purpose of illuminating material phenomena from multiple viewpoints. In the process, balance is achieved through separation and supplementarity.[35]

Lucia Moholy's Bauhaus photographs were widely distributed to the press, showing up in newspapers and journals in the years 1926–27. They appeared in *Das Kunstblatt*, for example, which simultaneously published positive and negative assessments of the institution, the building, and director Gropius.[36] They appeared in newspapers such as the *Arbeiter Illustrierte Zeitung* as well as in the more specialized architectural press; the American periodical *Architecture* published one photograph of the building taken by Moholy in 1929.[37] It would be a challenge to identify a survey of Western modern architecture published after 1926 that does *not* include her photographs of the Bauhaus, sometimes credited, other times without photographer's credit.

Closer to home, Bauhaus publicity materials were used to attract new students and draw attention to the institution and its faculty. Photographic images appeared on the invitation to the opening of the building, in the *bauhaus* magazine, on the Bauhaus prospectus of 1927, in the 1927 second edition of the first Bauhaus book (*Internationale Architektur*, originally published in 1925), on posters and publicity materials produced by the school, and in the Bauhaus book of 1930 dedicated to the buildings in Dessau. Until the Bauhaus moved in 1932, photographs then in circulation took on the burden of representing a functioning school that was also an increasingly famous institution. Among these materials, Herbert Bayer also made an important contribution to the image of the Bauhaus in circulation at the time.

In Bayer's miscellaneous invitations and announcements of the Bauhaus and its products, graphic and photographic presentation were highly integrated into hybrid texts combining photography, typography, and graphic motifs, a system that he had perfected in the *Musterkatalog* (sample catalog) of 1925, for which Lucia Moholy had provided many of the photographs (Figure 5.11). In Gropius's book the photographs suffered from a dearth of textual support; in Moholy's magazine layout, photographs and text did their work independent of one another. In the case of Bayer, by contrast, photographs were buried beneath a host of angled lines of text, subdivisions, ordering motifs, and graphic ornamentation.

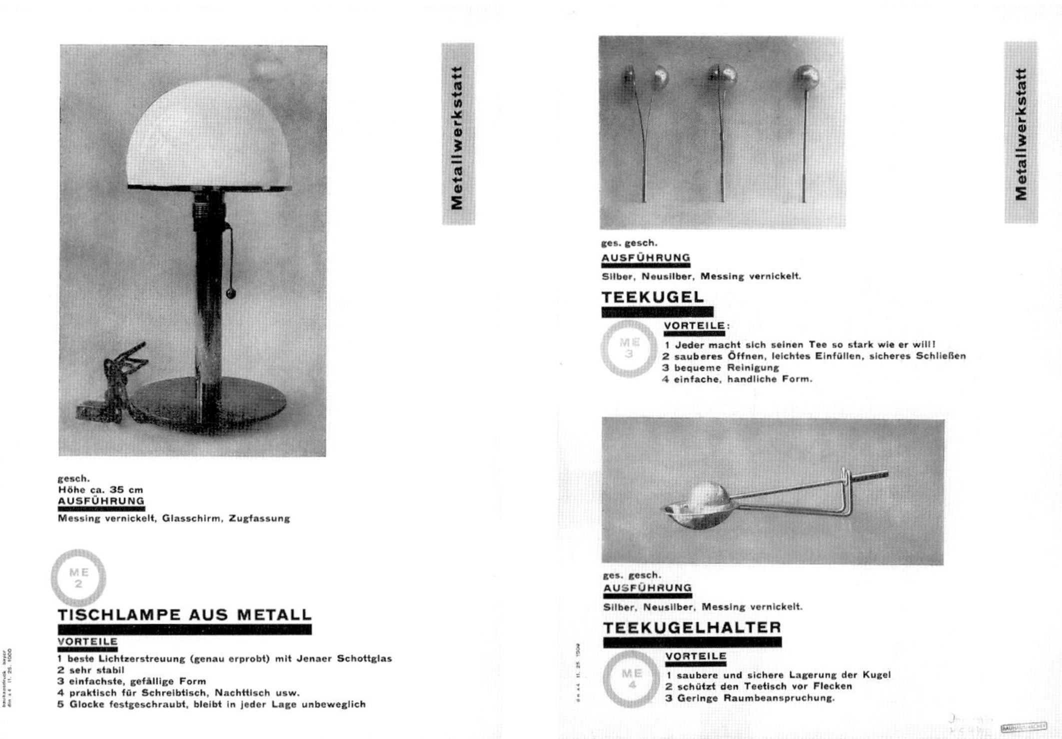

Figure 5.11. Lucia Moholy and Herbert Bayer, pages from the *Musterkatalog* of Bauhaus products, 1925. Photograph copyright 2012 Artists Rights Society (ARS), New York/VG Bild-Kunst, Bonn.

Bayer edited the first 1928 issue of *bauhaus* magazine; it came out in February, after Gropius had announced his resignation from the Bauhaus but before his contract had expired on April 1. Its cover features photographs of the Bauhaus building as a graphic motif supplementing a Bayer design. Pure geometric forms squash Gropius's earlier experiment in mass housing at Törten-Dessau and the competition drawings for Hannes Meyer's best-known project, the Petersschule Competition in Basel (1926) (Figure 5.12). The buildings appear not as objects depicted in photographs but rather as photographs in a newspaper—in other words, as photographs of photographs. This was perhaps a case of Bayer killing both of his professional fathers at once—his first teacher and employer, Gropius, and his new one, Meyer. In the back pages of the same issue, there is a captioned illustration identified as the reprint of a colored poster made up of multiple photographic prints of the Bauhaus building arranged in diagonal strips across the page. This pattern is then overlaid

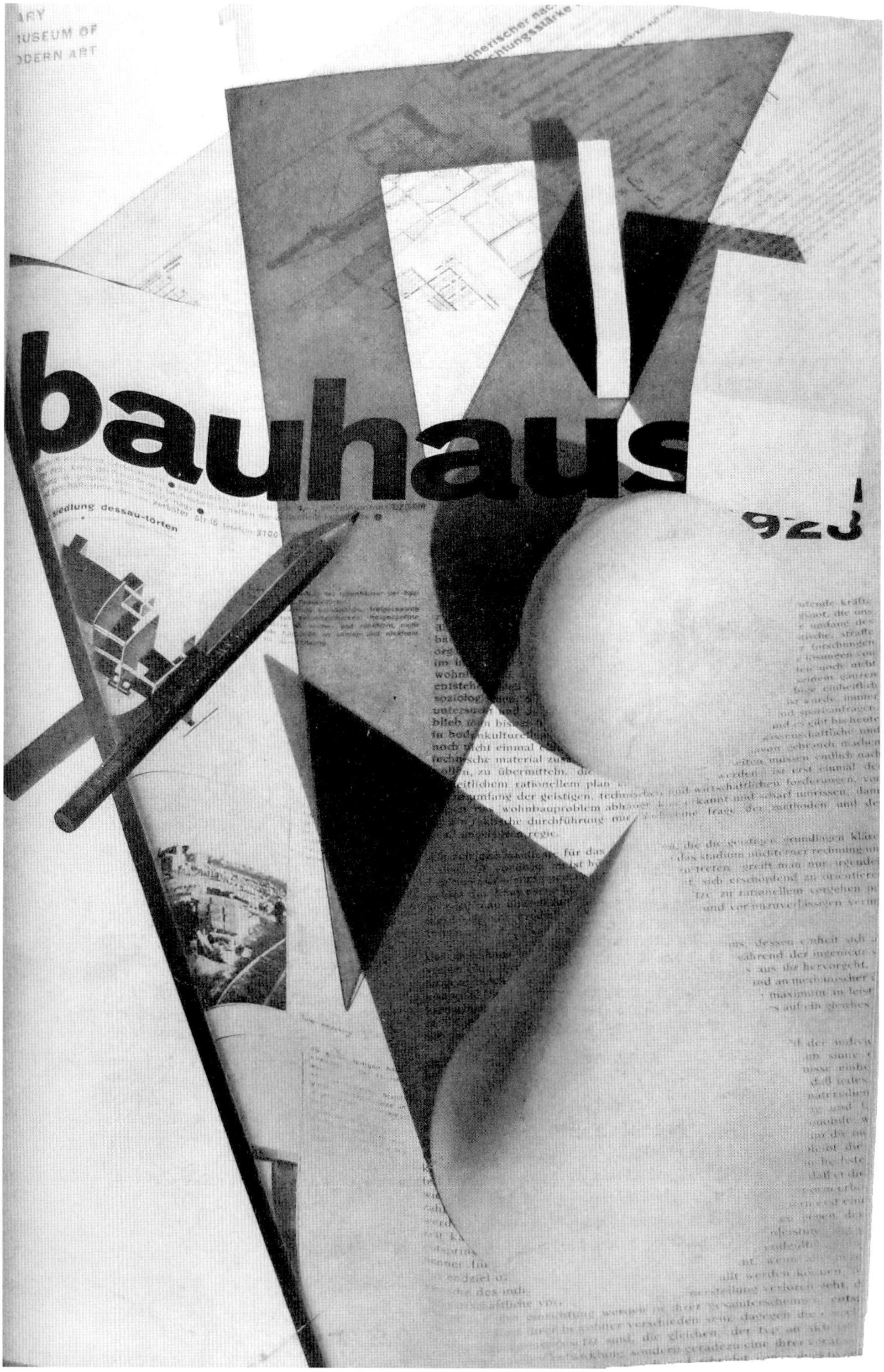

Figure 5.12. Front page of *bauhaus* 2, no. 1 (1928). Designer: Herbert Bayer.

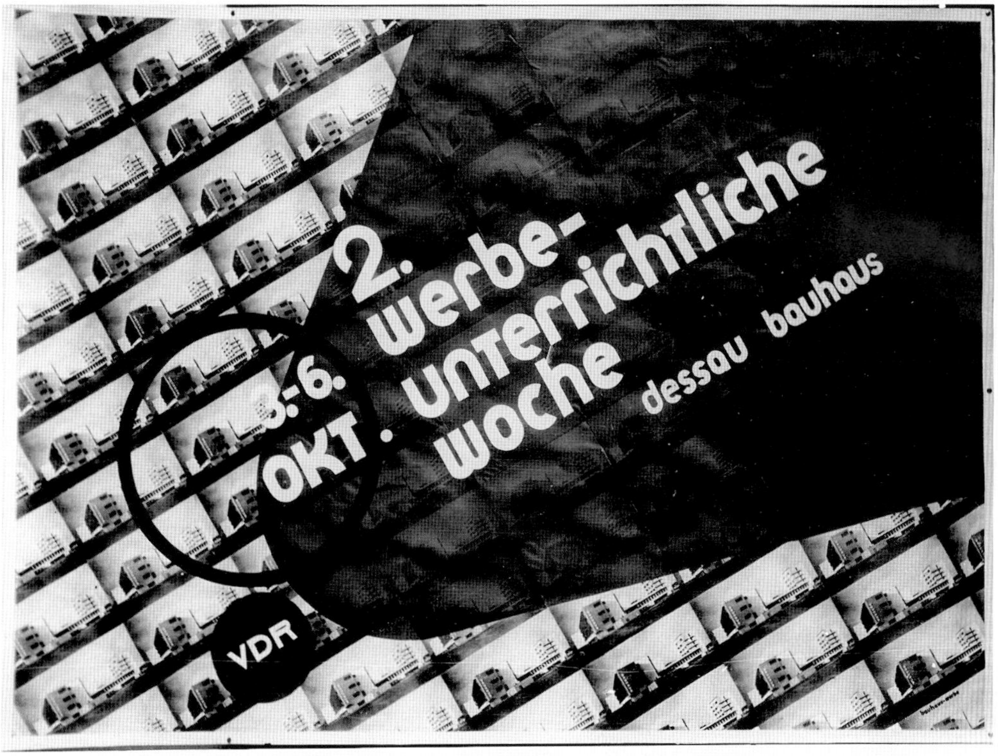

Figure 5.13. Advertising poster for the "second advertising instruction week" at the Bauhaus (original lost). Designer: Herbert Bayer. Harvard Art Museums/Busch-Reisinger Museum, Gift of Herbert Bayer, BR48.117. Photograph: Imaging Department, Harvard Art Museums; copyright President and Fellows of Harvard College.

with advertising for the Bauhaus's "second advertising instruction week" (Figure 5.13).[38] The original mock-up and all subsequent prints (if there were any) of this poster have been lost. The base photograph was taken by Klaus Hertig (identified from other Bauhaus publications). If Gropius gave the photographs too much voice, Bayer certainly did the opposite, reducing photography to graphic adjunct. His approach reflects a vibrant discourse on graphic design in Germany in which Bauhaus students and faculty had an active voice.

TEXT: *BAUHAUS(NEU)BAUTEN DESSAU*

Gropius's views on architectural photography unfolded simultaneously with the development of photography and the "New Vision" (Neues Sehen) of Moholy-Nagy, his right-hand man and colleague at the Bauhaus. Moholy-Nagy's exposition of "typophoto" laid out how text and image could work in dialogue, performing different functions and relaying different kinds of information. Moholy-Nagy did some of his most innovative work in texts, photographs, paintings, and sculpture at the

Bauhaus. The Bauhaus books that Moholy-Nagy designed, edited, and produced with the help of Moholy were also revolutionary. That his views on the liberative potential of photography within progressive art appear to have had limited effect on Gropius's views of architectural photography is striking. It suggests that Gropius, at least, understood this sort of photography to be limited to the sphere of reproduction, without the potential for productive work of its own. With this distinction in mind, we might take a closer look at Gropius's Bauhaus book, published two years after he had departed from Dessau in 1928.

Gropius's position changed radically in the two years that elapsed between his departure from the Bauhaus and the publication of Bauhaus book 12, *Bauhausbauten Dessau*. Having committed himself to the exploration of new building as an intellectual activity within an educational institution, Gropius left to transpose that work into commercial architectural practice. In this new phase, his previous work helped maintain his profile in German culture. He prepared the Bauhaus publication at this time. In his introduction, the architect carefully hedged his bets with respect to photography:

> the means of representation of buildings in a book are very restricted. photography does not allow the experience of space to be reproduced. the true scale relationships of a room or a building in relation to our firm, absolute body size create an exciting tension in the viewer that the reduced surface image simply cannot convey. finally, mass and space are the background for life itself, and they should serve it—the acts of movement that play out in them can be represented only in a translated form. I believed that the essence of these buildings, the ordering of their self-reflexive life functions, and the resulting spatial expression, could, for all these reasons, be conveyed to readers only if I provided numerous details, to convey through this change of sights the illusion of the conceived spatial sequence.[39]

Gropius emphasized the inherent inadequacies of photography for the accurate representation of space by projecting a provisional solution: a proliferation of photographs of a building might help compensate for the illusory nature of photographic communication of architecture. His words suggest that for photography—a medium incapable of conveying accurate spatial or scalar relationships—more of a faulty good would compensate for the medium's lack of fitness for its task. This scarcely appears logical, but Gropius's advocacy of the use of multiples was not unique. At the very least, the reproduction of many photographs would reveal the inadequacies of each one more fully.

Wilhelm Lotz proposed a similar solution to the problem of photographs of architecture (see chapter 4). In his article "Architekturfotos" in *Die Form* in 1929,

Lotz expressed a similar skepticism about the capacity of photography to represent architecture adequately. In the article, Lotz expanded upon the importance of different photographic genres. The problem for photography of architecture, Lotz noted, lay with the modern development of photography. The photographer was far too concerned with making "good and interesting pictures. The execution of an interesting exposure and a more interesting framing [Ausschnitt] is more important to him than a clear and objective representation of the object." Lotz blamed this on the "artistic pride of the photographer," seeking an interesting point of view and creating "a kind of spasmodic monumentalization of the object." "When this only concerns the production of a photograph," Lotz wrote, "it is quite different from when the photograph is to be the only medium of the impression of an object."[40] Lotz proposed that serial pictures might help solve the problem of accurate architectural representation.

Gropius's introduction to *Bauhausbauten Dessau* echoed Lotz's words in a different register. Both arguments hinged on divesting photography of visual authority, instead continually referring back to the absent architectural object by publishing multiple photographs of the same thing. More photographs of a building would reduce the value of any single one, thus transferring attention back to the building depicted; the building itself would be elusively revealed in photographs that "approached filmic representation."[41] Lotz recommended two ways of creating this filmic sequence: by approaching the building from one direction, in which the increasing size of the building is repeated from one exposure to the next; or by circling the building and taking sequential images, preferably indexed to solar orientation. Both used serial frames to depict dynamic movement through a simplified form of stop-action photographic animation, vaguely like the photography of Eadweard Muybridge or Étienne-Jules Marey. Bruno Taut's own house in Dahlewitz provided one of the demonstrations of this idea in Lotz's text (Figure 5.14); the best demonstration may be the large series of photographs of the Tugendhat House or Mendelsohn's book on his own domicile.

Gropius and Lotz shared ideas that were familiar to architecture specialists at the time. Any given picture presents partial information; the aggregation of many parts adds up to a single, if imperfect, whole. But Gropius's complaint is more substantive than this explanation suggests. His grudging acceptance of a syncopated filmic illusion of the experience of architecture sidesteps the essential problem that he articulated in the passage cited above: that architecture must be experienced in scale, that its effects depend on a bodily encounter between inhabitant and constructed space. Photographs of a building published in a book can never deliver adequate representations of such an experience, so that *Bauhausbauten Dessau* points to its own

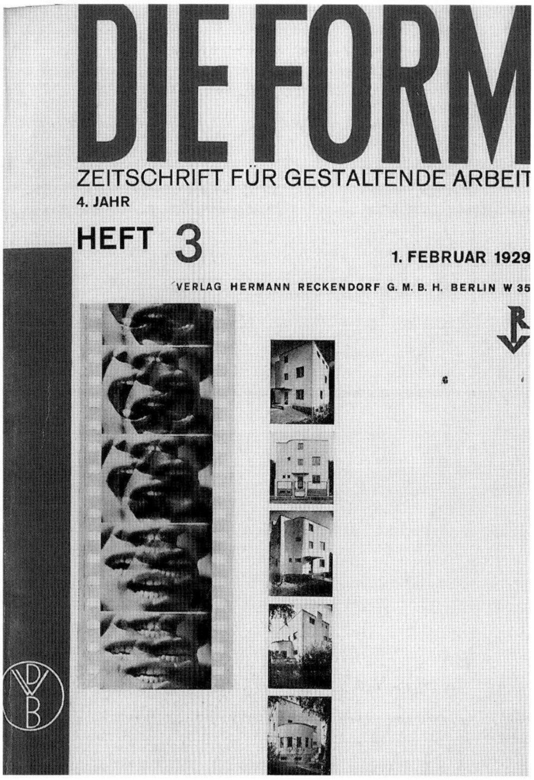

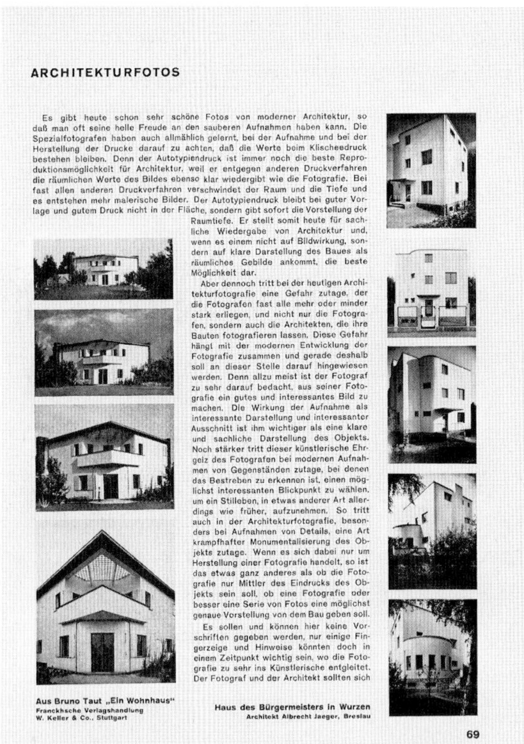

ARCHITEKTURFOTOS

Es gibt heute schon sehr schöne Fotos von moderner Architektur, so daß man oft seine helle Freude an den sauberen Aufnahmen haben kann. Die Spezialfotografen haben auch allmählich gelernt, bei der Aufnahme und bei der Herstellung der Drucke darauf zu achten, daß die Werte beim Klischeedruck bestehen bleiben. Denn der Autotypiendruck ist immer noch die beste Reproduktionsmöglichkeit für Architektur, weil er entgegen anderen Druckverfahren die räumlichen Werte des Bildes ebenso klar wiedergibt wie die Fotografie. Bei fast allen anderen Druckverfahren verschwindet der Raum und die Tiefe und es entstehen mehr malerische Bilder. Der Autotypiendruck bleibt bei guter Vorlage und gutem Druck nicht in der Fläche, sondern gibt sofort die Vorstellung der Raumtiefe. Er stellt somit heute für sachliche Wiedergabe von Architektur und, wenn es einem nicht auf Bildwirkung, sondern auf klare Darstellung des Baues als räumliches Gebilde ankommt, die beste Möglichkeit dar.

Aber dennoch tritt bei der heutigen Architekturfotografie eine Gefahr zutage, der die Fotografen fast alle mehr oder minder stark erliegen, und nicht nur die Fotografen, sondern auch die Architekten, die ihre Bauten fotografieren lassen. Diese Gefahr hängt mit der modernen Entwicklung der Fotografie zusammen und gerade deshalb soll an dieser Stelle darauf hingewiesen werden. Denn allzu meist ist der Fotograf zu sehr darauf bedacht, aus seiner Fotografie ein gutes und interessantes Bild zu machen. Die Wirkung der Aufnahme als interessante Darstellung und interessanter Ausschnitt ist ihm wichtiger als eine klare und sachliche Darstellung des Objekts. Noch stärker tritt dieser künstlerische Ehrgeiz des Fotografen bei modernen Aufnahmen von Gegenständen zutage, bei denen das Bestreben zu erkennen ist, einen möglichst interessanten Blickpunkt zu wählen, um ein Stilleben, in etwas anderer Art allerdings wie früher, aufzunehmen. So tritt auch in der Architekturfotografie, besonders bei Aufnahmen von Details, eine Art krampfhafter Monumentalisierung des Objekts zutage. Wenn es sich dabei nur um Herstellung einer Fotografie handelt, so ist das etwas ganz anderes als ob die Fotografie nur Mittler des Eindrucks des Objekts sein soll, ob eine Fotografie oder besser eine Serie von Fotos eine möglichst genaue Vorstellung von dem Bau geben soll.

Es sollen und können hier keine Vorschriften gegeben werden, nur einige Fingerzeige und Hinweise könnten doch in einem Zeitpunkt wichtig sein, wo die Fotografie zu sehr ins Künstlerische entgleitet. Der Fotograf und der Architekt sollten sich

Aus Bruno Taut „Ein Wohnhaus"
Franckhsche Verlagshandlung
W. Keller & Co., Stuttgart

Haus des Bürgermeisters in Wurzen
Architekt Albrecht Jaeger, Breslau

69

Figure 5.14. Bruno Taut's house in Dahlewitz, as illustrated in Wilhelm Lotz, "Architekturfotos," *Die Form* 4, no. 3 (1 February 1929): cover, 69.

inherent limitations as a way of adding value to its subject by rendering it ineffable, ungraspable in the available formats of mass communication. This removal of the possibility of full communication suggests that architecture could retain its status as authentic experience despite the incursions of media into its representational arena—a theme that recurs again and again in twentieth-century accounts. Moholy, Moholy-Nagy, and Bayer invested their efforts at the Bauhaus in discovering what new media had to offer the world of solid objects. Gropius's calculations, by contrast, were those of the consummate working professional who protected the market value of the good he produced by enhancing its nonmaterial value as cultural representation to the best of his ability.

Despite the declared inadequacies of photography, however, *Bauhausbauten Dessau* is more than anything else a picture book. It includes numerous photographic illustrations of the Dessau buildings and a much smaller selection of drawings, accompanied by Gropius's short introduction. In adopting this format, Gropius adopted a new norm in architectural publishing: Taut's and Mendelsohn's monographic photographic publications of their own houses in 1927 and 1932, respectively, provide comparanda for in-depth monographic publications of single buildings.[42] In addition, Gropius himself had published an earlier architectural picture book in his *Internationale Architektur* (1925), volume 1 of the Bauhaus books, even though the book was broadly focused on many buildings, not on one single building.[43]

In spite of these precedents, *Bauhausbauten Dessau* presents the reader at the outset with a contradiction that is difficult to resolve: photographs are inadequate to the representation of spatial products like buildings; nevertheless, the book uses photography overwhelmingly to illustrate architecture. But Gropius's specific disclaimer and the influential photographs contained in *Bauhausbauten Dessau* suggest that there was more at stake than the proclamations of photographic inadequacy suggest. The publishing program of the Bauhaus was filled with alternative formats for presenting information about spatial objects—other experiments of graphic designers at the institution in addition to those mentioned above are well-known. *Bauhausbauten Dessau*, by contrast, was among the most conventional in its layout. It contained none of the text–image combinations that were found in Moholy-Nagy's typophoto experiments, in Bayer's bold graphic design, or even in Moholy's more muted parallel presentation of text and image in adjacent textual-graphic layouts in the *bauhaus* magazine.

Gropius's foreword to his earlier book of 1925 clarifies his thoughts about photography of architecture yet further: "*Internationale Architektur* is a picture book of modern building art. It offers an overview of the creative activity of the leading modern architects of cultivated lands [Kulturländer] in a compressed form and makes contemporary architectonic creative development apparent." A footnote is appended to this statement, which reads: "To serve a wider lay public, the editor restricted himself in essence to illustrations of external building appearance. Typical plans and interiors will follow in a later volume."[44] Later on the same page, Gropius explained the period that preceded his own: "In the past, the art of building sank into a sentimental, aesthetically decorative conception that saw its goal as the use of motifs, ornament, and profiles from obsolete cultures to cover the exterior of buildings, without necessarily any relationship to the interior. The building was thus debased, becoming the carrier of external, dead ornamental form, instead of being a living organism." Gropius proceeded to link the living organicism of the building to progressive technology, new building materials, and new construction processes.[45] This book confronts us with another contradiction, equally as striking as the one that appeared in *Bauhausbauten Dessau*. If the external appearance of a building ideally proceeds from the building's internal genesis, how do photographs of building exteriors offer a way to understand this relationship? In this survey of international architecture, interiors and exteriors were specifically delaminated from one another, so that meaningful connections between them could no longer be made. Here, as in the introduction to *Bauhausbauten*, Gropius offered something with one hand only to take it away with the other. The reader must accept on faith the central claim for modern building made by the author.

What Gropius meant by reference to the inner truth versus the outer core of architecture is revealed in the essay he wrote for the Bauhaus exhibition of 1923. In his introduction to the catalog of this rich display of new artistic products, *Idee und Aufbau des Staatlichen Bauhauses* (Concept and realization of the state Bauhaus), Gropius noted the manner in which external appearance results from inner knowledge, how an exchange or a balance between internal metaphysical knowledge and external expression is achieved through the work of the hand. He described a "new world unity" that replaced the old, dualistic world picture (Weltbild):

> This new dawning knowledge of the unity of all things and appearances brings to all human creative work a common sense, based deep in ourselves. Nothing exists in itself, every entity becomes the analogy of a thought that pushes out of us into form, every work becomes the manifestation of our inner essence. Only such works retain a spiritual sense; mechanized work is lifeless and a task of dead machines. As long as machines are the end goal of the economy, however, instead of its means to free mental capacities from the burden of mechanical work, the individual remains unfree and the society cannot order itself. The solution depends on an altered inner approach of the individual to his work, not on the improvement of outer living conditions. The will to adjust to the new spirit is therefore of decisive meaning for new constructive work.[46]

Gropius's emphasis here on external appearance as the physical manifestation of internal force may recall earlier architectural writing about form by Karl Bötticher, whose articulation of a relationship between *core form* and *art form* in the middle of the nineteenth century was based on the premise that exterior form would translate and transform pure structural form into representation. But the twentieth century saw a new set of discourses on dynamic form arise that also may have influenced Gropius at this time. Biocentric discourse and philosophies of becoming from Nietzsche to Bergson entered art and architecture through the work of Alois Riegl, Wilhelm Worringer, and Aby Warburg.[47] Far more proximate to Gropius, however, were Moholy-Nagy on one hand and the Bauhaus painters on the other. Both were interested in the dynamic energy of form.[48]

Gropius articulated a similar notion in relation to modern architecture, and yet his writing appears embedded in neo-Platonic or neo-Kantian discourse. It may be that Bötticher is indeed the more salient source. In Gropius's statement, the outer shell of the building, the *Scheinform*, runs the risk of being the dead resultant of mechanical processes, a risk that Gropius seemed to see in photography as well. To understand outward appearance as an implicit index to internal organization was a core idea of modern architecture. Photographic negatives similarly captured the external appearance of things, with the implicit assumption that the sheer facticity of the process represented an absolute value. The surface of the photographic image here parallels the externality of three-dimensional form. But for Gropius, the photograph was only ever the product of a machine. Thus even if architecture might achieve the vitalism indicated in Gropius's soft monism ("the unity of all things and appearances"), the photograph would surely conceal that fact in its mechanistic shadow.

Gropius's resistance to the photographic image suggests that the three-dimensional representational image of building was hidden behind a veil of photographic appearance, not a truth manifestation. Photographs captured the two-dimensional image of an external form that was itself the concretion of something else—a three-dimensional image of internal forces or organic essence. In architectural photographs, building as representation was thus nested within photographic representation. This nesting obscured the parallelism of the two. To see outward manifestation (whether photograph or building) as representation was occluded by the frequent practice of making images of images—photographs of architectural representations. It is this nesting—the enclosure of one medium by another—that neutralized one practice (architecture) and made the other (photography) highly suspect. In his books, Gropius implicitly suggested that the representational identity of buildings *as images* was somehow canceled out by buildings' being rendered in two dimensions as *photographic images*. This is a paradoxical turn, in which the medium of truthful representation par excellence—photography—is recast as a deceptive, incredible process.

To recapitulate this argument: photographs of buildings cannot represent the spatial experience, or "essence," of architecture, which springs from the crystallization of internal ideas in external form, realized in an organic way through drawing and construction. Moreover, because of the spatial basis of architectural experience, as articulated throughout Gropius's early writings, a two-dimensional photograph captures only an image of an image—the external shell of a building whose essence lies in its organic internal spatiality. In the serial presentation of photographs, a compensatory illusion can be communicated two-dimensionally by a larger number of single views. This would appear to be an illogical proposition—more of a poor product is surely not better than less of it. But Gropius, like Lotz, may have felt that single views were like pennies; no amount of them would ever turn into the paper of a bank note, but enough of them would begin to approximate a similar value. In presenting new architecture to a lay public with these photographs, a picture book or an exhibition provided the logical format.

Alternately, when the presentation of new architecture was broadly organized around a group rather than around a single building, as in *Internationale Architektur*, it contained only a single external view of any given building. According to the logic suggested by Gropius and others, such external views were illusory and inadequate because they gave no clear indication of whether, or how, external appearance grew out of inner necessity. Such a presentation of material established a comparative framework for architecture: a kind of comparative sample set or cross section of new building approaches. Regardless of the shortcomings of architectural photographs, this comparative format of exterior views of buildings nevertheless constituted the most efficient means of spreading architectural ideas; it was thought to attract even the "hurried reader" to borrow Sigfried Giedion's phrase from 1928.[49] The instrument of comparison was photography, buttressed by captions and commentary.[50]

Gropius's idea of architectural essence, summarized in the 1923 *Staatlichen Bauhauses* catalog, reinforced the importance of the human hand in the facture of works of art, whether by an architect at a drawing board or a craftsman on a building site. Photography was barred from this notion of art making by its manner of production. Robin Kelsey's recent observation that nineteenth-century photographer William Henry Fox Talbot already understood how photography had to substitute the eye for the hand as the primary locus of art production leads us to ask whether Gropius was fighting a rearguard battle within the Bauhaus.[51] His posture on this matter is notable. With Moholy-Nagy at his side asserting the importance of photography for modern art, and Moholy and Bayer at his back producing invaluable publicity materials for architecture and the institution, Gropius nevertheless resisted the incursions of photographic technology into art or architecture making. If the eye was fundamental to contemporary architectural design, it was not, in his view, linked to "dead machines" such as the camera, but still worked in coordination with the artist's hand. "Art and Technology: A New Unity" was the slogan adopted at the Bauhaus from 1923. It appears, however, that this might have been a case of drawing one's enemy close—given Gropius's ostensible refusal and yet headlong embrace of photography as a communicative device used for relaying ideas about buildings to audiences in contemporary markets.[52]

Between the earliest appearance of Moholy's photographs of the Dessau Bauhaus in late 1926 in *bauhaus* 1 and the publication of *Bauhausbauten Dessau* in 1930, Gropius had left the school. He began constructing a historical account of the institution in which photographs played a crucial role, retroactively updating the account of his Bauhaus directorship in *Bauhausbauten Dessau* to answer criticisms of it made after 1928 by his successor, before Meyer's own 1930 departure from the institution. Meyer condemned Gropius's Bauhaus program for lack of rigor in relation to production and social ideals. Thus the account in *Bauhausbauten Dessau*, chronologically so close to the origin of the institution and its Dessau home, was nevertheless far enough from its beginnings to allow for distortions that plagued Bauhaus studies subsequently.[53] After 1928, Gropius struggled in the competitive world of Berlin architecture. Difficulties with projects for mass housing that began at this time increased the pressure on *Bauhausbauten Dessau* to maintain his centrality in German architectural debate in the volatile years after 1929. During 1928 and 1929 Gropius designed projects for three large housing settlements at Karlsruhe-Dammerstock, Berlin-Spandau-Haselhorst, and Berlin-Siemensstadt; he also collaborated with architects G. Stefan Fischer and Friedrich Paulsen on a fourth, a housing settlement to be located on a site located between Berlin and Potsdam. Of these, the Dammerstock Siedlung was partly built and was immediately criticized for its mechanistic approach to residential housing. In the words of critic Adolf Behne, this was evidence of "a spreading formalism under the label of science."[54] Although Gropius placed first in the Haselhorst competition, he ultimately received no commission. He built housing at Siemensstadt, but the fourth unbuilt project with Fischer and Paulsen, the so-called Gropius Stadt, was a public relations disaster as well as a failed building scheme. Gropius pulled out of the project in August 1929, two months before "Black Friday," acknowledging a flawed financial plan. Investors (prospective residents) lost their money in October when the stock market crashed, and Gropius was criticized for having lent his name and influence to the plan.[55] Sigfried Giedion later blamed the failure of these disastrous schemes for large housing construction on "a strong psychological opposition" on the part of German clients. Be that as it may, the problems besetting Gropius's architectural practice provide a context for understanding the importance of *Bauhausbauten Dessau* for his reputation and future.[56] The 1930 publication presented the building—rather than the institution it contained—as part of Gropius's own unfolding present.

The struggle for his professional practice in Berlin thus stands silently behind the presentation of this important building to the public in his 1930 book. The book was already historical and revisionist in its presentation, as Droste has pointed out. In this light, *Bauhausbauten Dessau* appears to lay claim to every development that ever took place at the Bauhaus in all of its sites, including Weimar, Dessau, the Bauhaus books, and the popular press, with the exception of one: thanks to the book's opening disclaimer, the only site that is not acknowledged is the fertile and productive site of architectural photography, one of the most interesting sites of Bauhaus production.

I refer to what could be termed the shop-window quality of things, a characteristic which the exhibition accentuates. . . . [T]he interest of the buyer has to be aroused by the external stimulus of the object, even the manner of its presentation. . . . The exhibition with its emphasis on amusement attempts a new synthesis between the principles of external stimulus and the practical functions of objects, and thereby takes the superadditum to its highest level. The banal attempt to put things in their best light, as in the cries of the street trader, is transformed into the interesting attempt to confer a new aesthetic significance from displaying objects together—something already happening in the relationship between advertising and poster art.

—GEORG SIMMEL,
"THE BERLIN TRADE EXHIBITION"

6. THE FUTURE IN THE PRESENT

ERSCHEINUNGSFORM AND "THE DWELLING," 1927

In May 1926 Ludwig Mies van der Rohe wrote a letter to the Werkbund journal *Die Form,* defending the recent exhibition of American architecture at the Akademie der Künste in Berlin. The editor of *Die Form,* Walter Curt Behrendt, published the letter near a rendering by Hugh Ferriss, one indicator of the wave of *Amerikanismus* (Americanism) sweeping Berlin at the time. No review of the exhibition appeared in the journal, but Behrendt had noted in February 1926, "Instead of a report about the exhibition *New American Architecture* that took place recently at the Academy of Art in Berlin, we present the essay by our New York collaborator, who can better inform us of the conceptions that presently govern American architecture than any exhibition could."[1] "Amerikanische Baukunst" was one of three chapters excerpted in *Die Form* 1 from Mumford's 1924 *Sticks and Stones,* a book that appeared in German as *Vom Blockhaus zum Wolkenkratzer* in 1925 (Figure 6.1).[2] Behrendt used the word *Architektur* in his reference to the Akademie exhibition; the title was actually "Neuer amerikanischer Baukunst." The term *Baukunst* (building art), unlike *Architektur,* was not burdened with centuries of antiquarian historical baggage but more recently endowed with notions of authenticity and *Sachlichkeit.* That Behrendt mistakenly used the more conventional term is striking, particularly in light of the clear distinction that progressive German architects had made between *Baukunst* and *Architektur* since the early 1920s.[3]

In *Die Form* in 1926, Mies countered criticism of the exhibition, addressing the editor directly. Preserving the erroneous title (whether intentionally or not), Mies noted:

> The exhibition "New American Architecture" constituted a compelling illustration of the views asserted by Mumford. But this speaks *for* the exhibition. One has also heard, especially in the Berlin press, the accusation that this exhibition was not put together following a definite plan, and that not all the top achievements of American building art are represented there. I must characterize it an advantage of this exhibition, that it carries through no particular and narrowly defined program, but rather leaves the visitor the opportunity to form his own opinion about American building art.[4]

Like many Germans, Mies had not visited North America, and he preferred the broad presentation offered in photographs, texts, and drawings to the travel accounts of his colleagues.[5] He noted:

> As interesting as it is to see how you yourself, how Mendelsohn, Paulsen, or Rading assess America, it seems to me equally necessary and desirable that everyone is able to form an image of the contemporary state of American building art for himself, and in this I saw the sense and worth of the Berlin exhibition.[6]

Mies was interested in the efficient delivery of new information in a lightly curated format. The broad array of exhibition material was valuable because of its volume and the lack of curatorial intervention (Figures 6.2a, 6.2b, 6.3a, and 6.3b). Mies had already benefited professionally from buildings that he saw in architectural publications; projects like his Kröller-Müller Villa (1912–13), Eliat House (1925), and Wolf House (1925–27) show Frank Lloyd Wright's influence, as does Mies's effort to

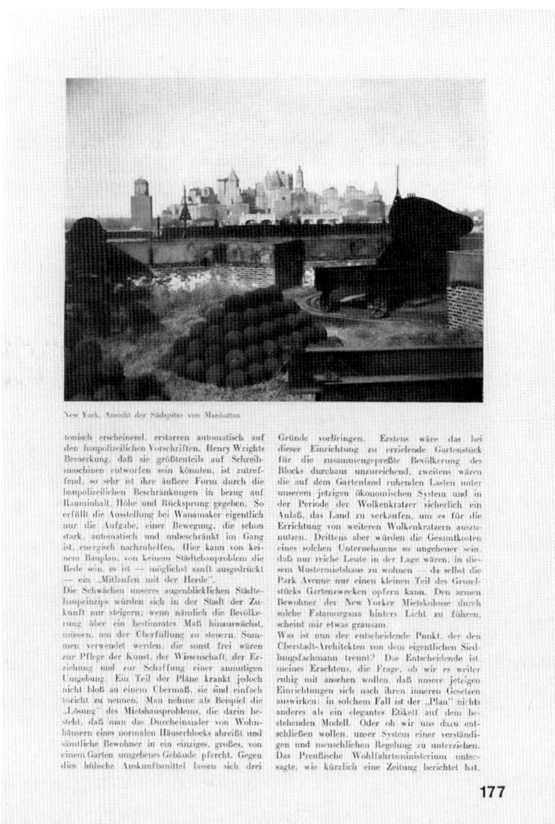

New York, Ansicht der Südspitze von Manhattan

tonisch erscheinend, erstarren automatisch auf den baupolizeilichen Vorschriften. Henry Wrights Bemerkung, daß sie größtenteils auf Schreibmaschinen entworfen sein könnten, ist zutreffend, so sehr ist ihre äußere Form durch die baupolizeilichen Beschränkungen in bezug auf Rauminhalt, Höhe und Rücksprung gegeben. So erfüllt die Ausstellung bei Wanamaker eigentlich nur die Aufgabe, einer Bewegung, die schon stark, automatisch und unbeschränkt im Gang ist, energisch nachzuhelfen. Hier kann von keinem Bauplan, von keinem Städtebauproblem die Rede sein, es ist — möglichst sanft ausgedrückt — ein „Mitlaufen mit der Herde".

Die Schwächen unseres augenblicklichen Städtebauprinzips würden sich in der Stadt der Zukunft nur steigern; wenn nämlich die Bevölkerung über ein bestimmtes Maß hinauswächst, müssen, um der Überfüllung zu steuern, Summen verwendet werden, die sonst frei wären zur Pflege der Kunst, der Wissenschaft, der Erziehung und zur Schaffung einer anmutigen Umgebung. Ein Teil der Pläne krankt jedoch nicht bloß an einem Übermaß, sie sind einfach töricht zu nennen. Man nehme als Beispiel die „Lösung" des Mietshausproblems, die darin besteht, daß man das Durcheinander von Wohnhäusern eines normalen Häuserblocks abreißt und sämtliche Bewohner in ein einziges, großes, von einem Garten umgebenes Gebäude pfercht. Gegen dies hübsche Auskunftsmittel lassen sich drei Gründe vorbringen. Erstens wäre das bei dieser Einrichtung zu erzielende Gartenstück für die zusammengepreßte Bevölkerung des Blocks durchaus unzureichend, zweitens wären die auf dem Gartenland ruhenden Lasten unter unserem jetzigen ökonomischen System und in der Periode der Wolkenkratzer sicherlich ein Anlaß, das Land zu verkaufen, um es für die Errichtung von weiteren Wolkenkratzern auszunutzen. Drittens aber würden die Gesamtkosten eines solchen Unternehmens so ungeheuer sein, daß nur reiche Leute in der Lage wären, in diesem Mustermietshaus zu wohnen — da selbst die Park Avenue nur einen kleinen Teil des Grundstücks Gartenzwecken opfern kann. Den armen Bewohner der New Yorker Mietskolosse durch solche Fatamorgana hinters Licht zu führen, scheint mir etwas grausam.

Was ist nun der entscheidende Punkt, der den Überstadt-Architekten von dem eigentlichen Siedlungsfachmann trennt? Das Entscheidende ist, meines Erachtens, die Frage, ob wir es weiter ruhig mit ansehen wollen, daß unsere jetzigen Einrichtungen sich nach ihren inneren Gesetzen auswirken: in solchem Fall ist der „Plan" nichts anderes als ein elegantes Etikett auf dem bestehenden Modell. Oder ob wir uns dazu entschließen wollen, unser System einer verständigen und menschlichen Regelung zu unterziehen. Das Preußische Wohlfahrtsministerium untersagte, wie kürzlich eine Zeitung berichtet hat,

177

Figure 6.1. *Die Form* 1, no. 8 (May 1926): 177.

a

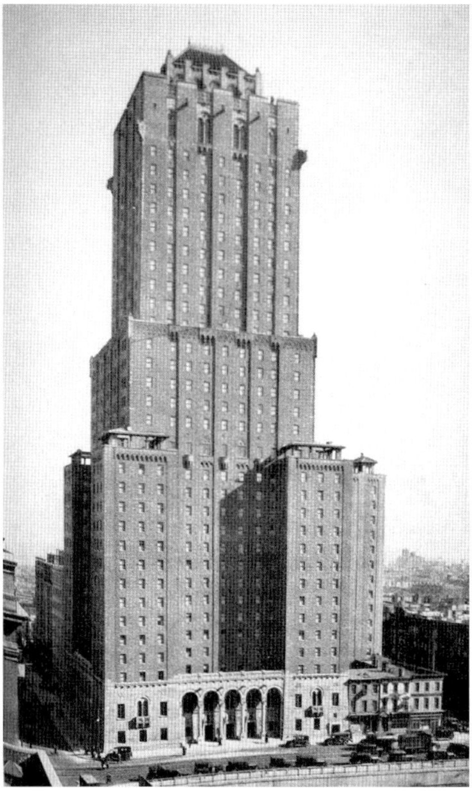

b

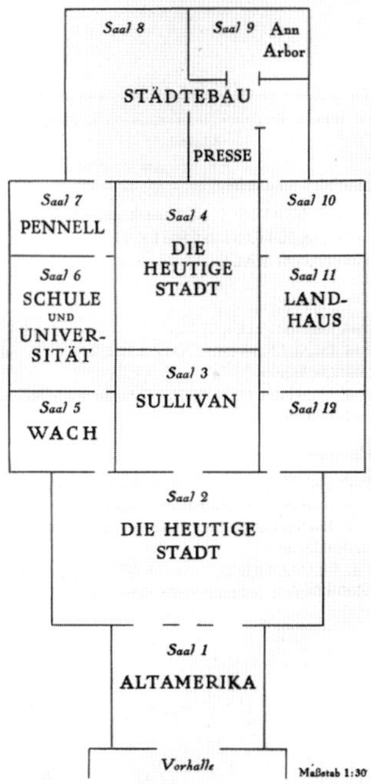

Figure 6.2. From *Ausstellung neuer amerikanischer Baukunst* (Berlin: Akademie der Künste, 1926): (a) The Shelton Hotel, New York; (b) plan of the exhibition.

keep Wright in the public eye in 1923.[7] His positive view of American architecture also favored the anticlassical, nativist approaches of Sullivan and H. H. Richardson,[8] both easy to associate with Chicago and the American heartland rather than the dystopic representations of New York circulating in the German press.[9] Mies's letter suggested that the eclecticism of the Akademie exhibition was precisely its strength, evoking a field of neutral objects from among which Berlin architects might choose their particular weapons. It provided a potential stockpile for German architecture culture.

Among the organizers, Edmund Schüler collected exhibition materials carried out during "repeated sojourns in the United States, with the support of the most important architects and institutes."[10] Irving Pond was active in Chicago-based preparations for the exhibition; Emil Lorch, of the "Ann Arbor-Universität," supplied a collection of student work. Hugo Wach was responsible for the installation in the Akademie galleries. The show did indeed have a curatorial voice; it was simply not the voice of Weimar modernists.

The exhibition was organized into categories—"the contemporary city," "the suburban house," and "city planning"—and three rooms dedicated to two-dimensional representation of architecture. Drawings by Hugh Ferriss and Joseph Pennell and a room of publications on American architecture joined Wach's aquarelles and drawings of a recent trip to the United States. One of the latter nearly matches a photograph in Erich Mendelsohn's *Amerika: Bilderbuch eines Architekten,* also of 1926 (Figures 6.3a, 6.3b). The central gallery (Saal 3) was entirely dedicated to Louis Sullivan, who had died in 1924; while no installation shot survives, the exhibition probably duplicated material from his 1920 exhibition in Chicago (Figure 6.4). Sullivan was singled out in the introduction to the catalog, where his 1906 essay "What Is Architecture?" was extracted in translation. An essay by Pond and one by Thomas Tallmadge further emphasized Chicago architecture.

In the introduction, this regional school of American architecture was character-

Figure 6.3. (a) *Thirty-ninth Street and Sixth Avenue, New York.* Renderer: Hugo Wach. From *Ausstellung neuer amerikanischer Baukunst.* (b) Plate from Erich Mendelsohn, *Amerika: Bilderbuch eines Architekten* (Berlin: Rudolf Mosse, 1926).

a

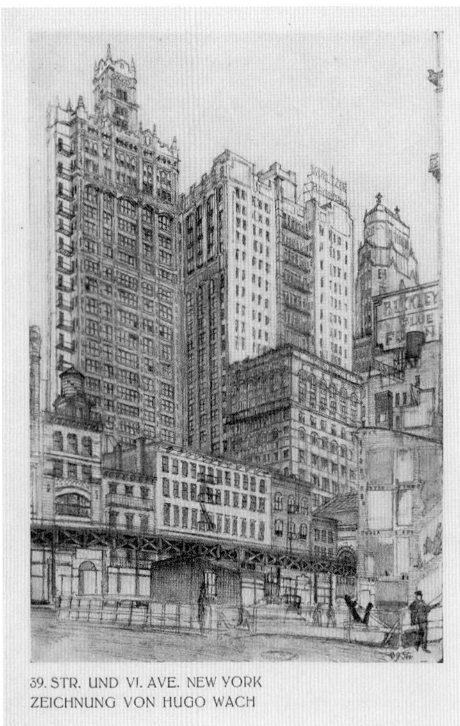

b

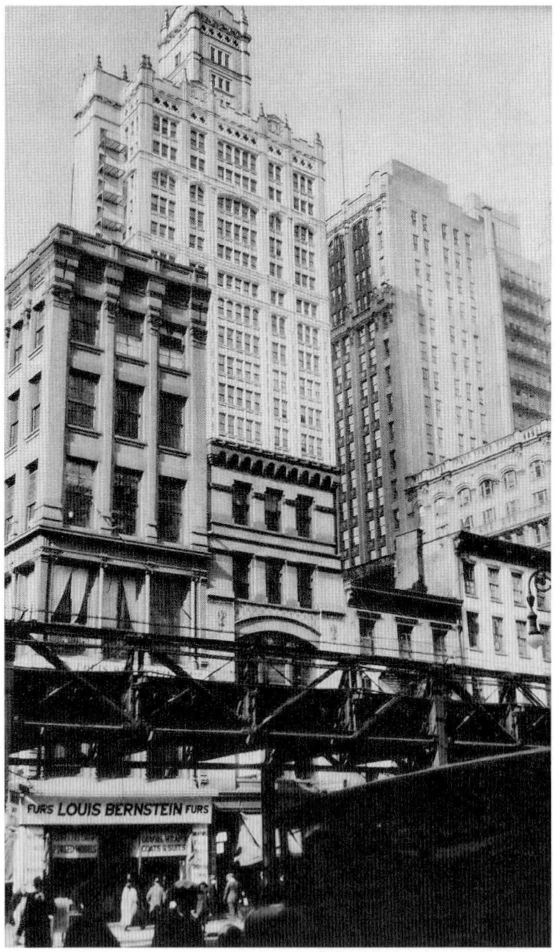

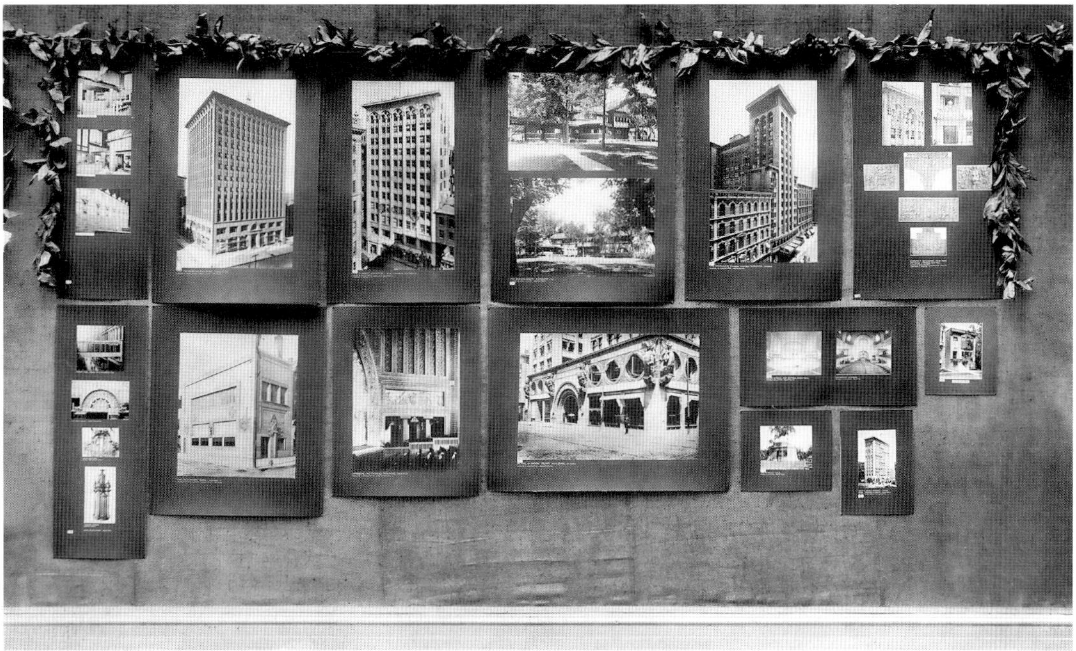

Figure 6.4. Louis Sullivan Exhibition, Chicago, 1920. Sullivaniana Collection, Ryerson and Burnham Archives, The Art Institute of Chicago. Courtesy of The Art Institute of Chicago.

ized as "authentic" modern architecture, and Sullivan was key to its development: "Hardly was the first ironwork used in building construction when he undertook to invent an intrinsic artistic form for it in his office buildings."[11] This theme, later picked up by Hitchcock, Pevsner, Giedion, and others, appealed to German architects; Sullivan is described as both hero and victim of American culture, a John the Baptist (presumably to Wright's Messiah) announcing the creed of modernism to a deaf public. "As he . . . raised his voice against weak imitation, as he began to proclaim the Evangelism of a deeply indigenous art for a time with serious goals, he found more enemies than believers. But the Prophet, who in the desert of old Chigacos *[sic]* could see the coming dawn of a new art, can serve us today as guide to the understanding of modern American building problems."[12] Sullivan's influence on German architecture was present much earlier, as Dietrich Neumann has pointed out; it extends back to 1911, when H. P. Berlage lectured and published on Sullivan and Wright.[13]

There is little other information about Mies's visit to the Akademie show. The material of the exhibition had evidently hit a nerve—Mies was not in the habit of spontaneous acts of publication, and indeed he owed at least one manuscript for publication at that very moment.[14] His interest in a show rich in drawings of architecture is hardly surprising, given his own interest in representation during these years. Sullivan's republished essay noted: "Architecture has three elementary concepts: the column, the architrave, and the dome. These are three types from which the language of building art has developed."[15] This may have resonated with Mies's own elementarist understanding of architecture; his embrace of the separation of structure and enclosure marks the beginning of a systematic grammar of architecture that he strove to develop into a poetic form and a technique.[16] Photographs of the Wainwright Building, the Guaranty Building, the Transportation Building from the 1893 Chicago exhibition, a number of the small bank buildings in the Midwest, the tombs, and several unbuilt projects were included in this remarkably extensive display.[17] This exhibition, relatively unknown today, provides a starting point from which to discuss the framework of architectural exhibitions and the compendious photographs that went with them. It makes a remarkable contrast to the architectural exhibitions sponsored by the Bauhaus and the German Werkbund in the same years.

In the history of exhibition architecture in Germany between 1907 and 1935, the Werkbund played an influential role as the sponsor of multiple exhibitions, of which "The Dwelling" in Stuttgart in 1927 was the most prominent.[18] Werkbund exhibitions focused on a variety of different media and themes; this chapter focuses primarily on the role of photography in German exhibitions at this time, using "The Dwelling" as an exemplary case study. The difference between exhibitions hosted in galleries and those that consisted of full-scale buildings on sites creates a division within exhibition architecture that structures the following discussion. Photographs played different roles in the two cases: in the first kind of exhibition, they provided content, as in the example described above; in the second type, photographs of constructed buildings were used to broadcast the results of the exhibition in published accounts. At the Stuttgart exhibition, the two worked in tandem, thanks to the fact that "The Dwelling" included full-scale constructions, a construction materials exhibition, and a gallery exhibition of international architecture.

Within the architectural exhibitions that became common in the early twentieth century, architectural photographs connected buildings to other buildings. With associated catalogs and other publications, architecture exhibitions were among the most efficient tools with which architects and critics could spread the compelling notion of a "movement" or a "campaign" for modernism. This was precisely what the 1926 exhibition in Berlin had failed to do, in Behrendt's eyes. While these exhibitions brought buildings into a comparative framework with one another through photography, the purpose and character of this framework varied. Whether in catalogs, journals, or books, or on the walls of a gallery, however, photographs of architecture were "photo texts," in which meanings were established using a different set of rules from those that pertained in scripted texts or that applied to buildings on sites.

Full-scale building exhibitions, by contrast, involved substantial commissions for architects and often allowed them a degree of freedom precluded in private or government commissions for permanent single buildings. Full-scale exhibitions might be combined with new housing initiatives sponsored by cities or regional governments. They provided laboratories within which architects tested new ideas and experimented with innovative construction methods. They were often funded by sources that were outside the conventional fiduciary exchanges between architects and clients, so that the nature of the commission and the architect's responsibility differed. These opportunities were frequently liberating to architects, providing an ad hoc form of research and development, formalized through the activities of the Werkbund. In 1927, for example, the National Research Society for Efficiency in Construction and Housing (Reichsforschungsgesellschaft für Wirtschaftlichkeit im Bau- und Wohnungswesen), a research entity linked to the state, operated in conjunction with the most important Werkbund housing exhibition to date, and a component of "The Dwelling": the Stuttgart Weissenhofsiedlung.[19]

GALLERY EXHIBITIONS OF ARCHITECTURE, 1926–27

Gallery exhibitions and associated publications featuring widely distributed architecture and planning projects grew more numerous in Germany in the wake of events like the 1910 Berlin planning competition, in which city plans from around the world were displayed and published within a comparative framework.[20] The industrialist Karl Ernst Osthaus sponsored a photographic exhibition of international architecture in 1911 from his German Museum for Art in Trade and Advertising (Deutsches Museum für Kunst in Handel und Gewerbe), an extensive collection of architectural photographs.[21] Walter Gropius worked on this exhibition and subsequently organized others, including the international architecture exhibition of photographs, drawings, and models at the Bauhaus exhibition of 1923.[22] The first Bauhaus book, *Internationale Architektur* (1925/1927) served as a catalog of this exhibition. In the same year, an exhibition sponsored by the professional organization of German architects (Bund Deutscher Architekten, or BDA) traveled to New York to display the work of the most established architects in Germany.[23] Similarly, the 1926 Berlin exhibition of American architecture also toured Germany the next year, opening in Hamburg and other German cities, with the same title: "Ausstellung neuer amerikanischer Baukunst."

Also in 1927, the "International Plan and Model Exhibition of New Building Art" (Internationale Plan- und Modellausstellung neuer Baukunst) opened as one component of "The Dwelling." Although the scene had changed, there were similarities to the 1923 Bauhaus show that had resulted in *Internationale Architektur.* Ludwig Hilberseimer edited the 1927 Stuttgart exhibition catalog, titled *Internationale neue Baukunst.* While architecture exhibitions were frequent in these years, a comparison of the contents of the American architecture exhibition of 1926 and of the two German exhibitions of 1923 and 1927 illustrates a range of conceptual themes that gallery exhibitions addressed and helps pinpoint photography's relationship to the development of architecture culture, whether nationalist or internationalist in focus.

The "Exhibition of New American Building Art" focused on commissions planned or executed for clients and consisted of an array of technical drawings, renderings, and photographs. It claimed to provide a cross section of American building activity by practice-oriented architects intended to promote American architecture abroad. Eclectic in building type, geography, and medium, the show had no formal theme; rather, it promoted American architecture as both an indigenous achievement and a potential export product. Defining its subject in relation to myths of native origin and autochthonous creation, the Akademie der Künste show did not promote an artistic movement unified by an aesthetic code. Seeking to raise the profile of American architects in Europe, Tallmadge and Pond also sought international recognition for work defined by national origin. From the German side, interest in the exhibition grew out of curiosity about new American building techniques at a time when earlier manifestations of *Amerikanismus* recurred following the introduction of the post–World War I Dawes Plan of 1924. The curatorial motivations behind the show were both practical and symbolic; Sullivan's organic functionalism appears to have struck a chord with young German architects like Mies, and other works in the show were enough to draw the close attention of an editor like Behrendt.[24]

All three exhibitions resulted in published catalogs, but in the case of the Bauhaus and Stuttgart shows, these publications were also books with lasting impacts on subsequent histories of modern architecture. As noted, the 1923 Bauhaus "Exhibition of International Architects" (Ausstellung internationaler Architekten) was the basis for *International Architecture (Internationale Architektur)* of 1925 (Bauhaus book 1). The book illustrated European and American buildings in models, photographs, and drawings. Nearly half of the projects were from German-speaking lands or by German architects; the rest were from France or Holland, with a small number of Eastern European projects, one Italian, one (unbuilt) Danish, one Belgian, and six American. The term *international* in the title of both exhibition and book was almost purely Eurocentric; the claim to anything broader rests on the handful of North American buildings that were included and on one photograph of a South American grain silo in the second edition of 1927—not insignificantly, a piece of industrial vernacular building (Figure 6.5).[25]

Both the 1923 Weimar Bauhaus exhibition and the Stuttgart Werkbund exhibition that followed in 1927 brought images of new architecture and engineering to German audiences. They were, however, framed at different moments in ongoing debate about the direction of German architecture. The activist internationalism of Bauhaus constructivism in 1923 gave way to a coalition of Werkbund officials and Neues Bauen architects in 1927. Both embraced international modernism, if in different registers. The Bauhaus in 1923 was an experimental site; the Stuttgart exhibition was also experimental but in a different way, making a claim on the formation of German architecture culture. Both coexisted with and confronted the followers of *Heimatstil,* those who pursued German traditional architecture that later became closely associated with National Socialism. The assertion of internationalism as a criterion for architecture was not a conciliatory gesture at the 1923 Bauhaus, with conservative advocates in the regional government opposing the school's mission, but it was tactical. Similarly, the internationalism of the 1927 Werkbund exhibition ran up against strong opposition from south German architects shut out of the local commissions that the exhibition offered. Throughout this period, the claims of modern

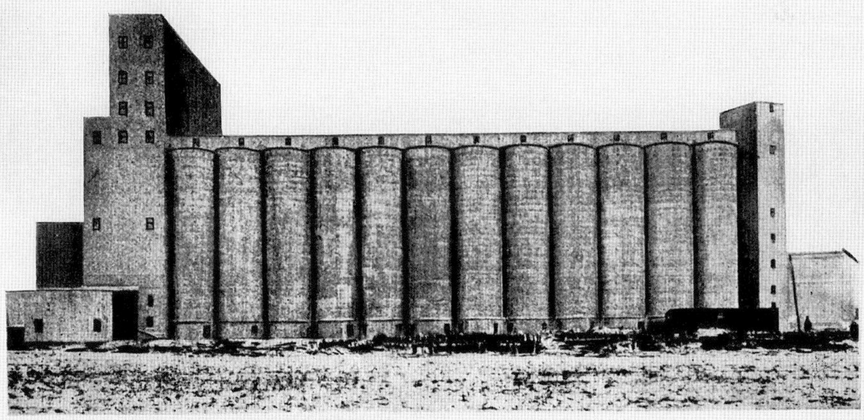

Kornsilo in Südamerika. Um 1910

Figure 6.5. Plate showing Latin American grain silo added to the 1927 edition of *Internationale Architektur* (first edition, 1925).

architects for the unity of their enterprise were perhaps as ideological as they were tendentious. Motivated by a firm belief in the democratizing potential of contemporary architecture and fueled by the belief that social relations as well as aesthetic products were mirrored in buildings, they were also more evidently vested in formal and stylistic consistency than the American architecture show, with its eclectic inclusivity of nearly anything that was built, or meant to be built, and American.[26]

"INTERNATIONAL PLAN AND MODEL EXHIBITION OF NEW BUILDING ART," 1927

The photographic campaign that formed an important part of "The Dwelling" was also tied to the changing status of the Neues Bauen in Germany at this time. "The Dwelling" opened to the public six months after the Bauhaus building in Dessau was completed. It had three parts: a full-scale building exhibition, a building materials exhibition, and an exhibition of international architecture. The first, a permanent housing settlement constructed on the Weissenhof hill (the Weissenhofsiedlung), was the largest and most significant part of the exhibition (Figures 2.9 and 6.6–6.11); the second was an exhibition of new construction materials, building

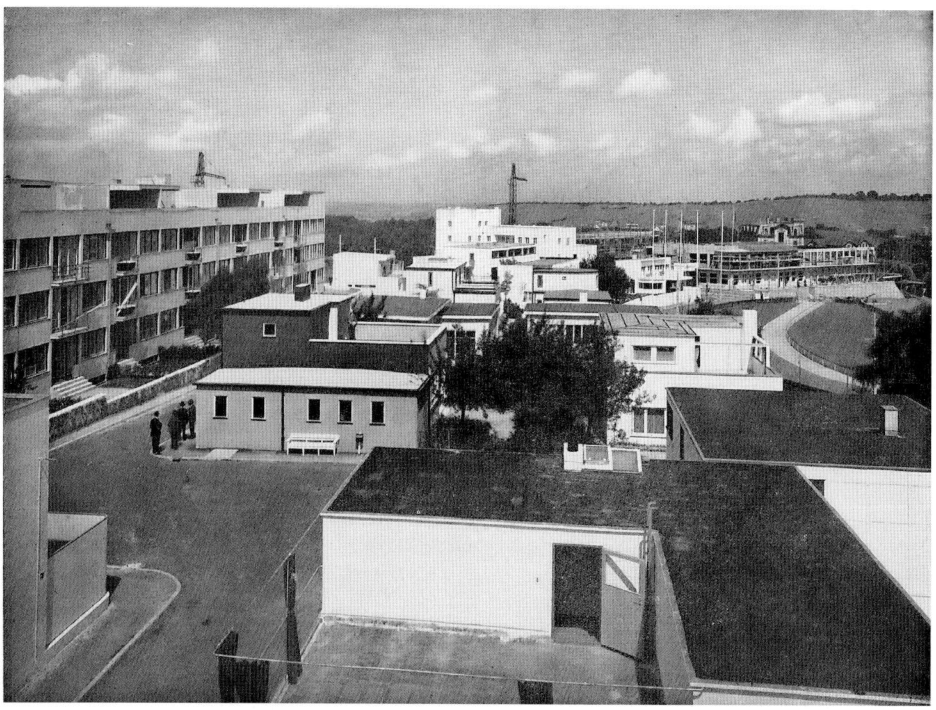

Figure 6.6. View of Weissenhofsiedlung, part of the German Werkbund exhibition, "The Dwelling," Stuttgart, 1927. Photograph: Dr. Lossen and Company.

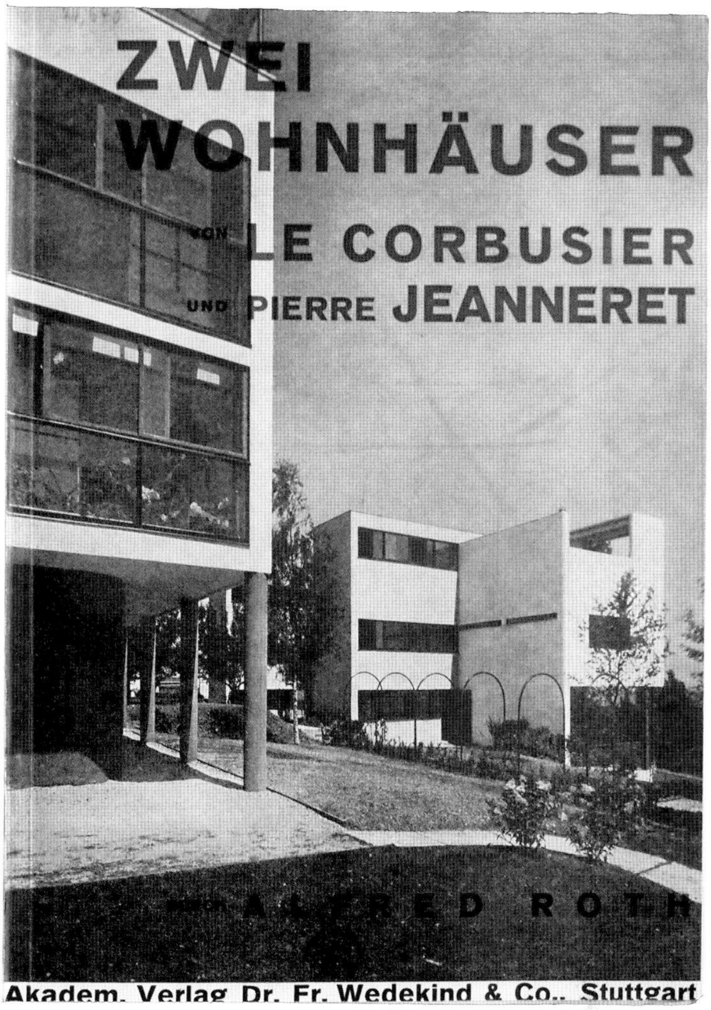

Figure 6.7. Alfred Roth, *Zwei Wohnhäuser von Le Corbusier und Pierre Jeanneret* (Stuttgart: Wedekind, 1927), cover.

products, and industrial design objects in a "materials show" (Materialienschau) in the Gewerbehalle in downtown Stuttgart (Figures 2.10, 2.11, 6.12). The third was the "International Plan and Model Exhibition of New Building Art," installed at the city exhibition hall near the New Palace, also in downtown Stuttgart (Figure 6.13).

The first two components of the exhibition were complementary: the materials show featured objects and materials that might be used in full-scale architecture. The third component, the plan and model exhibition, instead offered comparanda from international sites, contextualizing the Stuttgart exhibition and providing its buildings with company, if not history. The show included photographic enlargements of photographs and drawings from many sites. Although photography played an important role in all three components of the exhibition, here photographs were exhibition content, not tools to be used in documenting new materials or new buildings in the press.

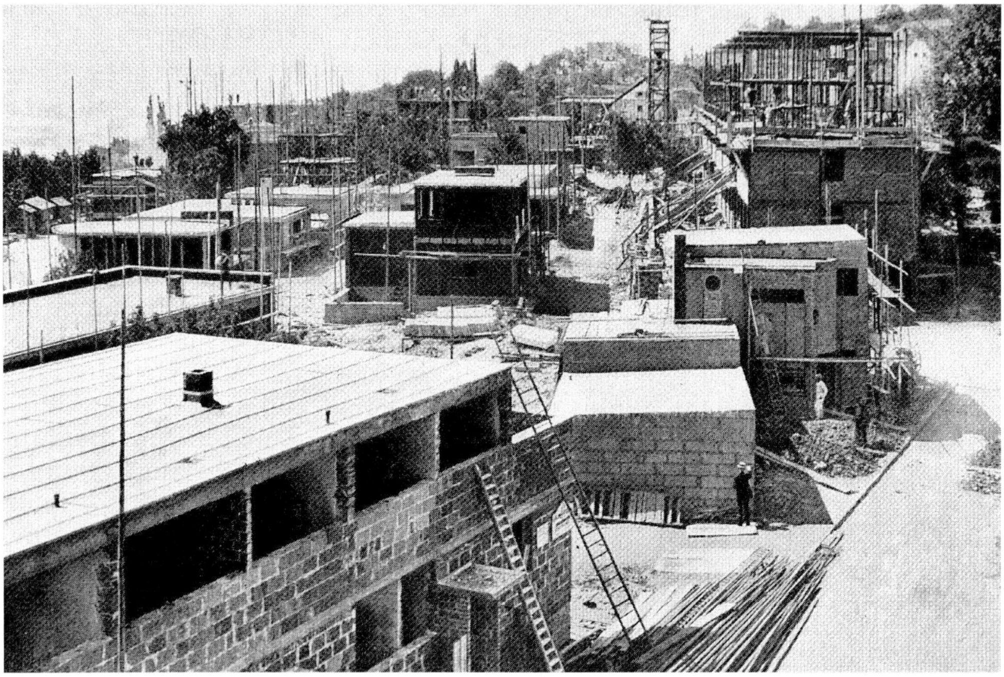

Figure 6.8. View of Weissenhofsiedlung, *Bau und Wohnung: Die Bauten der Weissenhofsiedlung in Stuttgart* (Stuttgart: Wedekind, 1927). Photograph: Dr. Lossen and Company.

The plan and model exhibition opened in Stuttgart in July 1927 and remained open until the end of October. It contained 150 different projects illustrated by 531 items; 129 architects participated, representing major European countries and the United States. A modified version of the show then traveled throughout Europe.[27] By the autumn of 1930, the exhibition materials were back in Stuttgart. Few plans but seventeen models were shown; the remainder were photographs and photomechanical enlargements of drawings. The traveling exhibition that opened in January in Zurich lacked models but was supplemented with additional contextual material from the "forerunners" of modern architecture—Tony Garnier and Adolf Loos among them. The traveling exhibition contained about half as many objects as the Stuttgart show. Both versions of the exhibition were aimed at a lay more than a professional public; hence the dearth of technical drawings. Drawings and photographs were rephotographed for the display, the result of a last-minute time crunch before the opening. Assistant Werner Gräff noted that when exhibition items did not arrive in time, a number of projects were taken from books and journals and blown up to the one-meter maximum height allowed by commercial rolls of photographic paper.[28]

Although the material displayed in Stuttgart included a heterogeneous array of objects (drawings, models, and photographs), the traveling exhibition was heavily

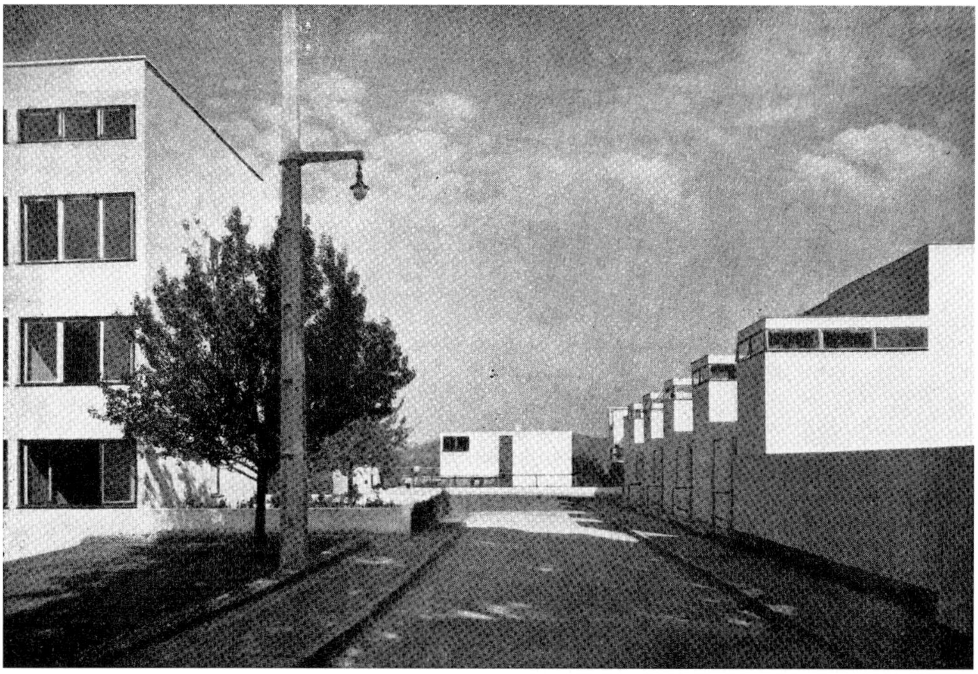

Figure 6.9. View of Weissenhofsiedlung, *Bau und Wohnung*. Photograph: Dr. Lossen and Company.

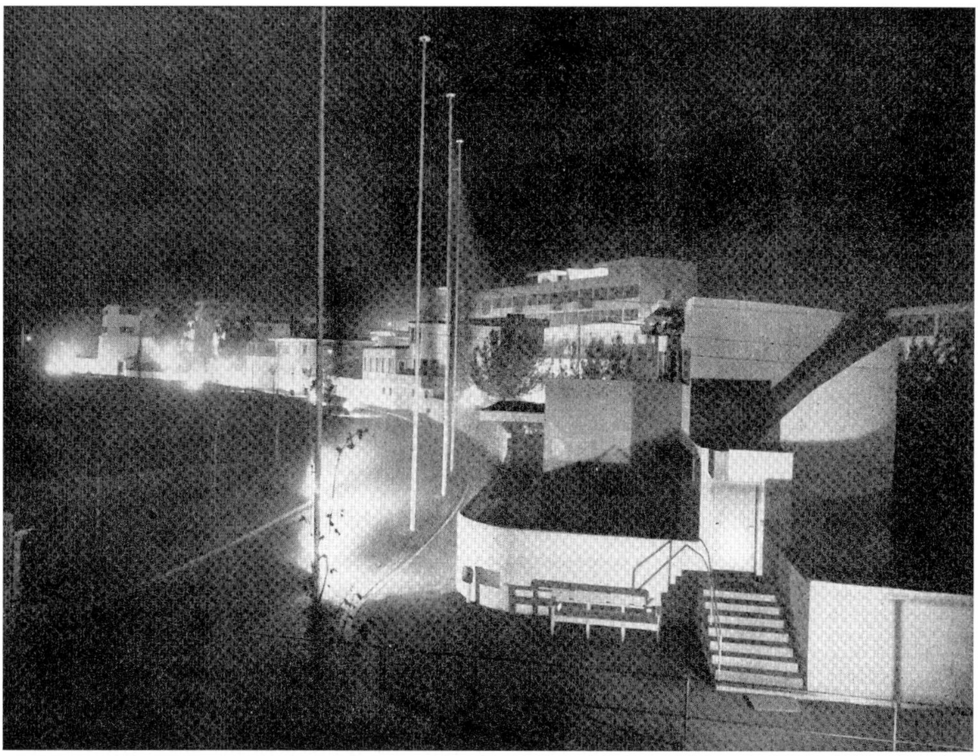

Figure 6.10. View of Weissenhofsiedlung, *Bau und Wohnung*. Photograph: Dr. Lossen and Company.

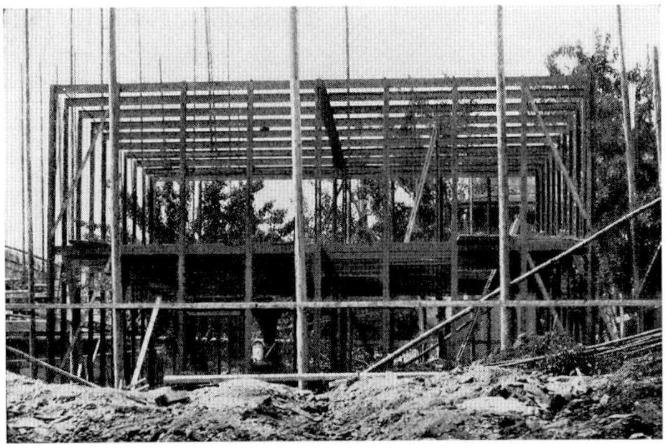

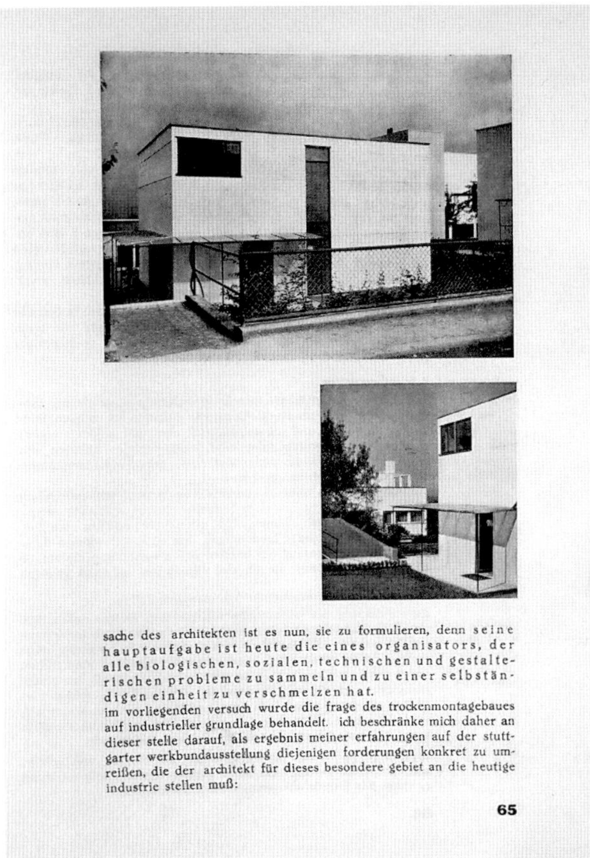

sache des architekten ist es nun, sie zu formulieren, denn seine hauptaufgabe ist heute die eines organisators, der alle biologischen, sozialen, technischen und gestalterischen probleme zu sammeln und zu einer selbständigen einheit zu verschmelzen hat.
im vorliegenden versuch wurde die frage des trockenmontagebaues auf industrieller grundlage behandelt. ich beschränke mich daher an dieser stelle darauf, als ergebnis meiner erfahrungen auf der stuttgarter werkbundausstellung diejenigen forderungen konkret zu umreißen, die der architekt für dieses besondere gebiet an die heutige industrie stellen muß:

65

Figure 6.11. Prefabricated house with metallic frame and dry-mounted wall panels, under construction and completed, "The Dwelling," 1927. From *Bau und Wohnung*.

photographic. It also influenced audiences throughout Europe and has been widely interpreted as one of the vehicles by which different versions of modern architecture were linked in a coordinated effort across various European lands. Belief in the common project of modern architecture was widespread in the late 1920s; it persisted even in 2002, when Karin Kirsch introduced the exhibition by noting, "As in an imaginary museum, examples of modern constructions [Bauwerke] from Europe and America were brought together in this part of the Werkbund exhibition, to make the similarity of the architecture and the mutually independent simultaneity of its appearance clear."[29] Kirsch's characterization reflects Hilberseimer's introduction to *Internationale neue Baukunst*, quoted in the epigraph to chapter 5. Hilberseimer identified an internal unity between buildings remote from one another, ascribing a unified set of ideas about culture to the "differentiated" production of diverse nations; he ignored the framing device of the exhibition itself as the breeder or incubator of unity. External form appears now as an index of internal coherence; Hilberseimer's words echo those of Walter Gropius in 1923.

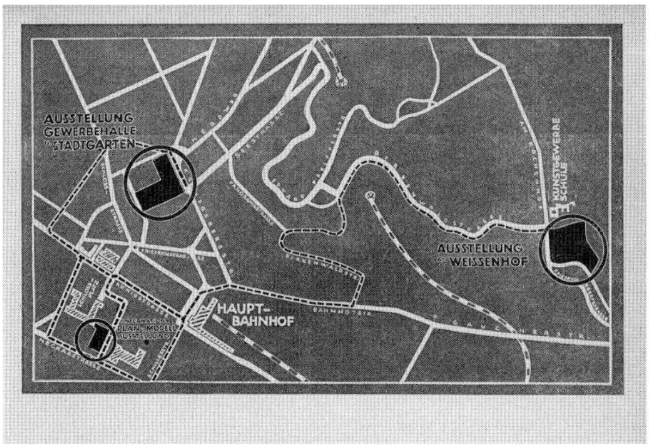

Figure 6.12. Plan, "The Dwelling," Stuttgart, 1927.

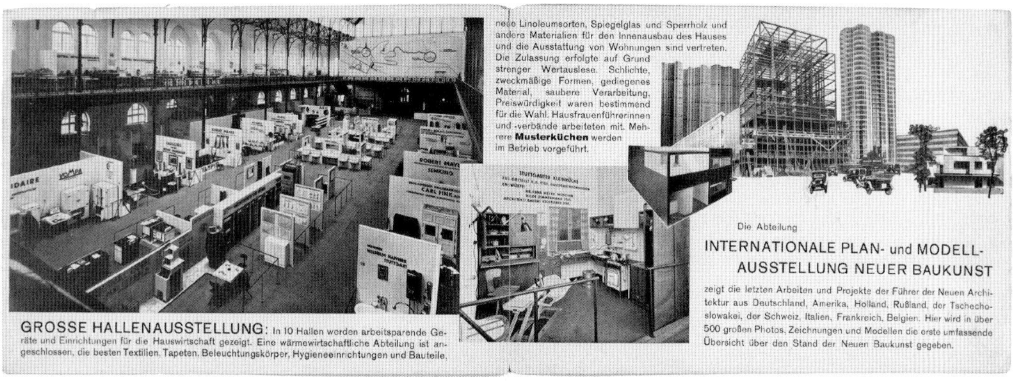

Figure 6.13. Exhibition brochure advertising the "Grosse Hallenausstellung" and the "Internationale Plan- und Modellausstellung neuer Baukunst," "The Dwelling," Stuttgart, 1927.

ERSCHEINUNGSFORM VERSUS PHOTOGRAPHIC CONVENTION

The viewer looking through the photographs of the 1927 exhibition or its catalog might easily draw connections between objects, seeing commonalities established by camera and book as well as by buildings themselves. To judge from the graphic layouts and consistency of presentation in both catalogs, this was true to a much greater degree than in the more eclectic American architecture show. Unifying effects that resulted from image capture, graphic design, and printing exploited by Hilberseimer, as by others involved in similar efforts, blur distinctions between object and representation. Modern architecture was endowed with the coherence and status of an international movement without regard to economic pressures acting on global building industries in the developed world. Broad comparative formats for presenting architecture to the public, such as the Stuttgart plan and model exhibition, used visible appearance as conveyed through photographs to help create affiliated visual networks that could instantiate the notion of the "modern movement" described by

Hilberseimer. These collections of photographic and representational material were not merely compendia. Rather, they were carefully readied ammunition, poised to be deployed on the battlefield for architectural prominence and social identity, and to bring into existence that which had only been imagined in a handful of buildings spread widely over Europe and North America: a form of modernism in which "spiritual" values might be allied with the forces of modernization. There is perhaps some measure of desperation in this effort to collate the efficiency that is embedded in capitalism itself with a meaningful architectural idea; the same desperation can be found in Le Corbusier's Domino House diagram—a diagram that can still be traced in the austere and inelegant concrete housing construction that fills the outskirts of global cities even today.

Emphasizing number and geography over thorough visual description, the plan and model show relied on the abstraction of photography to convey messages quickly using precisely the criteria that Gropius had both used and complained about in the 1923 text cited in the previous chapter: external form as the chief visible indicator of architectural identity.[30] Despite Hilberseimer's claims, the absence of technical drawings laid greater emphasis on exterior views as carriers of information.[31] Yet in this task photography also provided other means to help establish and maintain connections across a body of material that was situated in different countries, designed by different architects, and commissioned by different agents. The common format of one-meter photographs in the exhibition and the regular plate sizes in the published catalog provided the first of these, so that information was unified in size and potentially in print values. Added to this, the published photographs reflect the inventory of conventional views used by architectural photographers and already noted in chapter 4. Rules of thumb for image composition, framing, management of lighting conditions, lens choices, and printing also helped unify the disparate material of building within a common format.

In the publication documenting the exhibition, titled *Internationale neue Baukunst,* the majority of photographs show buildings from a raking angle, generally about 45 degrees off the geometry of the depicted subject, but occasionally from a larger or smaller angle. The visible similarity between similar compositions, often grouped on the same or facing pages, amplified any similarity between building forms in the objects depicted, establishing a double connection between different projects nevertheless affiliated by the label of the New Building. This can be seen in the juxtaposition of Erich Mendelsohn's Herpich facade with the photograph of the Bauhaus corner that was discussed at more length in chapter 5 (Figure 6.14). The interplay between conventional views and particular buildings was somewhat more complex than this, however, and merits brief discussion.

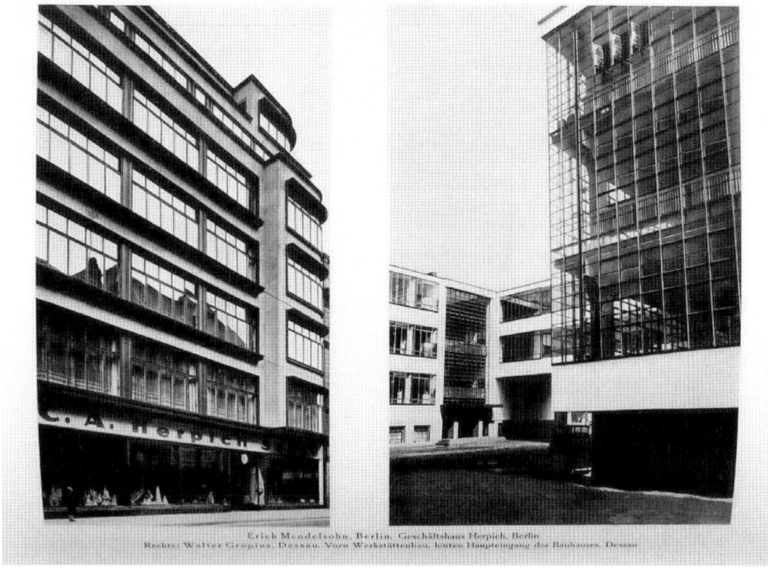

Figure 6.14. Facing plates of Mendelsohn and Gropius projects, from *Internationale neue Baukunst* (1927).

The oblique raking view of a building facade was among the most common formats for architectural photographs of building exteriors.[32] The standard conventions for photographing architecture were not entirely dependent on the formal characteristics of individual buildings. Nor were they necessarily immediately visible in pictures themselves. Gropius feared that superficial external form as represented through photographs might become synonymous with building itself, despite the fact that he advanced this very possibility by printing so many exterior views in his 1925 *Internationale Architektur.* The conventions of architectural photographs ensured that, just as external form became the signifier for individual buildings represented in pictures, a countervailing pressure tied buildings to other buildings with little regard for formal stylistic similarity—pressure exerted by the conventional use of and necessity for standardized views.

An inventory of conventional views used in architectural photography before World War II included three-quarter or oblique raking views, the straight-on view from the center of the image, the straight-on view from right or left, the worm's-eye version of these, or the bird's-eye version of the same. While Gropius feared that which he *could* see—external form as the chief indicator of architectural character—he neglected to note the threat of that which he *could not* see, at least not on the face of any individual picture. This was the "threat" constituted by the process of standardization that was intrinsic to photography and that permeated all of its products. The architectural objects captured in his survey, and in *Internationale neue Baukunst,* are tied together by an invisible yet implacable mesh made up of long-standing viewing convention and new technological capability. The buildings are bound within photographic images, and their bondage is shared by other photographs on the pages of these books.

This is not to argue that there were not similarities of construction and design between buildings executed in distant settings. Buildings constructed in the 1920s throughout Europe and parts of the United States certainly shared formal and constructive attributes. Whether these shared characteristics reflected an innate correspondence of ideas or simply a set of industries and technologies developing in similar directions guided by efficiency, economies of scale, and cost-benefit analysis is less clear. Left-leaning critics of the Neues Bauen took the latter view, protesting the conflation of capitalist abstraction with aesthetic abstraction and philosophical intention. But the way in which photographs were used to advance a campaign for modern architecture suggests that common practices of modern architects were considerably less important than the fact of a visible correspondence between buildings that could be corralled in systematic collections of photographs. In settings like the plan and model exhibition, arguments for common cause did not rest solely on technology, form, or conceptual intent. They rested also on photographic images that shared common visible features, to which common values might be attached, aggregated in standardized formats that might turn serendipity or necessity into intentionality. The importance of visible correspondence grew more important as time went on; in chapter 8 we will see what uses were made of it in future building projects.

"NEW BUILDING" AND EXHIBITION

Gallery exhibitions could present a unified view of modern buildings through skillful curation—careful selection of material, uniform photographic format, explanatory wall text, captions, and publicity materials. Single buildings became part of larger networks and advanced a campaign for building through visible similarity and shared location in space (whether within an exhibition gallery or a book). Full-scale building exhibitions, on the other hand, used publications to spread ideas to a wider public, to promote or enhance the stylistic unity of the exhibitions. Issues relating to stylistic unity recurred in Werkbund debates after the famous 1914 exhibition in Cologne. As Richard Pommer and Christian Otto noted in 1991, this exhibition was criticized for lack of stylistic unity; at the same time, and on that very occasion, Werkbund members rejected calls for standardization in design. The line between stylistic unity and artless conformity was still fuzzy a dozen years later, as exhibition director Mies tried to avoid both in the Stuttgart housing exhibition. There stylistic unity was created through the original massing model that Mies produced in 1925 (originally in clay) and through the design directives laid out for participating architects. The exhibition was referred to as a "preparatory model" (Modell-Vorarbeit) for industrialized building, an opportunity to explore prototypes for future innovation in technological and formal senses.[33] Mies placed the emphasis squarely on these two objectives: a visibly unified single entity composed of the work of many different authors as a symbolic representation of the Neues Bauen overall, and the exploration of new technological possibilities also within the unifying cloak of a spiritualized enterprise (architecture). Because the exhibition retained a provisional or experimental character, photography played an essential role in its canonization within histories of the modern movement.

The residential settlement reflected the period during which younger members of the Neues Bauen rose to prominence in the German Werkbund. The project, however, relied on a set of convictions and innovations that had not yet been successfully executed in building, except at a small scale. Many such innovations were essayed in the buildings of the Weissenhofsiedlung in a tentative and experimental fashion explicitly described by Mies. But the campaign of the New Building executed at the Stuttgart exhibition was still projective and prospective, asserting a reality that did not yet exist—either in terms of building technology or in terms of representation. The publications that spread the achievements of "The Dwelling" to a wide audience through books, journal publications, lectures, and the exhibition itself helped persuade the public that in fact "the victory of the new building style," to quote the title of a 1927 book by former *Die Form* editor Behrendt (who left the journal at the end of 1926), had already arrived. That it had not done so to the degree implied in publications of the event leads us to the photographic propaganda of the exhibition and the objectives of the photographers and architects involved in its production (Figures 6.6–6.11).

By 1926, the New Building had made significant inroads into the power structures of German cultural policy, a fact attested by Mies's ascent to the vice presidency of the Werkbund. While in this position, he was appointed design director of the Stuttgart exhibition. He was also appointed director of the later Barcelona exhibition of 1929, and of the 1931 Berlin Building Exhibition. Furthermore, Mies was not the only young architect rising within the ranks. By the mid-1920s, modernism had entered the mainstream of the German architecture world, with Ernst May and Martin Wagner planning large social housing developments in Frankfurt and Berlin. But German cultural policy began to change direction rapidly after the economic downturn of 1929, and most decisively after the election of a National Socialist government in 1933, showing that victory had been somewhat prematurely proclaimed. It is not surprising to find a negative photographic campaign launched by conservative architects against "The Dwelling," and particularly against the Weissenhofsiedlung after 1927. Conservative architects were equally as adept as modernists at

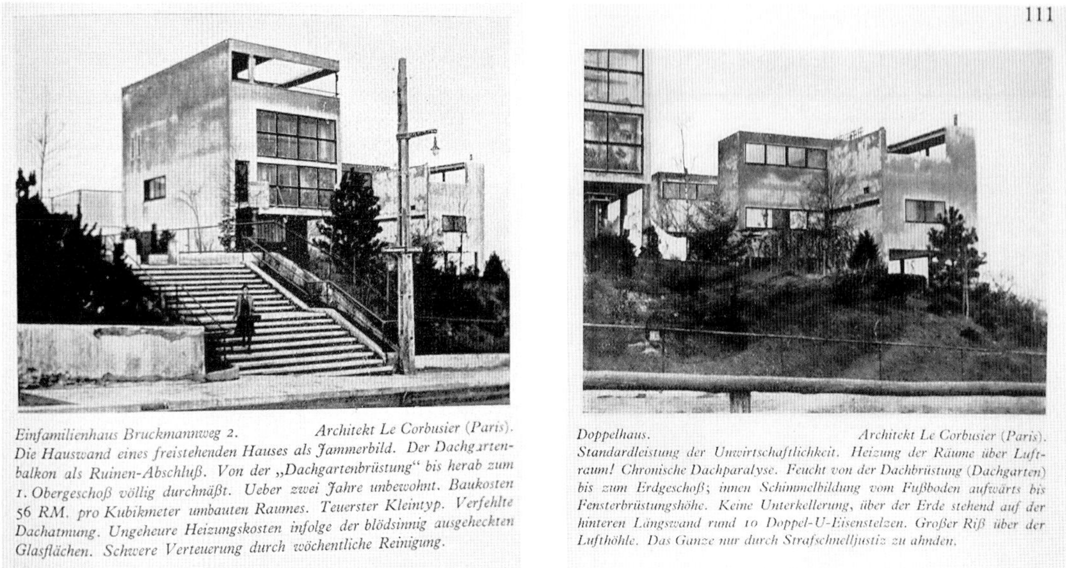

Figure 6.15. Weissenhofsiedlung in 1929: (a) "The wall of a freestanding house as a picture of confusion." (b) "Standardization of lack of economy." From *Deutsche Bauhütte* (1929).

using carefully selected photographs to advance a campaign attacking their enemies and advancing the cause of *Heimatstil* building (Figures 6.15a, 6.15b). Before we consider this point in more detail, discussion of the debates about innovation and quality that were central to the self-definition of the German Werkbund provides important background.

FULL-SCALE BUILDING EXHIBITIONS: THE WEISSENHOFSIEDLUNG

The Weissenhof exhibition was innovative in its combination of an exhibition of architecture with a planned settlement that showcased full-scale buildings as prototypes for new housing, although it was not unique. "The Dwelling" took the prosaic problem of housing and rendered it representational in the same sense that grander kinds of exhibition architecture had been representational for the better part of a century, as objects of display and carriers of symbolic value.[34]

The buildings at Weissenhof conjoined display architecture and a new construction program that encouraged technical innovation in the individual buildings, such as Walter Gropius's partially prefabricated houses (Figure 6.11). Mies also laid claim to the latitude generally granted to temporary exhibition architecture for the experimental construction at the settlement, even while he argued for the responsible use of established construction technologies in official press.[35] Much of his effort and that of Gustav Stotz went to ensuring that government resources allocated for research and development were used by architects interested in conceptual development, not merely building technology. Mies also vigorously fought off oversight that necessarily came with the use of public funds for research, to the extent that he was able to do so.

The full-scale exhibition on the Weissenhof hill collapsed architectural representation and utilitarian construction, transferring the image-based practices of architecture exhibitions onto the mundane program of housing.[36] Consistent with what we have seen at the Bauhaus, buildings at the Weissenhofsiedlung began to take on the status of images, as new ideas about formal expression distinguished building programs from established typologies. The Weissenhof experiment underlined the differences between the resulting image architecture and earlier referential architectural styles to a much greater degree than had been the case previously, thanks to the formal consistency between buildings, their close proximity to one another, and their mute appearance. It was not merely the case that architects substituted machine-age images for nineteenth-century historicist images, or for grand industrial objects like Behrens's Turbine Hall, in the design of public and semipublic buildings. The term *elementare Gestaltung* suggested that formal clarity governed external appearance, even as external appearance might well gesture to unconventional functional and historical precedents. In other words, a school might look like a factory in order to reflect (rhetorically or symbolically) on the character of education in twentieth-century Germany. The desire to render modern buildings transparent to program and structure and at the same time make them replete with semantic possibility—to make them signify—was a core modernist program. Its procedures resemble those of photography, equally intent on coding representation as truth and evidence. This was described in terms similar to *elementare Gestaltung* in more official Werkbund publications such as *Die Form,* where *Neugestaltung* replaced Mies's earlier formulation.[37] Despite the clear formal implications of the work of the Weissenhof, many critiques of the settlement were leveled at its "functionalism," as a value inseparable from engineering, objectivity (Sachlichkeit), and daily use. This conflation of agendas requires a little more unpacking.

Full-scale construction at the Weissenhof settlement allowed well-regarded "master" architects such as J. J. P. Oud, Le Corbusier, Walter Gropius, Peter Behrens, and Mies himself to investigate the potential of industrial production for finished buildings. For the most part, however, the buildings were *not* especially high-tech. Despite the fact that they were mostly site-built constructions that used traditional construction methods (with only a few exceptions), the final constructions were in many cases fraught with functional problems. Many of the buildings were conceived for industrialized construction processes that either did not yet exist or were still in preliminary stages of development, most graphically illustrated by

Ernst May's lift slab concrete panel construction on the experimental building site near the Weissenhofsiedlung.[38] The buildings were planned as models, or mock-ups, for fully industrialized architecture, a fact that was noted in statements for and critical responses to the settlement. That had always been the intention of the exhibition organizers: to put new construction techniques on display, so that they might gain visibility and be subject to further experimentation and deployment on building sites.

When the sketch of industrially produced architecture, however, met the tool of mechanical reproduction par excellence—the camera—a kind of chemical reaction occurred. The camera turned Weissenhof into everything it had been designed to predict. The buildings were presented in photographs as if they were industrially produced modern architecture. The Weissenhofsiedlung accomplished the "victory of the new building style" by blitzing the opposition with a juggernaut of mechanically reproduced images of site-built architecture. One of the tragicomic facts of this period of modernism is the tremendous abreaction of National Socialists to an architecture that had never really come "on line" in the sense implied by the term *industrial production.*[39] We can narrate that process a little more closely, since photography played a role in the countercampaign against Neues Bauen modernism as well.

The official photographs of the settlement were taken by the firm Dr. Lossen in Stuttgart and published in the monograph *Bau und Wohnung* as well as in Alfred Roth's *Zwei Wohnhäuser von Le Corbusier und Pierre Jeanneret,* both published by the Wedekind-Verlag in Stuttgart in 1927 and designed by Willi Baumeister. These two publications serve as exhibition catalogs to the Weissenhofsiedlung, although numerous other publications guided visitors through the settlement and advertised the exhibition to the public. In *Bau und Wohnung,* Mies introduced the *Siedlung* in text and in general photographic views, including some construction photographs. The book was then divided into sections by architect (arranged in alphabetical order), with separate page spreads for each building (or pair of buildings, in the cases in which an architect was assigned two) that were illustrated photographically. These sections included brief text, technical information, sketches, and photographs. The photographs lacked individual captions, so that the reader was offered "unmediated" access to the photographic images; the section heading (the name of the architect) served as overall caption for the photographs in any given section. Roth's fascinating *Zwei Wohnhäuser,* by contrast, gives a detailed presentation of the construction of the two houses by Le Corbusier and Jeanneret, with rich illustration (photographic and drawn) of the process of construction that went into both projects. Where the first publication gives a broad overview of the exhibition and its component parts, the second provides a close view of a single construction project.

Both are supplemented, then, by *Internationale neue Baukunst,* narrating the results of the plan and model exhibition. All three of these publications serve as a manner of exhibition catalog for "The Dwelling."

Responses from the press varied. Perhaps less interesting than those who were either for or against the event are those who remained critically positive. Siegfried Kracauer, for example, defended the Werkbund exhibition at Stuttgart from the political right and left as it opened in the summer of 1927. He was actually hedging his bets: elsewhere he expressed potential misgivings about the direction adopted by the Neues Bauen. Kracauer wrote about the innovative production of buildings, interior fittings, and textual/photographic representations, joining other progressive critics in positive assessments of the three component exhibitions.[40] His writing anticipated the counterreaction from the largely south German right wing.[41] It was to be expected that local opposition would be fierce, and we may understand Kracauer's nuanced writing as he entered a context in which he was obliged to be for the modernists, if only not to appear to be against them.

In the opening of his long article on the settlement in the *Frankfurter Zeitung* of July 31, Kracauer seemed to have his tongue in his cheek, as he celebrated the advanced condition of water faucets and bathroom fixtures, harbingers of the new architecture.[42] "The bathtubs don't have to be ashamed of the dining room anymore," Kracauer noted with gentle irony.[43] What attracted him most were the ineffable surfaces of the Glass Room (Figure 2.10), markers for an architecture that didn't yet exist, "contemporary constructive foreordinations of elements cleansed of bad superfluities."[44] Kracauer's use of the word "foreordinations" (Fügungen) correlates with Ludwig Mies van der Rohe's own explanations of the Stuttgart exhibition, although from a slightly different vantage point. Mies described the architecture and design installations as projective examples—prototypes—of an architecture that hadn't yet arrived. The notion of standing in the anticipation of an event figures in Kracauer's writings on architectural and nonarchitectural topics, such as "Those Who Wait" and "The Hotel Lobby." At Stuttgart it was both literally and figuratively true: the Weissenhofsiedlung, while it displayed new (and potentially more economical) construction technologies, was also very expensive. Like any prototype, it did not command the economies of scale on which its further articulation was premised. It was, very much, a foreordination, very similar to a prototype or a handmade readymade awaiting factory production.

As the 1930s advanced, right-wing architects found they had a number of targets at Weissenhof, arguing that construction standards had been sacrificed for the sake of Neues Bauen dogma. Experimental building was often criticized for poor quality in construction; photography could both prove and disprove the validity of this criticism as needed. An experimental project such as the Barcelona Pavilion that was provisionally built but soon dismantled might live a second life in photographs that were untroubled by problems that beset the building while it stood on-site. The Stuttgart exhibition reveals the contours of this dispute, since both sides published extensive pictures of its buildings. On one hand, "The Dwelling" represented the "victory of the new building style"; on the other, it represented the decline of German civilization in the face of alien building form and shabby construction.

Articles showing construction problems at the settlement appeared in right-wing publications. Rudolf Esterer, one of the apologists of the conservative *Heimatschutz* movement, described poor construction standards and new materials as mere symptoms of an overall corruption in traditional values represented by the new architecture when he wrote:

> Not glass, steel, and concrete, not all the new materials and ugly construction methods against which the *Heimatschutz* movement defended itself in vain, are responsible for the destruction and devastation of the picture of the homeland that we are still lamenting today, but rather the men of a culture-less time, who do not master the new materials technically, who cannot and will not take full command of the new construction methods, because their minds are directed toward other goals, to easy gain and hasty profit.[45]

Chief among the targets of the *Heimatschutz* architects was the Weissenhofsiedlung, but perhaps even more vulnerable was the Törten-Siedlung at Dessau, the experiment in industrialized building methods begun by Gropius at the Bauhaus but carried on by Hannes Meyer.[46] In these cases, the opponents of the Neues Bauen turned one of their most successful weapons against them, using photography to advance an attack on new construction methods in the press.

In the battle over construction standards that fueled contestation over the term *Qualitätsarbeit* (quality work), photography was a critical tool of argument; both sides used it with equal polemical intent. Close-up photographs detailing construction flaws were commonplace (Figures 6.15a, 6.15b), but more scandalous, on both sides of the battle, were attempts to use photographic technique to improve or degrade the architectural subject depicted. While both right- and left-wing groups argued over the meaning of terms like *Sachlichkeit,* both also deployed photography in self-consciously rhetorical fashion, to construct an argument that rested on the evidence of photographic images skillfully produced with quite specific objectives. These attempts were often rather unsophisticated, at least to the twenty-first-century viewer accustomed to the modalities of photography. And yet they were evidently successful at the time.

As the 1930s advanced, avant-garde architects and designers survived the negative propaganda onslaughts of their right-leaning colleagues partly to the extent that they were able to protect themselves from accusations of lowered building standards. Neues Bauen architects often sought to break existing technical barriers, which required experimentation and risk, either practically or conceptually. The Weissenhofsiedlung was a particular target thanks to its avowedly experimental aims and the usual budgetary shortfalls that rendered technical innovation difficult. There were problems at Weissenhof that translated into dramatic, accusatory photographs. In the 1930s, the greatest "offenders" who were members of the Neues Bauen generally fled, if not in direct response to the attacks of their right-wing colleagues at Stuttgart, then in response to the larger political situation that produced or allowed those attacks and that blossomed in the years following.[47]

Chapter 5 dwelled on the photographs of the Bauhaus within the history of German modernism and since. A different set of media-derived practices presented Weimar public audiences with large groups of photographs of affiliated modern buildings and designed objects. In these presentations, which included books, illustrated lectures, and exhibitions, the connections that could be established between photographs within a single venue were more important than any single photograph, conveying the idea of a movement for modern architecture unified by formal similarity as communicated through pictures. This unity might or might not bear up under scrutiny. Photographs of both the Bauhaus and "The Dwelling" provide a fuller understanding of the spectrum of techniques and effects that photographic architecture might deploy in Weimar-era debates and since.

The creation of a unified movement (a "neues Bauen") lay at the very heart of modern architects' aims in Germany. Photographs of buildings assembled from a variety of remote sites might emphasize their common features, thanks in part to photographic technologies and compositional convention. Using photography to bring disparate objects into comparative alignment in black-and-white pictures on a wall or in a book, architects and critics created photographic arrays that helped define the Neues Bauen. In the process, these arrays also presented proof that modern architecture was a widespread movement and not a collection of singularities or a set of uncoordinated responses to the pressure exerted by capital markets on building activity. By the same token, a widespread movement also required that its material be spread far and wide. In this process, it was also expedient to break a single entity into a maximum number of parts, to aid in spreading those parts as widely as possible.

Modern architects and publicists used photographic architecture along two axes: to transform perceptions of single landmark buildings like the Bauhaus through forceful aesthetic presentations and to demonstrate the purportedly global unification of related sets of objects that emerged from a common impulse to modernize on the part of people of many nations. In gallery exhibitions of architecture, photography provided a means to create affiliations between buildings that were remote from each other in space, aided by wall text or captioning, by framing, and by the copresence of many pictures within a single space (whether the gallery or the accompanying exhibition catalog, often the most important feature of an exhibition from a historical perspective).

In the case of a full-scale building exhibition, by contrast, when an ensemble of buildings was constructed on a single site, exhibition catalogs, monographs, and other publicity materials translated a spatial continuum in which many buildings formed a single environment into a series of disaggregated views. Three-dimensional objects that were copresent in space became two-dimensional atomized singularities that were then spread through the mass-printed page. In the first case, photography unified a disparate set of objects. In the second, photographs separated a single location into discrete bits, potentially spreading it over a wider terrain. In the process, events or monuments that occurred at a single location could be transmitted anywhere, amplified by their separation on the page. Thus photography was used both for gathering and for disseminating. This contradiction—that something that gathers also spreads—lies at the heart of architectural media, but it is only an apparent contradiction. Architecture and photography, although they share common attributes as discussed in preceding chapters, operate in fundamentally different ways. Individual photographic images can be swarmed and deployed for different purposes in ways that buildings cannot, and this flexibility—the ability to swarm in different directions with speed—made photography particularly effective as a form of visual persuasion in a predigital era. Against the stability of architecture as building, the mobility of architecture as media was breathtaking, and it continues to be so in the present.

Architectural photography opens up a space in which meaning can be construed according to predispositions of the perceiver in a manner that differs from the way in which we interpret buildings individually upon experiencing them in space. Photographs are also propaganda instruments liable to ideological construction distinct from the ideological constructions of the architecture they depict. They can be scripted by text and context at the source; the reader can also deviate from the intended script in favor of a different one engendered more by site of reception than by site of production. We have thus far examined sites of production. Now we might turn to sites of reception.

PART III IMAGEABILITY

The retention of the image, its development and multiplication, form an ordered succession of steps which composed the photographic act, taken as a whole. History determined, however, that this act would find its goal in reproduction, much the way the point of film as spectacle was established from the start. . . . So that photography's contribution, to use the terms of classical economy, is less on the level of *production*, properly speaking, than on that of *consumption*.

—HUBERT DAMISCH,
"FIVE NOTES FOR A
PHENOMENOLOGY OF THE
PHOTOGRAPHIC IMAGE"

7. PROMISE AND THREAT
AMERICAN PHOTOGRAPHS IN POSTWAR GERMANY

We might begin in Germany in 1947. After a suspension of three or sometimes four years, German architectural journals were just beginning to reappear, often under new names. New building had generally ceased; ruin clearance and the repair of heavily damaged cities were the order of the day. Those architects who had remained in Germany after the exodus of the post-1933 period and the war itself witnessed the juxtaposition of former achievements and current destruction. In a letter from Rudolf Schwarz to Ludwig Mies van der Rohe in May 1947, Schwarz wrote: "It's not going very well here, we have hardly the most necessary things, and sometimes not even, and the winter was hard. Many things that are unobserved trivialities in other lands have become rare luxuries about which one has nearly forgotten." In reference to Mies's work in Chicago, Schwarz noted: "Hopefully one will soon get to see something of your work in German periodicals or books (any foreign periodicals are not allowed to find their way to us). . . . In any case, for us building is the same as food and books, one can really only dream of them, and, if one rescues a spare scrap of paper, draw a little sketch."[1] Schwarz's letters relate the conditions under which architects resumed building in Germany. Places that had been central to the formation of modernism, its utopian aspirations, and its technical achievements were now decidedly peripheral. They would remain that way for some time.

Modern architecture had crossed and recrossed the Atlantic throughout the twentieth century. Photographs of American buildings had provided source material for European architects well before World War I, when grain silos and skyscrapers

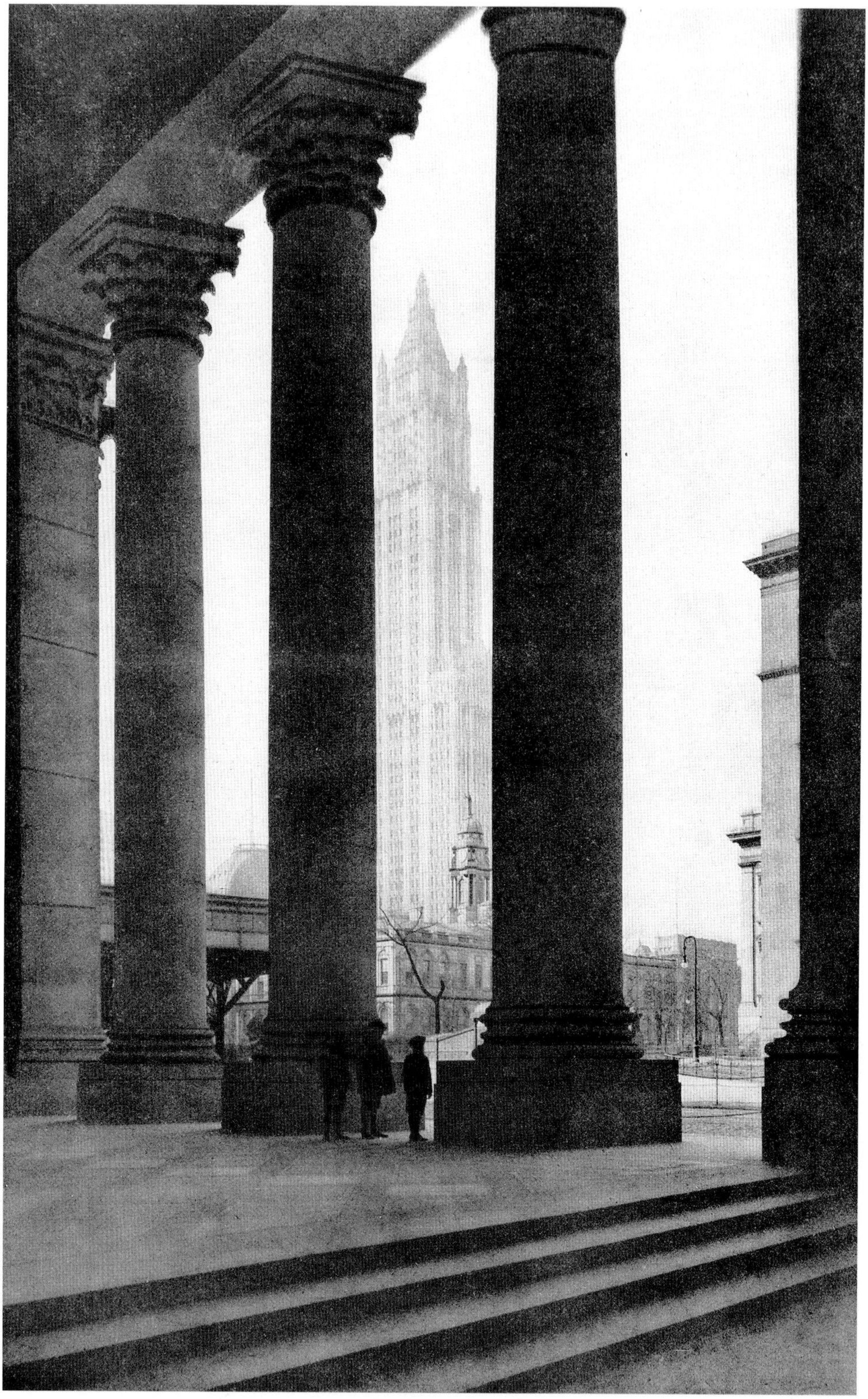

Figure 7.1. Plate 122 in Werner Hegemann, *Amerikanische Architektur & Stadtbaukunst: Ein Überblick über den heutigen Stand der Amerikanischen Baukunst in ihrer Beziehung zum Staedtebau abbildungen* (Berlin: E. Wasmuth, 1925/1927).

provided evidence of new building technologies, new forms, and new functions. Architects and editors published these photographs in a range of different accounts, from manifesto publications of the avant-garde to more conventional topographic accounts (Figures 7.1–7.3). Grain silos and other examples of American industrial architecture helped inspire a new formal language among European architects, who redirected functional markers for rhetorical and symbolic purposes. Profoundly impressed by American skyscrapers (the architecture of commerce), these architects quickly came to reject representational form for its superficial recitation of historical detail. Neo-Gothic or classicizing stone wrappers found in American examples dropped from the manifesto *Hochhäuser* of the Neues Bauen like so much sloughed-off skin (Figure 7.4). Yet European architects adapted representational form from bare-bones American factories for a range of program types, from factories to art schools, embracing the factory-symbol as signifier of the new. Such was the schizophrenia present in the formation of European modernism from the outset.[2]

Schwarz's postwar letters narrate a different moment. They testify to the information vacuum of post-1943 Germany, a vacuum that began to fill with images imported from abroad shortly after the war's end. If both new building and its publishing infrastructure had stopped in Germany, the same was not true elsewhere. Among the Allied nations, however, only those of North America were *not*

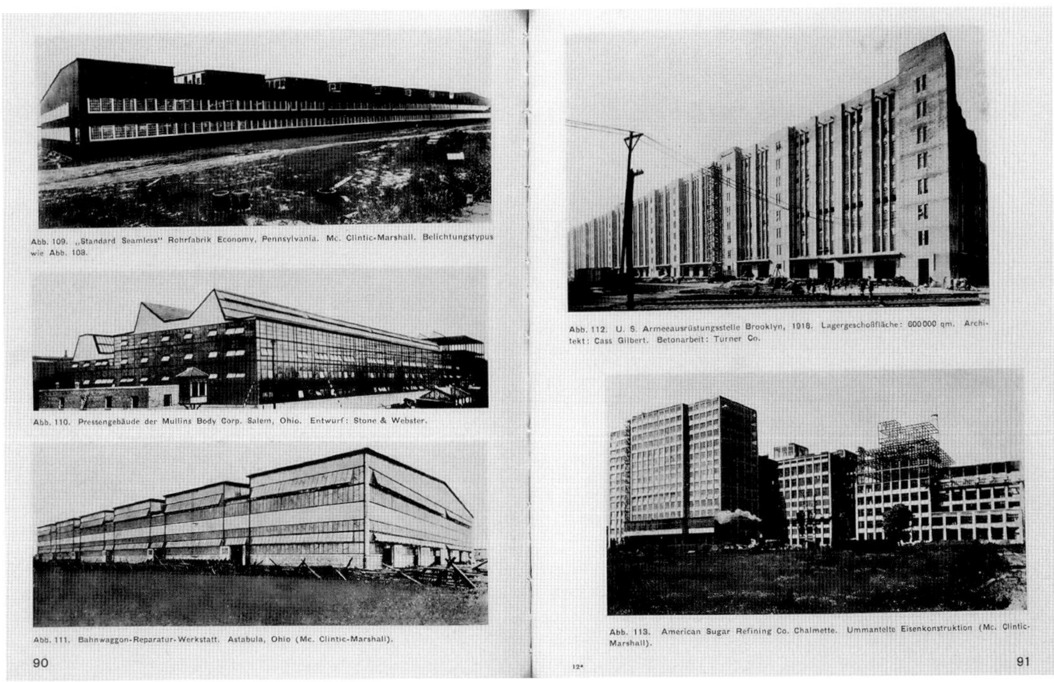
Abb. 109. „Standard Seamless" Rohrfabrik Economy, Pennsylvania. Mc. Clintic-Marshall. Belichtungstypus wie Abb. 108.

Abb. 110. Pressengebäude der Mullins Body Corp. Salem, Ohio. Entwurf: Stone & Webster.

Abb. 111. Bahnwaggon-Reparatur-Werkstatt. Astabula, Ohio (Mc. Clintic-Marshall).

90

Abb. 112. U. S. Armeeausrüstungsstelle Brooklyn, 1918. Lagergeschoßfläche: 600000 qm. Architekt: Cass Gilbert. Betonarbeit: Turner Co.

Abb. 113. American Sugar Refining Co. Chalmette. Ummantelte Eisenkonstruktion (Mc. Clintic-Marshall).

12*

91

Figure 7.2. Two-page spread showing photographs of industrial architecture in Richard Neutra, *Amerika, die Stilbildung des neuen Bauens in den Vereinigten Staaten* (Vienna: Scholl, 1930), 90–91.

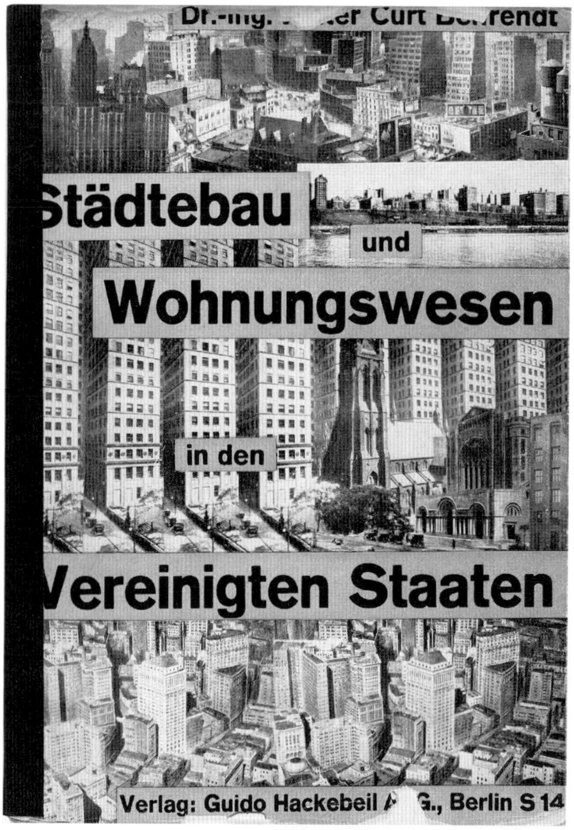

Figure 7.3. Walter Curt Behrendt, *Städtebau und Wohnungswesen in den Vereinigten Staaten* (Berlin: Guido Hackebeil, 1927), cover.

consumed with the need to repair basic infrastructure from wartime damage. Quite the contrary: the American economy, heated by World War II, was largely preoccupied with redirecting the productive capacities of industry after the war. The importance of the building industry can be seen in the steady increase in volume of steel production after 1946, fostering a new architectural language of metal sheathed in glass that replaced the ornamented masonry of earlier skyscrapers like the Chicago Tribune Tower with a close-fitting skin.[3] The immanence of steel construction replaced earlier narratives of historicism, partly as a result of the prominence of Mies, Marcel Breuer, and Walter Gropius in American architecture at this time.

This chapter focuses on the years after World War II, when a new kind of American architecture was exported to Europe, this time in the wake of extensive wartime destruction (Figure 7.5).[4] Émigré European architects like Mies, Gropius, and Breuer played important roles in this "return emigration."[5] German architects faced with massive destruction on the ground in their cities and countryside saw the return of former colleagues in photographs of buildings that metaphorically (sometimes literally) waved the banner of American economic and political power, acting on German audiences as both promise and threat as the Allied forces and the Soviet Union grappled for influence over the defeated country. While architectural photographs of American high-rise buildings traveled much of the world at this time, their effect on their former colleagues in defeated Germany contrasts the world of the producer with that of the consumer in a dramatic way. This contrast illuminates relays between architectural photography and new building; it provides a forced contrast that allows us to see the modes of photographic transmission of architecture with particular clarity.

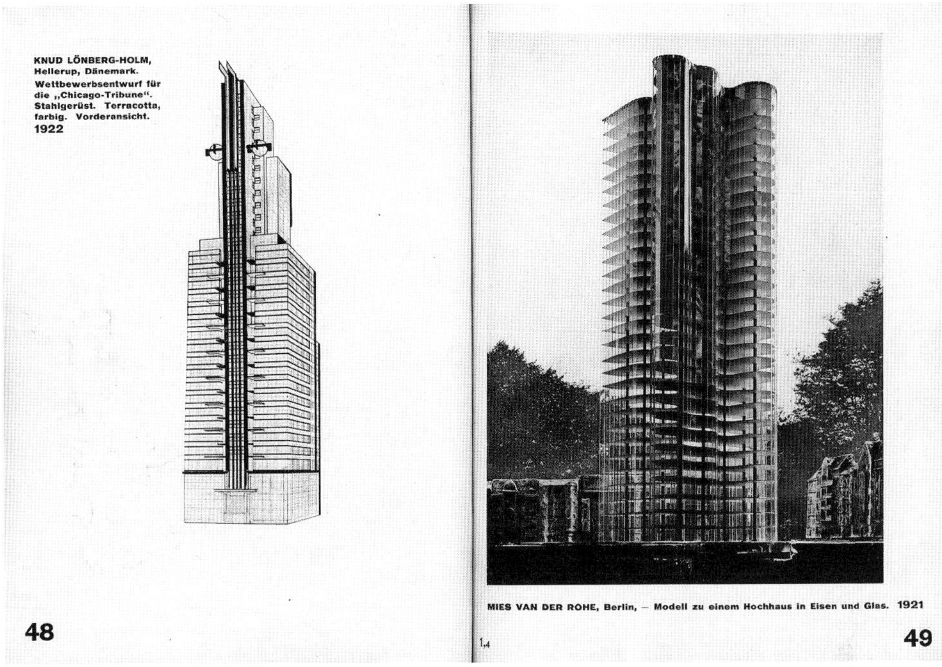

Figure 7.4. Plates from *Internationale Architektur* (1923) showing Chicago Tribune competition entry (Knud Lönberg-Holm) and Glass Skyscraper project (Ludwig Mies van der Rohe).

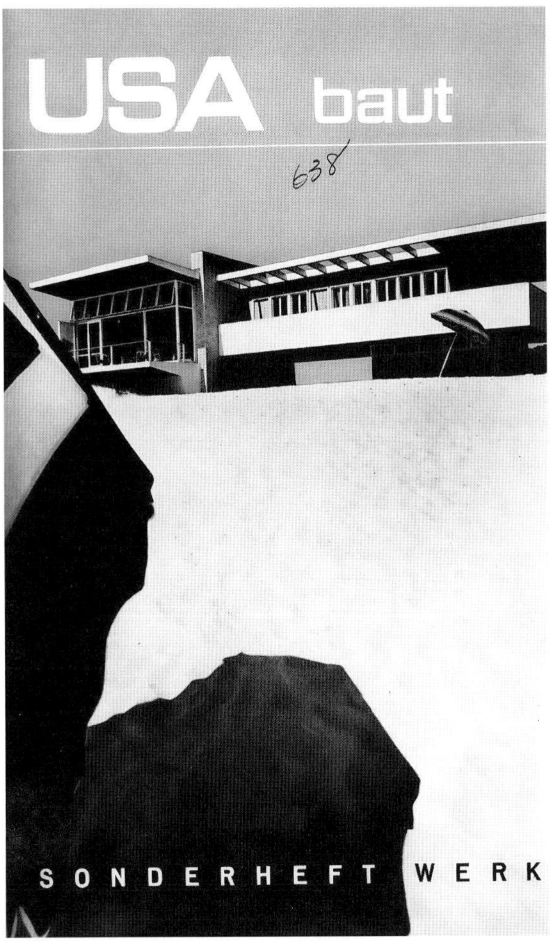

Figure 7.5. *USA Baut: Bildbericht der Ausstellung Moderne Amerikanische Architektur*, special issue of *Werk, 1945*, Alfred Roth, editor.

BAUHAUS-DEBATTE, 1953

German attitudes toward postwar modernism developed from the wreckage of 1945, as architects reengaged the legacy of modern architecture in Germany. The well-known "Bauhaus debate" unfolded in 1953 with Rudolf Schwarz's critique of modern architecture culture, and the Gropius Bauhaus especially, amid widespread interest in the legacy of both Gropius and Mies among German architects. Schwarz had expressed negative views of Neues Bauen modernism since the 1920s; his own approach to modern architecture was imbued instead with Catholic theology.[6] After the war, Schwarz's equally negative views of the Bauhaus and of National Socialist architecture, and his bitterness at the postwar situation in Germany, led him to critique technological modernity in a manner that he had already substantially formulated in the 1920s. This unfolded in *Von der Bebauung der Erde* in 1949; in his talk at the Darmstädter Gespräche, "Das Anliegen der Baukunst" (delivered in 1951, published in 1952); and again in the review of an exhibition of Hans Poelzig's work that took place in Krefeld in 1951. Finally, when asked to write an article on the topic "building and writing" (bauen und schreiben) for the periodical *Baukunst und Werkform* in late 1952, Schwarz gave full vent to his criticism of the Bauhaus legacy in general, and the influence of Gropius in particular.

Perhaps most incendiary in the 1952 publication of "Das Anliegen der Baukunst" was the fact that Schwarz referred to Gropius and his cohort as *Terroristen,* claiming that both the Bauhaus and National Socialist architectural policy reflected the same inorganic, antinatural, rationalist enterprise—architecture in the service of industrial capital. At a time when Gropius was triumphantly asserting the rectitude of his interwar work in Germany in light of wartime destruction and widespread condemnations of National Socialist cultural policy, Schwarz's remarks were bound to provoke a sharp response, particularly given the competitive market for new building commissions and reconstruction work that prevailed after the war. Gropius was especially attentive to his reputation in Germany at this time and lobbied aggressively for his own approach to architecture in a 1947 trip through Germany. Many former students and supporters of Gropius were also prominent in postwar German architecture and defended him in this debate. Schwarz was bound to meet with harsh criticism, although he was by no means isolated in his critique, then or earlier, as Winfried Nerdinger points out in a 1994 essay on this subject.[7]

Part of Schwarz's antirationalist protest writing was directed at architectural photography. Interpreting photography as a symptom of rationalized modernity and capitalism as a whole, Schwarz set up a polarity between buildings and pictures. In 1952, the publication of his 1951 Darmstadt address included the following judgment of architectural publication:

> In architecture, aesthetics have unfortunately assisted very little. . . . all these books have many pictures, and these pictures are photographed. This is so obvious to you all that you are probably amazed that I even mention it. Naturally pictures are photographed. But we must remind ourselves that earlier, decades ago, our books had not photographs but rather scale drawings. Only recently did the camera offer a ready instrument to the solitary, isolated aesthete; namely, the man who confronts a great work alone, and even—to my astonishment—remarks on things that are not there. The camera is a machine that is set up at a certain point and stares through one single eye. We are perhaps not all clear on how inadequate and fundamentally inappropriate this method is for encountering great architecture. These photographic games and all that stands behind them overlook the particular achievement of architecture, namely, making a collective whole out of many singularities. Many sacrifice themselves, giving themselves entirely into a community, and then suddenly a form blossoms that was fully foreclosed to the individual, who like a traveler with a travel guide can observe that which he can never create alone.[8]

Schwarz continued in 1953 with a condemnation of art historians:

> They stand on an aesthetic point and look from there out at the world. They have already revealed themselves by allowing so many photographs to be printed in their books, since the photographic machine is just what they need. It stares with one eye from one point at the architectonic all-world, while the real building master raises up an entire human community through one clarified common form, and thus obviously has something completely different in his mind. They speak not in our words, that are so beautiful and lasting, and are called wall, floor, roof, door, window, and so on, and that we would not exchange with optical plastic impressions for any price.[9]

Both presentations, that of 1951–52 and that of 1953, pit the authenticity of building against the inauthenticity of the printed photographic image. Orthographic drawings such as plans, sections, and elevations are also "our words," we might infer—that is, the architects' words—in the speech of architecture. In his earlier address, Schwarz ignored, somewhat paradoxically, the regularizing, rationalizing logic behind orthographic drawing, which had imposed a similar regime of order on architecture since the Renaissance, to the one that he decried in the twentieth century. Photography was both too subjective and too abstract in Schwarz's account. Photographs are taken from a single "egocentric" perspective; they are simultaneously manifestations of the cage, the *Gitterwerk* established by rationalization, and indicators of the imprisonment of the subject in a single point of view. As inconsistent in his choice of objects as he was nostalgic, Schwarz failed to make a clear distinction between perspectival representation and photography. His critique implies that photographs replaced orthographic drawing, not that they replaced perspective renderings. This assumption is as fascinating as it is revealing; he may well have been correct, in the sense that photographs assumed an inordinately central place in conveying ideas about architecture to mass audiences. And yet, photographs hardly replaced plans and sections; rather, they were used analogously, as objective representations of buildings, much in the manner of orthographic drawings but with different goals. Schwarz's critique assimilated two different things: a critique of photography and a critique of modern architecture. It lay at the heart of a vigorous debate carried out in the early 1950s.

AMERICAN ARCHITECTURE AND PHOTOGRAPHY AFTER 1945

Gropius, Mies, Breuer, Richard Neutra, Erich Mendelsohn, and other European architects who emigrated to the United States provided continuity to the unfolding history of modern architecture as it traveled across the Atlantic and the temporal gulf of National Socialism and the war years (1933–45). The buildings these architects designed and built after they arrived in the United States, however, bore little resemblance to their European work of the decades before. Numerous markers of difference in constructed buildings run counter to narratives of continuity that were rather based on individual authorship. Numerous examples might illustrate this point, such as a comparison of Gropius's Bauhaus *Meisterhäuser* with his regionally inspired domestic architecture in New England. Broadly speaking, modern architecture in the United States after World War II bore little resemblance to interwar modern architecture of the Weimar Republic or Eastern Europe. Differences can be found on many levels, including formal appearance—generally, they proceeded from a variety of causes. Building technologies, available materials, kinds of clients, capacities of contractors, and the nature of building codes or covenants were fundamentally different in the two contexts but increasingly consistent across the American continent. Despite evident differences between European and American modern architecture, however, continuity had to be asserted in order to promote individual artistic signature and successfully deploy the mechanisms of commercial markets. Paradoxically, photographs were used to establish the continuity of a single career, even as they also provided visible evidence of discontinuity. Thus the scripting of modern architecture as a coherent narrative also contained a mechanism for its own undoing.

The establishment of modern architecture in the United States after the war depended on the central importance of the architect as a figure with whom many things might be associated—artistic ability, market cachet, name recognition, experience, and centrality to earlier European architectural discourse. The last of these had become especially important after earlier events like the Museum of Modern Art show "Modern Architecture" and its accompanying manifesto, *The International Style,* both of 1932. Perhaps equally significant were issues of moral and political rectitude: non-Jewish émigrés were generally also escapees from National Socialism who in retrospect had backed the right side in the conflict between fascism and democratic principle, even before conflict had broken out. They could thus be seen as having acted on principle at a time when any potential reward for such action was unclear. They had apparently acted without regard to self-interest. In fact, Gropius, Mies, Breuer, Joseph Albers, and Herbert Bayer (all non-Jews, although Albers's wife, Anni, was Jewish) had the luxury of planning a "soft" landing in the United States, securing jobs at or in close proximity to American academic institutions. The same cannot be said for Jewish refugees such as Erich Mendelsohn, who also did not work on commissions for National Socialist institutions, as had Mies, Gropius, and Bayer.

Books, exhibitions, and journal articles produced in the United States in the 1940s and 1950s are filled with photographs that attest to difference, situated amid texts that attempted to repair the rift in modernist practices created between 1933 and 1945. In other words, such texts attempted to reestablish continuity simply by asserting its existence.[10] These texts provide insights into the role that photographic images played in the propagation and dissemination of a history of modern architecture that was activist and instrumental in advancing the careers of the émigrés themselves, just as the émigrés provided a direct connection to that history in the first place. The "International Style" gained legitimacy by claiming inheritance of the Neues Bauen and endorsing Corbusian formalism, regardless of the character of its present and future objects. European modernism provided American modernism with a heritage and a genealogy, at the same time serving the goals of American imperialism in the early stages of the Cold War.

We can turn to the photographs that Schwarz might have seen in the architectural press in the early 1950s and to buildings from American sites depicted there, many framed in steel. Architects such as Mies, who had grown interested in metal fabrication during the war, embraced the growing industrial production of structural steel with enthusiasm.[11] But metallic construction had a long history in American architecture already, particularly in Chicago architecture. Just as Mies and Le Corbusier had imposed a conceptual framework over construction systems that separated structural frame from spatial enclosure in the 1920s, so Mies's Chicago office imposed a new formal discipline on structural steel in buildings. This conceptual discipline was governed by external appearance rather than by constructional transparency. Although Mies had always favored the appearance of conceptual clarity over correspondence between inside and out (in contradistinction to structural rationalists and functionalists), it was in his American high-rise work that the discrepancy between appearance and structural reality could be most clearly articulated.

Many of Mies's American high-rise buildings, most notably the Seagram Building, were dedicated to the paradoxical display of something that was not there in a constructional sense (Figures 7.6, 7.7). Their exterior skin, with its phantom mullions acting as wind bracing, etched an immanent order on the exteriors of the buildings that nevertheless remained in the realm of the metaphysical—a depicted order, not a literal one. The building took on the status of an image: a representation of something imagined or desired. This, in turn, was imaged in photographs. Again, we find a trope repeatedly encountered in this study: the architectural photograph as the (flat) image of a (three-dimensional) image. In this case, the correspondence between outward visible signs on buildings—signs that implicate the buildings in ways that are not merely formal but imply something about construction as well—and photographic images produced an uncannily influential model, particularly for American high-rise construction.[12] The mythology of the steel frame has been levied against the

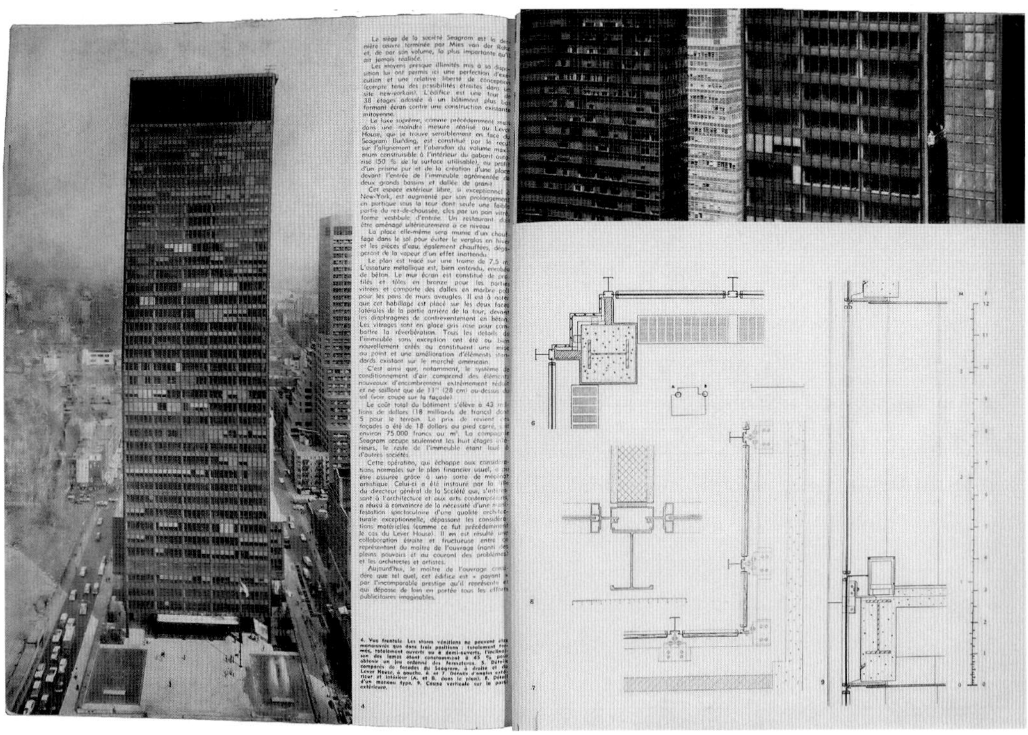

Figure 7.6. Seagram Building, New York, 1957. Architect: Ludwig Mies van der Rohe. From *L'Architecture d'Aujourd'hui* 79 (1958).

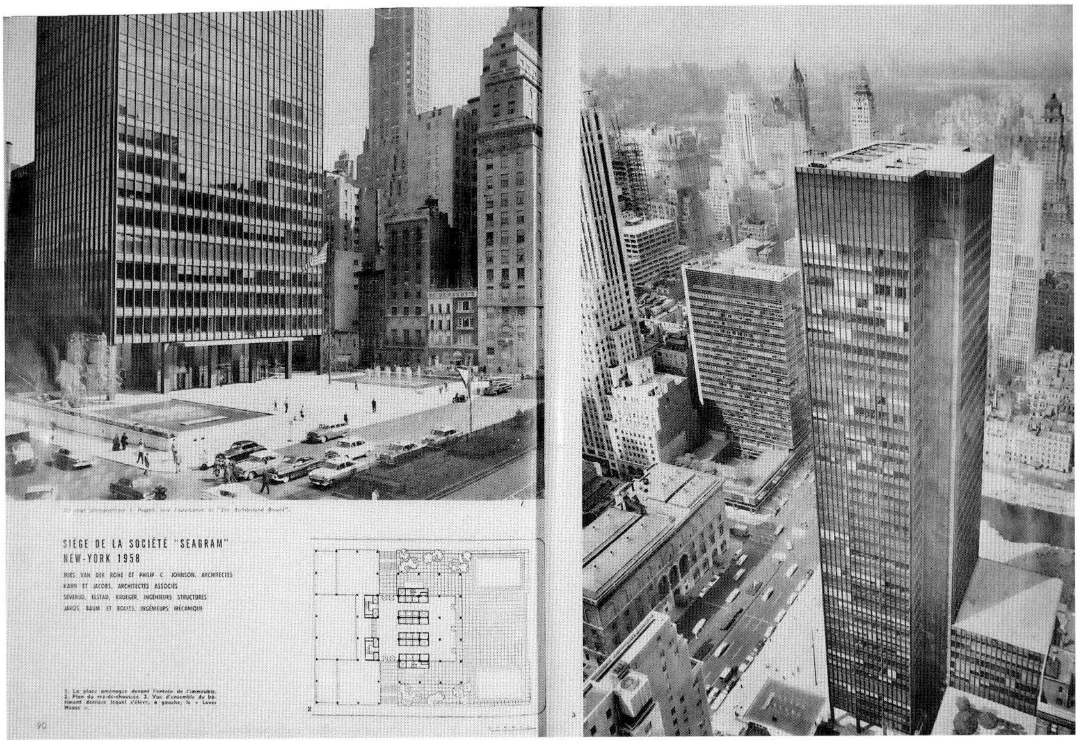

Figure 7.7. Seagram Building. From *L'Architecture d'Aujourd'hui* 79 (1958).

increasingly restrictive practices of construction, controlled by legal covenants and building codes. When these pictures traveled to a different context, however, they produced a different sort of discourse from that under way in the United States. As noted already: the image depicted in an image can be read in at least two ways, and often many more.

The wide circulation of architectural photographs of American buildings among international audiences coincided with the appearance of factory fabrication in the photographic image after the war. Both mark a new moment in the history of architecture and photography (Figure 7.8). Both photographic circulation and building construction were ever more closely tied to processes of serial reproduction and committed to increasingly sophisticated engineering as time went by. Simultaneously, a new historical phase commenced, with an altered balance of power between Europe and the United States. Photography played a specific role in the American political climate of the post–World War II years. Before we examine American modern architecture in a European "photographic return," an understanding of its initial context bears considering.

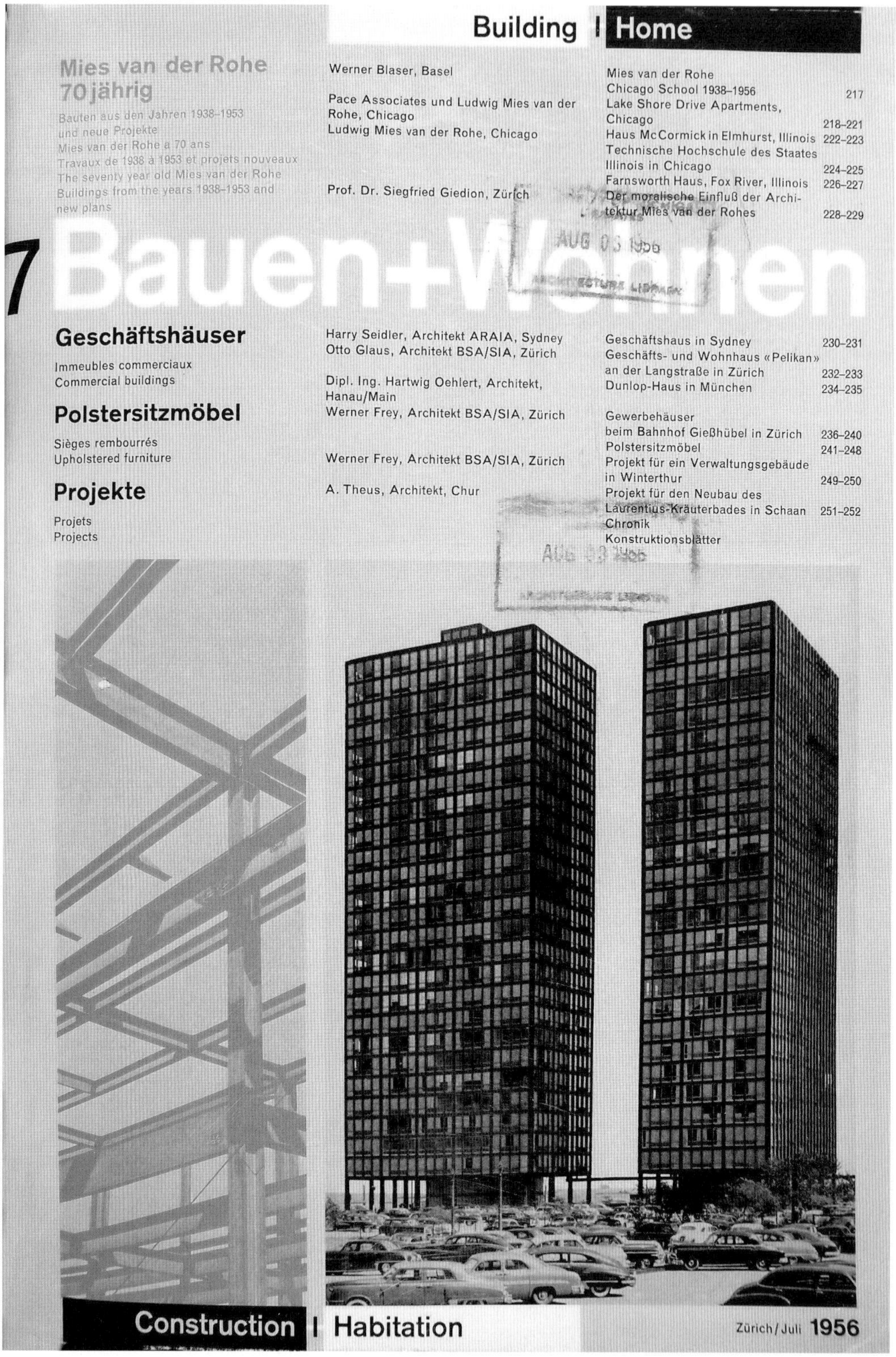

Building | Home

Mies van der Rohe 70 jährig

Bauten aus den Jahren 1938–1953 und neue Projekte
Mies van der Rohe a 70 ans
Travaux de 1938 à 1953 et projets nouveaux
The seventy year old Mies van der Rohe
Buildings from the years 1938–1953 and new plans

Werner Blaser, Basel — Mies van der Rohe

Chicago School 1938–1956 — 217

Pace Associates und Ludwig Mies van der Rohe, Chicago — Lake Shore Drive Apartments, Chicago — 218–221

Ludwig Mies van der Rohe, Chicago — Haus McCormick in Elmhurst, Illinois — 222–223

Technische Hochschule des Staates Illinois in Chicago — 224–225

Farnsworth Haus, Fox River, Illinois — 226–227

Prof. Dr. Siegfried Giedion, Zürich — Der moralische Einfluß der Architektur Mies van der Rohes — 228–229

7 Bauen+Wohnen

Geschäftshäuser

Immeubles commerciaux
Commercial buildings

Polstersitzmöbel

Sièges rembourrés
Upholstered furniture

Projekte

Projets
Projects

Harry Seidler, Architekt ARAIA, Sydney — Geschäftshaus in Sydney — 230–231

Otto Glaus, Architekt BSA/SIA, Zürich — Geschäfts- und Wohnhaus «Pelikan» an der Langstraße in Zürich — 232–233

Dipl. Ing. Hartwig Oehlert, Architekt, Hanau/Main — Dunlop-Haus in München — 234–235

Werner Frey, Architekt BSA/SIA, Zürich — Gewerbehäuser beim Bahnhof Gießhübel in Zürich — 236–240

Polstersitzmöbel — 241–248

Werner Frey, Architekt BSA/SIA, Zürich — Projekt für ein Verwaltungsgebäude in Winterthur — 249–250

A. Theus, Architekt, Chur — Projekt für den Neubau des Laurentius-Kräuterbades in Schaan — 251–252

Chronik

Konstruktionsblätter

Construction | Habitation

Zürich/Juli 1956

Figure 7.8. *Bauen und Wohnen* (July 1956), cover.

American construction altered during World War II through infusions of capital into technology-intensive industries like steel. Mies, Gropius, and Breuer built more during their American years, with larger projects getting built and fewer remaining on the drawing boards. Photographs of their Weimar architectural work did two things at least: broadly speaking, they provided track records for the architects, and more symbolically, they testified to a certain ideological propriety. Similarly, postemigration and postwar commissions, as they returned to Europe in pictures, testified to a scale and volume of practice commensurate with the earlier theoretical ambitions and history of the architects, but also now consonant with the blossoming Cold War and U.S. imperial expansion.[13] Although this effect worked best for German émigré architects in the United States, work by American architects was also exported in photographs—generally, however, under the rubrics established by the German masters. We might compare Mies's experience with those of other émigrés.

There are two distinct phases from this period, resulting in two different groups of pictures. During the transitional phase from roughly 1938 to 1956, the Mies office released photographs of German projects accompanied by many drawings and fewer but ever-increasing numbers of American projects (drawn, photographed, and photographed in models). Subsequently, from roughly 1956 until the architect's death in 1969, a large body of photographs of built work from the United States circulated in books and journals from Moscow to New York to Thailand. The 1956 German edition of Philip Johnson's monograph on the architect (the first edition had accompanied the MoMA show of 1947) included two additional chapters on completed American projects, supplementing the 1947 edition in which few had appeared.[14] In addition, an explosion of publication around 1955–56 in the international press changed Mies's professional profile, helping to place him fully into the international spotlight that eventually lead to the big Berlin commission at the end of his life, for the New National Gallery (Figure 7.8).[15] These later images looked nothing like the earlier German work, not merely because of changes in the buildings themselves but also because of subtle but substantial changes to photographic technologies that we might now briefly explore.

CAMERAS AND EQUIPMENT

Like building technologies, a number of photography's parameters changed between 1939 and 1945. This was in part the result of the high demand for cameras in these years. The difference between the wooden models in use before the war and the machined metal cameras in use after is visibly impressive, despite the fact that wooden view cameras subsequently continued to be used (and are often considered superior to metal). The year of Johnson's monographic Mies exhibition at MoMA and its accompanying catalog, 1947, was also the year in which a number of important technical milestones occurred in professional commercial photography. Lewis Kellsey's *Corrective Photography* announced changes in view camera photography that provided greater flexibility for photographing architecture. Kellsey was part owner of the Chicago-based Deardorff Company, which manufactured large-format field and studio view cameras, a firm that had grown significantly throughout the war years, thanks to government orders for large-format field cameras.[16] Similarly, smaller photographic companies, many based in Rochester, New York (the home of the Kodak Corporation), marketed the same product. The Sinar system for view cameras based on interchangeable components easily adjusted on-site was introduced to the market from its base in Switzerland at the same time. The Sinar system included interchangeable lenses that allowed a photographer to alter the focal length of the camera (the distance between lens and focusing plane, or negative) on-site.

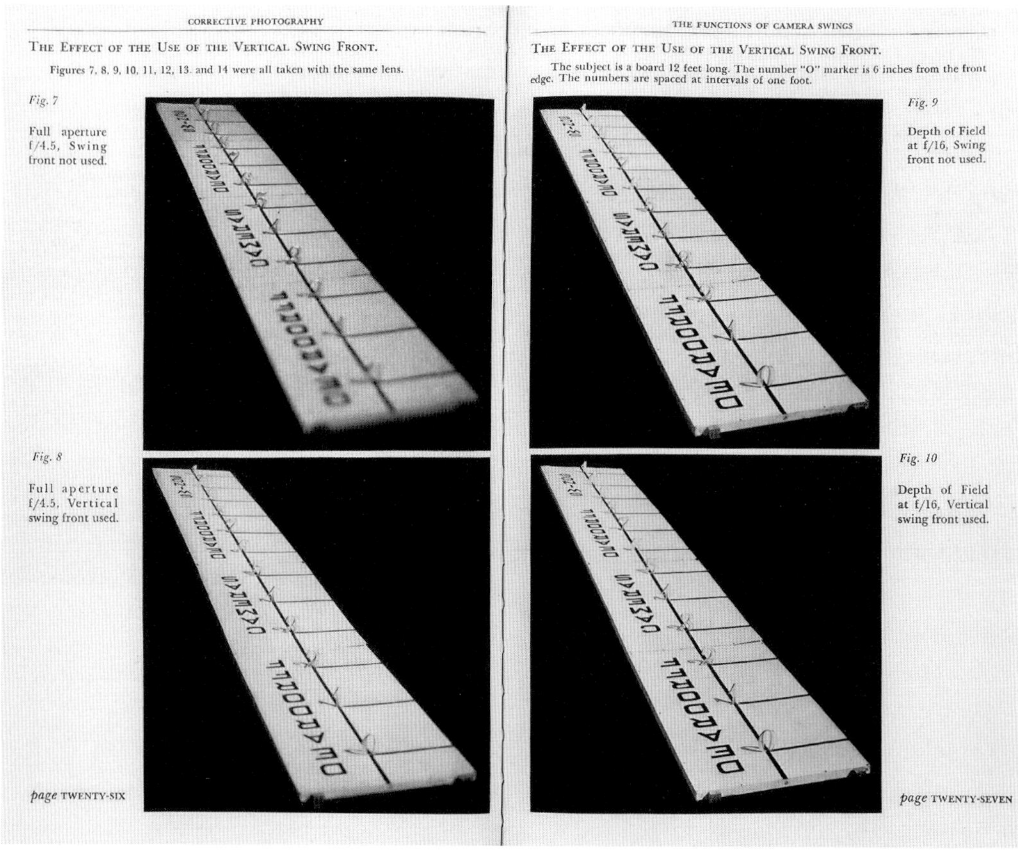
CORRECTIVE PHOTOGRAPHY

THE EFFECT OF THE USE OF THE VERTICAL SWING FRONT.

Figures 7, 8, 9, 10, 11, 12, 13, and 14 were all taken with the same lens.

Fig. 7

Full aperture f/4.5, Swing front not used.

Fig. 8

Full aperture f/4.5, Vertical swing front used.

page TWENTY-SIX

THE FUNCTIONS OF CAMERA SWINGS

THE EFFECT OF THE USE OF THE VERTICAL SWING FRONT.

The subject is a board 12 feet long. The number "O" marker is 6 inches from the front edge. The numbers are spaced at intervals of one foot.

Fig. 9

Depth of Field at f/16, Swing front not used.

Fig. 10

Depth of Field at f/16, Vertical swing front used.

page TWENTY-SEVEN

Figure 7.9. Lewis Kellsey, *Corrective Photography: An Elementary Illustrated Textbook on Camera Swings and How to Use Them* (Chicago: L. F. Deardorff, 1947), 26–27.

Bellows and camera backs were also interchangeable, making the camera easy to adapt to changing field conditions. At about the same time, Micro Precision Products brought similar technology to the market in England. In sum, within the five-year period following the end of the war, specialized photographic companies in Europe and the United States offered newly flexible ensembles of view camera photography to the commercial market—in one case, after the U.S. Army had agreed to destroy its wartime stock to prevent flooding the market with used equipment.[17]

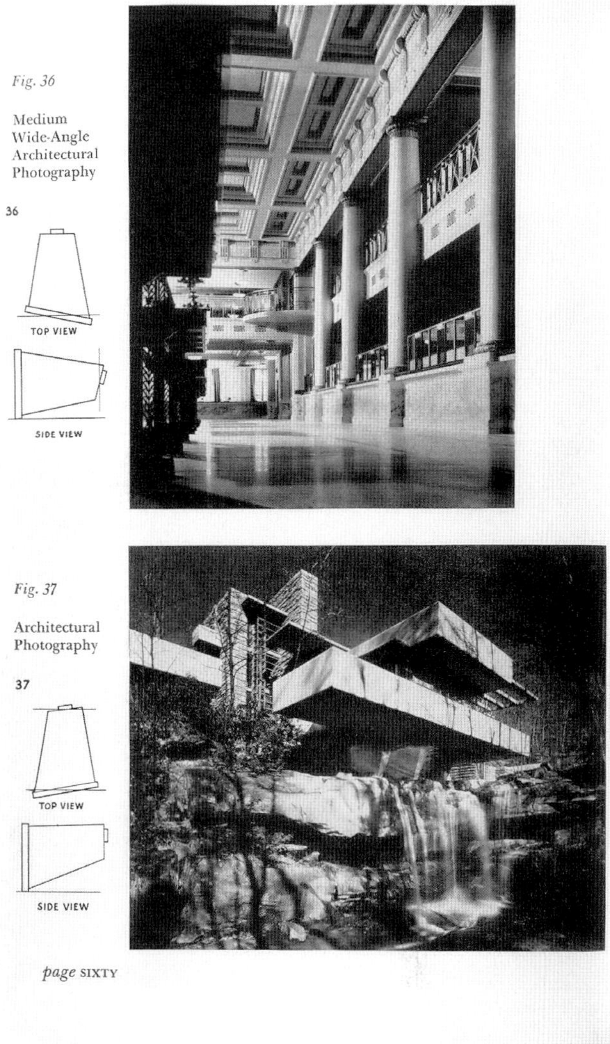

Figure 7.10. Plates from Kellsey, *Corrective Photography*, 60.

The most important postwar innovation announced in *Corrective Photography* was the invention of the front-swinging lens, which gave photographers greater depth of field. This technical innovation made it possible for the photographer to alter the orientation of the lens in relation to the camera back or negative holder. Photographers had long had the capacity to shift and swing the back of the camera, where the negative was housed as well. The flexibility of front shift controlled depth of field across angular surfaces. It enabled photographers to produce sharper pictures without focal distortion, because the lens orientation could be brought into closer correspondence to surfaces that ranged into the depth of the photograph at different angles. Plates from *Corrective Photography* explain the difference in graphic terms (Figures 7.9, 7.10).

These technological enhancements, from the greater flexibility of camera components to the visual effects produced by shift and swing lenses, were visible in

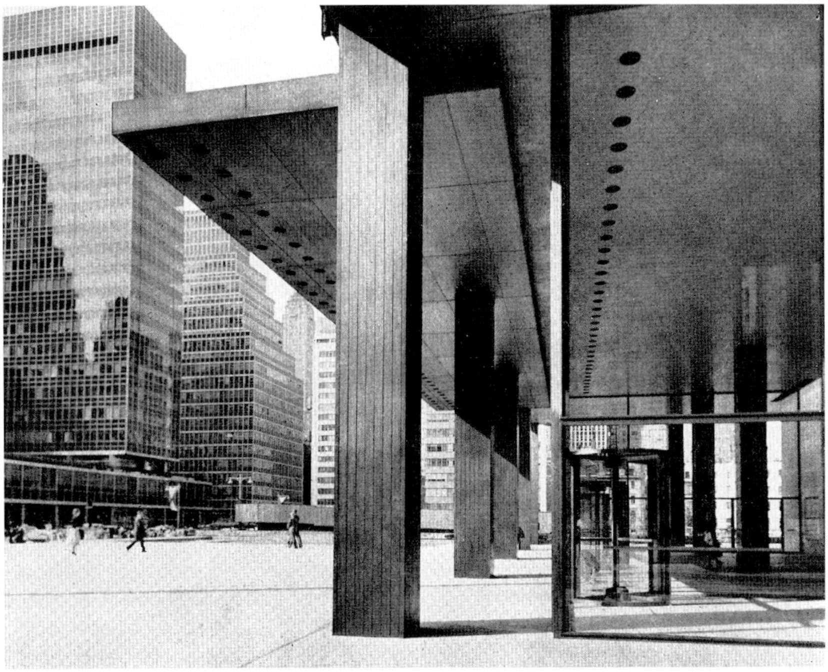

Figure 7.11. Entry to Seagram Building. From *L'Architecture d'Aujourd'hui* 79 (1958).

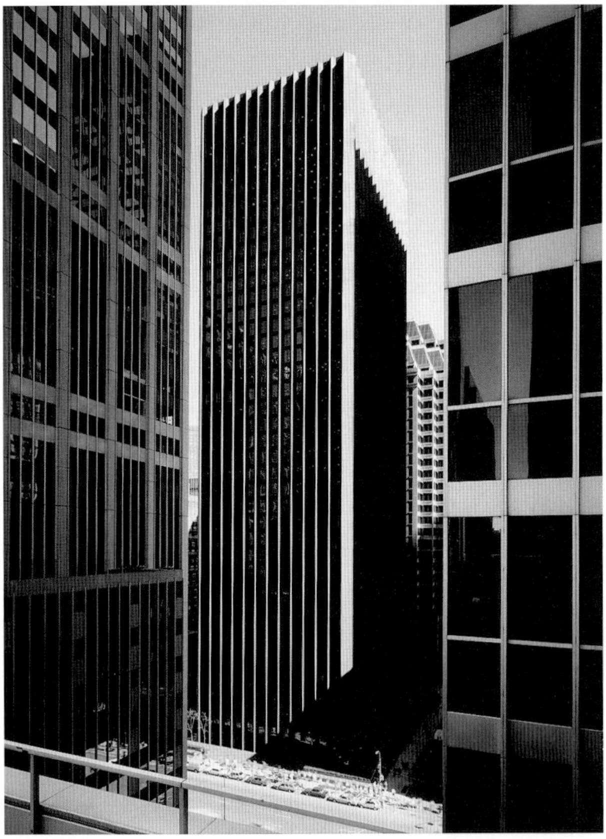

Figure 7.12. CBS Building, New York, 1965. Architect: Eero Saarinen. Photograph: Landov. Courtesy CBS/Landov.

architectural photographs. Generally, photographers grew more sophisticated in their ability to manipulate perspective and regularize the photographic process. One-point perspectives framed asymmetrically grew more frequent (Figure 7.11). In these photographs with two or more centers, one falls at the point of convergence of the lines of perspective and another corresponds roughly to the center of the field of the image. This was not new to postwar photography; a simpler version of the same kind of photograph appeared among the photographs of the Tugendhat House. There the photographer chose to alter the placement of the camera, presumably both to capture more information and to enliven the image (Figure 3.24). Postwar photographers used improved camera technologies to dramatize these asymmetrical one-point perspectives yet further. In contrast to earlier cameras, constrained by the combination of limited focal length (controlling the absolute size of the photograph) and depth of field, postwar cameras offered photographers far greater flexibility, making this image type more common and more visually compelling, thanks to enhanced depth of field. The most significant technological changes are often incremental, not related to initial invention but rather to stages in the acceleration that follows, as was the case with photography.

Front swing, with the greater depth of field it provided, helped photographers produce effects like those found in a closely framed view of Eero Saarinen's CBS Building (completed 1965) owned by Landov (Figure 7.12) or an overall view of Skidmore, Owings & Merrill's Union Carbide Headquarters Building (completed 1960) on Park Avenue by Ezra Stoller, as well as Mies's Seagram Building (completed 1957). The result is a crisper, more sharply focused photograph, one that rapidly became characteristic of postwar photography. Nevertheless, normative perspective composition remained the first choice of commercial photographers of architecture, despite innovations in photographic composition from the avant-gardes of the pre- and postwar years.

With interesting exceptions, the angled viewing of prewar avant-gardists shows up in American photographs of the postwar period in art photography and in populist stock photography for a general market more than it is found in commercial photography of architecture. Stock photo houses like Photo Researchers Incorporated marketed raking views of New York buildings similar to those produced in more radical versions by Aleksandr Rodchenko in Moscow before the war, or Berenice Abbott in New York before and after. In 1926 Erich Mendelsohn published a number of similar photographs taken by himself and others in *Amerika: Bilderbuch eines Architekten* (Figures 7.13, 7.14). Commercial architectural photographers in the United States, by contrast, went to considerable lengths to maintain the regime of standard perspective within most of their photographs, even as they became

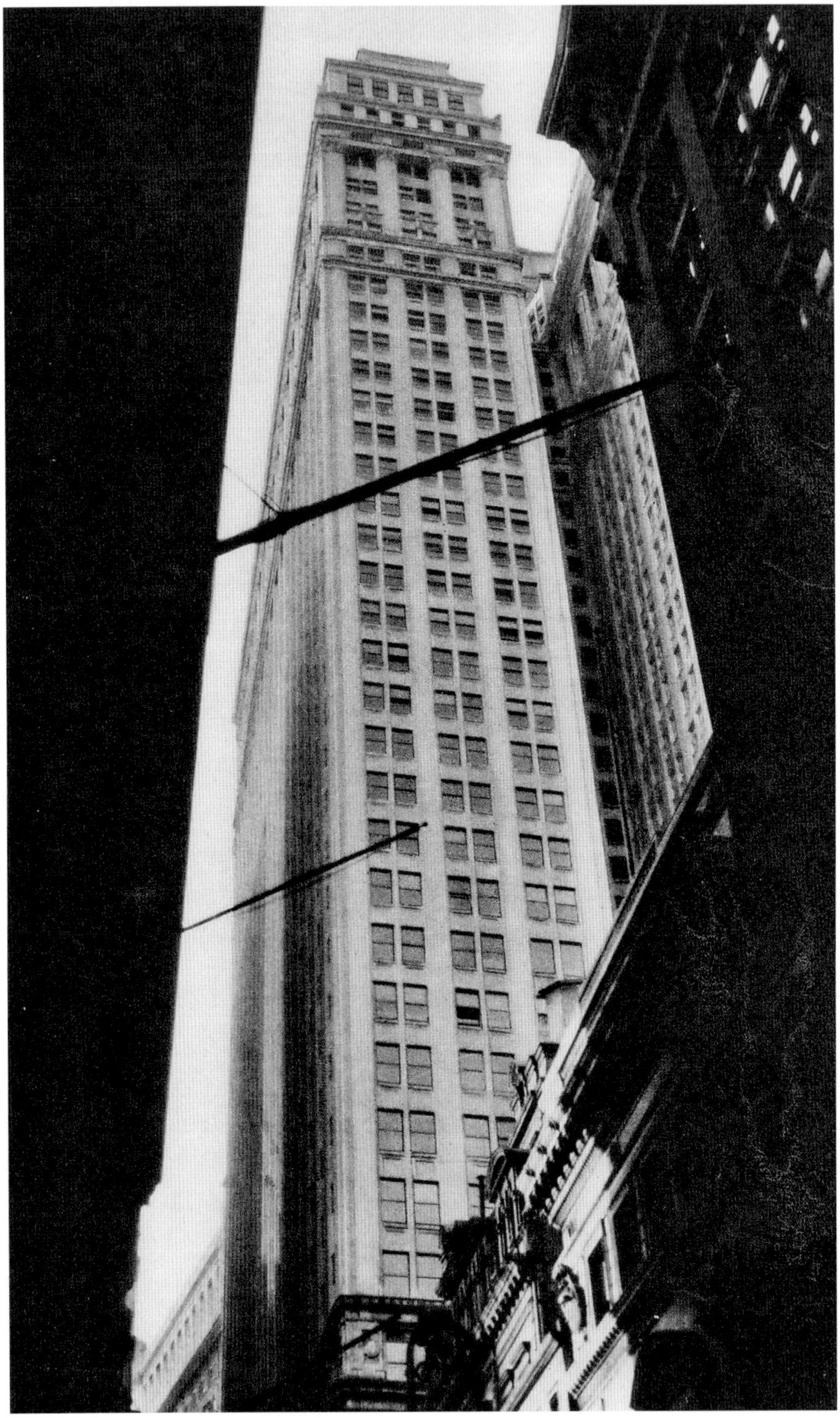

Figure 7.13. Equitable Trust Building, New York, as photographed by Erich Mendelsohn, in *Amerika: Bilderbuch eines Architekten* (Berlin: Rudolf Mosse, 1926).

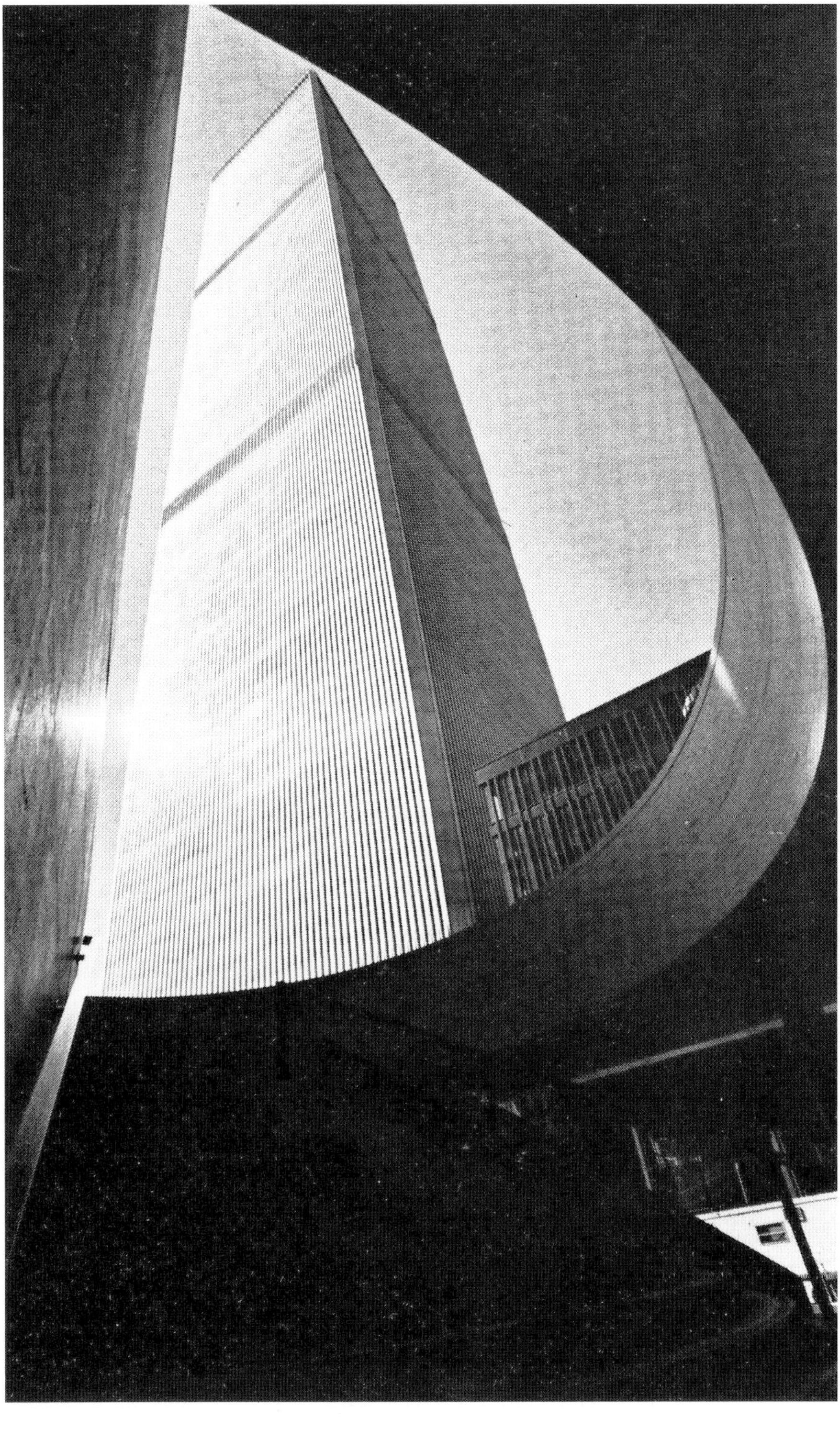

Figure 7.14. World Trade Center. Architect: Minoru Yamasaki. Photograph: Jan Lukas. From Manfredo Tafuri and F. Dal Co, *Modern Architecture* (Milan: Electa, 1976).

increasingly adept in its manipulation. In the case of high-rise buildings, there was no conflict in photographing architecture from high floors of neighboring skyscrapers, which give the appearance that the photographer may be floating in midair, well above the typical station point one meter above ground level.

How do these photographs differ from prewar architectural photographs, particularly those discussed in previous chapters? Photographs of postwar American architecture range from distant images of pristine object-buildings to close-ups of crisply rolled steel sections, as if just off the factory floor (Figure 7.8). The doubling of images (photographic and built) produces an effect of redundancy between industrialized architecture and industrialized photography. Perspective corrected by swing cameras but engendered by industrially produced rolled steel framing elements produced images with visual qualities radically different from those associated with earlier architecture. It is no longer abstract composition that governs these images of buildings, but instead a kind of hyperpresence of machine production as reflected in highly crafted photographs of I-beams, steel and glass detailing, or even cast concrete frameworks. Uniform visual fields substitute for illusions of depth.

These images convey a fiction of material presence that is in tension with similar rhetorics of presence and opticality in critical writing on abstract painting in the United States. In addition to Michael Fried's famous "Art and Objecthood," with its insistence that "presentness is grace," these photographs of architecture foreshadow Clement Greenberg's assessment of the common visual ambitions shared by architecture, sculpture, and painting in the same ten year period. In 1958, Greenberg wrote:

> The desire for "purity" works, as I have indicated, to put an even higher premium on sheer visibility and an even lower one on the tactile and its associations. . . . There is an attempt to overcome the distinctions between foreground and background; between formed space and space at large; between inside and outside; between up and down (many modernist buildings, like many modernist paintings, would look almost as well upside down or even stood on their sides). A related emphasis is on economy of physical substance. This manifests itself in the pictorial tendency to reduce all matter to two dimensions—to lines and surfaces that define or enclose space but hardly occupy it. Rendering substance entirely optical, and form, whether pictorial, sculptural, or architectural, as an integral part of ambient space—this brings anti-illusionism full circle. Instead of the illusion of things, we are now offered the illusion of modalities: namely, that matter is incorporeal, weightless, and exists only optically like a mirage. This kind of illusionism is stated in pictures whose paint surfaces and enclosing rectangles vibrate into the space around them; and in buildings that, apparently formed of lines alone, seem woven into the air.[18]

In architectural photographs by Ezra Stoller and other postwar photographers, enhanced depth of field as described above leads to equalized focus over the plane of the image. The new capacity of the camera to focus simultaneously on deep and shallow areas in a way that begins to equalize depth perception is not matched by the human eye. These images appear flattened, as all surfaces achieve nearly the same intensity.

The compensatory effect of architectural photographs that Hans Schmidt identified in 1902 (discussed in chapter 4) recurs here, where the photographer creates optical densification or intensification within the image itself to make up for the absence of spatial experience. Recalling how the wide-angle lens, for example, distorts perspectival space into a trumpet shape, a similar strategy here serves different goals. The wide-angle lens had intensified visual experience in the 1920s by enhancing the sense of depth, not diminishing it, precisely through the spatial exaggeration of the photograph—oversized foreground against tunnel-like background. In the case of the Seagram Building, by contrast, different camera technologies produced even focus throughout deep and shallow parts of the frame alike, flattening the photograph and the space it projects. A nearly complete reversal has occurred, between the immersive optical experience of the wide-angle lens of the late 1920s and this postwar photographic field condition, in which depth is neutralized by evenness of focus. This juxtaposition suggests how the tools of photography were used to depict architecture without being fully constrained by it. In both cases, photographic protocols reflect debates that were specific to two-dimensional media in conjunction with available photographic technology, imposing them on architecture through the photographic medium. There is no direct necessary correspondence between the photographer's intensification of two-dimensional representation and the spatial experience of a building. The relationship between the visual intensification provided by a skilled photographer and the building he or she depicts is as flexible as the Sinar itself.[19] Within this flexibility, certain arrangements are possible, others are not, and these are also temporally determined. Thus photographic architecture recasts its subject according to visual protocols of photography and the visual arts.

American photographers often refer to pictorial intensification—whether deep or shallow—as the effort to capture the "spirit" of the architecture. One of the best-known descriptions was actually written by a European architect. Richard Neutra's introduction to Julius Shulman's 1962 photography primer *Photographing Architecture and Interiors* suggests that the photographer must understand the architect's intention and translate it from three dimensions into two. The photographer "feels himself in, and gives what a camera can give."[20] We are thus returned to themes also described by Wilhelm Lotz in 1929 and noted in previous chapters; both suggest that camera recording of buildings is an approximate and correlative subjective practice, not a matter of objective documentation. Distortions produced by the camera appear permissible if they produce an intensified visual document relating a notion of "truth" about the building portrayed. But this intensification is imprecisely defined, suggesting that intensified optical experience might be correlated to bodily experience without offering any clear anchors or relays between these two affects. The architect usually sees this in terms of the camera's deficiencies: "Architectural photographers . . . apply themselves to the art of the befriended architect. They must select, to approximate *essential* memory images. . . . Technically, mechanically, chemically limited, [photography], naturally, can never be the same as the life object but it can approximate."[21] The correlation between intense opticality and haptic experience remains an interpretive matter, apparently not intended to attain any greater degree of specificity than that outlined by Neutra, or Shulman or Stoller or Joseph Molitor or Schmidt, or any others in their descriptions of their practice. It exists at the level of suggestion—hinted at by Greenberg, but generally left unarticulated as a specific goal for photography of buildings. And in this we seem not to have advanced from the same critiques made during the 1920s.

The optical intensification of photography combines with the doubling described above, in which highly industrialized cameras and highly industrialized architecture play against and reinforce each other in images. This is not to suggest that the *image* of technology and the trajectory of technological improvement in architecture were necessarily synchronized. What constituted "technological modernity" in photography or architecture at any given moment in time was not necessarily the same. We can only note the points of connection between the two media. Yet photography excelled at representing and intensifying an idea about technology for architecture, partly thanks to its own enhanced technical flexibilities. After the war, photographic images of American buildings, subject to optical intensification through photographic technique, constituted a different sort of "photo text" from that in use before.

The different histories of architecture and photography throughout the years surrounding World War II suggest a discrepancy between rates of development in the two fields. Technology change in building construction during wartime was controlled by highly specific needs.[22] Photographic technologies, by contrast, were characterized by accelerating change that was particularly intense as remote and aerial surveillance techniques intensified, putting pressure on a range of photographic developments. Pictures of rolled steel sections seemed to signify that the transformation of architecture into an industrialized practice had finally been completed "on the ground" thirty years after the Stuttgart settlement of 1927, at which this achievement had been prematurely announced. But at this historical juncture, photography processed pictures of architecture through a field condition of abstract formalist opticality. The technologies of photography, in other words, filtered the technologies of architecture through a set of photographic capacities.[23]

If Greenberg's comments on late modernist opticality can be mapped onto the photographic presentation of buildings, these must also be measured against their functionality as devices of propaganda and salesmanship. In other words, Greenberg's optical utopia might be summoned up by the hyperpresence of architecture in these photographs. But the complex of "discursive spaces" they occupied conditioned their reception. Not generally used as modernist manifestos, they worked efficiently as instruments for broadcasting and commerce. As new building products of the metal and glass industries, as cultural products of the architects who designed them, or as products of the corporations housed in the depicted buildings, these images were part of the apparatus of commercial advertising. At the same time, in discourse on architecture culture they offered proof of the victory of modern architecture over forces of both left- and right-wing extremism, the forces that had threatened the practitioners of the Neues Bauen in Germany before they emigrated. They were all these things at once.

Despite the unevenness of innovation described above, modernization was an accelerating process in the nineteenth and twentieth centuries, in architecture as well as in photography. This meant that the rate at which buildings became obsolescent sped up over the course of time. In Germany this process of acceleration was temporarily halted by events leading up to and following 1945, when new building came to a standstill and old buildings were destroyed. At the same time, wish images of a parallel world in the making in the United States streamed into the country in books, magazines, and slide lectures. The stylistic hegemony of postwar American modernism lies partly here, in the power of a set of photographic images circulated as if they represented an absolute standard for contemporary building. Other sorts of images, such as those from the Eastern bloc, did not circulate.[24] In general, if the fictionalization of Western modernity was one of the central tasks of twentieth-century architecture, then we might pay special attention to the illustrations of that process as they arrived back in the land of origin of many of the original leaders of modernism.

THE GERMAN RECEPTION

In a seminar at the Technical University in Berlin in 1967, Alison and Peter Smithson described Mies's significance for their practice,[25] noting that the Minerals and Metals Research Building "is the building that captured our personal interest when it was first published in England in 1947." In fact, the January 1946 issue of the *Architects'*

Journal included three photographs of the Chicago project taken by Mies's new photographers, the firm of Hedrich Blessing (Figure 8.12). The Smithsons continued, "Mies has without doubt moved even more towards the use of repetition because the culture he is working in is particularly good at quality control of serially produced metal objects, and as he has always loved metal he swims freely in this technology."[26] The Smithsons explicitly credited these 1946 photographs as the source of their Hunstanton Secondary Modern School (HSMS) in Norfolk, England. They absorbed factory production—with all its processes and infrastructures—as a defining characteristic of Mies's American work. How this necessarily partial view of Miesian architecture affected their subsequent work is explored in chapter 8. Here, the photographs of postwar American architecture that circulated in the international press are lifted away from conditions of building in the United States to landing sites in postwar Germany. We have already considered the effect of changed camera technologies; we might now turn to the more difficult question of photographic reception among German audiences.

The disjunction between Weimar and American work was both mediated and contravened by photography long before American firms under the leadership of Mies or Hugh Stubbins received large building commissions in Berlin beginning in the late 1950s.[27] Earlier photographs, such as those done for Mies by the Berliner Bildbericht and the Czech photographer Rudolf de Sandalo, continued to circulate in the architectural press throughout the postwar years. As new photographs joined them, neither the photographs nor the buildings they depicted looked similar to the earlier work. Despite this fact, modern architecture was presented as an organic evolution.

Information about American building reached Germany in the years after 1945 along three obvious avenues: visits by architects to American cities, the circulation of American exhibitions (on architecture and general subjects) throughout Europe in the wake of the Marshall Plan, and publications of photographs of American buildings in magazines, scholarly journals, and books, both German and foreign language. In these years, from 1945 through the early 1950s, the terms of subsequent debate had not yet hardened into the clear ideological divisions that would soon emerge in response to the war itself and to the political stakes between East and West.

Photographs of American life brought to Europe in the propaganda crusades of the Marshall Plan and the U.S. Information Agency (USIA) were portable and easy to transport.[28] The Marshall Plan exhibits began as modest affairs that traveled to German cities; the USIA projects were more elaborate. They ultimately merged with the world's fairs that continued a prewar tradition (dating back to the nineteenth century), now overlaid with the global politics of the Cold War. The famous

Khrushchev-Nixon "kitchen debate" of 1959 in Moscow, for example, took place on the crossroads between postwar propaganda and world's fair promotion. The exhibitions informed the general public about the advantages of American capitalism through displays of consumer goods and industrial power.

More specialized exhibitions also detailed the achievements of American architects in selected European venues. Traveling exhibitions (1945, 1949, and 1951), Walter Gropius's 1947 visit, the exhibition of Gropius and Mies at the Kestner-Gesellschaft in Hannover in 1951, and a range of other exhibitions on American work crisscrossed Europe in these years. Added to the exhibitions on American buildings were professional journals on architecture. By and large, journals in Germany that had ceased publication between 1943 and 1945 resumed in the early postwar years (from 1946 on), often under new names. *Deutsche Bauzeitung* and *Bauwelt* were both suspended during the war; the former resumed publication as *Bauzeitung* in 1946, the latter as *Neue Bauwelt* in 1947. These journals featured not only new American building but also discussions about the current direction of modern architecture and particularly the most pressing questions that faced German architects in relation to aspects of reconstruction.

German periodicals from 1946 through 1949 published articles about and photographs of American architecture as soon as they resumed production. Publication increased further in the early 1950s, as new construction in Europe also resumed, becoming relatively intense after 1957. Many focused on the American buildings published in German-language periodicals in the postwar years, and on the émigrés. *Baukunst und Werkform,* edited by Alfons Leitl and Ulrich Conrads in Darmstadt, and the Swiss *Bauen und Wohnen* published work by Richard Neutra, R.E. Windisch, Gropius, Mies, and many others in these years. Mies appeared in the European press from 1946 onward, with the density of publication increasing in the 1950s, particularly after the second German edition of his 1947 MoMA exhibition catalog of 1957.

Architects such as Erich Mendelsohn and Karl Schneider, major figures in Weimar architecture, were less frequently encountered, which suggests that historical significance in Germany mattered less than contemporary success in the United States to international architectural media. Young German architects claimed to have first learned about Mies through American projects at this time; absent from Germany since 1937, with much of his work elsewhere or intentionally suppressed by the architect himself, his name had to be reintroduced to an architecture scene that he had formerly dominated.[29] The postwar scene refracted a new history of interwar modernism that omitted figures whose postwar influence was diminished, tainted, or absent altogether. Thus postwar accounts of the history of modernism diminished the importance of Mendelsohn, Bruno Taut, Hannes Meyer, Hans Poelzig, and others who had played critical roles in defining interwar modernism. Instead, Mies, Gropius, Breuer, and Le Corbusier dominated these histories as they dominated the postwar scene.

Travel across the Atlantic had grown increasingly frequent after the war. Photographs by Hermann Mäckler, for example, from a visit to the United States were published in *Baukunst und Werkform* in 1949 (Mäckler participated in the debate about Schwarz's address two years later).[30] But the effect of seeing buildings in photographs is not negated by site visits, which simply add another level of experience to that provided by photographs, and vice versa. The two don't cancel each other out—or, rather, site visits don't cancel out the persistent visual effect of photographs. The conditions of either can be described independently because they function more or less independently—one as optical, the other as embodied experience.

Mies's postwar reputation in Europe grew as the photographic presence of his work increased. Although Johnson's catalog had been available from 1947, it appears not to have been accessible to German architects until significantly later.[31] An early article of 1947 was followed by more publications in 1949. After the 1951 joint Gropius–Mies exhibition at the Kestner-Gesellschaft (in Mies's case, largely imported from MoMA), Mies entered the competition for the Mannheim Theater in 1953, a competition for which he was celebrated.[32] As the 1950s progressed, Mies's earlier German work was overshadowed by his American projects, from the Illinois Institute of Technology (IIT) to the Seagram Building to the unbuilt 1958 office pavilion for Bacardi that would later evolve into the New National Gallery design.[33] A definitive language of steel and glass appeared as the most salient characteristic of this work in numerous architectural photographs published in the architectural press even before the buildings were completed.

Among the photographs published after the war, particularly in Mies's case, there were many construction photographs. Drawings and photographs of models of projects currently under construction on American sites also appeared, showing what distant architectural markets were consuming in more prosperous economies. Construction photographs gave the appearance of absolute currency; they even suggested that architectural progress might move in advance of its own images. The embrace of American modernism that runs throughout these publications leaves little room for Schwarz's ambivalence about the "glass cubes" (Glaswürfeln) of contemporary skyscraper architecture, to which we turn now.

In his 1951 Darmstadt talk, Schwarz lamented contemporary conditions of modern building, condemning architectural photography in particular for its abstraction and reification of elemental architectural relationships best represented in plan, section, and elevation (i.e., in drawings). As German architects struggled amid material shortages and reconstruction, Schwarz took an independent position that combined rejection of the Nazi past with unquestioning reversion to interwar modern architecture. First broadcast at the 1951 conference "Mensch und Raum" (the second of the Darmstädter Gespräche that took place between 1950 and 1975),[34] Schwarz's remarks triggered the "Bauhaus-Debatte" of 1953 when his "Bilde Künstler, rede nicht" appeared in *Baukunst und Werkform* in January of that year. In animated responses to Schwarz's article, architects debated the legacy of the Bauhaus in postwar Germany. *Baukunst und Werkform* published dissenting articles that fought back against Schwarz's critique.

BAUHAUS AND ARCHITECTURAL PHOTOGRAPHY, 1951–53

Schwarz's disavowal of Bauhaus functionalism drew a considerable reaction; Alfons Leitl published no fewer than seven rebuttals in the issue of *Baukunst und Werkform* that followed the one containing Schwarz's "Bilde Künstler, rede nicht"; he gave Schwarz space to respond to these commentaries in April 1953, and the dispute continued throughout the year in *Baukunst und Werkform* and other journals.[35] The Bauhaus-Debatte is well-known through Ulrich Conrads and Winfried Nerdinger's 1994 Bauwelt-Fundament anthology. Left out of this anthology, however, were specific responses to Schwarz's condemnation of the architectural photograph.

The first of these defenses of photography for building was written by Conrads himself and published in "Brief über Architektur und Fotografie," which appeared directly following Schwarz's 1953 article.[36] Leitl, editor of the journal, joined the two articles with a photographic essay consisting of work by the American topographic photographer Wright Morris (with no accompanying text) that were interleaved through both articles, and concluded the essay with a photograph of London suburbs from 1934 by the German émigré photographer Bill Brandt (Figure 7.15).[37] Although he kept the Bauhaus debate at arm's length, publishing opinion and counteropinion, Leitl felt entitled to defend his own industry from the outset, demonstrating the positive role that photographs of architecture played in constructing architectural discourse by showing, not telling.[38] He counterposed three opening epigraphs. An excerpt from André Malraux summarized an important point—that reproduction provides an "effective medium for the process of intellection to which we submit art"—at the same time that it confirmed Schwarz's claim, namely, that "art history . . . has become a history of that which can be photographed." This was followed by an excerpt from Schwarz's 1951 "Das Anliegen der Baukunst." A third heading titled "Der Photograph" included a parenthetical note to the Morris photographs interleaved throughout the following pages.[39] Conrads thus offered

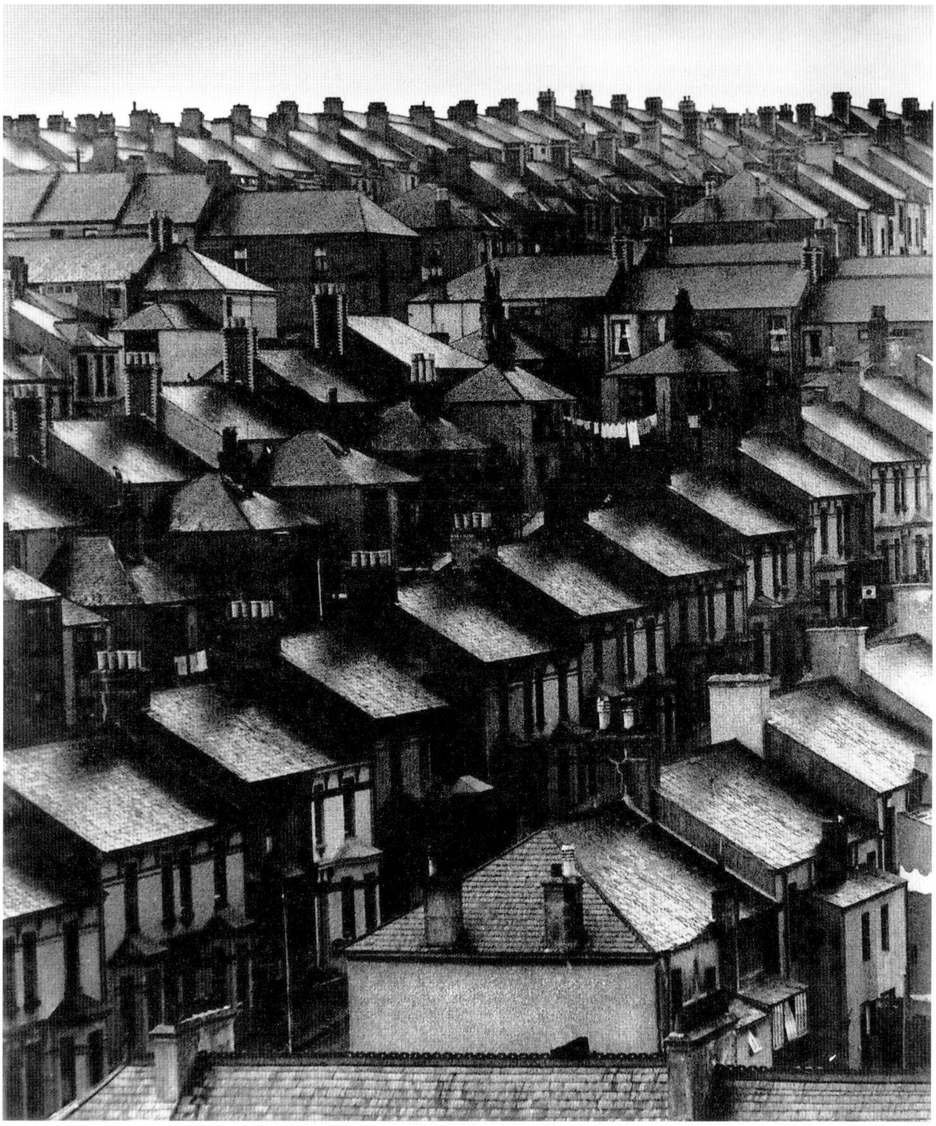

Figure 7.15. Bill Brandt, *Sky Lightens over London*, 1934.
From *Baukunst und Werkform* (1953). Copyright Bill Brandt Archive.

up the three poles of a debate: the photographer set against the architect and the historian.

Conrads argued for the importance and value of photography in constructing discourse and in the creation of a contemporary *Weltbild,* or world picture. Acknowledging the limitations of photography of architecture, including its tendency to abstraction (one of Schwarz's chief complaints), Conrads went on to claim that architectural photography abstracts too little, not too much, from the standpoint of the architect—"For the reproduction of that which is of meaning to the building master, the pencil has always given better service."[40] He challenged Schwarz's claims with the counterclaim that the real vehicle of abstraction is the drawing, not the photograph. *Abstraction* has different meanings in these two texts: for Schwarz, it referred to the reductions enforced by the generality of capitalism in cultural markets; for Conrads, it denoted the exclusion of aspects of building other than form subject to the controlling hand of the architect.

Conrads's main point, however, follows. Using the Morris photographs as proof, he noted, "Photography can speak of architecture."[41] Directly contradicting Schwarz with the use of his own metaphor, Conrads alluded to the memorability of the photographs of "abandoned buildings in towns and small cities in North America." He reflected on the value added by photography to our cognition of these buildings by noting how "all the more astonishing is the effectiveness [of this image], together with our inability to forget its 'common form.' Nothing is more possible to photograph than style, when ventured by a master photographer. . . . The 'staring eye' has given our thoughts immeasurable dynamic possibility, has gifted our feelings with the inklings of a greater reality, and our eyes the plurality of comparison, with which we can see where we are."[42] Thus Conrads outlined a positive agency for photography that rests precisely on its pictorialization of form and the interpretive frame within which photographs, not buildings, are viewed.

The second essay on architectural photography appeared later in 1953, written by the art historian Hans Gerhard Evers, also one of the organizers of the Darmstädter Gespräche. Noting the rapid changes in photographic technique (attested by the analysis above), Evers celebrated the present photographic moment as follows: "When I clarify to myself how incessantly things change, and how in thirty years what is here today will be here no longer, then . . . I want to love photography right away, quickly, so long as we still have it."[43] Also making a case for the positive agency of the medium, he picked up where Conrads left off, noting that it provides architects with a hybrid of real building and abstract representation that might influence new architecture in a positive direction.[44] Noting that abstraction is an inevitable process of representational systems (spelled out in slightly ironic tone through a rehearsal of basic semiotics), Evers went on: "Through abstraction, through dissolution into an ostensible nothing, that which is thought and meant, that which is seen internally, will be translated. The transformation [of architecture] into an intellectual/spiritual term reckons on others being able to grasp and decode it."[45] Furthermore, he noted, photography activates fantasy and provides a common text for discourse or communication:

> But that is precisely what is grand, that it abstracts! Thus can I send you a photograph, and you are capable of unfolding the world from it. It has to do with your

> own capacity and fantasy, with which you can recall color, and space, and size, not with a bit of cellulose and gelatin.
>
> That is just what is grand, and photography, which is generally comprehensible, has become a word speech better than English or Esperanto. Where would there be an image speech that is so generally understandable as this? Do you believe that today's architecture and its dissemination on the planet would be possible without books, newspapers, photographs?[46]

Evers defended architectural photography and publication against Schwarz's claim that it belonged to the realm of the art historian, and not the architect, that the real architect, "der wirkliche Baumeister," created environments and communal experiences that could not be represented in photographs. Evers's defense outlines the terms in which architectural photography operated as an export product in the years immediately following World War II—as a medium that allowed for projections of imagined postwar realities that had something to do with the logistical realities of faraway building projects but a great deal to do with contemporary social and material realities "on the ground" at the point of reception. Finally, Evers concluded with the claim that photography is an instrument of thought: "a reduction of the visible, but a key to the thinkable."[47] Thus the potential agency of photography was identified explicitly by German architects and critics, perhaps for the first time since Lucia Moholy argued similarly in 1927. The field condition of postwar American photography, received as a projection of longings for recovery in Europe, may well have elevated systematized vision and bureaucracy to the status of the heroic, in the process transforming it from one thing into quite another.

CONCLUSION

The contrast between senders and receivers of architectural photographs appeared graphically between postwar Germany and the United States. Such a gap between producer and consumer typically proceeds from incommensurate levels of economic, commercial, or industrial development. In economic terms, it echoes other versions of capitalism; the exploitation of geographic advantage for the sake of competitive market building. In this case, however, the uneven differential of geography proceeds from traumatic history: from catastrophe, moral or ethical failure, military defeat, vanquished foe versus triumphant victor. The process I have just narrated: Clear a site, brutally, in both a temporal and a physical sense; enclose the site with scaffolding bedecked with images of past glory (the Neues Bauen). Drop into it images of an alternate reality only tenuously connected to the local past. Then try to build some sort of provisional future. Photographs were in this case literally the "avant-garde" of the ideological project of the United States, simultaneously commercial, cultural, and philosophical. They smuggled ideological product in under the camouflage of an interwar dream. At the same time, their export values were not the same as their import values. German audiences weren't buying the product wholesale. Instead, they repurposed photographs of corporate skyscrapers for conditions that differed from those that pertained in America. The juggernaut of America as seen in photographs appeared as it really was: the threat of a new imperialism.

In postwar Germany architectural photography became one of the stakes in arguments about the immediate future of architecture as an expression of social or cultural value. Rudolf Schwarz's collapse of architectural photography with other abstractions of late capitalism was resisted in the German press; his opinions of interwar modernism were more vocally condemned, if somewhat unconvincingly. At the same time, the photographs flowing into German periodicals, or into the hands of German architects, show how photography had changed over the course of the war and how alterations to its subject matter—architecture—also meant that buildings were now different from what they had been in the Weimar and National Socialist years. In postwar Germany photographs of a new kind of modern building simultaneously announced the new and announced that its focus was no longer Europe generally and Germany specifically. Rather, the center of heat in Bauhaus modernism had migrated westward, it seemed, leaving Germans at the periphery both literally and figuratively. At the same time, this remoteness from the center of activity—a new condition for German architects—put added pressure on photography. Not only photography of new buildings but also photography of old ones became the subjects of heightened interest. In this condition, it became possible for architects to begin to ask what the productive effects of photography on architecture might be—how the agency of picture making might be enacted cyclically, in new architecture built with the information gathered from photographs clearly in mind. To have identified this question does not suggest that answers were immediately found: many postwar German buildings reflect their American counterparts and invite further examination of the role of the image in the formation of new building. At the same time, as some German architects questioned the effects of architectural photography, others had already embraced the implicit promise of photographic architecture for new building, as the next chapter will show.

Much more decisive is the unfathomable influence of Mies van der Rohe on the younger generation. This could accelerate to a dangerous level. What attracts these youths to sacrifice everything is the lack of compromise to which Mies van der Rohe aspires and which he is willing to adopt. This is not the only way to solve today's architectural problems. It is nevertheless remarkable, that in Mies van der Rohe's handling pure surface and constructive elements of an extreme avant-garde spirit meet the latest production methods, stimulating even more far-reaching solutions: magic and matter!

—SIGFRIED GIEDION,
"THE MORAL INFLUENCE OF
MIES VAN DER ROHE'S ARCHITECTURE"

8. THE PHOTOGRAPHIC ARCHITECTURE OF THE HUNSTANTON SCHOOL

The Hunstanton Secondary Modern School (Figure 8.1) in the village of Hunstanton in Norfolk, England, was published extensively in the architectural press even before it was finished. Construction photographs of the building show large white circles painted on its plate-glass walls to prevent humans and other animals from walking or flying into them as the steel frame of the building was slowly filled. Playful sketches were finger-etched on these white circles by the sculptor Eduardo Paolozzi (Figure 8.2).[1] The photographer was Paolozzi's friend and fellow member in the Independent Group Nigel Henderson, who used these pictograms when he depicted the unfinished building as a series of frontally layered screens established by the building's steel frame. Objects, people, walls seen through glass and graffiti appearing on the surface of glass fill pictures that interweave transparent surface, metallic frame, and open space throughout the depth of the photograph.[2] Spatial ambiguity recurs in a different manner in pictures where foreground objects appear artificially enlarged in contrast to those in the background that are equally artificially diminished, thanks to the effects of the wide-angle lens (Figure 8.3) (see chapter 3).

Henderson's Hunstanton photographs are unexpected reflections on a work in progress by his friends and colleagues Alison Smithson and Peter Smithson. They underline the ambiguity of space in two-dimensional representation, highlighting the multifaceted ways that photographic images shape ideas about architecture. Two features dominate these photographs: a steel frame and extensive surfaces of plate glass that appear both reflective and transparent. The visible (and thereby metaphorical)

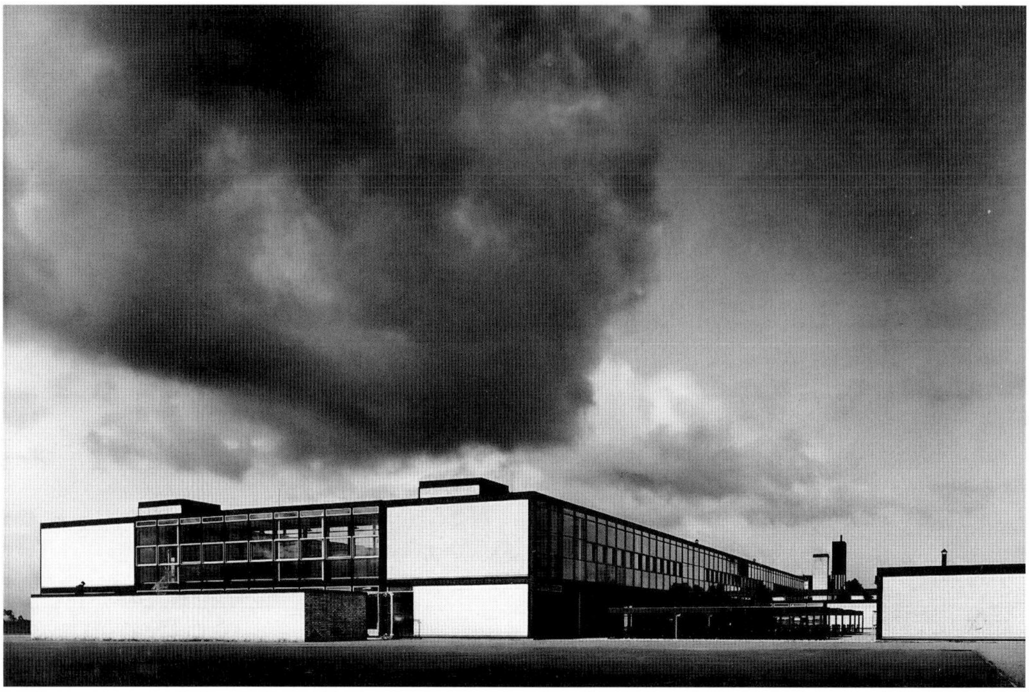

Figure 8.1. Hunstanton School, 1954. Architects: Alison and Peter Smithson. Photograph: Hugo Reginald de Burgh Galwey. Smithson Family Archive with kind permission of RIBA Library Photographs Collection.

Figure 8.2. Hunstanton School under construction, with Alison Smithson, 1953. Photograph: Nigel Henderson. Smithson Family Archive.

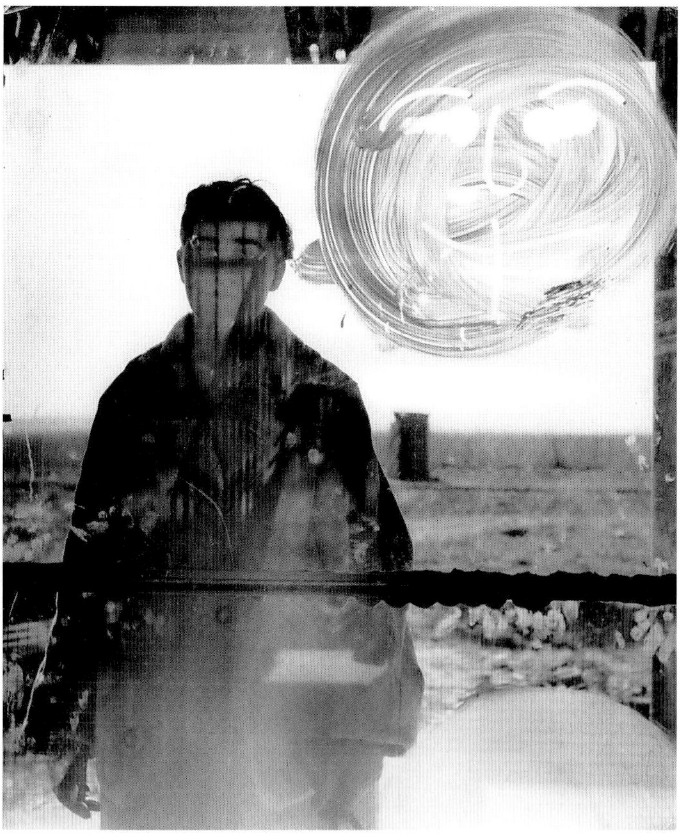

clarity provided by the building's frame is offset by the pictorial potential of its glass surfaces (surfaces used here for drawing pictograms). The copresence of the two suggests something like an architectural version of photographic indexicality, the chemical process by which light imprints an image onto photographic film. Hunstanton's steel structural frame appears similarly irreducible, just as its pictorial aspects (glass, geometric clarity, proportion) point to the building's status as an image despite or within its three-dimensional corporeality as a building. Henderson's photographs make the paradoxical copresence of image and structural object especially apparent and suggest that material weight and ephemeral appearance had come to leverage equal weight in postwar modern architecture. Following the struggles of German architects to come to terms with photographic transmission, the Smithsons, with their collaborator Henderson, found a way to negate the clear distinction between object and picture, remaining focused on the project now shared between them: architecture as a combination of thought, image, and concrete material.

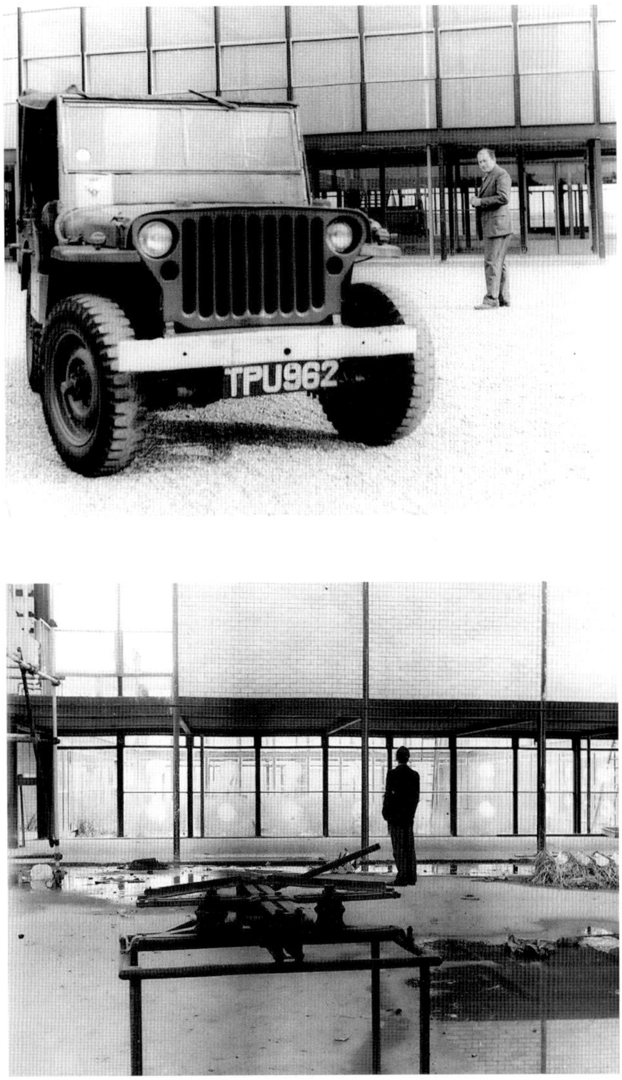

Figure 8.3. Hunstanton School under construction, 1953. Photographs: Nigel Henderson. Smithson Family Archive.

HUNSTANTON SCHOOL

Hunstanton School was built between 1951 and 1954 after a competition held in 1950. It was part of a general campaign for the construction of urgently needed new school buildings in the late 1940s and 1950s in the United Kingdom. The Smithsons, recent graduates of the University of Newcastle, won the commission on the judgment of the single assessor, schools architect Denis Clarke Hall. Construction commenced in March 1951; the project came to a halt for fourteen months because of a steel shortage, resuming in summer 1952. During the three-year span of construction, the Smithsons moved on to other work. They entered the Coventry Cathedral competition in 1951 and the competition for London housing at Golden Lane in 1952—both competitions brought them additional public attention.

In 1953, they began working with Henderson and Eduardo Paolozzi to curate the exhibition "Parallel of Life and Art" at the Institute of Contemporary Art in London. In addition, both Smithsons wrote about architecture, publishing letters and short articles in the architectural press from 1952. The design of Hunstanton was not substantially altered during this time, but the reputation of its young designers had grown by 1954, largely thanks to the school. More important, perhaps, decisions about how to photograph the finished building were made long after it had been designed; this was particularly significant in light of the rapid professional and artistic development of the young partnership. The Smithsons' architectural practice remained as dynamic after the school was finished as it had been during the construction period, when they entered the Coventry and Golden Lane competitions. Their work moved through a range of stylistic and conceptual approaches throughout the 1950s and 1960s, such that Hunstanton cannot be said to set a stylistic direction that they maintained in years to follow, even if certain preoccupations recurred with regularity. More important for the discussion to follow, the architects changed their views on contemporary architecture within the span of time it took for the job itself to be completed.

The school's complex of buildings sits on a podium with a two-story main building organized by a repeating bay structure ten feet by twenty or twenty-four feet that surrounds an open center where two grassy courtyards serve solely as light courts for the interior on either side of a large central hall. The second-floor classrooms are reached by ten individual sets of stairs that serve two or three classrooms each; the ground floor is largely taken up with offices, service spaces, hall, and caretaker apartment. The geometry of the central rectangular block leaves additional programmed spaces to be accommodated in separate volumes: the kitchen, storerooms, and service spaces are partially separated; the gymnasium also stands apart.

The glass perimeter of the building consists of steel frames welded directly to the main load-bearing structure mounted on concrete foundations. The steel was left visible but painted. End and partition walls were masonry unit construction with fair-faced brick of a yellow hue. Floors and roof were assembled from prefabricated reinforced concrete planks lifted into place by crane. The prefabricated floor slabs were inset between the steel structure with the help of a hydraulic jack that pried the steel apart until the concrete could be dropped into the web of the beam. Once the jack was removed, the steel returned to its original shape, trapping concrete members within a structural cage.[3] The construction system used small-gauge steel in a "plastic" structural system. The engineer, Ronald Jenkins of Ove Arup's office, developed the design in dialogue with Sir John Baker at Cambridge University, and with the assistance of Ronald Hobbs and a young draftsman hired just for this purpose, Jack Zunz. An early publication of the building in the *National Builder* in April 1953 explained its innovations:

> The orthodox method [of design], developed for bolted or riveted construction, penalises welded structures seriously. The plastic method of design, which is rational, being based on the real behaviour of the structure, overcomes this difficulty and is particularly applicable to welded structures where the joints between the members are designed to be rigid. . . . the orthodox method is liable to under-estimate seriously the collapse load of a rigidly jointed structure, such as a welded portal frame, and so to be extravagant.[4]

The plastic system transformed a welded steel cage into an integrated system functioning much like a timber balloon frame, as a single entity making use of smaller individual elements. This system of construction differed substantially from the steel construction frame then in use in Chicago in buildings by Ludwig Mies van der Rohe, a reference point for the Smithsons in this building.

PHOTOGRAPHIC EVIDENCE

Publications about the British school included an astounding array of photographs in an equally impressive variety of genres, from construction photographs to Nigel Henderson's quasi-surrealist tableaux to conventional architectural photographs, press photographs taken by photographers from local newspapers, and later critical reportage. These are supplemented by a significant array of unpublished photographs held in archives. The array of photographic genres was joined by an equally wide array of publication venues, from daily newspapers to the trade presses to advertising (Figures 8.4a, 8.4b). The published photographs in which the building appeared first are the primary focus here—these include the construction photographs that were preemptively published before the building was finished and the presentation photographs taken by professional architectural photographers once the school opened for students in the fall of 1954. The school has been photographed with other purposes in mind as well (Figure 8.5).

Photographs of the building under construction also served different purposes. A local photographic agency, Swain and Company, worked on commission from

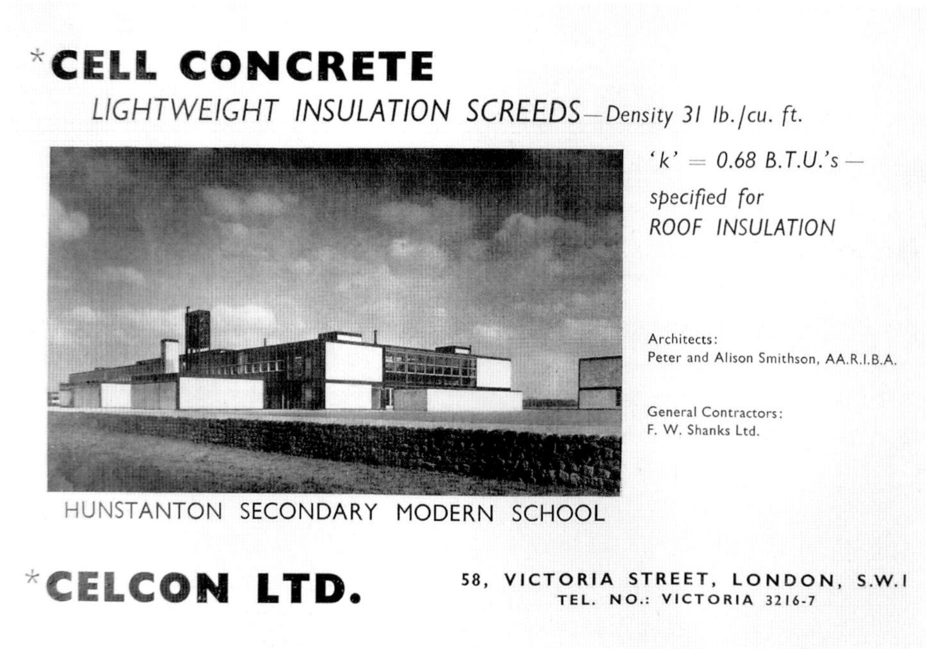

a

Figure 8.4. Advertisements featuring Hunstanton School: (a) advertisement for Celcon, 1954; (b) advertisement for Luxfer (glass products used by Pilkington Brothers), 1954. Smithson Family Archive with kind permission of RIBA Library Photographs Collection.

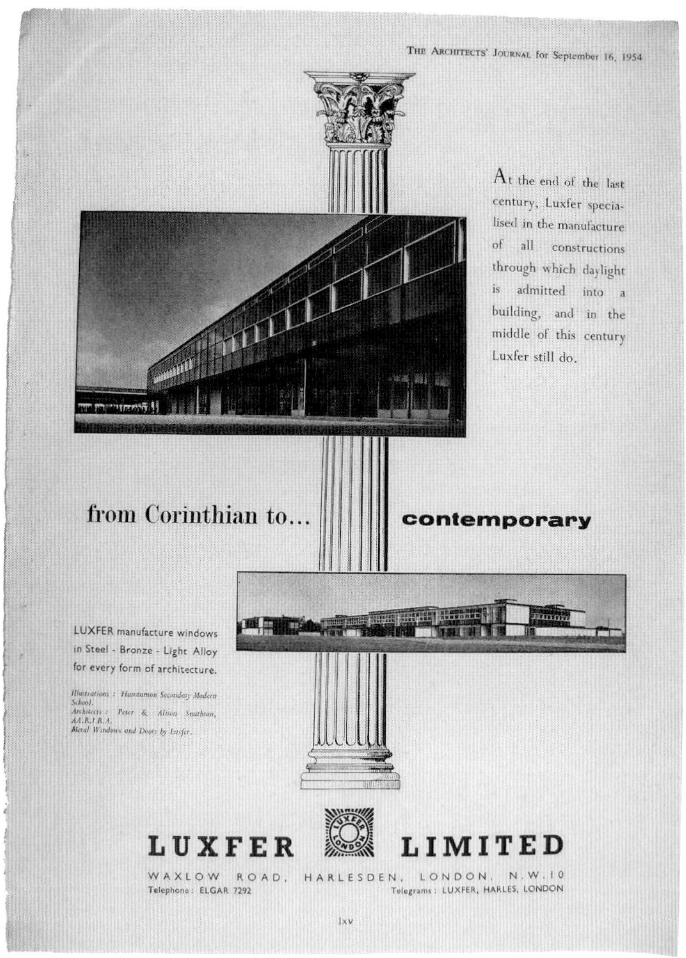

b

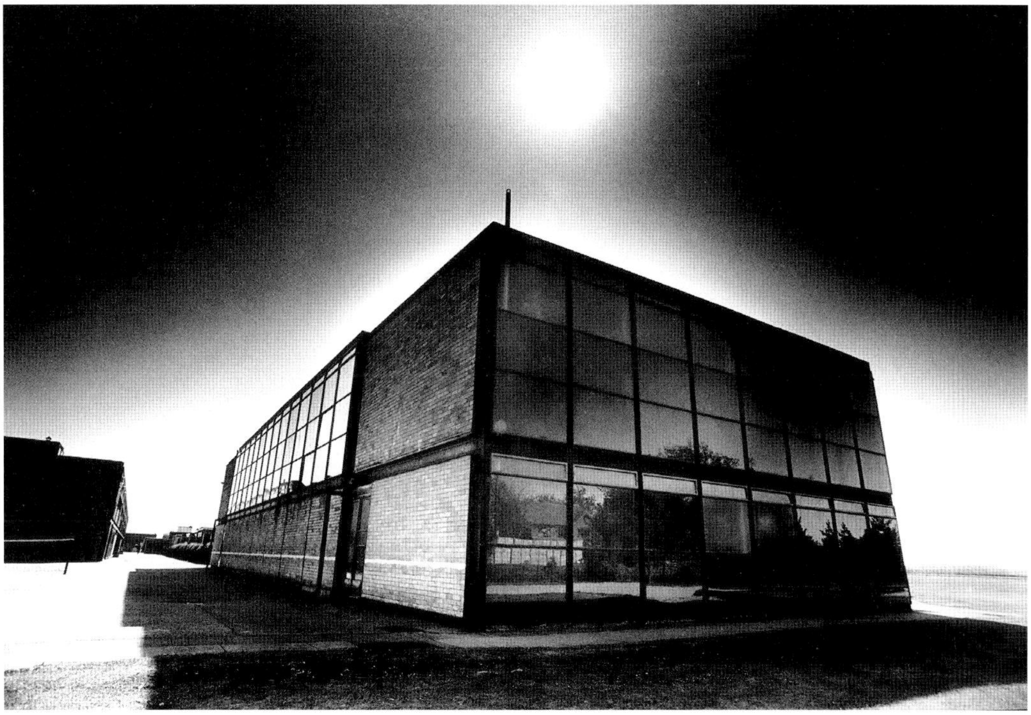

Figure 8.5. Hunstanton School as illustrated by Martin Pawley in the *Architects' Journal* (1984). Photograph: Douglis Firth. Architectural Press Archive/RIBA Library Photographs Collection.

the steel erectors Boulton and Paul as the building went up. These photos appeared in the trade presses and were republished in the Smithson monograph *The Charged Void* in 2001. The Smithsons themselves kept at least two photographic albums through which it is possible to follow the process of construction from start to finish; the series spans from the erection of the steel frame to the final installation of plate-glass panels (Figure 8.6).[5] The Hunstanton case is unusual in quantity and detail (although one finds an even greater volume of such photographs, generally taken by fewer agents, on certain construction sites of the 1970s). Some of the Hunstanton photographs were published in a preliminary conversation between the architects and the engineer Jenkins, an essential collaborator, in the *Architects' Journal* in September 1953.[6] Henderson's photographs of the school while it was still under construction had a completely different purpose and effect, as noted in the opening paragraphs of this chapter. Finally, Peter Smithson took his own photographs of the school both before and after it was finished; snapshots and journalistic images of the unfinished building are also present in significant numbers in prints held by archives and in the press cut sheets that the Smithsons kept with some care.

In addition to these preliminary photographs, two professional photographers under commission from outside agents (not the architects or client) photographed

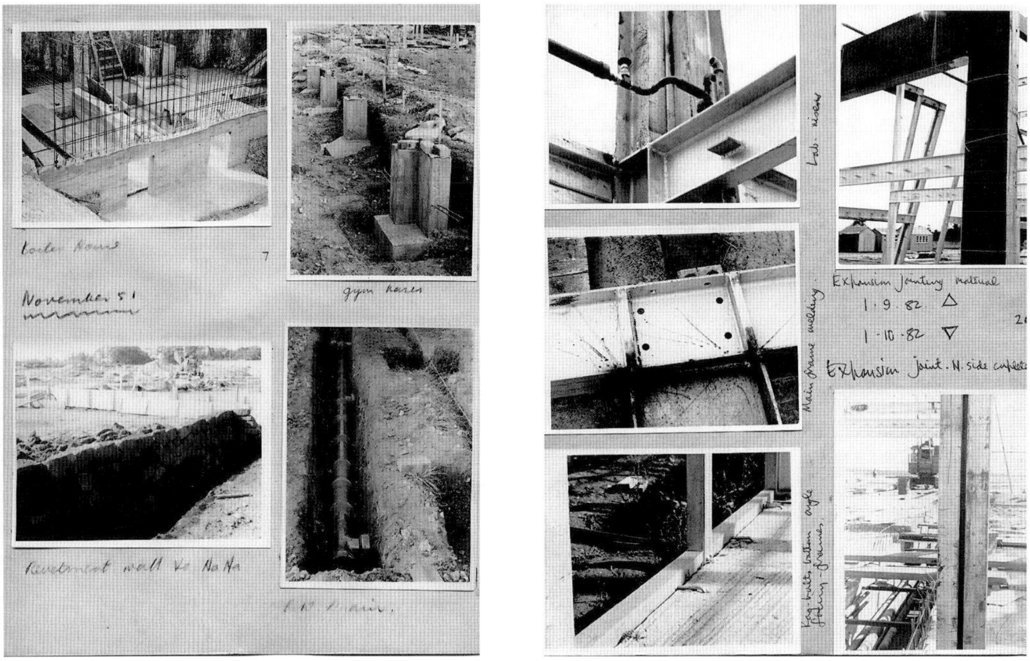

Figure 8.6. Construction photographs of Hunstanton School, 1952. Photographs: Swain and Company. Smithson Family Archive.

the completed Hunstanton School for publication in 1954. The freelance photographer John Maltby was an experienced professional who worked with Berthold Lubetkin's firm Tecton as well as with Owen Williams, the Odeon theater company, and a series of commercial products companies. His work was widely published in the British press. Maltby was commissioned by the firm of Pilkington Brothers, suppliers of the plate glass for the school; the firm used the photographs to advertise its products. Maltby's photographs were also widely published in other places, including the Smithsons' publications (Figures 8.7, 8.8).[7] Hugo Reginald de Burgh Galwey was a staff photographer for the Architectural Press; his photographs regularly appeared in the *Architectural Review* and the *Architects' Journal.* His photographic style was distinctive, with the camera leveled below standard height and the use of dramatic lighting that resulted in a noir aesthetic exaggerating the height of interior spaces, as in his dramatic photograph of the building's central hall (Figures 8.9, 8.10). Both photographers had distinctive "signatures"; Maltby resorted to fewer dramatic effects, but his photographs are compelling, perhaps because of their emphasis on composition rather than on lighting or camera position (Figure 8.11). The professional architectural photographs of the school merit comparison with the photographs that inspired its design in the first place, photographs by the firm Hedrich Blessing of the Minerals and Metals Research Building at the Illinois Institute of Technology, to which we now turn.

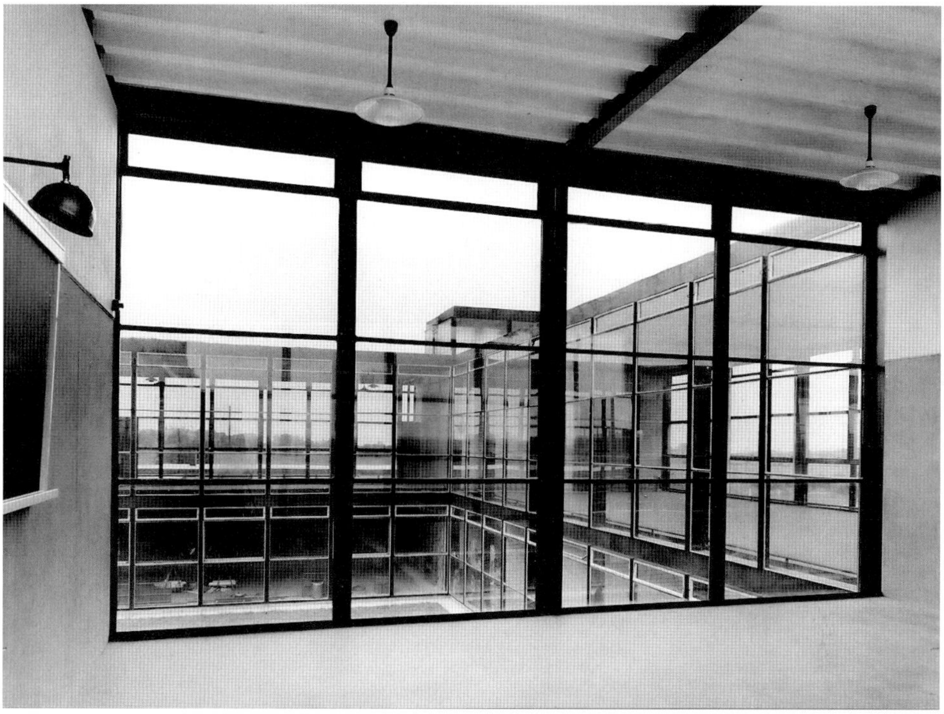

Figure 8.7. Hunstanton School, 1954. Photograph: John Maltby. Smithson Family Archive with kind permission of RIBA Library Photographs Collection.

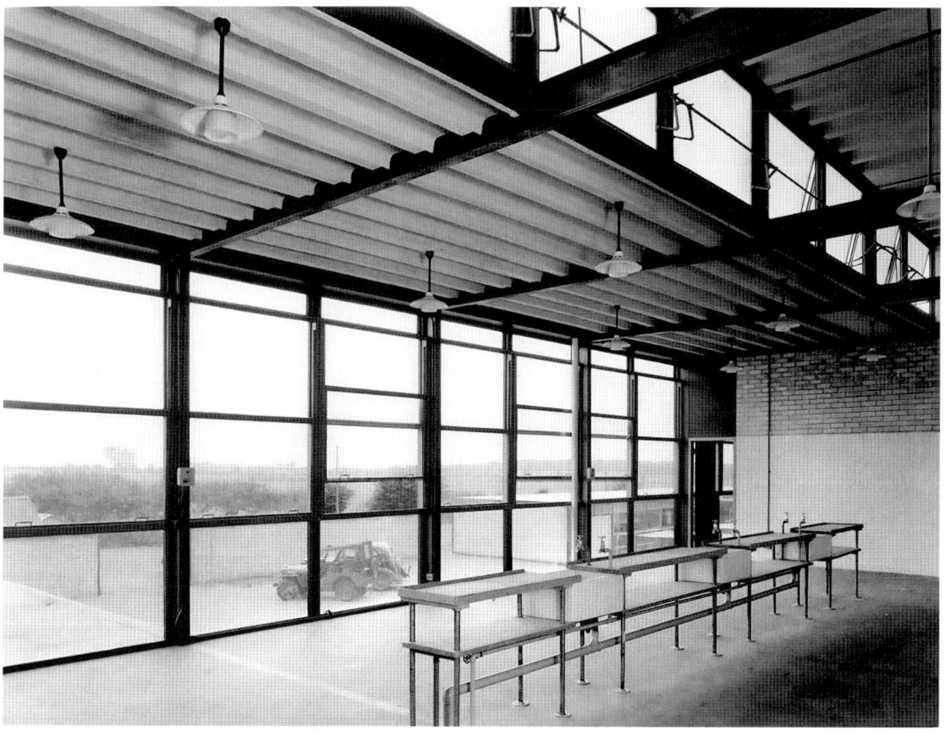

Figure 8.8. Hunstanton School, 1954. Photograph: John Maltby. Smithson Family Archive with kind permission of RIBA Library Photographs Collection.

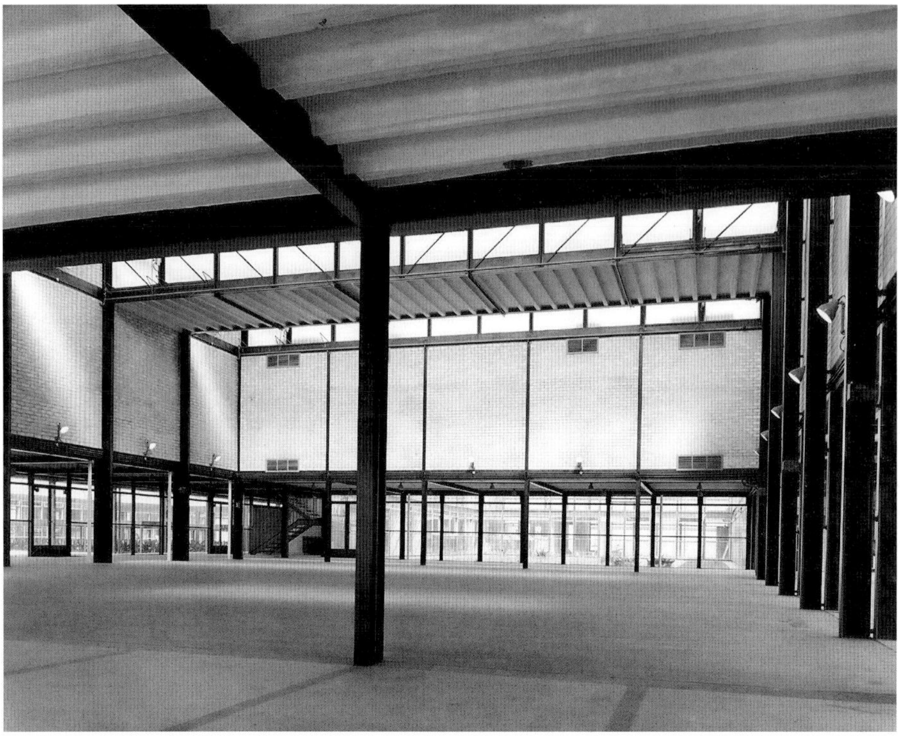

Figure 8.9. Hunstanton School, 1954. Photograph: Hugo Reginald de Burgh Galwey. Architectural Press Archive/RIBA Library Photographs Collection.

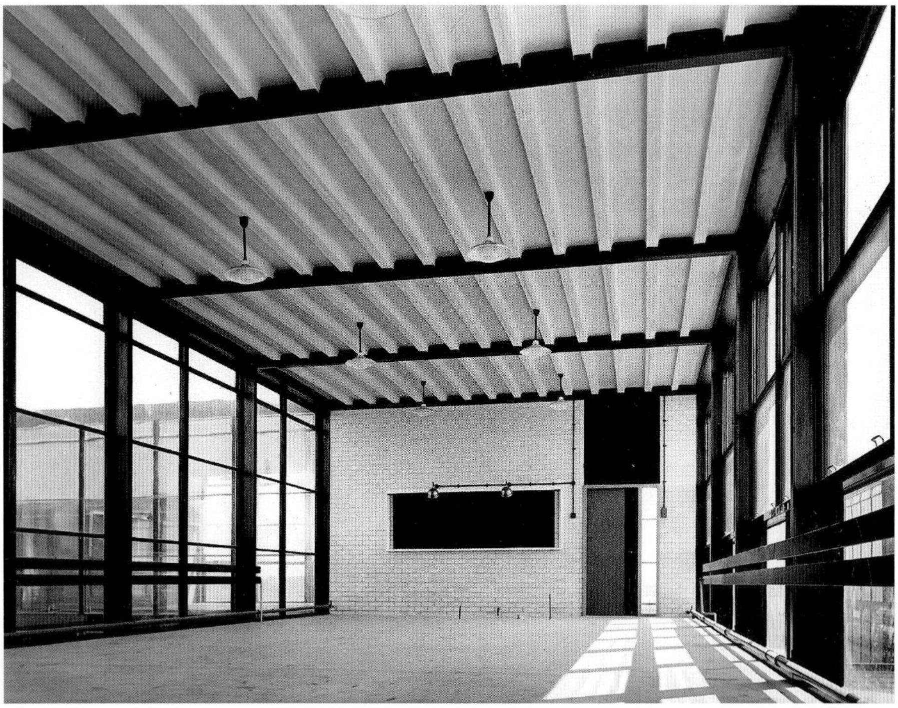

Figure 8.10. Hunstanton School, 1954. Photograph: Hugo Reginald de Burgh Galwey. Architectural Press Archive/RIBA Library Photographs Collection.

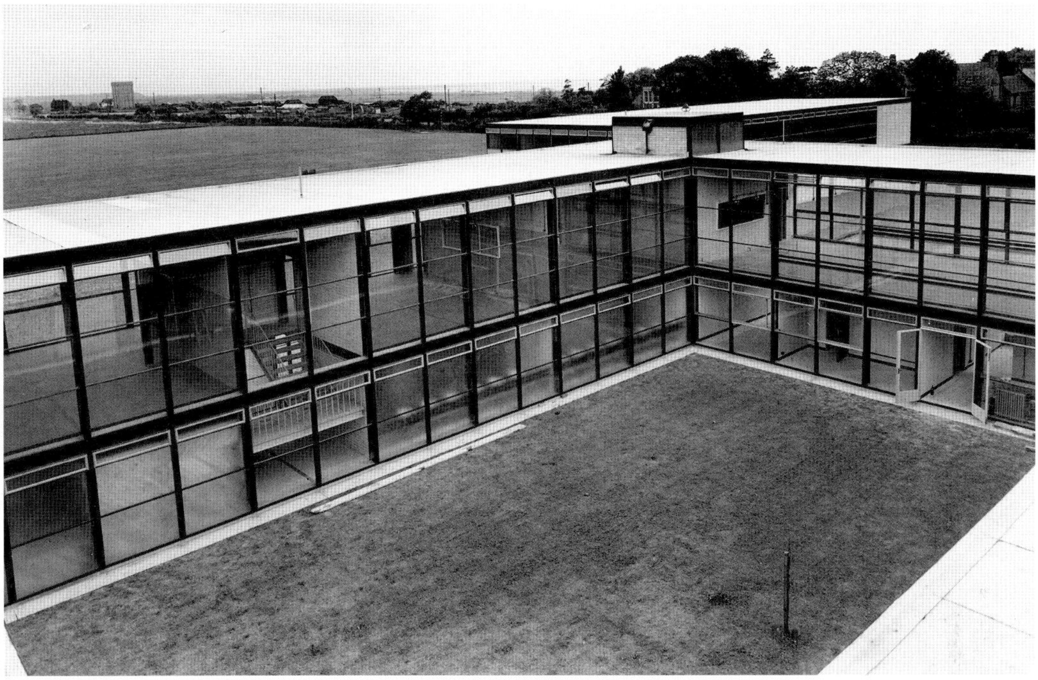

Figure 8.11. Hunstanton School, 1954. Photograph: John Maltby. Smithson Family Archive with kind permission of RIBA Library Photographs Collection.

MIES AND THE SMITHSONS

Peter Smithson described his first encounter with the photographs of the Illinois Institute of Technology published in the *Architects' Journal* in 1946 as "an act of publication that completely changed my life."[8] The exterior of the unbuilt Library and Administration Building for IIT accompanied the Minerals and Metals Building on the same two-page spread (Figure 8.12). The most extensive publication of the new building at Hunstanton in the *Architectural Review* in September 1954 included Philip Johnson's comment: "The plan is not only radical but good Mies van der Rohe, yet the architects have never seen Mies's work. . . . much of the excellence of their work is a tribute not only to themselves but also to the genius of Mies van der Rohe."[9] Mies's name provided the Smithsons with a genealogy that favored international modernism, later seen as mere camouflage for American cultural and economic imperialism. Another American source was not so well broadcast: the house in Pacific Palisades (1949) by Charles and Ray Eames, also built from small-gauge steel elements in a similarly transparent structural frame, was another inspiration to the Smithsons. Mies's influence was spread more widely in the press, but the Eames building bore more in common with the constructional paradigm of the school.[10] It was, perhaps, less useful for establishing intellectual and artistic coordinates in the minds of the architecture public at this time.

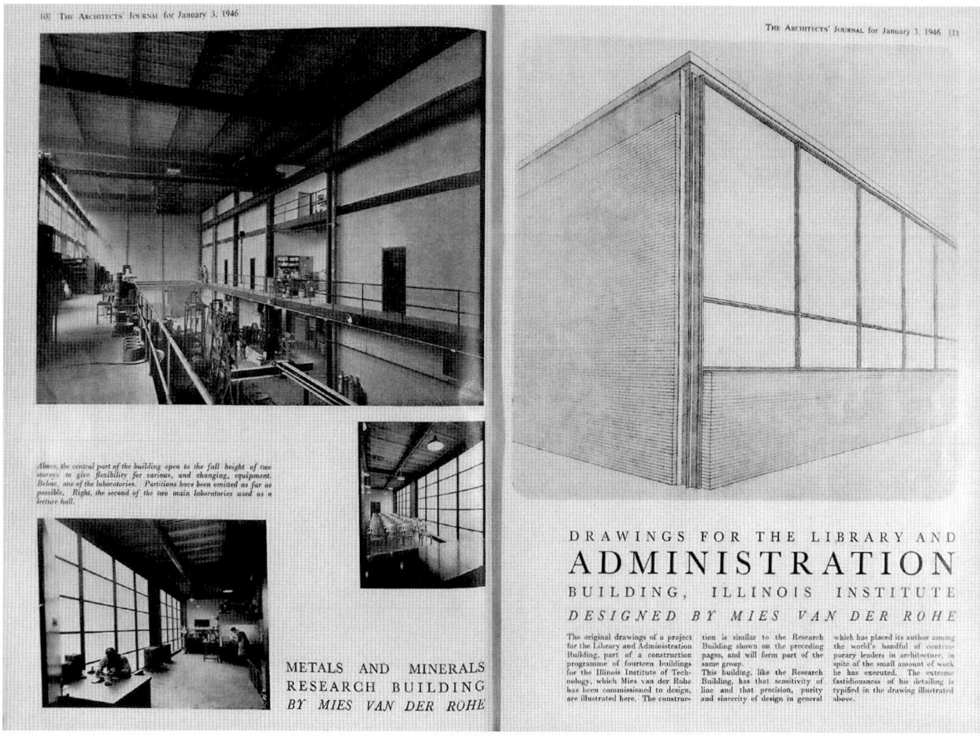
10] The Architects' Journal for January 3, 1946

The Architects' Journal for January 3, 1946 [11

Above, the central part of the building open to the full height of two storeys to give flexibility for various, and changing, equipment. Below, one of the laboratories. Partitions have been omitted as far as possible. Right, the second of the two main laboratories used as a lecture hall.

METALS AND MINERALS
RESEARCH BUILDING
BY MIES VAN DER ROHE

DRAWINGS FOR THE LIBRARY AND
ADMINISTRATION
BUILDING, ILLINOIS INSTITUTE
DESIGNED BY MIES VAN DER ROHE

The original drawings of a project for the Library and Administration Building, part of a construction programme of fourteen buildings for the Illinois Institute of Technology, which Mies van der Rohe has been commissioned to design, are illustrated here. The construction is similar to the Research Building shown on the preceding pages, and will form part of the same group.

This building, like the Research Building, has that sensitivity of line and that precision, purity and sincerity of design in general which has placed its author among the world's handful of contemporary leaders in architecture, in spite of the small amount of work he has executed. The extreme fastidiousness of his detailing is typified in the drawing illustrated above.

Figure 8.12. Minerals and Metals Research Building, Illinois Institute of Technology, in the *Architects' Journal* (January 1946). Architect: Ludwig Mies van der Rohe. Smithson Family Archive with kind permission of RIBA Library Photographs Collection.

In locating one source for their Hunstanton School in the 1946 photographs of IIT, the Smithsons identified factory production—with all its processes and infrastructures—as a base condition of Mies's American work and their own interests. Steel fabricated into frames on-site and then erected seriatim in the final buildings was also a defining feature of the school, with the substantial difference that the Smithsons used rigid frames of small-gauge elements in the plastic structural system described above, in contrast to Mies's larger-gauge steel bolted and riveted in moment connections.[11] Structural differences notwithstanding, the steel frame figures prominently in publications about Hunstanton School from 1953 to 1955, indicating one point of visual contact between the two buildings, even if the connection to the Eames house may have been equally or more important to their thinking. This visual contact between the Minerals and Metals Building and Hunstanton School may, in fact, be the only significant one. The most striking aspect of the Hunstanton building in relation to the Minerals and Metals Building, based on careful study of pictures, texts, and drawings and a visit to both sites, is the impression not of the similarity of the two buildings but of the substantial differences between them.[12]

Mies explored dualistic systems in several versions throughout his career based on the play of "freedom" against "order" that characterized so much of his thinking about buildings and society.[13] At Hunstanton School, by contrast, the architects focused their attention on producing a unitary system in which the structural frame led to, and to some extent determined, other decisions. The relationship between walls and steel structure in the IIT buildings thus gave way to a different hierarchy of construction. The window frames were welded directly to the frame in a literal treatment that also caused windows to crack with extreme fluctuations in temperature.[14] The legibility of the frame made the finished building a built manifesto for its designers. The Smithsons understood the signifying power of architecture as transcending the pragmatics of program, at least at this early stage of their careers. The reserve of the building in relation to its program suggests a leading and, when necessary, an adversarial role for postwar architecture, where buildings might demand an unprecedented attentiveness from users.[15] This contrasts with the approach of Charles and Ray Eames, whose gadget-like house in Pacific Palisades offered operational parallels but not similarity of aims.

The architects were well aware of the radical differences between their own building and Mies's buildings, and they indicated as much.[16] The fact of the buildings "looking alike" helped the Smithsons' building enter into an existing context where it might be received relationally, distinguishing itself by difference within an overarching framework of visible similarity.[17] The two commissions share an insistence on visible constructional clarity, even if Mies's understanding of that term was purely conceptual and the Smithsons' was hypostatized. Mies's buildings exhibit binary or dialogic relationships—frame talking to infill, infill talking to frame. The Smithsons' deployed a more open-ended schema—frame speaking to the world as transparency between material and meaning (function to emerge in relation to structure, not to determine it). The early "Five Projects" from Mies's Berlin years—the skyscraper projects and the Concrete Office Building (1923) most notably, as well as the workshop wing of the Bauhaus, with its floor slabs, structural columns, and mechanical systems exposed to view by a glass curtain wall—establish a genealogy that would have been available to the Smithsons through many sources. But the context is quite different.[18] In postwar Britain, one-to-one correspondence between construction and appearance was also intended to address the technocratic, compromised version of modernism that had followed the war. Their project has a kind of ethical urgency to it, as if transparency between architecture and society might have an effect, ameliorating recent crises or engendering a new relationship between users and construction by projective enactment.[19] It recalls Giedion's description of the "moral influence" of Miesian architecture on a younger generation quoted at the opening of this chapter.

Another difference characterizes the presentations of the two buildings. Both the 1946 *Architects' Journal* publication of IIT and the 1947 edition of Johnson's monograph on Mies were rich in drawings of IIT and relatively spare of photographs (if only by more recent standards for photographic illustration of architecture). The photographs of IIT published before 1954 were relatively few in number. By contrast, the photographs of Hunstanton are numerous, stacked up in serried ranks or crowded onto the pages of the 1954 *Architectural Review* and published widely in other journals (Figure 8.13, 8.14). The building was part of a phase of architectural development in which the photographic image had assumed sufficient importance in

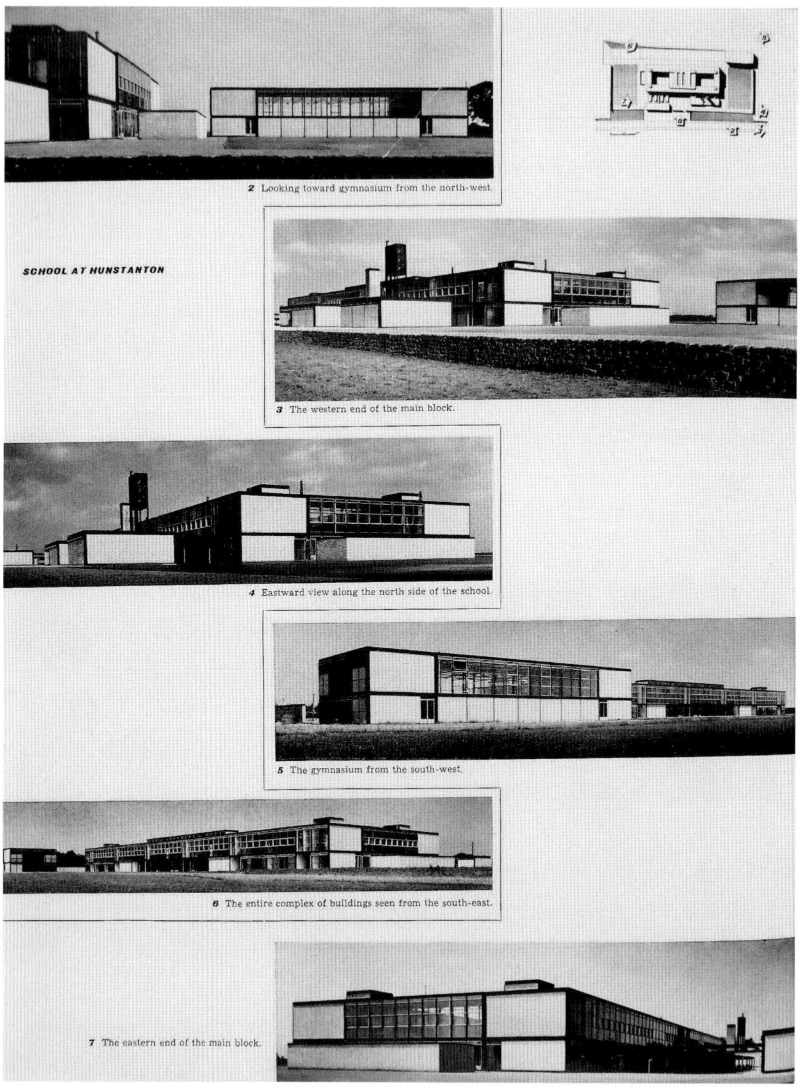

SCHOOL AT HUNSTANTON

2 Looking toward gymnasium from the north-west.

3 The western end of the main block.

4 Eastward view along the north side of the school.

5 The gymnasium from the south-west.

6 The entire complex of buildings seen from the south-east.

7 The eastern end of the main block.

Figure 8.13. Page from *Architectural Review* (1954). Smithson Family Archive with kind permission of RIBA Library Photographs Collection.

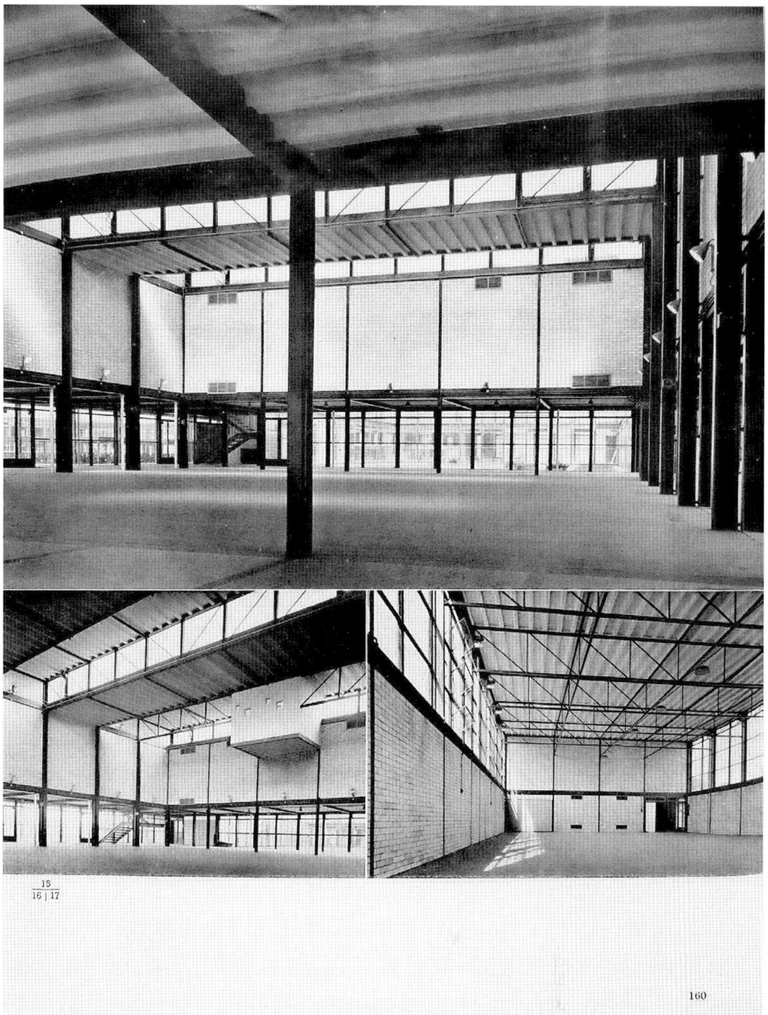

Figure 8.14. Page from *Architectural Review* (1954). Smithson Family Archive with kind permission of RIBA Library Photographs Collection.

the creation of markets and reputations to ensure that architects would seek widespread comprehensive coverage in journals and books. Thus an indirect effect of the transit between IIT and Hunstanton lies in the architects' implicit acceptance of photography and its print carriers as means for transmitting ideas metonymically or synecdochically—even ideas that were aimed at articulating insistently physical characteristics like structure and construction. So we have here the elements of a paradox: the flat surface of the photograph as the vehicle by which an insistently "real" experience of remote but "real" three-dimensional construction had to be conveyed. First, the photographs tell the viewer that the building looks like another building, and that this resemblance is intentionally visible; second, the volume of published photographs indicates the architects' embrace of photography as the primary system of information exchange for international modernism.

In this case, architectural photography was valuable because it enabled the architects to establish credentials within a competitive market without tying their hands as designers. It enabled them to establish visible similarities with existing buildings while pursuing a notably different sort of architecture. In addition, photography made it possible for these architects to enter into global networks of exchange that brought pictures of their work to distant audiences. These conditions differ from those of prephotographic periods only in the degree and intensity of the persuasion that photographs exert on architects and their audiences. This would seem to imply that photography was purely secondary, acting on architects in ways external to both photography and building, after the fact. But the Smithsons' work at Hunstanton and the concurrent work of Mies, Wittkower, and Reyner Banham raise another possibility.

POSTWAR BRITAIN

Two architectural historians who emigrated from Germany to Britain distinguished the architectural context within which the Hunstanton School was built: Nikolaus Pevsner (1902–83) and Rudolf Wittkower (1901–71). Pevsner's Reith Lectures of 1955, titled "The Englishness of English Art," capped the scholar's recent resuscitation of principles of picturesque planning ("townscape") and English proto-functionalism, perhaps first known to Pevsner through Hermann Muthesius's *Das englische Haus* of 1904.[20] Wittkower studied the influence of Renaissance architecture on Britain, rejecting the idea of indigenous or autochthonous building in favor of transmission networks through which architects adapted architecture from one context to another. The Smithsons specifically identified Wittkower's influential publications on the proportioning systems and societal role of Renaissance architecture in relation to their design for Hunstanton.[21] Advocacy for a proto-internationalism (before nationhood) in this effort fought the enemy within (Pevsner and the English picturesque) with the heroes of the recent war (Mies and Wittkower), vanquished from battles in Nazi Germany but victorious in the war for cultural heritage afterward. The recent world war (1939–45) and events in British and international architecture in the 1940s and early 1950s thus set the context within which the Smithsons began their professional careers.

Unlike their German counterparts, British architects had been and remained physically removed from two important centers of architectural activity after World War II. Distant from the blossoming American economy and its postwar building boom, they were also at a physical remove from the Continent, with its powerful history of modernist experiment recently suppressed by fascism and the war itself. The physical separation of Britain from its wartime allies was particularly noticeable during the immediate period of postwar austerity until about 1955, when Europe was under reconstruction but the British economy was still weak. In this period, architects came to depend even more fully on photographic images of buildings for information and ideas about architecture than had been the case previously, although the precedent of photographic presentation of architecture had long been set.

Although the profession relinquished apprenticeship models of training in favor of professional academic ones based on learning in studio and classroom from texts, pictures, and models well before World War II, the use of such instruments accelerated after the war,[22] as the internationalization of architectural networks favored increasingly rapid and extensive communication through images. This form of communication has long historical roots: in the nineteenth century, it can be correlated to the emergence of pedagogies that relied on stylistic comparison.[23] But its development in the years after World War II reflects a new historical period in which the dynamic relationship between photograph and architectural object began to change. This change was rendered more complex for architects in Britain by differences between the wealthy United States and the impoverished but subsidized countries of Marshall Plan Europe, in which considerable construction was taking place by the early 1950s; the United Kingdom was recovering from bombardment and seeking economic stability, and the countries of the Commonwealth were divesting themselves of British political authority while remaining tied to British markets.

Postwar austerity in the United Kingdom and Europe thus altered and intensified the importance of mass media that disseminated information about remote developments at a time when local initiatives might be retarded or suppressed by economic uncertainty. This was in stark contrast to the American scene, in which a booming economy churned out dramatic new technological and cultural material. For young Britons, particularly students, travel to distant sites was rendered more difficult for a brief but critical period.[24] During this time, the gradual erection of the "Iron Curtain" also made their access to the remarkable architectural achievements of interwar Eastern Europe increasingly difficult.[25] At the same time, the vigorous growth of the U.S. economy and of other global markets for European and British architecture enlarged the audiences that consumed magazines, journals, and books on architecture.[26] Increased commerce in photographs was coupled with regular traffic between architects in Commonwealth countries and the United Kingdom, where it is possible to examine the effects of photographic transmission with particular clarity.[27] It was not just that architects received their training in history and much of their familiarity with global contemporary architecture through images throughout the twentieth century, but rather that this condition became habitual and established after the war, when conditions shifted the balance between photograph and object to increase the importance of the former to an unprecedented degree. The primary locus of attention for information about buildings—the referent, as it were, for the architectural object—gradually began to shift from the building site to the page. This is not to claim that architects did not make site visits or learn from constructed architecture. Rather, it is to note that internal dynamics within the field had begun to favor the portable currency of photographs for conveying ideas about buildings to publics—and to young architects in training as part of this group.[28] We have been tracing the gradual shift of architectural photography and its media supports from adjuncts of architectural practice that helped promote products and reputations, even as they presented intractable problems to architects, to central instruments of architectural communication, commerce, and development. The distance between a building on-site and the same building in pictures grew larger as time went on, and the differences between the two became more pronounced. The architect was increasingly compelled to work on both buildings simultaneously—a pressure that was central to the formation of twentieth-century applied arts in many media, not only architecture.

Paradoxically, while this shift into bifurcated practice with a heavy emphasis on photographic buildings entailed a high degree of specialization and professionalization, it also signaled a new potential threat to professional independence. Increasing visual literacy throughout the nonprofessional population would ultimately lead to the erosion of the architect's status as "expert" and to the rise of postmodern populism, as the general public became more sophisticated about images and taste.[29] The effects of this divestment would not be seen until postmodernism had actually unfolded in architecture, when the power of images to shape architectural discourse was clearly demonstrated in texts such as Robert Venturi, Denise Scott Brown, and Steven Izenour's *Learning from Las Vegas* of 1972 and Charles Jencks's many publications.[30] These developments will be explored more fully in chapter 9. During the period under consideration here, the increased importance of photographs for architectural communication confronted architects and their critics with a problem that had been identified well before the war but that became increasingly hard to ignore as traffic in photographs increased. This was, of course, the problem of learning about three-dimensional objects from two-dimensional pictures, which critics regarded as a confusing compromise at best and as mendacious commercial practice at worst. As we have seen in previous chapters, the same issues played out in the early period of architectural photographic communication; in fact, they are still reprised today.

While young architects learned much of the history of buildings from pictures, many of them photographs, they were also simultaneously learning about the apparatuses by which photographs could circulate: exhibitions, lectures (with slides gathered from travel and from purchased sets), journals, magazines, and books. Information collapsed into infrastructure. The cognitive operations involved in translation from two to three dimensions and back again demanded that architects decode photographic images as spatial constructs and reencode spatial constructs into pictures.[31] In addition, young architects were challenged by increasingly complex professional networks in the distribution of architectural commissions, such as the quasi-informal networks maintained by powerful figures such as Leslie Martin on the British scene. None of this was new or unprecedented, but the networks of architecture were becoming considerably more complex as time went by.

Informal power structures made up of political and professional hierarchies governed local and regional markets within single nations, and increasingly international networks as well. Genealogies that linked young architects to interwar modernists and leading local practitioners thus made publication important to new practices. Young architects who depended on existing networks were therefore constrained to do two things at once. On one hand, they needed to innovate, to pioneer new approaches to building; on the other, they needed to engage and support contemporary work by older colleagues as a way of being accepted into ongoing discussions about architecture, including those that concerned potential commissions. Alison and Peter Smithson underlined a relationship to Mies collaterally, by asserting the importance of differences between their approach and that of the senior architect, yet their words were belied by the photographs of their first building, photographs that conveyed resemblance. They established an emergent practice in part by relating their work to one of the most important offices in contemporary architecture through visible similarity. In a similar way, other architects associated with the "New Brutalism" in the United Kingdom took the late work of Le Corbusier as a primary reference point.[32] Because the credo of the interwar avant-gardes required Britain's neo-avant-garde to reject past models and to embrace dissent combined with innovation, a paradoxical condition came to characterize the work of this generation of architects: they were both innovators and preservers of the status quo. This dual condition ultimately hastened the end of postwar late modernism. Instead, postmodernists could reclaim the conventional avant-garde mantle of rebellion, purportedly rejecting the dogma of the recent past and the hegemonic power structures of its architects. This required only the spirited performance of a rejection of modernism—a rejection that often turned out to be more than slightly illusory. In any case, postmodern rejection of late modernist precedent was never uniform or consistent.

RUDOLF WITTKOWER: THE LOCAL INFLUENCE OF THE GLOBAL

When Wittkower arrived in Britain he was appointed to an unpaid research position at the Warburg Institute, where he continued old work and began new research based on British collections. He and Fritz Saxl worked on British adaptations of Renaissance architecture in a photographic exhibition titled "English Art and the Mediterranean" mounted in 1941, one of a series of such exhibitions during the war years. The exhibition included 540 photographs spanning four thousand years and resulted in a large folio volume coauthored by Wittkower and Saxl titled *British Art and the Mediterranean,* which appeared in 1948, the year before Wittkower's *Architectural Principles in the Age of Humanism.* The exhibition provided British audiences with photographs of works of art that were inaccessible for the duration of the war.[33] Herbert Read's review in December 1941 echoed the Warburg Institute's approach to images, describing the curators' approach as "the art of visual education."[34] The 1948 book presented the same photographs with short texts on selected topics, organized chronologically from beginning to end. *British Art* highlighted the importance of photography for art historical study, continuing the ongoing project of the Warburg photographic archive in Britain, described as follows in the institute's 1934–35 annual report: "As the books give a picture of the history of the classical tradition in religion, art, literature and science, seen through the medium of words, so the collection of photographs will give a complementary picture through the medium of imagery."[35] Read commented further on this approach, noting that the Warburg method used relays of text and image to establish different realms of proof and argumentation: "The Warburg method begins with an idea, and is the realisation of that idea in the plastic medium of photography. . . . what emerges from this contemplation are certain generalisations which could certainly be expressed in words and are expressed in words, but which can be demonstrated and proved in illustrations and only in illustrations."[36] Architects in Britain found a historical echo of their own situation in the pages of *British Art and the Mediterranean,* faced as they were with the pressing need to communicate the substance of their work in photographs.

Wittkower wrote the second half of *British Art*; Saxl handled the early period from antiquity to circa 1500. Among Wittkower's short chapters, the one focusing on the role of the reception or entry hall in British architecture appears particularly relevant to the Smithsons' school at Hunstanton (Figures 8.14, 8.15). Wittkower described the English hall as "a new and genuine expression of the English mode of life in keeping with the social ambitions of the age."[37] The photographs of halls ranged from those of medieval houses (Penshurst Place, 1350, "in which the whole household lived and fed") to Palladian buildings (Kedleston by Robert Adam, 1772, a hall "of momentous importance, it was to become the prototype of classicistic museums all over the world"); they recall published photographs of the hall at Hunstanton by Maltby and Galwey. The main hall in the school was similarly a focus of the life of the institution, serving as main lobby, assembly space, and dining room.[38] Wittkower's Palladian precedents appear to have been in the young architects' minds as they designed their own neo-Palladian building.

Architectural Principles (1949) included Wittkower's previously published articles on harmonic proportion, on Palladio, and on Alberti, as well as new work on centrally planned Renaissance churches; all had been developed after his exile to Britain, during which he lived either in London or at the wartime home of the Warburg Institute in Denham. Wittkower related Renaissance architecture to scientific order, religious belief, and aesthetics by noting that important symbolic buildings were configured according to ideas about harmonic proportions and geometry. He also suggested that the means for perceiving this orderly union of science and art

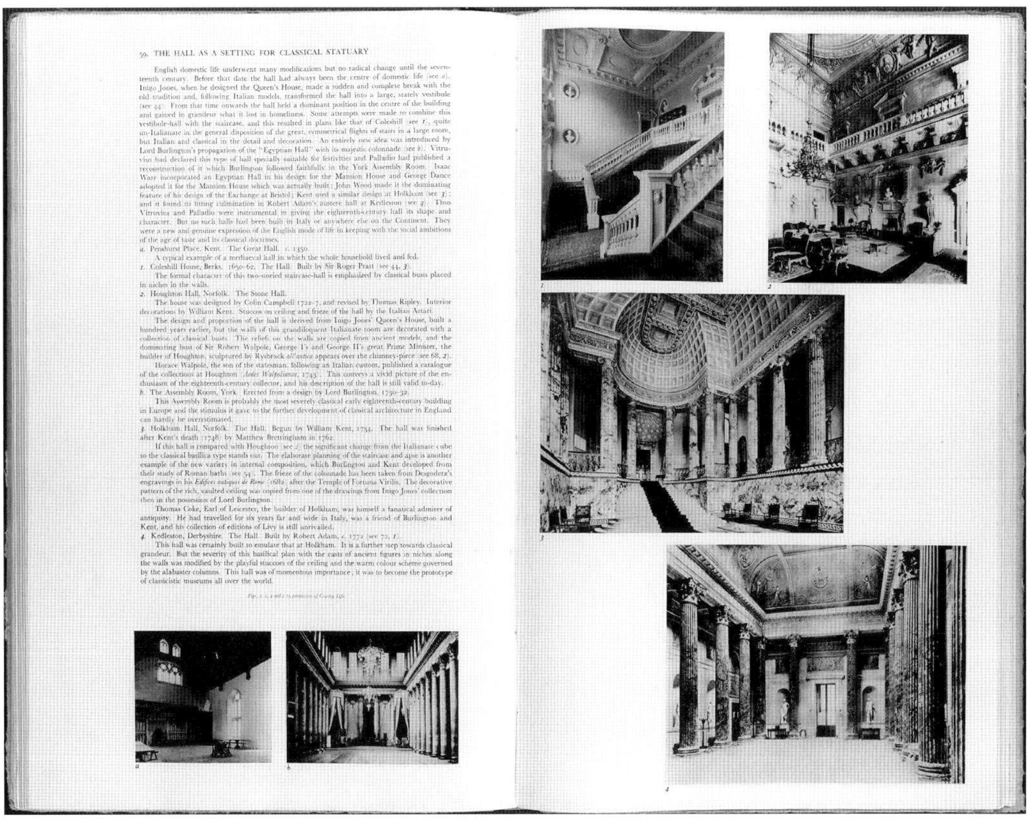

Figure 8.15. "The Hall as a Setting for Classical Statuary," Fritz Saxl and Rudolf Wittkower, *British Art and the Mediterranean* (London: Oxford University Press, 1948).

were made legible in the buildings themselves, not solely to those with the capacity to understand an architectural plan and/or elevation or to project the relationships transcribed in such representations through the perception of the object in situ, but rather because of the innate value of certain proportional harmonies. In relation to Santa Maria delle Carceri, he noted, "Its majestic simplicity, the undisturbed impact of its geometry, the purity of its whiteness are designed to evoke in the congregation a consciousness of the presence of God—of a God who has ordered the universe according to immutable mathematical laws, who has created a uniform and beautifully proportioned world, the consonance and harmony of which is mirrored in His temple below."[39] Santa Maria evokes the presence of God through form and haecceity, or "thisness."

A specialist might decode the perfection of the architecture in measured drawings, since precise geometric relationships were not intended to be legible in the building itself "on the ground."[40] Wittkower nevertheless published three photographs of Santa Maria to supplement the plan included in his description. It would have been axiomatic that readers do not understand photographs within a framework of technical legibility such as that which pertains to orthographic drawings, but rather consider photographs as tools of the experience of buildings. Furthermore, photographs combined with plans, sections, and elevations enable the reader to shuttle back and forth between multiple representations to understand buildings. The relationships that photographs depict are not the abstract orthographic relationships of plans and sections—but neither is our experience of them properly spatial. Photographic images are read like other kinds of images, but in ways that differ critically from the reading of measured drawings, renderings, or texts. The combination of veracity and myth that is imposed on architectural photographs is not to be found operating for other sorts of architectural representations, as Wittkower undoubtedly recognized. We expect them to supply an experience that is closer to spatial experience than anything that an orthographic drawing can supply. Wittkower's familiarity with Warburg Institute taxonomy (and his role in developing it) suggests that he considered photographs to be an alternate form of "text" supplementing written analysis, and used them accordingly.

Architectural Principles established a connection between formal aesthetics and societal values that showed how proportion and geometry could be seen as embodiments of a Renaissance ethos. The following quotation, from section I, "Alberti's Programme of the Ideal Church," also elucidates the Smithsons' project, not in terms of endorsing humanism, but rather in terms of architectural method: "Alberti here gives a complete picture of the humanist conception of ecclesiastical architecture, and it is apparent that for him humanism and religion were entirely compatible.

And let it be said emphatically: it is a serene, philosophical and almost puritanical architecture which his descriptions conjure up before us."[41] Wittkower pointed to the combination of "secular" humanism and religion in Alberti's buildings, undoing a long-held prejudice that divided Renaissance thought from religious devotion. He suggested that architecture might concretize or reify the ambitions of society in complex combinations that did not fit with received dogma—that were, quite literally, unprecedented. In suggesting that buildings could represent the society that built them in visible and unexpected ways, Wittkower provided young architects with an alternative to Pevsner's nationalistic British picturesque and a link to discourse on abstraction then so important to postwar artists and architects, even as the emphasis on visual perception that he stressed resonated with Pevsner's picturesque concerns.[42]

In their descriptions of the Hunstanton project, the Smithsons emphasized its relation to *Architectural Principles* and the publications that preceded it. The articles that Wittkower had published throughout the 1940s were also central to a wider set of debates on contemporary architecture at the Institute of Contemporary Art and in the British architectural press. In addition to questioning the direction that modern architecture might take after the 1951 Festival of Britain, architects also briefly embraced geometry and numerical proportion in architecture, largely in response to Wittkower and the appearance of Le Corbusier's *Le Modulor* at the same time. The Smithsons took part in this effort, writing in a letter to the *RIBA Journal* in 1952: "Dr. Wittkower is regarded by the younger architects as the *only* art-historian working in England capable of describing and analysing buildings in spatial and plastic terms, and not in terms of derivations and dates."[43] The overall project of *Architectural Principles* is bound up with the modernist desire for transparency among form, meaning, and function, illusory as this desire may have been. Wittkower's work had a powerful influence on the continuing project of modernism, with which it was historically continuous and to which its author was personally sympathetic.[44]

Wittkower's book was enlisted in attempts to reignite interwar modernist discourse after a period of intense denial. Wittkower had been resident in exile (and in some duress) for sixteen years before *Architectural Principles* appeared. He was not simply pursuing a neo-Kantian line of thought with the desire to refute the seemingly outmoded scholarly *Einfühlung* (empathy theory) of Geoffrey Scott in *The Architecture of Humanism* (1914).[45] Rather, he was responding to the far more proximate threat of anti-intellectual populism coupled with remnant fascist ideology. With the longing and sadness that must have characterized the conditions of the book's writing, Wittkower declared reason and order in the face of their evident opposites. These claims are not simply external to the text: they concern its very mode of argumentation.[46] They also help explain some of its subsequent effects on

British architecture, where the Smithsons and their cohort embarked on a parallel project for modernism at the end of the 1940s. Looking for a way out of the cul-de-sac of postwar British architecture, with its narrow horizons and resources, they pursued avenues that had been lost to view or blocked by the war. The importance of transparency and finitude emerges repeatedly from their writings about Hunstanton School—literal transparency within architecture itself, but also transparency between architecture and society. In a typescript for *The Architects' Yearbook* for 1955, they noted, "The idea behind this school was to try and prove that in every program there exists an inherent order which once discovered appears 'static, immutable, and entirely lucid.'" As the Smithsons tried to make modern architecture analogous in its relationship to its own historical moment, to the architecture of the Renaissance as described by Wittkower, they substituted new transcendental ethical values for Renaissance religious humanism. Their words imply that architecture might become the limpid crystallization of a postwar world in which restitution might be made between forces of reason and forces of modernization, as if machine production, accelerating technology, and critical and self-reflective artistic practice all might be recuperated with the aid of an updated anthropological model capable of holding them in check. Giedion's analysis of a "Mies effect," as seen in the epigraph to this chapter, claimed something similar.

Wittkower's book also indicated how young architects might make authoritative decisions about form. Like the discourses of structural rationalism and functionalism, the model interpolated from Wittkower's work implied something about visibility in finished buildings. You should be able to *see* the relationship between order and proportion and the finished form, even if specific numerico-geometric relationships are made explicit only in measured drawings. The Smithsons took this idea seriously in their own building, although they still grasped for appropriate motivations. The building's program was not the essential element; in an unpublished typescript dated 1954, Peter Smithson claimed instead that "form has a permanent validity," and that Hunstanton offered "a secret life of pure space, the permanent BUILT FORM which will persist when the School has given way to Museum or Warehouse, and which will continue to exist as Idea."[47] Smithson also noted in a 1953 text that "Hunstanton School tries to re-establish the finite order that is architecture." His and Alison's interpretation of Wittkower hinged on reasserting a didactically clear order for building, one that needed to be clear on-site and equally clear in photographs in order to respond to the perceived mandate of its own time. Keeping this notion of visibility in mind, a closer analysis of transmission between buildings and photographs might be useful.

GROWTH AND FORM

Before Galwey and Maltby photographed the completed school for publication, the architects had the furniture removed from the building, as they noted in the *Architectural Review* in 1954. They thus returned the building to a kind of protean or didactic state before photographs were taken, maintaining visual continuity between the construction photographs and the final photographs. It is not only that the steel frame is more clearly visible than would be the case if the schoolrooms were filled with desks and chairs and the legendary caretaker's curtains, as a few such photographs show (Figure 8.16), but also that the emphasis of the pictures lies fully on the architecture in a raw, newly finished state. In this way, the architects asserted control

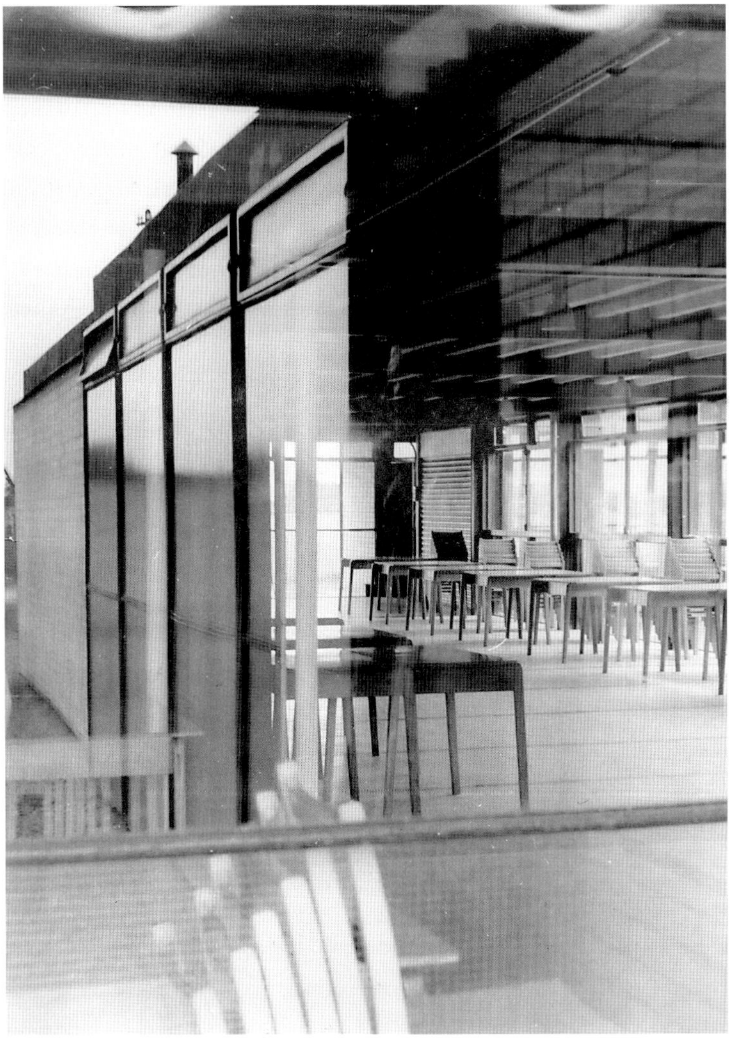

Figure 8.16. Hunstanton School, furnished. Photograph: David Wager. Smithson Family Archive.

over the photographs before the fact in a practicable way that their own professional expertise allowed.

As a result, the final publication pictures resemble published photographs of American buildings under construction that had appeared with increasing frequency in the European architectural press after 1946, as if to tease European architects with visions of American prosperity.[48] Photographs of Mies's unfinished Alumni Memorial Hall that were published in other venues recall the finished photographs of Hunstanton taken by Maltby and Galwey.[49] There are prewar and interwar modernist buildings that provide precedents for this—finished buildings that resemble buildings still under construction. These precedents reflect functionalist belief in transparency of means and gesture to the incomplete nature of any architectural project prior to inhabitation—the building remains literally unfinished until it is occupied.

By 1954, when the decision to photograph the building without furniture was made, the Smithsons had moved on from an earlier concern with the finitude of Wittkower's geometric formalism to a new set of concerns more closely related to ideas about growth and form that were circulating among artists, architects, critics, and others. Related themes of incompleteness or endlessness were taken up by the postwar neo-avant-garde, in particular by the Smithsons and Richard Llewelyn-Davies. The processual aspect of functionalist modernism, whether pre- or postwar, appears as a strange collation of Marxist materialism and philosophies of process or becoming from Hegel to Nietzsche to Bergson. The Smithsons at least had a passing familiarity with Bergson and knew D'Arcy Wentworth Thompson's *On Growth and Form* (1917) as well as the contemporary work of the German émigré architect Walter Segal, who pioneered collaborative prefabrication in the United Kingdom.

Continually evolving technology was interpreted as a positive value for postwar architecture, as noted in chapter 7. Construction photographs in the international press depicted the newest solutions to the challenge of steel frame construction, signaling a return to modern architectural principles that was long awaited in European architectural circles and validating technological innovation in modern architecture.[50] Photographs of steel beams and half-finished buildings remained benchmarks of technical and technological progress despite, or perhaps in direct response to, the effects of technology in the recent war.[51] In relation to this photographic currency, Nigel Henderson's photographs of Hunstanton subvert the notion of a purely technological motor of progress in architecture. But they also recall an important idea behind construction photographs as a category of architectural image: to define the absolutely new as that which will continue to develop beyond the moment captured in its image (as the building continues to be constructed). In the case of the Smithsons' building, however, this process-based, Bergsonian version of modernism contrasts with the didactic clarity of architecture reminiscent of Wittkower's Renaissance, which also suggests a complete and finite construct—a crystallization of a moment in time. So—a building projected into the future as an open construct that also crystallizes a moment in time as a way of representing social values of its time?—the paradoxes of Hunstanton multiply. The Smithsons appear to have been caught by a history unfolding in front of them.

RECURSION

The "bruteness" of Hunstanton's design suggests something like a reverse translation, the visitation of the technology of the photographic image on architecture itself. This would not *only* mean that it was made explicitly legible for reception through photographs. Despite the abstraction that the building and its pictures display, the quality most sought by the architects was that of hard, irreducible transparency between material, construction, and appearance—a kind of essential or irreducible architecture recalling the medieval doctrine of haecceity as well as contemporary phenomenology. Their notion of architectural transparency equally recalls both structural rationalism and hard-line functionalism without embracing either. It also implicitly relates to the photograph as an indexical sign in which appearance and reality correspond in the picture by virtue of an incontrovertible chemical process. As the architects sought new truths in a postwar world (following in the footsteps of their interwar predecessors), they appear to have landed on an idea to which architects had long been privy (the photograph as evidence and truthful representation) but that could now be integrated directly into architecture, into the fabric of building itself. Whether the Smithsons made a conscious choice to create a "photographic building"—one mimicking photographic processes—or not, links from their work extend back to the nineteenth century through the history of functionalism and structural rationalism, which the Smithsons had absorbed as basic discourses of modern architecture. Hunstanton School suggests that the logic of modern architecture shares something with photography understood as a technical procedure that also had objective social force, precisely because it combined truthfulness with appearance. That this did not turn out to be the case for photographic representation as it has subsequently been understood does not diminish the force of this idea, then or now.[52]

If Hunstanton was to be legible as a material construct to other architects *through photographs*, the qualities by which it would be read in photographs would have to be coded back into the building itself. This partly accounts for the emphatic quality of the architecture of Hunstanton School—for its extreme rigor and reduction to essentials—and for the intensification that took place in the transit from Chicago to Hunstanton. The building's didactic nature was overstated—intentionally or unconsciously—both in anticipation of its incipient translation into pictures and as a recursion of photography into building itself. If Banham had one interpretation of the Hunstanton-Wittkower nexus, it appears that the Smithsons had another. They first admired Banham but later protested his substitution of an "aesthetic" for what they always understood as an ethical project—the project of "re-establishing a finite order for architecture" and endowing it with social relevance and what they called "nobility."[53] But their desire to assert this fixed and "finite order" was challenged by architecture's increasingly symbolic role as a legible signifier (an "image") and by its ever-accelerating mobility in capitalism. The fixed construct so well articulated by Wittkower and the lack of fixity in postwar production of buildings and their photographs confronted the Smithsons with a contradiction that they were unable to resolve, although their attempts to do so sustained them throughout the 1960s. At Hunstanton and in later projects like "Patio and Pavilion" of 1956 they continued to seek a bare structure for others to settle and inhabit—as did Segal, John Habraken, and Lucien Kroll in different ways.[54] But as noted, the clarity and finality of the architectural image constructed at Hunstanton conflicted with the ideas of growth and form that lay behind the provision of an empty or naked structure as an invitation to settlement.[55] It is possible for pictures and buildings to go two separate ways, one getting filled up with the flotsam and jetsam of children's education, the other circulating continuously in classrooms, lecture halls, and publication, disseminating a "photographic architecture" only loosely related to a building aging on a site. But an examination of the Smithsons' building suggests that these two aims might also conflict, in that any remnant resistance to the power of media and image making that was implicit in the "ethical project" of New Brutalism is difficult to reconcile with the "imageable" architecture recognized by Banham in the building at Hunstanton, capable of communicating spatial concepts through photographs and incorporating photographic concepts into architecture. In fact, this reconciliation can be made, and was made.

Through the extremity of their solution at Hunstanton, the architects reasserted the importance of irreducible physical reality, now understood to be in complex play with ephemeral images. As their work contradicts the overweening power of images in the dissemination of architectural ideas, so it affirms their productive power through an assemblage such as the 1953 "Parallel of Life and Art." Just as an architecture "without rhetoric" would, above all, be one that could somehow refuse any distinction between a thing and its representation, so were the Smithsons deeply involved in representative images and optical perception—as featured in "Parallel," as received from Leo Steinberg, whose criticism they read, as described much later from a car in *AS in DS*, as photographed by Henderson and others, and as the means through which they absorbed heroic modern architecture and strove to reinvigorate and reinvent it.[56] Nigel Henderson's remarks delivered at the opening of "Parallel" elucidate this attitude toward photography. In describing the eclectic and varied array of photographs used in the exhibition, Henderson noted:

> We were fully conscious of the kind of distortions inherent in the photographic presentation [Henderson crossed out "re" at the start of this word] of diverse material phenomena, the misleading changes of scale, the glazing over of the particular terms of the medium of the occurrence. This may result at times in the perception of specious and unfruitful analyses . . . ; at others, one has at least a sense of genuine insight and enlarged understanding. . . . Moreover, the chemical basis of photography does allow of an extraordinary richness in the rendering of qualities of real things. It can be an immensely sensitive medium; and we have tried to reveal its subtlety and variety—to use it to its fullest extension. . . . we ourselves were concerned first of all with the subjective impression, the impact upon our senses rather than upon our intellects. This may explain our non-dogmatic attitude to the whole thing, and our appreciation of the need of the active participation of the spectators. We should like to bring about a situation in which people felt like undergoing a strong visual experience, without too much reliance on intellectual handrails for their support.[57]

Dichotomies between image and object are eliminated in the schema for Hunstanton School, where pictures and buildings (or other material phenomena) interpenetrate and enrich one another—and any notion of a conflict between them is here allowed to float away. The building is an image, and it is an ethical construct, and it works, if not always perfectly, with great force on many levels at once.

In the catalog for "Parallel of Life and Art," the authors cite A. Hyatt Mayor's 1946 article "The Photographic Eye" on modes of seeing and how they affect the production of art. The essay ends with an embedded quotation. About this quote included in his essay, Mayor writes, "These words were spoken by A. S. Eddington in 1927, in the ripe heyday of abstract art; they might have been written, changing 'science' to 'art,' by Klee or Picasso or Kandinsky." The words in question illuminate our understanding of "Parallel" as well:

> The physicist used to borrow the raw material of his world from the familiar world, but he does so no longer. The external world of physics has thus become a world of shadows. In removing our illusion we have removed the substance, for indeed we have seen that substance is one of the greatest of our illusions. The frank realisation that physical science is concerned with a world of shadows is an assertion of freedom for autonomous development.

Such may have been the Smithsons' realization as well.

A surviving image is an
image that, having lost its
original use value and meaning,
nonetheless comes back,
like a ghost, at a particular
historical moment: a moment
of "crisis," a moment when
it demonstrates its latency,
its tenacity, its vivacity, and
its "anthropological adhesion."

—GEORGES DIDI-HUBERMAN,
CONFRONTING IMAGES

9. FROM PHOTOGRAPHIC SURFACE TO IMAGE OBJECT

JAMES STIRLING'S POSTMODERNISM

One day in 1967, the architect James Stirling traveled to the construction site of the Cambridge History Faculty Library, where the architectural photographer Richard Einzig photographed him in the midst of his own work in progress. In the exposures taken that day, Stirling pops up like Kilroy here and there amid the roof trusses, trying out different angles for the camera in a series of photographs (Figure 9.1). These seemingly impromptu shots were followed by a series of elegant presentation photographs after the building had been completed (Figure 9.2). They import a convention (of the artist depicted in his own work) into architecture from the long history of art and the recent history of cinema (à la Alfred, rather than Henry-Russell, Hitchcock), but they also show the architect's evident pleasure in making buildings *and* images. They precede a later drawing type generally credited to Leon Krier. Krier brought a particular parodic signature to drawings in which the architect appeared in his own building (along with Krier himself).[1] But Stirling had already been there in photos, fully ten years before, himself providing the inspiration for Krier's parodies.

These kinds of photographs and drawings are part of a larger array of document types that came to be used regularly in architects' offices after World War II. A more specific taxonomy of representations intended for a variety of different purposes developed throughout the 1950s and 1960s in Western architectural practices, in part to better serve the different constituencies with whom architects interacted. Analytical diagrams, sketches, design development drawings, construction documents, presentation drawings for clients, and sometimes yet different sets of presentation

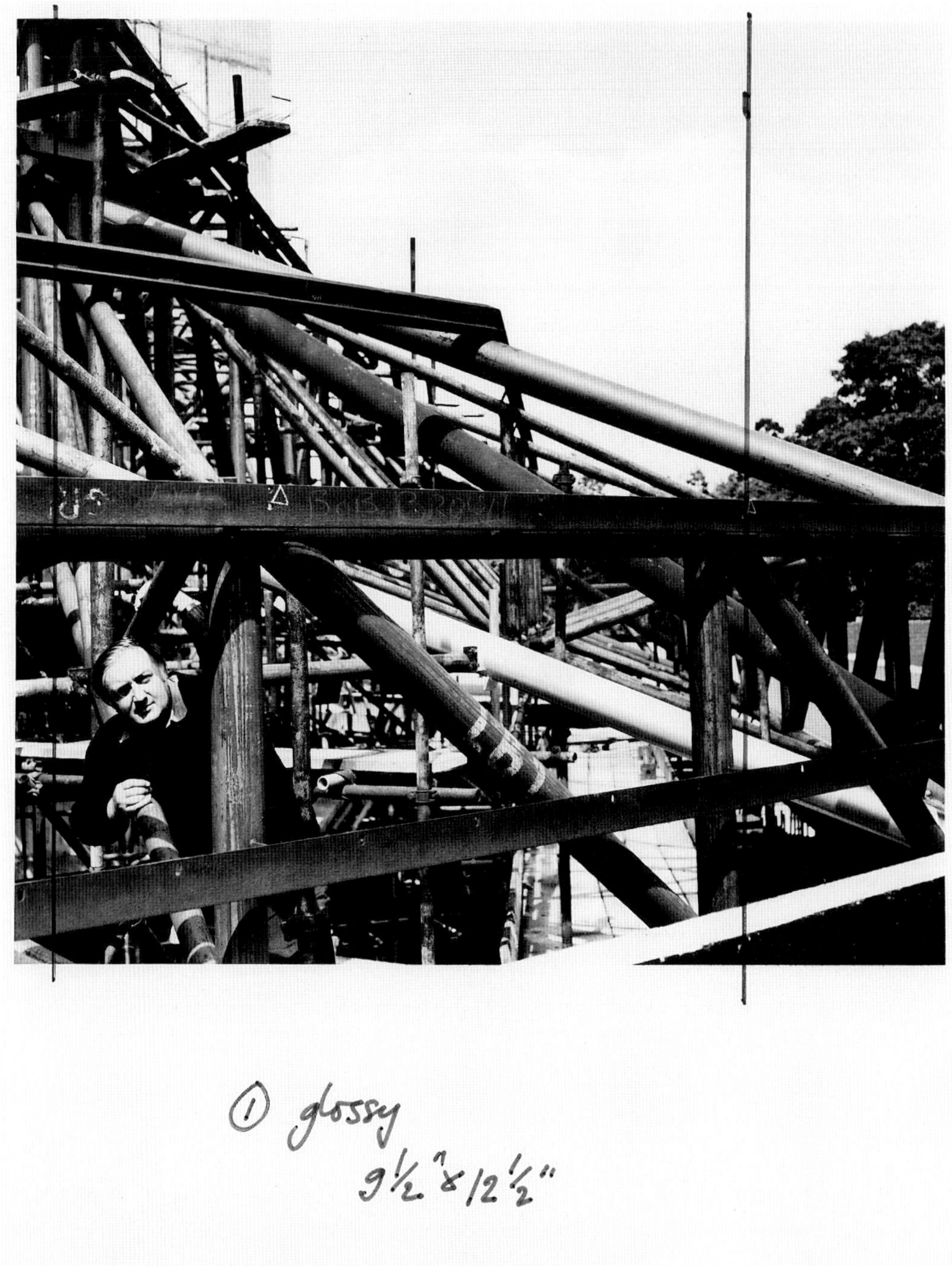

Figure 9.1. James Stirling in the roof of the Cambridge History Faculty Library. Photograph: Richard Einzig. James Stirling/Michael Wilford fonds; Collection Centre Canadien d'Architecture/Canadian Centre for Architecture, Montreal.

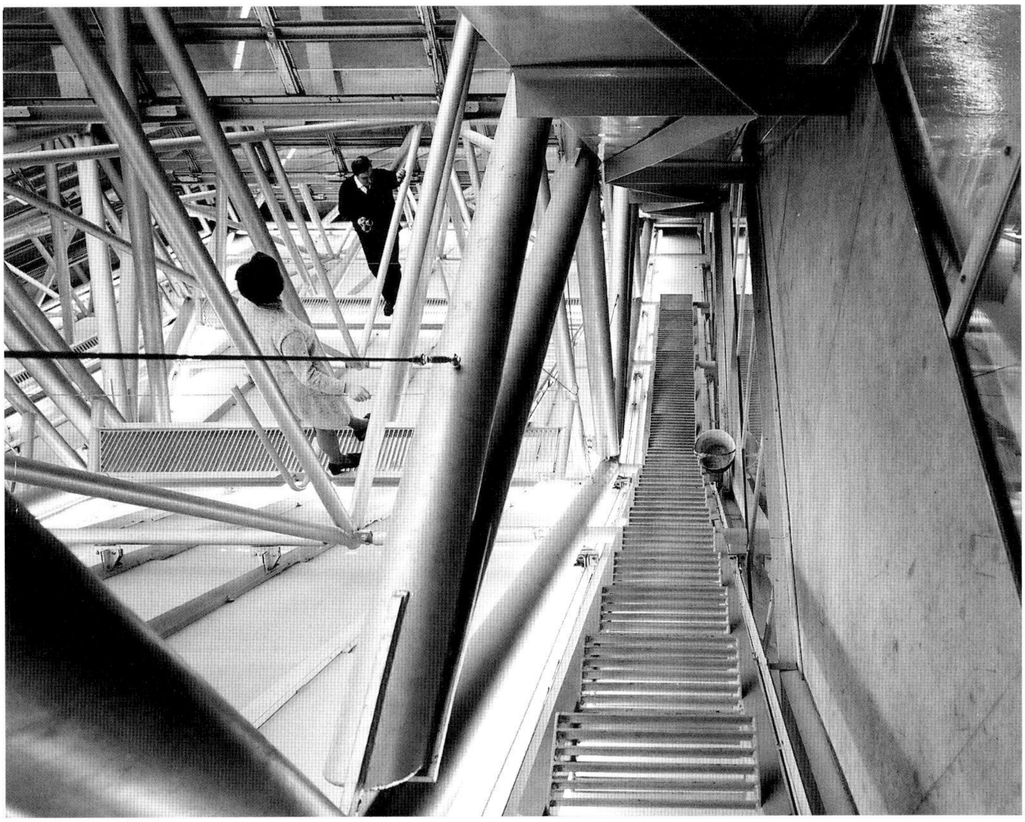

Figure 9.2. James Stirling in the roof of the Cambridge History Faculty Library. Photograph: Richard Einzig. James Stirling/Michael Wilford fonds; Collection Centre Canadien d'Architecture/Canadian Centre for Architecture, Montreal.

drawings for trade publications and for architectural school audiences appeared. Three-dimensional models, photographs of models, and photographs of building sites under construction and of finished buildings were also part of the wider array of representational artifacts that had become necessary to architectural practice. The whole adds up to a palette of different representations for different uses, one that dwarfs the office documentation of interwar practices in number and kind. The stratification of representational practices in architectural offices was of course matched by an increasing specialization of those offices, as they developed expertise in designing particular building types. The postwar period saw an acceleration of the professionalization of architecture generally; Stirling provides one demonstration of how this professionalization coincided with the production of media, and photographic images in particular.

This study of photography and architecture concludes by examining the generalized absorption of photographic images into architectural design—to a scale and degree that could come into existence only after mass-printed commercial photography became essential currency in the global architectural exchange. Like the Smithsons, Stirling absorbed the protocols of photography into his architectural thinking. Unlike the Smithsons' work, however, Stirling's work gives no evidence—nor does the archival record suggest—that the architect sought for transparency or immanence in taking representational protocols into the heart of his work. Nor did he look to Mies as a model in his early architectural work.[2] Rather, in Stirling's case, the prevalence of commercial photographic imaging in his immediate milieu merely reinforced a compositional method that he had adopted from the beginning of his practice and that drew heavily on a different German tradition: hard-line functionalism of the sort practiced most famously by Hannes Meyer. Stirling's inclusion in this study rests on this alternative Germanic and Eastern European tradition, which provided postwar architects, particularly British ones, with a stringent model of a stripped, economical architecture that was nonetheless rich in ideological as well as visual potential, even though this potential had never been fully tapped. In Stirling's case, his functionalist sources were absorbed into a method of accretion and absorption of history through images of all kinds, photographic and other. This method dovetailed with other protocols of the neo-avant-garde in Britain, most specifically neorealism and collage practice. Stirling's imagistic design method also grew from theories of dynamic growth that were sometimes associated with alternate functionalist ideas arising in British architecture more generally at this time.[3]

Early in his career, Stirling developed a design method that began with existing objects known to him in a variety of ways, many from published photographs. He modified this method over time into a distinctive formal language, his own parody, perhaps, of the idea of an "international style" for all users.[4] More important, the image objects that Stirling created constituted new resources for contemporary architecture in his day.[5] Whether Stirling responded to the pressures of name-brand marketing and authorial celebrity by creating a brand of his own or whether he simply borrowed the habits of celebrity marketing in order to pursue his own creative project in a more open fashion is a question that is possibly irrelevant and certainly difficult to answer here. The Stirling "signature" was crafted from many sources: some human, some photographic, some derived from other media instruments, and some from other objects. The architect photographed many himself and gathered others together in his offices.

Stirling was not the only architect to reflect on the status of the image in late twentieth-century architecture at this time—other examples come easily to mind. What distinguishes his work from that of Aldo Rossi, Peter Eisenman, or Robert Venturi and Denise Scott Brown, however, is the way in which images of other buildings—some photographic, others not—were reprocessed into new building in his work and how this reprocessing then became a design method in its own right. It might be said that mechanical reproduction, together with the theories of Reyner Banham, Charles Jencks, and Colin Rowe, enabled this architect to develop a design language that artfully reflected the forces brought to bear on architecture in his time.

James Stirling and Alison and Peter Smithson belonged to the same generation of architects. Stirling was born in 1924 (one year after Peter Smithson) and completed his architectural education after the war at Liverpool University under the tutelage of Rowe, a newly minted doctoral student of Rudolf Wittkower. Stirling's rise to prominence in British architecture postdated that of the Smithsons by a decade; he and his first partner, James Gowan, became architectural celebrities through their Leicester Engineering Building, completed nearly ten years after Hunstanton School, in 1963. Despite the fact that Stirling's interests ran parallel to those of the Smithsons, the two practices demarcate two fundamentally different directions in postwar British architecture. Some background on Stirling's views on interwar modernism on the Continent is helpful for understanding his approach to the photographic image.

Not long after World War II, Stirling had joined a group of other young architects in Britain who were critical of the bureaucracies that had led the immediate post-Blitz recovery of the late 1940s and the 1950s. Stirling focused his energy in at least two directions. In the first place, he explored Continental modernism as represented by Le Corbusier's 1920s residential architecture, in sharp contradistinction to the generalizing architecture of Ludwig Mies van der Rohe, who was then rapidly ascending as the force of American corporate modernism. Stirling's interest in Le Corbusier reflects a general movement in British architecture at this time; it also reflects the influence of Rowe and, through him, Wittkower.[6] Second, Stirling accomplished this revival with the aid of a design method that might be described as both *literal* and *literary* (he used the former term). On the fringes of the (loosely aggregated) Independent Group and Team 10 in London at the beginning of the 1950s, Stirling's overall project was not unique; his methods, however, were distinctive.[7] Like his contemporaries, from the Smithsons to Sandy Wilson, Stirling stood ready to revive the corpse of modernism and extend its life by charting new directions. Unlike most of his fellows, Stirling used the material closest to hand: the miscellaneous built objects of the modern and premodern landscape, overwhelmingly (although not exclusively) British; and the growing mass of published information on architecture, much of it photographic. Throughout the 1950s and 1960s, both with Gowan and on his own, he wove these disparate source references into narratives that embraced architecture as sequential spatial experience, yet staffed it with discrete spatial events, inverting formal relationships and syntaxes with dexterity.[8] Throughout these projects, the

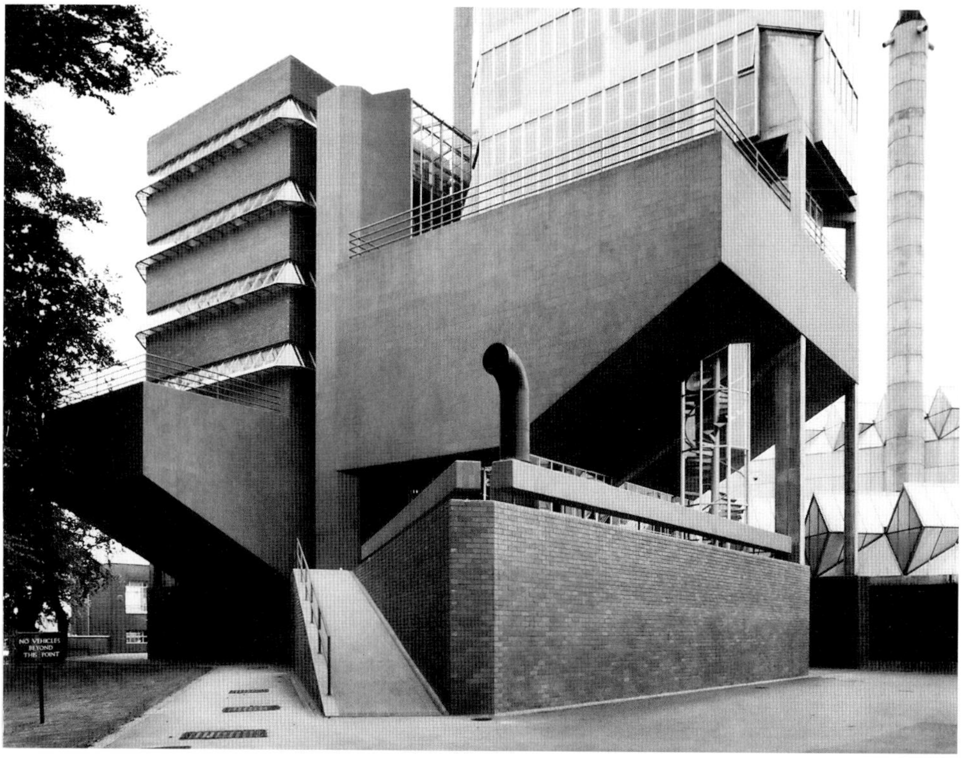

Figure 9.3. Leicester Engineering Building, Leicester University, 1959–63. Architects: James Stirling and James Gowan. Photograph: Y. Futagawa. James Stirling/Michael Wilford fonds; Collection Centre Canadien d'Architecture/Canadian Centre for Architecture, Montreal.

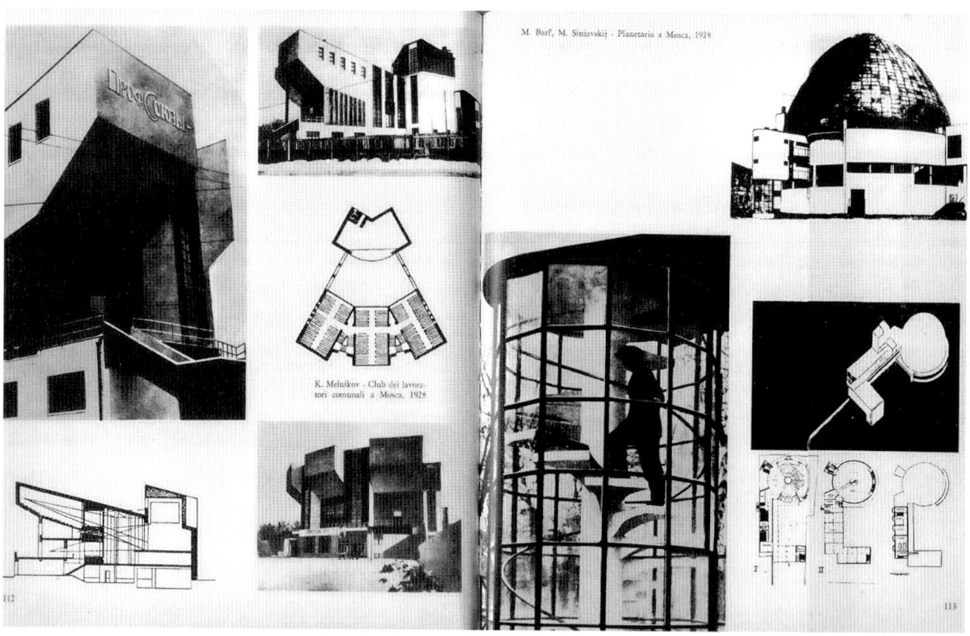

Figure 9.4. Two-page spread from Vittorio De Feo, *URSS: Architettura, 1917–1936* (Rome: Editori Riuniti, 1963), 112–13. Left: Rusakov Workers' Club, 1928–29. Architect: Konstantin Melnikov. Right: Moscow Planetarium, 1928. Architects: Mikhail Barsch and Mikhail Siniavskij.

influence of the photograph in architectural discourse reads through the thin veils of brick tile and glass with which Stirling covered his buildings (Figures 9.3, 9.4). The buildings emit two messages at once: they are functionalist, and they are narrative (representational). One of the things they narrate is the history of functionalism as a mythical ideal, another version of transparency between buildings and their fabrication—quite different from the transparency sought by the Smithsons, analyzed in chapter 8.

FUNCTIONALISM AND REPRESENTATION

Functionalism in modern architecture connected the formal appearance of buildings with their role as useful objects—as tools. Building form narrates the connection between outward appearance and inner workings. This was one of the ways in which building form might be "scripted" with a particular message—generally a message about usefulness or performance. The functional exterior is, in effect, the building's communicative image. Stirling exploited this aspect of functionalism, whether from organic or mechanistic schools, when he adapted ideas from nineteenth-century Beaux-Arts theorist Julien Guadet and arts and crafts architect W. R. Lethaby into his own "functionalist expression." The image objects that can be found in his early work, and then in Stirling and Gowan's projects (and later in Stirling's alone, and then Stirling and Wilford's), bore little resemblance to the thinly coded machine aesthetic of the 1920s. Instead, the aggregate volumes that were joined together around the spine of circulation in the University of Sheffield Arts and Architecture Building competition entry and that appear in the montaged blocks of the Leicester Engineering Building, to cite two examples, recall specific images: Konstantin Melnikov's Rusakov Workers' Club in Moscow of 1928, functionalist architecture of the 1920s, nineteenth-century British factories and commercial architecture, massed fields of red-brick row housing, and greenhouse architecture. The historical roots of these designs may extend back through Le Corbusier to Guadet and Auguste Choisy and to buildings like the Paris Opéra, an exemplar of Beaux-Arts functionalist massing. The method of assembly is part collage/montage and part narration—of improbable episodes, strange scale and material inversions, surreal juxtapositions, and humorous anecdotes.

Similar observations might be made about the work of Richard Hamilton, Eduardo Paolozzi, and even writers such as Thomas Pynchon. This method might best be described as one in which figures from the past are imposed on existing forms of late modernist production (whether art, architecture, literature, or some other medium). We might describe these as figurative fragments overlaid on remnant infrastructures of abstraction. Photographs of famous buildings like the Rusakov are transformed from part images back into montage elements embedded in the chassis of a project like that for the University of Sheffield, an unsuccessful competition entry of 1953.[9] Stirling's functional expression combined the two notions of use (or function) and representation. Lecture theaters are not simply functional containers; they are, rather, markers of programmatic *and* historical function—nods to past architectures and referential objects whose sequential mounted assembly tells a new story through functionalist aggregation. This idea of functionalism recalls the work of Banham and Rowe, who reconnected Le Corbusier to earlier roots—and attests Stirling's own familiarity with theorists like Guadet.[10] Stirling learned the history of functionalism from these two but also from publications—recycled for use in collage/montage. To understand his use of this term more clearly, we might look briefly at the Leicester Engineering Building in relation to work by contemporaries such as Paolozzi and Hamilton. Although the comparison with Hamilton may in many ways be the most telling, the parallel with Paolozzi is clearest and most dramatic, and that connection is briefly described here. We might first turn to the issue of expression and representation.

MONTAGE AND INTEGRATED SURFACE

The *Wittgenstein* series (1964) of prints by Eduardo Paolozzi figured prominently on the walls of Stirling's Belsize Park home, documents of an exchange between the two artists that probably dates from the mid-1960s, although the two were connected earlier by the Institute of Contemporary Arts, and both participated in the exhibition "This Is Tomorrow" in 1956. Paolozzi had returned to London from a two-year stint in Paris in 1949, bringing Continental *art brut* influences with him. He then worked independently but also collaborated with Henderson, the Smithsons, and Roland Jenkins in activities now associated with the Independent Group.

Upon his return from France, Paolozzi worked in a variety of media, although his primary activity was sculpture and graphic art. His *art brut* sculptures of the 1950s were complex but roughly cast pieces. They included everyday objects sucked into the vortex of lost wax castings and spit out again as solid objects in bronze, in works like *St. Sebastian Number I* of 1957 (Figure 9.5). Ben Highmore has explored this mode of work; he quotes Paolozzi in a 1959 interview: "In the finished casting, the original *objets trouvés* are no longer present at all, as they are in the Dada and Surrealist compositions of this kind. They survive in my sculptures only as ghosts of form that still haunt the bronze, details of its surface or its actual structure."[11] Paolozzi's work became smoother in the early 1960s, disciplined by a machine aesthetic in which all disparate objects had the same highly finished, machine-made surface, as in *Mechaniks Bench* or *Towards a New Laocoön*, both of 1963 (Figure 9.6).[12]

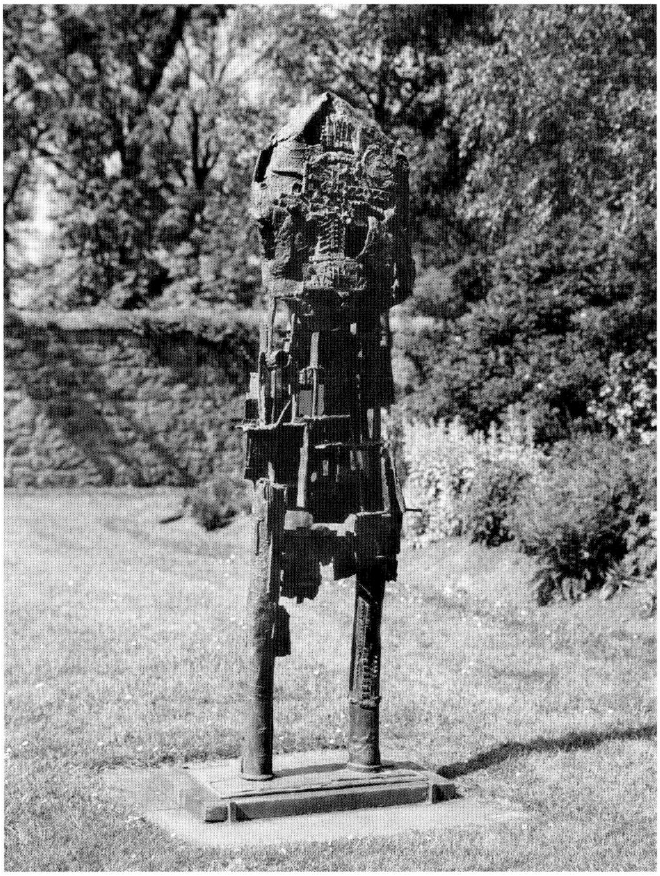

Figure 9.5. Eduardo Paolozzi, *St. Sebastian Number I*, 1957. Photograph from Scottish National Gallery of Modern Art. Photograph copyright 2012 Trustees of the Paolozzi Foundation; licensed by DACS/Artists Rights Society (ARS), New York.

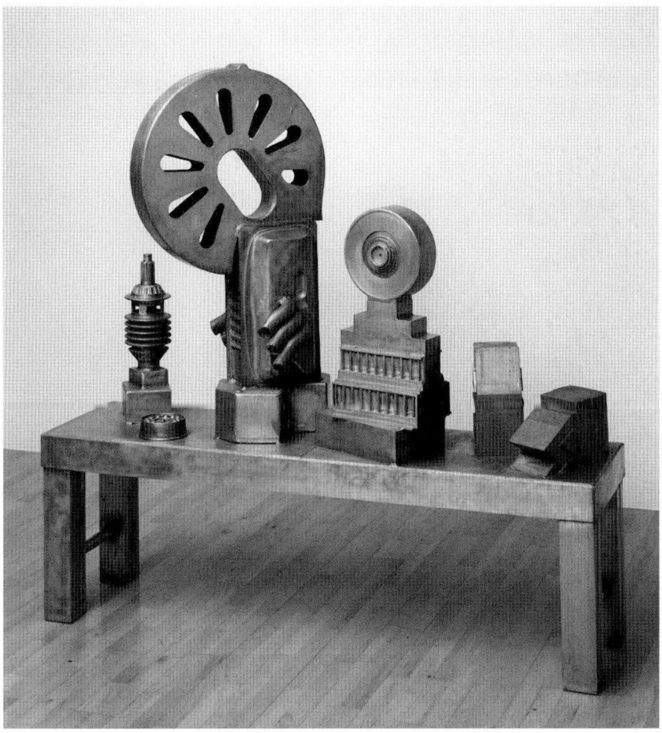

Figure 9.6. Eduardo Paolozzi, *Mechaniks Bench*, 1963. Photograph copyright 2012 Tate, London, and Trustees of the Paolozzi Foundation; licensed by DACS/Artists Rights Society (ARS), New York.

Stirling's writing records a similar transition. Although he never delved deeply into brutalist aesthetics in his own work, he processed brutalism as he found it in the postwar work of Le Corbusier. By the late 1950s, disturbed by the rough faces of Le Corbusier's Maison Jaoul, Stirling argued instead for the machine quality of smooth surfaces wrapping assemblages of disparate objects. The unified surface of these hybrid creations might then act as the locus of narration, with function, structure, and material all described by the architect as eminently pragmatic allocations *and* expressive opportunities.[13] Stirling adapted earlier Continental functionalism into a strategy for aggregative architectural representation—a strategy of montage or assembly. There are striking similarities in the fact that both artists treated montage/collage, paradoxically, as integration; in Stirling's case, the individuated objects of the Leicester Engineering Building, for example, were all wrapped in a skin of red brick, glazed tile, or glass, disciplining disparity through shiny, hard, architectural surface.[14] In a seminal essay on the building, Peter Eisenman has described the apparent refunctioning of brick, tile, and glass at Leicester as semantic ambiguity.[15] This inversion, in which materials are repurposed for new and unexpected uses, follows Dadaist and surrealist technique, but it also makes surface facture into the primary binder of disparate figurative parts.[16] Such a translation of collage fragments into assemblages of finished aggregate forms enclosed within a single surface constituted a fundamental reorganization of pre–World War II collage. Stirling's preference for smooth, shiny, enclosing surfaces recalls the surface of the eight-by-ten glossy print, or the printed surfaces of publications filled with architectural photographs.

The chapter on Guadet and his *Éléments et théories de l'architecture* (1901–4) in Banham's influential *Theory and Design in the First Machine Age* of 1960 provides a key to Stirling's functional expression. On composition as the aggregation of volumes, Banham quotes J. N. L. Durand: "Any complete building whatever is not, and cannot be, anything but the result of the assembly and putting together (composition) of a greater or lesser number of parts." Guadet, he noted, adopted a "particulate" approach: "The approach is particulate; small structural and functional members (elements of architecture) are assembled to make functional volumes, and these (elements of composition) are assembled to make whole buildings. To do this is to compose in the literal and derivational sense of the word, to put together."[17] Banham published these words in 1960, but his ideas were well-known to his contemporaries, both gleaned from and shared among members of his immediate architectural community, including Stirling. Stirling did more, however, than reinvent a way to make functionalist buildings into narrative devices (which they had always been); his innovations prompt some consideration.

In his work of the 1960s and beyond, Stirling connected a historical idea about building composition with history and collage/montage in his own architecture, embracing functional volumes derived not solely from notions of pure usage but also from historical evidence—from the polemical history of modernism and its British precursors. Buildings like the Leicester Engineering Building or the Sheffield design exemplify this approach. In a building such as the Florey Building at the Queen's College at Oxford University, by contrast, a different strategy was used. In this case, disparate historical references accrue to a single integrated building in which discrete functional volumes have begun to disappear. Instead, the distinction of parts that characterized the Sheffield competition project and the Leiceister Engineering Building dissolves into a single object where the borders of separate functional or montage elements become blurred together. Paolozzi's description above offers a way to think about these projects, where the "ghosts" of functionalist history appear as traces. References are overlaid on and integrated into the same object, so that multiple readings emerge from a single set of forms. This method, which Stirling had begun using earlier and pursued at Oxford, is worth exploring. It replaces the method of montage or assembly (to which Stirling would return later) with the demonstration of how a building might reflect and absorb a host of references—or iconic and noniconic images, perhaps—within a single object. Stirling's earlier approach to aggregated forms has here morphed into a design method in which preexisting objects and images are absorbed into new wholes. Both approaches to functional and historical reference define a phase of architectural practice in which the image had come to play a primary role in the three-dimensional realization of architecture, as explored below. In these sorts of projects, however, existent images began to turn into new ones in which past architecture was reprocessed and endowed with new life. Stirling was, again, not alone in this procedure, yet the results of his experimentation with image objects are particularly interesting.

REAL THINGS: THE FLOREY BUILDING

The Florey Building was built for the Queen's College of Oxford University between 1966 and 1971. It is a strange object, whether in drawings or on-site.[18] Its wraparound shape staggers backward as it rises from the ground, supported on angled *pilotis* like a building still under construction or, perhaps, an undergraduate resting on his punt poles in the river nearby. The history of the commission is a story of conflict and architectural tragedy, the building's theatrical shape a record of its own Shakespearean genesis. First, Stirling inserted a red-brick renegade into the midst of Britain's most elite academic precinct. We might call the result a Pyrrhic victory, thanks to architectural reductions that resulted from struggles over budget and architectural value between the architect and the resistant client. Florey is a

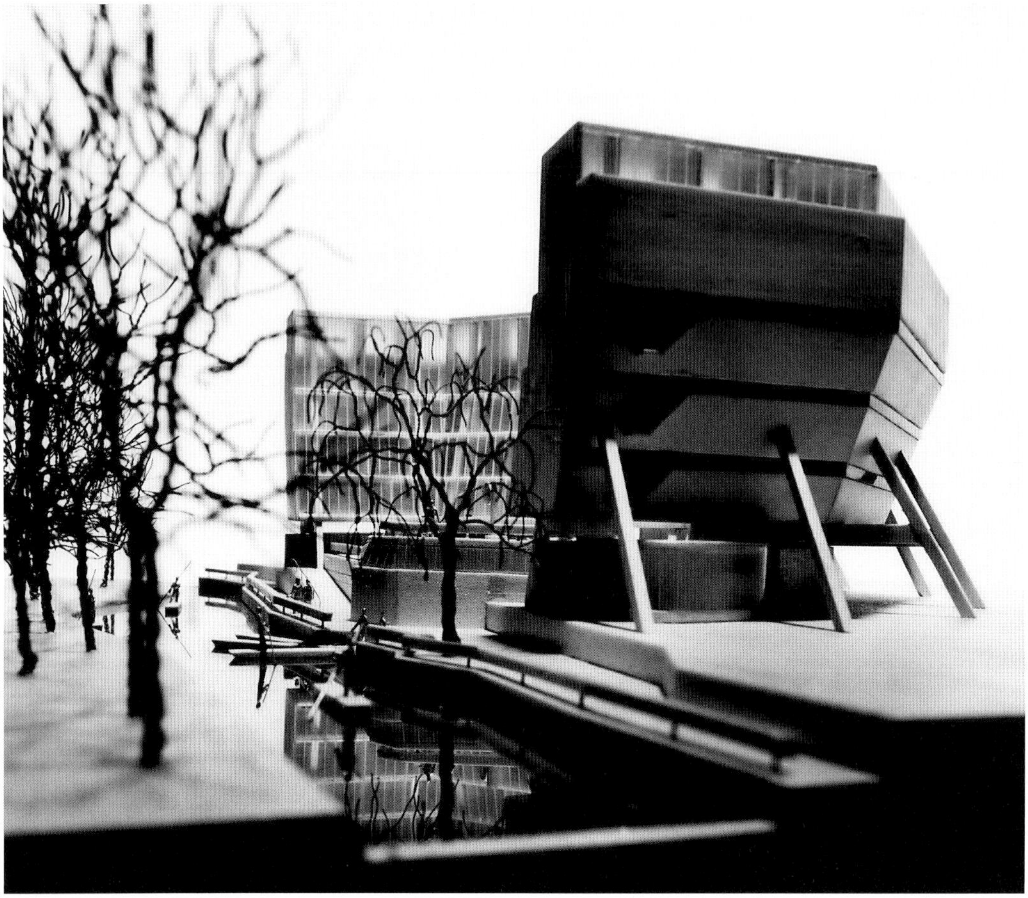

Figure 9.7. Model, the Florey Building, Queen's College, Oxford, 1966–71. Architect: James Stirling. James Stirling/Michael Wilford fonds; Collection Centre Canadien d'Architecture/Canadian Centre for Architecture, Montreal.

precarious building—both precarious looking and, until recently, existing precariously on its site.[19]

Florey also demonstrates Stirling's architectural method by the mid-1960s. His way of assembling parts of preexisting buildings and industrial objects into new buildings underwent a significant alteration after Leicester, although the parts can still be enumerated with some precision in buildings like this. The terraced profile of the section recalls several precedents (Figure 9.7). The building looks like a theater, but rather like a tall, cramped Elizabethan theater, although Stirling may also have been citing constructivist architecture, as he had done at Leicester. Nikolai Ladovsky's drawn project for a Communal House (1920) is a possible precedent. In addition to Elizabethan theaters, Russian utopian fantasies, and tipsy punters, the building speaks to the history of recent modern architecture. It is filled with arcane references to architecture culture.[20]

The stepped section found in a modified version in the Florey Building appeared in interwar modernism in sanatoriums and hospitals, as a way of maximizing sun exposure to rooms on different floors of a tall building. The same building type was used in schemes for mass housing for similar reasons. Marcel Breuer and Gustav Hassenpflug's 1929 project for a hospital building for 1,100 beds with a stepped section (Figure 9.8) appeared in Alberto Sartoris's *Gli elementi dell'architettura funzionali,* a basic sourcebook for Stirling (his much-used copy was cloaked in synthetic white fur).[21] But the Smithsons provide a more proximate source, and their influence is important for understanding Stirling's Florey project. In their work for the 1955 preparatory meeting at La Sarraz in preparation for the tenth CIAM conference (CIAM X) at Dubrovnik (the "Dubrovnik scroll"), the Smithsons included a stepped section, terraced housing complex organized in a gentle curving semicircle, part of

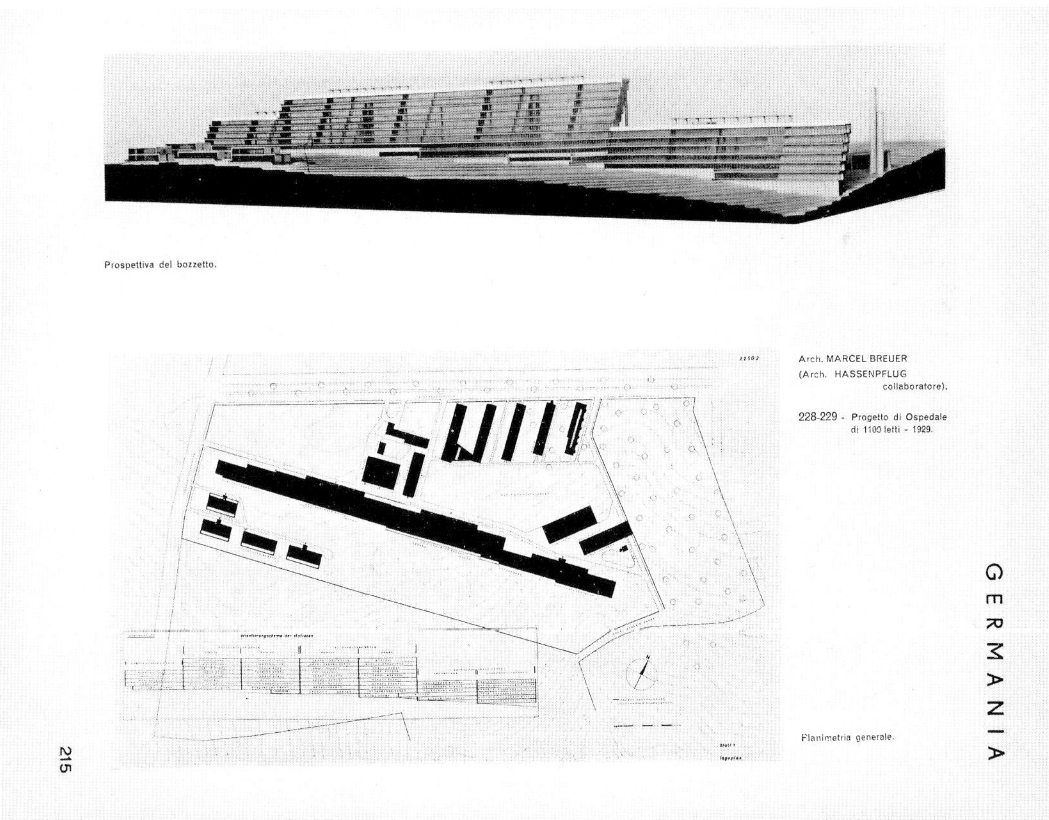

Figure 9.8. Project for a hospital building with 1,100 beds, 1929. Architects: Marcel Breuer and Gustav Hassenpflug. From Alberto Sartoris, *Gli elementi dell'architettura funzionali: Sintesi panoramica dell'architettura moderna* (Milan: Ulrico Hoepli, 1932). Marcel Breuer Estate.

the urban "scale of association." The section of this project, like that of Florey, tips back as it rises, buttressed by structural supports regularly arrayed along the curve. Each twelve-storied maisonette unit is part of a larger cluster in a landscape sketch in the Dubrovnik scroll, like an assembly of fragmented arcs.[22] The section of these buildings is remarkably similar to that of the Florey Building.

A perspective drawing of the continuous terrace that runs along the front of the units shows two figures in the foreground (Figure 9.9). It resembles Le Corbusier's similar sketch of the housing terraces of the Plan Obus for Algiers (1931), although the scale of Le Corbusier's project is considerably larger and the geometry less regular. From the Plan Obus scheme, one of four irregularly curved units may have been a reference for the Smithson design (Figure 9.10). In Le Corbusier's apartment buildings at Oued-Ouchaia (1933–34), however, a long, straight bar building has a section that otherwise resembles the Smithson scheme closely (Figure 9.11). The Smithsons appear to have collated the two Corbusian projects in their housing scheme for CIAM.[23] Their project recalls contemporary interest in mass housing in a long tradition of CIAM work dating back to 1929. In addition to these precedents, all of which accrue to Stirling's Florey Building in layered references that

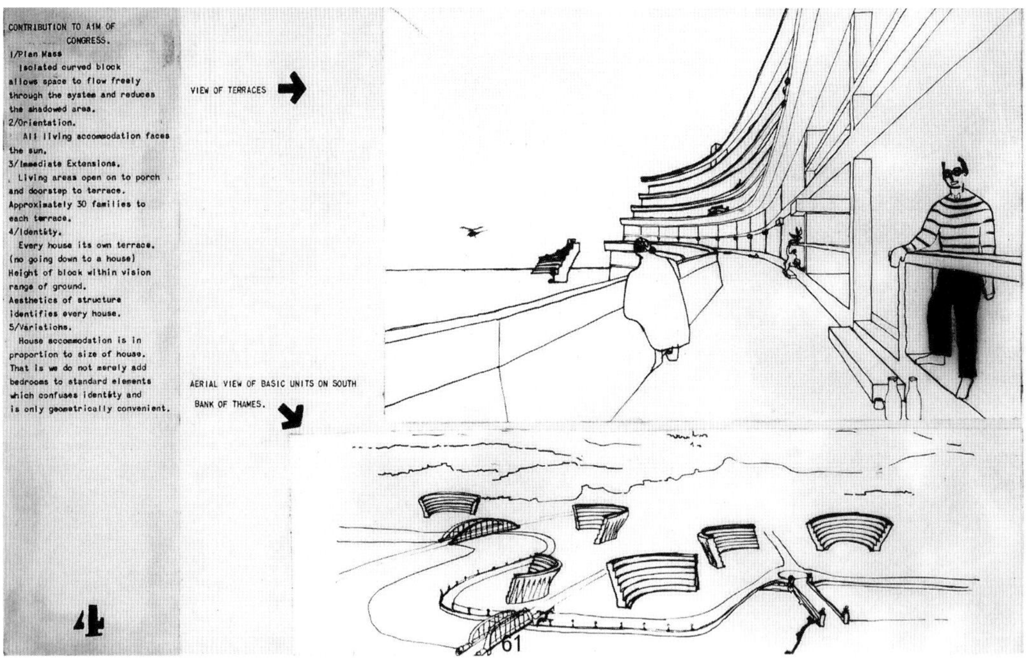

Figure 9.9. Perspective for CIAM X, Dubrovnik, Yugoslavia, 1956. Architects: Alison and Peter Smithson. NAi Collections and Archive, Rotterdam.

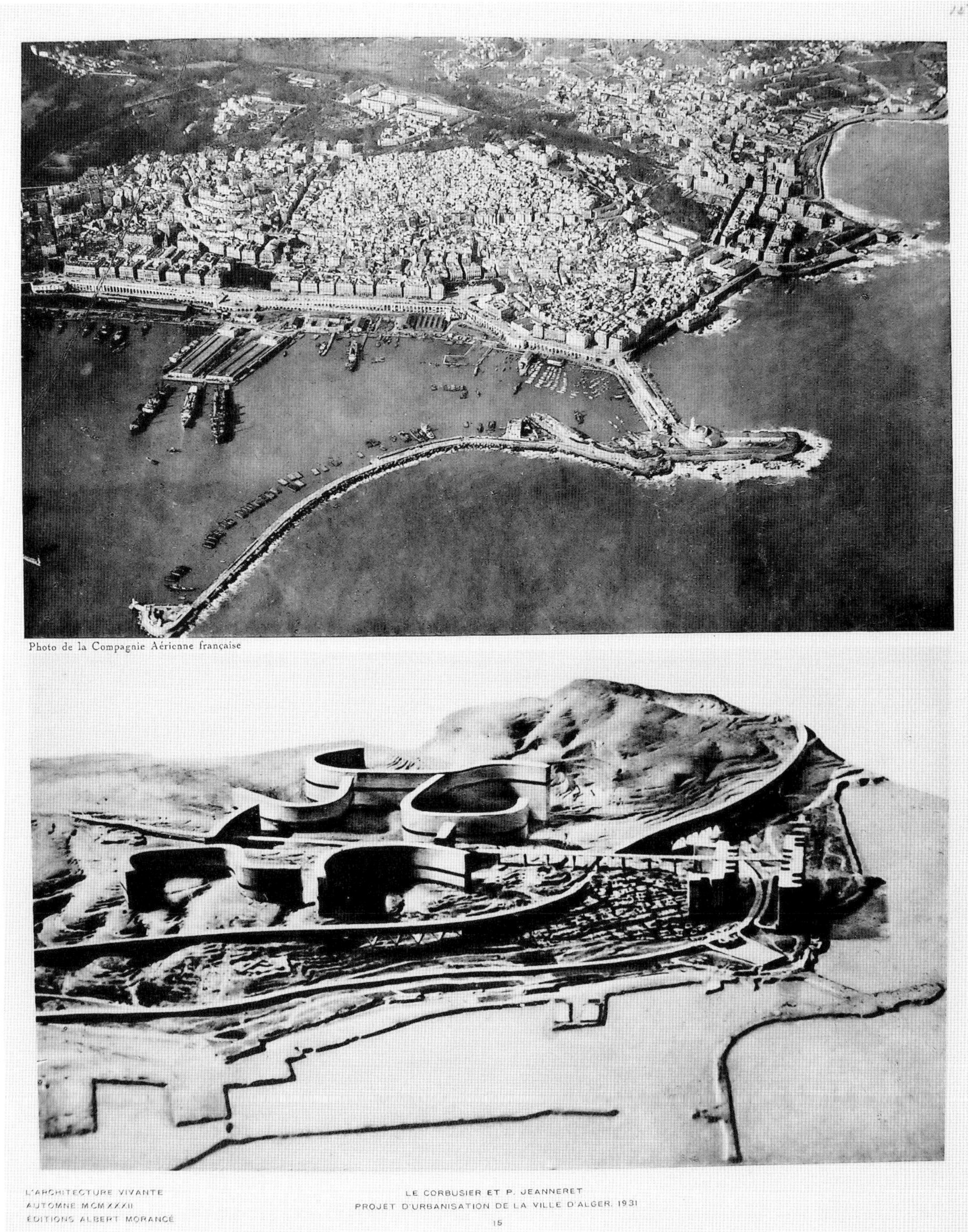

Figure 9.10. Plan Obus for Algiers, 1931. Architects: Le Corbusier and Pierre Jeanneret. From *L'Architecture Vivante*, Autumn 1932.

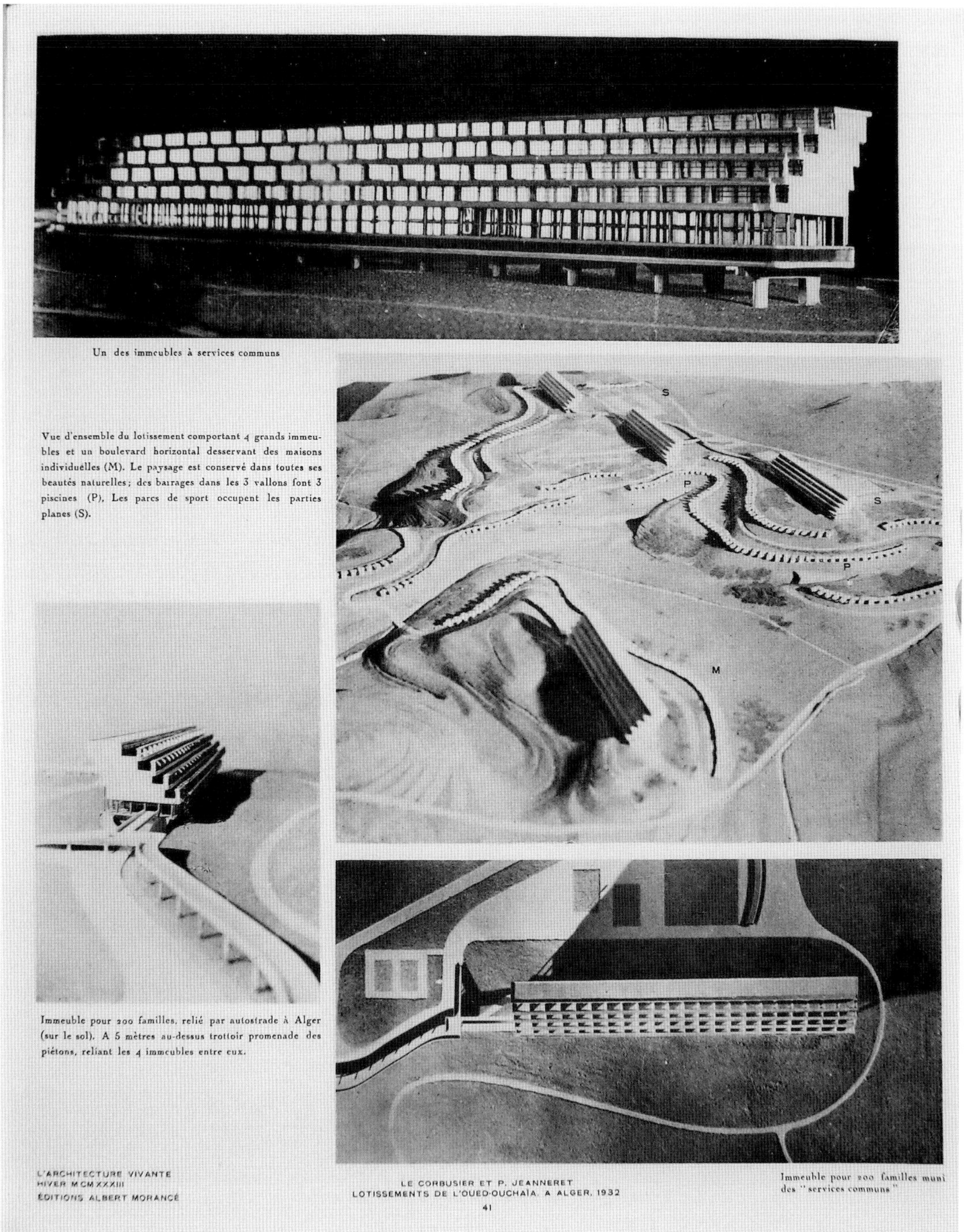
Un des immeubles à services communs

Vue d'ensemble du lotissement comportant 4 grands immeubles et un boulevard horizontal desservant des maisons individuelles (M). Le paysage est conservé dans toutes ses beautés naturelles; des barrages dans les 3 vallons font 3 piscines (P). Les parcs de sport occupent les parties planes (S).

Immeuble pour 200 familles, relié par autostrade à Alger (sur le sol). A 5 mètres au-dessus trottoir promenade des piétons, reliant les 4 immeubles entre eux.

Immeuble pour 200 familles muni des "services communs"

L'ARCHITECTURE VIVANTE
HIVER MCMXXXIII
ÉDITIONS ALBERT MORANCÉ

LE CORBUSIER ET P. JEANNERET
LOTISSEMENTS DE L'OUED-OUCHAÏA, A ALGER, 1932
41

Figure 9.11. Durand Housing, Oued-Ouchaia, Algeria, 1933–34. Architect: Le Corbusier. From *L'Architecture Vivante*, Winter 1933.

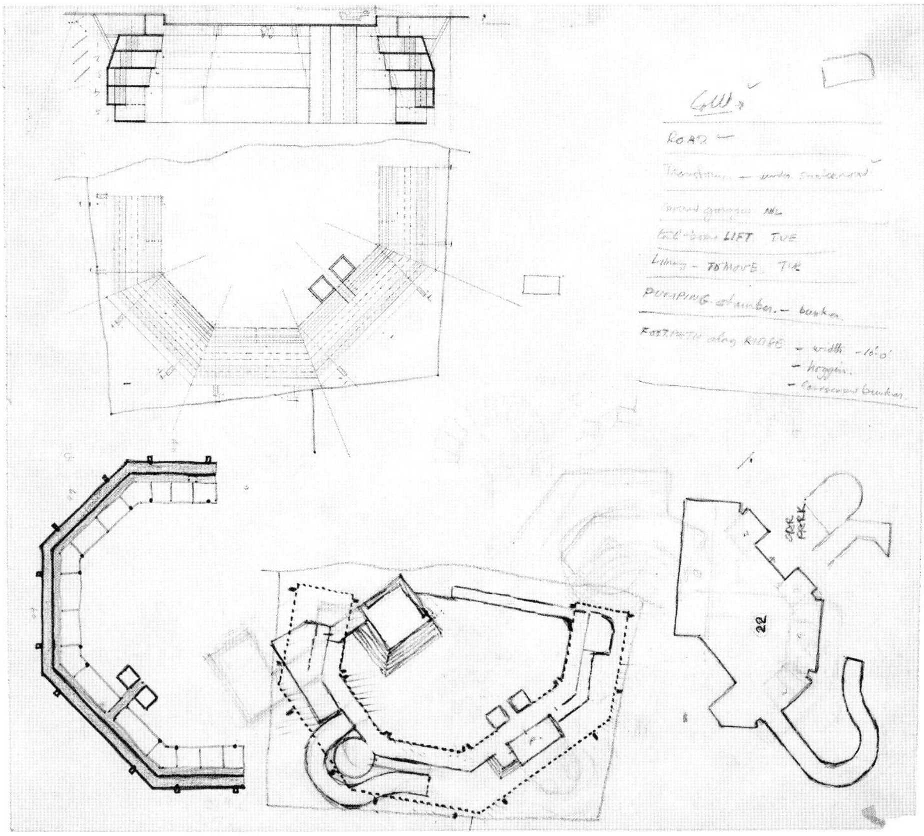

Figure 9.12. Design drawing for the Florey Building, Queen's College, Oxford, 1966–71. Architect: James Stirling. James Stirling/Michael Wilford fonds; Collection Centre Canadien d'Architecture/Canadian Centre for Architecture, Montreal.

were apparently too arcane for general audiences, Stirling himself emphasized the internal references to Oxbridge collegiate architecture, possibly as a camouflage for his modernist engagements.[24]

In contrast to the Smithsons' project, Stirling deregularized the geometry of the Oxford building; it is faceted, not curved (Figure 9.12). Nor is it symmetrical around a central axis. It recalls centralized theater architecture, or the Smithsons' curved housing, but at the same time resembles a series of units strung together and then wrapped into an *approximately* centralized building. Finally, Stirling quotes himself: in addition to the Selwyn College competition of 1959 with Gowan, Florey conjures the Cambridge History Faculty Library turned inside out, like a jacket with the sleeves pulled through to the wrong side. The catalog of references for this building surely extends further, but these examples suffice to illustrate the method, which resulted in a building that is as singular as it is multireferential. The density of references suggests a shift in the architect's frame of reference, from a context in which single buildings might merit response and reaction in the creation of new architecture to one where existing buildings (built and unbuilt) appear in series or multiples. This recalls the architect's training from precedents found in books and photographs rather than in buildings on sites.

The singularity of the Florey Building is directly connected to the multiplicity of references it contains: it is *like* but not *the same as* any one of them. This results in the paradox of a unique multireferential object, one whose character rests on simultaneous appropriation of and resistance to a multiplicity of other objects, one in which a range of images hover over a singular building, perhaps akin to the "ghosts of utopia" by which Reinhold Martin has described the postmodern period.[25] Stirling's approach to historical precedent was distinctive in its acceptance and appropriation of multiplicities of images. This distinction emerges further through comparison with the Smithsons.

IMAGES IN POSTWAR BUILDING

What is the difference between Alison and Peter Smithson referencing work by Le Corbusier in their own building project and Stirling quoting the Smithsons quoting Le Corbusier in his? The Smithsons were concerned with producing an architecture of reality, "without rhetoric," "as found," that was capable of representing the hard, brute, material realities of postwar life.[26] They had created precisely that sort of building in the Hunstanton Secondary Modern School (1949–54), and the term *New Brutalism* soon came into use as a descriptor, drawn partly from the immediacy of Jean Dubuffet's *art brut*. As Ben Highmore has pointed out, the Smithsons' conception of bare-bones, infrastructural architecture was intended to allow the automatic or unconscious aggregations of daily life to accrue (and these latter aggregations were supplied by Paolozzi and Nigel Henderson within Independent Group projects such as "Patio and Pavilion").

As noted in chapter 8, the Smithsons' efforts to produce this infrastructural architecture at Hunstanton were rendered considerably more complex by the pictorial qualities that inhered in their nonrhetorical architecture, particularly in the case of a rural secondary school that was widely consumed through a series of remarkable photographs.[27] Nonetheless, the Smithsons could be considered central participants in the effort to derive a realist program for modern architecture in their time, both thanks to their own declarations and thanks to the transparency of their work in relation to its tasks, from Hunstanton to the Economist Building. Their belief in the nonrhetorical "reality effect" in architecture was sincere, despite or because of their sensitivity to adjacent practices like photography.

By contrast, Stirling's architecture occasionally seems playful to the point of near frivolity, even in its hardest, most machined versions. To return briefly to CIAM X, the Smithsons adapted a pair of organizational ideas found in Corbusian mass housing as the basis for a pragmatic general solution to an immediate problem. Broadly speaking, they extended and corrected their elder. Stirling, by contrast, tinkered with a seemingly jerry-built machine, one that appears as if it might, but does not, lift off the ground, rather like an architectural version of one of Jean Tinguely's kinetic sculptures. The unexpectedness of the Florey Building, like many of Stirling's other projects, cannot be explained solely by an enumeration of its sources or its parts. A host of precedents simultaneously present yet absent in a single architectural object suggests instead a new operation for images in postwar building. Florey is like an amalgamated picture of architecture, or a series of pictures transformed into a single object. The building preserves its pictorial antecedents within its final form, as glancing references, or traces. This is not to suggest an excessive dependence of architecture on pictorial arts, but rather to note that the architectural fragments present in Stirling's buildings were more likely to be known to young architects in the 1950s *as images*—as a storehouse or database—than to be known from visits to buildings on sites. Stirling himself noted, "My education in modern architecture was a very literal one, i.e. from books—lectures—not the education of apprenticeship or direct experience which was the way with the generation older than mine."[28] The difference between Stirling's acceptance of this condition and the Smithsons' resistance to it marks a shift in architecture, despite the similar ages of the principal actors. In this period of architectural practice, photographic and other images became authoritative sources for designed objects. It was a period in which architects were compelled to pump three-dimensional information back into two-dimensional surface images through relays between sequences of pictures (either orthographic or photographic), through imagination and poetic license, and through conscious strategies of hybridization and pastiche. We might thus qualify existing histories of postmodernism; when Fredric Jameson noted, parenthetically, that "individual buildings are . . . objects only in photographs," he might also have noted that photographs become objects, often, in buildings, and that the period in question—the postwar period—involved substantial processual change in the ways in which buildings are conceived.[29]

How can we best understand the divide between the work of Stirling and that of the Smithsons? The difference between them relates to a quality of picture making that *inheres in* the former but *applies to* the latter. Stirling's architecture reflects a pictorial history of buildings reinstated in constructed objects, whether in aggregate, particulate forms or in synthetic formal objects; the Smithsons tried to use images, instead, to communicate qualities of hard material reality. Just as artists like Francis

Bacon, Hamilton, Paolozzi, Yves Klein, Raymond Hains, and Jacques de la Villeglé made realism a strategy of representation that shunned mimesis and incipient photorealism in favor of presentations of realist fragments, so Stirling produced an architecture that absorbed the realist fragments of a late modern world, offering them to the world of architecture, and the public at large, as reflections on cultural relations, politics, the performance of daily life, modernity, and—perhaps most of all—architecture's connection to imageability.

REYNER BANHAM

The term *imageability* brings Reyner Banham's ideas to bear on Stirling's images more fully, to relate them to Banham's theories of architecture and image in the mid-1950s. It is Banham's elusive concept of "memorability as image" as a counter and parallel to formal legibility that also best describes Stirling's working method in this phase of his practice, and in future.[30] Banham explained the relationship between the two, and while his views ultimately failed to persuade Alison and Peter Smithson (and vice versa), they were nevertheless influential in their time and since. From the historian's vantage point, Banham's work provides a diagnostic opportunity at a critical historical juncture, one that seems to enter into a resounding call and response with Stirling's work (Figure 9.13).

Just as the Smithsons were working out the principles of their architecture in the years between 1949 and 1953 at Hunstanton, so Banham was developing his early critical position. In the course of his 1955 essay "The New Brutalism," Banham defined the movement in relation to Hunstanton School, as already noted. By the end of the essay, he emended his third criterion, "formal legibility of plan," to "memorability as an image," partly based on his analysis of Hunstanton School. His conclusions were that contemporary (New Brutalist) architecture was based on (1) materials as found, (2) structure clearly displayed, and (3) "memorability as image," a concept that relates to the brand, trademark, or logo—the immediately recognizable sign as a communications device—and to the Gestalt theory of which such symbols partake.

We might look back to sources of Banham's ideas about New Brutalism briefly. Beginning with Wittkower's formal clarity, or "legibility," the Smithsons ended with the raw image of architecture then described by Banham. Describing an architectural approach in which appearance and conceptual structure would coalesce, Banham twice used the phrase "a coherent and apprehensible visible entity." Noting the importance of Wittkower's book to Hunstanton School's original conception, he effectively minimized Wittkower's significance to the final result by substituting memorability for the formal legibility described by the older historian. The differ-

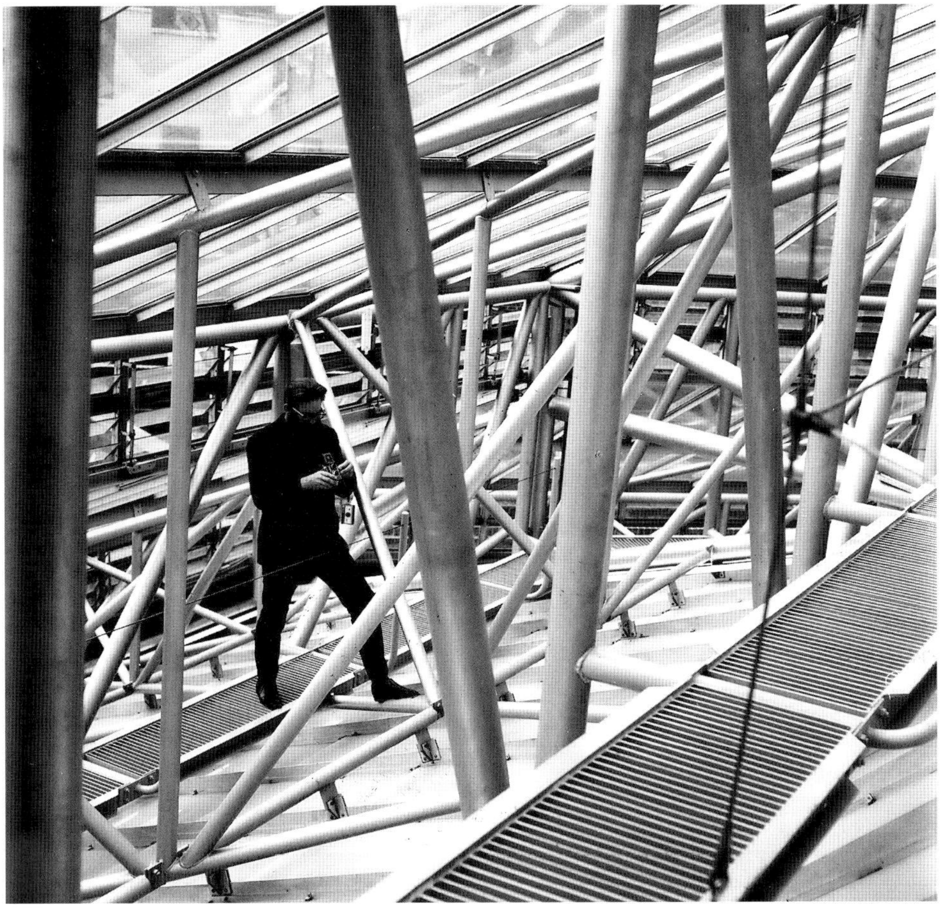

Figure 9.13. Reyner Banham in the roof of the Cambridge History Faculty Library. Architectural Press Archive/RIBA Library Photographs Collection.

ence between legibility and memorability hinges not on what is immediately visible but rather on what is not. Banham described a manner of visibility in which that which is no longer in view is nevertheless retained as an image, a powerful visual impression that lodges in the mind and sticks there. Through this formulation, Banham funneled some of his insights about commercial advertising directly into his theory of architecture, as well as architectural history. "Memorability as an image" is roughly similar to "branding," in which image recognition is portable and moves with the viewer. But Banham was talking about buildings themselves, and he used the word *image* comparatively—a building should perform *like an image*; it should be retained in the mind *as an image*.

If the concept of "legibility as image" thus sums up the ways in which the realm of images and the realm of solid construction in space had begun to overlap and interpenetrate in postwar modern architecture, it also describes the way that

Hunstanton was produced—both as authentic construction ("real architecture") and *as an image of authentic construction.* Derived from images, it would also be read from images, and it had the programmatic clarity of an image incorporated into its very structure. The quality of being imageable was embedded in the architecture not solely because it would be reproduced in books, magazines, and slide lectures, but also because the act of understanding architecture as part of culture had become inseparable from immediately graspable images—which in turn refracted back onto the design procedures of architects themselves.

Banham's theory of proactive projection into image emerged at the same time that he absorbed the Smithsons' work, but differently from their own understanding, as he himself noted in 1966.[31] Most important, Banham's formulation suggests a different kind of cognitive perception from that implied by Wittkower, one premised on repeatable memorable images that began to constitute the substrate of public consciousness in the age of photography and mass media, not on the formal legibility of a single building.[32] Banham's schema may have initially grown from the historian's concern for analyzing existing constructions (as his debt to Wittkower and his own art historical training show). But his broader intent was directly and unapologetically operative: as a critic, he theorized for architects.[33] And just as architects moved inexorably forward to generate new products for consuming markets, so Banham moved as well, leaving concern for the image in architecture behind when he turned to the question of networks and systems in the late 1960s. Before turning to the same moment in Stirling's work, we might look at the trajectory of his design work at this time.

STIRLING'S OBJECTS

A sketch among the drawings for the Olivetti Headquarters projected for Milton Keynes in 1974 but remaining unbuilt illustrates some of the volumetric objects that Stirling developed and then used in project after project at different scales (Figure 9.14). Just as the Florey was a "singular building," so can one identify a family of these forms in Stirling's practice at a wide range of scales. These "units" are a kind of image; more than simply formal objects, they are sometimes type objects (whether buildings, parts of buildings, or components of building), they recur throughout Stirling's history, and they come with references attached. These are, or become, "memorable images" through Stirling's inventive manipulations. They are increasingly a store of personalized image objects that relate to his previous use of images and objects drawn from the history of architecture as seen at the Leicester Engineering Building or the Sheffield competition entry. Stirling's design process was partly

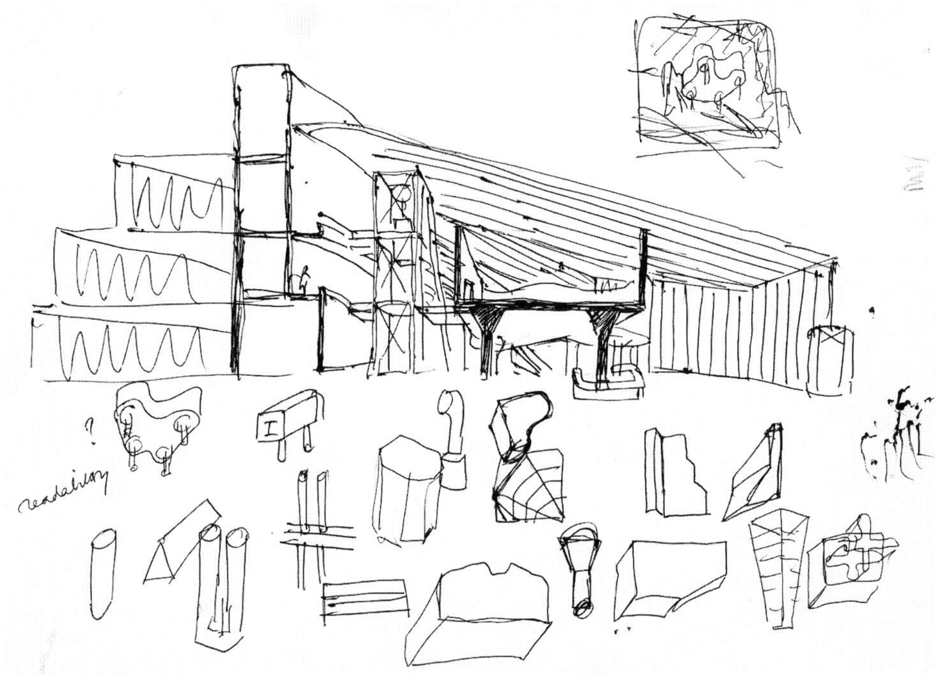

Figure 9.14. Sketch with architectural image objects, Olivetti Headquarters, Milton Keynes, England, 1974. Architect: James Stirling. James Stirling/Michael Wilford fonds; Collection Centre Canadien d'Architecture/Canadian Centre for Architecture, Montreal.

an ongoing project to define an image vocabulary of visibly recognizable image objects, but also increasingly of less recognizable objects created by the architect.[34]

Stirling maintained methodological continuity in his design process throughout his career. Anthony Vidler has noted that "analysis of the program, separation of its elements into volumetric units, and combination of the units through circulation" characterized Stirling's design process.[35] Against this overarching continuity we might also note the finer-grained changes to Stirling's design process that occurred over time. The "volumetric units" used in his early buildings perform like three-dimensional things reduced to flatness by drawing or photograph, then blown back up into three dimensions and placed on or within the framework of a building. These are just the sort of "memorable images" that Banham called for in 1955. They are also, quite literally, images from Stirling's own library—from Alberto Sartoris, from the British architectural press, from his childhood memories and his adult fact-finding expeditions. But both the source material and the architectural results changed over time.

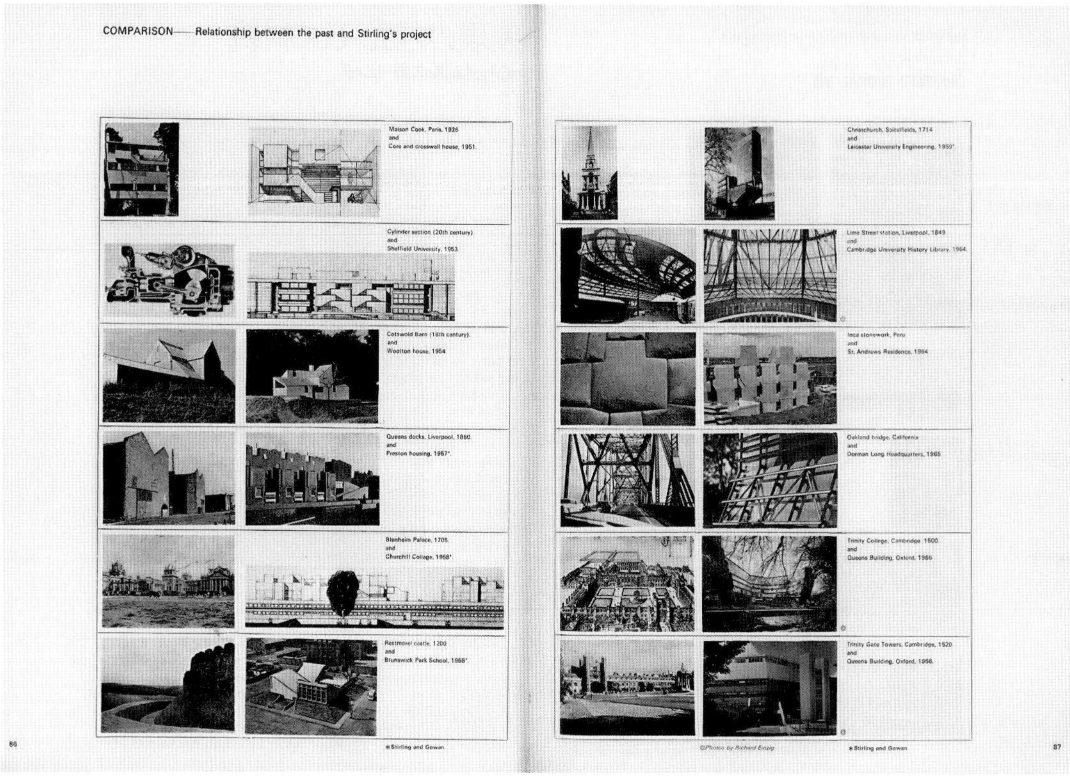

Figure 9.15. James Stirling, "Methods of Expression and Materials," *A+U* 2 (1975): 86–87.

Stirling himself commented on this aspect of his work frequently using the term "association." He declared himself concerned with "the *visual interpretation* of a plastic and social event" in an interview of 1960, also noting that it was the architect's "particular responsibility to find the correct *visual formation* of materials and structure and integrate these to an appropriate architectural solution." In a 1974 conference talk, Stirling noted:

> I believe that the shapes of a building should indicate—perhaps display the usage and way of life of its occupants. . . . The collection (in a building) of forms and shapes which the everyday public can *associate* with and be *familiar* with—and *identify* with—seems to me essential. These forms may derive from staircases, windows, corridors, rooms, entrances, etc., and the total building could be thought of as an assemblage of everyday elements *recognizable* to a normal man and not only an architect.[36]

Stirling's formal strategy recalls contemporary neorealist production in English and Continental art, some mentioned above. These comments also help explain the image objects shown in Figure 9.14. Just after this comment in his talk, Stirling displayed a set of paired slide comparisons of photographed architecture—the associational logic of his design being laid bare by these comparisons (Figure 9.15). Before pursuing this point, we must step back to the 1950s to follow the development of a concept that was central to British avant-garde production: the concept of endlessness.

ENDLESSNESS

Two years before the Sheffield competition, discourse on "endlessness" surfaced in British architecture. The best-known text, authored by Richard Llewelyn-Davies and titled "Endless Architecture," was first presented as a lecture in June 1951.[37] In this text, Llewelyn-Davies signaled a conceptual design idea that was also a modern trope par excellence. Precedents ranged from the Crystal Palace, talisman or token of industrial modernity itself, to Ludwig Mies van der Rohe's ongoing work at IIT in Chicago. The author characterized endlessness as intrinsic to twentieth-century modernity, derived from nineteenth-century industrialization and assembly-line production. A subset of this idea involves the more specific notion of extrusion, the process by which lengths of building material such as steel beams were produced in factory contexts. We might understand the adoption of these conceptual ideas—assembly-line building, or extruded architecture—in architecture as formal architectural expression. Buildings are not literally extruded—they are merely made to look as if they are. Endlessness had become a metaphor for industrial modernity, architecture its metonymic residue.

Stirling's numerous investigations of endless architecture began with Sheffield, but their full consideration lies outside the scope of a book on the photographic image in modern architecture. The theme emerged again and again in similar permutations in his early work. Generally, however, conceptually endless form was disciplined into singular architectural objects that were composed of multiple architectural images or image objects, as described above. At the Olivetti Headquarters in Haslemere, at Andrew Melville Hall, even at Derby and St. Andrew's Arts, the display of prefabrication or a systems approach is countered by the finite, object-like quality of the buildings. Stirling responded to the mandate of systems buildings by retrofitting systemic buildings into one-off surrealist building or image objects. Thus the aggregated image-building supersedes the repetitive structures of industry—or so one might conclude from this work. This retreat to form making has ideological overtones, but ones that Stirling regularly undercut with his overt dependence on material things as narrative devices.

A couple of projects did not readily conform to this approach. One of these is the office building for the Dorman Long steel corporation, designed in 1965.[38] The

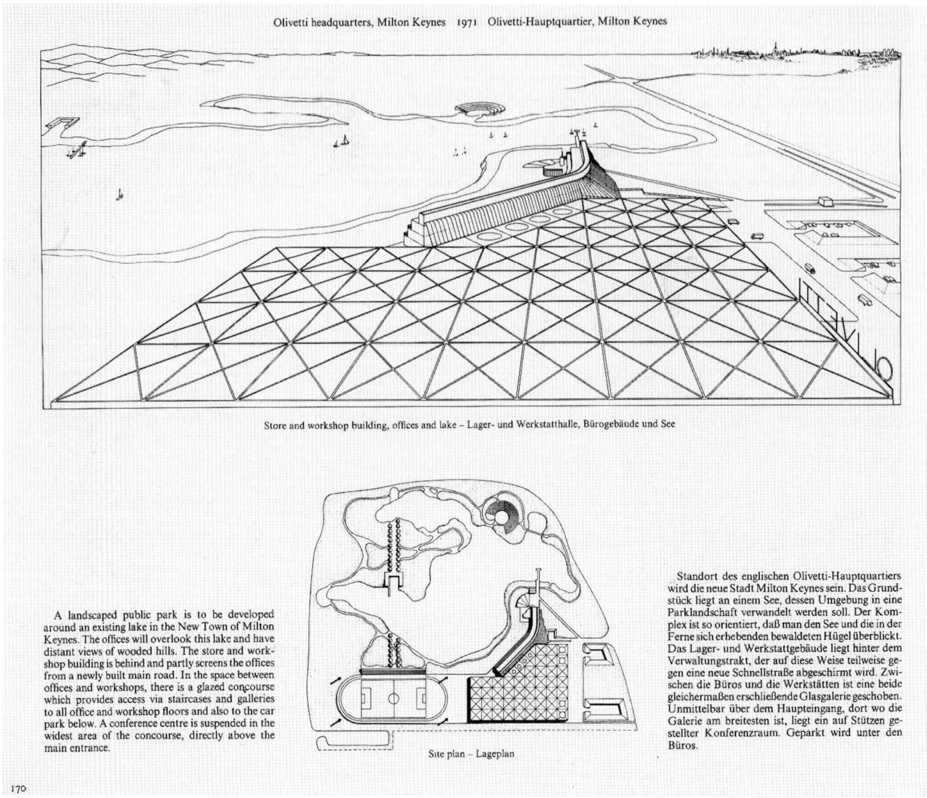

Figure 9.16. Plan and aerial perspective, Olivetti Headquarters, Milton Keynes, 1974. From *James Stirling: Buildings and Projects, 1950–1974* (New York: Oxford University Press, 1975). James Stirling/Michael Wilford fonds; Collection Centre Canadien d'Architecture/Canadian Centre for Architecture, Montreal.

second is the unbuilt Olivetti Headquarters for Milton Keynes, the project for which Stirling produced the image object sketch discussed above (Figure 9.14).[39] The building that Stirling designed for a lakeside site reflects the idea of endlessness in two senses (Figure 9.16). The main circulation spine of the office block at Olivetti Milton Keynes is, formally, extendable in both directions, despite its curving shape and the slight articulation around entry points and between offices and workshop. Second, the larger field of the workshop wing could grow along two axes, not just one. This is an adaptation of the factory type used at Leicester, with endlessness implicitly inhabiting its currently bounded forms, like an untapped potential or a missed opportunity. Here two versions of systems-based design are counterposed—spinal, linear buildings set against a horizontal field.[40] How did the two modes interact in relation to endlessness and the image qualities so present in Stirling's other buildings and noted at the beginning of this chapter? Moreover, how did extruded, systems-based design or endlessness relate to the image qualities found so insistently in Stirling's other buildings and noted at the outset—images of constructivist theaters, naval architecture, and English vernacular, and then images crafted by the architect's own hand? In Olivetti Milton Keynes, the two repetitive components of the design are accompanied by two unique elements—the curvilinear lobby in which Krier placed his own visage atop an antique herm in his famous rendering and the blob-like "convention center" supported on stilts accessed by a ramp and enclosed by a set of glass sheaths. Both look like homages to Hans Arp in plan. In a revision of the Leicester scheme, a "Stirling object" has replaced Melnikov's constructivist theaters. This object will recur in later projects, but earlier precedents for it are obscure or nonexistent (Figures 9.17, 9.18).

We might understand endlessness or extrusion as a reflection on the dynamic, process-based nature of architectural experience itself. Endlessness also reflects the iterative process of design that Stirling demonstrated in the countless small sketches commented on by Krier and others in his work, only some of which survive. It constitutes a reflection on design as process—as a mobile or dynamic procedure

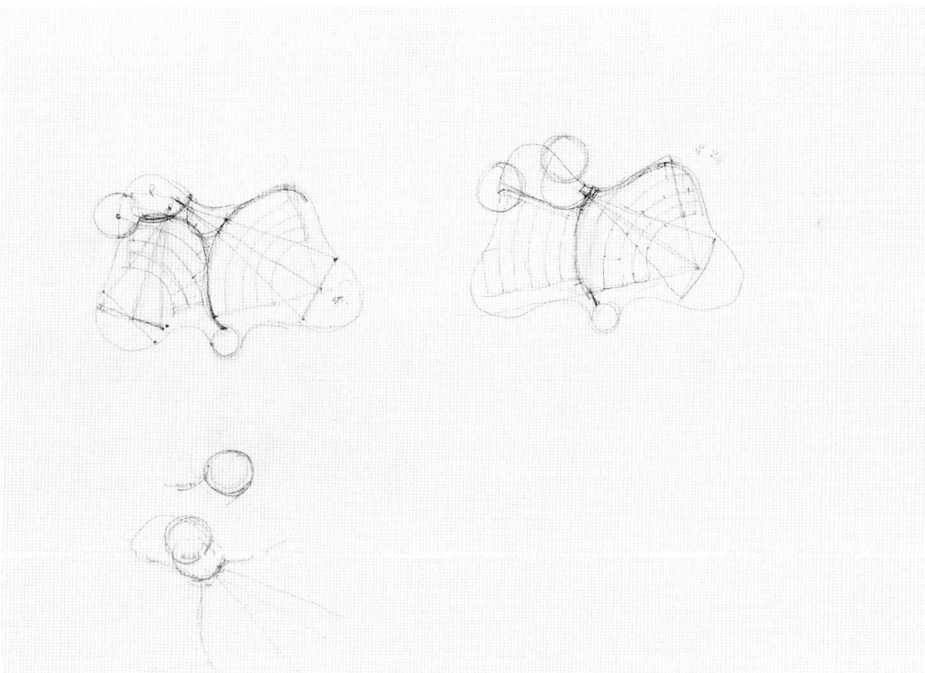

Figure 9.17. Preliminary sketches of lecture theaters, Olivetti Headquarters, Milton Keynes, 1974. James Stirling/Michael Wilford fonds; Collection Centre Canadien d'Architecture/Canadian Centre for Architecture, Montreal.

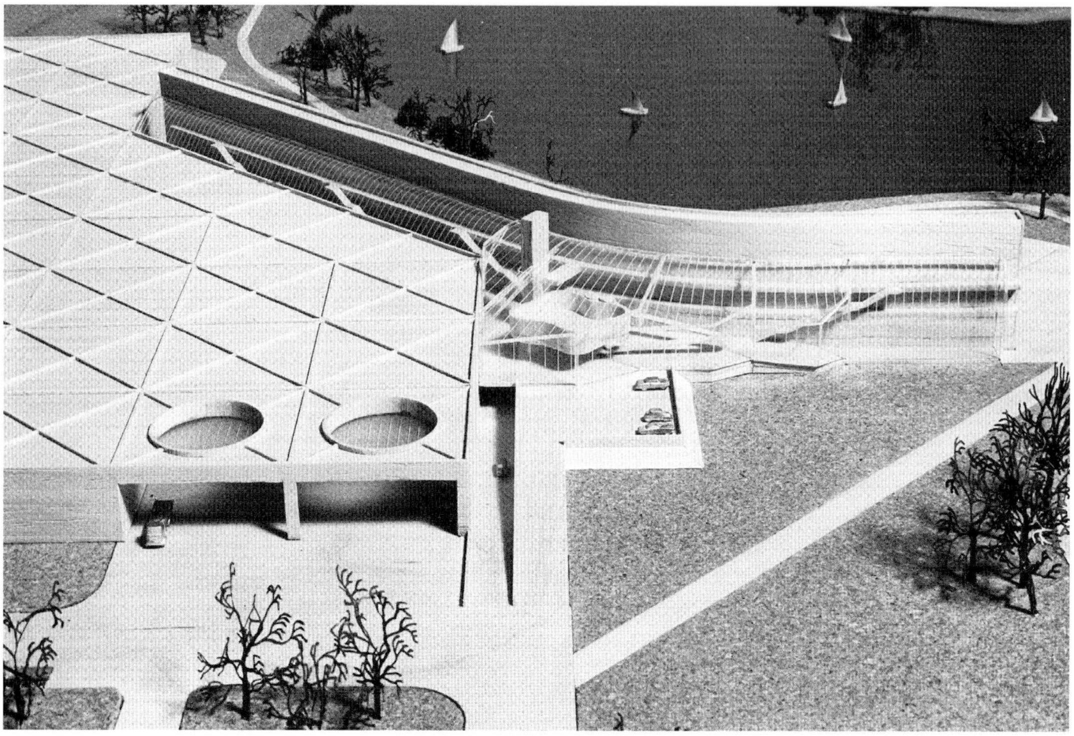

Figure 9.18. Model for Olivetti Headquarters, Milton Keynes, 1974. James Stirling/Michael Wilford fonds; Collection Centre Canadien d'Architecture/Canadian Centre for Architecture, Montreal.

without end, arrested for the purpose of construction. Finally, these image-buildings proffer a reflection on the fate of architecture in postindustrial Britain. If factory production and the empire that had accompanied it were increasingly part of England's past, then design that belonged to the regime of industry—like prefabrication and systems building—was itself something of a nostalgic reflex (Figure 9.19). Within the limited circle of architectural practice, Stirling took a seemingly *arrière-garde* position that was still never quite stable and always future oriented. In the process, he projected a role for the image in the future of architecture. The themes of extrusion, of process arrested, and of potential continuous growth (courtesy of D'Arcy Wentworth Thompson and others) stand out against the iterative volumetric approach of Stirling's other work—the combination of image objects discussed above.[41]

Architects' altered consciousness of the role of images in their work emerged in "postmodern architecture" in the late 1960s. Such a claim is clearly not revolutionary; image-based practices in a range of media are the trademark of postmodernism. Rather, we have probed that claim by complicating the definition of "image," at least insofar as it concerned architects, and by exploring an important historical fault line. Before Banham, the Smithsons, and Stirling, two-dimensional photographic images were part of the infrastructure of architectural marketing but only ambiguously part of the design process. After them, no such clear distinction can be made. Photographs were still part of the marketing apparatus of architecture—more so than ever. But in addition, image-based practices had infiltrated the way in which architects conceived of buildings to a greater degree than ever before. Postwar architects creatively adapted avant-garde and neorealist procedures that were also appearing in other media. In a general sense, these responded to consumer culture of the late 1950s. In a more specific sense, we see them finding ways to alter architectural design process in response to infrastructures like advertising and marketing as well as cross-medial artistic agendas. In Stirling's case, a clash between the static nature of the image as a singularity and the dynamic nature of architectural experience that found an echo in the very idea of dynamic, process-based systems building poses the larger problems of postwar architecture in terms of building design.

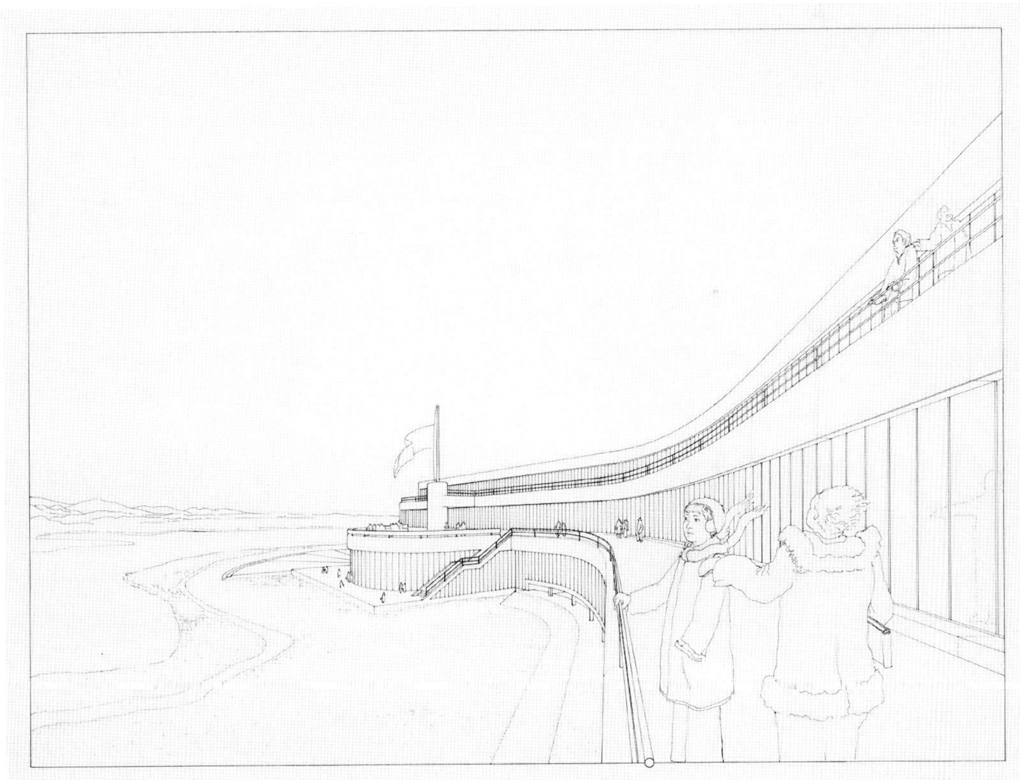

Figure 9.19. Perspective, Olivetti Headquarters, Milton Keynes, 1974. Renderer: Leon Krier. James Stirling/Michael Wilford fonds; Collection Centre Canadien d'Architecture/Canadian Centre for Architecture, Montreal.

The shift from Rudolf Wittkower's notion that buildings should be formally legible, both in their technical drawings and in their formal appearance, to Banham's notion of memorability of image has been noted. Banham's proposal suggests something beyond the immediate surface of the photographic image: that the image is in part a memory image—part of a recognizable category like a brand or logo (from architecture and elsewhere), to be used and reused in appropriate applications—the property of any interested parties in postwar circles. The typology debates that resurfaced in the 1970s partook of a similar set of ideas, much more firmly entrenched in the disciplinarity of architecture, not nondisciplinary postwar commercial culture. Stirling's experiments with "endless architecture" show how the iterative process of design and the experiential aspects of architecture were potentially in conflict with image-based marketing structures. These projects introduced dynamic instability into design process. Thus we find Stirling grappling with a problem that plagued and challenged architecture with increasing severity over the course of the twentieth century: the need to publicize, market, and sell buildings with a set of tools that appeared to be inherently inadequate to communication about space and form. But if the single image, often but not always photographic, was not adequate for conveying complex spatial experience to audiences, nevertheless it appears also to have provided architects like Stirling with a challenge, a glove thrown down in the endless duel between buildings and their pictorial avatars.

CONCLUSION

SURFACE DIVIDES

In July 1947, Ada Louise Huxtable sent an internal memo about the upcoming MoMA exhibition of Ludwig Mies van der Rohe's work. She wrote, "Using a new approach to the display of architecture, the photographs shown will be very large (the largest 20 × 14 feet) and so arranged that they can be viewed from a distance to give the effect of actual buildings."[1] Enlarged architectural photographs and drawings of Mies's German projects became space-defining architectural elements in the gallery (Figure C.1).[2] Of seven large photomurals used as or placed on wall planes, all showed work executed before Mies's 1937 emigration to the United States.

Wallis Miller has shown how the design of the exhibition gave Mies the opportunity to use wall-sized photographs of projects (built and unbuilt) as montage elements in the gallery, creating ambiguous relationships between surfaces and space.[3] The Glass Room installation of the 1927 Stuttgart exhibition shared the characteristic feature of picture-making planes arranged orthogonally in space but not to a rigid geometric scheme. Twenty years later, photographic wall panels replaced plate glass; a New York museum replaced a trade exhibition hall. This is a consequential difference: in 1927, the stakes for the new architecture lay with building materials suppliers, contractors, and public clients in the form of state governments, as well as the architectural profession. In 1947, the stakes for the new architecture, now conflated with "the International Style," lay with elite members of an American social and economic hierarchy. By contrast, the American architectural profession was, for many years, undecided about modern architecture.[4]

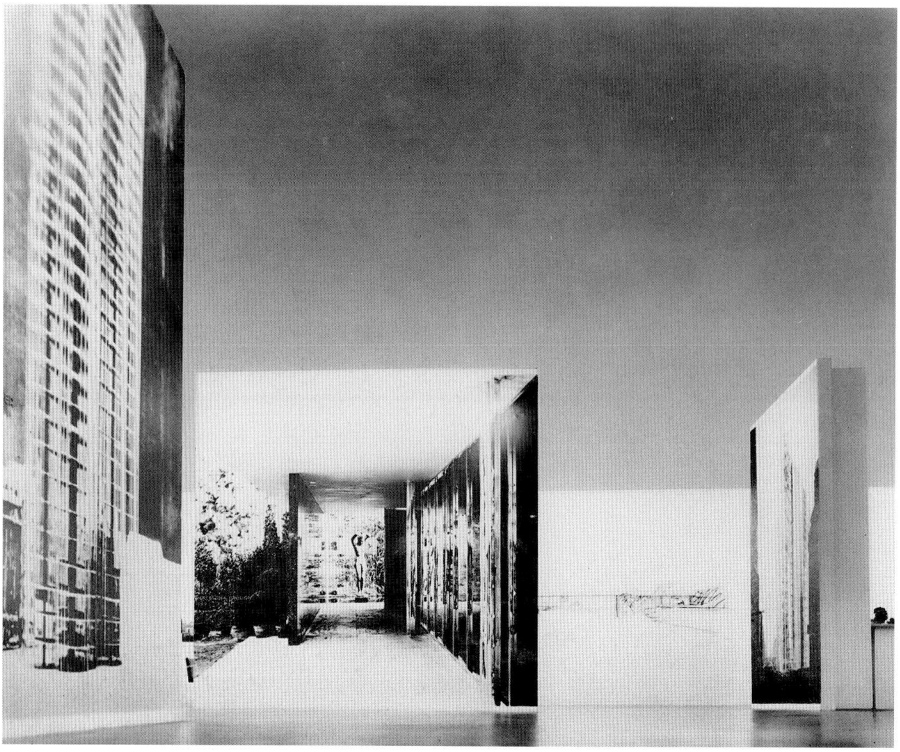

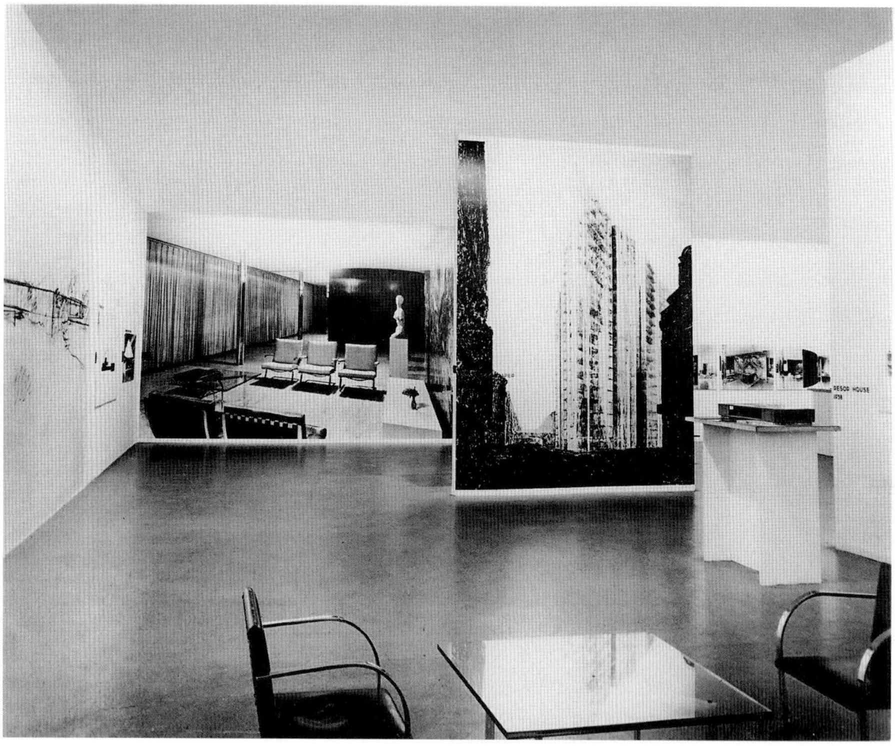

Figure C.1. Mies van der Rohe Exhibition, Museum of Modern Art, 1947. Curator: Philip Johnson. Exhibition designer: Ludwig Mies van der Rohe. Photographs: Soichi Sunami. Digital images copyright The Museum of Modern Art; licensed by SCALA/Art Resource, NY.

To those familiar with architectural modernism, the photographs in the MoMA show were already known from journal publications; the exhibition experience was partly a new—perhaps slightly shocking—encounter with old material. The brilliance of the show lay in its transformation of small-scale architectural propaganda of the type that had been in wide circulation for well over forty years into spatial (space-defining) matter itself through the technique of photomechanical enlargement.[5] There were precedents for this exhibition strategy in the large Werkbund exhibitions of the interwar years, and particularly in fascist propaganda shows in Germany and Italy, some of which Mies probably visited.[6] But Mies had already been working with large-scaled representations of architecture from the early 1920s and scarcely needed prompting in this direction.[7]

In the 1947 show architecture became photograph with minimal difference in scale between original and reproduction. But full-scale (human-scale) indexical images had been present in modern architecture since the advent of large surfaces of polished plate glass at the turn of the century, the very surfaces that inspired the Glass Room.[8] The most radical aspect of the show was not that building could be represented at full scale in a gallery. More important, in this show the half-page magazine illustration became as big as a building. The tools of architectural propaganda, generally transparent or even invisible as media per se, were blown up to monumental scale and placed within the museum, as if to underscore the fact that architectural media were in some sense *indistinguishable* from full-scale building. Mies, producer of poster-sized architectural renderings, was no doubt well aware of the effectiveness of using unexpected size to capture the attention of the public, transmitting the power of an architectural idea to an audience of specialists and nonspecialists alike. The buildings, transmitted through photographic or photomechanical reproduction, resumed their original shape in two dimensions only—as if to retain the trace of their own progress through history, from big to small to big again, but changed in the process.

The show thus combined visual spectacle with an internal discourse about architecture culture. But if the chief innovations were the enlarged architectural photographs that simulated full-scale construction, this has one effect in the space of a museum gallery and quite a different one in another photograph, printed on the pages of a book or a periodical, or even circulated electronically as we might see the image today. Huxtable claimed that the murals were "so arranged that they can be viewed from a distance to give the effect of actual buildings," one of the conceits of the exhibition. Yet the distance to which she refers is not just a measurable distance within the space of the gallery—it is rather also the kind of distance that

Walter Benjamin identified as coincident with the removal of aura from objects of art through the abstraction of reproduction. And it worked differently in further reproductions.

Within the space of the gallery, the planarity of the wall partition on which the photograph of the Barcelona Pavilion was printed would have remained obvious. But this photograph stood directly on axis with the entry to the gallery, and perhaps produced the effect that Huxtable claimed as one approached the doorway. It is also spatially ambiguous in the published photographs that relay its effects to us, as in the portrait of Mies in front of the same photograph in 1935 (Figure C.2).[9] When

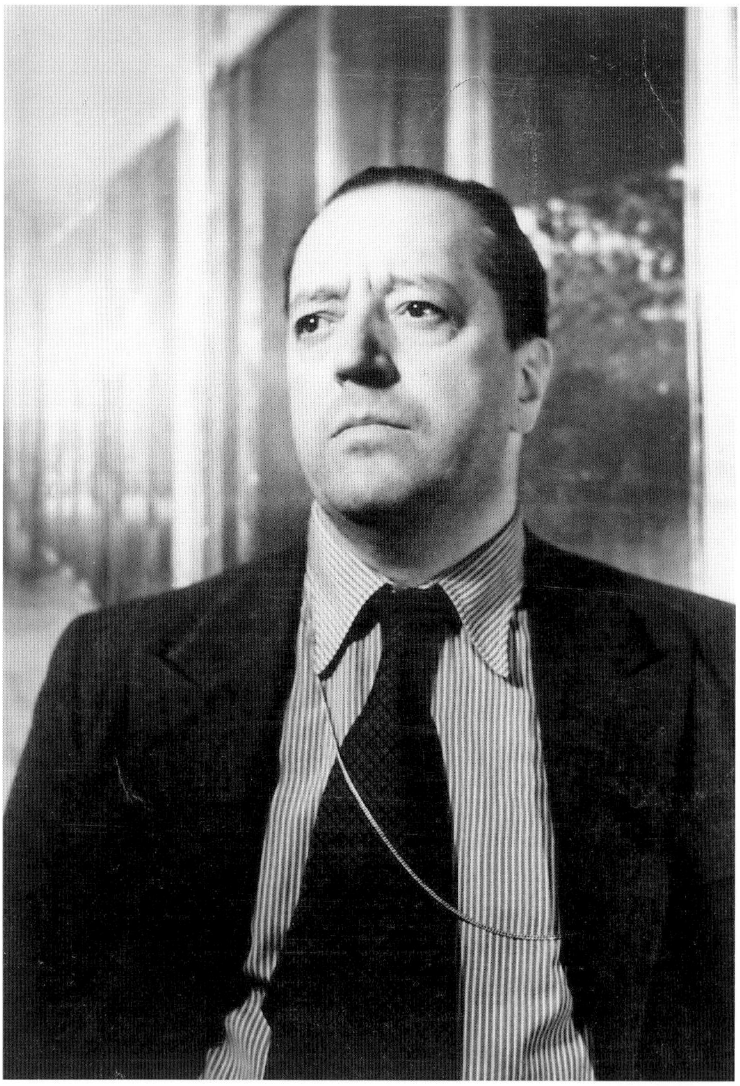

Figure C.2. Ludwig Mies van der Rohe in his studio on Am Karlsbad, Berlin, circa 1935. Copyright 2012 Artists Rights Society (ARS), New York/VG Bild-Kunst, Bonn.

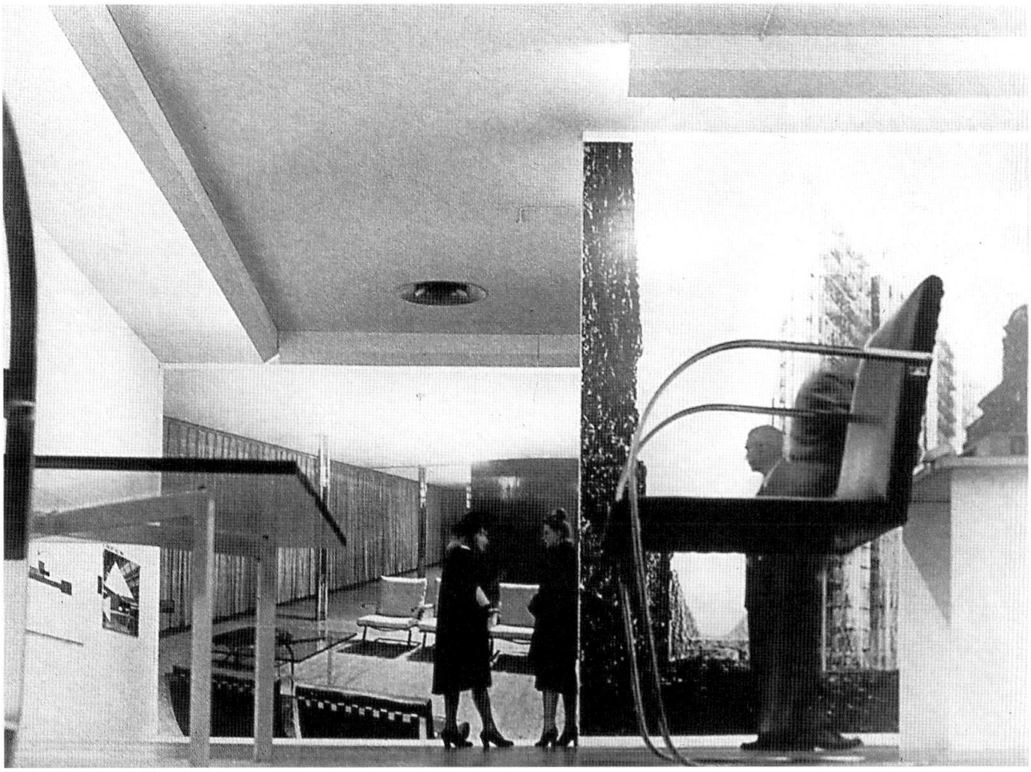

Figure C.3. Mies van der Rohe Exhibition, Museum of Modern Art, 1947. Photograph: Charles Eames. Digital images copyright The Museum of Modern Art; licensed by SCALA/Art Resource, NY.

we first see Figure C.1, the question is: Are we looking at a photograph of a photograph, or into a space? Here, at least two considerations arise. First, in the context of an architectural show, these full-scale photographs recalled the distance between the viewer and the building—a distance made up of time and geography, but also, in 1947, of politics and history; the German-period projects were all either remotely distant or nonexistent.[10] The large size of these murals points to their status as relics of a recent yet now remote past.

Second, in photographs of the exhibition (all that would remain after it closed its doors), the confusion that results when photographs are photographed would leave the viewer not quite certain about the spatial conditions of the picture. And indeed, in photographs of the installation, the equivalence between human figure and photographed space makes for a succession of alluring and disquieting images, particularly in the series shot by Charles Eames (Figure C.3). This surely was also an intentional effect: that the media of architecture would, in this particular case, provide some clues about the mutable nature of the spaces depicted within their cropped frames.

The 1947 exhibition provides a useful end point. In the accelerating history of the twentieth century, it lies roughly halfway between the beginning and the end of this book, when the photograph began to play an increasingly influential role in the administration of architecture. The exhibition took place as the Deardorff Company (and its competition) released new cameras made possible by wartime investment in imaging technologies, adding yet one more sophisticated imaging tool to the toolbox of the photographer of buildings. Despite the sophistication of the tools brought to bear on depicting architecture in photographs, a basic condition that pertains to the rest of the book surfaces graphically here. Modern architectural photographs were images of images. The gallery shots were then images of images of images. They demonstrate in space a condition of architectural media that often remains unseen: images of architecture published in the press rapidly become nested images, a *mise en abyme* sometimes referred to as the Droste effect, a theoretically unending series of images. Whether an original may exist or not, the chain of repetition rapidly eclipses the "first" image—either building or picture of building.

The conflation of photographic images of buildings and of buildings as representational "images" has led to confusion in the history of modernism that has also produced results. First confusion: Is it only photographs of building exteriors that function as images of images? The unclear border between inside and outside found at the Barcelona Pavilion that shows particularly well in the 1947 exhibition shot suggests that the answer is no. The interpenetration of inside and outside was a general condition of modern architecture and makes it difficult to draw firm distinctions between photographs of interiors and photographs of exteriors. Second confusion: If the presence of images in and of architecture is not at issue here, what have these things—images—produced in our thinking and acting about buildings?

Here, in conclusion, two further observations. First, the combination of a commercial instrument (the advertising photograph) and a cultural product (architecture) resulted in dynamic, productive exchanges between the two. Second, photographs had a particular kind of agency in the formation of modern architecture. Turning to the first observation, these pages reject any structural incompatibility between a commercial instrument and a culturally discursive medium. The two mutually coexist just as they have been mutually constitutive throughout the history of analog photography, if not the history of culture since antiquity.[11] But the fact of their mutual coexistence under capitalism is not an endorsement of this condition.[12] Rather, it underlines the important role that culture played in taming market forces for the purposes of mass consumption. Advertising photography was immensely useful to architecture in part precisely because of the way in which it could "take the rap" for the cruder aspects of marketing required by the architecture industry while at the same time enshrining buildings in "magical" auratic images.[13]

This book has repeatedly foregrounded a tension between the static architectural photograph and the phenomenon of movement or animation that is considered characteristic of architectural experience and is theoretically better captured in film than in photography. This tension between still and animated images recurred throughout twentieth-century architectural history and is still productive, even as any polarity between still image and animation breaks down in the face of increasingly sophisticated digital representations of architecture today.[14] Although the tension between photography and film has recurred here, a different tension has remained at center stage. The mandates of commercial practice have been posed in relation to architects' desires to bring their work into line with contemporary life in the most progressive and adventuresome ways, signified by engagement with the concept of avant-garde. Thus in relation to that which changes with increasing rapidity—the development of new media, currently called digital media—we can also look at that which changes less dramatically—the constraints within which business is conducted in capital markets, new modes of commercial interconnectivity notwithstanding.

The crossover between these two—commodity and art—lies at the heart of this study. There have been critical moments: Paul Zucker's identification of intermedial architecture as a component of the history of European architecture, Mies's (and others') discoveries of the immense propaganda power of photographic images and the immense creative power behind architectural montage, the Smithsons' skillful deployment of image in building and building in image, and Stirling's (and Banham's) reinvention of the image as a potent pictorial object of thought and then action. All of these moments of change in the history of a relationship (and many more that have not been narrated here) suggest how architecture and its market infrastructures could not be kept apart but interacted in mutually transformative ways. Not all transformations are good, but they are, at the very least, dynamic.

In this study of the interface between architecture and its markets through the architectural photographic image, no revivalist embrace of the interwar and postwar avant-gardes is conjured. Recycling myths of the avant-garde only distracts from a more urgent exercise: resituating history in relation to our own present and future, not that of a mythified past. Of what might this resituating consist? Many are embarked upon related projects already.[15] First, scholars and critics are coming to grips with the conditions of post-1989, post-2001 global society, in which avant-gardist polarities have increasingly disappeared. They are concerned not with the question of whether photographic images were important, but rather with a careful taxonomy of such images that recognizes how varied and flexible they have become and how potent they have been, construed both in relation to physical occupation and in terms of cognitive judgment.

This brings me back to the issue of design development in twentieth-century architecture. The book has mapped changing attitudes toward the photographic image as a productive force in this period. These include the idea of the photograph as a surface into which the viewer hurls him- or herself for a virtual experience of projected space, as in the case of the Tugendhat House photographs. This is the mode of cognition associated with empathy theory and subsequently with mass spectatorship.[16] A different attitude toward photographs saw them as surfaces resistant to penetration, integrated rather into the realm of daily experience and no longer separate from other phenomena of modernity. This notion of the repellent image surface follows on from the successors to empathy theory: estrangement and alienation as modern conditions. Some residue of that approach remains present in Hunstanton School, even as the Smithsons began to seek (immediately following the completion of the school) modes of communal association that would counter alienation effects that were particularly vivid after World War II. The image surface of Hunstanton School remains palpably present, acting as a brake on optical immersion, a continual, bracing reminder of building as a force in contemporary life—even as the commercial architectural photographs of that building draw the viewer in. A third notion of the image in architecture emerged in the final chapter, in the "image objects" of postmodernism, where the two-dimensional photographic image (of a building, of an image therefore) is blown back up into three dimensions and constructed in real space. Examined here in the case of James Stirling, the iterative nature of architecture's mediation in image and text led the architect to create a new set of objects with which he staffed his designs over many years. Photographic images (along with other kinds) led Stirling to craft an architectural vocabulary, just as Mies pursued spatial modes through planar montage, with pictorial planes as architectural elements. A tension between these latter two developments surfaces and is not resolved here. The associative condition of images for the latter, as for the Smithsons, seems incompatible with the discrete image objects of Stirling. Strikingly contemporary to one another, Stirling and the Smithsons nevertheless map two very different responses to the realism of the photographic image when it is visited upon architecture "proper." These are not the only two responses found in twentieth-century architecture; they are merely visible in high relief in the frame put around them here.[17]

We live with these legacies today, as well as others. As floods of pictures increasingly reduce the effectiveness of any single image, a variety of approaches have surfaced in relation to immersive media in general and screens in particular. Some of these approaches can be retroactively applied to photography, with caution. Common to both new and old media is an interest in connectivity, in the ways in which communicative devices relay ideas from one place to another, for use. But the question of image and action that was already present in the preface to this book insists. Are we meant to act on the basis of what we learn from photographic images? Or do they more precisely embed *inaction* in the optical experience that precedes and underpins judgment formation? Particularly in relation to the creation of architecture, urban space, and the built environment generally, how does traffic in images obscure or complicate the issues to which we need to respond today? Do images insulate us from pressure to act?

Recent biopolitical writing provides a framework for discussing the "ethical divide" of screens and image surfaces that bifurcate human action, imposing entirely different standards of judgment on either side of an invisible wall. Michel Foucault and Giorgio Agamben focus on the variable status of individual bodies in legal and social judgment. But in this case, consumers of photographic images or screen surfaces embrace bodily limits voluntarily. Part of the lure of the screen/image resides in the physical safety it seems to provide the body, the safety from which we experience bodily risk vicariously through its surface. We have the pleasure of investment without physical risk. We are, perhaps, indemnified from risk by the photographic image first, and the screen next. Decision making or judgment of any sort (aesthetic or otherwise) is affected by mode of cognition—it could not be otherwise—and in this case, the mode of cognition associated with image surfaces protects dispassionate judgment. We judge from safety about the risks made visible in images. In situations in which we face risk ourselves, such dispassionate judgment is precluded; we act in relation to physical risk in variable personal ways. In that sense, image environments are great equalizers: none of us is called to act, and therefore none can fail.

A distinction between action and judgment relates to the activities of architects directly, where screen images now convey that which designers are in the process of making. At a basic operational level, to construct the built environment is to act on behalf of others through the instrumentality of images. If these inherently encode a distinction between action and judgment about necessary action, then the very modality of design is inoculated by screen divides. In such a contradictory situation, the increasing importance of screen environments today merely reinforces an apparent impossibility. It may be that "kissing architecture" by impregnating buildings with images absorbs and enfolds this condition of image making. Is this a matter of securing the arena of action itself from any necessity for activist commitment? Encircled by flatness, we bury ourselves within the self-perpetuating prosperity of which the image is the infallible trace.

The work analyzed in this book occupies a period of modern architectural history that comes to seem more remarkable as we move further away from it in time. Increasingly sophisticated digital imaging techniques are removing the last traces of evidentiary authority from photographs of architecture, if not from the medium of photography overall. Photographic images of buildings can still be evidentiary—but they can also easily be fabricated within the space of a technical apparatus, appearing nearly identical to those that document constructed buildings. The surface of the image itself no longer tells us. When we look back into the history of architectural photography, this particular moment—of analog, print-based photography—is distinct precisely because there was still an evident belief in the documentary character of this genre. Architectural photographs were generally made as "documents," and received that way as well, partly because the mechanics of photographic production were overwhelmingly geared to the encoding of visual information (as distinct from but supplemented by interpretation). Photographs were doctored, by all the means narrated here and more as well, and yet they retained their status as evidence of something that "was there" on a site, "what Lacan calls the *Tuché,* the Occasion, the Encounter, the Real, in its indefatigable expression."[18] Images do not necessarily look different when produced with the most sophisticated imaging software available. But the ontology of the photographic image of architecture has changed since the 1980s. The photograph no longer indexes the real. It now equalizes the real and the imaginary, creating a different condition of being, in which the very idea of "reality" beyond the surface of the image and its cognitive reception has been effectively canceled. We can use this condition to inoculate ourselves against disruption and alterity, or we can use it in other ways.

ACKNOWLEDGMENTS

The help I received while writing this book extends in a series of ripples outward from the proofs before me and from the present back in time. Most proximate are those who helped with pressing tasks related to the book's production, either by reading and commenting on its content, providing me with the space (physical, financial, temporal) in which to write it, or assisting with the mechanics of production. At the University of Minnesota Press, I thank Pieter Martin, Kristian Tvedten, Daniel Ochsner, Laura Westlund, and Judy Selhorst for their commitment to this project and what it represents, and for their diplomatic balancing of authors' demands and publishers' realities. At the University of Michigan, Matt Biro, McLain Clutter, Caroline Constant, Geoff Eley, Robert Fishman, Andrew Herscher, Keith Mitnick, Alex Potts, Susan Siegfried, Achim Timmermann, and Rebecca Zurier have my deep gratitude for reading and commenting on the text. Rebecca Price has been such a positive force for research in Ann Arbor that it is impossible to praise her enough. For financial support, I thank the Department of the History of Art, the Taubman College of Architecture and Urban Planning, and the Humanities Institute. I owe Susan and Caroline in particular for so much assistance so unstintingly given—Caroline over many years, and Susan with particular intensity since I came to Ann Arbor. Alex has been a key force in the book's development, and I thank him and Doug Kelbaugh for lighting my path to Michigan and for treating scholarship so rigorously as open discourse. Andrew and Geoff fastened on the conjuncture of Dessau and Hunstanton in this study and persuaded me of its importance. Geoff's intellectual influence at the University of Michigan has altered my thinking about postwar British and interwar German material and the political debates around both. Other remarkable colleagues at a remarkable institution include Kerstin Barndt, Celeste Brusati, Kevin Carr, David Doris, Will Glover, Daniel Herwitz, Megan Holmes, Marty Powers, Mireille Roddier, and Johannes von Moltke (who is responsible for the presence of Siegfried Kracauer in this book). Michael Abrahamson, Candice Hamelin, Matt Heins, Joss Kiely, Grant Mandarino, Mick McCulloch, Faiza Moatassim, Johnathan Puff, Kristen Schroeder, and Maria Taylor also have my warmest thanks.

Far from Ann Arbor, Rachel Belash and Bob Burman played a key role in the book's completion, and I thank them with love and gratitude. Writing in New Mexico in their company was a sublime pleasure. Ed Dimendberg, Robert Elwall, Adrian Forty, Martin Hershenzon, Marco Iuliano, Reinhold Martin, Wallis Miller, Adrian Sudhalter, and Lynnette Widder read and commented perceptively on the manuscript or specific chapters. Ed gave me a crucial insight that subtly but meaningfully altered the book's final form. Adrian Forty's comments on an early draft made me cringe with shame, but all his remarks, both written and spoken, were delivered with the greatest generosity of spirit and have served as a model for me since. Reinhold's reading went directly to the manuscript's problems with a lightning speed that an author can only envy and be thankful for at once. Important assistance from Britt Eversole and Hannah Bennett, both at Princeton University, came at a critical last moment.

Those who provided me with a forum in which to present this material include Richard Anderson, Joseph Bedford, Mark Crinson, Elaine Harwood, John Harwood, Marco Iuliano, Vladimir Kulic, Juliana Maxim, Maria Antonella Pelizzari, François Penz, Alan Powers, Paolo Scrivano, Adrian Sudhalter, Robert Wiesenberger, and Lynnette Widder. In recent years, I have been grateful to many other friends and fellow travelers, among them Joseph Imorde, Lauren Kogod, Juliet Koss, the late Mary McAuliffe, Clara Oberle, Eeva-Lisa Pelkonen, Jeanette Redensek, Noa Steimatsky, and Victoria Walsh. Colleagues and friends who helped me define the book and its substance at an earlier stage include Rosemarie Bletter, a key force as my doctoral adviser. Jean-Louis Cohen has been a constant friend and interlocutor, and Barry Bergdoll gave me courage at a critical moment, and friendship and support since. Terry Riley unknowingly subsidized my research by hiring me to work on *Mies in Berlin*, which was as fascinating as it was rewarding. Barry and Terry deserve particular thanks for their sangfroid during surprising moments in the Mies Archive in the spring of 2000. My fellow fellows in the Berlin Program at the Free University in Berlin were wonderful discussants, and Michael Stöneberg and Simone Förster were invaluable and generous interlocutors during the research for this book. For assistance with archival research, I thank Pierre Adler, Mary Daniels, Ines Fernandez, Janos Frecot, Daniela Hammer-Tugendhat, Ivo Hammer, Lenka Kudelkova, Phyllis Lambert, Jonathan Makepeace, Jan Sapak, Soraya Smithson, Alexis Sornin, and Mirko Zardini. I thank Pat Avant-Kern, Julie Bohl, Julie Dawson, and, more than anyone, Elena Lavelle. Among the many former students who helped me immeasurably over the years of this project, five stand out: McLain Clutter, Britt Eversole, Enrique Ramirez, Molly Steenson, and Federica Vannuchi. Reaching further back, sessions at the Café Einstein with Wallis and Juliet were essential for developing the arguments contained here. I owe Eduard Sekler and Frank Kawasaki a great debt. Let me also thank all those who resist, for the rigor that they inadvertently engender.

Back at the center, I have another sort of debt altogether to the resolute Christopher Ratté, whose participation in the creation of this book cannot be overestimated. I thank the remarkable Helena and Leo Ratté for their silent (and audible) witnessing, and for their presence—and our communal copresence—in the world. I am proud to be their mother.

NOTES

INTRODUCTION

1. Banham, *A Concrete Atlantis,* 18. An earlier insight of Banham's is found in his *Theory and Design in the First Machine Age,* where he notes: "The Faguswerke at Alfeld . . . is frequently taken to be the first building of the Modern Movement properly so-called. . . . There can be little doubt that it owes this high esteem in part to Gropius's relationship to the historians of the Modern Movement, and also, in part to the accidents of photography" (79). Banham published this in 1960.
2. It was delivered to me, without their knowledge, by Beatriz Colomina and Jean-Louis Cohen. See Colomina, *Privacy and Publicity*; and Cohen, *Scenes of the World to Come.* In 2001, Hans Belting published *Bild-Anthropologie,* a book that would become important to me only in the last stages of editing this volume. See Belting, *An Anthropology of Images.*
3. From Banham's energetic boost, I went on to encounter the work of those who have made architectural photography a research focus. The late Robert Elwall, of the Royal Institute of British Architects, and Rolf Sachsse, foremost authority on architectural photography in Germany, are two leaders in the field whose work underpins this. A third exemplary precursor who focused on a different moment in the history of architecture is Mary N. Woods. These three are now in company with many others.
4. Elwall, *Photography Takes Command,* 9–18.
5. "It is no accident that the most *beautiful* photograph so far achieved is possibly the first image Nicéphore Niépce fixed in 1822, on the glass of the camera obscura—a fragile, threatened image, so close in its organization, its granular texture, and its emergent

aspect, to certain Seurats—an incomparable image which makes one dream of a photographic *substance* distinct from subject matter, and of an art in which light creates its own metaphor." Damisch, "Five Notes for a Phenomenology of the Photographic Image," 72.

6. To those who would shift the genesis of modern architecture further back in time—to John Soane, perhaps—photography historians might respond with Josiah Wedgwood, who pioneered photography before adequate knowledge of chemistry allowed images to be fixed in permanent or semipermanent fashion. See Batchen, "A Philosophical Window" and *Burning with Desire.*
7. Mallgrave, *The Architect's Brain,* 62–64. Schinkel invented an architecture that manifested the authority of classical order in visible external appearance, partly by depicting (but not always literally enacting) principles of rational construction. Fox Talbot invented a new technical procedure that manifested the authority of a natural process in visible external appearance, regulated by chemical reactions to light. These two ideas were not identical, but they ran in parallel. Architects invoked scientific principles as constructional guides and as metaphors; photographers used them literally in the production of images and strategically in the creation of a new field. On connections between external appearance (Ausserlichkeit) and architecture in the same period, connections not adequately taken up here, see Jarzombek, "The Cunning of Architecture's Reason." On Schinkel, also see Arburg, "Fassadenzauber oder schöner Schein?"; and Scholl, "Die schöne Kunst der Konstruktion."
8. Fox Talbot, *The Pencil of Nature,* 1.
9. Jacques Rancière asks, "Does not the term 'image' contain several functions whose problematic alignment precisely constitutes the labor of art?" He goes on to define images as "operations that couple and uncouple the visible and its signification or speech and its effect, which create and frustrate expectations," further designating them "dissemblances" that use resemblance as subterfuge. See Rancière, *The Future of the Image,* 1–31. For earlier claims about the status of photographic images as pictures, see Snyder and Allen, "Photography, Vision, Representation"; see also later work by Joel Snyder.
10. "A *surviving image* is an image that, having lost its original use value and meaning, nonetheless comes back, like a ghost, at a particular historical moment: a moment of 'crisis,' a moment when it demonstrates its latency, its tenacity, its vivacity, and its 'anthropological adhesion.'" Didi-Huberman, *Confronting Images,* xxii.
11. Levine, *Modern Architecture.*
12. For discussion of similar issues drawn from a much larger historical terrain, see Blau and Kaufman, *Architecture and Its Image*; for an American focus, see Pai, *The Portfolio and the Diagram.*
13. Colomina, *Privacy and Publicity,* 14.
14. Belting, *An Anthropology of Images.* Belting indicates important references for his own work in the new introduction written for English readers and in chapter 1, "An Anthropology of Images: Picture, Medium, Body."
15. Ibid., 5.
16. This study does not cover the subsequent development of digital photography. While we

have not totally exhausted the camera in recent years, nevertheless the terms of discussion have been altered substantively by predictive computer graphics that allow architects to "photograph" buildings in advance of their construction. Thus the notion of photography as evidence no longer corresponds to that of analog photography, although the idea still reverberates in discussions of architectural photography. The dynamic relationship between buildings and digital imagery that currently pertains can best be analyzed once a fuller picture of an earlier historical condition is better understood.

17. See Keller, "Durandelle, the Paris Opéra, and the Aesthetic of Creativity."
18. On architecture and language, see Forty, *Words and Buildings.*
19. Photography also began to be used to regulate architecture on sites, as an administrative tool that allowed clients and architects to keep tabs on the progress of construction without being on-site. In the nineteenth century, the presence of photography on buildings sites was intermittent and selective, being reserved for only a small fraction of large commissions usually associated with government-funded projects.
20. There are numerous texts that might be cited here; the identification of architecture's representational status was the subject of philosophical reflection throughout the nineteenth century. Here I underline the conflation between a notion of architectural representation and the highly literal photographic representation of buildings that broke onto the cultural scene noticeably after 1895, overtaking philosophical discourse and blasting it into irrelevance by sheer force of visual impact. For one strand of discourse, see Jarzombek, "The Cunning of Architecture's Reason."
21. See Levine, "Architectural Reasoning in the Age of Positivism"; Levine, *Modern Architecture.*
22. For discussion of photographic impulses that occurred before the invention of the practice, see Batchen, *Burning with Desire.*
23. Bergdoll, *Karl Friedrich Schinkel,* 177–80.
24. See Gutschow, "The Culture of Criticism."
25. For basic reference on the history of construction, see Elliott, *Technics and Architecture.*
26. On the photographs of Mies's Barcelona Pavilion, see Dodds, *Building Desire*; on El Lissitzky, see Perloff and Reed, *Situating El Lissitzky.*
27. See Kelsey, "Photography, Chance, and *The Pencil of Nature.*"
28. See Bergdoll, *Karl Friedrich Schinkel,* 216.
29. Daston and Galison, "The Image of Objectivity." Also see Daston and Galison, *Objectivity,* particularly 125–38. Barry Bergdoll has explored a broader set of epistemological connections between nineteenth-century architecture and natural history. See Bergdoll, "Of Crystals, Cells, and Strata." Also see Picon and Ponte, *Architecture and the Sciences*; Forty, "'Spatial Mechanics' Scientific Metaphors," in *Words and Buildings,* 86–101; Galison and Thompson, *The Architecture of Science*; Yanni, *Nature's Museums.*
30. For just one example, see "Are You Being Served?"
31. This flexibility appears to be common to bureaucratic infrastructures produced by expansive market economies generally (photography and its media of circulation included): "Colonial governance is marked precisely by a calculus of extreme sensitivity to situational circumstance. Rather than betray their own alienness, the codes of imperial power

sought to be inextricably entwined with the native's own mode of cognition." Dutta, *The Bureaucracy of Beauty*, 12.

32. For a demonstration in support of this claim, see Zimmerman, "From Legible Form to Memorable Image."

1. *BILDARCHITEKTUREN*

1. Brunet, *Visions de l'ouest*; Kelsey, *Archive Style*.
2. Lavin, *Kissing Architecture*.
3. The Microsoft Lab's new product lines, the Stanford Humanities Lab, and the MIT Media Lab all offer similar constellations that allow users to explore how screens and physical experience might interpenetrate. In popular culture, however, interactivity between screen and viewer generally occurs in more predictable ways.
4. This obligation had surfaced only in the eighteenth and nineteenth centuries, as a result of the increasing rationalization of architectural discourse.
5. For one example, see Lipsius, "On the Aesthetic Treatment of Iron in Tall Buildings."
6. Romba, *Iron Construction and Cultural Discourse*; Mallgrave and Contandriopoulos, *Architectural Theory*; Frampton, *Studies in Tectonic Culture*.
7. See Geretsegger and Peintner, *Otto Wagner 1841–1918*, 160–65.
8. On the persistence of disruptive tactics in aesthetic practices, see Rancière, *The Future of the Image*, 22–31; and Rancière, *The Politics of Aesthetics*, 9–11.
9. Frederic Schwartz narrates some of these developments in several chapters of *Blind Spots*.
10. Kracauer, "Kult der Zerstreuung." For English translation, see Kracauer, "Cult of Distraction."
11. See Gortcheva, "Modern Spaces and Cinema."
12. Kracauer, "Cult of Distraction," 328.
13. Worringer, *Abstraktion und Einfuhlung*. Also see Koss, "On the Limits of Empathy."
14. Behrendt, *Die einheitliche Blockfront als Raumelement im Stadtbau*.
15. Frankl, *Die Glasmalerei des fünfzehnten Jahrhunderts in Bayern und Schwaben*. On Behne also see Schwartz, "Form Follows Fetish," 57.
16. Zucker, *Raumdarstellung u. Bildarchitekturen bei den Florentiner Malern der ersten Hälfte des Quattrocento*. Zucker produced two dissertations, in effect: the first limited itself to the second half of the Quattrocento and was the thesis for which he received his degree; the second was broader and more ambitious in scope, but otherwise devoted to the same topic. Both appeared in 1913 and led Zucker to a position at the Schinkel Museum (where he assisted Max Georg Zimmermann) and to an assistantship with Richard Borrmann.
17. Müller-Wulckow, *Die Konstruktion der Bildarchitekturen in der deutschen Graphik des 15. Jahrhunderts*. Müller-Wulckow completed his dissertation at Strasbourg; his four-volume Blue Books on modern building, widely available much later, include *Buildings of Work and Transportation*, *Housing and Residential Settlements*, *Buildings of the Community*, and *The German Dwelling of the Present*.
18. These architectural historians became known for scholarship that appeared after World War I. Kracauer and Zucker were students of Borrmann; Kracauer would go on to be-

come a correspondent at the *Frankfurter Zeitung* and Zucker a prominent figure in Berlin academic life before National Socialism forced his departure from Germany. Zucker's scholarly output remained high after he left Germany, however, and his work was read in architectural schools throughout the 1970s and 1980s. Behne was a student of Adolph Goldschmidt at the University of Berlin and later the foremost advocate of architectural expressionism as well as an early chronicler and analyst of the modern movement. He was also a founding member of the Novembergruppe and the Arbeitsrat für Kunst and a prolific writer. Frankl studied with Berthold Riehl and then Heinrich Wölfflin in Munich, becoming a historian of Gothic architecture.

19. Behne, for example, turned to space as the essential medium of architecture par excellence in his *Eine Stunde Architektur.* Here I depend on the nuanced argument of Juliet Koss in *Modernism after Wagner*, 71–72.

20. Perhaps most remarkable is how many of the major advocates of modern architecture or modernism more generally number among the group who produced these studies. Behne, Behrendt, and Zucker all played major roles in the formation of contemporary architecture in the 1920s; Müller-Wulckow was perhaps most important in its dissemination, since his Blue Books were inexpensive, widely available, popular booklets meant to spread ideas about modern building more broadly than the specialized trade publications in which Neues Bauen members often published their work. On these kinds of publications, see Imorde, "'Das billige Bild.'"

21. Zucker, *Raumdarstellung und Bildarchitekturen im florentiner Quattrocento,* 140. Unless otherwise noted, all translations are my own.

22. "Eine Betrachtung von Bildarchitekuren, von gemalten Architekturen, muß notwendigerweise immer in eine Art Zwischenland der Kunst führen—Einflüsse werden festzustellen sein von einem Zweig der bildenden Kunst, der Architektur, auf einen anderen, die Malerei—und vielleicht lassen sich auch rückschließend Beziehungen aufweisen, die von den gemalten Architekturen zu wirklich entstandenen Bauwerken führen. Gerade die Analyse eines solchen Grenzgebietes wird stilkritisch besonders fruchtbar sein, denn es werden sich hier Ansätze zu Entwickelungen zeigen, die durch die technischen Bedingungen der Schwesterkunst erschwert oder unmöglich gemacht worden sind. . . . Es ist also möglich und wahrscheinlich, daß die charakteristischen innerlichen Merkmale eines Stiles sich unter Bedingungen schon aussprechen, unter denen dieser Stil noch nicht imstande ist, sich seine eigenen Ausdrucksformen gleich in voller Instensität zu schaffen—daß sich in zwitterartigen Gebilde eine neue kommende Gesinnung schon ausspricht, daß dabei die Übergänge zwischen den einzelnen Kunstzweigen verwischt werden und die gleichsam 'beweglichste' Kunst als erste die neuen Stilmerkmale ausprägt." Ibid., 1.

23. Gutschow, "The Culture of Criticism," 66.

24. Behne, *Der Inkrustationsstil in Toscana,* 108–9. See also Rupp, *Inkrustationsstil der romanischen Baukunst zu Florenz.*

25. Behne, *Der Inkrustationsstil in Toscana,* 130.

26. See Gutschow, "The Culture of Criticism," 66.

27. Behrens's crematorium was footnoted in the dissertation. Also see Behne, "Peter Behrens und die toskanische Architektur des 12. Jahrhunderts." In the latter work, in reference to the crematorium and the AEG pavilion of 1908, Behne wrote: "Where are the motifs

that Peter Behrens used in the creation of these buildings? In Florence and Pisa in Tuscan architecture of the twelfth and thirteenth centuries." (Wo liegen die Motive, die Peter Behrens bei der Gestaltung dieser Bauten angeregt haben? In Florenz und Pisa in der toskanischen Architektur des 12. und 13. Jahrhunderts) (45). Also see Anderson, "Behrens's Changing Concept of Life as Art," in *Peter Behrens and a New Architecture for the Twentieth Century.*

28. For a historical sourcebook, see Frank, *The Theory of Decorative Art.*
29. Kracauer's career spanned a number of different activities. He was initially trained as a professional architect. After completing his doctorate, he became an architectural historian or a *Bauforscher,* an architect trained to do historical research. After World War I, he also became a journalist, gravitating eventually toward film criticism. He is often described as a cultural critic, based on his journalism and subsequent publications in a wide variety of genres, from fiction to biography to history.
30. A general survey of Kracauer's early writing reveals methodologies indebted to the history of architecture and the decorative arts as exemplified in his dissertation. Much of Kracauer's work had little to do with buildings per se, but in his analysis of the material conditions of twentieth-century culture, he applied a formal and materialist approach to nonmaterial phenomena. Gerwin Zohlen refers to this as the "Metaphorisierung der Architektur." See Zohlen, "Schmugglerpfad," 340. Michael Podro uses a similar term to describe Gottfried Semper's attitudes toward surface. Podro refers to Semper's "sense of architectural metaphor" in *The Critical Historians of Art,* 47.
31. Borrmann was an archaeologist whose fieldwork began at the site of Olympia in Greece. His book on architectural ceramics detailed planar surface ornament ("painterly" ornament) in addition to modeled architectural details ("plastic" ornament). Borrmann, *Die Keramik in der Baukunst.* Kracauer's thesis topic also reflects Borrmann's interest in local building types in Berlin and Brandenberg.
32. Henrik Reeh has written the most extensive analysis of this document to date; see *Ornaments of the Metropolis,* chap. 2. In general, this early text did not fit within Reeh's project, unless otherwise noted.
33. "Sie schliessen den Hof ab und fassen die Gebäudeflügel architektonisch zusammen, ohne den Durchblick auf den Hauptbau zu hindern." Kracauer, *Die Entwicklung der Schmiedekunst,* 40.
34. A process for extruding sheets of plate glass was invented simultaneously in Europe and the United States. Émile Fourcault invented an extruded sheet glass production process in Belgium in 1905 and produced the material commercially from 1914. See Phillips, *Glass,* 206.
35. Kracauer's dissertation work was connected to scholarship on architectural ornament from the second half of the nineteenth century and a growing literature on the regional architecture of Berlin and Brandenburg. See Mebes, *Um 1800.* A striking parallel for Kracauer's dissertation, for example, is the wrought-iron ornamental grillwork of the Woodland Chapel by Erik Gunnar Asplund.
36. Semper's theories of surface cladding connected ornamentation and material expression to remnant evidence of technological constraints that was maintained long after the

constraints had disappeared. As Podro has pointed out, however, Semper's schema was complex, in that material constraints provided only one influence on formal articulation. Podro, *The Critical Historians of Art,* 45–47. Outside Germany, Hittorf in France and Owen Jones in England had also studied surface ornamentation as index to conditions of its origin; both are well-known for theories of ornament, and Hittorf particularly for investigating the highly colored surface painting of ancient Greek temples. For a general treatment of these issues, see Bergdoll, *European Architecture 1750–1890.*

37. Riegl saw the history of ornament as a way to make explicit certain time-dependent cultural preoccupations that he characterized as *Kunstwollen,* a force uniting artistic ideas of abiding communal interest at a given historical conjuncture. And while Schwartz has pointed to Kracauer's simultaneous dependence on and distance from Riegl in "The Mass Ornament," other writings (including the dissertation) attest a productive engagement with Riegl's work. See Riegl, *Stilfragen.*
38. His textual references were narrowly focused on the history of Berlin architecture and of wrought-iron architectural detail in Europe. Borrmann's influence is evident in frequent citations of *Die Bau- und Kunstdenkmäler von Berlin* of 1893.
39. Simmel, "Das Problem des Stiles"; Simmel, "Psychologie des Schmuckes." Also see Belke and Renz, *Siegfried Kracauer, 1889–1966,* 11–12; Schwartz, *Blind Spots,* 139.
40. "Das Monogramm in der Mitte . . . verliert als Schmuckteil die Bedeutung, die ihm im Baroock zukam. Wie bei diesem Gitter im besonderen, so allgemein. Es wird zu einem den vielen Schnörkeln gleichgeordneten Zierat, während es früher, im Barock, ein Schmuckzentrum bildete und gleichsam der ornamentale Punkt der Gitterfläche war. Die typische Form der barocken Krone wird zu naturalistischem Muschelwerk aufgelöst." Kracauer, *Die Entwicklung der Schmiedekunst,* 54. See the "ornamentation of the surface" on p. 74.
41. On similar themes in Riegl's work, see Iversen, *Alois Riegl,* particularly the chapters titled "The Aesthetics of Disintegration" and "The Articulation of Ornament."
42. Contrast this group with a historian such as Sigfried Giedion. He belonged to the same generation and, like many of these historians, was instrumental in the formation of modern architecture.
43. Schwartz, *Blind Spots,* 137–235.
44. On the formation of art history, see Lang, *Chaos and Cosmos*; Zimmermann, *The Art Historian*; Mansfield, *Art History and Its Institutions*; Brush, *The Shaping of Art History*; Podro, *The Critical Historians of Art*; Dilly, *Kunstgeschichte als Institution.* Also see Michael Ann Holly's introduction to *Panofsky and the Foundations of Art History,* 21–45. For an assessment of the role photography played in the establishment of art history as a discipline, see Bohrer, "Photographic Perspectives." Kathryn Brush notes that Goldschmidt included photographs in his 1889 dissertation. Brush, *The Shaping of Art History,* 51.
45. Giedion, *Space, Time and Architecture.*
46. Against which we might balance the postwar work of L. Moholy-Nagy at the Chicago Institute of Design.
47. Mies and Reich directed the entire exhibition, but it was Reich who was in charge of the materials display overall. Although she had a greater role in the design of the exhibits,

Mies's interest in plate glass meant that he was closely involved with the design of this particular installation. See Tegethoff, *Mies van der Rohe: Die Villen und Landhausprojekte,* 66–67.

48. On glass, see Mies van der Rohe, "What Would Concrete, What Would Steel Be without Mirror Glass?" 314. Also see chapter 2 for a discussion of Naum Gabo's sculpted figurine enclosed in a similar glass vitrine in Lissitzky's Abstrakt Kabinett in Hannover.
49. "In der Hallen-Ausstellung befindet sich ein merkwürdiger von Mies van der Rohe und Lilly Reich erdachter Raum. Seine Wände sind aus milchigen und dunkelfarbigen Glasplatten zusammengesetzt. Ein Glaskasten, durschscheinend, die Nachbarräume dringen herein. Jedes Gerät und jede Bewegung in ihnen zaubert Schattenspiele auf die Wand, körperlose Silhouetten, die durch die Luft schweben und sich mit den Spiegelbildern aus dem Glasraum selber vermischen. Die Beschwörung dieses ungreifbaren gläsernen Spuks, der sich kaleidoskopartig wandelt wie die Lichtreflexe, ist ein Zeichen dafür, daß das neue Wohnhaus nicht eine letzte Erfüllung bedeutet, daß es nicht genügen kann, Wasserhähnchen zufrieden zu stellen und eisernen Oefen der Dekoration abzuschlagen[?]. Wie kitschig[?] immer die abgeschlagenen[?] Zierate waren: [der Rest] ersetzt das mit ihnen Gemeinte nicht. Wahrscheinlich sind die neuen Häuser ihrem Gehalt nach Reste, das heißt, zeitgemäße konstruktive Fügungen der von schlechtem Üerberfluß gereinigten Elemente; und gewiß sind diese Restkompositionen allein in der gegenwärtigen Gesellschaft zu verantworten. Aber es ware gut, wenn aus ihnen mehr noch, als es heute geschieht, die Trauer über die Entsagung spräche, die sie üben müssen; jene scurrile Trauer, die an den in die Glasfläche gebannten Erscheinungen haftet. Denn die Hausgerippe sind sich nicht Selbstzweck, sondern der notwendige Durchgang zu einer Fülle, die keiner Abzüge mehr bedarf und heute nur negativ durch die Trauer bezeugt werden kann. Sie werden erst Fleisch ansetzen, wenn der Mensch aus dem Glas steigt." Siegfried Kracauer, "Das neue Bauen," 2.
50. On Ernst Bloch, see Schwartz, *Blind Spots,* 120–26; on Schwarz, see Conrads, *Die Bauhaus-Debatte 1953.*
51. See Gutschow, "From Object to Installation in Bruno Taut's Exhibit Pavilions."
52. Worringer, *Form Problems of the Gothic,* 15.
53. Schwartz, *Blind Spots*; Reeh, *Ornaments of the Metropolis.*
54. Lungstrum, "The Display Window"; later revised in Ward, *Weimar Surfaces.* For the Glass Room photographs, Mies van der Rohe Archive, Museum of Modern Art; also see Reuter et al., "Mies and the Photographers I," 238, 247.

2. PHOTOGRAPHY INTO BUILDING

1. Stierli, "Mies Montage"; Sachsse, "Mies Montiert"; Lambert, "Collage and Montage," in *Mies in America,* 204–11; Lepik, "Mies and Photomontage, 1910–1938"; Sudhalter, "Mies van der Rohe and Photomontage in the 1920s."
2. For an impressively exhaustive, if not comprehensive, contribution to Mies studies, see Robbers, "Modern Architecture in the Age of Cinema."
3. For other sources on these photographs, see Reuter and Schulte, *Mies and Modern Living*; Dodds, *Building Desire*; Quetglas, *Fear of Glass*; Evans, "Mies van der Rohe's Paradoxical Symmetries"; Bonta, *Architecture and Its Interpretation.*

4. The sketch is not preserved, but it is referred to in correspondence about the Weissenhofsiedlung publication. See Mies to Gustav Stotz, September 23, 1927, Weissenhof correspondence files, Mies van der Rohe Archive, Museum of Modern Art. It is perhaps not so significant whether Mies directed photographers of his buildings to take particular views (although he did on occasion), or whether he simply selected from a batch of photographs after the fact. We are forced by the historical record to default to the knowledge that the photographs selected for publication were approved by his office.
5. Lambert, "Mies Immersion," in *Mies in America*, 204–11.
6. Evans, "Mies van der Rohe's Paradoxical Symmetries"; Mertins, "Architectures of Becoming."
7. Mertins invokes Henri Bergson to describe the pavilion as a kind of life-form, the subject and beneficiary of evolutionary processes, seemingly organically unstable, "a space of expectancy and emergence." Mertins, "Architectures of Becoming," 133.
8. Gough, "Constructivism Disoriented." For related work, see Elcott, "Rooms of Our Time."
9. Margarita Tupitsyn connects the two *Demonstrationsräume* to Lissitzky's photocollage of 1926, *Runner in the City*, an image that combines photographic manipulation with filmic consciousness in a dynamic, striated representation of the modern urban subject. Tupitsyn, *El Lissitzky*.
10. See note 1 above.
11. The German Pavilion established a gateway between the grandiose, eclectic architecture of the exhibition proper and the picturesque Spanish "village," the Pueblo Español, on the hill behind the pavilion site. For further detail, see Solà-Morales et al., *Mies van der Rohe*.
12. The commission for the German Pavilion was in Mies's office in the late summer of 1928, and the building was constructed from March to May 1929. The hurried schedule was complicated by a brief work stoppage and a subsequent budget shortfall that led to several cost-cutting measures. Planned as a project employing new building technologies, much of the pavilion's construction had to be adapted to the resources of 1929 Barcelona, based largely in nineteenth-century methods. Subsequently considered a manifesto for the new architecture, the project was part of Mies's ongoing effort to develop a paradigm for the steel-framed building, in this case challenged by a difficult schedule, an insufficient budget, and a number of technological compromises. Conceptually clear, Mies's first essay into a new structure/enclosure paradigm was still, of necessity, a constructional hybrid.
13. Curtis, "Mies's Choice."
14. Images of the pavilion and the pavilion itself are remarkably absorbent of multiple interpretations. The building has been related to a Greek temple, a picturesque landscape, and a machine for simultaneously producing and destroying symmetry. Modernist critics saw it as the quintessential example of spatial abstraction in architecture. More recent interpretations have emphasized transactions between building and site or building and user. The reconstructed Barcelona Pavilion sits astride a body of historiographical material that virtually ensures its continued status as a "canonical" building. Its relationship to that material is still evolving.
15. Neumann, "Der Barcelona Pavillon."

16. In a 1969 lecture, Grete Tugendhat cited the Weissenhofsiedlung in Stuttgart as a precedent for her selection of Mies. The Perls/Fuchs House in Berlin has been cited as another precedent; the clients also visited the recently completed Wolf House in Guben before selecting their architect.
17. The elements of the bourgeois home nevertheless remain—dining room, living room, study/library, music room, conservatory—reinforced by the furniture and textiles designed by Mies and Lilly Reich, in some cases explicitly for this commission.
18. In comparison to the transparency and openness of the main level of the Tugendhat House, the family bedrooms are carefully screened from viewers at street level. With a terrace overlooking the site below, the bedrooms paradoxically occupy the building's most private zone. In addition, they are conventionally discrete, a series of closed rooms for sleeping and bathing. Similarly, the service spaces on the floor below are concealed and separated behind another stretch of milk-glass wall on the main level. The house thus carefully screened the private life of its owners. According to the testimony of the Tugendhats, the grandeur of the living space accommodated itself well to the private needs of the family. See Tugendhat and Tugendhat, "Die Bewohner des Hauses Tugendhat äußern sich."
19. Bergdoll, "The Nature of Mies's Space." Interesting parallels can be found in Le Corbusier's siting of buildings. See Constant, "From the Virgilian Dream to Chandigarh."
20. For a sequence of articles on this subject, see *Die Form* 6 (1931): Walter Riezler, "Das Haus Tugendhat in Brünn" (September); Justus Bier, "Kann man im Haus Tugendhat wohnen?" (October); Riezler's commentary on Bier (October); Roger Ginsburger's exchange with Riezler (November); Grete Tugendhat and Fritz Tugendhat, "Die Bewohner des Hauses Tugendhat äußern sich" (November); and Ludwig Hilberseimer's commentary (November). The persistence of this debate is evident in Hammer-Tugendhat and Tegethoff, *Ludwig Mies van der Rohe*. Bruno Taut commented on the Exhibition House at the Berlin Building Exhibition: "Mies's house . . . is certainly very 'beautiful,' even paradisiacally beautiful; it is the house of the Superman, the 'blond beast,' to cite Nietzsche loosely, of the completely isolated individual being, the individual as such." Taut, Comments on the Exhibition House.
21. See Mallgrave and Ikonomou, *Empathy, Form, and Space*. Also see Jarzombek, *The Psychologizing of Modernity.*
22. Tafuri and Dal Co, *Modern Architecture,* 112.
23. For one interpretation of this relationship, see Dorner, "Zur abstrakten Malerei."
24. See Roth, *Zwei Wohnhäuser von Le Corbusier und Pierre Jeanneret* (a reprint of a special issue of *Bau und Wohnung*). Le Corbusier sent the French text for translation by Alfred Roth, for publication as "Fünf Punkte zu einer neuen Architektur," in June 1927. See Pommer and Otto, *Weissenhof 1927 and the Modern Movement in Architecture,* 87, 229n40; also see Moos, *Le Corbusier,* 69–71. Le Corbusier had actually published a preliminary version of the five points in 1926 in *Journal de Psychologie Normale et Pathologique*. Le Corbusier, "Architecture d'époque machiniste" (see Moos, *Le Corbusier,* 71n3). It would also be possible to argue that the separation of structure and enclosure predates the appearance of the five points and rightly belongs together with the Domino House diagram of 1914.

25. Although his interest in chance sprang from rather different sources, one might note here a possible debt to Marcel Duchamp, who had already identified chance procedure as an important mode of artistic practice in his *Three Standard Stoppages* of 1913–14 and other works.
26. Here see Museum for a Small City (1942–43), variations on the Courtyard House (as worked up in the 1930s in Germany, and then reworked with students in Chicago in the 1940s), and Project for a Concert Hall (1941–42), three projects that preserve the final traces of this exploration in Mies's American period. For basic reference on the American period, consult Lambert, *Mies in America.*
27. Neumeyer, *The Artless Word,* 171–77.
28. See Dorner, "Zur abstrakten Malerei"; and Dorner, "Glasraum in der Gewerbehalle auf der Werkbundausstellung 'Die Wohnung' Stuttgart 1927."
29. A small cabinet enclosed a sculpted figurine by Naum Gabo in the Abstrakt Kabinett, built into one corner of the room. It resembled a small-scale version of the larger-than-life-sized Lehmbruck bust in Mies's Glass Room.
30. As a showroom for the German glass industry (an industry in which Mies had had a special interest at least since 1921), the Glass Room used colored-glass spatial dividers indirectly illuminated by a top-lit fabric ceiling similar to that used in Adolphe Appia's stage set installations at Heinrich Tessenow's Festhalle at Hellerau (1910–12), but also to El Lissitzky's *Demonstrationsraum* for Dresden's Internationale Kunstausstellung of 1926, a project that immediately preceded the Abstrakt Kabinett.
31. The Gabo sculpture, far smaller in scale than the Lehmbruck, occupied a small vitrine at chest height. The Lehmbruck sculpture, while also contained within a glass box within the Glass Room, was continuous with the visitor's space, and the statue was slightly larger than life-size.
32. There is no precise parallel for the inaccessible enclosed space in the Glass Room project. Instead, at the Barcelona Pavilion, Mies enclosed a physically inaccessible slab of space within milk-glass walls. This was intended to function as a kind of lighting device, a "light box" for the otherwise unlit building. Similar milk-glass apertures at Tugendhat let onto service space; there the notion of a spatial vitrine has instead gravitated to the outer walls, where it encloses the accessible winter garden. This motif was repeated in unbuilt projects such as the Gericke House of 1932. These renditions of glass-walled spaces relate to the *Schaufenster* (show window) of Weimar commercial architecture and the *Wintergarten* of the nineteenth century.
33. Schinkel generally provided spaces into which one might look before entering, thus previewing a future moment in the architectural circuit. See Bergdoll, *Karl Friedrich Schinkel*; Stemshorn, *Mies & Schinkel*
34. For a comment on the "shopwindow quality of things," see Simmel, "Berliner Gewerbeausstellung." My thanks to Kerstin Barndt for this reference; see Barndt, "'Dioramas of a New World.'"
35. Korn, *Glas im Bau und als Gebrauchsgegenstand.* In 1924, Meyer presented his Co-op Vitrine for a trade fair staged in Basel and Ghent. See Hays, "Co-op Vitrine and the Representation of Mass Production."
36. Ebeling, *Space as Membrane,* 34.

37. Mertins and Jennings, *G*.
38. For a fuller investigation, see Koss, *Modernism after Wagner.*
39. Mertins, "Architecture, Worldview, and World Image in *G*."
40. This serves as a counterpoint to the subsequent discussions in chapters 5 and 6.
41. These included the Barcelona Pavilion (1929), the Nolde House (1929), the Golf Club for Krefeld (1930), the Tugendhat House (1930), the Henke House Addition (1930), the Berlin Building Exhibition House (1931), the Gericke House (1932), the Ulrich Lange House (1935), the German Pavilion at Brussels (1934), the Hubbe House (1935), and the Museum for a Small City (1942).
42. Phillips's intermedial application of musical modes to the work of another great modernist has been critical to this study in more than one way. See Phillips, *The Poetic Modes of Octavio Paz,* 2–5.
43. Ibid., 3.
44. Because they were not built, other projects from this period reflect these and other spatial modes that remain largely conjectural, but important. It is impossible to compare the unbuilt schemes with their (nonexistent) photographs, a primary task of this study.
45. Many of Mies's students and colleagues commented on this "discovery" in later years. Peter Carter, one of Mies's former employees, noted in 1974 in relation to the 1928 commission for the Barcelona Pavilion: "While he was concentrating upon the planning of this pavilion he suddenly became aware, as if after years of rumination, that structural elements and space-defining elements could be separate entities, and by being so would release a new and significant architectural force. . . . With the successful application of these ideas to the different functions of the Barcelona Pavilion and the Tugendhat House, Mies van der Rohe was convinced that he had arrived at a sound general principle upon which to develop his future work." Carter, *Mies van der Rohe at Work,* 20.
46. See Lang, *Chaos and Cosmos*, 80–81.
47. The theologian-philosopher Romano Guardini had a significant influence on Mies. See Neumeyer, *The Artless Word.*
48. Mies also drew on architectural convention for his 1920s work. Karl Bötticher's writing on tectonic-formal relationships, a schema in which "core-form" (Kernform) performs structural work in a building and "art-form" (Kunstform) sheathes that structure, expressively echoes in the pavilion's sheathed columns. Ebeling referenced architecture's role in industrial transformation and surely drew on this precedent, as well as on the biological theories of Raoul Francé. In any case, Bötticher's theories relate to Mies's articulated design system. Although such evidence is never definitive, Mies's library contains the 1852 edition of Bötticher's *Tektonik der Hellenen.* See Ludwig Mies van der Rohe Collection, Rare Books, Richard J. Daley Library, University of Illinois at Chicago, http://library.uic.edu/home/collections/manuscripts-and-rare-books/rare-books-at-the-richard-j.-daley-library (accessed September 11, 2013). Mies also owned two copies of Alois Riegl's *Stilfragen* and the posthumous volume of Riegl's lectures *Die Entstehung der Barockkunst in Rom.* Gottfried Semper theorized structural framework as distinct from "curtain" walls or textile spatial enclosure, exemplified in Semper's "four elements"; this was also part of the familiar history of tectonics from the late nineteenth century in Ger-

many. Connections between Semperian theory and the marble and glass sheets that were so characteristic of Mies's architecture should also be noted.

49. See Scharnholz, "Wolf House, Gubin, 1925–27"; Zimmerman, "Eliat House Project, 1925."
50. This is partly the case because so many of the projects in which Mies investigated this system of design remained unbuilt. The computer animations created for *Mies in Berlin* provide a means to understand the correlation between spatial choreographies and viewing moments in buildings like the Hubbe House and the Glass Room. But they were constructed as fly-throughs rather than walk-throughs, altering the pace (speeding it up) and the point of view (raising it above average human height).
51. Kleinmann and Van Duzer, *Mies van der Rohe*; and Kleinmann and Van Duzer, "Eisen und Mörtel."
52. For discussion of Mies's and Schinkel's plan methodologies, see Bergdoll, "Schinkel and Mies: Urban Perspective"; Bergdoll, "Schinkel and Mies: Nature's Perspective"; Stemshorn, *Mies & Schinkel*; Bergdoll, "The Nature of Mies's Space"; Tegethoff, "Catching the Spirit"; Neumeyer, "Space for Reflection"; Johnson, "Schinkel and Mies."
53. For example, see Schulze, *Mies van der Rohe,* 70–71; and Tafuri, "The Stage as 'Virtual City.'"
54. Quoted in Beacham, *Adolphe Appia,* 42.
55. This attitude toward theater reform contrasts dramatically with the efforts of Georg Fuchs in Munich, who also sought to change the setting of the stage, but starting from a rather different point. See Koss, *Modernism after Wagner,* chap. 5.
56. Mies van der Rohe, "Bauen."
57. Loos, "Regarding Economy."
58. Discussing the calls for theatrical reform of the late nineteenth and early twentieth centuries in Europe, Tafuri noted, "It is Appia himself who wonders how this materialization of souls in space, this private ritual, can be translated into everyday behavior." Tafuri quoted Appia, who had called for "the *Salle,* cathedral of the future, which, in a free, vast, and flexible space, will bring together the most diverse manifestations of our social and artistic life—the perfect place for dramatic art to flourish, *with or without an audience,*" in the pages of *Music and the Art of the Theatre.* Passing briefly over references to the Arbeitsrat für Kunst's "cathedral of the future," Tafuri paused on Mies, with the comment, "That . . . Appia firmly declares that the spectators are superfluous seems rather to foreshadow . . . the 'metaphoric' theaters of Mies." Tafuri, "The Stage as 'Virtual City,'" 98. For the Appia quotation, see Adolphe Appia, *Music and the Art of the Theatre,* 5.
59. The passage goes on: "In that space, a place of *absence,* empty, conscious of the impossibility of restoring 'synthesis,' once the 'negative' of the metropolis has been understood, man, the spectator of a spectacle that is really 'total' because it is nonexistent, is obliged to perform a pantomime that reproduces the wandering in the urban labyrinth of sign-beings among signs having no sense, a pantomime he must attempt daily. In the absoluteness of silence, the audience of the Barcelona Pavilion can thus be 'reintegrated' with that *absence.* . . . In a place that refuses to present itself as space and that is destined to vanish

like a circus tent, Mies gives life to a language composed of empty and isolated signifiers, in which things are portrayed as mute events. . . . The utopia no longer resides in the city, nor does its spectacular metaphor, except as a game or a productive structure disguised as the imaginary." Tafuri, "The Stage as 'Virtual City,'" 111–12.

60. An exchange between Mies and Frank Lloyd Wright suggests that Mies also felt this way. On October 25, 1947, Wright apologized for his negative comments on the 1947 MoMA show on Mies's work: "Then I said the BP was your best contribution to the original 'Negation' and you seemed to be still back there where I was then." Wright felt that modernism had bogged down on that line and noted that the "show struck me as reactionary." Mies responded on November 25: "I feel that you use this word for qualities that I find positive and essential." Container 60, Frank Lloyd Wright folder, Ludwig Mies van der Rohe Papers, Manuscripts Division, Library of Congress.
61. Correspondence between Mies and Van Doesburg was especially warm and enthusiastic in the early 1920s, as letters held by the Library of Congress and the Museum of Modern Art's Mies Archive attest. See Van Doesburg file, Ludwig Mies van der Rohe Papers, Manuscripts Division, Library of Congress.
62. See Giertz, *Kultus ohne Götter.*
63. See Schlemmer, *Die Bühne im Bauhaus*; Koss, *Modernism after Wagner,* chap. 7; Moynihan and Odom, "Oskar Schlemmer's 'Bauhaus Dances'"; Manning and Benson, "Interrupted Continuities." For a comparative treatment of Schlemmer and Wigman, see Scheyer, *The Shapes of Space.*
64. Moynihan and Odom, "Oskar Schlemmer's 'Bauhaus Dances,'" 58.
65. Mies's access to the Hellerau circle in the years before World War I introduced him to Appia's work. Familiar with the work of Jaques-Dalcroze and Appia in the Hellerau Institute through his fiancée, Ada Bruhn, a student of eurhythmics there during the term of their engagement, he also knew the dancer Mary Wigman, who studied at Hellerau with Ada, then with Laban in Munich, and who remained friends with the Mies couple over many years. On Mary Wigman, see Delius, *Mary Wigman.* The future wife of Hans Prinzhorn was also close to Bruhn and Wigman, and Mies remained in close contact with Prinzhorn through the 1920s. See Schulze, *Mies van der Rohe,* 70–71; and Prinzhorn file, Ludwig Mies van der Rohe Papers, Manuscripts Division, Library of Congress.
66. Bücher, *Arbeit und Rhythmus.* Bücher was an economic historian of the Wilhelmine and Weimar years, studying economic history in connection with anthropological concerns. *Arbeit und Rhythmus* surveys a wide range of material, organized by song type ("different types of worker songs"), ethnicity ("worker songs as bonding larger groups"), and economic implications ("Rhythm as economic development principle"). Sample groups ranged from New Zealand Totowaka to African Americans to Lettlanders and Estonians. The book was reprinted in 1899, 1902, 1909, and 1924.
67. Drost's book included contributions from August Schmarsow, Alois Riegl, Wilhelm Worringer, Theodor Lipps, and Kurt Koffka. While Mies may not have read the work of these theorists (although his reading tastes were quite varied), nevertheless his library contained the works of Riegl, Worringer, and Lipps, and the prevalence of interest in the subject in the years before and after World War I is worth noting.
68. Evans goes on to relate this treatment to two specific forms of spatial perception: the

spatial conception of the blind (a space that exists only within the compass of human locomotion) and what Evans describes as "the shape of space made for extended vision." Evans, "Mies van der Rohe's Paradoxical Symmetries."

69. Manfredo Tafuri, José Quetglas, K. Michael Hays, and Detlef Mertins have elaborated on the surface effects of the building, each articulating a slightly different understanding. See Mertins, "Architectures of Becoming."
70. Mertins and Jennings, *G*. Also see Stierli, "Mies Montage."
71. On Richter, see Foster, *Hans Richter*; Turvey, "Dada between Heaven and Hell"; Lawder, *The Cubist Cinema*. For a recent discussion of Mies's connection to Richter, see Mertins, "Architectures of Becoming."
72. *Universal space* is the term often applied to Mies's later, clear-span projects such as the New National Gallery in Berlin. It is important to note that a similar term was in use much earlier to describe a completely different sort of work, and that Mies was part of this development.
73. Richter and Eggeling authored *Universelle Sprache* in 1920 (all copies lost) and used it to solicit funding for their film experiments. See also Museum of Modern Art, Hans Richter, *Rhythmus 21*, http://www.moma.org/collection/object.php?object_id=91477 (accessed September 11, 2013).
74. In a letter of April 4, 1966, Richter requested a plan of the Brick Country House from Mies to use for his new book, "den ich als erstes 1921/22 bei Ihnen sah." On June 25, Mies responded affirmatively: "Naturally you can use my plan of the BCH for your book." Container 6, personal correspondence 1930–69, folder R, Ludwig Mies van der Rohe Papers, Manuscripts Division, Library of Congress.
75. "Der Rhythmus ist die Grundform, das Skelett eines Films—sofern er Kunst ist. . . . Hierbei sind zu berücksichtigen: 1. Die Länge eines jeden Montagestücks 2. die Richtung der Bewegungen 3. das Tempo 4. Schließlich ihre Gewalt, die je nach Größe Ton und Form von verschiedener Wirkung ist. Rhythmus im Film bedeutet nicht weniger, als die künstlerisch klar geregelte Folge der Bewegungen." Richter, *Filmgegner von heute, Filmfreunde von morgen*, 34, 42.
76. Lawder, *The Cubist Cinema*, 52.
77. Turvey, "Dada between Heaven and Hell," 30.
78. Detlef Mertins discusses rhythm in the avant-garde context of both the Glass Room and the Barcelona Pavilion. He sees this as a generalized reference, noting, "As in Richter's films, the elements and spaces assume coherence and unity through the rhythm with which they move the observer through and around them." This effect is then countered by simultaneity: "Yet at the same time, something of van Doesburg's simultaneity also remains in effect—combining synchronic and diachronic conceptions of rhythm and unity." See Mertins, "Architectures of Becoming," 131–32.
79. Turvey, "Dada between Heaven and Hell," 33.
80. Appia, "Eurhythmics and Light," 131–32. Connections between Appia and other pedagogical projects in Germany at this time might be further explored—for example, Friedrich Froebel's earlier emphasis on sensory perception in children's education. This connection was pointed out to me by Rosemarie Bletter. One might also look at the work of the psychologist Hans Prinzhorn in a similar regard.

81. See the use of rhythm in Walter Riezler's initial discussion of the Tugendhat House, in "Das Haus Tugendhat in Brünn," 321. See also Grete Tugendhat's use of the same word in her defense against the critique of the house in Tugendhat and Tugendhat, "Die Bewohner des Hauses Tugendhat äußern sich."
82. See Bergdoll, "The Nature of Mies's Space"; Bergdoll, *Karl Friedrich Schinkel,* chap. 3.
83. Tim Benton has explored similar terrain in the case of Le Corbusier. See Benton, *Le Corbusier*; also see Herschdorfer, *Le Corbusier and the Power of Photography.*

3. ARCHITECTURAL ABSTRACTION

1. Lotz, "Architekturfotos." Basic source material on the Tugendhat House includes Barta, *Wohnen in Mies van der Rohes Villa Tugendhat*; Hammer-Tugendhat and Tegethoff, *Ludwig Mies van der Rohe*; Stiller, *Das Haus Tugendhat*; Tegethoff, *Im Brennpunkt der Moderne*; Tegethoff, *Mies van der Rohe: The Villas and Country Houses.* Although this linear description would almost certainly never have been published in its entirety, nevertheless a monograph on the house would have included many of the photographs.
2. There are no extant images of the northern side of the house in the Mies Archive at the Museum of Modern Art. The lack of views of this side of the building could stem from two causes: the northern facade contains the garage and service wing of the house, and the view from the north shows a radically foreshortened building, since the garage masks the long wing that runs perpendicular to it behind, leaving only a small part of the wing visible from the street approach.
3. Lotz, "Architekturfotos."
4. The same point can be made with respect to the 1931 Exhibition House at the Berlin Building Exhibition and the Henke House addition in Essen (1930). Mies designed a series of unbuilt commissions that also followed similar design principles.
5. I am grateful to Lauren Kogod for first alerting me to the relationship between the spatial zoning of the Tugendhat House and earlier theories of domestic planning from Hermann Muthesius, Karl Scheffler, and others.
6. The bibliography on Czech architecture in Moravia includes Kudělka and Chatrný, *For New Brno*; Kubová, *L'Avant-Garde architecturale en Tchécoslovaquie, 1918–1939*; Šlapeta, *Die Brünner Funktionalisten*; Kudělka, *Brnenská architektura 1919–1928.*
7. It is possible that the all-glass gasworks pavilion by Fuchs made an impression on Mies when he was at the beginning of the process of designing the Barcelona Pavilion.
8. Archivists in the city architectural archive report no evidence that Mies visited the "Exhibition of Contemporary Culture" or that he had any special acquaintance with Fuchs. Like Mies's Tugendhat files, the files that passed from the local building contractor into the possession of the city sometime during the Cold War years were apparently destroyed. The city owns drawings, but no other files. Dr. Lenka Kudělková, Muzeum Města Brna (Brno City Museum), and Jan Sapák, Brno, personal conversations with author, April 2003.
9. For discussions of the Tugendhat House in relation to local architectural culture, see Sapák, "Umfeld und Entstehung eines berühmten Hauses"; and Templ, "Streiflichter auf die Baukultur in Brünn und Querverbindung nach Wien."
10. Rudolf de Sandalo senior died in Brno in 1932; his son Rudolf de Sandalo took over the

office, also opening an office in Prague by 1937, and in Berlin by 1941. His last recorded work is found in publications of the work of Fritz Breuhaus de Groot, in which the photographer's credit reads "Sandalo, Schömberg." A chronology of the life of the elder de Sandalo is found in the archives of the Muzeum Města Brna.

11. See Birgus, *Czech Photographic Avant-Garde, 1918–1948.*
12. *Forum Zeitschrift für Architektur, freie und angewandte Kunst,* published in Bratislava from 1931 to 1938, included numerous de Sandalo photographs; Atelier de Sandalo advertised itself in the pages of *Index: Leták kulturní informace,* published in Brno, 1929–39, as "photographers of modern architecture" (Fota modernich architektur).
13. The local competition included the photographers Karel Stoklas, Herbert Orth, and Evzen Petruj. For information on Brno modernism, see Kudělka and Chatrný, *For New Brno.*
14. Another image of the locker room at the baths frames architecture through architecture, a technique commonly used by Köster for Mendelsohn's work. In this case, however, de Sandalo has framed the lavatory with its seat up, through an adjacent doorway.
15. The extent of this series makes the lack of similar photos from Tugendhat notable. No photograph of the mechanism that operated the house's sinking window (Versenkfenster) exists, for example. Perhaps these images were of no interest to Mies and have therefore not survived.
16. Also in Birgus, "Czech Avant-Garde Art and the World," 19.
17. Fuchs, *Masarykův studentský Domov Brno.*
18. This material may have originally been stored at Eduard Ludwig's parents' barn in Brandenburg before the onset of World War II, but the recent sale of that material makes this improbable. A more likely explanation is that the Tugendhat files were kept at Lilly Reich's office after Mies's departure from Germany, possibly as a result of her close involvement in the project, the importance of her contribution, and continuing publication demands. They would then have been destroyed in her atelier in the 1940s. Notably, the photo files (Reich may well have had her own) escaped this fate and came to Chicago with the rest. The de Sandalo atelier retained the negatives, and Mies frequently referred requests for prints to the photographer directly, at least through the 1930s.
19. This group includes a view along the passageway toward the stairs on the entry floor, a view of Fritz Tugendhat's bedroom, views of the nanny's bedroom, views of Hannah Weiss's bedroom (Weiss was Grete Tugendhat's daughter from her first marriage), a view of the master bathroom, a view down the length of the winter garden, a view of the pantry, a view of the kitchen, and a short series of views of the upper terrace, including images of the Tugendhat children at play.
20. As noted, there are no extant views of the street facade from the north, and there is only one view from the northern corner of the garden, known from a copy print probably shot from a published example by Mies's first Chicago photographers, Williams and Meyer. See photo files, Mies van der Rohe Archive, Museum of Modern Art.
21. See references to Willi Warstat in chapter 4.
22. Barthes, commenting on the seemingly evidentiary nature of the photograph, further noted: "The absence of code disintellectualizes the message because it seems to found in nature the signs of culture. This is without a doubt an important historical paradox: the

more technology develops the diffusion of information (and notably of images), the more it provides the means of masking the constructed meaning under the appearance of the given meaning." Barthes, "Rhetoric of the Image," 45–46.

23. Numerous examples might be offered here; for the present discussion, Mies's own perspective sketches, dated after the Tugendhat and Barcelona commissions, mimic the space of these earlier photographs, constituting "wide-angle sketches." See sketches for the Krefeld Gold Club of 1930, the Gericke House of 1932, and the Hubbe House and Court House Studies of the years following 1934, all in Drexler, *The Mies van der Rohe Archive,* vols. 4 and 6.
24. I thank Adrian Forty for his insightful discussion of this point.
25. For a brief account of the shifting camera back, see Liebermann, "Thoughts of an Art Historian/Photographer on His Two Disciplines."
26. Significant changes wrought by the interim phases of use might be considered radical enough to constitute different "versions" of this building over its life. This chapter focuses primarily on the first constructed version of the building and on its first photographic version. Future work might take up additional versions over the life of the building or its photography. Sarah Dreller has conducted an investigation into the second phase of photography of the Farnsworth House, for example; her investigation might be said to articulate a new photographic version of that building, distinct from the one that accompanied its first construction and revelatory of a new historical interpretation adequate to its own moment in time. See Dreller, "Curtained Walls."
27. See Bois, "The Iconoclast."
28. See chapter 4 for discussion of the inverted image of the camera's ground-glass focusing field.
29. For contributions to the debate, see chapter 2, note 20.
30. For more on this debate, see Cohen, "Roger Ginsburger."
31. Fritz Tugendhat, letter to the editor, *Die Form* 6, no. 11 (1931): 438.
32. One might mention here Mies's own visual appreciation of his architecture. George Nelson paraphrased Mies's experience at the Tugendhat House in a 1935 interview for *Pencil Points*: "Miës *[sic]* hates and despises cheap materials, but for once he indulged his tastes. An onyx wall, selected after months of searching for the right material, the curved macassar wall, the hundred feet of plate glass window and silk curtains to cover them—all these were things he really enjoyed working with. Into his search for the onyx wall he put a fantastic amount of time and money . . . but in the end he got his wall, which was all that interested him. Today, when he makes an occasional visit to Brno, he settles his bulk into one of the comfortable metal chairs, looks at his creation with contentment and says, 'Now there is a *wall*!'" Nelson, "Architects of Europe Today, 7," 456.
33. My thanks to photographic historian Thomas Drysdale for information about the effects of different lens varieties on the representation of space, and on lens and camera types in common use in Weimar Germany.
34. For a fuller understanding of film theory in the 1920s, see the entire text of Teige's interesting essay "Zur Ästhetik des Films."
35. "Gerade diese Fläche muß gesprengt werden, um hinter ihr die neue Tiefe, das raumzeit-

liche Filmkontinuum zu entdecken. Dort und nirgends anders liegt die schöpferische Sphäre des gestaltenden Films! Der poly-dimensionale Raum, den die Bildhauer seit Michelangelos 'Grablegung' vergeblich zu gestalten versucht haben, wird einmal mittels raffinierter Filmtechnik lebendig werden." Van Doesburg, "Film als reine Gestaltung," 249. Barthes blasted this notion apart in his "Rhetoric of the Image" as follows: "The distinction between film and photograph is not a simple difference of degree but a radical opposition. Film can no longer be seen as animated photographs: the *having-been-there* gives way before a *being-there* of the thing" (45).

36. "Die neue Tiefe" might also be translated as "the new depth"; I use the more old-fashioned noun "deep" for its spatial connotations, less present in the vector "depth."
37. In his 1927 essay "Perspective as Symbolic Form," Panofsky described the problematic nature of perspective but also commented on contemporary theorizations of perspectival space and the so-called fourth dimension, embraced by El Lissitzky and others in these years. See also Christopher Wood's introduction in Panofsky, *Perspective as Symbolic Form.*
38. See Barr, "Introduction."
39. Oechslin and Harbers, *Sigfried Giedion und die Fotografie.*
40. For a fuller survey of this concept in photography, see Kellein and Lame, *Abstrakte Fotografie.*
41. See Naginski, "Romanticism's Piranesi." Naginski discusses the relations between the projected spaces of Piranesi's drawings and the historiographical response to those spaces in the nineteenth century as they resonated with contemporary concerns. She thus connects an old source to a series of relatively contemporary concerns, as sketched here. In addition, we might cite Bruno Taut as the most pertinent exemplar of drawing as a tool for envisioning an "abstract" architecture, in his crystalline Alpine Architecture projects. See Bletter, "Bruno Taut and Paul Scheerbart's Vision"; Schirren, *Bruno Taut.*
42. See Mallgrave and Ikonomou, *Empathy, Form, and Space.*
43. For the first half of this story, see Crary, *Techniques of the Observer*; and Crary, *Suspensions of Perception.* Mysticism, theosophy, and embodied cultlike practices also influenced modernism. For a pertinent case, see Giertz, *Kultus ohne Götter.* Also see Lang, *Chaos and Cosmos.*

4. TYPE-PHOTO

1. Haus, "Photogenic Architecture."
2. "Profession," in this case, designates a practice that was located somewhere between craft and machine technology. Photography was as much artisanal as it was industrial at this time.
3. Michael Pidgley locates the transmission of picturesque pictorial conventions in landscape photography as early as the 1840s. See Pidgley, "Picturesque."
4. Nilsen, *Architecture in Nineteenth-Century Photographs*; Elwall, *Photography Takes Command*; Pare, *Photography and Architecture, 1839–1939.*
5. Keller, "Durandelle, the Paris Opéra, and the Aesthetic of Creativity." For the earlier yet parallel case of Édouard Baldus, see Bergdoll, "A Matter of Time."

6. Elwall, *Photography Takes Command.*
7. The originality of Henry Hobson Richardson's work can be understood in relation to the historicist precedents he gathered from photographic images, with which his work was in spirited dialogue, as Mary Woods has shown. Woods quotes the editors of *American Architect*: "The rapid dissemination of accurate representations of new buildings cannot but have a great effect on popularizing the work of men of conspicuous talent, and while we may expect to see architectural fashions succeed each other as rapidly during the next century as they have in this, they are likely to be led, like the Richardsonian Romanesque, by architects, and not by rhetoricians." Woods, "The Photograph as Tastemaker," 155.
8. The autotype process goes back to 1881; halftone printing to 1895. See Heidtmann, *Wie das Photo ins Buch kam.*
9. Woods, "The Photograph as Tastemaker." For two early examples of photographs published in a journal in 1856, see Lipstadt, "The Building and the Book in César Daly's *Revue Générale de l'Architecture.*"
10. Lipstadt, "The Building and the Book in César Daly's *Revue Générale de l'Architecture.*"
11. The phrase "reactionary modernist" refers to Herf, *Reactionary Modernism.*
12. For the most dramatic example, see photographs of the interior of Loos's Khuner House, in which the view out a picture window has been switched from upslope to downslope. Loos's most explicit denunciations of photography are found in an interview that he gave to Bohuslav Markalous, editor of the Czech journal *Wohnungskultur,* in 1924 or 1925. See Loos, "Regarding Economy." Also see Colomina, *Privacy and Publicity,* 269–73.
13. Banham, *A Concrete Atlantis*; Colomina, *Privacy and Publicity*; Cohen, *Scenes of the World to Come.*
14. This too, however, was not a unidirectional effect; the art status of photography has only grown more pronounced throughout the history of the medium, and the quality of photographic images has kept pace with the medium's artistic ambitions. See Giedion, *Walter Gropius* (1931); Giedion, *Walter Gropius: Work and Teamwork* (1954); Giedion, *Walter Gropius* (1992).
15. Supplementary volumes of a series titled Sonderheften der Architektur des XX. Jahrhunderts were also edited by Creutz, including *Wilhelm Kreis.* Frank Lloyd Wright's Wasmuth volume of 1911 was also part of this series, despite radical differences in its format. See Powers, "The Architectural Book," 168. Earlier books that used photography to argue a case for architecture include Paul Schultze-Naumburg's Kulturarbeiten series (1902–6), where photography was a tool of argument. Here I focus, however, on commercial publications whose primary purpose was to argue through photographs, rather than on text illustrations that buttressed written arguments. Also see Stöneberg, *Arthur Köster, Architekturfotographie 1926–1933*; Jaeger, *Neue Werkkunst*; Sachsse, *Photographie als Medium der Architekturinterpretation.*
16. See Sachsse, *Bild und Bau,* 66–74; also see Heidtmann, *Wie das Photo ins Buch kam,* 74–75; Powers, "The Architectural Book," 168.
17. Robert Elwall notes the appearance of "ink photos" in British periodicals from the mid-1870s, and their supersession by the halftone. Elwall, *Building with Light,* 95.
18. According to Frank Heidtmann, photoxylography was in widest use around 1865, the

Woodbury print around 1864, collotype in 1869, heliogravure in 1879, and halftone printing in 1890. Other authors give 1881 as the date for the invention of halftone printing. See Heidtmann, *Wie das Photo ins Buch kam*; Twyman, *Printing 1770–1970*, chap. 6, especially 102–4.

19. Boyer, "*La Mission Héliographique*"; Sachsse, *Bild und Bau*, 36–42.
20. See, for example, projects such as the Wheeler Survey and the work of photographers such as Peter Emerson and Eadweard Muybridge. Also see Kelsey and Stimson, *The Meaning of Photography.*
21. Heidtmann notes that in the 1860s, 32 new journals began with photographic illustration; by the 1880s that number had increased to 103. Heidtmann, *Wie das Photo ins Buch kam*, 84.
22. Froschauer, "*An die Leser!*"
23. See chapter 5 for discussion of the affiliation of a building and its logo.
24. For one analysis of this transition, see Brown, *The Corporate Eye.*
25. On the materiality of early architectural photography, see Sachsse, *Bild und Bau*, 60–62.
26. See McArthur, *The Picturesque*, 20–21; Puttfarken, *The Discovery of Pictorial Composition.* Also see Lieberman, "Thoughts of an Art Historian/Photographer on the Relationship of his Two Disciplines," especially 240; and Robinson and Herschman, *Architecture Transformed*, 1–5.
27. Carpo, *Architecture in the Age of Printing*; Wittman, *Architecture, Print Culture, and the Public Sphere in Eighteenth-Century France.*
28. Warstat, *Allgemeine Ästhetik der photographischen Kunst auf psychologischer Grundlage*, 20–27.
29. Institutions such as the Bauhaus and the Leipzig Hochschule für Graphik und Buchkunst did not begin to teach commercial photography until later, the former in 1928 and the latter in the early 1920s.
30. Michael Stöneberg has noted the many instances in which his primary subject, Arthur Köster, resisted the standard recommendations for architectural photography in favor of creative composition or unexpected lighting. Stöneberg, *Arthur Köster, Architekturfotografie 1926–1933.*
31. Similarly representative books from the perspective of British photographers might be Abney's *A Treatise on Photography* (1897) and Story's *The Story of Photography* (1902), both of which include sections on architectural photography.
32. Indeed, glass plate negatives could be repurposed dramatically: many of photographer Arthur Köster's negatives were washed and installed in broken window frames after World War II, and he was surely not alone in this practice. Michael Stöneberg, personal conversation with author, summer 2004.
33. "It requires a certain amount of practice to form a correct pictorial estimate of an inverted image, and it is probably by turning the head in such a position that the line joining the eyes is nearly vertical, a more correct idea can be formed than by keeping it in the usual position. At first no diaphragm should be in the lens, as the general sweep of light and shade can be better studied. When this is satisfactory and the lines of the picture are the best that can be obtained, a diaphragm may be inserted with an aperture of the

largest size which will admit of a good general focus being obtained." Abney, *A Treatise on Photography,* 255–56.

34. "Bilder, welche von nur sehr selten zu erreichenden Standpunkten aus aufgenommen sind, haben immer für den Beschauer etwas Unnatürliches." Schmidt, *Die Architektur-Photographie,* 60.

35. "So möchten wir hier ergänzend, jedoch nicht berichtigend hinzufügen, dass bei Strassen, Säulengängen, Interieurs, überhaupt bei sich stark in die Tiefe ziehenden Objekten, manchmal auch eine Aufstellung der Camera so, dass die optische Achse parallel der Halbierungslinie des Objektes läuft, sehr brauchbare Bilder giebt. Man vermeide es dann aber unbedingt, die Camera genau in jene Linie zu stellen. Man sehe vielmehr darauf, dass dieselbe wesentlich seitlich davon abgestellt wird, widrigenfalls man in beiden Bildhäften genau symmetrische Aufnahmen erhält, die einen ungemein langweiligen Eindruck machen." Ibid., 64.

36. "Der gänzliche Mangel einer solchen macht sich ungemein störend geltend, indem das Ganze keinen Halt in sich zeigt. . . . Ein Bild muss stets einen passenden Abschluss haben, und darf nie eine Wölbung [arch or vault] ohne Stütze sein." Ibid., 65.

37. "Für die Herstellung von Architekturaufnahmen eignet sich am besten ein mäßig bedeckter Himmel. Greller Sonnenschein wirft zu schwere Schatten, welche zahlreiche Details in Dunkel hüllen, deren Studium den eigentlichen Zweck der Aufnahme bildete." E. Wach, "Architekturaufnahmen," 187.

38. See notes 14, 15, and 16 for other sources on architectural photography used in this discussion. See also Lotz, "Architekturfotos."

39. "Da die Photographie nicht die Farbe des Originals wiedergibt, so kann sie zum größten Teil nur durch den Verlauf der Linien wirken. Eine hübsche Perspektive ist also für den Gesamtwert eines photographischen Bildes weitausschlaggebender als bei einem Gemälde der Fall ist." Schmidt, *Die Architektur-Photographie,* 38. Schmidt reemphasized the importance of composition later in his book, noting the dependence of good composition on the careful choice of standpoint. He considered this choice more decisive for a good architectural photograph than any of the darkroom techniques available for manipulating an existing exposure. See ibid., 64.

40. "Namentlich in der Architektur-Photographie können wir nicht durch feine Verteilung von Licht und Schatten wirken, da wir dieselbe, im Gegensatz zur Porträt-Photographie, hier nur wenig in der Hand haben, müssen also in besonderem Grade bestrebt sein durch die Perspektive zu wirken." Ibid., 38.

41. "Manche glauben, zu einem jeden Bilde gehört eine Staffage, besonders eine oder mehrere Personen, und seien es nur einige passende Schulkinder. Wie sehr solches Beiwerk ein sonst gelungenes Bild in seiner Wirkung gänzlich verderben kann, weiß ein jeder. Gewiß, zuweilen ist eine Belebung einer Straße, eines Platzes sehr ansprechend, aber es muß auch wirklich eine Belebung, es dürfen nicht mehr oder weniger aufdringlich sich breit machende Menschen sein. Lieber keine Staffage, als eine solche, die allzusehr nach Mache aussieht." Franck, "Aufnahmen von Bauwerken, Städteansichten usw," 230. Similarly, in 1927, Maximilian von Karnitschnigg recommended avoiding staffage if it threatened to compete with the image itself, and especially in the case of interior photography: "One

must remember that the purpose of the exposure is architecture and not the representation of some person. The use of people as staffage in interior photographs is absolutely reprehensible." The paragraph reads: "Findet man nicht an Ort und Stelle eine wirklich ganz zum Bilde passende Staffage, so verzichte man lieber auf eine solche. Auch vermeide man es, Staffagen in einer derartigen Größe aufzunehmen, daß dadurch eine Konkurrenz der Motive entsteht. Man bedenke immer, daß ja die Architektur den Zweck der Aufnahme bildet und nicht die Wiedergabe irgendeiner Person. Völlig verwerflich ist die Verwendung von Personen als Staffagen bei der Aufnahme von Innenräumen." Karnitschnigg, "Moderne Architekturphotographie," 3, 44.

42. Ezra Stoller has noted that the photographer who poses figures with their backs to the camera achieves a similar effect. Nägele, "An Interview with Ezra Stoller."
43. An interesting example of this sort of inclusion of figures is found in Bruno Taut's 1927 *Ein Wohnhaus,* a monograph on the house he built for his family in Dahlewitz, outside Berlin. In this publication Taut's daughter and other figures demonstrate the uses of various spaces in the house, including cooking and showering, in photographs by Köster. The Bauhaus film in which Ise Gropius and her sister Ellen Frank played the role of inhabitants of the Master House in Dessau provides another example, as do photographs of Marlene Poelzig's house for her family in Berlin-Charlottenburg, including photographs with the Poelzig children playing inside and out.
44. The prolific and highly successful architectural photographer Arthur Köster constitutes another important exception. Köster sometimes used scale figures in his photographs, along with other pictorial and narrative devices. On Köster, see Stöneberg, *Arthur Köster, Architekturfotographie 1926–1933.* On Köster's collaboration with Erich Mendelsohn, see Förster, *Masse braucht Licht*; Stöneberg, *Arthur Köster*, 338–45.
45. "Unterschiede aber, die ohne weiteres jedermann auffallen, treten in Erscheinung, sobald es sich um die Wiedergabe der dritten, der Tiefendimension durch das Auge einerseits und durch die photographische Platte anderseits handelt. Es ist gewiß schon einem jeden Photographen aufgefallen, daß die photographische Kamera nicht so weit in die Ferne trägt, wie das menschliche Auge. Jeder Photograph wird—wenigstens in den Anfängen seiner Laufbahn—die Erfahrung gemacht haben, daß Gegenstände, die seinem Auge noch gar nicht so sehr weit entfernt zu sein schienen, auf der photographischen Platte ganz unverhältnismäßig stark in die Ferne gerückt erschienen." Warstat, *Allgemeine Ästhetik der photographischen Kunst auf psychologischer Grundlage,* 21.
46. Warstat's critique was by no means original, nor was it even particularly new. The limitations of photography had long been noted. See, for example, the critique of Francis Wey in 1853: "First of all, the accuracy of perspective is only relative: we have corrected it, but we have not completely rectified it. Secondly, heliography deceives us with regard to the relationship among tones. It pales blue tints, pushes green and red toward black, and has difficulty capturing delicate shades of white." Quoted in McCauley, *A. E. E. Disdéri and the Carte de Visite Portrait Photograph,* 194. See also Jay, "Photo-unrealism," for a discussion of this issue.
47. Jakobson, "The Contours of the Safe Conduct," 195.
48. Even the Barcelona Pavilion, massively successful overall, had one highly negative critic,

who wrote in the *Deutsche Bauzeitung*; not surprisingly, he had his own photographer. Equally unsurprisingly, the photographs show only the poorly constructed roof of the pavilion.

49. Arindam Dutta describes a similar flexibility for bureaucracy in colonial encounters. The comparison is apt: the publicity of architecture was a proliferating network par excellence, with certain similarities to bureaucratic organization. There was no single imperial entity guiding this network, but rather many forces pulling in a similar direction, proliferating an economy for global architecture that required flexibility above all, for portability to multiple sites. Dutta, *The Bureaucracy of Beauty,* 1–37.
50. Lotz, "Architekturfotos," 69.
51. Friedberg, *The Virtual Window from Alberti to Microsoft.*
52. The same divergence can be observed in relations between architects and the building industry.
53. Köster photographed the Wolf House of 1925–26 and the Monument to the November Revolution of 1926 for Mies. His work for Mies fell at the beginning of a long career during which Köster became the premier architectural photographer of the Neues Bauen. But his pictures for Mies give little indication of his future work, although they are technically sophisticated large-format photographs of remarkable crispness.
54. Förster, *Masse braucht Licht*; Stöneberg, *Arthur Köster, Architekturfotografie 1926–1933.*
55. Sachsse, *Bild und Bau,* 82.

5. AURA DEFERRED

1. The school had left the city of Weimar following political opposition and the withdrawal of funds by the conservative government of the state of Thuringia in 1924. The institution found a new sponsor in the city government of Dessau, largely thanks to the interest of the mayor, Fritz Hesse. Resident in the city from early 1925, the Bauhaus first reconstituted itself in temporary quarters pending completion of a new building. From the beginning of its seven years in Dessau, Bauhaus director Walter Gropius paid particular attention to the public image of the school and the creation of publicity materials for the press.
2. Giedion, *Space, Time and Architecture,* 402–3. Giedion's book was based on his Norton Lectures at Harvard University of 1940. Giedion's comparison between the Bauhaus and cubism would have been recognizable to the American cultural elite who had been familiar with the latter since the Armory Show (1913).
3. This was so even though that paradigm was neither without contradiction nor entirely stable over the years after 1926. On the instabilities of the Bauhaus image between 1926 and 1968, see Moholy, "Das Bauhaus Bild." Moholy notes that by 1967, James Marston Fitch was heralding the Bauhaus as synonymous with "Gropius-Architektur."
4. "die ecke des werkstattbaues läßt das konstruktionsgerüst der betonpfeiler und massivdecken klar erkennen. zum erstenmal wurde hier das problem der auflösung der wand durch ausspannen einer durchgehenden glashaut vor das tragende bauskelett bis zur letzten konsequenz durchgeführt. die auskragung der decken über das kellergeschoß ergibt

doppelte vorteile: die statisch günstiget und daher ökonomische verkürzung der abstände von außenpfeilern zu mittelpfeilern im innern und die ausnutzbarkeit der gesamten glasfront auch vor den pfeilern für arbeitsplätze der werkstätten. niedrige heizkörper vor der ganzen breite der glaswand. fenstervorhänge unter den decken entlang der gesamten glaswand gegen sonnenstrahlen." Gropius, *Bauhausbauten Dessau,* 47.

5. The Steiff factory near Munich, built in 1903–4, featured full glass curtain walls, as did Gropius's own Fagus factory of 1911; Albert Kahn's Highland Park plant for Henry Ford was built in 1910.
6. Barthes, "Rhetoric of the Image."
7. Moholy understood that her negatives had been lost in Germany and only learned much later that they had survived in Gropius's possession and that he had in fact distributed them to colleagues at his own discretion. See Moholy, "The Missing Negatives." For more information on Moholy, see Schuldenfrei, "Images in Exile."
8. For literary theoretical comparanda, see Genette, *Paratexts.*
9. Roland Barthes's analysis of the advertising image breaks it down into linguistic message, coded iconic message (connoted), and uncoded iconic message (denoted). In books devoted to architecture, however, the caption is often supplemented with much longer textual interpretation that differs from the advertising images on which Barthes based his analysis. In architectural publishing, the linguistic message contains constituent parts—in this case, caption and interpretive text, with the latter firmly leashed to the image that it purports to explicate. See Barthes, "Rhetoric of the Image."
10. Simone Brott reflects on this definition of the image in *Architecture for a Free Subjectivity.* Also see Rancière, *The Future of the Image.*
11. Anderson, *Peter Behrens and a New Architecture for the Twentieth Century*; Buddensieg, *Industriekultur*; Behrens, "*Wer aber will sagen, was Schönheit sei?*"
12. See Schwartz, *The Werkbund.*
13. For Gropius's analysis of factory architecture, see his texts on the subject from 1911 through 1913, including the review "Zur Wanderausstellung moderner Fabrikbauten."
14. Rudolf Mosse began an advertising company in Berlin in 1867, expanding into publishing in 1872 with the founding of the Berliner Tageblatt. See "Mosse Family," in Leo Baeck Institute, *Catalog of the Archival Collections.*
15. Hake, "Visualising the Urban Masses." For a similar point about "the city on paper," see Zurier, *Picturing the City.*
16. See chapter 6 for discussion of the juxtaposition of Mendelsohn and Gropius in Hilberseimer, *Internationale Neue Baukunst.*
17. After opening in Weimar in 1919, the Bauhaus moved to Dessau in 1925. The move was precipitated by political negotiations with Weimar officials. Opposition to the Bauhaus crystallized behind newly elected conservative members of the city government who cut off funding to the institution after its much-heralded open house and exhibition of 1923, in which Bauhaus products and artwork were displayed for public audiences. Recent literature on the Bauhaus is extensive, partly fueled by (and partly fueling) a major exhibition jointly organized by museums in Berlin and New York in 2009. In addition to the sources listed below, see Barbican Art Gallery, *Bauhaus*; Bauhaus-Archiv Berlin et

al., *Bauhaus*; Bergdoll and Dickerman, *Bauhaus 1919–1933*; Saletnik and Schuldenfrei, *Bauhaus Construct.* A growing body of work on Bauhaus influence includes Colini and Eckardt, *Bauhaus and the City*; Neef, *An bord der Bauhaus.*

18. Gropius listed the following architects as assisting on the Bauhausbau commission: Karl Fieger, Friedrich Hirz, Max Krajewski, Fritz Levedag, Otto Meyer-Ottens, Ernst Neufert, Heinz Nösselt, Richard Paulick, Herbert Schipke, Bernhard Sturtzkopf, Franz Throll, Walter Tralau, Hans Volger. Gropius, *Bauhausbauten Dessau,* 12.
19. Wick, *Teaching at the Bauhaus*; Droste, "Unterrichtsstruktur und Werkstattarbeit am Bauhaus unter Hannes Meyer."
20. Meyer, "My Expulsion from the Bauhaus," 165.
21. Bauhaus Dessau Foundation and Kentgens-Craig, *The Dessau Bauhaus Building 1926–1999.*
22. See Droste, "The Successor's Disinheritance."
23. For an array of these images, see Bauhaus Dessau Foundation and Kentgens-Craig, *The Dessau Bauhaus Building 1926–1999,* 114–18.
24. Droste has noted Gropius's ambivalence toward Meyer's work, as well as the degree to which he laid claim to selected achievements of his successor in his book. See Droste, "The Successor's Disinheritance."
25. Born in Prague in 1894, Lucia Schulz studied art history and philosophy at the University of Prague (she did not complete a degree) and then worked for publishers in Germany from 1914, in Leipzig from 1917 to 1920. She spent the summers of 1918 and 1919 in the artists' colony at Worpswede, where she first took up photography. She and László Moholy-Nagy met in the spring of 1920 and married in January 1921; she continued to work for a Berlin publisher until her husband joined the faculty of the Bauhaus in 1923. Until their move to Weimar, Moholy was the primary financial support of the couple, while László prepared for his solo exhibition at Der Sturm in 1922. See Moholy, *Marginalien zu Moholy Nagy/Moholy Nagy, Marginal Notes,* 11/55; also see Sachsse, *Lucia Moholy: Bauhaus Fotografin,* 12; Sachsse, *Lucia Moholy.*
26. Moholy-Nagy, "Produktion-Reproduktion"; Moholy-Nagy, "Typofoto."
27. Moholy, *Marginalien zu Moholy Nagy,* 55.
28. As she noted in 1972, "When Moholy-Nagy was appointed Master at the 'Staatliche' . . . Bauhaus, I decided to set aside my literary and philosophical leanings and adjust myself to the largely visual approach awaiting us in the new surroundings." Ibid., 61. On the Leipzig institution, see Sachsse, "Beginnen wir!"
29. Moholy-Nagy, *Von Material zu Architektur.* According to Moholy, she was in charge of book production—the assembly of final manuscripts and layouts, and their shepherding through the reprographic processes that preceded printing and binding. There is, however, virtually no evidence of this activity of hers as "producer" of the Bauhaus series, because this sort of work was not regarded as editing or publishing itself, but rather as something more menial. What she did for the Bauhaus books was, apparently, not "work" in the sense of "work for hire" and for pay—either in cash or in the author's capital that accrued to Walter Gropius and László Moholy-Nagy. In effect, we have to take it on faith that Moholy's role as "producer" was dependent on her expertise as "reproducer" for these books.

30. With the exception of a small number of projects, her later photographic work was concentrated on portraits and some landscape or genre images. For more information on the extent of Moholy's photography at the Bauhaus, see Hartmann, "Anmerkungen zum fotographischen Nachlaß."
31. Moholy soon met Theodor Neubauer, a leftist union leader who introduced her to Communist Party and Reichstag member Clara Zetkin, whom she photographed. Neubauer became her life partner until his arrest by the National Socialists in 1933, after which time she fled the country.
32. For other images similarly composed, see Figures 4.4, 7.1, 7.12–7.14, and 8.9. For published images of the Bauhaus, see Sachsse, *Lucia Moholy: Bauhaus Fotografin*; Sachsse, *Lucia Moholy*.
33. Photographic historian Michael Stöneberg notes her relative inexperience as a photographer, which he characterizes positively as "nonchalance" with respect to photographic convention. Stöneberg, *Arthur Köster, Architekturfotografie 1926–1933*, 362–63.
34. This pictorial convention goes all the way back to William Henry Fox Talbot's earliest images of architecture—a precedent with which Moholy was certainly familiar by 1939, when she published *A Hundred Years of Photography,* and probably earlier, through her interest in photography dating back to 1915 in Prague.
35. See Sachsse, *Lucia Moholy: Bauhaus Fotografin*; Sachsse, *Lucia Moholy*.
36. Paul Westheim, editor of *Das Kunstblatt,* was especially skeptical of Gropius and his ability to set a path for contemporary architecture, referring to the Bauhaus director thus: "In the parlance of radio broadcasting, he has the equipment of a receiver, not a sender" (radiotechnisch gesprochen, er hat die Anlage zum Empfänger, nicht zum Sender). He also noted that Gropius was "not an idea giver, at best an idea reproducer" (nicht Ideengeber, bestenfalls Ideenweitergeber). See Westheim, "Für und wider," 368–69.
37. Lowenstein, "Germany's Bauhaus Experiment."
38. "2. werbe-unterrichtliche Woche Dessau-Bauhaus." *bauhaus* 2, no. 1 (1928): n.p.
39. "die mittel der darstellung von bauten in einem buch sind sehr beschränkt. die fotografie vermag das erlebnis des raumes nicht wiederzugeben. die wahren maßverhältnisse eines raumes oder eines baukörpers im verhältnis zu unserer feststehenden, absoluten körpergröße erzeugen vor dem bauwerk selbst im beschauer erregende spannungen, die das verkleinerte flächenabbild überhaupt nicht zu vermitteln vermag. schließlich sind masse und raum auch gehäuse und hintergrund für das leben selbst, dem sie dienen sollen, —die bewegungsvorgänge, die sich in ihnen abspielen, sind nur in übertragenem sinne darstellbar. ich glaubte, das wesentliche dieser bauten, die ordnung der sich in ihnen abspielenden lebensfunktionen und den daraus resultierenden räumlichen ausdruck, aus allen diesen gründen nur dadurch wiedergeben zu können, daß ich den leser nacheinander an zahlreichen bildausschnitten vorüberführe, um ihm durch diesen wechsel der sichten die illusion des gedachten räumlichen ablaufs zu vermitteln." Gropius, *Bauhausbauten Dessau,* 11.
40. Lotz, "Architekturfotos."
41. Ibid. Lotz's short essay appears to have been leveled at Moholy-Nagy and the Werkbund exhibition "Film und Foto," which also opened in 1929. He concluded by noting: "Wenn man sich rüstet, in Stuttgart eine Fotoausstellung zu machen, sollte man solche

Gesichtspunkte berücksichtigen und nach Möglichkeiten suchen. Man sollte vor allen Dingen an die Aufgabe der Fotografie als Mittler des Eindrucks des Objekts denken."

42. Taut, *Ein Wohnhaus*; Mendelsohn, *Neues Haus—Neue Welt.*
43. Earlier examples of similar publications were often sponsored by commercial clients, as in Max Creutz's series for the Tietz department store and other enterprises in the years before World War I, and demonstrate how well established this precedent was when *Bauhausbauten Dessau* was planned.
44. "Die 'Internationale Architektur' ist ein Bilderbuch moderner Baukunst. Es will in knapper Form Überblick über das Schaffen führender moderner Architekten der Kulturländer geben und mit der heutigen architektonischen Gestaltsentwicklung vertraut machen." The note reads: "Um einem breiteren Laienpublikum zu dienen, beschränkte sich der Herausgeber im wesentlichen auf Abbilder äußerer Bauerscheinungen. Typische Grundrisse und Innenräume werden in einem späteren Bande folgen." Gropius, "Vorwort," in *Internationale Architektur*, 5. Photographs of the Bauhaus appeared in the expanded second edition of *Internationale Architektur* in 1927. The anticipated additional volume never appeared.
45. For the related theme of biocentric discourse, see Botar and Wünsche, *Biocentrism and Modernism.*
46. "Diese neuaufdämmernde Erkenntnis der Einheit aller Dinge und Erscheinungen bringt aller menschlichen Gestaltungsarbeit einen gemeinsamen, tief in uns selbst beruhenden Sinn. Nichts besteht mehr an sich, jedes Gebilde wird zum Gleichnis eines Gedankens, der aus uns zur Gestaltung drängt, jede Arbeit zur Manifestation unseres inneren Wesens. Nur solche Arbeit behält geistigen Sinn, mechanisierte Arbeit ist leblos und Aufgabe der toten Maschine. Solange aber die Wirtschaft, die Maschine Selbstzweck sind, anstatt Mittel, die Geisteskräfte zunehmend von mechanischer Arbeitslast zu befreien, bleibt der Einzelne unfrei und die Gesellschaft kann sich nicht ordnen. Die Lösung hängt von der veränderten innerlichen Einstellung des Einzelnen zu seinem Werk, nicht von Verbesserungen der äußeren Lebensumstände ab. Der Wille zur Umstellung auf den neuen Geist ist deshalb von entscheidender Bedeutung für neue aufbauende Arbeit." Gropius, *Idee und Aufbau des Staatlichen Bauhauses*, 7.
47. Papapetros, "On the Biology of the Inorganic."
48. Botar, "Prolegomena to the Study of Biomorphic Modernism"; Asendorf, "Bodies in Force Fields."
49. Giedion, "Preliminary Remark," in *Bauen in Frankreich Bauen in Eisen Bauen in Eisenbeton.*
50. On the relationship between photographic image and text, see Barthes, "Rhetoric of the Image"; Goodman, *Languages of Art.*
51. "If . . . the crux of artistic production was a matter of seeing, then photography as an art would be at no disadvantage when compared to painting. Talbot construes the art of all pictorial art as an opportunism of sight. Discovering a picturesque scene requires aesthetic sensibility and inspiration; transposing it to a surface, whether canvas or photographic paper, is merely a matter of mechanical industry." Kelsey, "Photography, Chance, and *The Pencil of Nature*," 21.

52. Fortunately, Moholy-Nagy had his opposite number in architecture: Ludwig Mies van der Rohe. Mies took the notion of typophoto and the potential of photography seriously and transported them into the heart of architectural practice, as we saw in previous chapters.
53. Droste, "The Successor's Disinheritance."
54. Quoted in Nerdinger, *Walter Gropius*, 114.
55. Ibid., 122.
56. Giedion, *Walter Gropius* (1992), 82.

6. THE FUTURE IN THE PRESENT

1. "Anstatt eines Berichtes über die Ausstellung Neuer Amerikanischer Architektur, die vor kurzem, in der Akademie der Künste zu Berlin stattfand, bringen wir diesen Aufsatz unseres Newyorker Mitarbeiters, der über die Auffassungen, die gegenwärtig die amerikanische Architektur beherrschen, besser unterrichtet, als es jene Ausstellung vermochte.—Die Schriftleitung." *Die Form* 1, no. 5 (February 1926): 102.
2. Mumford, *Vom Blockhaus zum Wolkenkratzer.*
3. Mies had adopted *Baukunst* in *G* several years earlier. See Mertins and Jennings, *G.*
4. "Beim Durchlesen des Mumforschen Artikels mußte ich feststellen, daß gerade die Ausstellung 'Neue amerikanische Architektur' eine schlagende Illustration zu den von Mumford geäußerten Auffassungen bildet. Das spricht doch für die Ausstellung. Auch hat man, besonders in der Berliner Presse, dieser Ausstellung zum Vorwurf gemacht, daß sie nicht nach einem bestimmten Plan zusammegestellt sei, und daß in ihr nicht alle Spitzenleistungen amerikanischer Baukunst vertreten wären. Ich muß es als einen Vorzug dieser Ausstellung bezeichnen, daß sie keinen bestimmtes und eng begrenztes Programm durchführte, sondern dem Besucher die Möglichkeit ließ, sich selbst ein Urteil über die amerikanische Baukunst zu bilden." Mies, letter to the editor, *Die Form* 1, no. 8 (May 1926): 179, reprinted in Neumeyer, *The Artless Word,* 251.
5. Behrendt, Adolf Rading, Heinrich Paulsen, Werner Hegemann, Erich Mendelsohn, Edmund Schüler, Martin Wagner, and many others traveled to the United States in the mid-1920s.
6. "So interessant es ist zu sehen, wie Sie selbst, wie Mendelsohn, Paulsen oder Rading Amerika beurteilen, so notwendig und wünschenswert schien es mir zu sein, daß jeder sich selbst ein Bild von dem augenblicklichen Zustand amerikanischer Baukunst machen konnte, und darin sah ich den Sinn und auch den Wert der Berliner Ausstellung." Mies, letter to the editor, *Die Form,* reprinted in Neumeyer, *The Artless Word,* 179.
7. See letter from Mies to H. P. Berlage, December 1923, asking for publication rights to Berlage's essay on Wright for *Der Neubau.* Ludwig Mies van der Rohe Papers, Manuscripts Division, Library of Congress. The exhibition did not include work by Frank Lloyd Wright, who was slated for a solo exhibition at a later date, but evidently provided a broader array of materials appropriate to this task that also reflected the positive aspects of *Amerikanismus.*
8. See Münsterburg, *Die Amerikaner,* 184.
9. Erich Mendelsohn's *Amerika* articulated the dystopia of the American city in text cap-

tions that accompanied the photographs. There is a growing literature on German interest in America; selected sources include Neumann, *Die Wolkenkratzer Kommen!*; and Zimmermann, *Der Schrei nach dem Turmhaus*; in addition to Cohen's *Scenes of the World to Come.*

10. Liebermann, "Vorwort," n.p. The exhibition was organized by K. O. Bertling, director of the Amerika-Institut in Berlin, Geheimrat Schüler, and Professor Hugo Wach of the Akademie, himself an exhibitor in the show. Leading architects Bruno Paul, Hans Poelzig, and the painter Max Liebermann were members of the Akademie; the honorary advisory board also included Peter Behrens, Paul Bonatz, Josef Hoffmann, Heinrich Tessenow, Wach, and a number of others, who may have been nominally consulted in the organization of the exhibition.
11. "Kaum waren im Hausbau die ersten Eisenkonstruktionen verwendet, unternahm er es, in seinem Geschäftshäusern . . . dem Hochhaus künstlerische Eigenformen zu erfinden." *Ausstellung neuer amerikanischer Baukunst,* 1.
12. "Als er . . . seine Stimme erhob gegen schwächliche Nachahmung, als er begann, das Evangelium einer vertieften eigenen Kunst für eine Zeit mit ernsten eigenen Zielen zu verkündigen, fand er mehr Feinde als Gläubige. Aber der Seher, der in der Wüste des älteren Chigacos *[sic]* den Anbruch einer neuen Kunst vorahnen konnte, kann uns noch heute als Wegweiser zum Verständnis moderner amerikanischer Architekturprobleme dienen." Ibid.
13. The title of Mies's Friedrichstrasse competition entry, Wabe (honeycomb), referred to Sullivan's essay "The Tall Office Building Artistically Considered." See Neumann, *Die Wolkenkratzer kommen!,* 55.
14. Mies had promised, but failed to deliver, a volume on *Baukunst* for the psychologist Hans Prinzhorn (also a personal friend), who planned a series of books under the heading "Das Weltbild: Eine Bücherei des lebendigen Wissens," to be published by the Müller/Kiepenheuer Verlag in Potsdam. Container 3, Ludwig Mies van der Rohe Papers, Manuscripts Division, Library of Congress.
15. "Die Architektur hat drei elementare Denkformen, den Pfeiler, den Querbalken und den Bogen. Sie sind die drei Typen, aus denen sich die Baukunst als eine Sprache entwickelt hat." Sullivan, "Was ist Architektur?," 9.
16. While the notion of architecture as a language is common enough to be virtually generic in architectural theory, nevertheless, the timing is striking, as is the conjuncture between Mies's "spiritual" search (commenced around the same time) and Sullivan's poetic imagination. See Mies's untitled lecture manuscript of March 1926, possibly based on a presentation in Bremen of late November 1925. When Mies delivered his lecture, "Geist der neuen Baukunst," he had no text, as he explained in a letter. "My talk is not so carefully written down that I would like to deposit it in your library. But should I sometime write it down, then I will happily place a copy at your disposal." Mies Archive, Museum of Modern Art, reprinted in Neumeyer, *The Artless Word,* 252–56. Neumeyer dates the subsequent text to 1926.
17. All of the built works were illustrated with several views, including overall views and details of stairs, elevator cages, and other interiors. The medium of each item was not called

out; rather, the type of view was indicated: "Innenansicht," "Treppenhaus," "Haupteingang," and so on. See *Ausstellung neuer amerikanischer Baukunst,* 35–37.

18. Wallis Miller is writing a comprehensive analytical history of German architecture exhibitions in the nineteenth and twentieth centuries; also see Cramer and Gutschow, *Bauausstellungen*; Lampugnani, "Ausstellungen von Architektur." Cramer and Gutschow use the term "Bauausstellung" to differentiate the full-scale exhibition from "Architekturausstellung," the gallery show of architectural representations.
19. This exhibition has been researched extensively; its photographic components make it a subject of interest here. For publications on the Weissenhofsiedlung, see Kirsch, *Die Weißenhofsiedlung*; Pommer and Otto, *Weissenhof 1927 and the Modern Movement in Architecture*; Kirsch, *Briefe zur Weißenhofsiedlung.* Also see *Amtlicher Katalog Werkbund-Ausstellung Die Wohnung.* On the plan and model exhibition, see Hilberseimer, *Internationale neue Baukunst.*
20. Hegemann, *Der städtebau nach den ergebnissen der Allgemeinen städtebau-ausstellung in Berlin, nebst einem anhang.*
21. See Röder, "Propaganda für ein neues Bauen"; Müller, "Zur Geschichte des 'Deutschen Museums für Kunst in Handel und Gewerbe.'" On Osthaus, see Kuenzli, "The Birth of the Modernist Art Museum."
22. The contents of the exhibition are described in Bergdoll, "Bauhaus Multiplied." Also see Passarge's 1923 review "The Bauhaus Exhibition in Weimar"; Breuer, "Advertisements for His Own Architecture and Neues Bauen"; Gropius, *Internationale Architektur.*
23. See Bund Deutscher Architekten, *Internationale Architektur Ausstellung, New York 1925.*
24. Advance publicity was carried on in Hannover at the regular meeting of the Werkbund administration in late November 1925. In the invitation to the meeting, an illustrated lecture by Vetterlein titled "Bauliche Eindrucke aus Amerika" (Impressions of building from America) prepared the way. Meeting minutes record Mies's attendance at this event. Container 3, Ludwig Mies van der Rohe Papers, Manuscripts Division, Library of Congress.
25. The South American grain silo was also published in Banham, *A Concrete Atlantis.*
26. There were disbelievers among the critics of the Bauhaus and the Neues Bauen, from the left as well as the right. See Bloch, "Berlin."
27. The traveling exhibition went to Zurich, Basel, Berlin, Rotterdam, Stockholm, Göteborg, Stettin, Vienna, Prague, Breslau, Amsterdam, Hannover, Kiel, Aachen, Dortmund, and Graz. For these and other details on the contents of the exhibition, see Kirsch, "Internationales Neues Bauen 1927/2002." Kirsch does not mention the Berlin venue, where the exhibition opened as part of the Große Berliner Kunstausstellung in May 1928; it was advertised in *bauhaus* 2/3, 2. jahrgang (1928): back page.
28. Kirsch, "Internationales Neues Bauen 1927/2002," 63.
29. Ibid., 62. For similar reflections on the International Style exhibition at the Museum of Modern Art in 1932, see Rosa, "Architectural Photography and the Construction of Modern Architecture."
30. The Russian critic V. Schtscherbakov lamented this emphasis on exterior formal appear-

ance in his comments on Le Corbusier's projects at Weissenhof, seeing it as the neglect of "logic, comfort, functionality, and economy." See Cohen, "Ambivalente Aura," 73.

31. When the show traveled to Switzerland, additional technical drawings were added to render the exhibition more useful to a professional audience. See Kirsch, "Internationales Neues Bauen 1927/2002," 62.
32. For discussion of the conventions of architectural photography, see chapter 4.
33. Pommer and Otto, *Weissenhof 1927 and the Modern Movement in Architecture,* 56, 210n3.
34. Pommer and Otto note that earlier housing experimentation at architecture exhibitions had been oriented to technical issues: "These exhibitions were devoted to industry, not art; and the model dwellings were reproducible types, like industrial products." Ibid., 36. Also, on exhibitions before 1927, see "Gebaute Ausstellungen," in Cramer and Gutschow, *Bauausstellungen,* 16–36.
35. Pommer and Otto, *Weissenhof 1927 and the Modern Movement in Architecture,* 88.
36. Jacques Rancière comments on this condition within a broader framework of modernism in *The Future of the Image.*
37. Lane, *Architecture and Politics in Germany, 1918–1945,* 130, 251nn22–23.
38. Perhaps not coincidentally, May was not included in the main exhibition site at Weissenhof but given a site on the grounds set aside for construction experimentation adjacent to the settlement. His radical functionalism was perhaps not reconcilable with Mies's interest in *elementarer Gestaltung.* See Pommer and Otto, *Weissenhof 1927 and the Modern Movement in Architecture,* 50.
39. Compare the subsequent Stuttgart exhibitions of 1933 (Kochenhof Siedlung, "Deutsches Holz für Hausbau und Wohnung,") and 1934 ("Im Vogelsang") with the 1927 exhibition. Cramer and Gutschow, *Bauausstellungen,* 174–86.
40. Pommer and Otto, *Weissenhof 1927 and the Modern Movement in Architecture*; Kirsch, *The Weissenhofsiedlung.* Also see *Bau und Wohnung.* For the counterreaction, see Pommer and Otto, *Weissenhof 1927*; and Plarre, *Die Kochenhofsiedlung, das Gegenmodell zur Weissenhofsiedlung.*
41. The local Stuttgarter who was included, Richard Döcker, was a modernist in a traditionalist part of the country; he could not be counted on, nor did he have the power, to hand commissions to his local colleagues.
42. Kracauer, "Das neue Bauen," 2. He was perhaps nodding to Adolf Loos, long an admirer of the advanced state of American and English plumbing. If architecture did not provide enough purchase for Kracauer's investigations, this was almost certainly connected to the top-down power structures of the profession until the tipping point of 1926, when control of the Werkbund and the BDA passed into the hands of younger architects more or less free of the control of the old Wilhelmine power brokers. At this point, and only then, could architects begin to engage contemporary mass culture in ways that might seem relevant to a population (and a journalist) growing increasingly enamored of the movie screen and the illustrated press. Mies van der Rohe became vice president of the Werkbund in 1926 and was given the task of organizing the Stuttgart exhibition that struck Kracauer so forcefully. By 1931, Kracauer, like Ernst Bloch and Behne, exposed

the radical project of the Neues Bauen as one unknowingly complicit with and obedient to the reductive rationalization of capitalism. See Zimmerman, "Siegfried Kracauer's Architectures."

43. "Die Badewannen brauchen sich der Speisezimmer nicht mehr zu schämen." Ibid. Also see Ward, *Weimar Surfaces*; Pisani, "Kracauer sul Weissenhof Stoccarda 1927."
44. "Zeitgemäße konstruktive Fügungen der von schlechtem Überfluß gereinigten Elemente." Kracauer, "Das neue Bauen," 2.
45. "Nicht Glas, Eisen, und Beton, nicht all die neuen Materialien und häßlichen Konstruktionsweisen, gegen die sich die Heimatschutzbewegung vergebens wehrte, sind verantwortlich für die Zerstörung und Verwüstungen im Heimatbild, die wir heute noch beklagen, sondern die Menschen einer kulturlosen Zeit, die die neuen Materialien technisch nicht meistern, die neuen Konstruktionsweisen, nicht beherrschen konnten und wollten, weil ihr Sinn auf andere Ziele, auf leichten Erwerb und raschen Gewinn, gerichtet war." Esterer, *Heimatschutz und neue Baugesinnung*, 22. Also see Otto, "Modern Environment and Historical Continuity," 150, 155.
46. For negative press on the Törten-Siedlung, see "Zur Propaganda neuer Versuchsbauten." For negative press on the Weissenhofsiedlung, see Felix Schuster in *Schwäbische Merkur*, nos. 410, 434, 470, 482, 506, 518 (September 3–November 5, 1927); Hegemann, "Stuttgarter Schildbürgerstreiche und Berliner Bauausstellung 1930"; *Innen-Dekoration* 40 (June 1929); "Eine zeitgemäße Aufdeckung."
47. Notably, an avant-garde designer like Wilhelm Wagenfeld remained. His research on glass products was concerned with manufacture and product quality, and thus protected him from persecution; technological innovation was always eagerly received by the National Socialists, whether it would then be clothed in historicist architectural language or not.

7. PROMISE AND THREAT

1. Letter from R. Schwarz to Mies van der Rohe, May 1947, Ludwig Mies van der Rohe Papers, Manuscripts Division, Library of Congress. In fact, Schwarz was building during these years; his 1947 church reconstructions make a dramatic contrast with his earlier work. See Hasler, *Architektur als Ausdruck*; Pehnt, *Bewohnte Bilder*. See note 31 below.
2. For differing analyses, see two recent accounts of architectural modernism: Levine, *Modern Architecture*; Payne, *From Ornament to Object*.
3. For an economic profile of the U.S. steel industry in the years before and after World War II, see Tiffany, "The Roots of Decline."
4. On the attributes of this new American postwar architecture, see Friedman, *American Glamour and the Evolution of Modern Architecture*; Martin, *The Organizational Complex*.
5. Lynnette Widder and Richard Anderson organized a conference by this title at Columbia University in 2008, in which material from this chapter was first presented. My thanks to both organizers, but especially to Lynnette for her comments on this chapter. Information about the conference is available at http://calendar.columbia.edu/sundial/webapi/get.php?vt=detail&id=19787&con=embedded&br=ais (accessed September 19, 2013).
6. Schwarz studied the work of Romano Guardini and introduced Mies to this theologian-philosopher. For background on this relationship, see Neumeyer, *The Artless Word*.

7. Nerdinger, "Das Bauhaus zwischen Mythisierung und Kritik."
8. "Auf die Architektur angewendet, hat die Ästhetik aber leider sehr wenig gefördert. . . . alle diese Bücher haben viele Bilder, und diese Bilder sind fotografiert. Das ist für Sie vielleicht so selbstverständlich, daß Sie wahrscheinlich staunen, warum ich darauf hinweise. Natürlich sind die Bilder fotografiert. Wir müssen uns aber erinnern, daß früher, vor Jahrzehnten, in unseren Lehrbüchern keine fotografierten Bilder waren, sondern maßstäbliche Zeichnungen, und daß erst seit kurzem im fotografischen Apparat sich ein Instrument anbietet, das dem einsamen, isolierten Ästheten so richtig zur Hand liegt, nämlich dem Manne, der sich allein einem großen Werk gegenüberstellt und daran eben—meinetwegen bewundernd—Bemerkungen macht, aber gegenübersteht, der nicht darin ist; der Fotoapparat ist eine Maschine, die an einem bestimmten Punkt aufgestellt wird und nur durch ein einziges Auge einen großen Raum anstiert. Wir haben uns vielleicht alle noch nicht klargemacht, wie inadequat und im Grunde unwürdig diese Methode ist, großen Architekturen zu begegnen. . . . Diese Fotografiererei und alles, was dahintersteht, übersieht die eigentliche Leistung der Architektur: nämlich viele einzelne hineinzutun in irgend etwas: viele einzelne opfern sich, geben sich ganz hinein in eine Gemeinschaft, und dann erblüht ihnen plötzlich eine Form, die dem einzelnen völlig verschlossen wäre, die er wohl als Reisender mit dem Reiseführer besehen kann, die er aber niemals hervorbringen würde." Schwarz, "Das Anliegen der Baukunst," 64–65.
9. "Sie stehen auf einem ästhetischen Standpunkt und besehen von da aus die Welt. Sie verraten das schon dadurch, daß sie in ihre Bücher so viele Fotografien drucken lassen, denn die fotographische Maschine ist ja das, was sie brauchen: Sie stiert mit einem Auge von einem Punkt aus ins architektonische Weltall, während doch der wirkliche Baumeister eine Menschengemeinde in eine gemeinsame, ganz geklärte Form hebt, also offenbar etwas ganz anderes im Sinn hat. Sie sprechen auch nicht in unseren Worten, die doch so schön und ewiggültig sind und Wand, Boden, Decke, Tür, Fenster usw. lauten und die wir um keinen Preis gegen optisch plastiche Empfindungen tauschen." Schwarz, "Bilde Künstler, rede nicht," 11.
10. In Mies's case, continuity with European work is said to rest on the bridge of the Krefeld factories and the Museum for a Small City—the first forecasting American concerns before Mies's emigration, and the second continuing German ones in the United States. These are indeed transitional projects. They might perhaps be the exceptions that prove the rule.
11. On wartime production and architecture, see Cohen, *Architecture in Uniform*.
12. For a discussion of the development of high-rise curtain wall design in Mies's office, see Lambert, *Mies in America*. For two insightful articles on the Seagram Building, see Martin, "Atrocities"; Scott, "An Army of Soldiers or a Meadow." Lambert's *Building Seagram* unfortunately came out after this volume had gone to press.
13. See "Mies van der Rohe: Arbeiten der letzten beiden Jahre"; Weber, "Mies van der Rohe in Chicago."
14. One of these chapters also appeared in the second English edition of 1953.
15. This 1962 commission followed unbuilt German commissions of the previous years, the Mannheim Theater competition of 1953 and the Schaefer Museum for Schweinfurt in the

early 1960s among them. In the years following the architect's death, a different sort of publication began to emerge.

16. "The business was incorporated in 1945 and during the war period we sold many cameras to the government. In 1949 the Air Force gave us our largest order for 353 8 × 10 View cameras, carrying cases, tripods, focusing clothes, and lenses. After the war we discontinued the Triamapro and the small 4 × 5 camera which was brought out about 1940. . . . Our most prosperous years were 1956 and 1957 and left us in a very strong position, but from 1958 to 1970 business was very poor." "History of Deardorff," http://www.craigcamera.com/deardorf.htm (accessed September 19, 2013).
17. Ibid.
18. Greenberg, "Sculpture in Our Time," 60.
19. See chapter 4, note 49.
20. Neutra, "The Photographer and Architect," ix.
21. Ibid., vii–ix.
22. A case in point: when Detroit architect Albert Kahn could no longer procure steel for wartime uses, he developed a rapid method of concrete construction that he dubbed "Warspeed construction." See "Factory Construction"; "Warspeed System of Construction in Concrete."
23. For an insightful study of this topic in a different context, see Brown, *The Corporate Eye.*
24. Journals that appeared in the late 1940s had to be approved by the administration of the occupying forces for the zone in which the editorial office was based. See, for example, the colophon page of *Architektur und Wohnform* 57, nos. 1/2 (1948): "Veröffentl. unter der Zulassungs-Nr. US-W-1030 d. Nachrichtenkontrolle d. Militär-Regierung."
25. They characterized his American work as "present[ing] us with a new softly smiling face of our discipline" (ein neues, leise lächelndes Gesicht unserer Disziplin darbietet). Smithson and Smithson, *Mies van der Rohe,* n.p. A published version of this statement appeared in *Architectural Design* in 1969, and another in Smithson and Smithson, *Without Rhetoric,* 19–44, revised in their *Changing the Art of Inhabitation,* 17.
26. "Dieses Gebäude weckte unser Interesse an Mies, als es zum erstenmal 1946 in England veröffentlicht wurde. . . . Mies ist zweifellos noch mehr dazu übergegangen, sich der Wiederholung zu bedienen, weil der technische Stand seiner Umwelt sie begünstigt. Die Qualitätskontrolle von seriell produzierten identischen Metallteilen ist besonders gut. Mies hat Metall seit jeher geliebt, und deshalb kann er sich dieser Technik frei bedienen." The Smithsons also note: "Certainly the skin of Mies's Colonnade Apartments (1959–60) would be unachievable outside the world of U.S. technology. See in it how he has moved from the poetry of 'assembled' components—rolled sections and bricks—of one of the early buildings at IIT, the Metal and Mineral Research Building (1942–43) . . . to the unique extrusions of aluminum and neoprene of the Colonnade skin. Mies is working through the available technologies, and at New Jersey a very high level of formal sophistication is achieved on the same budget as 'conventional speculative builders projects.'" Ibid.
27. Hugh Stubbins completed the Kongresshalle in 1956–57, and Mies the New National Gallery in 1968.

28. American architects such as Jack Masey (graduate of Yale School of Architecture and former employee of *Architectural Forum*) designed the exhibits. See Masey and Morgan, *Cold War Confrontations.*
29. See the recollections of Peter von Seidlein in Hilpert, *Mies van der Rohe im Nachkriegsdeutschland.*
30. Mäckler, "Praeceptor Germaniae et Europae?"
31. In his letter to Mies of May 1947, Schwarz wrote, "Hoffentlich wird man recht bald etwas von Ihren Arbeiten in deutschen Zeitschriften oder Büchern zu sehen bekommen (irgendwelche ausländische Veröffentlichungen dürfen ja nicht zu uns eingeführt werden), dass man sich daran freuen kann." In October 1948: "Können Sie uns nicht einmal eine Veröffentlichung Ihrer Werke schicken? Wir würden uns sehr darüber freuen." Ludwig Mies van der Rohe Papers, Manuscripts Division, Library of Congress.
32. Despite the overwhelming effect of the gigantic metal-and-glass model that arrived in Mannheim in a huge custom-made crate, he did not win. According to Sigfried Giedion, the Germans simply were not ready for Mies's design, which one architect had referred to as a "veredelte Werkhalle." Giedion, "Der moralische Einfluss der Architektur Mies van der Rohes"; Eckhard, "Strukturwandel im Theater!" Also see Sachsse, *Bild und Bau,* 218.
33. Zimmerman, "New National Gallery," 358.
34. Martin Heidegger, José Ortega y Gasset, and other public intellectuals spoke in the same forum, eclipsing Schwarz's seemingly practical concerns about the iniquities of photographing buildings. See Bartning, *Mensch und Raum.* These talks were revived around 1995 and now feature speakers such as Bruno Latour and Slavoj Žižek. See http://www.neuedarmstaedtergespraeche.de (accessed September 20, 2013).
35. Leitl, "Anmerkungen zur Zeit"; Schwarz, "Was dennoch besprochen werden muß." For other contributions to the debate, see Conrads, *Die Bauhaus-Debatte 1953.*
36. Schwarz, "Bilde Künstler, rede nicht"; Conrads, "Brief über Architektur und Fotografie."
37. On Wright Morris, also see Lieberman, "Thoughts of an Art Historian/Photographer on the Relationship of His Two Disciplines."
38. The heading for the photographs reads: "Der Photograph: (läßt sich mit den Bildern auf den Seiten 8, 13, 19, 29, 22, 23 dieses Heftes zitieren.) Wright Morris." *Baukunst und Werkform* 6, no. 1 (1953): 18. The photograph by Brandt on page 25 appears as a coda or afterthought—perhaps in the context of "return emigrations" such as those of Mies or Gropius, since Brandt had himself emigrated from Germany in 1933.
39. "Wirkungkräftiges Mittel für den Intellektualisierungsprozeß, dem wir die Kunst unterwerfen" and "die Kunstgeschichte . . . ist eine Geschichte des Photographierbaren geworden." Conrads, "Brief über Architektur und Fotografie," 22.
40. "Für die Wiedergabe dessen, was für den Baumeister von Bedeuting ist, hat immer der Zeichenstift einen besseren Dienst geleistet." Ibid.
41. "Die Photographie von Architektur sprechen kann." Ibid.
42. "Um so erstaunlicher die Wirkung und unser Nicht-vergessen-können ihrer 'gemeinsamer Form.' Nichts is photographierbarer als Stil, den meisterlichen Photographen vorausgesetzt. . . . Das 'starre Auge' hat unserem Denken unausgemessene Bewegungsmöglich-

keiten, unserem Gefühl Ahnungen von einer größeren Wirklichkeit geschenkt, unseren Augen aber die Vielfalt des Vergleichbaren, damit wir sehen, wo wir sind." Ibid., 24.

43. "Wenn ich mich klar mache, wie unaufhörlich sie sich verändert, und wie sie in dreißig Jahren nicht mehr da sein wird, was sie heute ist, dann . . . möchte die Fotografie geradezu lieben, rasch, solange wir sie noch haben." Evers, "Brief über die Architektur-Fotografie," 522.

44. "Immer, sehen Sie, rechnet die Fotografie mit der tätigen Phantasie"; and "Hand aufs Herz: wenn unser Architekt die Fotografie von einem Bauwerk eines Kollegen sieht, das er in Wirklichkeit nicht kennt, könnte es ihm nie und niemals passieren, daß er es in der Fotografie passabel fände, und hernach, wenn er hinkommt, wäre er enttäuscht? Das würde dann bedeuten: daß die Fotografie in ihm Vorstellungskräfte entfaltet hätte, schöpferisches geistiges Leben, zu dem die wirkliche Architektur keinen ausreichenden Anlaß bot." Ibid., 524–25.

45. "Durch die Abstraktion, durch das Verschwinden in ein scheinbares Nichts wird das Gemeinte und Gedachte, das Innerlich-Geschaute übertragbar. Die Verwandlung in den geistigen Begriff rechnet damit, daß jemand anderer ihn wieder auffassen und auflösen kann." Ibid., 524.

46. "Aber das ist doch gerade das Großartige an ihr, daß sie abstrahiert! Dadurch kann ich Ihnen eine Fotografie schicken, und Sie sind imstande, aus ihr die Welt zu entfalten. Es handelt sich doch nicht um das bißchen Zellulose und Gelatine, sondern um Ihre eigene Fähigkeit und Phantasie, mit der Sie Farben und Räume und Größen daraus wiedergewinnen. Das ist doch gerade das Großartige and der Fotografie, daß sie allgemein verständlich ist, daß sie eine Weltsprache geworden ist, besser als Pidgin-Englisch und Esperanto. Wo wäre denn eine Bildsprache, die so allgemein verstanden werden kann wie sie? Glauben Sie . . . daß die heutige Architektur und ihre Ausbreitung auf der Erde möglich wäre ohne Bücher, Zeitschriften, Fotografien?" Ibid.

47. "Eine Reduzierung des Sichtbaren, aber ein Schlüssel zum Denkbaren." Ibid., 527.

8. THE PHOTOGRAPHIC ARCHITECTURE OF THE HUNSTANTON SCHOOL

1. Soraya Smithson, personal conversation with author, June 2011.

2. "During the construction of Hunstanton we saw layering of structure at the naked stage, layering of reflection at the glazed stage." Smithson and Carolin, "Reflections on Hunstanton," 38. On Henderson, see Walsh, *Nigel Henderson.*

3. "The original intention was to cut away a small portion from the upper edge of the R.S.J.s to allow the floor slabs to be dropped in, but it was found that the steel members could be jacked apart sufficiently—an inch or two—in their centres to make this unnecessary. The floor units were edged in and slid along into position. . . . When the hydraulic jack was removed, the frames returned to their original form." See "Welded Steel Fabrication Used at Hunstanton Secondary Modern School."

4. Baker, "The Theory behind Plastic Design." Also see Baker, *The Steel Skeleton.* My sincere thanks to Sir Jack Zunz for this timely reference.

5. Modern architects had begun to record the process of construction in photographs at least from the late 1920s (as distinct from clients and photographers, who were doing it

much earlier), whether to protect against potential litigation, to keep all parties apprised of the progress of construction, or to have a visual archive of construction methods and decisions made on-site.

6. "Secondary School at Hunstanton."
7. My gratitude goes to the late Robert Elwall, curator of photographs at the Royal Institute for British Architecture, for this information; also see Elwall, *Building with Light*; Elwall, *John Maltby.*
8. "How the tear sheets got into my hands I do not know. Certainly it seems unlikely that I tore them out in the first week of the first year of peace. But I certainly read them in London in 1948." See "The Smithsons." Also see Smithson and Carolin, "Reflections on Hunstanton," 35; and Smithson and Smithson, *Changing the Art of Inhabitation,* 41–42. Although the *Architects' Journal* article included no photographs of the building's exterior, the Smithsons would have seen those in the monograph by Philip Johnson that was already in their possession.
9. Johnson, "School at Hunstanton, Norfolk."
10. My thanks to Joan Ockman for reminding me of this important connection. On the Eames house, see Albrecht, *The Work of Charles and Ray Eames,* especially Colomina, "Reflections on the Eames House." Also see Steele, *Eames House*; Colomina, "The Eames House," in *Domesticity at War,* 83–110.
11. The phrase quoted above, "the orthodox method is liable to under-estimate seriously the collapse load of a rigidly jointed structure, such as a welded portal frame, and so to be extravagant," may well refer to Mies's work and system of design. See Baker, "The Theory behind Plastic Design."
12. Stalder, "'New Brutalism,' 'Topology,' and 'Image.'" Also see my essay "Photographic Images from Chicago to Hunstanton." On the differences between two phases of Mies's practice, also see Zimmerman, *Ludwig Mies van der Rohe.*
13. On Mies's philosophical affiliations, see Neumeyer, *The Artless Word.*
14. Cruickshank, "Hunstanton School, Norfolk, 1954."
15. This contrasts dramatically with the assertions of Walter Benjamin in the interwar period that architecture is experienced in a state of distraction; while it is unlikely that the Smithsons had access to any work by Benjamin, it is equally unlikely that the contrasts between these conceptions of architecture are totally unrelated. For her investigation of the existentialist roots of this kind of architecture, see Goldhagen, "Freedom's Domiciles."
16. For one example, see "Secondary School at Hunstanton," 323.
17. This strategy recalls their growing interest in "multi-evocative" images, in partnership with other Independent Group members. See Walsh, "Reordering and Redistributing the Visual."
18. Other influences included Hannes Meyer and modernist functionalism as disseminated by Alberto Sartoris and others. On the visual archive of functionalist design available to the Smithsons, see Sartoris, *Gli elementi dell'architettura funzionale*; and Sartoris, *Encyclopédie de l'architecture nouvelle.* In the Smithsons Archive at Harvard University's Loeb Library an undated published letter from Walter Segal on "the New Brutalism" lays out Hannes Meyer's influence in satirical terms: "No finishes for Meyer, and no gar-

ments. Naked stand his buildings in the Continental sun; and naked they are inside. . . . to Bernau school, the new shrine built for the trade unions went the brutalist pilgrims." It is unclear whether Segal knew that by the time of his writing (probably about 1955) the ADGB Trade Union Officers Training School in Bernau had been substantially altered by the National Socialist government, for which it had also served as an officer training school, minus the trade unions.

19. "Thoughts in Progress"; also see Highmore, "Rough Poetry." For a response, see Pezolet, "'Signs of Inhabitation.'"
20. Pevsner, *The Englishness of English Art*; Muthesius, *Das englische Haus.*
21. Wittkower, *Architectural Principles in the Age of Humanism*; Saxl and Wittkower, *British Art and the Mediterranean.*
22. Peter Smithson referred to this change in relation to his own experience in an article of 1997: "In September 1939, I was a 16 year old with School Certificate and good only at English and drawing. My father knew the local architect in Stockton-on-Tees and asked him what I should do. He replied that the system of articled pupilage was dying and suggested that I should go to the architecture school in Newcastle." Later in the same essay Smithson referred to visits to Scandinavian architects in 1947 by noting, "Today, every school has its journal but then, communication was person to person, within a much smaller community of architects." Smithson and Carolin, "Reflections on Hunstanton," 32, 34.
23. On an earlier period, see Carpo, *Architecture in the Age of Printing*; on late nineteenth-century pedagogical method, see Çelik, "Kinaesthetic Impulses."
24. Offset against this difficulty was the experience of war itself, which brought young British soldiers to Europe and Asia under particularly charged conditions. See Peter Smithson's reflections on the war in Smithson and Carolin, "Reflections on Hunstanton," 32, 34.
25. The number of canonical modern buildings that fell into states of disrepair (or were demolished) after the war should also be mentioned. Young architects in the immediate postwar decades had the remarkable experience of studying buildings in pristine black-and-white photographs while the objects themselves stood in total disrepair on sites nearby.
26. Reyner Banham signals the increase of a general public for architecture in British popular media, noting in regard to skirmishes in the popular press in 1952: "These events of the summer of 1952 were of some consequence, since the *Observer's* commitment to regular weekly criticism was one of the first signs of increasing architectural awareness in the daily and weekly press. Unfortunately, no talent capable of exploiting the opportunity offered has so far appeared, and the *Observer's* experience with its architectural correspondents has been as unsatisfactory as those correspondents' performance, from Jordan's ill-judged 'Guide to the Isms of Modern Architecture' to Ian Nairn's equally unfortunate attempts to influence local politics over planning decisions." Banham, "Revenge of the Picturesque," 266.
27. For traffic between the Southern and Northern Hemispheres, see Clark and Walker, *Looking for the Local.* My thanks to Andrew Leach for pointing out this important connection.

28. Compare, for example, early issues of *American Architect* from the 1880s with mid-1920s issues of *Die Form* with postwar issues of the *Architectural Review.* Increased image circulation, however, is *not* inversely related to travel to and from architectural sites; looking at images and visiting sites are two different perceptual experiences, complementary and mutually influential.
29. The relationship between this trend and the simultaneous emergence of a discourse of political and architectural autonomy among European intellectuals is no coincidence, although its consequences merit fuller consideration. See Aureli, *The Project of Autonomy*; Castoriadis, *World in Fragments,* 32–43.
30. John Gold makes a related point about general (nonprofessional) media attention to architecture, noting, "Whereas newspapers and the broadcast media showed hardly any interest in architectural matters in 1954, by 1972 many architects might have fervently hoped for rather less extensive coverage." Gold, *The Practice of Modernism,* 12. The emergence of widespread media coverage within the professional press, however, is also a broader phenomenon of postwar architecture. Also see Venturi, Brown, and Izenour, *Learning from Las Vegas*; Stadler and Stierli, *Las Vegas Studio*; Stierli, *Las Vegas im Rückspiegel*; Vinegar, *I Am a Monument*; Vinegar and Golec, *Relearning from Las Vegas.*
31. This is by no means the same skill required in reading from plan to section/elevation, or from plan to photograph. Architects are often ignorant of the technical aspects of photography, particularly lens types, which have profound effects on visual perception and spatial cognition through two-dimensional images. In addition, architectural photography requires translation *after* design has taken place or *before* it has occurred. And while architects had always had to consider their markets and marketing through a variety of means, the postwar period was particularly demanding in this regard.
32. Forty, "Le Corbusier's British Reputation"; Murray and Osley, *Le Corbusier and Britain.*
33. Saxl and Wittkower, *British Art and the Mediterranean.*
34. Read, "English Art and the Mediterranean." A concurrent effort in a similar direction was André Malraux's "museum without walls," published first in 1947. See Malraux, *Le Musée imaginaire,* published in English in 1949 as *The Museum without Walls.*
35. Warburg Institute, annual report, 1934–35. Also see Mann, "Two-Way Traffic."
36. Read, "English Art and the Mediterranean."
37. Saxl and Wittkower, *British Art and the Mediterranean,* 59.
38. During a recent visit to the school by architectural historians, the hall's stage was decorated for a production of *The Wizard of Oz,* which the cast rehearsed in front of the guests, providing a ludicrous and entertaining spectacle.
39. Wittkower, *Architectural Principles in the Age of Humanism,* 20.
40. "It is obvious that such mathematical relations between plan and section cannot be correctly perceived when one walks about in a building. Alberti knew that, of course, quite as well as we do. We must therefore conclude that the harmonic perfection of the geometrical scheme represents an absolute value, independent of our subjective and transitory perception." Ibid., 8.
41. Ibid., 9.
42. See Pevsner, *Visual Planning and the Picturesque.*
43. The letter continues, "and this is no insular phenomenon, for Dr. Giedion at a lecture at

the I.C.A. earlier in the year stated that during 1950, at seminars in both Zurich and at the M.I.T., the most discussed books of the year were *Le Modulor* and *The Architectural Principles in the Age of Humanism [sic],* both concerned with proportion. Dr. Wittkower was furthermore the only representative from this country invited to the recent International Congress on Proportion at Milan when mathematicians, artists and architects met to discuss this vital subject. It seems strange that the most important work on architecture published in England since the war (in 1949) can be reviewed in a professional journal almost three years later by a person wholly ignorant of the state of the profession and apparently more than eager to alienate one of the few people outside the profession who see buildings as works of art and not as possible future literary projections of their own erudition." Alison Smithson and Peter Smithson, letter to the editor, *RIBA Journal* 59 (February 1952): 140. In the 1962 edition of *Architectural Principles,* Wittkower himself noted the influence of his book on Walter Paatz, Ezra D. Ehrenkrantz, P. H. Scholfield, Reyner Banham, and Roberto Pane. British interest in proportion in architecture died out quickly, however, as Peter Smithson asserted in 1958. See "Report of a Debate on the Motion 'That Systems of Proportion Make Good Design Easier and Bad Design More Difficult.'"

44. Banham noted connections between Wittkower's book and contemporary British architecture in 1968; also see Millon, "Rudolf Wittkower, *Architectural Principles in the Age of Humanism*"; Payne, "Rudolf Wittkower and Architectural Principles in the Age of Modernism."
45. See Wittkower's first footnote in reference to Scott. Wittkower, *Architectural Principles in the Age of Humanism,* 1.
46. A similar condition can be found in Walter Benjamin's famous "Work of Art" essay, in which Benjamin makes assertions as if they represent factual realities. This is neither intentional duplicity nor incorrectness; rather, it reflects a belief in the power of textual representation to make claims and project the future. See Benjamin, "The Work of Art in the Age of Its Technological Reproducibility."
47. Mies expressed a similar idea in relation to his New National Gallery in "Mies in Berlin," RIAS interview transcript, excerpted in "Mies Speaks." Also see Aldo Rossi's *The Architecture of the City,* originally published in 1966: "In almost all European cities there are large palaces, building complexes, or agglomerations that constitute whole pieces of the city. . . . When one visits a monument of this type . . . one is always surprised by a series of questions intimately associated with it. In particular, one is struck by the multiplicity of functions that a building of this type can contain over time, and how these functions are entirely independent of the form. At the same time, it is precisely the form that impresses us, we live it and experience it, and in turn it structures the city" (29)
48. Mies's Alumni Memorial Hall appeared in a photograph taken immediately after construction; the steel frame of his Chemistry Building was shown in a completed state, but before interior or exterior walls had been added. See Johnson, *Mies van der Rohe,* 151, 158.
49. *Bauzeitschrift: Wohnen, arbeiten, sich erholen* 1, no. 2 (1947): n.p.
50. "Those who think 'Mies is all the same,' or who confuse a Braun toast-maker with a record-player, will find that their children—who at seven can date Volkswagens by the

small yearly detail changes—do not have these problems. By anyone truly embedded in our culture, a building by Mies can be placed with ease, certainly dated within three years by the dozens of signs to do with changing building technique and the refinement of the formal idea." Smithson and Smithson, *Without Rhetoric*, 42.

51. For conflicted debates on these issues, see Conrads, *Die Bauhaus-Debatte 1953*.
52. Tagg, *The Burden of Representation*.
53. "Alison and Peter Smithson's review of Banham's Bumper Book on Brutalism," for *Architects' Journal* (December 28, 1966), typescript, Loeb Library, Harvard University.
54. Colomina, "Friends of the Future," 26; Highmore, "Rough Poetry," 278. The related projects of Aldo van Eyck and Herman Hertzberger, and their debt to Johannes Duiker, deserve note as well.
55. Sources of this interest include Bergson's *Creative Evolution* and Thompson's *On Growth and Form*.
56. See Steinberg, "The Eye Is Part of the Mind"; Mayor, "The Photographic Eye." These two texts provided epigraphs for the catalog of the 1953 "Parallel of Life and Art" exhibition. Also see Smithson, *AS in DS*. For commentary on the images obtained from the DS, see Colomina, "Unbreathed Air," in *Domesticity at War*, 206–8.
57. Nigel Henderson Papers, Tate Gallery Archive, TGA 9211.5.1.5.

9. FROM PHOTOGRAPHIC SURFACE TO IMAGE OBJECT

1. Krier placed himself off to the side of the image, taking the form of an antique herm (an ancient statue type that often consists of a rectangular shaft of stone, a head, and a phallus). In antiquity, the herm was associated with wisdom. See "Herma," *Wikipedia*, http://en.wikipedia.org/wiki/Herma (accessed September 24, 2013).
2. Stirling came to symbolize the anti-Mies, as his No. 1 Poultry office building rose on a site adjacent to the canceled Mansion House Square scheme for a Mies high-rise in London.
3. Two opposite indicators here are D'Arcy Wentworth Thompson's *On Growth and Form* of 1917 (reprinted 1942) and Richards's 1958 *The Functional Tradition in Early Industrial Buildings*. On Stirling's functionalist roots, also see Szmidt, *The Polish School of Architecture, 1942–1945*.
4. "International style," and "universal space" are two (related) aspects of modernism that Stirling rejected, whether in interwar or postwar versions. According to Mark Crinson, this method owed a great deal to James Gowan. See Crinson, *Stirling and Gowan*, 245–46.
5. I have used the term *image object* spontaneously, deriving it from an analysis of Stirling's work, but I find that it has a history: "Image Objects are simple graphical elements which are assembled together to create more complex artworks like icons, cursors, buttons, sprites and more." Axialis Software, "What Is an Image Object?" http://www.axialis.com/tutorials/tutorial-imageobjects.html (accessed September 24, 2013). Or "A wrapper for image data and its associated meta-information. . . . An ImageObject is a wrapper containing ImageData." DocBook.org, "ImageObject," http://www.docbook.org/tdg/en/html/imageobject.html (accessed September 24, 2013). Image objects are also related to object-oriented ontology; see Harman, *Tool Being*.

6. In a 1968 essay, Reyner Banham described the position of young progressive architects in 1954: "It was to Continental modern architecture and, above all, to Le Corbusier, that they looked for exemplars of a sane and rational design method (as they saw it) to set against the empiricism and compromises of the Picturesque. Le Corbusier, even more than Mies van der Rohe, was seen as the great living exponent of a European classical tradition. That the origins of this tradition were seen to lie in the Renaissance, rather than Greece or Rome, is a tribute, above all, to Professor Wittkower's *Architectural Principles in the Age of Humanism* . . . and the associated essays on Italian and Anglo-Palladian architecture in various journals. The effect of such massive methodology applied to topics that had hitherto been reserved for the amateur attentions of professors at the Bartlett School, or the compilers of country-house profiles in *Country Life,* was galvanic." Banham identified the unreason of picturesque planning rather than the unreason of Continental political events here. Banham, "Revenge of the Picturesque," 268–69. For a more recent consideration of the unstated effects of war and postwar recovery on British architecture in general and the Smithsons in particular, see Highmore, "Rough Poetry."
7. On Team 10, see the excellent compilation and exhibition catalog *Team 10, 1953–81,* edited by Max Risselada and Dirk van den Heuvel; on the Independent Group, see Massey, *The Independent Group*; Robbins, *The Independent Group.* Also see Crinson and Zimmerman, *Neo-avant-garde and Postmodern.*
8. On Stirling and Gowan, see Crinson *Stirling and Gowan.* For new work on James Gowan, see Woodman, *James Gowan.*
9. Describing the three competition entries that he found worthy of consideration (his own, Colin St. John Wilson's, and Peter Smithson's, with no mention of Peter's spouse and partner Alison), all unpremiated, Stirling noted: "Sandy's [Wilson's] scheme is impressive, but . . . in the matter of principle is the same as the winners . . . inasmuch as it is regarded entirely legitimate to give an overall single expression to a block which has such highly diverse accommodation,—by using a glass curtain wall in front . . . so 'disguising' the nature (function) of the accommodation behind, i.e. staff rooms.—ramped lecture theaters,—lavatories, etc.—this is similar to the principal *[sic]* whereby Mies can combine the Farnsworth house + the drive-in restaurant, inflate to a gigantic size and make it a national theatre. The glass curtain wall is legitimate where the accommodation behind is similar i.e. offices—'uno' and 'lever house' *[sic]*—as the use of an emphatic overall expression where a slab is cellular i.e. Marseilles Unité but not unbuilt Sheffield where hardly any two elevations were of the same size or similar function." James Stirling notebook, James Stirling Family Archive. Also see Crinson, *James Stirling.*
10. Another connection between Stirling and an earlier history of functionalism can be traced to his training at the Liverpool School of Architecture under Lionel Budden, successor to the previous dynamic head of the school, Charles Reilly. Stirling also had access to recent modernist functionalism from the Polish School of Architecture, housed in Liverpool throughout the war. Although the Polish students and faculty had departed before his arrival in 1945, an extensive catalog of student work remained and can still be found in Stirling's library, as others have noted. See Szmidt, *The Polish School of Architecture 1942–1945.*

11. Quoted in Highmore, "'Image-Breaking, God-Making,'" 91. For a new study of Paolozzi, see Kitnick, "Eduardo Paolozzi and Others, 1947–1958."
12. These two works of 1963 deploy numerous repeated forms arrayed differently in space. The repetition of elements is also a feature of Stirling's work over a very long trajectory. See Kirkpatrick, *Eduardo Paolozzi*; and *Eduardo Paolozzi: Recent Sculpture, Drawings and Collage.*
13. Crinson, *James Stirling.* Also see Girouard, *Big Jim,* 83.
14. For a fuller discussion of this idea, see Zimmerman, "James Stirling Re-assembled."
15. Eisenman, "Real and English."
16. Stirling himself referred to glass in his buildings as skin, as at Leicester, when he noted in a 1975 lecture, "The iceberg formation is sheathed in glass which is thought of as a sort of skin more like polythene than sheet-plate. . . . the glass . . . is used again as a sort of skin to cover the whole surface of the building at the back." James Stirling, Hornbostel lecture 1974, emended typescript 1975, James Stirling Fonds, Canadian Centre for Architecture.
17. Banham, *Theory and Design in the First Machine Age,* 16, 20.
18. For details on Florey, see Lawrence, "Remaining Modern." Also see Crinson, *Stirling and Gowan.*
19. For details on the commission, see Girouard, *Big Jim,* 148–49. Girouard notes Nikolaus Pevsner's pronounced dislike of Stirling's Oxbridge commissions. Also see Stirling, Hornbostel lecture 1974, emended typescript 1975.
20. Charles Jencks later claimed to have urged Stirling to discard arcane self-reference in favor of more accessible populist reference, presumably without abandoning his combinative method. Jencks, personal conversation with author, summer 2007.
21. Sartoris, *Gli elementi dell'architettura funzionali,* 215.
22. The Smithson scheme was also published in the *Architectural Review* in 1957; Stirling might have known it already as a consequence of his own connections to Team 10.
23. Le Corbusier and Jeanneret, *Oeuvre Complète de 1929–1934,* 140–43, 160–66. Stepped sections occur frequently in Le Corbusier's work, sometimes on the top floors of apartment buildings like that at Porte Molitor and sometimes more comprehensively, as in the museum for the city of Paris (1935).
24. On this topic, see Lawrence, "Remaining Modern."
25. Martin, *Utopia's Ghost.*
26. See Lichtenstein and Schregenberger, *As Found.*
27. See Highmore, "Rescuing Optimism from Oblivion"; Highmore, "Rough Poetry"; Zimmerman, "Photographic Images from Chicago to Hunstanton."
28. Stirling, Hornbostel lecture 1974, emended typescript 1975, 3. This particular hybrid condition belongs to the immediate postwar years; the situation today is yet more complex.
29. Jameson, "Architecture and the Critique of Ideology," 36.
30. Banham, "The New Brutalism." On Banham, see Whiteley, *Reyner Banham.*
31. Banham, *The New Brutalism.*
32. The relationship between Banham and Wittkower requires historical stratification, since Banham's opinions were known to change over time, particularly after the declarations

of postmodernism. At issue here is his relationship to Wittkower's work in the initial formulation of New Brutalism in 1955 and the subsequent disagreements as to its characteristics and theoretical underpinnings.

33. By 1966, when Banham published his book-length study of the movement, his analytical schema was suppressed in favor of a stylistic one. He noted his earlier attempt to "father some of my own pet notions on the movement." See Banham, "Memoirs of a Survivor," in *The New Brutalism,* 134.
34. Elements from Aldo Rossi's monument at Segrate, shown on the left side of the image in Figure 9.14, are independent geometric objects. But since they also reference Rossi's work, their geometric neutrality is immediately compromised by association with a specific historical milieu.
35. Vidler, *James Frazer Stirling,* 78.
36. My emphasis. See Stirling, "Methods of Expression and Materials."
37. Llewelyn-Davies, "Endless Architecture."
38. Here the mute qualities of a conceptually endless building are on display in increments that could be added to over time. Here endlessness passes over into extrusion—a conceptual idea becomes a formal and procedural one. At Dorman Long, the potential extrusion of the building rather reflects the material steel itself—infinitely extrudable, in theory at least. The design also reflects both client needs and external design constraints; it is cited by the architect as a kind of countermodel in publications like "Anti-structure" (1969) and "Methods of Expression and Materials" (1975), where Stirling acknowledges his boredom with such technology-driven design. In other words, he was not interested in endlessness per se.
39. Milton Keynes, one of the "New Towns" laid out after the war, was planned by Richard Llewelyn-Davies, the author of "Endless Architecture," and was intended for possible future extension over the landscape.
40. Each piece compromises the potential extension of the other: the office spine collides into the factory floor; in addition, the location of the lake blocks the office wing on the other end. Characteristically, the blank end wall of an "endless" extrusion caps it without completing it.
41. Later, Stirling's office found other ways to introduce dynamic instabilities into projects, once discourse on endlessness and systems building had died out in Britain (by the mid-1970s). From an interest in process-based buildings such as Olivetti Milton Keynes, focus shifted to narrative and procession in projects like the Düsseldorf museum—a dramatic about-face. Endlessness as a process of fabrication gave way to the endlessness of the path, the postwar *dérive* replacing the pre- and interwar assembly line.

CONCLUSION

1. Correspondence dated July 23, 1947, registrar's files, Museum of Modern Art.
2. The wall murals included photographs of the model of the Glass Skyscraper of 1922, the Monument to Karl Liebknecht and Rosa Luxemburg of 1926, the Barcelona Pavilion, and the Tugendhat House; drawings included the 1921 Friedrichstrasse Skyscraper and the 1923 Concrete Office Building. Other projects were exhibited in drawings or in smaller formats and in models, interspersed with Mies's glass-and-chrome furniture

throughout the space of the gallery. My thanks to Wallis Miller for providing me with a list of the show's contents, also available at MoMA.

3. Wallis Miller, public lecture, American Academy Berlin, fall 2003. Miller is currently at work on a detailed study of architecture exhibitions in nineteenth- and twentieth-century Germany. Mies had already used this technique extensively, most notably in the German Pavilion at Barcelona and in the Tugendhat House, both on display at MoMA.
4. On Philip Johnson's early sponsorship of Mies's work, see Grawe, *Call for Action*, 69–76.
5. Dietrich Neumann has documented Mies's patent applications for photographic wallpaper. See Neumann, "'. . . Wallpaper with Arctic Landscapes . . .'"
6. Eversole, "The Procession of an Architect"; Sachsse, "Messen und Ausstellungen als Hort der Moderne im NS-Staat."
7. See the portrait photographs of Mies with a large print of the Barcelona Pavilion image that was later used at full scale in the 1947 MoMA show in the background, in Reuter and Schulte, *Mies and Modern Living*, 32, 34. Also, the interior photographic murals in the electricity pavilion at the Barcelona exhibition are relevant comparanda here.
8. See Phillips, *Glass*, 206–13. Plate glass was produced by cutting and rolling out hand-blown cylinders until 1899, and with machine-blown cylinders by 1903. Manufacture of rolled plate glass began in 1917, and continuous processes of rolling glass were invented in the early 1920s. From 1903, lengths of up to forty feet could be produced, although maximum widths were limited to roughly eight feet. That dimension had increased to nearly eleven feet by 1941.
9. For a particularly compelling example, see the photomontage "Neue Stadt" in Reuter and Schulte, *Mies and Modern Living*, fig. 215.
10. The inclusion of the Monument to the November Revolution can surely be taken as an ideologically exemplary project for immediate post–World War II America, situating Mies in the camp of the antifascists. His attitude toward the Nazi government had been conciliatory, and had not entitled him to this status. And a few years later, any connection to the left wing would again prove problematic in the political climate of the United States.
11. Many scholars have recently underscored the varying functions of images in registers once thought incompatible. For two examples, see Kelsey, *Archive Style*; Joselit, "Notes on Surface."
12. Reinhold Martin has associated this coexistence with "the military-industrial complex," noting: "The system's phantasmagorias—with built architecture also counted prominently among these—likewise constitutes an indelibly real system of images, with indelibly real consequences. . . . Far from simply staging a spectacle that screens out the structural logic of corporate power by coaxing the spectator-user into a state of passive distraction, architecture works here actively to integrate spaces and subjects into naturalized organizations, specifically to the degree that it is 'reduced' to corporate image." Martin, *The Organizational Complex*, 4.
13. Flusser, *Für eine Philosophie der Fotografie.*
14. Papapetros, *On the Animation of the Inorganic.*

15. See Aggregate, *Governing by Design.*
16. See Koss, *Modernism after Wagner*; Papapetros, *On the Animation of the Inorganic.*
17. There are many other postmodern architects whose work lends itself to comparative analysis in relation to the photographic image and a more generalized idea of images. Most obvious are Aldo Rossi and Robert Venturi/Denise Scott Brown; the latter partnership has been analyzed extensively in recent years, and hence has not been included here. See Moos, *Venturi, Rauch, and Scott Brown*; Moos, *Venturi, Scott Brown & Associates.* Also see Stierli, *Las Vegas im Rückspiegel*; Vinegar, *I Am a Monument*; Vinegar and Golec, *Relearning from Las Vegas.*
18. Barthes, *Camera Lucida,* 4.

BIBLIOGRAPHY

ARCHIVAL SOURCES

City of Barcelona Municipal Archives
City of Brno Archives, Muzeum Města Brna
Ludwig Mies van der Rohe Archive, Museum of Modern Art, New York
Ludwig Mies van der Rohe Papers, Manuscripts Division, Library of Congress
Royal Institute of British Architects Library Photographs Collection
Smithson Family Archive
James Stirling Family Archive
James Stirling Fonds, Canadian Centre for Architecture, Montreal
Tate Gallery Archive

Abney, William de Wiveleslie. *A Treatise on Photography.* 9th ed. London: Longmans, Green, 1897.

Aggregate. *Governing by Design: Architecture, Economy, and Politics in the Twentieth Century.* Pittsburgh: University of Pittsburgh Press, 2012.

Albrecht, Donald, ed. *The Work of Charles and Ray Eames: A Legacy of Invention.* New York: Harry N. Abrams, 1997.

Amtlicher Katalog Werkbund–Ausstellung Die Wohnung. Stuttgart: Deutscher Werkbund, 1927.

Anderson, Stanford. *Peter Behrens and a New Architecture for the Twentieth Century.* Cambridge: MIT Press, 2000.

Appia, Adolphe. "Eurhythmics and Light" (1912). In *Adolphe Appia: Theatre Artist,* by Richard Beacham. Cambridge: Cambridge University Press, 1987.

———. *Music and the Art of the Theatre.* Translated by Robert W. Corrigan and Mary Douglas Dirks. Coral Gables, Fla.: University of Miami Press, 1962.

Arburg, Hans-Georg von. "Fassadenzauber oder schöner Schein? Architektur als Modellfall einer Ästhetik der Oberfläche um 1800 (Schinkel, Moritz, Goethe." *Zeitschrift für Kunstgeschichte* 70 (2007): 381–408.

"Are You Being Served?" *Building Design,* July 1, 1999. http://www.bdonline.co.uk.

Asendorf, Christoph. "Bodies in Force Fields: Design between the Wars." In *From Energy to Information: Representation in Science and Technology, Art, and Literature,* edited by Bruce Clark and Linda Dalrymple Henderson, 195–212. Stanford, Calif.: Stanford University Press, 2002.

Aureli, Pier Vittorio. *The Project of Autonomy: Politics and Architecture within and against Capitalism.* New York: Princeton Architectural Press, 2008.

Ausstellung neuer amerikanischer Baukunst. Berlin: Akademie der Künste, 1926.

Baker, J. F. *The Steel Skeleton.* 2 vols. Cambridge: Cambridge University Press, 1954–56.

———. "The Theory behind Plastic Design." *National Builder,* April 1953, 281.

Banham, Reyner. *A Concrete Atlantis: U.S. Industrial Building and European Modern Architecture, 1900–1925.* Cambridge: MIT Press, 1986.

———. "The New Brutalism." *Architectural Review* 118 (1955): 354–61.

———. *The New Brutalism: Ethic or Aesthetic?* New York: Reinhold, 1966.

———. "Revenge of the Picturesque: English Architectural Polemics, 1945–1965." In *Concerning Architecture: Essays on Architectural Writers and Writing Presented to Nikolaus Pevsner,* edited by John Summerson, 265–73. London: Allen Lane, 1968.

———. *Theory and Design in the First Machine Age.* 2nd ed. Cambridge: MIT Press, 1980.

Barbican Art Gallery. *Bauhaus: Art as Life.* London: Koenig Books, 2012.

Barndt, Kerstin. "'Dioramas of a New World': Siegfried Kracauer and Weimar Exhibition Culture." In *Culture in the Anteroom: The Legacies of Siegfried Kracauer,* edited by Gerd Gemünden and Johannes von Moltke, 162–78. Ann Arbor: University of Michigan Press, 2012.

Barr, Alfred. "Introduction." In *The International Style,* by Henry-Russell Hitchcock and Philip Johnson, 15–16. New York: Museum of Modern Art, 1932.

Barta, Ilsebill. *Wohnen in Mies van der Rohes Villa Tugendhat: Fotografiert von Fritz Tugendhat, 1930–38.* Vienna: Mobiliendepots, 2002.

Barthes, Roland. *Camera Lucida: Reflections on Photography.* Translated by Richard Howard. New York: Hill & Wang, 1981.

———. "Rhetoric of the Image." In *Image-Music-Text.* Translated by Stephen Heath, 32–51. New York: Hill & Wang, 1977.

Bartning, Otto, ed. *Mensch und Raum: Darmstädter Gespräch.* Darmstadt: Neue Darmstädter Verlagsanstalt, 1952.

Batchen, Geoffrey. *Burning with Desire: The Conception of Photography.* Cambridge: MIT Press, 1999.

———. “A Philosophical Window.” *History of Photography* 26, no. 2 (Summer 2002): 100–112.

Bauhaus-Archiv Berlin/Museum für Gestaltung, Stiftung Bauhaus Dessau, and Klassik Stiftung Weimar, eds. *Bauhaus: A Conceptual Model.* Ostfildern: Hatje Cantz, 2009.

Bauhaus Dessau Foundation and M. Kentgens-Craig. *The Dessau Bauhaus Building 1926–1999.* Boston: Birkhäuser, 1998.

Bau und Wohnung: Die Bauten der Weissenhofsiedlung in Stuttgart. Stuttgart: Franz Wedekind, 1927.

Beacham, Richard. *Adolphe Appia: Theatre Artist.* Cambridge: Cambridge University Press, 1987.

Behne, Adolf. *Eine Stunde Architektur.* Stuttgart: Franz Wedekind, 1928.

———. *Der Inkrustationsstil in Toscana.* Berlin: Emil Ebering, 1912.

———. “Peter Behrens und die toskanische Architektur des 12. Jahrhunderts.” *Kunstgewerbeblatt,* no. 3 (1911): 45–50.

Behrendt, Walter Curt. *Die einheitliche Blockfront als Raumelement im Stadtbau: Ein Beitrag zur Stadtbaukunst der gegenwart.* Berlin: Ernst Cassirer, 1911.

———. *Städtebau und Wohnungswesen in den Vereinigten Staaten.* Berlin: Guido Hackebeil, 1927.

Behrens, Peter. *“Wer aber will sagen, was Schönheit sei?” Grafik, Produktgestaltung, Architektur.* Edited by Hans-Georg Pfeifer. Düsseldorf: Beton-Verlag, 1990.

Belke, Ingrid, and Irina Renz. *Siegfried Kracauer, 1889–1966.* Marbach am Neckar: Deutsche Schillergesellschaft/Schiller-Nationalmuseum, 1994.

Belting, Hans. *An Anthropology of Images: Picture, Medium, Body.* Translated by Thomas Dunlap. Princeton, N.J.: Princeton University Press, 2011.

Benjamin, Walter. “The Work of Art in the Age of Its Technological Reproducibility” (second version). In *Selected Writings.* Vol. 3, *1935–1938.* Edited by Howard Eiland and Michael W. Jennings. Cambridge, Mass.: Harvard University Press, 2006.

Benton, Tim. *Le Corbusier: Secret Photographer.* Baden: Lars Müller, 2013.

Bergdoll, Barry. “Bauhaus Multiplied: Paradoxes of Architecture and Design in and after the Bauhaus.” In *Bauhaus 1919–1933: Workshops for Modernity,* edited by Barry Bergdoll and Leah Dickerman, 48–51. New York: Museum of Modern Art, 2009.

———. *European Architecture 1750–1890.* New York: Oxford University Press, 2000.

———. *Karl Friedrich Schinkel: An Architecture for Prussia.* New York: Rizzoli, 1994.

———. “A Matter of Time: Architects and Photographers in Second Empire France.” In *The Photographs of Édouard Baldus,* edited by Malcolm Daniel, 99–119. New York: Metropolitan Museum of Art, 1994.

———. “The Nature of Mies’s Space.” In *Mies in Berlin,* edited by Terence Riley and Barry Bergdoll. New York: Museum of Modern Art, 2001.

———. “Of Crystals, Cells, and Strata: Natural History and Debates on the Form of a New Architecture in the Nineteenth Century.” *Architectural History* 50 (2007): 1–29.

———. “Schinkel and Mies: Nature’s Perspective.” *A+U* 388, no. 1 (2003): 12–14.

———. “Schinkel and Mies: Urban Perspective.” In *Building Berlin,* special issue, *A+U* 384, no. 9 (2002): 20–22.

Bergdoll, Barry, and Leah Dickerman, eds. *Bauhaus 1919–1933: Workshops for Modernity.* New York: Museum of Modern Art, 2009.

Bergson, Henri. *Creative Evolution.* Translated by A. Phillips. New York: Holt, 1911.

Bier, Justus. "Kann man im Haus Tugendhat wohnen?" *Die Form* 6, no. 10 (1931): 392–93.

Birgus, Vladimír. "Czech Avant-Garde Art and the World." In *Czech Photographic Avant-Garde, 1918–1948,* edited by Vladimír Birgus, 13–34. Cambridge: MIT Press, 2002.

———, ed. *Czech Photographic Avant-Garde, 1918–1948.* Cambridge: MIT Press, 2002.

Blau, Eve, and Edward Kaufman, eds. *Architecture and Its Image: Four Centuries of Architectural Representation.* Montreal: Canadian Centre for Architecture, 1989.

Bletter, Rosemarie. "Bruno Taut and Paul Scheerbart's Vision: Utopian Aspects of German Expressionist Architecture." Ph.D. diss., Columbia University, 1974.

Bloch, Ernst. "Berlin: Functions in Hollow Space." In *Heritage of Our Times.* Translated by Neville Plaice and Stephen Plaice. Cambridge: Polity Press, 1991.

Bohrer, Frederick N. "Photographic Perspectives: Photography and the Institutional Formation of Art History." In *Art History and Its Institutions: Foundations of a Discipline,* edited by Elizabeth Mansfield, 246–59. London: Routledge, 2002.

Bois, Yve-Alain. "The Iconoclast." In *Piet Mondrian, 1872–1894,* 313–40. Milan: Leonardo Arte, 1994.

Bonta, Juan Pablo. *Architecture and Its Interpretation: A Study in Expressive Systems in Architecture.* London: Lund Humphries, 1979.

Borrmann, Richard. *Die Bau- und Kunstdenkmäler von Berlin.* Berlin: J. Springer, 1893.

———. *Die Keramik in der Baukunst.* Stuttgart: Arnold Bergsträsser, 1897.

Botar, Oliver. "Prolegomena to the Study of Biomorphic Modernism: Biocentrism, László Moholy-Nagy's 'New Vision,' and Ernö Kállai's Bioromantik." Ph.D. diss., University of Toronto, 2001.

Botar, Oliver A. I., and Isabel Wünsche, eds. *Biocentrism and Modernism.* Burlington, Vt.: Ashgate, 2011.

Boyer, M. Christine. "*La Mission Héliographique*: Architectural Photography, Collective Memory and the Patrimony of France, 1851." In *Picturing Place: Photography and the Geographical Imagination,* edited by Joan M. Schwartz and James R. Ryan, 21–54. London: I. B. Tauris, 2003.

Breuer, Gerda. "Advertisements for His Own Architecture and Neues Bauen: Walter Gropius and Photography." In *Walter Gropius: Amerikareise 1928 = American Journey 1928,* edited by Gerda Breuer and Annemarie Jaeggi, 75–125. Berlin: Bauhaus-Archiv, 2008.

Brott, Simone. *Architecture for a Free Subjectivity.* Burlington, Vt.: Ashgate, 2011.

Brown, Elspeth H. *The Corporate Eye: Photography and the Rationalization of American Commercial Culture, 1884–1929.* Baltimore: Johns Hopkins University Press, 2005.

Brunet, François. *Visions de l'ouest: Photographies de l'exploration américaine, 1860–1880.* Paris: Musée d'art américain Giverny, 2007.

Brush, Kathryn. *The Shaping of Art History: Wilhelm Vöge, Adolph Goldschmidt, and the Study of Medieval Art.* Cambridge: Cambridge University Press, 1996.

Bücher, Karl. *Arbeit und Rhythmus.* Leipzig: Teubner, 1896.

Buddensieg, Tilmann. *Industriekultur: Peter Behrens and the AEG, 1907–1914*. Translated by Iain Boyd Whyte. Cambridge: MIT Press, 1984.

Bund Deutscher Architekten. *Internationale Architektur Ausstellung, New York 1925*. Berlin: Bund Deutscher Architekten, 1925.

Carpo, Mario. *Architecture in the Age of Printing: Orality, Writing, Typography, and Printed Images in the History of Architectural Theory*. Translated by Sarah Benson. Cambridge: MIT Press, 2001.

Carter, Peter. *Mies van der Rohe at Work*. New York: Praeger, 1974.

Castoriadis, Cornelius. *World in Fragments: Writings on Politics, Society, Psychoanalysis, and the Imagination*. Translated and edited by David Ames Curtis. Stanford, Calif.: Stanford University Press, 1997.

Çelik, Zeynep. "Kinaesthetic Impulses: Aesthetic Experience, Bodily Knowledge, and Pedagogical Practices in Germany, 1871–1918." Ph.D. diss., Massachusetts Institute of Technology, 2008.

Clark, Justine, and Paul Walker. *Looking for the Local: Architecture and the New Zealand Modern*. Wellington: University of Victoria Press, 2000.

Cohen, Jean-Louis. "Ambivalente Aura: Der Weißenhof in der europäischen Kritik." In *Internationales Neues Bauen 1927/2002*. Stuttgart: Institut für Auslandsbeziehungen, 2002.

———. *Architecture in Uniform: Designing and Building for the Second World War*. Montreal: Canadian Centre for Architecture, 2011.

———. "Roger Ginsburger: Agent double et critique radical entre France et Allemagne." In *Das Bauhaus und Frankreich*, edited by Isabelle Ewig, Thomas W. Gaehtgens, and Matthias Noell, 349–63. Berlin: Akademie Verlag, 2002.

———. *Scenes of the World to Come: European Architecture and the American Challenge, 1893–1960*. Paris: Flammarion, 1995.

Colini, Laura, and Frank Eckardt, eds. *Bauhaus and the City: A Contested Heritage for a Challenging Future*. Würzburg: Königshausen & Neumann, 2011.

Colomina, Beatriz. *Domesticity at War*. Cambridge: MIT Press, 2007.

———. "Friends of the Future: A Conversation with Peter Smithson." *October* 94 (Autumn 2000): 3–30.

———. *Privacy and Publicity: Modern Architecture as Mass Media*. Cambridge: MIT Press, 1994.

———. "Reflections on the Eames House." In *The Work of Charles and Ray Eames: A Legacy of Invention*, edited by Donald Albrecht. New York: Harry N. Abrams, 1997.

Conrads, Ulrich, ed. *Die Bauhaus-Debatte 1953: Dokumente einer verdrängten Kontroverse*. Braunschweig: Vieweg, 1994.

———. "Brief über Architektur und Fotografie." *Baukunst und Werkform* 6, no. 1 (1953): 22–24.

Constant, Caroline. "From the Virgilian Dream to Chandigarh: Le Corbusier and the Modern Landscape." *Architectural Review* 181, no. 1079 (January 1987): 66–72.

Cramer, Johannes, and Niels Gutschow. *Bauausstellungen: Eine Architekturgeschichte des 20. Jahrhunderts*. Stuttgart: W. Kohlhammer, 1984.

Crary, Jonathan. *Suspensions of Perception: Attention, Spectacle, and Modern Culture.* Cambridge: MIT Press, 1999.

———. *Techniques of the Observer: On Vision and Modernity in the Nineteenth Century.* Cambridge: MIT Press, 1990.

Creutz, Max, ed. *Wilhelm Kreis: Kaufhausneubau L. Tietz A.G. in Elberfeld.* Berlin: Ernst Wasmuth, 1912.

Crinson, Mark, ed. *James Stirling: Early Unpublished Writings on Architecture.* London: Routledge, 2009.

———. *Stirling and Gowan: Architecture from Austerity to Affluence.* New Haven, Conn.: Yale University Press, 2012.

Crinson, Mark, and Claire Zimmerman, eds. *Neo-avant-garde and Postmodern: Postwar Architecture in Britain and Beyond.* New Haven, Conn.: Yale University Press for Yale Center for British Art, 2010.

Cruickshank, Dan. "Hunstanton School, Norfolk, 1954." *RIBA Journal* 104, no. 1 (1997): 50–57.

Curtis, Penelope. "Mies' Choice: Georg Kolbe in the Barcelona Pavilion (1929)." In *Patio and Pavilion: The Place of Sculpture in Modern Architecture,* 10–27. Los Angeles: J. Paul Getty Museum, 2008.

Damisch, Hubert. "Five Notes for a Phenomenology of the Photographic Image." *October* 5 (Summer 1978): 70–72.

Daston, Lorraine, and Peter Galison. "The Image of Objectivity." *Representations* 40 (Fall 1992): 81–128.

———. *Objectivity.* New York: Zone Books, 2007.

Delius, Rudolf von. *Mary Wigman.* Dresden: C. Reissner, 1925.

Didi-Huberman, Georges. *Confronting Images: Questioning the Ends of a Certain History of Art.* University Park: Pennsylvania State University Press, 2005.

Dilly, Heinrich. *Kunstgeschichte als Institution: Studien zur Geschichte einer Disziplin.* Frankfurt: Suhrkamp, 1979.

Dodds, George. *Building Desire: On the Barcelona Pavilion.* New York: Routledge, 2005.

Doesburg, Theo van. "Film als reine Gestaltung." *Die Form* 4, no. 10 (1929): 241–50.

Dorner, Alexander. "Glasraum in der Gewerbehalle auf der Werkbundausstellung 'Die Wohnung' Stuttgart 1927." *Die Form* 3, no. 4 (1928): 114–17.

———. "Zur abstrakten Malerei (Erklärung zum Raum der Abstakten in der hannoverschen Gemäldegalerie)." *Die Form* 3, no. 4 (1928): 110–14.

Dreller, Sarah. "Curtained Walls: Architectural Photography, the Farnsworth House, and the Opaque Mythology of Transparency." Paper delivered at Newberry Library, Chicago, 2010.

Drexler, Arthur, ed. *The Mies van der Rohe Archive.* Vols. 4, 6. New York: Garland, 1986, 1992.

Droste, Magdalena. "The Successor's Disinheritance: The Conflict between Hannes Meyer and Walter Gropius." In *Bauhaus Conflicts, 1919–2009: Controversies and Counterparts,* edited by Philipp Oswalt, 68–83. Ostfildern: Hatje Cantz, 2009.

———. "Unterrichtsstruktur und Werkstattarbeit am Bauhaus unter Hannes Meyer." In *Hannes Meyer 1889–1954: Architekt, Urbanist, Lehrer.* Berlin: Ernst & Sohn, 1989.

Dutta, Arindam. *The Bureaucracy of Beauty: Design in the Age of Its Global Reproducibility.* New York: Routledge, 2007.

Ebeling, Siegfried. *Space as Membrane.* Translated by Pamela Johnson, edited by Spyros Papapetros. London: Architectural Association, 2010. Originally published as *Der Raum als Membran: Ist ein analytisch-kritischer Beitrag zu Fragen zukünftiger Architektur die über das nackte Bedürfnis hinausgeht und hiermit sich legen möchte in die gestaltende Hand aller Wissenschaft.* Dessau: C. Dünnhaupt, 1926.

Eckhard, H. P. "Strukturwandel im Theater! Bau eines Theaters in Mannheim." *Die Bauzeitung* 58, no. 3 (1953): 95–103.

Eduardo Paolozzi: Recent Sculpture, Drawings and Collage. Newcastle-upon-Tyne: Hatton Gallery, 1965.

Eisenman, Peter. "Real and English: The Destruction of the Box I." *Oppositions* 4 (1974): 5–33.

Elcott, Noam M. "Rooms of Our Time: László Moholy-Nagy and the Stillbirth of Multimedia Museums." In *Screen/Space: The Projected Image in Contemporary Art,* edited by Tamara Trodd, 25–52. New York: Manchester University Press, 2011.

Elliott, Cecil D. *Technics and Architecture: The Development of Materials and Systems for Buildings.* Cambridge: MIT Press, 1992.

Elwall, Robert. *Building with Light: The International History of Architectural Photography.* London: Merrell, 2004.

———. *John Maltby.* London: RIBA, 2000.

———. *Photography Takes Command: The Camera and British Architecture, 1890–1939.* London: RIBA, 1994.

Esterer, Rudolf. *Heimatschutz und neue Baugesinnung.* Dresden: Landesverein Sächsischer Heimatschutz, 1931.

Evans, Robin. "Mies van der Rohe's Paradoxical Symmetries" (1990). In *Translations from Drawing to Building, and Other Essays,* 232–76. Cambridge: MIT Press, 1997.

Evers, Hans Gerhard. "Brief über die Architektur-Fotografie." *Baukunst und Werkform* 7, nos. 7/8 (1954): 522–27.

Eversole, Britt. "The Procession of an Architect: Giuseppe Terragni." Unpublished manuscript, n.d.

"Factory Construction: New Warspeed Method of Concrete Roof and Girder Construction." *Architectural Forum* 77, no. 4 (October 1942).

Flusser, Vilém. *Für eine Philosophie der Fotografie.* Göttingen: European Photography, 1983.

Förster, Simone. *Masse braucht Licht: Arthur Kösters Fotografien der Bauten von Erich Mendelsohn: Ein Beitrag zur Geschichte der Architekturfotografie der 1920er Jahre.* Berlin: Dissertation.de, 2008.

Forty, Adrian. "Le Corbusier's British Reputation." In *Le Corbusier: Architect of the Century,* edited by Michael Raeburn and Victoria Wilson, 35–41. London: Arts Council of Great Britain, 1987.

———. *Words and Buildings: A Vocabulary of Modern Architecture.* New York: Thames & Hudson, 2000.

Foster, Stephen, ed. *Hans Richter: Activism, Modernism, and the Avant-Garde.* Cambridge: MIT Press, 1998.

Fox Talbot, William Henry. *The Pencil of Nature*. 1844–46. Reprint, Chicago: KWS, 2011.

Frampton, Kenneth. *Studies in Tectonic Culture*. Cambridge: MIT Press, 1995.

Franck, Carl. "Aufnahmen von Bauwerken, Städteansichten usw." *Photographische Rundschau und Mitteilungen: Zeitschrift für Freunde der Photographie* 52 (1915): 227–31.

Frank, Isabelle. *The Theory of Decorative Art*. New Haven, Conn.: Yale University Press, 2000.

Frankl, Paul. *Die Glasmalerei des fünfzehnten Jahrhunderts in Bayern und Schwaben*. Strasbourg: Heitz & Mündel, 1912.

Friedberg, Anne. *The Virtual Window from Alberti to Microsoft*. Cambridge: MIT Press, 2006.

Friedman, Alice. *American Glamour and the Evolution of Modern Architecture*. New Haven, Conn.: Yale University Press, 2010.

Froschauer, Eva. *"An die Leser!" Baukunst darstellen und vermitteln: Berliner Architekturzeitschriften um 1900*. Berlin: Wasmuth, 2009.

Fuchs, Bohuslav. *Masarykuv studentsky Domov Brno*. Brno, 1930.

Galison, Peter, and Emily Thompson, eds. *The Architecture of Science*. Cambridge: MIT Press, 1999.

Genette, Gérard. *Paratexts: Thresholds of Interpretation*. Cambridge: Cambridge University Press, 1997.

Geretsegger, Heinz, and Max Peintner. *Otto Wagner 1841–1918*. Vienna: Residenz Verlag, 1983.

Giedion, Sigfried. *Bauen in Frankreich Bauen in Eisen Bauen in Eisenbeton*. Leipzig: Klinkhardt & Biermann, 1928.

———. "Der moralische Einfluss der Architektur Mies van der Rohes." *Bauen und Wohnen* 7 (July 1956): 228–29.

———. *Space, Time and Architecture: The Growth of a New Tradition*. Cambridge, Mass.: Harvard University Press, 1941.

———. *Walter Gropius*. Paris: G. Crés, 1931.

———. *Walter Gropius*. 1954. Reprint, New York: Dover, 1992.

———. *Walter Gropius: Work and Teamwork*. New York: Reinhold, 1954.

Giertz, Gernot. *Kultus ohne Götter: Emile Jaques-Dalcroze und Adolphe Appia*. Munich: Kitzinger, 1975.

Girouard, Mark. *Big Jim: The Life and Work of James Stirling*. London: Chatto and Windus, 1998.

Gold, John. *The Practice of Modernism: Modern Architects and Urban Transformation, 1954–1972*. London: Routledge, 2007.

Goldhagen, Sarah Williams. "Freedom's Domiciles: Three Projects by Alison and Peter Smithson." In *Anxious Modernisms: Experimentation in Postwar Architectural Culture*, edited by Sarah Williams Goldhagen and Réjean Legault, 75–95. Cambridge: MIT Press, 2000.

Goldschmidt, Adolph. *Lubecker Malerei und Plastik bis 1530 mit 43 Lichtdrucktafeln von Joh. Nohring in Lubeck*. Lubeck, 1889.

Goodman, Nelson. *Languages of Art: An Approach to the Theory of Symbols*. Indianapolis: Bobbs-Merrill, 1968.

Gortcheva, Nora. "Modern Spaces and Cinema: Movie Theaters and City Films in Wilhelmine and Weimar Berlin." Ph.D. diss., Yale University, 2011.

Gough, Maria. "Constructivism Disoriented: El Lissitzky's Dresden and Hannover *Demonstrationsräume.*" In *Situating El Lissitzky: Vitebsk, Berlin, Moscow,* edited by Nancy Perloff and Brian Reed, 77–124. Los Angeles: Getty Research Institute, 2003.

Grawe, Gabriele Diana. *Call for Action: Mitglieder des Bauhauses in Nordamerika.* Weimar: VDG, 2002.

Greenberg, Clement. "Sculpture in Our Time" (1958). In *Collected Essays and Criticism.* Vol. 4, *Modernism with a Vengeance, 1957–1969.* Edited by John O'Brian. Chicago: University of Chicago Press, 1993.

Gropius, Walter. *Bauhausbauten Dessau.* 1930. Reprint, Mainz: Florian Kupferberg, 1974.

———. *Idee und Aufbau des Staatlichen Bauhauses.* Munich: Bauhausverlag, 1923.

———. *Internationale Architektur.* Munich: Albert Langen Verlag, 1925.

———. *Internationale Architektur.* 2nd ed. Munich: Albert Langen Verlag, 1927.

———. "Zur Wanderausstellung moderner Fabrikbauten" (1911). In *Walter Gropius.* Vol. 3, *Ausgewählte Schriften.* Edited by Hartmut Probst and Christian Schädlich, 26–27. Berlin: Verlag für Architektur und technische Wissenschaften, 1988.

Gutschow, Kai. "The Culture of Criticism: Adolf Behne and the Development of Modern Architecture in Germany, 1910–1914." Ph.D. diss., Columbia University, 2005.

———. "From Object to Installation in Bruno Taut's Exhibit Pavilions." *Journal of Architectural Education* 59, no. 4 (2006): 63–70.

Hake, Sabine. "Visualising the Urban Masses: Modern Architecture and Architectural Photography in Weimar Berlin." *Journal of Architecture* 11, no. 5 (2006): 523–30.

Hammer-Tugendhat, Daniela, and Wolf Tegethoff, eds. *Ludwig Mies van der Rohe: The Tugendhat House.* Vienna: Springer, 2000.

Harman, Graham. *Tool Being: Heidegger and the Metaphysics of Objects.* Chicago: Open Court, 2002.

Hartmann, Sabine. "Anmerkungen zum fotographischen Nachlaß." In *Lucia Moholy: Bauhaus Fotografin,* edited by Rolf Sachsse, 113–16. Berlin: Bauhaus-Archiv, 1995.

Hasler, Thomas. *Architektur als Ausdruck: Rudolf Schwarz.* Zurich: gta, 2000.

Haus, Andreas. "Photogenic Architecture." *Daidalos* 66 (December 1997): 84–91.

Hays, K. Michael. "Co-op Vitrine and the Representation of Mass Production." In *Modernism and the Posthumanist Subject: The Architecture of Hannes Meyer and Ludwig Hilberseimer,* 25–53. Cambridge: MIT Press, 1992.

Hegemann, Werner. *Amerikanische Architektur & Stadtbaukunst: Ein Überlick über den heutigen Stand der Amerikanischen Baukunst in ihrer Beziehung zum Staedtebau abbildungen.* Berlin: E. Wasmuth, 1925/1927.

———. *Der städtebau nach den ergebnissen der Allgemeinen städtebau-ausstellung in Berlin, nebst einem anhang: Die Internationale städtebau-ausstellung in Düsseldorf.* Berlin: Wasmuth, 1911–13.

———. "Stuttgarter Schildbürgerstreiche und Berliner Bauausstellung 1930." *Wasmuths Monatshefte zur Baukunst* (1928): 8–12.

Heidtmann, Frank. *Wie das Photo ins Buch kam.* Berlin: Arno Spitz, 1984.

Herf, Jeffrey. *Reactionary Modernism: Technology, Culture, and Politics in Weimar and the Third Reich.* Cambridge: Cambridge University Press, 1984.

Herschdorfer, Nathalie, ed. *Le Corbusier and the Power of Photography.* London: Thames & Hudson, 2012.

Highmore, Ben. "'Image-Breaking, God-Making': Paolozzi's Brutalism." *October* 136 (Spring 2011): 87–104.

———. "Rescuing Optimism from Oblivion." In *Team 10, 1953–81: In Search of a Utopia of the Present,* edited by Max Risselada and Dirk van den Heuvel, 271–75. Rotterdam: NAi, 2005.

———. "Rough Poetry: *Patio and Pavilion* Revisited." *Oxford Art Journal* 29, no. 2 (2006): 269–90.

Hilberseimer, Ludwig, ed. *Internationale neue Baukunst.* 1927. Reprinted as *Neues Bauen International 1927/2002.* Stuttgart: Institut für Auslandsbeziehungen, 2002.

Hilpert, Thilo. *Mies van der Rohe im Nachkriegsdeutschland: Das Theaterprojekt—Mannheim, 1953.* Leipzig: A. E. Seeman, 2001.

Holly, Michael Ann. *Panofsky and the Foundations of Art History.* Ithaca, N.Y.: Cornell University Press, 1984.

Imorde, Joseph. "'Das billige Bild': Hochkunst als Massenware." Intermedia Design Center, Fachhochschule Trier (summer 2010), and Museum für Gegenwartskunst Siegen (summer 2011).

Iversen, Margaret. *Alois Riegl: Art History and Theory.* Cambridge: MIT Press, 1993.

Jaeger, Roland. *Neue Werkkunst: Architektenmonographien der zwanziger Jahre.* Berlin: Gebrüder Mann, 1998.

Jakobson, Roman. "The Contours of the Safe Conduct." In *Semiotics of Art: Prague School Contributions,* edited by Ladislav Matejka and Irwin R. Titunik, 188–95. Cambridge: MIT Press, 1976.

Jameson, Fredric. "Architecture and the Critique of Ideology." In *Ideologies of Theory: Essays 1971–1986.* Vol. 2, *Syntax of History.* Minneapolis: University of Minnesota Press, 1988.

Jarzombek, Mark. "The Cunning of Architecture's Reason." *Footprint* 1 (Autumn 2007): 31–46.

———. *The Psychologizing of Modernity: Art, Architecture, History.* Cambridge: Cambridge University Press, 2000.

Jay, Martin. "Photo-unrealism: The Contribution of the Camera to the Crisis of Ocularcentrism." In *Vision and Textuality,* edited by Stephen Melville and Bill Readings, 344–60. Durham, N.C.: Duke University Press, 1995.

Johnson, Philip. *Mies van der Rohe.* New York: Museum of Modern Art, 1947.

———. "Schinkel and Mies" (1962). In *Writings/Philip Johnson.* Edited by Robert A. M. Stern. New York: Oxford University Press, 1979.

———. "School at Hunstanton, Norfolk." *Architectural Review* 116 (September 1954): 148–62.

Joselit, David. "Notes on Surface: Toward a Genealogy of Flatness." *Art History* 23, no. 1 (2000): 19–34.

Karnitschnigg, Maximilian R. von. "Moderne Architekturphotographie." *Photofreund* 7 (1927): 3, 42–44.

Kellein, Thomas, and Angela Lame. *Abstrakte Fotografie*. Ostfildern: Hatje Cantz, 2000.

Keller, Ulrich. "Durandelle, the Paris Opéra, and the Aesthetic of Creativity." *Gazette des Beaux-Arts* 111 (January/February 1988): 109–18.

Kellsey, Lewis. *Corrective Photography: An Elementary Illustrated Textbook on Camera Swings and How to Use Them*. Chicago: L. F. Deardorff, 1947.

Kelsey, Robin. *Archive Style: Photographs and Illustrations for U.S. Surveys, 1850–1890*. Berkeley: University of California Press, 2007.

———. "Photography, Chance, and *The Pencil of Nature*." In *The Meaning of Photography*, edited by Robin Kelsey and Blake Stimson, 15–33. Williamstown, Mass.: Sterling and Francine Clark Art Institute, 2008.

Kelsey, Robin, and Blake Stimson, eds. *The Meaning of Photography*. Williamstown, Mass.: Sterling and Francine Clark Art Institute, 2008.

Kirkpatrick, Diane. *Eduardo Paolozzi*. Greenwich, Conn.: New York Graphic Society, 1970.

Kirsch, Karin. *Briefe zur Weißenhofsiedlung*. Stuttgart: Deutsche Verlags–Anstalt, 1997.

———. "Internationales Neues Bauen 1927/2002: Ein imaginäres Museum der frühen Modernen Architektur. Versuch einer Dokumentation." In *Internationales Neues Bauen 1927/2002*, 62–71. Stuttgart: Institut für Auslandsbeziehungen, 2002.

———. *The Weissenhofsiedlung: Experimental Housing Built for the Deutscher Werkbund, Stuttgart, 1927*. New York: Rizzoli, 1989.

———. *Die Weißenhofsiedlung: Werkbund–Ausstellung "Die Wohnung"—Stuttgart 1927*. Stuttgart: Deutsche Verlags–Anstalt, 1987.

Kitnick, Alex. "Eduardo Paolozzi and Others, 1947–1958." Ph.D. diss., Princeton University, 2010.

Kleinmann, Kent, and Leslie van Duzer. "Eisen und Mörtel: Anmerkungen zu Haus Lange und Haus Esters." *Bauwelt* 91, no. 41 (2000): 16–19.

———. *Mies van der Rohe: The Krefeld Villas*. New York: Princeton Architectural Press, 2005.

Korn, Arthur. *Glas im Bau und als Gebrauchsgegenstand*. Berlin: E. Pollack, 1929.

Koss, Juliet. *Modernism after Wagner*. Minneapolis: University of Minnesota Press, 2010.

———. "On the Limits of Empathy," *Art Bulletin* 88, no. 1 (March 2006): 139–57.

Kracauer, Siegfried. "Cult of Distraction." In *The Mass Ornament: Weimar Essays*. Translated and edited by Thomas Y. Levin, 323–28. Cambridge, Mass.: Harvard University Press, 1995.

———. *Die Entwicklung der Schmiedekunst in Berlin, Potsdam und einigen Städten der Mark vom 17. Jahrhundert bis zum Beginn des 19. Jahrhunderts*. 1915. Reprint, Berlin: Gebrüder Mann, 1997.

———. "Kult der Zerstreuung: Über die Berlinier Lichtspielhäuser." *Frankfurter Zeitung* 70, no. 167 (March 4, 1926): feuilleton 1–2.

———. "Das neue Bauen. Zur Stuttgarter Werkbund-Ausstellung: 'Die Wohnung.'" *Frankfurter Zeitung* 72, no. 561 (July 31, 1927).

Kubová, Alena. *L'Avant-Garde architecturale en Tchécoslovaquie, 1918–1939*. Liège: Mardaga, 1992.

Kudělka, Zdeněk. *Brněnská architektura 1919–1928*. Brno: Nakladatelství Blok, 1970.

Kudělka, Zdeněk, and Jindřich Chatrný, eds. *For New Brno: The Architecture of Brno, 1919–1939*. Brno: Muzeum Města Brna, 2000.

Kuenzli, Katherine. "The Birth of the Modernist Art Museum: The Folkwang as *Gesamtkunstwerk*." *Journal of the Society of Architectural Historians* 72, no. 4 (2013): 503–29.

Lambert, Phyllis. *Building Seagram*. New Haven, Conn.: Yale University Press, 2013.

———, ed. *Mies in America*. Montreal: Canadian Centre for Architecture, 2001.

Lampugnani, Vittorio Magnago. "Ausstellungen von Architektur: Eine fragmentarische historische Übersicht für Europa und die USA." In *Internationale Bauausstellung Berlin 1984*. Berlin: Quadriga, 1981.

Lane, Barbara Miller. *Architecture and Politics in Germany, 1918–1945*. Cambridge, Mass.: Harvard University Press, 1968.

Lang, Karen. *Chaos and Cosmos: On the Image in Aesthetics and Art History*. Ithaca, N.Y.: Cornell University Press, 2006.

Lavin, Sylvia. *Kissing Architecture*. Princeton, N.J.: Princeton University Press, 2011.

Lawder, Standish. *The Cubist Cinema*. New York: New York University Press, 1975.

Lawrence, Amanda Reeser. "Remaining Modern: The Architecture of James Stirling, 1955–1971." Ph.D. diss., Harvard University, 2007.

Le Corbusier. "Architecture d'époque machiniste." *Journal de Psychologie Normale et Pathologique* 22 (1926): 325–50.

Le Corbusier and Pierre Jeanneret. *Oeuvre complète de 1929–1934*. Zurich: H. Girsberger, 1935.

Leitl, Alfons. "Anmerkungen zur Zeit: Debatte um Rudolf Schwarz." *Baukunst und Werkform* 6, nos. 2/3 (1953): 59–95.

Leo Baeck Institute. *Catalog of the Archival Collections*. Tübingen: J. C. B. Mohr, 1990.

Lepik, Andres. "Mies and Photomontage, 1910–1938." In *Mies in Berlin*, edited by Terence Riley and Barry Bergdoll, 324–29. New York: Museum of Modern Art, 2001.

Levine, Neil. "Architectural Reasoning in the Age of Positivism: The Neo-Grec Idea of Henri Labrouste's Bibliothèque Ste.-Geneviève." Ph.D. diss., Yale University, 1975.

———. *Modern Architecture: Representation and Reality*. New Haven, Conn.: Yale University Press, 2009.

Lichtenstein, Claude, and Thomas Schregenberger. *As Found: The Discovery of the Ordinary*. Zurich: Lars Müller, 2001.

Lieberman, Ralph. "Thoughts of an Art Historian/Photographer on the Relationship of His Two Disciplines." In *Art History through the Camera's Lens*, edited by Helene E. Roberts, 217–49. Amsterdam: Gordon & Breach, 1995.

Liebermann, Max. "Vorwort." In *Ausstellung neuer amerikanischer Baukunst*. Berlin: Akademie der Künste, 1926.

Lipsius, Constant. "On the Aesthetic Treatment of Iron in Tall Buildings" (1878). In *Architectural Theory*. Vol. 2, *An Anthology from 1871–1905*, edited by Harry Francis Mallgrave and Christina Contandriopoulos, 69–70. Malden, Mass.: Blackwell, 2006.

Lipstadt, Hélène. "The Building and the Book in César Daly's *Revue Générale de l'Architecture.*" In *Architectureproduction,* edited by Beatriz Colomina, 25–55. New York: Princeton Architectural Press, 1988.

Llewelyn-Davies, Richard. "Endless Architecture." *Architectural Association Journal* 67 (November 1951): 106–12.

Loos, Adolf. "Regarding Economy" (interview with Bohuslav Markalous). In *Raumplan versus Plan Libre: Adolf Loos and Le Corbusier, 1919–1930,* edited by Max Risselada, 137–41. New York: Rizzoli, 1987.

Lotz, Wilhelm. "Architekturfotos." *Die Form* 4, no. 3 (1929): 69–70.

Lowenstein, Milton. "Germany's Bauhaus Experiment." *Architecture* 60, no. 1 (1929): 1–6.

Lungstrum, Janet Ward. "The Display Window: Designs and Desires of Weimar Consumerism." *New German Critique* 76 (Winter 1999): 115–60.

Mäckler, Hermann. "Praeceptor Germaniae et Europae?" *Baukunst und Werkform* 6, nos. 2/3 (1953): 65–66, 68.

Mallgrave, Harry Francis. *The Architect's Brain: Neuroscience, Creativity, and Architecture.* Chichester: Wiley-Blackwell, 2010.

Mallgrave, Harry Francis, and Christina Contandriopoulos, eds. *Architectural Theory.* Vol. 2, *An Anthology from 1871–1905.* Malden, Mass.: Blackwell, 2006.

Mallgrave, Harry Francis, and Eleftherios Ikonomou, eds. *Empathy, Form, and Space: Problems in German Aesthetics, 1873–1893.* Santa Monica, Calif.: Getty Center for the History of Art and the Humanities, 1994.

Malraux, André. *Le Musée imaginaire.* Vol. 1 of *La Psychologie de l'art.* Geneva: Skira, 1947.

Mann, Nicholas. "Two-Way Traffic: The Warburg Institute as a Microcosm of Cultural Exchange between Britain and Europe." In *The British Contribution to the Europe of the Twenty-First Century: The British Academy Centenary Lectures,* edited by Basil Markesinis, 94–104. Oxford: Hart, 2002.

Manning, Susan Allene, and Melissa Benson. "Interrupted Continuities: Modern Dance in Germany." *The Drama Review: TDR* 30, no. 2 (1986): 30–45.

Mansfield, Elizabeth, ed. *Art History and Its Institutions: Foundations of a Discipline.* London: Routledge, 2002.

Martin, Reinhold. "Atrocities. Or, Curtain Wall as Mass Medium." *Perspecta* 32 (2001): 67–75.

———. *The Organizational Complex: Architecture, Media, and Corporate Space.* Cambridge: MIT Press, 2003.

———. *Utopia's Ghost: Architecture and Postmodernism, Again.* Minneapolis: University of Minnesota Press, 2010.

Masey, Jack, and Conway Lloyd Morgan, *Cold War Confrontations: US Exhibitions and Their Role in the Cultural Cold War.* Baden: Lars Müller, 2008.

Massey, Anne. *The Independent Group: Modernism and Mass Culture in Britain, 1945–59.* Manchester: Manchester University Press, 1995.

Mayor, A. Hyatt. "The Photographic Eye." *Metropolitan Museum of Art Bulletin,* n.s., 5, no. 1 (Summer 1946): 19–26.

McArthur, John. *The Picturesque: Architecture, Disgust, and Other Irregularities.* London: Routledge, 2007.

McCauley, Elizabeth Anne. *A. E. E. Disdéri and the Carte de Visite Portrait Photograph.* New Haven, Conn.: Yale University Press, 1985.

Mebes, Paul. *Um 1800: Architektur und Handwerk im letzten Jahrhundert ihrer traditionelle Entwicklung.* Munich: F. Bruckmann, 1908.

Mendelsohn, Erich. *Amerika: Bilderbuch eines Architekten.* Berlin: Rudolf Mosse, 1926.

———. *Neues Haus—Neue Welt.* Berlin: Rudolf Mosse, 1932.

Mertins, Detlef. "Architecture, Worldview, and World Image in *G*." In *G: An Avant-Garde Journal of Art, Architecture, Design, and Film, 1923–1926,* translated by Steven Lindberg, edited by Detlef Mertins and M. Jennings, 71–96. Santa Monica, Calif.: Getty Research Institute, 2010.

———. "Architectures of Becoming." In *Mies in Berlin,* edited by Terence Riley and Barry Bergdoll. New York: Museum of Modern Art, 2001.

Mertins, Detlef, and Michael W. Jennings, eds. *G: An Avant-Garde Journal of Art, Architecture, Design, and Film, 1923–1926.* Translated by Steven Lindberg. Santa Monica, Calif.: Getty Research Institute, 2010.

Meyer, Hannes. "My Expulsion from the Bauhaus: An Open Letter to Lord Mayor Hesse of Dessau" (1930). In *The Bauhaus: Weimar, Dessau, Berlin, Chicago,* by Hans M. Wingler, 163–65. Cambridge: MIT Press, 1978.

"Mies Speaks." *Architectural Review* 144 (December 1968): 451–52.

"Mies van der Rohe: Arbeiten der letzten beiden Jahre." *Baukunst und Werkform,* May 1951, 9–20.

Mies van der Rohe, Ludwig. "Bauen." In *G: An Avant-Garde Journal of Art, Architecture, Design, and Film, 1923–1926,* translated by Steven Lindberg, edited by Detlef Mertins and Michael W. Jennings. Santa Monica, Calif.: Getty Research Institute, 2010.

———. "What Would Concrete, What Would Steel Be without Mirror Glass?" (1933). In *The Artless Word: Mies van der Rohe on the Building Art,* translated by Fritz Neumeyer, 314. Cambridge: MIT Press, 1991.

Millon, Henry A. "Rudolf Wittkower, *Architectural Principles in the Age of Humanism*: Its Influence on the Development and Interpretation of Modern Architecture." *Journal of the Society of Architectural Historians* 31, no. 2 (1972): 83–91.

Moholy, Lucia. "Das Bauhaus Bild." *werk* 6 (1968): 397–402.

———. *A Hundred Years of Photography.* Harmondsworth: Penguin, 1939.

———. *Marginalien zu Moholy Nagy/Moholy Nagy, Marginal Notes.* Krefeld: Scherpe Verlag, 1972.

———. "The Missing Negatives." In *Lucia Moholy: Bauhaus Fotografin,* edited by Rolf Sachsse, 108–10. Berlin: Bauhaus-Archiv, 1995.

Moholy-Nagy, László. "Produktion–Reproduktion." *De Stijl* 5, no. 7 (July 1922): 98–100. Reprinted as "Production–Reproduction." In *Moholy-Nagy: Photographs and Photograms,* by Andreas Haus, translated by Frederic Samson, 46–47. New York: Pantheon, 1980.

———. "Typofoto." In *Malerei Fotografie Film,* 36–38. Munich: Albert Langen, 1927.

———. *Von Material zu Architektur.* Bauhausbuch no. 14. Munich: Albert Langen, 1929.

Moos, Stanislaus von. *Le Corbusier: Elements of a Synthesis.* Cambridge: MIT Press, 1979.

———. *Venturi, Rauch, and Scott Brown: Buildings and Projects.* New York: Rizzoli, 1987.

———. *Venturi, Scott Brown & Associates: Buildings and Projects, 1986–1998*. New York: Monacelli Press, 1999.

Moynihan, D. S., and Leigh George Odom. “Oskar Schlemmer’s ‘Bauhaus Dances’: Debra McCall’s Reconstructions.” *The Drama Review: TDR* 28, no. 3 (1984): 46–58.

Müller, Sebastian. “Zur Geschichte des ‘Deutschen Museums für Kunst in Handel und Gewerbe.’” In *Karl Ernst Osthaus: Leben und Werk,* edited by Herta Hesse-Freilinghaus et al., 259–342. Recklinghausen: Aurel Bongers, 1971.

Müller-Wulckow, Walter. *Die Konstruktion der Bildarchitekturen in der deutschen Graphik des 15. Jahrhunderts*. Strasbourg, 1911; Frankfurt 1914. http://hdl.handle.net/2027/uc1.b2646345.

Mumford, Lewis. *Vom Blockhaus zum Wolkenkratzer: Eine Studie über amerikanische Architektur und Zivilisation*. Berlin: Bruno Cassirer, 1925.

Münsterburg, Hugo. *Die Amerikaner.* 2nd expanded ed. Berlin: Mittler, 1912.

Murray, Irena, and Julian Osley. *Le Corbusier and Britain*. London: Routledge, 2009.

Muthesius, Hermann. *Das englische Haus*. Berlin: Wasmuth, 1904–5.

Nägele, Daniel. “An Interview with Ezra Stoller.” *History of Photography* 22 (Summer 1998): 105–15.

Naginski, Erika. “Romanticism’s Piranesi.” In *The Built Surface*. Vol. 1, *Architecture and the Pictorial Arts from Antiquity to the Enlightenment,* edited by Christy Anderson, 237–259. Aldershot: Ashgate, 2002.

Neef, Sonja, ed. *An bord der Bauhaus: Zur Heimatlosigkeit der Moderne*. Bielefeld: Transcript, 2009.

Nelson, George. “Architects of Europe Today, 7: Van der Rohe, Germany.” *Pencil Points* 16, no. 9 (September 1935): 453–60.

Nerdinger, Winfried. “Das Bauhaus zwischen Mythisierung und Kritik.” In *Die Bauhaus-Debatte 1953: Dokumente einer verdrängten Kontroverse,* edited by Ulrich Conrads, 7–19. Braunschweig: Vieweg, 1994.

———. *Walter Gropius*. Berlin: Bauhaus-Archiv, 1985.

Neumann, Dietrich. “Der Barcelona Pavillon.” In *Mythos Bauhaus: Zwischen Selbsterfindung und Enthistorisierung,* edited by Anja Baumhoff and Magdalena Droste, 227–44. Berlin: Reimer, 2009.

———. “‘. . . Wallpaper with Arctic Landscapes . . .’: Mies van der Rohe’s Patents for Wallpaper Design and Printing Technology, 1937–50.” In *Mies and Modern Living: Interiors, Furniture, Photography,* edited by Helmut Reuter and Birgit Schulte. Ostfildern: Hatje Cantz, 2008.

———. *Die Wolkenkratzer Kommen! Deutsche Hochhaüser der zwanziger Jahre*. Braunschweig: Vieweg, 1995.

Neumeyer, Fritz. *The Artless Word: Mies van der Rohe on the Building Art.* Translated by Mark Jarzombek. Cambridge: MIT Press, 1991.

———. “Space for Reflection: Block versus Pavilion.” In *Mies van der Rohe: Critical Essays,* edited by Franz Schulze, 148–70. New York: Museum of Modern Art, 1989.

Neutra, Richard. *Amerika, die Stilbildung des neuen Bauens in den Vereinigten Staaten*. Vienna: Scholl, 1930.

Neutra, Richard J. “The Photographer and Architect.” In *Photographing Architecture and Interiors,* by Julius Shulman, vi–ix. 1962. Reprint, Los Angeles: Balcony Press, 2000.

Nilsen, Micheline. *Architecture in Nineteenth-Century Photographs: Essays on Reading a Collection.* Burlington, Vt.: Ashgate, 2011.

Oechslin, Werner, and Guido Harbers, eds. *Sigfried Giedion und die Fotografie: Bildinszenierungen der Moderne.* Zurich: gta, 2010.

Otto, Christian F. "Modern Environment and Historical Continuity: The Heimatschutz Discourse in Germany." *Art Journal* 43, no. 2 (1983): 148–57.

Pai, Hyungmin. *The Portfolio and the Diagram: Architecture, Discourse, and Modernity in America.* Cambridge: MIT Press, 2002.

Panofsky, Erwin. *Perspective as Symbolic Form.* New York: Zone Books, 1991.

Papapetros, Spyros. *On the Animation of the Inorganic: Art, Architecture, and the Extension of Life.* Chicago: University of Chicago Press, 2012.

———. "On the Biology of the Inorganic: Crystallography and Discourses of Latent Life in the Art and Architectural Historiography of the Early Twentieth Century." In *Biocentrism and Modernism,* edited by Oliver A. I. Botar and Isabel Wünsche, 77–106. Burlington, Vt.: Ashgate, 2011.

Pare, Richard, ed. *Photography and Architecture, 1839–1939.* Montreal: Canadian Centre for Architecture, 1982.

Passarge, Walter. "The Bauhaus Exhibition in Weimar" (1923). In *The Bauhaus: Weimar, Dessau, Berlin, Chicago,* by Hans M. Wingler, 67. Cambridge: MIT Press, 1978.

Payne, Alina. *From Ornament to Object: Genealogies of Architectural Modernism.* New Haven, Conn.: Yale University Press, 2012.

———. "Rudolf Wittkower and Architectural Principles in the Age of Modernism." *Journal of the Society of Architectural Historians* 53, no. 3 (1994): 322–42.

Pehnt, Wolfgang. *Bewohnte Bilder: Rudolf Schwarz, 1897–1961.* Ostfildern: Hatje Cantz, 1997.

Perloff, Nancy, and Brian Reed, eds. *Situating El Lissitzky: Vitebsk, Berlin, Moscow.* Los Angeles: Getty Research Institute, 2003.

Pevsner, Nikolaus. *The Englishness of English Art.* New York: Praeger, 1956.

———. *Visual Planning and the Picturesque.* Edited by Mathew Aitchison. Los Angeles: Getty Research Institute, 2010.

Pezolet, Nicola. "'Signs of Inhabitation': The Critical Legacies of Patio and Pavilion." *Thresholds* 35 (2009): 44–49.

Phillips, C. J. *Glass: The Miracle Maker.* 2nd ed. New York: Pitman, 1948.

Phillips, Rachel. *The Poetic Modes of Octavio Paz.* London: Oxford University Press, 1972.

Picon, Antoine, and Alessandra Ponte, eds. *Architecture and the Sciences: Exchanging Metaphors.* New York: Princeton Architectural Press, 2003.

Pidgley, Michael. "Picturesque." In *The Oxford Companion to Western Art,* edited by Hugh Brigstocke, 572–73. Oxford: Oxford University Press, 2001.

Pisani, Daniele. "Kracauer sul Weissenhof Stoccarda 1927." *Casabella* 67 (July–August 2003): 48–59.

Plarre, Stephanie. *Die Kochenhofsiedlung, das Gegenmodell zur Weissenhofsiedlung: Paul*

Schmitthenners Siedlungsprojekt in Stuttgart von 1927 bis 1933. Stuttgart: Hohenheim, 2001.

Podro, Michael. *The Critical Historians of Art.* New Haven, Conn.: Yale University Press, 1982.

Pommer, Richard, and Christian F. Otto. *Weissenhof 1927 and the Modern Movement in Architecture.* Chicago: University of Chicago, 1991.

Powers, Alan. "The Architectural Book: Image and Accident." In *This Is Not Architecture,* edited by Kester Rattenbury, 157–73. London: Routledge, 2002.

Puttfarken, Thomas. *The Discovery of Pictorial Composition: Theories of Visual Order in Painting, 1400–1800.* New Haven, Conn.: Yale University Press, 2000.

Quetglas, José. *Fear of Glass: Mies van der Rohe's Pavilion in Barcelona.* Basel: Birkhäuser, 2001.

Rancière, Jacques. *The Future of the Image.* Translated by Gregory Elliott. London: Verso, 2007.

———. *The Politics of Aesthetics: The Distribution of the Sensible.* Translated by Gabriel Rockhill. London: Continuum, 2004.

Read, Herbert. "English Art and the Mediterranean." *The Listener* 26, no. 675 (December 18, 1941): 819.

Reeh, Henrik. *Ornaments of the Metropolis: Siegfried Kracauer and Modern Urban Culture.* Cambridge: MIT Press, 2004.

"Report of a Debate on the Motion 'That Systems of Proportion Make Good Design Easier and Bad Design More Difficult.'" *RIBA Journal* 64 (September 1957): 460–61.

Reuter, Helmut, and Birgit Schulte, eds. *Mies and Modern Living: Interiors, Furniture, Photography.* Ostfildern: Hatje Cantz, 2008.

Reuter, Helmut, Wolf Tegethoff, and Rolf Sachsse, "Mies and the Photographers I." In *Mies and Modern Living: Interiors, Furniture, Photography,* edited by Helmut Reuter and Birgit Schulte. Ostfildern: Hatje Cantz, 2008.

Richards, J. M. *The Functional Tradition in Early Industrial Buildings.* London: Architectural Press, 1958.

Richter, Hans, in collaboration with Werner Gräff. *Filmgegner von heute, Filmfreunde von morgen.* Berlin: Verlag Herman Reckendorf, 1929.

Riegl, Alois. *Die Entstehung der Barockkunst in Rom.* Edited by Arthur Burda and Max Dvořák. Vienna: A. Schroll, 1908.

———. *Stilfragen: Grundlegungen zu einer Geschichte der Ornamentik.* Berlin: G. Siemens, 1893.

Riezler, Walter. "Das Haus Tugendhat in Brünn." *Die Form* 6, no. 9 (1931): 321–32.

Risselada, Max, and Dirk van den Heuvel, eds. *Team 10, 1953–81: In Search of a Utopia of the Present.* Rotterdam: NAi, 2005.

Robbers, Lutz. "Modern Architecture in the Age of Cinema: Mies van der Rohe and the Moving Image." Ph.D. diss., Princeton University, 2012.

Robbins, David, ed. *The Independent Group: Postwar Britain and the Aesthetics of Plenty.* Cambridge: MIT Press, 1990.

Robinson, Cervin, and Joel Herschman. *Architecture Transformed: A History of the Photography of Buildings from 1839 to the Present.* Cambridge: MIT Press, 1987.

Röder, Sabine. "Propaganda für ein neues Bauen: Die 'Photographien- und Diapositivzentrale' des Deutschen Museums für Kunst in Handel und Gewerbe." In *Katalog Moderne Baukunst 1900–1914: Die Photosammlung des Deutschen Museums für Kunst in Handel und Gewerbe*, 8–18. Krefeld: Stadt Krefeld, 1993.

Rohde, David. "Held by the Taliban." *New York Times*, October 17–22, 2009. http://www.nytimes.com.

Romba, Katherine. *Iron Construction and Cultural Discourse: German Architectural Theory 1890–1918*. Saarbrücken: Verlag Dr. Müller, 2009.

Rosa, Joseph. "Architectural Photography and the Construction of Modern Architecture." *History of Photography* 22, no. 2 (1998): 99–104.

Rossi, Aldo. *The Architecture of the City*. Translated by Diane Ghirardo and Joan Ockman. Cambridge: MIT Press, 1982.

Roth, Alfred. *Zwei Wohnhäuser von Le Corbusier und Pierre Jeanneret*. Special issue of *Bau und Wohnung*. 1927. Reprint, Stuttgart: Karl Krämer, 1977.

Rupp, Fritz. *Inkrustationsstil der romanischen Baukunst zu Florenz*. Stuttgart: Heitz, 1919.

Sachsse, Rolf. "Beginnen wir! Die photographischen Abteilung der Hochschule für Graphik und Buchkunst in Leipzig zwischen 1890 und 1950." In *Fotografie: Arbeiten von Absolventen und Studenten 1980–1993*, edited by Joachim Jansong. Leipzig: Hochschule für Graphik und Buchkunst, 1993.

———. *Bild und Bau: Zur Nutzung technischer Medien beim Entwerfen von Architektur.* Braunschweig: Vieweg & Sohn, 1997.

———. *Lucia Moholy*. Düsseldorf: Marzona, 1985.

———, ed. *Lucia Moholy: Bauhaus Fotografin*. Berlin: Bauhaus-Archiv, 1995.

———. "Messen und Ausstellungen als Hort der Moderne im NS-Staat." In *Die Erziehung zum Wegsehen: Fotografie im NS-Staat*, 58–68. Hamburg: Philo Fine Arts, 2003.

———. "Mies Montiert." *ARCH + Zeitschrift für Architektur und Städtebau* 61 (June 2002): 58–61.

———. *Photographie als Medium der Architekturinterpretation: Studien zur Geschichte der deutschen Architekturphotographie im 20. Jahrhundert*. Munich: Saur, 1984.

Saletnik, Jeffrey, and Robin Schuldenfrei, eds. *Bauhaus Construct: Fashioning Identity, Discourse and Modernism*. London: Routledge, 2009.

Sapák, Jan. "Umfeld und Entstehung eines berühmten Hauses." In *Das Haus Tugendhat: Ludwig Mies van der Rohe, Brünn, 1930*, edited by Adolf Stiller, 63–76. Vienna: Verlag Anton Pustet, 1999.

Sartoris, Alberto. *Gli elementi dell'architettura funzionale: Sintesi panoramica dell'architettura moderna*. Milan: Ulrico Hoepli, 1932.

———. *Encyclopédie de l'architecture nouvelle*. 3 vols. Milan: Ulrico Hoepli, 1948–57.

Saxl, Fritz, and Rudolf Wittkower. *British Art and the Mediterranean*. London: Oxford University Press, 1948.

Scharnholz, Lars. "Wolf House, Gubin, 1925–27." In *Mies in Berlin*, edited by Terence Riley and Barry Bergdoll. New York: Museum of Modern Art, 2001.

Scheyer, Ernst. *The Shapes of Space: The Art of Mary Wigman and Oskar Schlemmer*. New York: Dance Perspectives Foundation, 1970.

Schirren, Matthias. *Bruno Taut: Alpine Architektur—eine Utopie.* Munich: Prestel, 2004.

Schlemmer, Oskar. *Die Bühne im Bauhaus.* Mainz: Kupferberg, 1965.

Schmidt, Hans. *Die Architektur-Photographie: Unter besonderer Berücksichtigung der Plastik und des Kunstgewerbes.* Berlin: Verlag von Gustav Schmidt, 1902.

Scholl, Christian. "Die schöne Kunst der Konstruktion: Charakterisierung als Mittel der Darstellung in der Architektur Karl Friedrich Schinkels." *Zeitschrift für Kunstgeschichte* 68 (2005): 71–90.

Schuldenfrei, Robin. "Images in Exile: Lucia Moholy's Bauhaus Negatives and the Construction of the Bauhaus Legacy." *History of Photography* 37, no. 2 (2013): 182–203.

Schulze, Franz. *Mies van der Rohe: A Critical Biography.* Chicago: University of Chicago Press, 1985.

Schwartz, Frederic J. *Blind Spots: Critical Theory and the History of Art in Twentieth-Century Germany.* New Haven, Conn.: Yale University Press, 2005.

———. "Form Follows Fetish: Adolf Behne and the Problem of *Sachlichkeit.*" *Oxford Art Journal* 21, no. 2 (1998): 47–77.

———. *The Werkbund: Design Theory and Mass Culture before the First World War.* New Haven, Conn.: Yale University Press, 1996.

Schwarz, Rudolf. "Das Anliegen der Baukunst." In *Darmstädter Gespräch 1951: Mensch und Raum,* edited by Otto Bartning. Darmstadt: Neue Darmstädter Verlagsanstalt, 1952.

———. "Bilde Künstler, rede nicht." *Baukunst und Werkform* 6, no. 1 (1953): 9–17.

———. "Was dennoch besprochen werden muß." *Baukunst und Werkform* 6, no. 4 (1953): 191–99.

Scott, Felicity. "An Army of Soldiers or a Meadow: The Seagram Building and the 'Art of Modern Architecture.'" *Journal of the Society of Architectural Historians* 70, no. 3 (2011): 330–53.

Scott, Geoffrey. *The Architecture of Humanism: A Study in the History of Taste.* London: Constable, 1914.

"Secondary School at Hunstanton." *Architects' Journal* 118 (September 10, 1953): 323–28.

Simmel, Georg. "Berliner Gewerbeausstellung." *Die Zeit* (Vienna), July 25, 1896, 59–60. Reprinted as "The Berlin Trade Exhibition," translated by Sam Whimster. *Theory, Culture & Society* 8, no. 3 (1991): 119–23.

———. "Das Problem des Stiles." *Dekorative Kunst* 11 (1908).

———. "Psychologie des Schmuckes." *Der Morgen* 2, no. 15 (1908): 454–59.

Šlapeta, Vladimír. *Die Brünner Funktionalisten: Moderne Architektur in Brünn.* Innsbruck: Institut für Raumgestaltung, 1985.

Smithson, Alison. *AS in DS: An Eye on the Road.* Delft: Delft University Press, 1983.

Smithson, Alison, and Peter Smithson. *Changing the Art of Inhabitation.* London: Artemis, 1994.

———. *The Charged Void: Architecture.* New York: Monacelli Press, 2001.

———. *Mies van der Rohe.* Berlin: Technische Universität, 1968.

———. *Without Rhetoric: An Architectural Aesthetic, 1955–1972.* Cambridge: MIT Press, 1974.

Smithson, Peter, and Peter Carolin. "Reflections on Hunstanton." *Architectural Research Quarterly* 2, no. 4 (1997): 32–43.

"The Smithsons: Adding a Fringe to the Fabrics—Bath Projects." *Architects' Journal* 178 (November 30, 1983): 38.

Snyder, Joel, and Neil Walsh Allen. "Photography, Vision, Representation." *Critical Inquiry* 2, no. 1 (1975): 143–69.

Solà-Morales, Ignasi de, Cristian Cirici, and Fernando Ramos. *Mies van der Rohe: Barcelona Pavilion.* Barcelona: G. Gili, 1993.

Stadler, Hilar, and Martino Stierli. *Las Vegas Studio: Images from the Archives of Robert Venturi and Denise Scott Brown.* Zurich: Scheidegger & Spiess, 2008.

Stalder, Laurent. "'New Brutalism,' 'Topology,' and 'Image': Some Remarks on the Architectural Debates in England around 1950." *Journal of Architecture* 13, no. 3 (2008): 261–83.

Steele, James. *Eames House: Charles and Ray Eames.* London: Phaidon, 1994.

Steinberg, Leo. "The Eye Is Part of the Mind." *Partisan Review* 20 (1953): 192–212.

Stemshorn, Max. *Mies und Schinkel: Das Vorbild Schinkels im Werk Mies van der Rohe.* Tübingen: Wasmuth, 2002.

Stierli, Martino. *Las Vegas im Rückspiegel: Die Stadt in Theorie, Fotografie, und Film.* Zurich: gta, 2010.

———. "Mies Montage." *AA Files* 61 (2010): 54–72.

Stiller, Adolf, ed. *Das Haus Tugendhat: Ludwig Mies van der Rohe, Brünn, 1930.* Salzburg: Verlag Anton Pustet, 1999.

Stirling, James. "Anti-structure" *Zodiac* 18 (1969).

———. *James Stirling: Buildings and Projects, 1950–1974.* New York: Oxford University Press, 1975.

———. "Methods of Expression and Materials." *A+U* 2 (1975): 86–89.

Stöneberg, Michael. *Arthur Köster, Architekturfotografie 1926–1933: Das Bild vom "Neuen Bauen."* Berlin: Gebrüder Mann, 2009.

Story, Alfred Thomas. *The Story of Photography.* New York: Appleton, 1902.

Sudhalter, Adrian. "Mies van der Rohe and Photomontage in the 1920s." Paper presented at a seminar on Mies, New York University, Institute of Fine Arts, 1997.

Sullivan, Louis H. "Was ist Architektur? Eine Studie am amerikanischenn Volk." In *Ausstellung neuer amerikanischer Baukunst.* Berlin: Akademie der Künste, 1926.

Szmidt, Boleslaw, ed. *The Polish School of Architecture 1942–1945.* Liverpool: University of Liverpool School of Architecture, 1945.

Tafuri, Manfredo. "The Stage as 'Virtual City': From Fuchs to the Totaltheater." In *The Sphere and the Labyrinth: Avant-Gardes and Architecture from Piranesi to the 1970s.* Translated by Pellegrino d'Acierno and Robert Connolly, 93–117. Cambridge: MIT Press, 1990.

Tafuri, Manfredo, and Francesco Dal Co. *Modern Architecture.* Milan: Electa, 1976.

Tagg, John. *The Burden of Representation: Essays on Photographies and Histories.* Amherst: University of Massachusetts Press, 1988.

Taut, Bruno. Comments on the Exhibition House at the Berlin Building Exhibition. *Bauwelt* 63, no. 33 (1977): 11.

———. *Ein Wohnhaus.* Berlin: Gebrüder Mann, 1927.

Tegethoff, Wolf. "Catching the Spirit: Mies's Early Work and the Impact of the 'Prussian Style.'" In *Mies in Berlin,* edited by Terence Riley and Barry Bergdoll, 134–54. New York: Museum of Modern Art, 2001.

———. *Im Brennpunkt der Moderne: Mies van der Rohe und das Haus Tugendhat in Brünn.* Munich: HypoVereinsbank, 1998.

———. *Mies van der Rohe: Die Villen und Landhausprojekte.* Krefeld: Kaiser Wilhelm Museum, 1981.

———. *Mies van der Rohe: The Villas and Country Houses.* Translated by Russell M. Stockman, edited by William Dyckes. New York: Museum of Modern Art, 1985.

Teige, Karel. "Zur Ästhetik des Films." *Kunst für Alle* 9 (1925): 332–39.

Templ, Stephan. "Streiflichter auf die Baukultur in Brünn und Querverbindung nach Wien." In *Das Haus Tugendhat: Ludwig Mies van der Rohe, Brünn, 1930,* edited by Adolf Stiller, 77–83. Vienna: Verlag Anton Pustet, 1999.

Thompson, D'Arcy Wentworth. *On Growth and Form.* 1917. Reprint, Cambridge: Cambridge University Press, 1942.

"Thoughts in Progress: The New Brutalism." *Architectural Design* 27 (1957): 111–13.

Tiffany, Paul A. "The Roots of Decline: Business–Government Relations in the American Steel Industry, 1945–1960." *Journal of Economic History* 44, no. 2 (1984): 407–19.

Tugendhat, Grete, and Fritz Tugendhat. "Die Bewohner des Hauses Tugendhat äußern sich." *Die Form* 6, no. 11 (1931): 437–39.

Tupitsyn, Margarita. *El Lissitzky: Beyond the Abstract Cabinet: Photography, Design, Collaboration.* New Haven, Conn.: Yale University Press, 1999.

Turvey, Malcolm. "Dada between Heaven and Hell: Abstraction and Universal Language in the *Rhythm* Films of Hans Richter." *October* 105 (Summer 2003): 13–36.

Twyman, Michael. *Printing 1770–1970: An Illustrated History of Its Development and Uses in England.* London: Eyre and Spottiswode, 1970.

Venturi, Robert, Denise Scott Brown, and Steven Izenour. *Learning from Las Vegas.* Cambridge: MIT Press, 1972.

Vidler, Anthony. *James Frazer Stirling: Notes from the Archive.* New Haven, Conn.: Yale Center for British Art, 2010.

Vinegar, Aron. *I Am a Monument: On* Learning from Las Vegas. Cambridge: MIT Press, 2008.

Vinegar, Aron, and Michael J. Golec, eds. *Relearning from Las Vegas.* Minneapolis: University of Minnesota Press, 2009.

Wach, E. "Architekturaufnahmen." *Photographische Rundschau und Mitteilungen: Zeitschrift für Freunde der Photographie* 51 (1914): 184–87, 197–98.

Walsh, Victoria. *Nigel Henderson: Parallel of Life and Art.* London: Thames & Hudson, 2001.

———. "Reordering and Redistributing the Visual: The Expanded 'Field' of Pattern-Making in *Parallel of Life and Art* and Hammer Prints." *Journal of Visual Culture* 12, no. 2 (2013): 222–44.

Ward, Janet. *Weimar Surfaces: Urban Visual Culture in 1920s Germany.* Berkeley: University of California Press, 2001.

"Warspeed System of Construction in Concrete." *Architectural Record* 92, no. 6 (December 1942).

Warstat, Willi. *Allgemeine Ästhetik der photographischen Kunst auf psychologischer Grundlage.* Halle a.S.: Wilhelm Knapp, 1909.

Weber, Hugo. "Mies van der Rohe in Chicago." *Bauen und Wohnen* 9 (1951): 1–12.

"Welded Steel Fabrication Used at Hunstanton Secondary Modern School." *National Builder,* April 1953, 281.

Westheim, Paul. "Für und wider. Architekturbetrachtungen: Gropius." *Das Kunstblatt* 9 (1925): 368–74.

Whiteley, Nigel. *Reyner Banham: Historian of the Immediate Future.* Cambridge: MIT Press, 2002.

Wick, Rainer K. *Teaching at the Bauhaus.* Ostfildern: Hatje Cantz, 2000.

Wittkower, Rudolf. *Architectural Principles in the Age of Humanism.* 1949. Reprint, London: Alec Tiranti, 1952.

Wittman, Richard. *Architecture, Print Culture, and the Public Sphere in Eighteenth-Century France.* London: Routledge, 2007.

Woodman, Ellis. *James Gowan: Modernity and Reinvention.* London: Black Dog, 2008.

Woods, Mary N. "The Photograph as Tastemaker: The *American Architect* and H.H. Richardson." *History of Photography* 14 (April–June 1990): 155–63.

Worringer, Wilhelm. *Abstraktion und Einfuhlung: Ein Beitrag zur Stilpsychologie.* Munich: R. Piper, 1908.

———. *Form Problems of the Gothic.* New York: G. E. Steichert, 1918.

Yanni, Carla. *Nature's Museums: Victorian Science and the Architecture of Display.* Baltimore: Johns Hopkins University Press, 1999.

"Eine zeitgemäße Aufdeckung." *Deutsche Bauhütte* 36, nos. 9, 10, 11 (1932): 109–11; 122–23; 138–41.

Zimmerman, Claire. "Eliat House Project, 1925." In *Mies in Berlin,* edited by Terence Riley and Barry Bergdoll, 200–203. New York: Museum of Modern Art, 2001.

———. "From Legible Form to Memorable Image: Architectural Knowledge from Rudolf Wittkower to Reyner Banham." *Candide* 5 (Spring 2012): 93–116.

———. "James Stirling Re-assembled." *AA Files* 56 (November 2007): 30–41.

———. *Ludwig Mies van der Rohe.* Cologne: Taschen, 2007.

———. "New National Gallery." In *Mies in Berlin,* edited by Terence Riley and Barry Bergdoll. New York: Museum of Modern Art, 2001.

———. "Photographic Images from Chicago to Hunstanton." In *Neo-avant-garde and Postmodern: Postwar Architecture in Britain and Beyond,* edited by Mark Crinson and Claire Zimmerman, 203–28. New Haven, Conn.: Yale University Press for Yale Center for British Art, 2010.

Zimmermann, Florian, ed. *Der Schrei nach dem Turmhaus.* Berlin: Argon, 1988.

Zimmermann, Michael F., ed. *The Art Historian: National Traditions and Institutional Practices.* Williamstown, Mass.: Sterling and Francine Clark Art Institute, 2003.

Zohlen, Gerwin. "Schmugglerpfad: Siegfried Kracauer, Architekt und Schriftsteller." In *Siegfried Kracauer: Neue Interpretationen,* edited by Thomas Y. Levin and Michael Kessler, 325–44. Tübingen: Stauffenburg, 1990.

Zucker, Paul. *Raumdarstellung u. Bildarchitekturen bei den Florentiner Malern der ersten Hälfte des Quattrocento.* Leipzig: Klinkhardt & Biermann, 1912.

———. *Raumdarstellung und Bildarchitekturen im florentiner Quattrocento.* Leipzig: Klinkhardt & Biermann, 1913.

Zurier, Rebecca. *Picturing the City: Urban Vision and the Ashcan School.* Berkeley: University of California Press, 2006.

"Zur Propaganda neuer Versuchsbauten." *Deutsche Bauhütte* 33, no. 12 (1929): 193–96.

INDEX

Page numbers in italics refer to figures.

Claire Zimmerman is associate professor of art history and architecture at the University of Michigan in the College of Literature, Science, and the Arts, and the Taubman College of Architecture and Urban Planning. She is the author of *Ludwig Mies van der Rohe* and coeditor of *Neo-avant-garde and Postmodern: Postwar Architecture in Britain and Beyond*.